Large-Scale Kernel Machines

Neural Information Processing Series
Michael I. Jordan and Thomas Dietterich, editors

Advances in Large Margin Classifiers
Alexander J. Smola, Peter L. Bartlett, Bernhard Schölkopf,
and Dale Schuurmans, eds., 2000

Advanced Mean Field Methods: Theory and Practice
Manfred Opper and David Saad, eds., 2001

Probabilistic Models of the Brain: Perception and Neural Function
Rajesh P. N. Rao, Bruno A. Olshausen, and Michael S. Lewicki, eds., 2002

Exploratory Analysis and Data Modeling in Functional Neuroimaging
Friedrich T. Sommer and Andrzej Wichert, eds., 2003

Advances in Minimum Description Length: Theory and Applications
Peter D. Grunwald, In Jae Myung, and Mark A. Pitt, eds., 2005

Nearest-Neighbor Methods in Learning and Vision: Theory and Practice
Gregory Shakhnarovich, Piotr Indyk, and Trevor Darrell, eds., 2006

New Directions in Statistical Signal Processing: From Systems to Brains
Simon Haykin, José C. Prncipe, Terrence J. Sejnowski, and John McWhirter, eds., 2007

Predicting Structured Data
Gökhan Bakır, Thomas Hofmann, Bernard Scholköpf, Alexander J. Smola,
Ben Taskar, and S.V.N. Vishwanathan, eds., 2007

Toward Brain-Computer Interfacing
Guido Dornhege, José del R. Millán, Thilo Hinterberger, Dennis McFarland,
and Klaus-Robert Müller, eds., 2007

Large-Scale Kernel Machines
Léon Bottou, Olivier Chapelle, Dennis DeCoste, and Jason Weston, eds., 2007

Large-Scale Kernel Machines

Léon Bottou
Olivier Chapelle
Dennis DeCoste
Jason Weston

The MIT Press
Cambridge, Massachusetts
London, England

Typeset by the authors using LaTeX 2_ε
Library of Congress Control No. 2007000980
Printed and bound in the United States of America

Library of Congress Cataloging-in-Publication Data
Large-scale kernel machines / edited by Léon Bottou ... [et al.].
    p. cm. — (Neural information processing series)
  Includes bibliographical references and index.
  ISBN 978-0-262-02625-3 (hardcover : alk. paper)
  1. Data structures (Computer science)   2. Machine learning   I. Bottou, Léon.
  QA76.9.D35L38 2007
  005.7'3—dc22
                                        2007000980

    10 9 8 7 6 5 4 3 2 1

Contents

Series Foreword   ix

Preface   xi

1 Support Vector Machine Solvers   1
Léon Bottou, Chih-Jen Lin

   1.1   Introduction 1
   1.2   Support Vector Machines 3
   1.3   Duality 6
   1.4   Sparsity 10
   1.5   Early SVM Algorithms 12
   1.6   The Decomposition Method 16
   1.7   A Case Study: LIBSVM 20
   1.8   Conclusion and Outlook 26
       Appendix 27

2 Training a Support Vector Machine in the Primal   29
Olivier Chapelle

   2.1   Introduction 29
   2.2   Links between Primal and Dual Optimization 30
   2.3   Primal Objective Function 32
   2.4   Newton Optimization 34
   2.5   Experiments 39
   2.6   Advantages of Primal Optimization 44
   2.7   Conclusion 48
       Appendix 49

3 Fast Kernel Learning with Sparse Inverted Index   51
Patrick Haffner, Stephan Kanthak

   3.1   Introduction 51
   3.2   Sequential Kernel Learning 53
   3.3   Sparse Matrix-Vector Multiplication 54
   3.4   Complexity Analysis 60
   3.5   Speeding Up SVM Training 65

3.6   Feature Selection 67
3.7   Large-Scale Experiments 67
3.8   Concluding Remarks 70

4   Large-Scale Learning with String Kernels   **73**
Sören Sonnenburg, Gunnar Rätsch, Konrad Rieck

4.1   Introduction 74
4.2   String Kernels 74
4.3   Sparse Feature Maps 79
4.4   Speeding up SVM Training and Testing 83
4.5   Benchmark Experiments 85
4.6   Extensions 92
4.7   Conclusion 103

5   Large-Scale Parallel SVM Implementation   **105**
Igor Durdanovic, Eric Cosatto, Hans-Peter Graf

5.1   Introduction 106
5.2   Accelerating SVMs: Previous Approaches 107
5.3   The Sequential Algorithm 111
5.4   Spread-Kernel Optimization (Full Data) (SKOFD) 119
5.5   Spread-Kernel Optimization (Split Data) (SKOSD) 121
5.6   Networking Overhead 123
5.7   Theoretical Model 126
5.8   Experimental Results 129
5.9   Conclusion 136

6   A Distributed Sequential Solver for Large-Scale SVMs   **139**
Elad Yom-Tov

6.1   Introduction 139
6.2   A Distributed Solution of the SVM Problem Using a Sequential Solver 144
6.3   Metrics for Comparing SVMs 145
6.4   Simulation 147
6.5   A Model of the Computational Time 151
6.6   Concluding Remarks 154

7   Newton Methods for Fast Semisupervised Linear SVMs   **155**
Vikas Sindhwani, S. Sathiya Keerthi

7.1   Introduction 155
7.2   Modified Finite Newton Linear l_2-SVM 157
7.3   Fast Multiswitch Transductive SVMs 161
7.4   Semisupervised SVMs Based on Deterministic Annealing 164
7.5   Empirical Study 167
7.6   Conclusion 174

8 The Improved Fast Gauss Transform with Applications to Machine Learning **175**

Vikas Chandrakant Raykar, Ramani Duraiswami

8.1 Computational Curse of Nonparametric Methods 175
8.2 Bottleneck Computational Primitive: Weighted Superposition of Kernels 176
8.3 Structured Matrices and ϵ-Exact Approximation 177
8.4 Motivating Example: Polynomial Kernel 178
8.5 Sum of Gaussian Kernels: The Discrete Gauss Transform 179
8.6 Bringing Computational Tractability to the Discrete Gauss Transform 180
8.7 Multi-index Notation 182
8.8 The Improved Fast Gauss Transform 184
8.9 IFGT vs. FGT 189
8.10 Numerical Experiments 191
8.11 Fast Multivariate Kernel Density Estimation 196
8.12 Conclusions 199
     Appendix 201

9 Approximation Methods for Gaussian Process Regression **203**

Joaquin Quiñonero-Candela, Carl Edward Rasmussen, Christopher K. I. Williams

9.1 Introduction 203
9.2 Gaussian Process Regression 204
9.3 Sparse Approximations Based on Inducing Variables 206
9.4 Fast Matrix Vector Multiplication Approximations 217
9.5 Selecting the Inducing Variables 218
9.6 Approximate Evidence and Hyperparameter Learning 220
9.7 Classification 222
9.8 Conclusions 223

10 Brisk Kernel Independent Component Analysis **225**

Stefanie Jegelka, Arthur Gretton

10.1 Introduction 225
10.2 Independent Component Analysis 227
10.3 Independence Measures Based on RKHS Covariance Operators . . 228
10.4 Gradient Descent on the Orthogonal Group 232
10.5 Complexity Analysis 238
10.6 Experiments 239
10.7 Conclusions and Future Directions 248
     Appendix 249

11 Building SVMs with Reduced Classifier Complexity   **251**
S. Sathiya Keerthi, Olivier Chapelle, Dennis DeCoste

11.1 Introduction 251
11.2 The Basic Optimization 255
11.3 Selection of New Basis Element 257
11.4 Hyperparameter Tuning 263
11.5 Comparison with Kernel Matching Pursuit 264
11.6 Additional Tuning 267
11.7 Comparison with Standard SVM Training 270
11.8 Conclusion 270
    Appendix 273

12 Trading Convexity for Scalability   **275**
Ronan Collobert, Fabian Sinz, Jason Weston, Léon Bottou

12.1 Introduction 275
12.2 The Concave-Convex Procedure 276
12.3 Nonconvex SVMs 277
12.4 Experiments with Nonconvex SVMs 281
12.5 Nonconvex Transductive SVMs 285
12.6 Experiments with TSVMs 292
12.7 Conclusion 299

13 Training Invariant SVMs Using Selective Sampling   **301**
Gaëlle Loosli, Léon Bottou, Stéphane Canu

13.1 Introduction 301
13.2 Online Algorithm with Selective Sampling 304
13.3 Invariance 308
13.4 Application 313
13.5 Conclusion 320

14 Scaling Learning Algorithms toward AI   **321**
Yoshua Bengio, Yann LeCun

14.1 Introduction 321
14.2 Learning Models Toward AI 324
14.3 Learning Architectures, Shallow and Deep 329
14.4 Fundamental Limitation of Local Learning 337
14.5 Deep Architectures 345
14.6 Experiments with Visual Pattern Recognition 347
14.7 Conclusion 358

References   **361**

Contributors   **389**

Index   **393**

Series Foreword

The yearly Neural Information Processing Systems (NIPS) workshops bring together scientists with broadly varying backgrounds in statistics, mathematics, computer science, physics, electrical engineering, neuroscience, and cognitive science, unified by a common desire to develop novel computational and statistical strategies for information processing and to understand the mechanisms for information processing in the brain. In contrast to conferences, these workshops maintain a flexible format that both allows and encourages the presentation and discussion of work in progress. They thus serve as an incubator for the development of important new ideas in this rapidly-evolving field. The series editors, in consultation with workshop organizers and members of the NIPS Foundation Board, select specific workshop topics on the basis of scientific excellence, intellectual breadth, and technical impact. Collections of papers chosen and edited by the organizers of specific workshops are built around pedagogical introductory chapters, while research monographs provide comprehensive descriptions of workshop-related topics, to create a series of books that provides a timely, authoritative account of the latest developments in the exciting field of neural computation.

Michael I. Jordan and Thomas G. Dietterich

Preface

The methods of conventional statistics were developed in times where both dataset collection and modeling were carried out with paper and pencil. The appearance of computers first displaced the pencil for model calculation. Machine learning gained prominence by exploiting this new opportunity, enabling the construction of efficient high-dimensional models using comparatively small training sets

Another change of similar magnitude is underway. Pervasive and networked computers have reduced the cost of collecting and distributing large-scale datasets. We now need learning algorithms that scale linearly with the volume of the data, while maintaining enough statistical efficiency to outperform algorithms that simply process a random subset of the data.

For the sake of the argument, assume that there are only two categories of computers. The first category, the "makers," directly mediate human activity. They implement the dialogue between sellers and buyers, run the accounting department, control industrial processes, route telecommunications, etc. The makers generate and collect huge quantities of data. The second category, the "thinkers," analyze this data, build models, and draw conclusions that direct the activity of the makers. Makers produce datasets whose size grows linearly with their collective computing power. We can roughly write this size as nd where n is a number of examples and d the number of features per example. The computational needs of state-of-the-art learning algorithms typically grow like $n^2 d$ or nd^2. If thinkers were to use these algorithms, their collective computing power would have to vastly exceed that of the makers. This is economically infeasible. The Googles of this world cannot deploy vastly more resources than all their customers together: their advertisement income cannot exceed the wealth of those who receive the messages, because the advertisers would never sell enough to recoup their expense.

The title "Large-Scale Kernel Machines" may appear to be a contradiction in terms. Kernel machines are often associated with dual techniques that implement very large parameter spaces at the expense of scalability in the number of examples. However, as was made clear during the NIPS 2005 workshop, kernel machines can scale nicely by cleverly approximating the conventional optimization problem solved during learning. Because we derive these large-scale systems from relatively well understood kernel machines, we can assess more soundly the impact of their increased scalability on their statistical efficiency.

This book offers solutions to researchers and engineers seeking to solve practical learning problems with large-scale datasets. Algorithms are described in detail;

experiments have been carried out on realistically large datasets. Many contributors have made their code and data available online.

This book is also intended for researchers seeking to increase our conceptual understanding of large-scale learning. Large-scale learning research so far has mostly been empirical. Many useful algorithms lack firm theoretical grounds. This book gathers information that can help address the discrepancy between advances in machine learning mathematics and advances in machine learning algorithms.

The first chapter provides a very detailed description of state-of-the-art support vector machine (SVM) technology. It also reviews the essential concepts discussed in the book. The second chapter compares primal and dual optimization techniques. The following chapters progress from well understood techniques to more and more controversial approaches. This is, of course, a very subjective assessment since most chapters contain both aspects. This progression includes:

- Fast implementation of known algorithms, leveraging special kernels, sparse data, or parallel computers. Some chapters describe experimental setups that should be considered as masterpieces of engineering.

- Approximations that are amenable to theoretical guarantees, such as multipole approximations and fast matrix-vector multiplication.

- Algorithms that perform very well in practice but are difficult to analyze theoretically. This part includes three very effective methods to improve the scalability of kernel machines: greedy selection, nonconvex optimization, and selective sampling.

Finally, we invited the authors of the final chapter to rationalize their mistrust in kernel algorithms for large-scale problems. They consider problems that animals perform effortlessly, such as perception and control. They argue convincingly that local kernel representations are inefficient for these problems. Meanwhile, this argument might not apply to other relevant tasks, such as mining transaction logs. This analysis suggests that this class of problems is different enough to justify a specific scientific approach.

Léon Bottou, Olivier Chapelle, Dennis DeCoste, and Jason Weston,
December 1, 2006.

1 Support Vector Machine Solvers

Léon Bottou
Chih-Jen Lin

Considerable efforts have been devoted to the implementation of an efficient optimization method for solving the support vector machine dual problem. This chapter proposes an in-depth review of the algorithmic and computational issues associated with this problem. Besides this baseline, we also point out research directions that are exploited more thoroughly in the rest of this book.

1.1 Introduction

The support vector machine (SVM) algorithm (Cortes and Vapnik, 1995) is probably the most widely used kernel learning algorithm. It achieves relatively robust pattern recognition performance using well-established concepts in optimization theory.

Despite this mathematical classicism, the implementation of efficient SVM solvers has diverged from the classical methods of numerical optimization. This divergence is common to virtually all learning algorithms. The numerical optimization literature focuses on the asymptotic performance: how quickly the accuracy of the solution increases with computing time. In the case of learning algorithms, two other factors mitigate the impact of optimization accuracy.

1.1.1 Three Components of the Generalization Error

The generalization performance of a learning algorithm is indeed limited by three sources of error:

- The *approximation error* measures how well the exact solution can be approximated by a function implementable by our learning system,

■ The *estimation error* measures how accurately we can determine the best function implementable by our learning system using a finite training set instead of the unseen testing examples.

■ The *optimization error* measures how closely we compute the function that best satisfies whatever information can be exploited in our finite training set.

The estimation error is determined by the number of training examples and by the capacity of the family of functions (e.g., Vapnik, 1982). Large families of functions have *smaller approximation errors* but lead to *higher estimation errors*. This compromise has been extensively discussed in the literature. Well-designed compromises lead to estimation and approximation errors that scale between the inverse and the inverse square root of the number of examples (Steinwart and Scovel, 2007).

In contrast, the optimization literature discusses algorithms whose error decreases exponentially or faster with the number of iterations. The computing time for each iteration usually grows linearly or quadratically with the number of examples.

It is easy to see that exponentially decreasing optimization errors are irrelevant in comparison to the other sources of errors. Therefore it is often desirable to use poorly regarded optimization algorithms that trade asymptotic accuracy for lower iteration complexity. This chapter describes in depth how SVM solvers have evolved toward this objective.

1.1.2   Small-Scale Learning vs. Large-Scale Learning

There is a budget for any given problem. In the case of a learning algorithm, the budget can be a limit on the number of training examples or a limit on the computation time. Which constraint applies can be used to distinguish small-scale learning problems from large-scale learning problems.

■ *Small-scale learning problems* are constrained by the number of training examples. The generalization error is dominated by the approximation and estimation errors. The optimization error can be reduced to insignificant levels since the computation time is not limited.

■ *Large-scale learning problems* are constrained by the total computation time. Besides adjusting the approximation capacity of the family of function, one can also adjust the number of training examples that a particular optimization algorithm can process within the allowed computing resources. Approximate optimization algorithms can then achieve better generalization error because they process more training examples (Bottou and LeCun, 2004). Chapters 11 and 13 present such algorithms for kernel machines.

The computation time is always limited in practice. This is why some aspects of large-scale learning problems always percolate into small-scale learning problems. One simply looks for algorithms that can quickly reduce the optimization error comfortably below the expected approximation and estimation errors. This has been the main driver for the evolution of SVM solvers.

1.1.3   Contents

The present chapter contains an in-depth discussion of optimization algorithms for solving the dual formulation on a single processor. Algorithms for solving the primal formulation are discussed in chapter 2. Parallel algorithms are discussed in chapters 5 and 6. The objective of this chapter is simply to give the reader a precise understanding of the various computational aspects of sparse kernel machines.

Section 1.2 reviews the mathematical formulation of SVMs. Section 1.3 presents the generic optimization problem and performs a first discussion of its algorithmic consequences. Sections 1.5 and 1.6 discuss various approaches used for solving the SVM dual problem. Section 1.7 presents the state-of-the-art LIBSVM solver and explains the essential algorithmic choices. Section 1.8 briefly presents some of the directions currently explored by the research community. Finally, the appendix links implementations of various algorithms discussed in this chapter.

1.2   Support Vector Machines

The earliest pattern regognition systems were linear classifiers (Nilsson, 1965). A pattern $\mathbf{x}$ is given a class $y = \pm 1$ by first transforming the pattern into a feature vector $\Phi(\mathbf{x})$ and taking the sign of a linear discriminant function $\hat{y}(\mathbf{x}) = \mathbf{w}^\top \Phi(\mathbf{x}) + b$.

The hyperplane $\hat{y}(\mathbf{x}) = 0$ defines a decision boundary in the feature space. The problem specific feature vector $\Phi(\mathbf{x})$ is usually chosen by hand. The parameters $\mathbf{w}$ and b are determined by running a learning procedure on a training set $(\mathbf{x}_1, y_1) \cdots (\mathbf{x}_n, y_n)$.

Three additional ideas define the modern SVMs.

1.2.1   Optimal Hyperplane

The training set is said to be linearly separable when there exists a linear discriminant function whose sign matches the class of all training examples. When a training set is linearly separable there usually is an infinity of separating hyperplanes.

Vapnik and Lerner (1963) propose to choose the separating hyperplane that maximizes the margin, that is to say the hyperplane that leaves as much room as possible between the hyperplane and the closest example. This optimum hyperplane is illustrated in figure 1.1.

The following optimization problem expresses this choice:

$$\min \; \mathcal{P}(\mathbf{w}, b) = \frac{1}{2}\mathbf{w}^2$$
$$\text{subject to } \forall i \quad y_i(\mathbf{w}^\top \Phi(\mathbf{x}_i) + b) \geq 1 \tag{1.1}$$

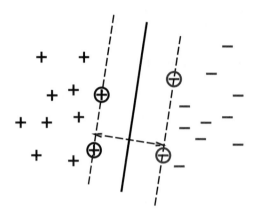

Figure 1.1   The optimal hyperplane separates positive and negative examples with the maximal margin. The position of the optimal hyperplane is solely determined by the few examples that are closest to the hyperplane (the support vectors.)

Directly solving this problem is difficult because the constraints are quite complex. The mathematical tool of choice for simplifying this problem is the Lagrangian duality theory (e.g., Bertsekas, 1995). This approach leads to solving the following dual problem:

$$\max \; \mathcal{D}(\boldsymbol{\alpha}) = \sum_{i=1}^{n} \alpha_i - \frac{1}{2} \sum_{i,j=1}^{n} y_i \alpha_i \, y_j \alpha_j \, \Phi(\mathbf{x}_i)^\top \Phi(\mathbf{x}_j)$$

$$\text{subject to} \quad \begin{cases} \forall i \quad \alpha_i \geq 0, \\ \sum_i y_i \alpha_i = 0. \end{cases} \tag{1.2}$$

Problem (1.2) is computationally easier because its constraints are much simpler. The direction $\mathbf{w}^*$ of the optimal hyperplane is then recovered from a solution $\boldsymbol{\alpha}^*$ of the dual optimization problem (1.2).

$$\mathbf{w}^* = \sum_i \alpha_i^* y_i \Phi(\mathbf{x}_i).$$

Determining the bias b^* becomes a simple one-dimensional problem. The linear discriminant function can then be written as

$$\hat{y}(\mathbf{x}) = \mathbf{w}^{*\top} \mathbf{x} + b^* = \sum_{i=1}^{n} y_i \alpha_i \, \Phi(\mathbf{x}_i)^\top \Phi(\mathbf{x}) + b^*. \tag{1.3}$$

Further details are discussed in section 1.3.

1.2.2 Kernels

The optimization problem (1.2) and the linear discriminant function (1.3) only involve the patterns $\mathbf{x}$ through the computation of dot products in feature space. There is no need to compute the features $\Phi(\mathbf{x})$ when one knows how to compute the dot products directly.

Instead of hand-choosing a feature function $\Phi(\mathbf{x})$, Boser et al. (1992) propose to directly choose a kernel function $K(\mathbf{x}, \mathbf{x}')$ that represents a dot product $\Phi(x)^\top \Phi(\mathbf{x}')$ in some unspecified high-dimensional space.

The *reproducing kernel Hilbert spaces* theory (Aronszajn, 1944) precisely states which kernel functions correspond to a dot product and which linear spaces are implicitly induced by these kernel functions. For instance, any continuous decision boundary can be implemented using the radial basis function (RBF) kernel $K_\gamma(x, y) = e^{-\gamma \|x-y\|^2}$. Although the corresponding feature space has infinite dimension, all computations can be performed without ever computing a feature vector. Complex nonlinear classifiers are computed using the linear mathematics of the optimal hyperplanes.

1.2.3 Soft Margins

Optimal hyperplanes (section 1.2.1) are useless when the training set is not linearly separable. Kernel machines (section 1.2.2) can represent complicated decision boundaries that accomodate any training set. But this is not very wise when the problem is very noisy.

Cortes and Vapnik (1995) show that noisy problems are best addressed by allowing some examples to violate the margin constraints in the primal problem (1.1). These potential violations are represented using positive slack variables $\boldsymbol{\xi} = (\xi_i \dots \xi_n)$. An additional parameter C controls the compromise between large margins and small margin violations.

$$
\begin{aligned}
\max_{\mathbf{w},b,\boldsymbol{\xi}} \; \mathcal{P}(\mathbf{w}, b, \boldsymbol{\xi}) &= \frac{1}{2}\mathbf{w}^2 + C\sum_{i=1}^{n}\xi_i \\
\text{subject to} \quad & \begin{cases} \forall i \quad y_i(\mathbf{w}^\top \Phi(\mathbf{x}_i) + b) \geq 1 - \xi_i \\ \forall i \quad \xi_i \geq 0 \end{cases}
\end{aligned}
\tag{1.4}
$$

The dual formulation of this soft-margin problem is strikingly similar to the dual formulation (1.2) of the optimal hyperplane algorithm. The only change is the appearance of the upper bound C for the coefficients $\boldsymbol{\alpha}$.

$$
\begin{aligned}
\max \; \mathcal{D}(\boldsymbol{\alpha}) &= \sum_{i=1}^{n}\alpha_i - \frac{1}{2}\sum_{i,j=1}^{n} y_i\alpha_i\, y_j\alpha_j\, K(\mathbf{x}_i, \mathbf{x}_j) \\
\text{subject to} \quad & \begin{cases} \forall i \quad 0 \leq \alpha_i \leq C \\ \sum_i y_i\alpha_i = 0 \end{cases}
\end{aligned}
\tag{1.5}
$$

1.2.4   Other SVM Variants

A multitude of alternative forms of SVMs have been introduced over the years(see Schölkopf and Smola, 2002, for a review). Typical examples include SVMs for computing regressions (Vapnik, 1995), for solving integral equations (Vapnik, 1995), for estimating the support of a density (Schölkopf et al., 2001), SVMs that use different soft-margin costs (Cortes and Vapnik, 1995), and parameters (Schölkopf et al., 2000; C.-C. Chang and Lin, 2001). There are also alternative formulations of the dual problem (Keerthi et al., 1999; Bennett and Bredensteiner, 2000). All these examples reduce to solving quadratic programming problems similar to (1.5).

1.3   Duality

This section discusses the properties of the SVM quadratic programming problem. The SVM literature usually establishes basic results using the powerful Karush-Kuhn-Tucker theorem (e.g., Bertsekas, 1995). We prefer instead to give a more detailed account in order to review mathematical facts of great importance for the implementation of SVM solvers.

The rest of this chapter focuses on solving the soft-margin SVM problem (1.4) using the standard dual formulation (1.5),

$$\max \; \mathcal{D}(\boldsymbol{\alpha}) = \sum_{i=1}^{n} \alpha_i - \frac{1}{2} \sum_{i,j=1}^{n} y_i \alpha_i \, y_j \alpha_j \, K_{ij}$$

$$\text{subject to} \quad \begin{cases} \forall i \quad 0 \le \alpha_i \le C, \\ \sum_i y_i \alpha_i = 0, \end{cases}$$

where $K_{ij} = K(\mathbf{x}_i, \mathbf{x}_j)$ is the matrix of kernel values.

After computing the solution $\boldsymbol{\alpha}^*$, the SVM discriminant function is

$$\hat{y}(\mathbf{x}) = \mathbf{w}^{*\top}\mathbf{x} + b^* = \sum_{i=1}^{n} \alpha_i^* K(\mathbf{x}_i, \mathbf{x}) + b^*. \tag{1.6}$$

The optimal bias b^* can be determined by returning to the primal problem, or, more efficiently, using the optimality criterion (1.11) discussed below.

It is sometimes convenient to rewrite the box constraint $0 \le \alpha_i \le C$ as a box constraint on the quantity $y_i \alpha_i$:

$$y_i \alpha_i \in [A_i, B_i] = \begin{cases} [\,0, C\,] & \text{if } y_i = +1, \\ [-C, 0\,] & \text{if } y_i = -1. \end{cases} \tag{1.7}$$

In fact, some SVM solvers, such as SVQP2 (see appendix), optimize variables $\beta_i = y_i \alpha_i$ that are positive or negative depending on y_i. Other SVM solvers, such as LIBSVM (see section 1.7), optimize the standard dual variables α_i. This chapter

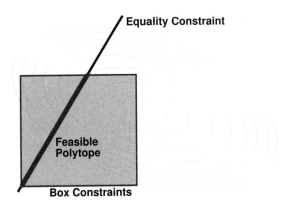

Figure 1.2 Geometry of the dual SVM problem (1.5). The box constraints $A_i \leq \alpha_i \leq B_i$ and the equality constraint $\sum \alpha_i = 0$ define the feasible polytope, that is, the domain of the $\boldsymbol{\alpha}$ values that satisfy the constraints.

follows the standard convention but uses the constants A_i and B_i defined in (1.7) when they allow simpler expressions.

1.3.1 Construction of the Dual Problem

The difficulty of the primal problem (1.4) lies with the complicated inequality constraints that represent the margin condition. We can represent these constraints using positive Lagrange coefficients $\alpha_i \geq 0$.

$$\mathcal{L}(\mathbf{w}, b, \boldsymbol{\xi}, \boldsymbol{\alpha}) = \frac{1}{2}\mathbf{w}^2 + C \sum_{i=1}^{n} \xi_i - \sum_{i=1}^{n} \alpha_i \left(y_i (\mathbf{w}^\top \Phi(\mathbf{x}_i) + b) - 1 + \xi_i \right).$$

The formal dual objective function $\underline{\mathcal{D}}(\boldsymbol{\alpha})$ is defined as

$$\underline{\mathcal{D}}(\boldsymbol{\alpha}) \quad = \quad \min_{\mathbf{w}, b, \boldsymbol{\xi}} L(\mathbf{w}, b, \boldsymbol{\xi}, \boldsymbol{\alpha}) \quad \text{subject to} \quad \forall i \ \ \xi_i \geq 0. \tag{1.8}$$

This minimization no longer features the complicated constraints expressed by the Lagrange coefficients. The $\xi_i \geq 0$ constraints have been kept because they are easy enough to handle directly. Standard differential arguments[1] yield the analytical expression of the dual objective function.

$$\underline{\mathcal{D}}(\boldsymbol{\alpha}) = \begin{cases} \sum_i \alpha_i - \frac{1}{2} \sum_{i,j} y_i \alpha_i \, y_j \alpha_j \, K_{ij} & \text{if } \sum_i y_i \alpha_i = 0 \text{ and } \forall i \ \alpha_i \leq C, \\ -\infty & \text{otherwise.} \end{cases}$$

---

1. This simple derivation is relatively lenghty because many cases must be considered.

The dual problem (1.5) is the maximization of this expression subject to positivity constraints $\alpha_i \geq 0$. The conditions $\sum_i y_i \alpha_i = 0$ and $\forall i \; \alpha_i \leq C$ appear as constraints in the dual problem because the cases where $\underline{\mathcal{D}}(\boldsymbol{\alpha}) = -\infty$ are not useful for a maximization.

The differentiable function

$$\mathcal{D}(\boldsymbol{\alpha}) = \sum_i \alpha_i - \frac{1}{2} \sum_{i,j} y_i \alpha_i \, y_j \alpha_j \, K_{ij}$$

coincides with the formal dual function $\underline{\mathcal{D}}(\boldsymbol{\alpha})$ when $\boldsymbol{\alpha}$ satisfies the constraints of the dual problem. By a slight abuse of language, $\mathcal{D}(\boldsymbol{\alpha})$ is also referred to as the dual objective function.

The formal definition (1.8) of the dual function ensures that the following inequality holds for any $(\mathbf{w}, b, \boldsymbol{\xi})$ satisfying the primal constraints (1.4) and for any $\boldsymbol{\alpha}$ satisfying the dual constraints (1.5):

$$\mathcal{D}(\boldsymbol{\alpha}) = \underline{\mathcal{D}}(\boldsymbol{\alpha}) \leq \mathcal{L}(\mathbf{w}, b, \boldsymbol{\xi}, \boldsymbol{\alpha}) \leq \mathcal{P}(\mathbf{w}, b, \boldsymbol{\xi}) \; . \tag{1.9}$$

This property is called *weak duality*: the set of values taken by the primal is located above the set of values taken by the dual.

Suppose we can find $\boldsymbol{\alpha}^*$ and $(\mathbf{w}^*, b^*, \boldsymbol{\xi}^*)$ such that $\mathcal{D}(\boldsymbol{\alpha}^*) = \mathcal{P}(\mathbf{w}^*, b^*, \boldsymbol{\xi}^*)$. Inequality (1.9) then implies that both $(\mathbf{w}^*, b^*, \boldsymbol{\xi}^*)$ and $\boldsymbol{\alpha}^*$ are solutions of the primal and dual problems. Convex optimization problems with linear constraints are known to have such solutions. This is called *strong duality*.

Our goal is now to find such a solution for the SVM problem.

1.3.2 Optimality Criteria

Let $\boldsymbol{\alpha}^* = (\alpha_1^* \dots \alpha_n^*)$ be a solution of the dual problem (1.5). Obviously $\boldsymbol{\alpha}^*$ satisfies the dual constraints. Let $\mathbf{g}^* = (g_1^* \dots g_n^*)$ be the derivatives of the dual objective function in $\boldsymbol{\alpha}^*$.

$$g_i^* = \frac{\partial \mathcal{D}(\boldsymbol{\alpha}^*)}{\partial \alpha_i} = 1 - y_i \sum_{j=1}^{n} y_j \alpha_j^* \, K_{ij} \tag{1.10}$$

Consider a pair of subscripts (i, j) such that $y_i \alpha_i^* < B_i$ and $A_j < y_j \alpha_j^*$. The constants A_i and B_j were defined in (1.7).

Define $\boldsymbol{\alpha}^\varepsilon = (\alpha_1^\varepsilon \dots \alpha_n^\varepsilon) \in \mathbb{R}^n$ as

$$\alpha_k^\varepsilon = \alpha_k^* + \begin{cases} +\varepsilon \, y_k & \text{if } k = i, \\ -\varepsilon \, y_k & \text{if } k = j, \\ 0 & \text{otherwise.} \end{cases}$$

The point $\boldsymbol{\alpha}^\varepsilon$ clearly satisfies the constraints if ε is positive and sufficiently small. Therefore $\mathcal{D}(\boldsymbol{\alpha}^\varepsilon) \leq \mathcal{D}(\boldsymbol{\alpha}^*)$ because $\boldsymbol{\alpha}^*$ is solution of the dual problem (1.5). On the other hand, we can write the first-order expansion

$$\mathcal{D}(\boldsymbol{\alpha}^\varepsilon) - \mathcal{D}(\boldsymbol{\alpha}^*) = \varepsilon \left(y_i g_i^* - y_j g_j^* \right) + o(\varepsilon).$$

Therefore the difference $y_i g_i^* - y_j g_j^*$ is necessarily negative. Since this holds for all pairs (i, j) such that $y_i \alpha_i^* < B_i$ and $A_j < y_j \alpha_j^*$, we can write the following *necessary optimality criterion*:

$$\exists \rho \in \mathbb{R} \text{ such that } \max_{i \in I_{\text{up}}} y_i g_i^* \ \leq \ \rho \ \leq \ \min_{j \in I_{\text{down}}} y_j g_j^*, \tag{1.11}$$

where $I_{\text{up}} = \{\, i \mid y_i \alpha_i < B_i \,\}$ and $I_{\text{down}} = \{\, j \mid y_j \alpha_j > A_j \,\}$.

Usually, there are some coefficients α_k^* strictly between their lower and upper bounds. Since the corresponding $y_k g_k^*$ appear on both sides of the inequality, this common situation leaves only one possible value for ρ.

We can rewrite (1.11) as

$$\exists \rho \in \mathbb{R} \text{ such that } \forall k, \quad \begin{cases} \text{if } \ y_k g_k^* > \rho \ \text{ then } \ y_k \alpha_k^* = B_k, \\ \text{if } \ y_k g_k^* < \rho \ \text{ then } \ y_k \alpha_k^* = A_k, \end{cases} \tag{1.12}$$

or, equivalently, as

$$\exists \rho \in \mathbb{R} \text{ such that } \forall k, \quad \begin{cases} \text{if } \ g_k^* > y_k \rho \ \text{ then } \ \alpha_k^* = C, \\ \text{if } \ g_k^* < y_k \rho \ \text{ then } \ \alpha_k^* = 0. \end{cases} \tag{1.13}$$

Let us now pick

$$\mathbf{w}^* = \sum_k y_k \alpha_k^* \Phi(\mathbf{x}_k), \quad b^* = \rho, \quad \text{and} \quad \xi_k^* = \max\{0, g_k^* - y_k \rho\}. \tag{1.14}$$

These values satisfy the constraints of the primal problem (1.4). A short derivation using (1.10) then gives

$$\mathcal{P}(\mathbf{w}^*, b^*, \boldsymbol{\xi}^*) - \mathcal{D}(\boldsymbol{\alpha}^*) = C \sum_{k=1}^n \xi_k^* - \sum_{k=1}^n \alpha_k^* g_k^* = \sum_{k=1}^n \left(C \xi_k^* - \alpha_k^* g_k^* \right).$$

We can compute the quantity $C \xi_k^* - \alpha_k^* g_k^*$ using (1.14) and (1.13). The relation $C \xi_k^* - \alpha_k^* g_k^* = -y_k \alpha_k^* \rho$ holds regardless of whether g_k^* is less than, equal to, or greater than $y_k \rho$. Therefore

$$\mathcal{P}(\mathbf{w}^*, b^*, \boldsymbol{\xi}^*) - \mathcal{D}(\boldsymbol{\alpha}^*) = -\rho \sum_{i=1}^n y_i \alpha_i^* = 0. \tag{1.15}$$

This strong duality has two implications:

■ Our choice for $(\mathbf{w}^*, b^*, \boldsymbol{\xi}^*)$ minimizes the primal problem because inequality (1.9) states that the primal function $\mathcal{P}(\mathbf{w}, b, \boldsymbol{\xi})$ cannot take values smaller than $\mathcal{D}(\boldsymbol{\alpha}^*) = \mathcal{P}(\mathbf{w}^*, b^*, \boldsymbol{\xi}^*)$.

■ The optimality criteria (1.11—1.13) are in fact *necessary and sufficient*. Assume that one of these criteria holds. Choosing $(\mathbf{w}^*, b^*, \boldsymbol{\xi}^*)$ as shown above yields the strong duality property $\mathcal{P}(\mathbf{w}^*, b^*, \boldsymbol{\xi}^*) = \mathcal{D}(\boldsymbol{\alpha}^*)$. Therefore $\boldsymbol{\alpha}^*$ maximizes the dual because inequality (1.9) states that the dual function $\mathcal{D}(\boldsymbol{\alpha})$ cannot take values greater than $\mathcal{D}(\boldsymbol{\alpha}^*) = \mathcal{P}(\mathbf{w}^*, b^*, \boldsymbol{\xi}^*)$.

The necessary and sufficient criterion (1.11) is particularly useful for SVM solvers (Keerthi et al., 2001).

1.4   Sparsity

The vector $\boldsymbol{\alpha}^*$ solution of the dual problem (1.5) contains many zeros. The SVM discriminant function $\hat{y}(\mathbf{x}) = \sum_i y_i \alpha_i^* K(\mathbf{x}_i, \mathbf{x}) + b^*$ is expressed using a sparse subset of the training examples called the support vectors (SVs).

From the point of view of the algorithm designer, sparsity provides the opportunity to considerably reduce the memory and time requirements of SVM solvers. On the other hand, it is difficult to combine these gains with those brought by algorithms that handle large segments of the kernel matrix at once (chapter 8). Algorithms for sparse kernel machines, such as SVMs, and algorithms for other kernel machines, such as Gaussian processes (chapter 9) or kernel independent component analysis (chapter 10), have evolved differently.

1.4.1   Support Vectors

The optimality criterion (1.13) characterizes which training examples become support vectors. Recalling (1.10) and (1.14),

$$g_k - y_k\rho = 1 - y_k \sum_{i=1}^{n} y_i\alpha_i K_{ik} - y_k b^* = 1 - y_k\,\hat{y}(\mathbf{x}_k). \tag{1.16}$$

Replacing in (1.13) gives

$$\begin{cases} \text{if } y_k\,\hat{y}(\mathbf{x}_k) < 1 & \text{then } \alpha_k = C, \\ \text{if } y_k\,\hat{y}(\mathbf{x}_k) > 1 & \text{then } \alpha_k = 0. \end{cases} \tag{1.17}$$

This result splits the training examples into three categories:[2]

■ Examples $(\mathbf{x}_k, y_k)$ such that $y_k\,\hat{y}(\mathbf{x}_k) > 1$ are not support vectors. They do not appear in the discriminant function because $\alpha_k = 0$.

■ Examples $(\mathbf{x}_k, y_k)$ such that $y_k\,\hat{y}(\mathbf{x}_k) < 1$ are called *bounded support vectors* because they activate the inequality constraint $\alpha_k \leq C$. They appear in the discriminant function with coefficient $\alpha_k = C$.

---

2. Some texts call an example k a *free support vector* when $0 < \alpha_k < C$ and a *bounded support vector* when $\alpha_k = C$. This is *almost* the same thing as the above definition.

- Examples $(\mathbf{x}_k, y_k)$ such that $y_k\, \hat{y}(\mathbf{x}_k) = 1$ are called *free support vectors*. They appear in the discriminant function with a coefficient in range $[0, C]$.

Let $\mathcal{B}$ represent the best error achievable by a linear decision boundary in the chosen feature space for the problem at hand. When the training set size n becomes large, one can expect about $\mathcal{B}n$ misclassified training examples, that is to say $y_k\hat{y} \leq 0$. All these misclassified examples[3] are bounded support vectors. Therefore the number of bounded support vectors scales at least linearly with the number of examples.

When the hyperparameter C follows the right scaling laws, Steinwart (2004) has shown that the total number of support vectors is asymptotically equivalent to $2\mathcal{B}n$. Noisy problems do not lead to very sparse SVMs. Chapter 12 explores ways to improve sparsity in such cases.

1.4.2 Complexity

There are two intuitive lower bounds on the computational cost of any algorithm that solves the SVM problem for arbitrary kernel matrices K_{ij}.

- Suppose that an oracle reveals which examples are not support vectors ($\alpha_i = 0$), and which examples are bounded support vectors ($\alpha_i = C$). The coefficients of the R remaining free support vectors are determined by a system of R linear equations representing the derivatives of the objective function. Their calculation amounts to solving such a system. This typically requires a number of operations proportional to R^3.

- Simply verifying that a vector $\boldsymbol{\alpha}$ is a solution of the SVM problem involves computing the gradient $\mathbf{g}$ of the dual and checking the optimality conditions (1.11). With n examples and S support vectors, this requires a number of operations proportional to $n\,S$.

Few support vectors reach the upper bound C when it gets large. The cost is then dominated by the $R^3 \approx S^3$. Otherwise the term $n\,S$ is usually larger. The final number of support vectors therefore is the critical component of the computational cost of solving the dual problem.

Since the asymptotic number of support vectors grows linearly with the number of examples, the computational cost of solving the SVM problem has both a quadratic and a cubic component. It grows at least like n^2 when C is small and n^3 when C gets large. Empirical evidence shows that modern SVM solvers come close to these scaling laws.

---

3. A sharp-eyed reader might notice that a discriminant function dominated by these $\mathcal{B}n$ misclassified examples would have the wrong polarity. About $\mathcal{B}n$ additional well-classified support vectors are needed to correct the orientation of $\mathbf{w}$.

1.4.3   Computation of the Kernel Values

Although computing the n^2 components of the kernel matrix $K_{ij} = K(\mathbf{x}_i, \mathbf{x}_j)$ seems to be a simple quadratic affair, a more detailed analysis reveals a much more complicated picture.

▪ *Computing kernels is expensive* — Computing each kernel value usually involves the manipulation of sizable chunks of data representing the patterns. Images have thousands of pixels (e.g., Boser et al., 1992). Documents have thousands of words (e.g., Joachims, 1999a). In practice, computing kernel values often accounts for more than half the total computing time.

▪ *Computing the full kernel matrix is wasteful* — The expression of the gradient (1.10) only depend on kernel values K_{ij} that involve at least one support vector (the other kernel values are multiplied by zero). All three optimality criteria (1.11, 1.12, and 1.13) can be verified with these kernel values only. The remaining kernel values have no impact on the solution. To determine which kernel values are actually needed, efficient SVM solvers compute no more than 15% to 50% additional kernel values (Graf, personal communication). The total training time is usually smaller than the time needed to compute the whole kernel matrix. SVM programs that precompute the full kernel matrix are not competitive.

▪ *The kernel matrix does not fit in memory* — When the number of examples grows, the kernel matrix K_{ij} becomes very large and cannot be stored in memory. Kernel values must be computed on the fly or retrieved from a cache of often accessed values. The kernel cache hit rate becomes a major factor of the training time.

These issues only appear as "constant factors" in the asymptotic complexity of solving the SVM problem. But practice is dominated by these constant factors.

1.5   Early SVM Algorithms

The SVM solution is the optimum of a well-defined convex optimization problem. Since this optimum does not depend on the details of its calculation, the choice of a particular optimization algorithm can be made on the sole basis[4] of its computational requirements. High-performance optimization packages, such as MINOS and LOQO (see appendix), can efficiently handle very varied quadratic programming workloads. There are, however, differences between the SVM problem and the usual quadratic programming benchmarks.

▪ Quadratic optimization packages were often designed to take advantage of sparsity in the quadratic part of the objective function. Unfortunately, the SVM kernel matrix is rarely sparse: sparsity occurs in the *solution* of the SVM problem.

---

4. Defining a learning algorithm for a multilayer network is a more difficult exercise.

- The specification of an SVM problem rarely fits in memory. Kernel matrix coefficients must be cached or computed on the fly. As explained in section 1.4.3, vast speedups are achieved by accessing the kernel matrix coefficients carefully.

- Generic optimization packages sometimes make extra work to locate the optimum with high accuracy. As explained in section 1.1.1, the accuracy requirements of a learning problem are unusually low.

Using standard optimization packages for medium-sized SVM problems is not straightforward (section 1.6). In fact, all early SVM results were obtained using adhoc algorithms.

These algorithms borrow two ideas from the optimal hyperplane literature (Vapnik, 1982; Vapnik et al., 1984). The optimization is achieved by performing successive applications of a very simple *direction search*. Meanwhile, *iterative chunking* leverages the sparsity of the solution. We first describe these two ideas and then present the *modified gradient projection* algorithm.

1.5.1   Iterative Chunking

The first challenge was, of course, to solve a quadratic programming problem whose specification does not fit in the memory of a computer. Fortunately, the quadratic programming problem (1.2) has often a sparse solution. If we knew in advance which examples are support vectors, we could solve the problem restricted to the support vectors and verify a posteriori that this solution satisfies the optimality criterion for all examples.

Let us solve problem (1.2) restricted to a small subset of training examples called the *working set*. Because learning algorithms are designed to generalize well, we can hope that the resulting classifier performs honorably on the remaining training examples. Many will readily fulfill the margin condition $y_i \hat{y}(\mathbf{x}_i) \geq 1$. Training examples that violate the margin condition are good support vector candidates. We can add some of them to the working set, solve the quadratic programming problem restricted to the new working set, and repeat the procedure until the margin constraints are satisfied for all examples.

This procedure is not a general-purpose optimization technique. It works efficiently *because* the underlying problem is a learning problem. It reduces the large problem to a sequence of smaller optimization problems.

1.5.2   Direction Search

The optimization of the dual problem is then achieved by performing *direction searches* along well-chosen successive directions.

Assume we are given a starting point $\boldsymbol{\alpha}$ that satisfies the constraints of the quadratic optimization problem (1.5). We say that a direction $\mathbf{u} = (u_1 \ldots u_n)$ is a *feasible direction* if we can slightly move the point $\boldsymbol{\alpha}$ along direction $\mathbf{u}$ without violating the constraints.

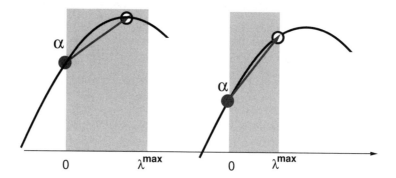

Figure 1.3 Given a starting point $\boldsymbol{\alpha}$ and a feasible direction $\mathbf{u}$, the direction search maximizes the function $f(\lambda) = \mathcal{D}(\boldsymbol{\alpha} + \lambda\mathbf{u})$ for $\lambda \geq 0$ and $\boldsymbol{\alpha} + \lambda\mathbf{u}$ satisfying the constraints of (1.5).

Formally, we consider the set Λ of all coefficients $\lambda \geq 0$ such that the point $\boldsymbol{\alpha} + \lambda\mathbf{u}$ satisfies the constraints. This set always contains 0. We say that u is a feasible direction if Λ is not the singleton $\{0\}$. Because the feasible polytope is convex and bounded (see figure 1.2), the set Λ is a bounded interval of the form $[0, \lambda^{\max}]$.

We seek to maximizes the dual optimization problem (1.5) restricted to the half-line $\{\boldsymbol{\alpha} + \lambda\mathbf{u}, \lambda \in \Lambda\}$. This is expressed by the simple optimization problem

$$\lambda^* = \arg\max_{\lambda \in \Lambda} \mathcal{D}(\boldsymbol{\alpha} + \lambda\mathbf{u}).$$

Figure 1.3 represent values of the $\mathcal{D}(\boldsymbol{\alpha} + \lambda\mathbf{u})$ as a function of λ. The set Λ is materialized by the shaded areas. Since the dual objective function is quadratic, $\mathcal{D}(\boldsymbol{\alpha} + \lambda\mathbf{u})$ is shaped like a parabola. The location of its maximum λ^+ is easily computed using Newton's formula:

$$\lambda^+ = \frac{\left.\frac{\partial \mathcal{D}(\boldsymbol{\alpha}+\lambda\mathbf{u})}{\partial \lambda}\right|_{\lambda=0}}{\left.\frac{\partial^2 \mathcal{D}(\boldsymbol{\alpha}+\lambda\mathbf{u})}{\partial \lambda^2}\right|_{\lambda=0}} = \frac{\mathbf{g}^\top \mathbf{u}}{\mathbf{u}^\top \mathbf{H} \mathbf{u}},$$

where vector $\mathbf{g}$ and matrix $\mathbf{H}$ are the gradient and the Hessian of the dual objective function $\mathcal{D}(\boldsymbol{\alpha})$,

$$g_i = 1 - y_i \sum_j y_j \alpha_j K_{ij} \quad \text{and} \quad H_{ij} = y_i y_j K_{ij}.$$

The solution of our problem is then the projection of the maximum λ^+ into the interval $\Lambda = [0, \lambda^{\max}]$,

$$\lambda^* = \max\left(0, \min\left(\lambda^{\max}, \frac{\mathbf{g}^\top \mathbf{u}}{\mathbf{u}^\top \mathbf{H} \mathbf{u}}\right)\right). \tag{1.18}$$

This formula is the basis for a family of optimization algorithms. Starting from an initial feasible point, each iteration selects a suitable feasible direction and applies the direction search formula (1.18) until reaching the maximum.

1.5.3 Modified Gradient Projection

Several conditions restrict the choice of the successive search directions $\mathbf{u}$.

- The equality constraint (1.5) restricts $\mathbf{u}$ to the linear subspace $\sum_i y_i u_i = 0$.
- The box constraints (1.5) become sign constraints on certain coefficients of $\mathbf{u}$. Coefficient u_i must be non-negative if $\alpha_i = 0$ and non-positive if $\alpha_i = C$.
- The search direction must be an ascent direction to ensure that the search makes progress toward the solution. Direction $\mathbf{u}$ must belong to the half-space $\mathbf{g}^{\top}\mathbf{u} > 0$ where $\mathbf{g}$ is the gradient of the dual objective function.
- Faster convergence rates are achieved when successive search directions are conjugate, that is, $\mathbf{u}^{\top}\mathbf{H}\mathbf{u}' = 0$, where $\mathbf{H}$ is the Hessian and $\mathbf{u}'$ is the last search direction. Similar to the conjugate gradient algorithm (Golub and Van Loan, 1996), this condition is more conveniently expressed as $\mathbf{u}^{\top}(\mathbf{g} - \mathbf{g}') = 0$ where $\mathbf{g}'$ represents the gradient of the dual before the previous search (along direction $\mathbf{u}'$).

Finding a search direction that simultaneously satisfies all these restrictions is far from simple. To work around this difficulty, the optimal hyperplane algorithms of the 1970s (see Vapnik, 1982, addendum I, section 4) exploit a reparametrization of the dual problem that squares the number of variables to optimize. This algorithm (Vapnik et al., 1984) was in fact used by Boser et al. (1992) to obtain the first experimental results for SVMs.

The modified gradient projection technique addresses the direction selection problem more directly. This technique was employed at AT&T Bell Laboratories to obtain most early SVM results (Bottou et al., 1994; Cortes and Vapnik, 1995).

The four conditions on the search direction would be much simpler without the box constraints. It would then be sufficient to project the gradient $\mathbf{g}$ on the linear subspace described by the equality constraint and the conjugation condition. Modified gradient projection recovers this situation by leveraging the chunking procedure. Examples that activate the box constraints are simply evicted from the working set!

Algorithm 1.1 illustrates this procedure. For simplicity we omit the conjugation condition. The gradient $\mathbf{g}$ is simply projected (lines 8–10) on the linear subspace corresponding to the inequality constraint. The resulting search direction $\mathbf{u}$ might drive some coefficients outside the box constraints. When this is the case, we remove these coefficients from the working set (line 11) and return to the projection stage.

Modified gradient projection spends most of the computing time searching for training examples violating the optimality conditions. Modern solvers simplify this step by keeping the gradient vector $\mathbf{g}$ up to date and leveraging the optimality condition (1.11).

Algorithm 1.1 Modified gradient projection

1: $\boldsymbol{\alpha} \leftarrow \mathbf{0}$
2: $\mathcal{B} \leftarrow \emptyset$
3: **while** there are examples violating the optimality condition, **do**
4:      Add some violating examples to working set $\mathcal{B}$.
5:      **loop**
6:          $\forall k \in \mathcal{B} \;\; g_k \leftarrow \partial \mathcal{D}(\boldsymbol{\alpha})/\partial \alpha_k$ using (1.10)
7:          **repeat**   *% Projection–eviction loop*
8:              $\forall k \notin \mathcal{B} \;\; u_k \leftarrow 0$
9:              $\rho \leftarrow \text{mean}\{\, y_k g_k \mid k \in \mathcal{B} \,\}$
10:            $\forall k \in \mathcal{B} \;\; u_k \leftarrow g_k - y_k \rho$ *% Ensure $\sum_i y_i u_i = 0$*
11:              $\mathcal{B} \leftarrow \mathcal{B} \setminus \{\, k \in \mathcal{B} \mid (u_k > 0 \text{ and } \alpha_k = C) \text{ or } (u_k < 0 \text{ and } \alpha_k = 0) \,\}$
12:          **until** $\mathcal{B}$ stops changing
13:          **if** $\mathbf{u} = \mathbf{0}$ **exit loop**
14:          Compute λ^* using (1.18)   *% Direction search*
15:          $\boldsymbol{\alpha} \leftarrow \boldsymbol{\alpha} + \lambda^* \mathbf{u}$
16:      **end loop**
17: **end while**

1.6   The Decomposition Method

Quadratic programming optimization methods achieved considerable progress between the invention of the optimal hyperplanes in the 1960s and the definition of the contemportary SVM in the 1990s. It was widely believed that superior performance could be achieved using state-of-the-art generic quadratic programming solvers such as MINOS or LOQO (see appendix).

Unfortunately the designs of these solvers assume that the full kernel matrix is readily available. As explained in section 1.4.3, computing the full kernel matrix is costly and unneeded. Decomposition methods (Osuna et al., 1997b; Saunders et al., 1998; Joachims, 1999a) were designed to overcome this difficulty. They address the full-scale dual problem (1.5) by solving a sequence of smaller quadratic programming subproblems.

Iterative chunking (section 1.5.1) is a particular case of the decomposition method. Modified gradient projection (section 1.5.3) and shrinking (section 1.7.3) are slightly different because the working set is dynamically modified during the subproblem optimization.

1.6.1   General Decomposition

Instead of updating all the coefficients of vector $\boldsymbol{\alpha}$, each iteration of the decomposition method optimizes a subset of coefficients α_i, $i \in \mathcal{B}$ and leaves the remaining coefficients α_j, $j \notin \mathcal{B}$ unchanged.

Starting from a coefficient vector $\boldsymbol{\alpha}$ we can compute a new coefficient vector $\boldsymbol{\alpha}'$ by adding an additional constraint to the dual problem (1.5) that represents the frozen coefficients:

$$\max_{\boldsymbol{\alpha}'} \; \mathcal{D}(\boldsymbol{\alpha}') = \sum_{i=1}^{n} \alpha'_i - \frac{1}{2} \sum_{i,j=1}^{n} y_i \alpha'_i \, y_j \alpha'_j \, K(\mathbf{x}_i, \mathbf{x}_j)$$

$$\text{subject to} \quad \begin{cases} \forall i \notin \mathcal{B} \quad \alpha'_i = \alpha_i, \\ \forall i \in \mathcal{B} \quad 0 \le \alpha'_i \le C, \\ \sum_i y_i \alpha'_i = 0. \end{cases} \tag{1.19}$$

We can rewrite (1.19) as a quadratic programming problem in variables α_i, $i \in \mathcal{B}$ and remove the additive terms that do not involve the optimization variables $\boldsymbol{\alpha}'$:

$$\max_{\boldsymbol{\alpha}'} \; \sum_{i \in \mathcal{B}} \alpha'_i \left(1 - y_i \sum_{j \notin \mathcal{B}} y_j \alpha_j \, K_{ij} \right) - \frac{1}{2} \sum_{i \in \mathcal{B}} \sum_{j \in \mathcal{B}} y_i \alpha'_i \, y_j \alpha'_j \, K_{ij} \tag{1.20}$$

$$\text{subject to} \quad \forall i \in \mathcal{B} \;\; 0 \le \alpha'_i \le C \;\; \text{and} \;\; \sum_{i \in \mathcal{B}} y_i \alpha'_i = - \sum_{j \notin \mathcal{B}} y_j \alpha_j.$$

Algorithm 1.2 Decomposition method

1: $\forall k \in \{1 \ldots n\} \quad \alpha_k \leftarrow 0$ *% Initial coefficients*
2: $\forall k \in \{1 \ldots n\} \quad g_k \leftarrow 1$ *% Initial gradient*

3: **loop**
4:      $G^{\max} \leftarrow \max_i y_i g_i \;\; \text{subject to} \;\; y_i \alpha_i < B_i$
5:      $G^{\min} \leftarrow \min_j y_j g_j \;\; \text{subject to} \;\; A_j < y_j \alpha_j$
6:      **if** $G^{\max} \le G^{\min}$ **stop.**   *% Optimality criterion (1.11)*

7:      Select a working set $\mathcal{B} \subset \{1 \ldots n\}$ *% See text*

8:      $\boldsymbol{\alpha}' \leftarrow \; \arg\max_{\boldsymbol{\alpha}'} \; \sum_{i \in \mathcal{B}} \alpha'_i \left(1 - y_i \sum_{j \notin \mathcal{B}} y_j \alpha_j \, K_{ij} \right) - \frac{1}{2} \sum_{i \in \mathcal{B}} \sum_{j \in \mathcal{B}} y_i \alpha'_i \, y_j \alpha'_j \, K_{ij}$

   $\text{subject to} \;\; \forall i \in \mathcal{B} \;\; 0 \le \alpha'_i \le C \;\; \text{and} \;\; \sum_{i \in \mathcal{B}} y_i \alpha'_i = - \sum_{j \notin \mathcal{B}} y_j \alpha_j$

9:      $\forall k \in \{1 \ldots n\} \quad g_k \leftarrow g_k - y_k \sum_{i \in \mathcal{B}} y_i (\alpha'_i - \alpha_i) K_{ik}$ *% Update gradient*

10:     $\forall i \in \mathcal{B} \quad \alpha_i \leftarrow \alpha'_i$ *% Update coefficients*
11: **end loop**

Algorithm 1.2 illustrates a typical application of the decomposition method. It stores a coefficient vector $\boldsymbol{\alpha} = (\alpha_1 \ldots \alpha_n)$ and the corresponding gradient vector $\mathbf{g} = (g_1 \ldots g_n)$. This algorithm stops when it achieves[5] the optimality criterion (1.11). Each iteration selects a working set and solves the corresponding subproblem using any suitable optimization algorithm. Then it efficiently updates the gradient by evaluating the difference between the old gradient and the new

---

5. With some predefined accuracy, in practice. See section 1.7.1.

gradient and updates the coefficients. All these operations can be achieved using only the kernel matrix rows whose indices are in $\mathcal{B}$. This careful use of the kernel values saves both time and memory, as explained in section 1.4.3

The definition of (1.19) ensures that $\mathcal{D}(\boldsymbol{\alpha}') \geq \mathcal{D}(\boldsymbol{\alpha})$. The question is then to define a *working set selection scheme* that ensures that the increasing values of the dual reach the maximum.

- Like the modified gradient projection algorithm (section 1.5.3) we can construct the working sets by eliminating coefficients α_i when they hit their lower or upper bound with sufficient strength.

- Joachims (1999a) proposes a systematic approach. Working sets are constructed by selecting a predefined number of coefficients responsible for the most severe violation of the optimality criterion (1.11). Section 1.7.2.2 illustrates this idea in the case of working sets of size two.

Decomposition methods are related to *block coordinate descent* in bound-constrained optimization (Bertsekas, 1995). However the equality constraint $\sum_i y_i \alpha_i = 0$ makes the convergence proofs more delicate. With suitable working set selection schemes, asymptotic convergence results state that any limit point of the infinite sequence generated by the algorithm is an optimal solution (e.g., C.-C. Chang et al., 2000; C.-J. Lin, 2001; Hush and Scovel, 2003; List and Simon, 2004; Palagi and Sciandrone, 2005). Finite termination results state that the algorithm stops with a predefined accuracy after a finite time (e.g., C.-J. Lin, 2002).

1.6.2 Decomposition in Practice

Different optimization algorithms can be used for solving the quadratic programming subproblems (1.20). The Royal Holloway SVM package was designed to compare various subproblem solvers (Saunders et al., 1998). Advanced solvers such as MINOS or LOQO have relatively long setup times. Their higher asymptotic convergence rate is not very useful because a coarse solution is often sufficient for learning applications. Faster results were often achieved using SVQP, a simplified version of the modified gradient projection algorithm (section 1.5.3): the outer loop of algorithm 1.1 was simply replaced by the main loop of algorithm 1.2.

Experiments with various working set sizes also gave surprising results. The best learning times were often achieved using working sets containing very few examples (Joachims, 1999a; Platt, 1999; Collobert, 2004).

1.6.3 Sequential Minimal Optimization

Platt (1999) proposes to always use the smallest possible working set size, that is, two elements. This choice dramatically simplifies the decomposition method.

- Each successive quadratic programming subproblem has two variables. The equality constraint makes this a one-dimensional optimization problem. A single direction search (section 1.5.2) is sufficient to compute the solution.

▪ The computation of the Newton step (1.18) is very fast because the direction **u** contains only two nonzero coefficients.

▪ The asymptotic convergence and finite termination properties of this particular case of the decomposition method are very well understood (e.g., Keerthi and Gilbert, 2002; Takahashi and Nishi, 2005; P.-H. Chen et al., 2006; Hush et al., 2006).

The sequential minimal optimization (SMO) algorithm 1.3 selects working sets using the maximum violating pair scheme. Working set selection schemes are discussed more thoroughly in section 1.7.2. Each subproblem is solved by performing a search along a direction **u** containing only two nonzero coefficients: $u_i = y_i$ and $u_j = -y_j$. The algorithm is otherwise similar to algorithm 1.2. Implementation issues are discussed more thoroughly in section 1.7.

Algorithm 1.3 SMO with maximum violating pair working set selection

1: $\forall k \in \{1 \dots n\}$ $\alpha_k \leftarrow 0$ *% Initial coefficients*
2: $\forall k \in \{1 \dots n\}$ $g_k \leftarrow 1$ *% Initial gradient*

3: **loop**
4:     $i \leftarrow \arg\max_i y_i g_i$ subject to $y_i \alpha_i < B_i$
5:     $j \leftarrow \arg\min_j y_j g_j$ subject to $A_j < y_j \alpha_j$ *% Maximal violating pair*
6:     **if** $y_i g_i \leq y_j g_j$ **stop.**   *% Optimality criterion* (1.11)
7:     $\lambda \leftarrow \min \left\{ B_i - y_i \alpha_i,\ y_j \alpha_j - A_j,\ \dfrac{y_i g_i - y_j g_j}{K_{ii} + K_{jj} - 2K_{ij}} \right\}$ *% Direction search*
8:     $\forall k \in \{1 \dots n\}$ $g_k \leftarrow g_k - \lambda y_k K_{ik} + \lambda y_k K_{jk}$ *% Update gradient*
9:     $\alpha_i \leftarrow \alpha_i + y_i \lambda$ $\alpha_j \leftarrow \alpha_j - y_j \lambda$ *% Update coefficients*
10: **end loop**

The practical efficiency of the SMO algorithm is very compelling. It is easier to program and often runs as fast as careful implementations of the full fledged decomposition method.

SMO prefers sparse search directions over conjugate search directions (section 1.5.3). This choice sometimes penalizes SMO when the soft-margin parameter C is large. Reducing C often corrects the problem with little change in generalization performance. Second-order working set selection (section 1.7.2.3) also helps.

The most intensive part of each iteration of algorithm 1.3 is the update of the gradient on line 8. These operations require the computation of two full rows of the kernel matrix. The *shrinking* technique (Joachims, 1999a) reduces this calculation. This is very similar to the decomposition method (algorithm 1.2) where the working sets are updated on the fly, and where successive subproblems are solved using SMO (algorithm 1.3). See section 1.7.3 for details.

1.7   A Case Study: LIBSVM

This section explains the algorithmic choices and discusses the implementation details of a modern SVM solver. The LIBSVM solver (version 2.82; see appendix) is based on the SMO algorithm, but relies on a more advanced working set selection scheme. After discussing the stopping criteria and the working set selection, we present the shrinking heuristics and their impact on the design of the cache of kernel values.

This section discusses the dual maximization problem

$$\max \ \mathcal{D}(\boldsymbol{\alpha}) = \sum_{i=1}^{n} \alpha_i - \frac{1}{2} \sum_{i,j=1}^{n} y_i\alpha_i \, y_j\alpha_j \, K(\mathbf{x}_i, \mathbf{x}_j)$$

$$\text{subject to} \quad \begin{cases} \forall i \quad 0 \le \alpha_i \le C, \\ \sum_i y_i\alpha_i = 0 \end{cases}$$

Let $\mathbf{g} = (g_1 \ldots g_n)$ be the gradient of the dual objective function,

$$g_i = \frac{\partial \mathcal{D}(\boldsymbol{\alpha})}{\partial \alpha_i} = 1 - y_i \sum_{k=1}^{n} y_k\alpha_k \, K_{ik}.$$

Readers studying the source code should be aware that LIBSVM was in fact written as the minimization of $-\mathcal{D}(\boldsymbol{\alpha})$ instead of the maximization of $\mathcal{D}(\boldsymbol{\alpha})$. The variable `G[i]` in the source code contains $-g_i$ instead of g_i.

1.7.1   Stopping Criterion

The LIBSVM algorithm stops when the optimality criterion (1.11) is reached with a predefined accuracy ϵ,

$$\max_{i \in I_{\text{up}}} y_i g_i - \min_{j \in I_{\text{down}}} y_j g_j < \epsilon, \tag{1.21}$$

where $I_{\text{up}} = \{ i \mid y_i\alpha_i < B_i \}$ and $I_{\text{down}} = \{ j \mid y_j\alpha_j > A_j \}$ as in (1.11).

Theoretical results establish that SMO achieves the stopping criterion (1.21) after a finite time. These finite termination results depend on the chosen working set selection scheme. (See Keerthi and Gilbert, 2002; Takahashi and Nishi, 2005; P.-H. Chen et al., 2006; Bordes et al., 2005, appendix).

Schölkopf and Smola (2002, section 10.1.1) propose an alternate stopping criterion based on the duality gap (1.15). This criterion is more sensitive to the value of C and requires additional computation. On the other hand, Hush et al. (2006) propose a setup with theoretical guarantees on the termination time.

1.7.2 Working Set Selection

There are many ways to select the pair of indices (i, j) representing the working set for each iteration of the SMO algorithm.

Assume a given iteration starts with coefficient vector $\boldsymbol{\alpha}$. Only two coefficients of the solution $\boldsymbol{\alpha}'$ of the SMO subproblem differ from the coefficients of $\boldsymbol{\alpha}$. Therefore $\boldsymbol{\alpha}' = \boldsymbol{\alpha} + \lambda \mathbf{u}$ where the direction $\mathbf{u}$ has only two nonzero coefficients. The equality constraint further implies that $\sum_k y_k u_k = 0$. Therefore it is sufficient to consider directions $\mathbf{u}^{ij} = (u_1^{ij} \ldots u_n^{ij})$ such that

$$
u_k^{ij} = \begin{cases} y_i & \text{if } k = i, \\ -y_j & \text{if } k = j, \\ 0 & \text{otherwise.} \end{cases} \tag{1.22}
$$

The subproblem optimization then requires a single direction search (1.18) along direction $\mathbf{u}^{ij}$ (for positive λ) or direction $-\mathbf{u}^{ij} = \mathbf{u}^{ji}$ (for negative λ). Working set selection for the SMO algorithm then reduces to the selection of a search direction of the form (1.22). Since we need a feasible direction, we can further require that $i \in I_{\text{up}}$ and $j \in I_{\text{down}}$.

1.7.2.1 Maximal Gain Working Set Selection

Let $\mathcal{U} = \{ \mathbf{u}^{ij} \mid i \in I_{\text{up}}, \, j \in I_{\text{down}} \}$ be the set of the potential search directions. The most effective direction for each iteration should be the direction that maximizes the increase of the dual objective function:

$$
\begin{aligned}
\mathbf{u}^* = \underset{\mathbf{u}^{ij} \in \mathcal{U}}{\arg\max} \quad & \underset{0 \leq \lambda}{\max} \; \mathcal{D}(\boldsymbol{\alpha} + \lambda \mathbf{u}^{ij}) - \mathcal{D}(\boldsymbol{\alpha}) \\
\text{subject to} \quad & \begin{cases} y_i \alpha_i + \lambda \leq B_i, \\ y_j \alpha_j - \lambda \geq A_j. \end{cases}
\end{aligned} \tag{1.23}
$$

Unfortunately the search of the best direction $\mathbf{u}^{ij}$ requires iterating over the $n(n-1)$ possible pairs of indices. The maximization of λ then amounts to performing a direction search. These repeated direction searches would virtually access all the kernel matrix during each SMO iteration. This is not acceptable for a fast algorithm.

Although maximal gain working set selection may reduce the number of iterations, it makes each iteration very slow. Practical working set selection schemes need to simplify problem (1.23) in order to achieve a good compromise between the number of iterations and the speed of each iteration.

1.7.2.2   *Maximal Violating Pair Working Set Selection*

The most obvious simplification of (1.23) consists in performing a first-order approximation of the objective function

$$\mathcal{D}(\boldsymbol{\alpha} + \lambda \mathbf{u}^{ij}) - \mathcal{D}(\boldsymbol{\alpha}) \approx \lambda\, \mathbf{g}^{\top} \mathbf{u}^{ij},$$

and, in order to make this approximation valid, to replace the constraints by a constraint that ensures that λ remains very small. This yields problem

$$\mathbf{u}^{*} = \underset{\mathbf{u}^{ij} \in \mathcal{U}}{\arg\max}\ \underset{0 \le \lambda \le \epsilon}{\max}\ \lambda\, \mathbf{g}^{\top} \mathbf{u}^{ij}.$$

We can assume that there is a direction $\mathbf{u} \in \mathcal{U}$ such that $\mathbf{g}^{\top}\mathbf{u} > 0$ because we would otherwise have reached the optimum (see section 1.3.2). Maximizing in λ then yields

$$\mathbf{u}^{*} = \underset{\mathbf{u}^{ij} \in \mathcal{U}}{\arg\max}\ \mathbf{g}^{\top} \mathbf{u}^{ij}. \tag{1.24}$$

This problem was first studied by Joachims (1999a). A first look suggests that we may have to check the $n(n-1)$ possible pairs (i, j). However, we can write

$$\underset{\mathbf{u}^{ij} \in \mathcal{U}}{\max}\ \mathbf{g}^{\top}\mathbf{u}^{ij} = \underset{i \in I_{\mathrm{up}}\ j \in I_{\mathrm{down}}}{\max}\ (y_i g_i - y_j g_j) = \underset{i \in I_{\mathrm{up}}}{\max}\ y_i g_i - \underset{j \in I_{\mathrm{down}}}{\min}\ y_j g_j.$$

We recognize here the usual optimality criterion (1.11). The solution of (1.24) is therefore the *maximal violating pair* (Keerthi et al., 2001)

$$
\begin{aligned}
i &= \underset{k \in I_{\mathrm{up}}}{\arg\max}\ y_k g_k, \\
j &= \underset{k \in I_{\mathrm{down}}}{\arg\min}\ y_k g_k.
\end{aligned} \tag{1.25}
$$

This computation require a time proportional to n. Its results can immediately be reused to check the stopping criterion (1.21). This is illustrated in algorithm 1.3.

1.7.2.3   *Second-Order Working Set Selection*

Computing (1.25) does not require any additional kernel values. However, some kernel values will eventually be needed to perform the SMO iteration (see algorithm 1.3, lines 7 and 8). Therefore we have the opportunity to do better with limited additional costs.

Instead of a linear approximation of (1.23), we can keep the quadratic gain

$$\mathcal{D}(\boldsymbol{\alpha} + \lambda \mathbf{u}^{ij}) - \mathcal{D}(\boldsymbol{\alpha}) = \lambda(y_i g_i - y_j g_j) - \frac{\lambda^2}{2}(K_{ii} + K_{jj} - 2K_{ij})$$

but eliminate the constraints. The optimal λ is then

$$\frac{y_i g_i - y_j g_j}{K_{ii} + K_{jj} - 2K_{ij}},$$

and the corresponding gain is

$$\frac{(y_i g_i - y_j g_j)^2}{2(K_{ii} + K_{jj} - 2K_{ij})} \ .$$

Unfortunately the maximization

$$\mathbf{u}^* = \underset{\mathbf{u}^{ij} \in \mathcal{U}}{\arg \max} \frac{(y_i g_i - y_j g_j)^2}{2(K_{ii} + K_{jj} - 2K_{ij})} \quad \text{subject to} \quad y_i g_i > y_j g_j \tag{1.26}$$

still requires an exhaustive search through the the $n(n-1)$ possible pairs of indices. A viable implementation of the second-order working set selection must heuristically restrict this search.

The LIBSVM solver uses the following procedure (Fan et al., 2005a):

$$
\begin{aligned}
i &= \underset{k \in I_{\text{up}}}{\arg \max} \ y_k g_k \\
j &= \underset{k \in I_{\text{down}}}{\arg \max} \ \frac{(y_i g_i - y_k g_k)^2}{2(K_{ii} + K_{kk} - 2K_{ik})} \quad \text{subject to} \quad y_i g_i > y_k g_k \ .
\end{aligned}
\tag{1.27}
$$

The computation of i is exactly as for the maximal violating pair scheme. The computation of j can be achieved in time proportional to n. It only requires the diagonal of the kernel matrix, which is easily cached, and the ith row of the kernel matrix, which is required anyway to update the gradients (algorithm 1.3, line 8).

We omit the discussion of $K_{ii} + K_{jj} - 2K_{ij} = 0$. See (Fan et al., 2005a) for details and experimental results. The convergence of this working set selection scheme is proved in (P.-H. Chen et al., 2006).

Note that the first-order (1.24) and second-order (1.26) problems are only used for selecting the working set. They do not have to maintain the feasibility constraint of the maximal gain problem (1.23). Of course the feasibility constraints must be taken into account during the computation of $\boldsymbol{\alpha}'$ that is performed after the determination of the working set. Some authors (Lai et al., 2003; Glasmachers and Igel, 2006) maintain the feasibility constraints during the working set selection. This leads to different heuristic compromises.

1.7.3   Shrinking

The *shrinking* technique reduces the size of the problem by temporarily eliminating variables α_i that are unlikely to be selected in the SMO working set because they have reached their lower or upper bound (Joachims, 1999a). The SMO iterations then continue on the remaining variables. Shrinking reduces the number of kernel values needed to update the gradient vector (see algorithm 1.3, line 8). The hit rate of the kernel cache is therefore improved.

For many problems, the number of free support vectors (section 1.4.1) is relatively small. During the iterative process, the solver progressively identifies the partition of the training examples into nonsupport vectors ($\alpha_i = 0$), bounded support vectors ($\alpha_i = C$), and free support vectors. Coefficients associated with nonsupport vectors and bounded support vectors are known with high certainty and are good candidates for shrinking.

Consider the sets[6]

$$J_{\text{up}}(\boldsymbol{\alpha}) = \{\, k \mid y_k g_k > m(\boldsymbol{\alpha}) \,\} \qquad \text{with} \quad m(\boldsymbol{\alpha}) = \max_{i \in I_{\text{up}}}\ y_i g_i, \quad \text{and}$$

$$J_{\text{down}}(\boldsymbol{\alpha}) = \{\, k \mid y_k g_k < M(\boldsymbol{\alpha}) \,\} \quad \text{with} \quad M(\boldsymbol{\alpha}) = \min_{j \in I_{\text{down}}}\ y_j g_j.$$

With these definitions, we have

$$k \in J_{\text{up}}(\boldsymbol{\alpha}) \quad \Longrightarrow \quad k \notin I_{\text{up}} \quad \Longrightarrow \quad \alpha_k = y_k B_k, \quad \text{and}$$
$$k \in J_{\text{down}}(\boldsymbol{\alpha}) \quad \Longrightarrow \quad k \notin I_{\text{down}} \quad \Longrightarrow \quad \alpha_k = y_k A_k.$$

In other words, these sets contain the indices of variables α_k that have reached their lower or upper bound with a sufficiently "strong" derivative, and therefore are likely to stay there.

▪ Let $\boldsymbol{\alpha}^*$ be an arbitrary solution of the dual optimization problem. The quantities $m(\boldsymbol{\alpha}^*)$, $M(\boldsymbol{\alpha}^*)$, and $y_k\, g_k(\boldsymbol{\alpha}^*)$ do not depend on the chosen solution (P.-H. Chen et al., 2006, theorem 4). Therefore the sets $J_{\text{up}}^* = J_{\text{up}}(\boldsymbol{\alpha}^*)$ and $J_{\text{down}}^* = J_{\text{down}}(\boldsymbol{\alpha}^*)$ are also independent of the chosen solution.

▪ There is a finite number of possible sets $J_{\text{up}}(\boldsymbol{\alpha})$ or $J_{\text{down}}(\boldsymbol{\alpha})$. Using the continuity argument of (P.-H. Chen et al., 2006, theorem 6), both sets $J_{\text{up}}(\boldsymbol{\alpha})$ and $J_{\text{down}}(\boldsymbol{\alpha})$ reach and keep their final values J_{up}^* and J_{down}^* after a finite number of SMO iterations.

Therefore the variables α_i, $i \in J_{\text{up}}^* \cup J_{\text{down}}^*$ also reach their final values after a finite number of iterations and can then be safely eliminated from the optimization. In practice, we cannot be certain that $J_{\text{up}}(\boldsymbol{\alpha})$ and $J_{\text{down}}(\boldsymbol{\alpha})$ have reached their final values J_{up}^* and J_{down}^*. We can, however, tentatively eliminate these variables and check later whether we were correct.

▪ The LIBSVM *shrinking* routine is invoked every $\min(n, 1000)$ iterations. It dynamically eliminates the variables α_i whose indices belong to $J_{\text{up}}(\boldsymbol{\alpha}) \cup J_{\text{down}}(\boldsymbol{\alpha})$.

▪ Since this strategy may be too aggressive, *unshrinking* takes place whenever $m(\boldsymbol{\alpha}^k) - M(\boldsymbol{\alpha}^k) < 10\epsilon$, where ϵ is the stopping tolerance (1.21). The whole gradient vector $\mathbf{g}$ is first reconstructed. All variables that do not belong to $J_{\text{up}}(\boldsymbol{\alpha})$ or $J_{\text{down}}(\boldsymbol{\alpha})$ are then reactivated.

The reconstruction of the full gradient $\mathbf{g}$ can be quite expensive. To decrease this cost, LIBSVM maintains an additional vector $\bar{\mathbf{g}} = (\bar{g}_1 \dots \bar{g}_n)$

$$\bar{g}_i \;=\; y_i \sum_{\alpha_k = C} y_k \alpha_k\, K_{ik} \;=\; y_i C \sum_{\alpha_k = C} y_k\, K_{ik}.$$

---

6. In these definitions, J_{up}, J_{down}, and g_k implicitly depend on $\boldsymbol{\alpha}$.

during the SMO iterations. This vector needs to be updated whenever an SMO iteration causes a coefficient α_k to reach or leave the upper bound C. The full gradient vector $\mathbf{g}$ is then reconstructed using the relation

$$g_i = 1 - \bar{g}_i - y_i \sum_{0 < \alpha_k < C} y_k \alpha_k \, K_{ik}.$$

The shrinking operation never eliminates free variables ($0 < \alpha_k < C$). Therefore this gradient reconstruction only needs rows of the kernel matrix that are likely to be present in the kernel cache.

1.7.4   Implementation Issues

Two aspects of the implementation of a robust solver demand particular attention: numerical accuracy and caching.

1.7.4.1   Numerical Accuracy

Numerical accuracy matters because many parts of the algorithm distinguish the variables α_i that have reached their bounds from the other variables. Inexact computations could unexpectedly change this partition of the optimization variables with catastrophic consequences.

Algorithm 1.3 updates the variables α_i without precautions (line 9). The LIBSVM code makes sure, when a direction search hits the box constraints, that at least one of the coefficients α_i or α_j is exactly equal to its bound. No particular attention is then necessary to determine which coefficients of $\boldsymbol{\alpha}$ have reached a bound.

Other solvers use the opposite approach (e.g., SVQP2) and always use a small tolerance to decide whether a variable has reached its lower or upper bound.

1.7.4.2   Data Structure for the Kernel Cache

Each entry i of the LIBSVM kernel cache represents the ith row of the kernel matrix, but stores only the first $l_i \leq n$ row coefficients $K_{i1} \ldots K_{i l_i}$. The variables l_i are dynamically adjusted to reflect the known kernel coefficients.

Shrinking is performed by permuting the examples in order to give the lower indices to the active set. Kernel entries for the active set are then grouped at the beginning of each kernel matrix row. To swap the positions of two examples, one has to swap the corresponding coefficients in vectors $\boldsymbol{\alpha}$, $\mathbf{g}$, $\bar{\mathbf{g}}$ and the corresponding entries in the kernel cache.

When the SMO algorithm needs the first l elements of a particular row i, the LIBSVM caching code retrieves the corresponding cache entry i and the number l_i of cached coefficients. Missing kernel values are recomputed and stored. Finally, a pointer to the stored row is returned.

The LIBSVM caching code also maintains a circular list of recently used rows. Whenever the memory allocated for the cached rows exceeds the predefined maximum, the cached coefficients for the least recently used rows are deallocated.

1.8　Conclusion and Outlook

This chapter has presented the state-of-the-art technique to solve the SVM dual optimization problem with an accuracy that comfortably exceeds the needs of most machine learning applications. Like early SVM solvers, these techniques perform repeated searches along well-chosen feasible directions (section 1.5.2). The choice of search directions must balance several objectives:

- Search directions must be *sparse*: the SMO search directions have only two nonzero coefficients (section 1.6.3).

- Search directions must leverage the *cached kernel values*. The decomposition method (section 1.6) and the shrinking heuristics (section 1.7.3) are means to achieve this objective.

- Search directions must offer good chances to increase the dual objective function (section 1.7.2).

This simple structure provides opportunities for large-scale problems. Search directions are usually selected on the basis of the gradient vector which can be costly to compute. Chapter 13 uses an *approximate* optimization algorithm that partly relies on chance to select the successive search directions (Bordes et al., 2005).

Approximate optimization can yield considerable speedups because there is no point in achieving a small optimization error when the estimation and approximation errors are relatively large. However, the determination of stopping criteria in dual optimization can be very challenging (Tsang et al., 2005; Loosli and Canu, 2006). In chapter 2, the approximate optimization of the primal is claimed to be more efficient. In chapter 11, very direct greedy algorithms are advocated.

Global approaches have been proposed for the approximate representation (Fine and Scheinberg, 2001) or computation (chapter 8) of the kernel matrix. These methods can be very useful for nonsparse kernel machines (chapters 9 and 10). In the case of support vector machines, it remains difficult to achieve the benefits of these methods without partly losing the benefits of sparsity.

This chapter has solely discussed support vector machines with arbitrary kernels. Specific choices of kernels can also lead to dramatic speedups (chapters 7, 3, and 4).

Acknowledgments

Part of this work was funded by NSF grant CCR-0325463. Chih-Jen Lin thanks his students for proofreading the paper.

Appendix

1.A   Online Resources

- LIBSVM (`http://www.csie.ntu.edu.tw/~cjlin/libsvm/`) has been presented in section 1.7. It implements SVM classification, SVM regression, and one-class SVM using both the C-SVM and ν-SVM formulations. It handles multiclass problems using the one-vs.-one heuristic.

- SVM*light* (`http://svmlight.joachims.org`) is a very widely used solver for SVM classification, SVM regression, SVM ranking, and transductive SVM (Joachims, 1999a). It implements algorithms for quickly computing leave-one-out estimates of the generalization error. It offers more options than LIBSVM at the price of some additional complexity.

- SimpleSVM (`http://asi.insa-rouen.fr/~gloosli/simpleSVM.html`) implements the simple SVM algorithm (Vishwanathan et al., 2003) in MATLAB. It offers acceptable performance because it properly caches the kernel values instead of precomputing the full kernel matrix.

- SVQP and SVQP2 (`http://leon.bottou.org/projects/svqp`) are two compact C++ libraries for solving the SVM problem. SVQP2 is a self-contained SMO implementation with state-of-the-art performance. It implements hybrid maximum gain working set selection (Glasmachers and Igel, 2006) and has a mode for solving SVMs without bias. SVQP is a relatively old implementation of the modified gradient projection (section 1.5.3) to be used with the decomposition method.

- Royal Holloway SVM (`http://svm.dcs.rhbnc.ac.uk/dist/index.shtml`) is an older solver based using the decomposition method around the SVQP, MINOS, or LOQO solvers (Saunders et al., 1998).

- MINOS (`http://www.sbsi-sol-optimize.com/asp/sol_products_minos.htm`) is a generic quadratic programming package that was often used by early SVM implementations.

- LOQO (`http://www.princeton.edu/~rvdb/loqo`) is a generic quadratic programming package using advanced interior point and primal-dual optimization methods (Vanderbei, 1999).

The kernel machines (`http://www.kernel-machines.org/software.html`) site lists a large number of software packages for kernel machines. Considerable variability should be expected in the quality of the software packages and the accuracy of the claims.

2   Training a Support Vector Machine in the Primal

Olivier Chapelle

Most literature on support vector machines (SVMs) concentrates on the dual optimization problem. In this chapter, we would like to point out that the primal problem can also be solved efficiently, both for linear and nonlinear SVMs, and that there is no reason to ignore this possibility. On the contrary, from the primal point of view new families of algorithms for large-scale SVM training can be investigated.

2.1   Introduction

The vast majority of textbooks and articles introducing support vector machines (SVMs) first state the primal optimization problem, and then go directly to the dual formulation (Vapnik, 1998; Burges, 1998; Cristianini and Shawe-Taylor, 2000; Schölkopf and Smola, 2002). A reader could easily obtain the impression that this is the only possible way to train an SVM.

In this chapter, we would like to reveal this as being a misconception, and show that someone unaware of duality theory could train an SVM. Primal optimizations of linear SVMs have already been studied by Keerthi and DeCoste (2005) and Mangasarian (2002). One of the main contributions of this chapter is to complement those studies to include the nonlinear case.[1] Our goal is not to claim that the primal optimization is better than the dual, but merely to show that they are *two equivalent ways of reaching the same result*. Also, we will show that when the goal is to find an *approximate* solution, primal optimization is superior.

---

1. Primal optimization of nonlinear SVMs has also been proposed in (Y.-J. Lee and Mangasarian, 2001b, section 4), but with a different regularizer.

Given a training set $\{(\mathbf{x}_i, y_i)\}_{1 \le i \le n}, \mathbf{x}_i \in \mathbb{R}^d, y_i \in \{+1, -1\}$, recall that the primal SVM optimization problem is usually written as

$$\min_{\mathbf{w}, b} \; ||\mathbf{w}||^2 + C \sum_{i=1}^{n} \xi_i^p \quad \text{under constraints} \quad y_i(\mathbf{w} \cdot \mathbf{x}_i + b) \ge 1 - \xi_i, \;\; \xi_i \ge 0, \; (2.1)$$

where p is either 1 (hinge loss) or 2 (quadratic loss). At this point, in the literature there are usually two main reasons mentioned for solving this problem in the dual:

1. The duality theory provides a convenient way to deal with the constraints.

2. The dual optimization problem can be written in terms of dot products, thereby making it possible to use kernel functions.

We will demonstrate in section 2.3 that those two reasons are not a limitation for solving the problem in the primal, mainly by writing the optimization problem as an unconstrained one and by using the representer theorem. In section 2.4, we will see that performing a Newton optimization in the primal yields exactly the same computational complexity as optimizing the dual; that will be validated experimentally in section 2.5. Finally, the possible advantages of a primal optimization are presented in section 2.6. But we will start now with some general discussion about primal and dual optimization.

2.2   Links between Primal and Dual Optimization

As mentioned in the introduction, primal and dual optimization have strong connections and we illustrate some of them through the example of regularized least squares (RLS).

Given a matrix $X \in \mathbb{R}^{n \times d}$ representing the coordinates of n points in d dimensions and a target vector $\mathbf{y} \in \mathbb{R}^n$, the primal RLS problem can be written as

$$\min_{\mathbf{w} \in \mathbb{R}^d} \; \lambda \mathbf{w}^\top \mathbf{w} + ||X\mathbf{w} - \mathbf{y}||^2, \tag{2.2}$$

where λ is the regularization parameter. This objective function is minimized for $\mathbf{w} = (X^\top X + \lambda I)^{-1} X^\top \mathbf{y}$ and its minimum is

$$\mathbf{y}^\top \mathbf{y} - \mathbf{y}^\top X (X^\top X + \lambda I)^{-1} X^\top \mathbf{y}. \tag{2.3}$$

Introducing slack variables $\xi = X\mathbf{w} - \mathbf{y}$, the dual optimization problem is

$$\max_{\boldsymbol{\alpha} \in \mathbb{R}^n} \; 2\boldsymbol{\alpha}^\top \mathbf{y} - \frac{1}{\lambda} \boldsymbol{\alpha}^\top (X X^\top + \lambda I) \boldsymbol{\alpha}. \tag{2.4}$$

The dual is maximized for $\boldsymbol{\alpha} = \lambda (X X^\top + \lambda I)^{-1} \mathbf{y}$ and its maximum is

$$\lambda \mathbf{y}^\top (X X^\top + \lambda I)^{-1} \mathbf{y}. \tag{2.5}$$

The primal solution is then given by the Karush-Kuhn-Tucker (KKT) condition,

$$\mathbf{w} = \frac{1}{\lambda} X^\top \boldsymbol{\alpha}. \tag{2.6}$$

Now we relate the inverses of $XX^\top + \lambda I$ and $X^\top X + \lambda I$ thanks to the *Woodbury formula* (Golub and Van Loan, 1996, p. 51),

$$\lambda (XX^\top + \lambda I)^{-1} = I - X(\lambda I + X^\top X)^{-1} X^\top . \tag{2.7}$$

With this equality, we recover that primal (2.3) and dual (2.5) optimal values are the same, i.e., that the duality gap is zero.

Let us now analyze the computational complexity of primal and dual optimization. The primal requires the computation and inversion of the matrix $(X^\top X + \lambda I)$, which is in $O(nd^2 + d^3)$. On the other hand, the dual deals with the matrix $(XX^\top + \lambda I)$, which requires $O(dn^2 + n^3)$ operations to compute and invert. It is often argued that one should solve either the primal or the dual optimization problem depending on whether n is larger or smaller than d, resulting in an $O(\max(n,d)\min(n,d)^2)$ complexity. But this argument does not really hold because one can always use (2.7) in case the matrix to invert is too big.[2] So both for primal and dual optimization, the complexity is $O(\max(n,d)\min(n,d)^2)$.

The difference between primal and dual optimization comes when computing approximate solutions. Let us optimize both the primal (2.2) and dual (2.4) objective functions by conjugate gradient and see how the primal objective function decreases as a function of the number of conjugate gradient steps. For the dual optimization, an approximate dual solution is converted to an approximate primal one by using the KKT condition (2.6).

Intuitively, the primal optimization should be superior because it directly minimizes the quantity we are interested in. Figure 2.1 confirms this intuition. In some cases, there is no difference between primal and dual optimization (left), but in some other cases, the dual optimization can be slower to converge (right).[3] In the appendix 2.A, we try to analyze this phenomenon by looking at the primal objective value after one conjugate gradient step. We show that the primal optimization always yields a lower value than the dual optimization, and we quantify the difference.

The conclusion from this analysis is that even though primal and dual optimization are equivalent, both in terms of the solution and time complexity, when it comes to *approximate solution, primal optimization is superior* because it is more focused on minimizing what we are interested in: the primal objective function. In

---

2. Note that primal optimization with the Woodbury formula is in general not equivalent to dual optimization (even though they have the same complexity). Indeed, the dual problem involves the conjugate of the loss function. RLS is a special case because $t \to \frac{1}{2}t^2$ is self-conjugate.
3. As discussed above the time complexity is the same for finding the exact solution. But with approximate methods, this is not necessarily the case.

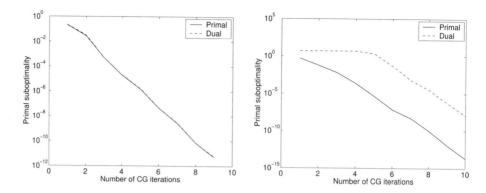

Figure 2.1 Plots of the primal suboptimality, (2.2)-(2.3), for primal and dual optimization by conjugate gradient (**pcg** in **MATLAB**). n points are drawn randomly from a spherical Gaussian distribution in d dimensions. The targets are also randomly generated according to a Gaussian distribution. λ is fixed to 1. *Left*: $n = 10$ and $d = 100$. *Right*: $n = 100$ and $d = 10$.

general, there is indeed no guarantee that an approximate dual solution yields a good approximate primal solution.

2.3 Primal Objective Function

Coming back to SVMs, let us rewrite (2.1) as an unconstrained optimization problem:

$$||\mathbf{w}||^2 + C \sum_{i=1}^{n} L(y_i, \mathbf{w} \cdot \mathbf{x}_i + b), \qquad (2.8)$$

with $L(y, t) = \max(0, 1 - yt)^p$ (see figure 2.2). More generally, L could be any loss function.

Let us now consider nonlinear SVMs with a kernel function k and an associated reproducing kernel Hilbert space $\mathcal{H}$. The optimization problem (2.8) becomes

$$\min_{f \in \mathcal{H}} \lambda ||f||^2_{\mathcal{H}} + \sum_{i=1}^{n} L(y_i, f(\mathbf{x}_i)), \qquad (2.9)$$

where we have made a change of variable by introducing the regularization parameter $\lambda = 1/C$. We have also dropped the offset b for the sake of simplicity. However, all the algebra presented below can be extended easily to take it into account (see appendix 2.B).

Suppose now that the loss function L is differentiable with respect to its second argument. Using the reproducing property $f(\mathbf{x}_i) = \langle f, k(\mathbf{x}_i, \cdot) \rangle_{\mathcal{H}}$, we can differentiate (2.9) with respect to f and at the optimal solution f^*, the gradient vanishes,

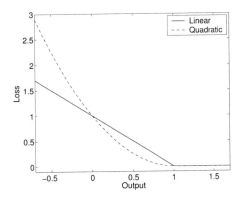

Figure 2.2   SVM loss function, $L(y, t) = \max(0, 1 - yt)^p$ for $p = 1$ and 2.

yielding

$$2\lambda f^* + \sum_{i=1}^{n} \frac{\partial L}{\partial t}(y_i, f^*(\mathbf{x}_i))k(\mathbf{x}_i, \cdot) = 0, \tag{2.10}$$

where $\partial L/\partial t$ is the partial derivative of $L(y, t)$ with respect to its second argument. This implies that the optimal function can be written as a linear combination of kernel functions evaluated at the training samples. This result is also known as the *representer theorem* (Kimeldorf and Wahba, 1970).

Thus, we seek a solution of the form:

$$f(\mathbf{x}) = \sum_{i=1}^{n} \beta_i k(\mathbf{x}_i, \mathbf{x}). \tag{2.11}$$

We denote those coefficients β_i and not α_i as in the standard SVM literature to stress that they should *not* be interpreted as Lagrange multipliers.

Let us express (2.9) in term of β_i,

$$\lambda \sum_{i,j=1}^{n} \beta_i \beta_j k(\mathbf{x}_i, \mathbf{x}_j) + \sum_{i=1}^{n} L\left(y_i, \sum_{j=1}^{n} k(\mathbf{x}_i, \mathbf{x}_j)\beta_j\right), \tag{2.12}$$

where we used the kernel reproducing property in

$$||f||_{\mathcal{H}}^2 = \sum_{i,j=1}^{n} \beta_i \beta_j < k(\mathbf{x}_i, \cdot), k(\mathbf{x}_j, \cdot) >_{\mathcal{H}} = \sum_{i,j=1}^{n} \beta_i \beta_j k(\mathbf{x}_i, \mathbf{x}_j).$$

Introducing the kernel matrix K with $K_{ij} = k(\mathbf{x}_i, \mathbf{x}_j)$ and K_i the ith column of K,

(2.12) can be rewritten as

$$\Omega(\boldsymbol{\beta}) := \lambda \boldsymbol{\beta}^\top K \boldsymbol{\beta} + \sum_{i=1}^{n} L(y_i, K_i^\top \boldsymbol{\beta}). \tag{2.13}$$

As long as L is differentiable, we can optimize (2.13) by gradient descent. Note that this is an unconstrained optimization problem.

2.4   Newton Optimization

The unconstrained objective function (2.13) can be minimized using a variety of optimization techniques such as conjugate gradient. Here we will only consider Newton optimization as the similarities with dual optimization will then appear clearly.

We will focus on two loss functions: the quadratic penalization of the training errors (figure 2.2) and a differentiable approximation to the linear penalization, the Huber loss.

2.4.1   Quadratic Loss

Let us start with the easiest case, the L_2 penalization of the training errors,

$$L(y_i, f(\mathbf{x}_i)) = \max(0, 1 - y_i f(\mathbf{x}_i))^2.$$

For a given value of the vector $\boldsymbol{\beta}$, we say that a point $\mathbf{x}_i$ is a *support vector* if $y_i f(\mathbf{x}_i) < 1$, i.e., if the loss on this point is nonzero. Note that this definition of support vector is different[4] from $\beta_i \neq 0$. Let us reorder the training points such that the first n_{sv} points are support vectors. Finally, let I^0 be the $n \times n$ diagonal matrix with the first n_{sv} entries being 1 and the others 0,

$$I^0 \equiv \begin{pmatrix} 1 & & & & & & & \\ & \ddots & & & 0 & & & \\ & & 1 & & & & & \\ & & & 0 & & & & \\ & 0 & & & \ddots & & \\ & & & & & 0 \end{pmatrix}.$$

---

4. From (2.10), it turns out at the optimal solution that the sets $\{i,\ \beta_i \neq 0\}$ and $\{i,\ y_i f(\mathbf{x}_i) < 1\}$ will be the same. To avoid confusion, we could have defined this latter as the set of *error vectors*.

The gradient of (2.13) with respect to $\boldsymbol{\beta}$ is

$$
\begin{aligned}
\nabla &= 2\lambda K\boldsymbol{\beta} + \sum_{i=1}^{n_{\mathsf{sv}}} K_i \frac{\partial L}{\partial t}(y_i, K_i^\top \boldsymbol{\beta}) \\
&= 2\lambda K\boldsymbol{\beta} + 2\sum_{i=1}^{n_{\mathsf{sv}}} K_i y_i (y_i K_i^\top \boldsymbol{\beta} - 1) \\
&= 2(\lambda K\boldsymbol{\beta} + KI^0(K\boldsymbol{\beta} - Y)),
\end{aligned}
\tag{2.14}
$$

and the Hessian,

$$
H = 2(\lambda K + KI^0 K).
\tag{2.15}
$$

Each Newton step consists of the following update,

$$
\boldsymbol{\beta} \leftarrow \boldsymbol{\beta} - \gamma H^{-1}\nabla,
$$

where γ is the step size found by line search or backtracking (Boyd and Vandenberghe, 2004, section 9.5). In our experiments, we noticed that the default value of $\gamma = 1$ did not result in any convergence problem, and in the rest of this section we only consider this value. However, to enjoy the theoretical properties concerning the convergence of this algorithm, backtracking is necessary.

Combining (2.14) and (2.15) as $\nabla = H\boldsymbol{\beta} - 2KI^0 Y$, we find that after the update,

$$
\begin{aligned}
\boldsymbol{\beta} &= (\lambda K + KI^0 K)^{-1} KI^0 Y \\
&= (\lambda I_n + I^0 K)^{-1} I^0 Y
\end{aligned}
\tag{2.16}
$$

Note that we have assumed that K (and thus the Hessian) is invertible. If K is not invertible, then the expansion is not unique (even though the solution is), and (2.16) will produce one of the possible expansions of the solution. To avoid these problems, let us simply assume that an infinitesimally small ridge has been added to K.

Let I_p denote the identity matrix of size $p \times p$ and K_{sv} the first n_{sv} columns and rows of K, i.e., the submatrix corresponding to the support vectors. Using the fact that the lower left block $\lambda I_n + I^0 K$ is 0, the inverse of this matrix can be easily computed, and finally, the update (2.16) turns out to be

$$
\begin{aligned}
\boldsymbol{\beta} &= \begin{pmatrix} (\lambda I_{n_{\mathsf{sv}}} + K_{\mathsf{sv}})^{-1} & 0 \\ 0 & 0 \end{pmatrix} Y, \\
&= \begin{pmatrix} (\lambda I_{n_{\mathsf{sv}}} + K_{\mathsf{sv}})^{-1} Y_{\mathsf{sv}} \\ 0 \end{pmatrix}.
\end{aligned}
\tag{2.17}
$$

If the current solution is far from the optimal one, the set sv might be large and some computational ressources wasted on trying to invert (2.17). We will present later (algorithm 2.1) a way to avoid this problem.

2.4.1.1   *Link with Dual Optimization*

The update rule (2.17) is not surprising if one has a look at the SVM dual optimization problem:

$$\max_{\boldsymbol{\alpha}} \ \sum_{i=1}^{n} \alpha_i - \frac{1}{2} \sum_{i,j=1}^{n} \alpha_i \alpha_j y_i y_j (K_{ij} + \lambda \delta_{ij}), \quad \text{under constraints } \alpha_i \geq 0.$$

Consider the optimal solution: the gradient with respect to all $\alpha_i > 0$ (the support vectors) must be 0,

$$\mathbf{1} - \text{diag}(Y_{\text{sv}})(K_{\text{sv}} + \lambda I_{n_{\text{sv}}})\text{diag}(Y_{\text{sv}})\boldsymbol{\alpha} = 0,$$

where $\text{diag}(Y)$ stands for the diagonal matrix with the diagonal being the vector Y. Thus, up to a sign difference, the solutions found by minimizing the primal and maximizing the dual are the same: $\beta_i = y_i \alpha_i$.

2.4.1.2   *Complexity Analysis*

Only a couple of iterations are usually necessary to reach the solution (rarely more than five), and this number seems independent of n. The overall complexity is thus the complexity of one Newton step, which is $O(nn_{\text{sv}} + n_{\text{sv}}^3)$. Indeed, the first term corresponds to finding the support vectors (i.e., the points for which $y_i f(\mathbf{x}_i) < 1$) and the second term is the cost of inverting the matrix $K_{\text{sv}} + \lambda I_{n_{\text{sv}}}$. It turns out that this is the same complexity as in standard SVM learning (dual maximization) since those two steps are also necessary. Of course n_{sv} is not known in advance and this complexity analysis is an a posteriori one. In the worse case, the complexity is $O(n^3)$.

It is important to note that in general this time complexity is also a lower bound (for the *exact* computation of the SVM solution). Chunking and decomposition methods, for instance (Joachims, 1999a; Osuna et al., 1997b), do not help since there is fundamentally a linear system of size n_{sv} to be be solved.[5] Chunking is only useful when the K_{sv} matrix cannot fit in memory. Keep in mind that we did not take into account the complexity of computing entries of the kernel matrix: in practice, training time of different SVM solvers can differ significantly based on the kernel cache strategy (see also chapter 1).

---

5. We considered here that solving a linear system (either in the primal or in the dual) takes cubic time. This time complexity can, however, be improved.

2.4.2 Huber/Hinge Loss

The hinge loss used in SVMs is not differentiable. We propose to use a differentiable approximation of it, inspired by the Huber loss (cf. figure 2.3):

$$L(y, t) = \begin{cases} 0 & \text{if } \quad yt > 1 + h, \\ \frac{(1+h-yt)^2}{4h} & \text{if } \quad |1 - yt| \leq h, \\ 1 - yt & \text{if } \quad yt < 1 - h. \end{cases} \tag{2.18}$$

where h is a parameter to choose, typically between 0.01 and 0.5.

Note that we are not minimizing the hinge loss, but *this does not matter*, since, from a machine learning point of view, there is no reason to prefer the hinge loss anyway. If really one wants to approach the hinge loss solution, one can make $h \rightarrow 0$, similarly to (Y.-J. Lee and Mangasarian, 2001b).

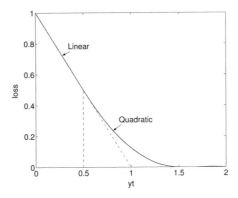

Figure 2.3 The Huber loss is a differentiable approximation of the hinge loss. The plot is (2.18) with $h = 0.5$.

The derivation of the Newton step follows the same line as for the L_2 loss and we will not go into the details. The algebra is just a bit more complicated because there are three different parts in the loss (and thus three different categories of points):

- n_{sv} of them are in the quadratic part of the loss.
- $n_{\bar{sv}}$ are in the linear part of the loss. We will call this category of points the support vectors "at bound," in reference to dual optimization where the Lagrange multipliers associated with those points are at the upper bound C.
- The rest of the points have zero loss.

We reorder the training set in such a way that the points are grouped in the three categories above. As in the previous section, I^0 corresponds to the points in the first category. For the points in the second category, let I^1 be a diagonal matrix with the first n_{sv} 0 elements followed by $n_{\bar{\text{sv}}}$ 1 elements (and 0 for the rest).

The gradient is

$$\nabla = 2\lambda K\beta + \frac{KI^0(K\beta - (1+h)Y)}{2h} - KI^1Y,$$

and the Hessian

$$H = 2\lambda K + \frac{KI^0 K}{2h}.$$

Thus,

$$\nabla = H\beta - K\left(\frac{1+h}{2h}I^0 + I^1\right)Y,$$

and the new β is

$$
\begin{aligned}
\beta &= \left(2\lambda I_n + \frac{I^0 K}{2h}\right)^{-1}\left(\frac{1+h}{2h}I^0 + I^1\right)Y \\
&= \begin{pmatrix} (4h\lambda I_{n_{\text{sv}}} + K_{\text{sv}})^{-1}((1+h)Y_{\text{sv}} - K_{\text{sv},\bar{\text{sv}}}Y_{\bar{\text{sv}}}/(2\lambda)) \\ Y_{\bar{\text{sv}}}/(2\lambda) \\ 0 \end{pmatrix} \equiv \begin{pmatrix} \beta_{\text{sv}} \\ \beta_{\bar{\text{sv}}} \\ 0 \end{pmatrix}.
\end{aligned} \quad (2.19)
$$

Again, one can see the link with the dual optimization: letting $h \to 0$, the primal and the dual solution are the same, $\beta_i = y_i \alpha_i$. This is obvious for the points in the linear part of the loss (with $C = 1/(2\lambda)$). For the points that are right on the margin, their output is equal to their label,

$$K_{\text{sv}}\beta_{\text{sv}} + K_{\text{sv},\bar{\text{sv}}}\beta_{\bar{\text{sv}}} = Y_{\text{sv}}.$$

But since $\beta_{\bar{\text{sv}}} = Y_{\bar{\text{sv}}}/(2\lambda)$,

$$\beta_{\text{sv}} = K_{\text{sv}}^{-1}(Y_{\text{sv}} - K_{\text{sv},\bar{\text{sv}}}Y_{\bar{\text{sv}}}/(2\lambda)),$$

which is the same equation as the first block of (2.19) when $h \to 0$.

2.4.2.1   *Complexity Analysis*

Similar to the quadratic loss, the complexity is $O(n_{\text{sv}}^3 + n(n_{\text{sv}} + n_{\bar{\text{sv}}}))$. The $n_{\text{sv}} + n_{\bar{\text{sv}}}$ factor is the complexity for computing the output of one training point (number of nonzero elements in the vector β). Again, the complexity for dual optimization is the same since both steps (solving a linear system of size n_{sv} and computing the outputs of all the points) are required.

2.4.3   Other Losses

Some other losses have been proposed to approximate the SVM hinge loss (Y.-J. Lee and Mangasarian, 2001b; J. Zhang et al., 2003; J. Zhu and Hastie, 2005). However, none of them has a linear part and the overall complexity is $O(n^3)$ which can be much larger than the complexity of standard SVM training. More generally, the size of the linear system to solve is equal to n_{sv}, the number of training points for which $\frac{\partial^2 L}{\partial t^2}(y_i, f(\mathbf{x}_i)) \neq 0$. If there are some large linear parts in the loss function, this number might be much smaller than n, resulting in significant speedup compared to the standard $O(n^3)$ cost.

2.5 Experiments

The experiments in this section can be considered as a sanity check to show that primal and dual optimization of a nonlinear SVM have similar time complexities. However, for linear SVMs, the primal optimization is definitely superior (Keerthi and DeCoste, 2005) as illustrated below.[6]

Some MATLAB code for the quadratic penalization of the errors and taking into account the bias b is available online at `http://www.kyb.tuebingen.mpg.de/bs/people/chapelle/primal`.

2.5.1 Linear SVM

In the case of quadratic penalization of the training errors, the gradient of the objective function (2.8) is

$$\nabla = 2\mathbf{w} + 2C \sum_{i \in \mathsf{sv}} (\mathbf{w} \cdot \mathbf{x}_i - y_i)\mathbf{x}_i,$$

and the Hessian is

$$H = I_d + C \sum_{i \in \mathsf{sv}} \mathbf{x}_i \mathbf{x}_i^\top.$$

The computation of the Hessian is in $O(d^2 n_{\mathsf{sv}})$ and its inversion in $O(d^3)$. When the number of dimensions is relatively small compared to the number of training samples, it is advantageous to optimize directly on $\mathbf{w}$ rather than on the expansion coefficients. In the case where d is large, but the data is sparse, the Hessian should not be built explicitly. Instead, the linear system $H^{-1}\nabla$ can be solved efficiently by conjugate gradient (Keerthi and DeCoste, 2005).

Training time comparison on the Adult dataset (Platt, 1999) in presented in figure 2.4. As expected, the training time is linear for our primal implementation, but the scaling exponent is 2.2 for the dual implementation of LIBSVM (comparable to the exponent 1.9 reported by Platt (1999)). This exponent can be explained

---

6. For a dual optimizer to be competitive, it needs to make use of the fact that the kernel matrix is low rank. For instance, the Lagrangian SVM (Mangasarian and Musicant, 2001) relies on the Woodbury formula (2.7) to train linear SVMs.

as follows : n_{sv} is very small (Platt, 1999, table 12.3) and $n_{\bar{\mathrm{sv}}}$ grows linearly with n (the misclassified training points). So for this dataset the complexity of $O(n_{\mathrm{sv}}^3 + n(n_{\mathrm{sv}} + n_{\bar{\mathrm{sv}}}))$ turns out to be about $O(n^2)$.

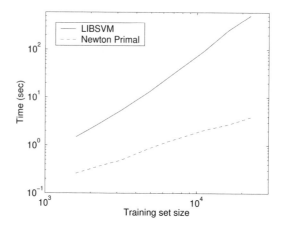

Figure 2.4   Time comparison of the sequential minimal optimization solver LIBSVM with the direct Newton optimization on the normal vector $\mathbf{w}$.

It is noteworthy that, for this experiment, the number of Newton steps required to reach the exact solution was seven. More generally, this algorithm is usually extremely fast for linear SVMs.

2.5.2 L_2 Loss

We now compare primal and dual optimization for nonlinear SVMs. To avoid problems of memory management and kernel caching and to make time comparison as straightforward as possible, we decided to precompute the entire kernel matrix. For this reason, the Adult dataset used in the previous section is not suitable because it would be difficult to fit the kernel matrix in memory (about 8G).

Instead, we used the USPS dataset consisting of 7291 training examples. The problem was made binary by classifying digits 0 to 4 versus 5 to 9. An RBF kernel with bandwidth $\sigma = 8$ was chosen,

$$K(\mathbf{x}_i, \mathbf{x}_j) = \exp\left(-\frac{\|\mathbf{x}_i - \mathbf{x}_j\|^2}{2\sigma^2}\right).$$

We consider in this section the hard-margin SVM by fixing λ to a very small value, namely 10^{-8}.

The training for the primal optimization is performed as follows (see algorithm 2.1): we start from a small number of training samples, train, double the number of samples, retrain, and so on. In this way, the set of support vectors is rather well identified (otherwise, we would have to invert an $n \times n$ matrix in the first Newton step).

Algorithm 2.1 SVM primal training by Newton optimization

Function: $\beta = \text{PRIMALSVM}(K,Y,\lambda)$
  $n \leftarrow \text{length}(Y)$ % *Number of training points*
  if $n > 1000$ **then**
    $n_2 \leftarrow n/2$ % *Train first on a subset to estimate the decision boundary*
    $\beta \leftarrow \text{PRIMALSVM}(K_{1..n_2,1..n_2}, Y_{1..n_2}, \lambda)]$
    sv $\leftarrow$ nonzero components of β
  else
    sv $\leftarrow \{1, \ldots, n\}$.
  end if
  repeat
    $\beta_{\text{sv}} \leftarrow (K_{\text{sv}} + \lambda I_{n_{\text{sv}}})^{-1} Y_{\text{sv}}$
    Other components of $\beta \leftarrow 0$
    sv $\leftarrow$ indices i such that $y_i[K\beta]_i < 1$
  until sv has not changed

The time comparison is plotted in figure 2.5: the running times for primal and dual training are almost the same. Moreover, they are directly proportional to n_{sv}^3, which turns out to be the dominating term in the $O(nn_{\text{sv}} + n_{\text{sv}}^3)$ time complexity. In this problem n_{sv} grows approximately like $\sqrt{n}$. This seems to be in contradiction to the result of Steinwart (2003), which states than the number of support vectors grows linearly with the training set size. However, this result holds only for noisy problems, and the USPS dataset has a very small noise level.

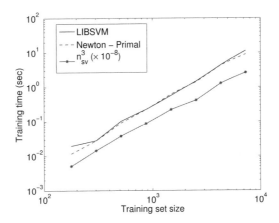

Figure 2.5 With the L_2 penalization of the slacks, the parallel between dual optimization and primal Newton optimization is striking: the training times are almost the same (and scale in $O(n_{\text{sv}}^3)$). Note that both solutions are *exactly the same.*

Even though we ignored the time spent on computing the kernel matrix, it is noteworthy that algorithm 2.1 only needs the compute submatrix K_{ij}, $1 \leq i \leq n$, $i \in$ sv. So the number of kernel evaluations would typically be of the order of nn_{sv}, as for dual methods (see chapter 1). If this matrix does not fit in memory, *shrinking* can be used. But if K_{sv} is also too big, then one has to resort to approximations (see section 2.6).

2.5.3   Huber Loss

We perform the same experiments as in the previous section, but introduce noise in the labels: for a randomly chosen 10% of the points, the labels are flipped. In this kind of situation the L_2 loss is not well suited, because it penalizes the noisy examples too much. However, if the noise were, for instance, Gaussian in the inputs, then the L_2 loss would have been very appropriate.

We will study the time complexity and the test error when we vary the parameter h. Note that the solution will not usually be exactly the same as for a standard hinge loss SVM (it will only be the case in the limit $h \to 0$). The regularization parameter λ was set to 1/8, which corresponds to the best test performance.

In the experiments described below, a line search was performed in order to make Newton converge more quickly. This means that instead of using (2.19) for updating $\boldsymbol{\beta}$, the following step was made,

$$\boldsymbol{\beta} \leftarrow \boldsymbol{\beta} - tH^{-1}\nabla,$$

where $t \in [0,1]$ is found by one-dimensional minimization. This additional line search does not increase the complexity since it is just $O(n)$. Indeed, given the direction $\mathbf{u} = H^{-1}\nabla$, let us the write the objective function (2.13) along this line as

$$g(t) := \Omega(\boldsymbol{\beta} + t\mathbf{u}) = \lambda(\boldsymbol{\beta}^\top K\boldsymbol{\beta} + 2t\mathbf{u}^\top K\boldsymbol{\beta} + t^2\mathbf{u}^\top K\mathbf{u}) + \sum_{i=1}^{n} L(y_i, K_i^\top \boldsymbol{\beta} + tK_i^\top \mathbf{u}).$$

This function g takes $O(n)$ operations to evaluate once $K\boldsymbol{\beta}$ and $K\mathbf{u}$ have been precomputed. Its minimum is easily found after couple of 1D Newton steps. For the L_2 loss described in the previous section, this line search was not necessary and full Newton steps were taken ($t = 1$).

2.5.3.1   *Influence of h*

As expected, the left-hand side of figure 2.6 shows that the test error is relatively unaffected by the value of h, as long as it is not too large. For $h = 1$, the loss looks more like the L_2 loss, which is inappropriate for the kind of noise we generated.

Concerning the time complexity (right-hand side of figure 2.6), there seems to be an optimal range for h. When h is too small, the problem is highly nonquadratic (because most of the loss function is linear), and a lot of Newton steps are necessary.

On the other hand, when h is large, n_{sv} increases, and since the complexity is mainly in $O(n_{sv}^3)$, the training time increases (cf. figure 2.7).

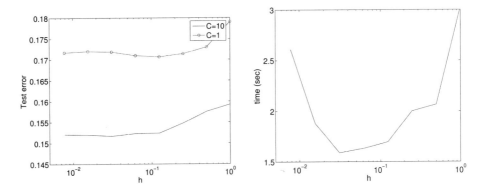

Figure 2.6 Influence of h on the test error and the training time. Left: $n = 500$. Right: $n = 1000$.

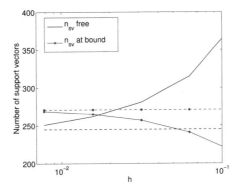

Figure 2.7 When h increases, more points are in the quadratic part of the loss (n_{sv} increases and $n_{\bar{sv}}$ decreases). The dashed lines are the LIBSVM solution. For this plot, $n = 1000$.

2.5.3.2   *Time comparison with LIBSVM*

Figure 2.8 presents a time comparison of both optimization methods for different training set sizes. As for the quadratic loss, the time complexity is $O(n_{sv}^3)$.

However, unlike figure 2.5, the constant for LIBSVM training time is better. This is probably the case because the loss function is far from quadratic and the Newton optimization requires more steps to converge (on the order of 30). But we believe that this factor can be improved on by not inverting the Hessian from scratch in each iteration or by using a more direct optimizer such as conjugate gradient descent.

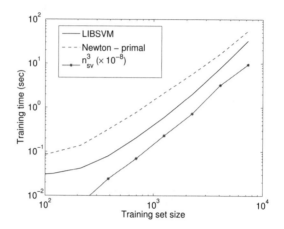

Figure 2.8 Time comparison between LIBSVM and Newton optimization. Here n_{sv} has been computed from LIBSVM (note that the solutions are not exactly the same). For this plot, $h = 2^{-5}$.

2.6   Advantages of Primal Optimization

As explained throughout this chapter, primal and dual optimizations are very similar, and it is not surprising that they lead to the same computational complexity, $O(nn_{sv} + n_{sv}^3)$. So is there any reason to use one rather than the other?

We believe that primal optimization might have advantages for *large-scale optimization*. Indeed, when the number of training points is large, the number of support vectors is also typically large and it becomes intractable to compute the exact solution. For this reason, one has to resort to *approximations* (Bordes et al., 2005; Bakır et al., 2005; Collobert et al., 2002a; Tsang et al., 2005; see also chapters 11 and 13 of this book). But introducing approximations in the dual may not be wise. There is indeed no guarantee that an approximate dual solution yields a good approximate primal solution. Since what we are eventually interested in is a good primal objective function value, it is more straightforward to directly minimize it (cf. the discussion at the end of section 2.2).

Below are some examples of approximation strategies for primal minimization. One can probably come up with many more, but our goal is just to give a flavor of what can be done in the primal.

2.6.1 Conjugate Gradient

One could directly minimize (2.13) by conjugate gradient descent. For squared loss without regularizer, this approach has been investigated in (Ong, 2005). The hope is that on a lot of problems a reasonable solution can be obtained with only a couple of gradient steps.

In the dual, this strategy is hazardous: there is no guarantee that an approximate dual solution corresponds to a reasonable primal solution. We have indeed shown in section 2.2 and appendix 2.A that for a given number of conjugate gradient steps, the primal objective function was lower when optimizing the primal than when optimizing the dual.

However, one needs to keep in mind that the performance of a conjugate gradient optimization strongly depends on the parameterization of the problem. In section 2.2, we have analyzed an optimization in terms of the primal variable $\mathbf{w}$, whereas in the rest of the chapter, we used the reparameterization (2.11) with the vector $\boldsymbol{\beta}$. The convergence rate of conjugate gradient depends on the condition number of the Hessian (Shewchuk, 1994). For an optimization on $\boldsymbol{\beta}$, it is roughly equal to the condition number of K^2 (2.15), while for an optimization on $\mathbf{w}$, this is the condition number of K.

So optimizing on $\boldsymbol{\beta}$ could be much slower. There is fortunately an easy fix to this problem: preconditioning by K. In general, preconditioning by a matrix M requires the ability to compute efficiently $M^{-1}\nabla$, where ∇ is the gradient (Shewchuk, 1994, section B5). But in our case, it turns out that one can factorize K in the expression of the gradient (2.14) and the computation of $K^{-1}\nabla$ becomes trivial. With this preconditioning (which comes at no extra computational cost), the convergence rate is now the same as for the optimization on $\mathbf{w}$. In fact, in the case of RLS of section 2, one can show that the conjugate gradient steps for the optimization on $\mathbf{w}$ and for the optimization on $\boldsymbol{\beta}$ with preconditioning are identical.

Pseudocode for optimizing (2.13) using the Fletcher-Reeves update and this preconditioning is given in algorithm 2.2. Note that in this pseudocode $\mathbf{g}$ is exactly the gradient given in (2.14) but "divided" by K. Finally, we would like to point out that algorithm 2.2 has another interesting interpretation: it is indeed equivalent to performing a conjugate gradient minimization on $\mathbf{w}$ (cf (2.8)), while maintaining the solution in terms of $\boldsymbol{\beta}$, i.e. such that $\mathbf{w} = \sum \beta_i \mathbf{x}_i$. This is possible because at each step of the algorithm, the gradient (with respect to $\mathbf{w}$) is always in the span of the training points. More precisely, we have that the gradient of (2.8) with respect to $\mathbf{w}$ is $\sum (\mathbf{g}_{new})_i \mathbf{x}_i$.

Let us now have an empirical study of the conjugate gradient behavior. As in the previous section, we considered the 7291 training examples of the USPS dataset. We monitored the test error as a function of the number of conjugate gradient iterations. It can be seen in figure 2.9 that

■ A relatively small number of iterations (between 10 and 100) are enough to reach a good solution. Note that the test errors at the right of the figure (corresponding

---

Algorithm 2.2 Optimization of (2.13) (with the L_2 loss) by preconditioned conjugate gradients

---

Let $\beta = 0$ and $\mathbf{d} = \mathbf{g}_{old} = -Y$
repeat
    Let t^* be the minimizer of (2.13) on the line $\beta + t\mathbf{d}$.
    $\beta \leftarrow \beta + t^* \mathbf{d}$.
    Let $\mathbf{o} = K\beta - Y$ and $\mathsf{sv} = \{i, o_i y_i < 1\}$. Update I^0.
    $\mathbf{g}_{new} \leftarrow 2\lambda\beta + I^0 \mathbf{o}$.
    $\mathbf{d} \leftarrow -\mathbf{g}_{new} + \frac{\mathbf{g}_{new}^\top K \mathbf{g}_{new}}{\mathbf{g}_{old}^\top K \mathbf{g}_{old}} \mathbf{d}$.
    $\mathbf{g}_{old} \leftarrow \mathbf{g}_{new}$.
until $\|\mathbf{g}_{new}\| \leq \varepsilon$

---

to 128 iterations) are the same as for a fully trained SVM: the objective values have almost converged at this point.

■ The convergence rate depends, via the condition number, on the bandwidth σ. For $\sigma = 1$, K is very similar to the identity matrix and one step is enough to be close to the optimal solution. However, the test error is not so good for this value of σ and one should set it to 2 or 4.

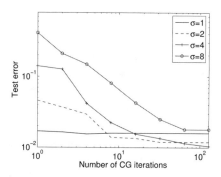

Figure 2.9 Optimization of the objective function (2.13) by conjugate gradient for different values of the kernel width.

It is noteworthy that the preconditioning discussed above is really helpful. For instance, without it, the test error is still 1.84% after 256 iterations with $\sigma = 4$.

Finally, note that each conjugate gradient step requires the computation of $K\beta$ (2.14) which takes $O(n^2)$ operations. If one wants to avoid recomputing the kernel matrix at each step, the memory requirement is also $O(n^2)$. Both time and memory requirements could probably be improved to $O(n_{\mathsf{sv}}^2)$ per conjugate gradient iteration by directly working on the linear system (2.19). But this complexity is probably still too high for large-scale problems. Here are some cases where the matrix vector multiplication can be done more efficiently.

Sparse kernel If a compactly supported radial basis function (RBF) kernel (Schaback, 1995; Fasshauer, 2005) is used, the kernel matrix K is sparse. The time and memory complexities are then proportional to the number of nonzero elements in K. Also, when the bandwidth of the Gaussian RBF kernel is small, the kernel matrix can be well approximated by a sparse matrix.

Low rank Whenever the kernel matrix is (approximately) low rank, one can write $K \approx AA^{\top}$ where $A \in \mathbb{R}^{n \times p}$ can be found through an incomplete Cholesky decomposition in $O(np^2)$ operations. The complexity of each conjugate iteration is then $O(np)$. This idea has been used in (Fine and Scheinberg, 2001) in the context of SVM training, but the authors considered only dual optimization. Note that the kernel matrix is usually low rank when the bandwidth of the Gaussian RBF kernel is large.

Fast multipole methods Generalizing both cases above, fast multipole methods (chapter 8) and KD-trees provide an efficient way of computing the multiplication of an RBF kernel matrix with a vector (Greengard and Rokhlin, 1987; Gray and Moore, 2001; C. Yang et al., 2005; de Freitas et al., 2006; Y. Shen et al., 2006). These methods have been successfully applied to kernel ridge regression and Gaussian processes, but do not seem to be able to handle high dimensional data. See (D. Lang et al., 2005) and chapter 8 for an empirical study of the time and memory requirements for these methods.

2.6.2   Reduced Expansion

Instead of optimizing on a vector $\boldsymbol{\beta}$ of length n, one can choose a small subset of the training points to expand the solution on and optimize only those weights. More precisely, the same objective function (2.9) is considered, but unlike (2.11), it is optimized on the subset of the functions expressed as

$$f(\mathbf{x}) = \sum_{i \in S} \beta_i k(\mathbf{x}_i, \mathbf{x}), \tag{2.20}$$

where S is a subset of the training set. This approach is pursued in chapter 11 where the set S is greedily constructed and in (Y.-J. Lee and Mangasarian, 2001a) where S is selected randomly. If S contains k elements, these methods have a complexity of $O(nk^2)$ and a memory requirement of $O(nk)$.

2.6.3   Model Selection

Another advantage of primal optimization is when some hyperparameters are optimized on the training cost function (Chapelle et al., 2002; Grandvalet and Canu, 2002). If $\boldsymbol{\theta}$ is a set of hyperparameters and $\boldsymbol{\alpha}$ the dual variables, the standard way of learning $\boldsymbol{\theta}$ is to solve a minmax problem (remember that the maximum of the dual is equal to the minimum of the primal):

$$\min_{\theta} \max_{\alpha} \quad \text{Dual}(\alpha, \theta),$$

by alternating between minimization on θ and maximization on α (see for instance Grandvalet and Canu, 2002, for the special case of learning scaling factors). But if the primal is minimized, a *joint optimization* on β and θ can be carried out, which is likely to be much faster.

Finally, to compute an approximate *leave-one-out* error, the matrix $K_{sv} + \lambda I_{n_{sv}}$ needs to be inverted (Chapelle et al., 2002); but after a Newton optimization, this inverse is already available in (2.17).

2.7   Conclusion

In this chapter, we have studied the primal optimization of nonlinear SVMs and derived the update rules for a Newton optimization. From these formulae, it appears clear that there are strong similarities between primal and dual optimization. Also, the corresponding *implementation is very simple* and does not require any optimization libraries.

The historical reasons for which most of the research in the last decade has been about dual optimization are unclear. We believe that it is because SVMs were first introduced in their hard-margin formulation (Boser et al., 1992), for which a dual optimization (because of the constraints) seems more natural. In general, however, soft-margin SVMs should be preferred, even if the training data is separable: the decision boundary is more robust because more training points are taken into account (Chapelle et al., 2000).

We do not pretend that primal optimization is better in general; our main motivation was to point out that primal and dual are two sides of the same coin and that there is no reason to look always at the same side. And by looking at the primal side, some new algorithms for finding approximate solutions emerge naturally. We believe that an approximate primal solution is in general superior to a dual one since an approximate dual solution can yield a primal one which is arbitrarily bad.

In addition to all the possibilities for approximate solutions mentioned in this chapter, the primal optimization also offers the advantage of tuning the hyperparameters simultaneously by performing a conjoint optimization on parameters and hyperparameters.

Acknowledgments

We are grateful to Adam Kowalczyk and Sathiya Keerthi for helpful comments.

Appendix

2.A Primal Suboptimality

Let us define the following quantities,

$$
\begin{aligned}
A &= \mathbf{y}^\top \mathbf{y}, \\
B &= \mathbf{y}^\top X X^\top \mathbf{y}, \\
C &= \mathbf{y}^\top X X^\top X X^\top \mathbf{y}.
\end{aligned}
$$

After one gradient step with exact line search on the primal objective function, we have $\mathbf{w} = \frac{B}{C+\lambda B} X^\top \mathbf{y}$, and the primal value (2.2) is

$$
\frac{1}{2} A - \frac{1}{2} \frac{B^2}{C + \lambda B}.
$$

For the dual optimization, after one gradient step, $\boldsymbol{\alpha} = \frac{\lambda A}{B+\lambda A} \mathbf{y}$ and by (2.6), $\mathbf{w} = \frac{A}{B+\lambda A} X^\top \mathbf{y}$. The primal value is then

$$
\frac{1}{2} A + \frac{1}{2} \left(\frac{A}{B + \lambda A} \right)^2 (C + \lambda B) - \frac{AB}{B + \lambda A}.
$$

The difference between these two quantities is

$$
\frac{1}{2} \left(\frac{A}{B + \lambda A} \right)^2 (C + \lambda B) - \frac{AB}{B + \lambda A} + \frac{1}{2} \frac{B^2}{C + \lambda B} = \frac{1}{2} \frac{(B^2 - AC)^2}{(B + \lambda A)^2 (C + \lambda B)} \geq 0.
$$

This proves that if one does only one gradient step, one should do it on the primal instead of the dual, because one will get a lower primal value this way.

Now note that by the Cauchy-Schwarz inequality $B^2 \leq AC$, and there is equality only if $X X^\top \mathbf{y}$ and $\mathbf{y}$ are aligned. In that case the above expression is zero: the primal and dual steps are as efficient. That is what happens on the left side of figure 2.1: when $n \ll d$, since X has been generated according to a Gaussian distribution, $X X^\top \approx dI$ and the vectors $X X^\top \mathbf{y}$ and $\mathbf{y}$ are almost aligned.

2.B Optimization with an Offset

We now consider a joint optimization on $\begin{pmatrix} b \\ \boldsymbol{\beta} \end{pmatrix}$ of the function

$$
f(\mathbf{x}) = \sum_{i=1}^{n} \beta_i k(\mathbf{x}_i, \mathbf{x}) + b.
$$

The augmented Hessian (cf. (2.15)) is

$$
2 \begin{pmatrix} 1^\top I^0 1 & 1^\top I^0 K \\ K I^0 1 & \lambda K + K I^0 K \end{pmatrix},
$$

where 1 should be understood as a vector of all 1.

This can be decomposed as

$$2 \begin{pmatrix} -\lambda & 1^\top \\ 0 & K \end{pmatrix} \begin{pmatrix} 0 & 1^\top \\ I^0 1 & \lambda I + I^0 K \end{pmatrix}.$$

Now the gradient is

$$\nabla = H\beta - 2 \begin{pmatrix} 1^\top \\ K \end{pmatrix} I^0 Y$$

and the equivalent of the update equation (2.16) is

$$\begin{pmatrix} 0 & 1^\top \\ I^0 1 & \lambda I + I^0 K \end{pmatrix}^{-1} \begin{pmatrix} -\lambda & 1^\top \\ 0 & K \end{pmatrix}^{-1} \begin{pmatrix} 1^\top \\ K \end{pmatrix} I^0 Y$$

$$= \begin{pmatrix} 0 & 1^\top \\ I^0 1 & \lambda I + I^0 K \end{pmatrix}^{-1} \begin{pmatrix} 0 \\ I^0 Y \end{pmatrix}. \quad (2.21)$$

So instead of solving (2.17), one solves

$$\begin{pmatrix} b \\ \beta_{sv} \end{pmatrix} = \begin{pmatrix} 0 & 1^\top \\ 1 & \lambda I_{n_{sv}} + K_{sv} \end{pmatrix}^{-1} \begin{pmatrix} 0 \\ Y_{sv} \end{pmatrix}.$$

3 Fast Kernel Learning with Sparse Inverted Index

Patrick Haffner
Stephan Kanthak

When dealing with very large datasets, a key issue in classification algorithms consists in finding the examples which are critical for defining the separation between the two classes. This information retrieval view of machine learning is exploited in this chapter: we show that an inverted index representation can be used to speedup kernel-based sequential optimization algorithms on sparse data. It is applied to support vector machines (SVM) sequential optimization algorithms (SMO). Instead of dot products over sparse feature vectors, our computation incrementally merges lists of training examples and minimizes access to the data. Caching and shrinking are also optimized for sparsity. On very large natural language tasks (tagging, translation, text classification) with sparse feature representations, a 20- to 80-fold speedup over LIBSVM is observed using the same SMO algorithm. Theory and experiments explain what type of sparsity structure is needed for this approach to work, and why its adaptation to maximum entropy sequential optimization is inefficient.

3.1 Introduction

Kernel-based methods, such as support vector machines (SVMs) (Cortes and Vapnik, 1995; Vapnik, 1998), represent the state of the art in classification techniques. However, their application is limited by the scaling behavior of their training algorithm, which, in most cases, scales quadratically with the number of training examples. This scaling issue may be one of the reasons why other techniques, such as maximum entropy, or maxent (Berger et al., 1996), are often chosen for natural language applications. Maxent learning times usually scale linearly with the number of examples (Haffner, 2005). Their optimization techniques operate in the feature space (also called the primal space) and seem particularly appropriate for sparse data. Recent advances in linear SVM optimization (Joachims, 2006) also provide a linear scaling property for SVMs. However, this chapter focuses on nonlinear SVMs and other kernel-based methods.

In this chapter, data is called *sparse* when the number of active or nonzero features in a training vector is much lower than the total number of features. It is a very common property of language data. For instance, in the bag of n-gram input, features represent the occurrence of a word or token n-gram in a given sentence. In every sentence, only a small portion of the total n-gram vocabulary will be present. This type of input can be used for text classification (Joachims, 1998), machine translation, text annotation and tagging.[1]

Scaling up kernel algorithms (beyond the linear case) has recently been the subject of extensive research with improved algorithms (Fan et al., 2005a), parallelization (Graf et al., 2005), and techniques based on online or active sampling (Bordes et al., 2005). Variations on the perceptron algorithm (Crammer et al., 2004) can also be considered as fast online approximations of SVMs. All these *iterative* algorithms have produced considerable speedups, but none of them reconsider the central computation step, i.e., the computation of kernel products.

In most iterative algorithms, the kernel computation can be folded into a matrix-vector multiplication. This chapter shows that, for a large class of kernels, this multiplication can be optimized for sparse data. The methods presented here can be combined with most other SVM speedups. Usually, the data is represented as a set of examples, where each example is a list of features. The *transpose* representation, known as the *inverse index* in information retrieval, views the data as a set of features, where each feature is a list of examples. Based on this transpose representation, this chapter shows how to speed up the kernel computation in an existing kernel iterative algorithm. Note that the entire kernel learning problem can also be described as a linear system whose optimization can be simplified with matrix approximation. Such global approaches (C. Yang et al., 2005) have been demonstrated on nonsparse low-dimension data.

section 3.2 introduces kernel learning and provides a generic description of the algorithm for matrix-vector multiplication. section 3.3 describes the traditional approaches to this multiplication and introduces new transpose methods. section 3.4 provides a theoretical and experimental complexity analysis. section 3.5 describes in more detail the implementation in the case of SVMs. section 3.7 outlines large-scale experiments on text and language learning problems: natural language understanding, tagging, and machine translation.

---

1. MALLET, `http://mallet.cs.umass.edu`.

3.2 Sequential Kernel Learning

Machine learning algorithms often consist of sequential procedures where a new example is added and the score of all training examples is modified accordingly. In particular, kernel-based algorithms rely on the computation of kernels between pairs of examples to solve classification or clustering problems. Most of them require an iterative learning procedure. The most common of these procedures is the sequential minimal optimization (SMO, see chapter 1 for a review) used for SVMs, but many other procedures are possible (for instance, the perceptron algorithm).

The kernel classifier is represented as a list of support vectors $\mathbf{x}_k$ and their respective multipliers α_k (in the classification case, the label $y_k \in \{-1, 1\}$ gives the sign of α_k). The classifier score for vector $\mathbf{x}$ is $f(\mathbf{x}) = \sum_k \alpha_k K(\mathbf{x}, \mathbf{x}_k)$. Each iteration consists of addition or modification of one (perceptron), two (SMO), or more (other SVM algorithms) support vectors. At each iteration, we want to find the best candidate support vector to add or update. For that purpose, we need to keep an update of the scores of all training examples or a large subset of these training examples (called the active set). When adding factor $\delta\alpha_k$ to the multiplier α_k of support vector $\mathbf{x}_k$, these scores must be incremented as follows:

$$\forall i; f(\mathbf{x}_i) = f(\mathbf{x}_i) + \delta\alpha_k K(\mathbf{x}_i, \mathbf{x}_k) \tag{3.1}$$

For each modification of a support vector multiplier, the main required computation is the kernels $K(\mathbf{x}, \mathbf{x}_k)$ between the support vector $\mathbf{x}_k$ and each vector of the active set.

Given the algorithm, one usually attempts to optimize the computation of each kernel individually. In the case of sparse data, this has led to a considerable amount of work. When the kernel relies on a simple dot product over finite dimension vectors, an efficient solution is well-known (Platt, 1999). But sparse data can also come from complex structures, and kernels have also been proposed for such structures, for instance, strings (Lodhi et al., 2002) and more generally finite-state automata (Cortes et al., 2004).

This focus on the optimization of a single kernel does not take into account the fact that an entire line of kernels must be computed at the same time. However, in the case of very sparse data, this suggest a very different speedup strategy. Take a sequential optimization algorithm which adds a single training vector to the set of support vectors: one must look for the vectors in the training set whose score needs to be updated after this addition. Only vectors which share features with the added support vector need to have their score updated, and their proportion can be small if the data is extremely sparse.

This suggests that, in this case, the most time-consuming part of the learning process amounts to retrieving the small proportion of training vectors which have features in common with the added support vector, and, as in information retrieval, the concept of inverted index can be useful.

For instance, suppose that our new support vector corresponds to the sentence

Table 3.1 Notation and Matrix-SVM correspondences

Symbol	Type	Matrix	SVM training
N_r	Number	rows	train samples
N_c	Number	columns	total features
$\mathbf{x}$	Vector	multiplicand	input
$\mathbf{y}$	Vector	product	dot product

"I want to check my bill," and that we reduced it to a vector with three active features ("want," "check," "bill"), ignoring function words such as "I," "to," and "my". The inverted index approach would retrieve the list of vectors including these three words and merge them. Thus, rather than computing the kernels with every possible example, one would rather focus on examples which contain "want," "check," and "bill."

To formalize this intuition, it is convenient to define a matrix multiplication framework, which is presented in the rest of this section.

The kernel can often be expressed as a function of the dot product $K(\mathbf{x}_1, \mathbf{x}_2) = \phi(\langle \mathbf{x}_1, \mathbf{x}_2 \rangle)$. This includes most major vector kernels (Vapnik, 1998): polynomial, Gaussian, and sigmoid kernels. For instance, in the polynomial case, $\phi(t) = (at+b)^p$. The Gaussian kernel can be written as

$$K(\mathbf{x}_1, \mathbf{x}_2) = \exp -\frac{1}{\sigma^2}(\|\mathbf{x}_1\| + \|\mathbf{x}_2\| - 2\langle \mathbf{x}_1, \mathbf{x}_2 \rangle), \tag{3.2}$$

where the norms $\|\mathbf{x}_1\|$ and $\|\mathbf{x}_2\|$ are computed in advance. This dot product computation cannot be used on nonvectorial data, for instance, in the case of kernels for sequential or graph data (Cortes et al., 2004). An example of a vectorial kernel not reducible to a dot product is the Laplacian kernel.

In summary, for a large class of vectorial kernels, one must compute, for each vector $\mathbf{x}_i$ in the active set, the dot product $y_i = \langle \mathbf{x}_i, \mathbf{x}_k \rangle$. By defining the matrix $\mathbf{M}$ with rows $\mathbf{M}_i = \mathbf{x}_i$, we obtain the matrix-vector multiplication $\mathbf{y} = \mathbf{M}\mathbf{x}_k$. As described in table 3.1, the notation in the rest of the chapter has both a "matrix multiplication" and "SVM training" interpretation and departs from the traditional SVM notation.

3.3   Sparse Matrix-Vector Multiplication

Sparse matrix-vector multiplication algorithms are well studied (Toledo, 1997; Im, 2000) and the choice of algorithm depends on the type of sparsity found in the matrix or in the vector and on the type of targeted processor or parallelization. Efficient algorithms have been described for sparse matrices with dense contiguous sub-blocks and in most cases the vector is assumed to be dense. We found this

---

Algorithm 3.1 Sparse matrix-vector multiplication

```
sMxV(M, x)
    for (i=0; i<Nr; i++) do
        y[i] = DOT(M[i], x);
return y

DOT(v1, v2)
    dot = 0;
    for (j=0; j<|v1|; j++) do
        dot += v1[j].val * v2[v1[j].idx];
        DOT_ACCESS++;
        DOT_MULADD++;
return dot
```

---

literature of little help for our problem, where no block pattern can be found, where the vector itself is very sparse, and where we do not want to tune the algorithm to a specific hardware platform. This section is organized as follows. Subsection 3.3.1 describes, using our notation, the technique most commonly used in sparse kernel learning. Then subsections 3.3.2 and 3.3.3 show how the use of the inverted index results in a new set of algorithms. Finally, subsection 3.3.4 offers comparisons with previous work for other applications than kernel learning.

3.3.1 Sequence of Dot Products

As described in the previous section, the typical implementation of the sparse matrix-vector multiplication can be described as a sequence of dot products between each row of the matrix $\mathbf{v_1} = \mathbf{M}_i$ and the vector $\mathbf{v_2} = \mathbf{x}$, so that $y_i = \langle \mathbf{M}_i, \mathbf{x} \rangle$. This implementation is shown in algorithm 3.1. $\mathbf{v_1}$ is encoded as a sorted table of index-value pairs, where only the indices of the nonzero components are kept. $|\mathbf{v_1}|$ is the number of nonzero components in $\mathbf{v_1}$, i.e., the size of $\mathbf{v_1}$ encoded as a table of index-value pairs. The number of operations for DOT is $|\mathbf{v_1}|$, and the total complexity for the matrix $\mathbf{M}$ is $\sum_i |\mathbf{M}_i|$. The main drawback is that a potentially very large dense vector $\mathbf{x}$ must be loaded in the processor cache and must remain there for the whole sequence of dot products.

In the case of sparse implementations for support vectors (Platt, 1999; Joachims, 1999a), a fully sparse algorithm is preferred. The dot product DOT is replaced with SDOT, as shown in algorithm 3.2. This algorithm relies on the fact that $\mathbf{v_1}$ and $\mathbf{v_2}$ are both sparse.

To measure complexity, we introduce the counters SDOT_ACCESS, which counts how many times indices are accessed, and SDOT_MULADD, which counts how many times values are multiplied and added to the product. In this algorithm, we must make the distinction between memory access and multiply-add operations, as they are counted differently. Performance analysis using callgrind (a profiler plug-in for the valgrind debugging suite) on a Linux platform shows that

- the most costly operation is memory access;

Algorithm 3.2 Sparse-sparse dot product

```
SDOT(v1, v2)
    dot = 0, j1 = 0, j2 = 0;
    while (j1 < |v1| and j2 < |v2|) do
        idx1 = v1[j1].idx;
        idx2 = v2[j2].idx;
        SDOT_ACCESS++;
        if (idx1 == idx2) then
            dot += v1[j1].val * v2[j2].val;
            j1++, j2++;
            SDOT_MULADD++;
        else if (j1 > j2) then
            j2++;
        else
            j1++;

return dot
```

- after accessing the index slot of an index-value pair, the cost of accessing the value slot is negligible;

- the actual cost of the multiply-add is low, as it can be pipelined after the memory access.

In the DOT algorithm, the multiply-add operation also requires accessing the v1 and v2 tables. In contrast, the multiply-add in the SDOT algorithm does not require any memory access, as the values are already in the processor cache because of the previous access to the indices.

To simplify our analysis, we consider memory access operations as our main performance determiner, and systematically track them. It shall be noted that the type of memory access operations which DOT_ACCESS and SDOT_ACCESS count are not exactly the same. Because of the influence of the processor architecture, no detailed analysis will be provided, and we will assume that their complexity is comparable. In this example, SDOT requires more memory access than DOT.

The problem with computations in DOT and SDOT is that they are performed even when the vectors do not overlap and the resulting product turns out to be zero. Looking at figure 3.1, the DOT and SDOT algorithms need to access the features values represented by every circle.

3.3.2   Using the Inverted Index

The inverted index, or *transpose*, approach to matrix-vector multiplication is the following. Figure 3.1 shows that only the columns of the matrix that correspond to components that are nonzero in $\mathbf{x}$ contribute to the result $\mathbf{y}$ and suggests an algorithm whose complexity would be a function of $|\mathbf{x}|$. A transpose representation of the matrix, where columns are accessed first, is required.

Instead of going through each row $\mathbf{M}_i$, the procedure goes through each column $\mathbf{M}_{.,j}$. Instead of computing each component of $\mathbf{y} = \mathbf{M}\mathbf{x}$ separately, successive

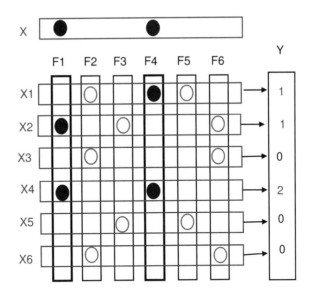

Figure 3.1 *Visual description of the matrix-vector multiplication.* The matrix has are six rows corresponding to vectors {X1,...,X6} and six columns corresponding to features {F1,...,F6}. Nonzero elements have value 1 and are represented by a circle. The result Y of the multiplication appears in the right column, where each element is a dot product that counts the number of circles shared by X and Xi. Both the `DOT` and `SDOT` dot products need to access every nonzero feature in each vector, even when this feature is not used by the other vector and when the product of the two features is zero. The transpose approach only considers columns F1 and F4: the six dot products in column Y are obtained by merging the lists represented by columns F1 and F4. The total number of operations is only proportional to the number of (full) circles in these columns. Compare this with the traditional dot product algorithm that has to access every single circle. Note that while `SDOT` will not apply multiply-add to white circles, an access operation is still needed.

refinements of **y** are computed iteratively over the columns of **M** that correspond to nonzero values of **x** (see algorithm 3.3).

The transpose sparse matrix-vector multiplication algorithm critically relies on function `TADD` that performs a componentwise addition between $\mathbf{v_1} = \mathbf{y}$ and $\mathbf{v_2} = \mathbf{M}_{.,j}$ weighted by $w = x_j$.

All the algorithms presented so far produce a dense **y** vector as a result. As we will see in section 3.5.1, a table of index-value pairs would be much more efficient for further processing. To obtain this table, the transformation shown in figure 3.2 and described in algorithm 3.4 is required. This apparently simple `VEC2LIST` operation is much more expensive than it looks. The critical operation is simply to access each **y** element, and must be performed N_r times.

Another price to pay with dense **y** vectors is that they do not always hold in the processor cache. In the case of SVMs, the size of the **y** vector corresponds to the number of training examples. 500,000 examples would require a vector of 2MB

Algorithm 3.3 Transpose matrix-vector multiplication

```
TsMxV(M, x)
 | y = 0;
 | for (i=0; i<|x|; i++) do
 |  └ y = TADD(y, M[.][x[i].idx], x[i].val);
 return y

TADD(v1, v2, w)
 | for (j=0; j<|v2|; j++) do
 |  | v1[v2[j].idx] += w * v2[j].val;
 |  | TADD_ACCESS++;
 |  └ TADD_MULADD++;
 return v1
```

Algorithm 3.4 Dense vector to index-value table

```
VEC2LIST(y)
 | y' = 0;
 | pos = 0;
 | for (i=0; i<N_r; i++) do
 |  | VEC2LIST_ACCESS++;
 |  | if (y[i] != 0) then
 |  |  | y'[pos].idx = i;
 |  |  | y'[pos].val = y[i];
 |  └  └ pos++;
 return y'
```

(using 4 byte floats) which do not fit in the secondary cache of current processors.

3.3.3   List-Merging Algorithms

In order to avoid any transformation from dense vectors to index-value tables, the TADD function is modified to exploit sparsity by also encoding the **y** vector as an index-value table. Initially, **y**′ is an empty list, and an incremental process merges **y**′ with the list $\mathbf{M}_{.,j}$. In this case, TMRG becomes the merging of two sorted lists with addition of the values when the same index is found in both lists (see algorithm 3.5). TMRG has the same number of MULADD operations as TADD but also requires COPY operations, which can be costly. The counter TMRG_ACCESS=TMRG_MULADD+TMRG_COPY accounts for memory access to the lists v1, v2, and y'.

Looking at this code, one could think that a function TMRG($\mathbf{v_1}, \mathbf{v_2}$) that modifies $\mathbf{v_1}$ in-place would save the TMRG_COPY operations and be more efficient. Our simulations show that this is not the case, as $\mathbf{v_1}$ would have to be a list object supporting INSERT and REMOVE operations. The added complexity from these operations offsets the gains from the in-place TMRG. Here is an important caveat: $|\mathbf{y}'(i)|$ can grow quite large, especially if some feature j is shared by many examples, and $|\mathbf{M}_{.,j}|$ grows as large as the number of examples. It is important to sort the matrix columns so that the ones with small $|\mathbf{M}_{.,j}|$ are added first to prevent $|\mathbf{y}'(i)|$ from growing very large immediately.

Algorithm 3.5 Sparse list-merging algorithm

```
TMRG(v1, v2, w)
    j1 = 0, j2 = 0, j = 0;
    y' = 0;
    while (j1 < |v1| and j2 < |v2|) do
        idx1 = v1[j1].idx;
        idx2 = v2[j2].idx;
        TMRG_ACCESS++;
        if (idx1 == idx2) then
            y'[j].val = v1[j1].val + w * v2[j2].val;
            y'[j].idx = idx1;
            j++, j1++, j2++;
            TMRG_MULADD++;
        else if (j1 > j2) then
            y'[j].val = w * v2[j2].val;
            y'[j].idx = idx2;
            j++, j2++;
            TMRG_MULADD++;
        else
            y'[j].val = v1[j1].val;
            y'[j].idx = idx1;
            j++, j1++;
            TMRG_COPY++;
    return y'
```

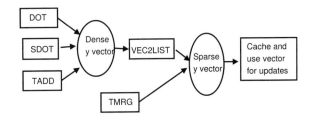

Figure 3.2 Possible sequences of algorithms to obtain a sparse kernel line that will be used by the caching algorithm (section 3.5.1).

A drawback of the transpose algorithms applied to SVM training is that they require a double storage of the training data matrix. The original matrix is required to fetch the support vector to be added ($\mathbf{x}$), and the transpose matrix stores the inverted indices $\mathbf{M}_{.,j}$. This adds complexity to the code, and increases the memory requirements. In practice, this increased memory is negligible compared to the memory required for the kernel cache.

Figure 3.2 summarizes our choice of algorithms, and how they depend on each other.

3.3.4   Previous Work

The TADD and TMRG algorithms are well-known, and the TADD algorithm has been applied to kernel classifier testing (the PKI algorithm in (Kudo and Matsumoto,

Table 3.2 Average case estimates of the profiling counters introduced in Algorithms 3.1, 3.2, 3.3 and 3.5. They are reported as a fraction of their maximum value, which is the number of elements in the dense matrix $N_c N_r$. They are a function of the sparsity ration α. Simplifications are made with the assumption that $\frac{1}{N_c} \ll \alpha \ll 1$. The number of columns in $\mathbf{M}$ is denoted N_c, and when $\mathbf{x}$ is dense, $|\mathbf{x}| = N_c$.

	Dense $\mathbf{x}$ Dense $\mathbf{M}$	Dense $\mathbf{x}$ Sparse $\mathbf{M}$	Sparse $\mathbf{x}$ Sparse $\mathbf{M}$
DOT_ACCESS	1	α	α
DOT_MULADD	1	α	α
SDOT_ACCESS	1	1	2α
SDOT_MULADD	1	α	α^2
TADD_ACCESS	1	α	α^2
TADD_MULADD	1	α	α^2
TMRG_ACCESS	1	1	$\frac{1}{2}\alpha^3 N_c$
TMRG_MULADD	1	α	α^2
TMRG_COPY	0	1	$\frac{1}{2}\alpha^3 N_c$
VEC2LIST_ACCESS	$1/N_c$	$1/N_c$	$1/N_c$

2003)). However, to our knowledge, they have never been applied to kernel training. The inverted index is mostly used in information retrieval. While sparse matrix multiplication has also been studied for information retrieval (Goharian et al., 2000), the main goal was to use existing multiplication algorithms (SDOT in this chapter), and it does not seem to rely on the inverse index. A matrix multiplication algorithm applied to the transpose "sparse column" representation is described in (Goharian et al., 2003), but found to be slower as it does not exploit the sparsity of the query vector.

3.4 Complexity Analysis

This section attempts to predict the complexity of the algorithms based on sparsity hypotheses on $\mathbf{M}$ and $\mathbf{x}$, followed by experiments on the SVM and maximum entropy training problems.

3.4.1 Statistical Predictions

Table 3.2 compares all algorithms on various configurations, where $\mathbf{M}$ or $\mathbf{x}$ is sparse. Sparsity is measured with a ratio α, which is the proportion of nonzero elements in a matrix with N_c columns and N_r rows. α is much smaller than 1, but bounded by the assumption that the average number of features per example, which is αN_c, is much larger than 1. The predicted *complexity ratio* is the fraction of the maximum number of operations $N_c N_r$ actually performed. They are obtained from simple common sense reasoning, except the TMRG_COPY line, which requires theorems 3.2 and 3.3. TMRG_ACCESS is the approximate sum of TMRG_MULADD and TMRG_COPY.

When both $\mathbf{M}$ and $\mathbf{x}$ are dense, it is trivial to verify that all four algorithms DOT, SDOT, TADD, and TMRG require exactly one MULADD and ACCESS operation for each element of the matrix and have a complexity ratio of 1.

When $\mathbf{x}$ is dense and $\mathbf{M}$ is sparse, we observe that DOT or TADD can have a much better behavior with a number of MULADD and ACCESS operations equal to $\alpha N_r N_c$. In this case, as no nonzero values are skipped, the number of MULADD is exactly the number of nonzero components in the matrix. The complexity of both SDOT and TMRG is $O(N_r N_c)$, due to SDOT_ACCESS and TMRG_COPY operations. This observation (confirmed by experiments in table 3.4) suggests that the scope of this study is limited to sparse $\mathbf{x}$ vectors.

When both $\mathbf{x}$ and $\mathbf{M}$ are sparse, transpose algorithms, which use the sparsity of $\mathbf{x}$, are clear winners, with an overall complexity ratio which is always significantly lower than α.

A more detailed analysis of the TADD and TMRG algorithms is required here. First, both TADD and TMRG require exactly the same number $\alpha^2 N_r N_c$ of MULADD operations, that is the product between the number αN_c of nonzero elements in $\mathbf{x}$ and the average number of nonzero elements in a column, which is αN_r. However, this α^2 complexity ratio is usually negligible compared to other operations required by the two algorithms.

- In the case of TADD, we need to mention the cost of the VEC2LIST transformation, which is required for the DOT, SDOT, and TADD algorithms, but only becomes critical for the TADD algorithm. The N_r VEC2LIST_ACCESS operations yield a factor of $\frac{1}{N_c}$ after division by $N_c N_r$. As one can assume that the average number of features per example, αN_c, is significantly larger than 1, we have $\frac{1}{N_c} \ll \alpha$ and therefore TADD is significantly faster than DOT and SDOT.

- TMRG mostly requires ACCESS operations, which lead to either MULADD and COPY operations. TMRG_COPY is very complex to track. The average case predictions reported in table 3.2 are obtained in section 3.4.2. As they are based on the assumption that $\alpha N_c \gg 1$, we have TMRG_COPY $\gg$ TMRG_MULADD and TMRG_MULADD $\approx$ TMRG_COPY. If we assume that $\alpha^3 N_c \ll \alpha$, TMRG is significantly faster than DOT and SDOT.

The interesting question is how TADD and TMRG compare to each other, which mainly reduces to a comparison between VEC2LIST_ACCESS $= \frac{1}{N_c}$ and TMRG_ACCESS $= \frac{1}{2}\alpha^3 N_c$. If we introduce the critical factor

$$\rho = \frac{1}{2}\alpha^3 N_c^2, \tag{3.3}$$

one should prefer TADD is $\rho > \rho_0$ and TMRG otherwise. The threshold ρ_0 is the ratio between the cost of a single VEC2LIST_ACCESS and the cost of a single TMRG_ACCESS. From the following observations, we estimate that $\frac{1}{4} \le \rho_0 \le \frac{1}{2}$:

- VEC2LIST_ACCESS requires a single read-access operation.

- `TMRG_ACCESS` requires one to two read-access operations, and one write-access operation. This write-access operation is actually performed after `TMRG_MULADD` and `TMRG_COPY`, but its total count is exactly the same as `TMRG_ACCESS`.[2]

From an SVM training viewpoint, this represents the following trade off:

- Higher sparsity (and lower α) promotes `TMRG`.
- A large number N_c of features can significantly slow down `TMRG`, as it implies a lot of list merging, and an increasingly large number of `TMRG_COPY` operations

This theoretical study will verify remarkably well on our experiments in table 3.5.

Note we rely on the fact that the proportion of nonzero components is the same for each column, that is, the number of examples containing a given feature is the same. In case of a nonuniform distribution, one should sort the columns according to the increasing proportion of nonzero components. Therefore, the growth of the accumulated $\mathbf{y}'$ vector would mostly happen during the last calls of `TMRG`, and the number of `TMRG_COPY` operations could be smaller.

3.4.2 Complexity of the `TMRG` Algorithm

This subsection focuses on the number of `TMRG_COPY` operations. The lists merged by `TMRG` grow larger as this algorithm is called iteratively: this causes a growing number of `TMRG_COPY` operations which cannot be predicted exactly. Therefore, our best chance is to obtain the expected number of operations under some simple statistical assumptions.

Lemma 3.1. *The proportion α of nonzero components is assumed to be exactly the same in $\mathbf{x}$ and each row of the matrix, and these components are assumed to be uniformly and independently distributed. Then, the average number of `TMRG_COPY` operations for the nth call to `TMRG` is $N_r(1 - (1-\alpha)^{n-1})(1-\alpha)$.*

Proof At each call of `TMRG`, because of distribution independence, a proportion $1-\alpha$ of the nonzero features accumulated so far will go through `TMRG_COPY`. For the same reason, the number of zero features after each call of `TMRG` is reduced by a factor of $1 - \alpha$. This means that after $n - 1$ calls to `TMRG`, the number of nonzero features is $N_r(1 - (1-\alpha)^{n-1})$, thus the number of `TMRG_COPY` operations for the nth call to `TMRG` is $N_r(1-\alpha)(1 - (1-\alpha)^{n-1})$. ∎

Using lemma 3.1, we can prove the following results

Theorem 3.2. *If $\alpha N_r \gg 1$, approximately $N_r N_c$ `TMRG_COPY` operations are required to multiply a dense vector to a sparse matrix.*

---

2. Under the assumption $\alpha N_c \gg 1$, our model considers the actual time spent in multiply-adds to be negligible. This is confirmed by computer simulations, and vindicates the idea that sparse kernel learning is about finding the right examples, not computing kernels.

Proof We just need to sum up the number of `TMRG_COPY` operations for each call to `TMRG`, and our first approximation relies on $\alpha N_r \gg 1$.

$$\sum_{n=1}^{N_c} N_r(1-\alpha)(1-(1-\alpha)^{n-1}) = N_r(1-\alpha)\left(N_c - \frac{1-(1-\alpha)^{N_r}}{\alpha}\right) \tag{3.4}$$

$$\approx N_r(1-\alpha)(N_c - \frac{1}{\alpha}) \tag{3.5}$$

$$\approx N_r N_c. \tag{3.6}$$

$\blacksquare$

Theorem 3.3. *If $\alpha N_c \gg 1$ and $\alpha^2 N_c \ll 1$, approximately $\frac{1}{2}\alpha^3 N_r N_c^2$ `TMRG_COPY` operations are required to multiply a sparse vector to a sparse matrix.*

Proof Noting $\nu = \alpha N_c$, we have

$$\sum_{n=1}^{\nu}(1-(1-\alpha)^{n-1}) = \nu - \frac{1}{\alpha}(1-(1-\alpha))^{\nu} \tag{3.7}$$

$$= \nu - \frac{1}{\alpha}\left(1 - e^{\nu \log(1-\alpha)}\right). \tag{3.8}$$

A second-order expansion of $\log(1-x)$ is followed by a second-order expansion of $e^x - 1$. For the expansion of $e^{-\nu\alpha}$, we assume that $\nu\alpha \ll 1$ (or $\alpha^2 N_c \ll 1$).

$$\sum_{n=1}^{\nu}(1-(1-\alpha)^{n-1}) \approx \nu - \frac{1}{\alpha}\left(1 - e^{-\nu(\alpha+\frac{1}{2}\alpha^2)}\right) \tag{3.9}$$

$$\approx \nu - \frac{1}{\alpha}\left(\nu(\alpha + \frac{1}{2}\alpha^2) - \frac{1}{2}(\nu\alpha)^2\right) \tag{3.10}$$

If we assume that $\nu \gg 1$ ($\alpha N_c \gg 1$), and thus $\nu\alpha^2 \ll (\nu\alpha)^2$, we finally obtain

$$\sum_{n=1}^{\nu}(1-(1-\alpha)^{n-1}) \approx \frac{1}{2}\alpha\nu^2 = \frac{1}{2}\alpha^3 N_c^2 \tag{3.11}$$

To obtain the number of operations, we multiply this result by $N_r(1-\alpha) \approx N_r$. $\blacksquare$

3.4.3   Computer simulations with SVM learning

Experiments determine the number of operations performed by each algorithm on a specific task and the type of sparsity structure for which the `TADD` and `TMRG` algorithms prove efficient. The data we used is a subset of the VoiceTone dataset (presented in section 3.7) with 9093 training examples and 5282 features.

Table 3.3 explains why, in the case of SVMs, the `TADD` and `TMRG` algorithms are far superior to the `SDOT` algorithm. The problem lies with a very large number of `SDOT_ACCESS` operations. One verifies that `TMRG`, `SDOT`, and `TADD` have exactly the same number of `MULADD` operations for the same data. As predicted, sorting the features

Table 3.3 Time and number of operations required for each algorithm/data configuration. The algorithms with dot products (`DOT` and `SDOT`) use features corresponding to word bigrams in alphabetical order (Abc). The algorithm with merges (`TMRG`) starts with the same data. A second run sorts the feature by frequency (+Sort). The counters are described in Algorithms 3.1, 3.2, 3.3 and 3.5.

Algo	Data	Time	Operations (Millions)		
			MULADD	ACCESS	COPY
DOT	Abc	20s	732	732	
SDOT	Abc	25s	72	1379	
TADD	Abc	11s	72		
TMRG	Abc	10s	72	118	46
TMRG	+Sort	9s	72	103	31

so that the frequent ones are only merged last reduces the number of `TMRG_COPY` operations.

The `DOT` algorithm also avoids `SDOT_ACCESS` operations, but the number of `DOT_MULADD` operations becomes very large. On this relatively small dataset, as the entire dense vector can hold in the processor cache, `DOT` is slightly faster than `SDOT`. However, this will not be the case on larger datasets.

3.4.4 Computer Simulations with Maxent Learning

While SVM optimization is usually sequential in the dual space (i.e., examples), algorithms such as Adaboost and maximum entropy (Maxent) tend to rely on optimization procedures which are sequential in the primal space (i.e., features). It would be interesting to adapt our transpose methods to primal sequential optimization procedures such as iterative scaling (Berger et al., 1996) or the L1-regularized sequential algorithm (Dudik et al., 2004).

In the case of conditional maxent, we estimate for each training sample $\mathbf{x}$ the Gibbs score $q(y|\mathbf{x}) = \frac{1}{Z(\mathbf{x})} \exp^{\sum_k \lambda_k f_k(\mathbf{x})}$. Each iteration consists in identifying the feature f_k for which updating λ_k would bring the largest decrease in the loss function. The most expensive computations stem from computing the quantities $q_k(y) = \sum_{\mathbf{x}} q(y|\mathbf{x}) f_k(\mathbf{x})$.

This dot product between dense vector $q(y|.)$ and sparse vector $f_k(.)$ can be further optimized by looking at the differences only, so that

$$\delta q_k(y) = \sum_{\mathbf{x}} \delta q(y|\mathbf{x}) f_k(\mathbf{x}),$$

where δ corresponds to the modification caused by the previous feature update. $\delta q(y|.)$ is sparse, because $\delta q(y|\mathbf{x}) = 0$ for examples $\mathbf{x}$ that do not contain this previous feature. We construct the transpose data matrix $\mathbf{M}^T$ where each row

Table 3.4 Time and number of operations required for each algorithm in a Maxent learning problem. Notation is the same as in table 3.3.

Alg	Time	Operations (millions)		
		MULADD	ACCESS	COPY
DOT	47s	3249	3249	
SDOT	294s	431	91028	
TADD	36s	431		
TMRG	225s	431	46305	45974

corresponds to a feature $f_i(.)$ and each column to a training vector $\mathbf{x}_j$. The sparse matrix-vector multiplication $\delta q(y) = \mathbf{M}^T \delta q(y|.)$ is suitable for transpose methods.

Table 3.4 compares matrix-vector multiplication methods for the same VoiceTone data subset using a L1-regularized maxent algorithm (Dudik et al., 2004).[3] While TMRG improves over SDOT, the best approaches are DOT (where $\delta q(y|.)$ is used as a dense vector) and TADD. The very large number of TMRG_COPY operations cripples the TMRG algorithm, and is caused by the fact that $\delta q(y|.)$ is not very sparse, as predicted by table 3.2. As a matter of fact, $\delta q(y|.)$ is dense when the last updated feature is the bias term, which occurs in every training vector.

In summary, this section shows that the transpose methods introduced in this chapter can be applied to learning algorithms other than those which are kernel-based, but that these methods are only effective for specific types of sparsity.

3.5 Speeding Up SVM Training

We have shown in the previous sections that on sparse data, transpose methods considerably speed up the core operation of a typical SVM iteration, which is a matrix-vector multiplication required for kernel computation. However, code profiling shows that on problems where the data is ultrasparse, the speedup is so considerable that the proportion of time spent in kernel computation, which is usually above 50%, becomes small compared to other steps in the learning procedure, such as the updating of the scores in (3.1). It becomes therefore critical to adapt all the other steps of the learning algorithms, in particular by systematizing the use of the index-value table representation. As explained in chapter 1, most SVM software packages accelerate the computation by *caching* the kernel values and *shrinking* the active set as learning progresses. See chapter 1.

---

3. This algorithm is faster than GIS, and, on sparse data, compares favorably to L-BFGS methods (Malouf, 2002).

3.5.1   Sparse and More Efficient Cache

This acceleration assumes that a large proportion of kernels between examples is zero.[4] As shown above, the list $\mathbf{y}'$ of dot products between some support vector and each vector of the active set is encoded as a list of index-value pairs, and we assume that $|\mathbf{y}'|$ is much smaller than the active training set size N_r. While it naturally follows the application of the TMRG algorithm (see algorithm 3.5), this sparse list can be obtained after any matrix-vector multiplication by removing all the zero elements of the vector $\mathbf{y}$.

The gains from this sparse representation amount to a reduction of $\frac{N_r}{|\mathbf{y}'|}$ in some computational and memory requirements. Among the computations that scale proportionally to N_r and are thus significantly reduced, we have the updating of the scores (see (3.1)) and the transformation of the dot product into the final kernel function. This transformation can be expensive: for instance an exponential is required for the Gaussian kernel. To save memory, only $|\mathbf{y}'|$ index-value pairs need to be stored in the cache instead of N_r values. The *sparse cache* algorithm relies on operations over lists that are very similar to the TMRG algorithm.

3.5.2   Transpose Shrinking

The reduction of the size of the active training set N_r during learning is a commonly used technique. Traditional shrinking algorithms require maintaining a list of active vectors, and removing some columns in the cache matrix. Using transpose methods, efficient shrinking requires removing elements from each inverted index, that is, each column $\mathbf{M}_{.,j}$. Frequent removal of examples from the active list can be costly: for each feature j, one must check if the example appears in its transpose list $\mathbf{M}_{.,j}$. In order to minimize list removal operations, it is important to follow the following sequence of operations:

- Group a significant number N_x of examples to be removed before performing a shrinking step.

- If each example is encoded as a list of features, merge these lists into a consolidated list.

- For each feature j in this list, remove examples listed in N_x from list $\mathbf{M}_{.,j}$. This list removal operation is in $O(N_x + |\mathbf{M}_{.,j}|)$.

The algorithms that implement *transpose shrinking* are significantly more complex than traditional shrinking, and the *unshrinking* procedure is extremely costly. Parallelization algorithms that split the training set (Graf et al., 2005) may be

4. It can also be a constant factor $\phi(0)$ which typically results from the application of the transform function ϕ to a zero dot product. $\phi(0)$ can be subtracted from all kernel products without impacting the overall score output by the classifier, as the sum is $\sum_i \alpha_i y_i \phi(0) = 0$.

more appropriate in the context of our transpose methods, but have not been implemented for the work presented in this chapter.

3.6   Feature Selection

The previous algorithms are mostly efficient when a large number of dot products are zero. However, a sparse feature representation does not necessarily result in a sparse kernel matrix. While other features are sparse, one feature can appear with a nonzero coefficient in every example. As a consequence, every dot product is nonzero.

More generally, *frequent* features that are shared by a large proportion of examples are problematic. In text information retrieval, it is known that words that appear in a large number of documents (high document frequency or DF) carry little information. This motivates reweighting the feature corresponding to this word by a factor inversely proportional to the DF.

A more sophisticated approach that applies to binary features is the information gain (IG). It measures the number of bits of information obtained for output prediction by the classifier from knowing the presence or the absence of a feature. It is equivalent to the weighted mutual information. Removing the low IG features was shown (Y. Yang and Pedersen, 1997) to perform a feature selection which is very similar to removing low DF features.

Our goal is to remove the *low-information-high-frequency* features, and none of the established techniques were found to be appropriate. We propose to focus on the amount of information a feature brings to an example that uses this feature, rather than on the total information. This view of feature selection attempts to balance the computational cost of a feature (represented by the DF) and its benefit (represented by the IG). We only keep the features for which the ratio IG/DF exceeds a specified threshold. This algorithm will be referred to as IG-IDF.

3.7   Large-Scale Experiments

Experiments focus on binary classification. As most of our problems have more than two classes, we choose a specific class (usually the most common or most difficult) and try to detect its presence or absence. In a multiclass setting, this would correspond to a one-vs.-other scheme.

3.7.1   Description of the Data

The MNIST OCR dataset has been extensively studied on a large variety of learning approaches (LeCun et al., 1998a). The input vector is a list of 30×30 pixels ranging

Table 3.5 Key characteristics of the four datasets used in the experiments, and comparisons of LIBSVM and LLAMA training speeds. VoiceToneS applies the IG-IDF algorithm to the VoiceTone data.

Dataset	Training size	Testing size	Number of features	NonZero features α (%)	Critical ratio ρ	Training time (sec) LIBSVM SDOT	LLAMA TMRG	TADD
MNIST-7	60000	10000	900	16.7	2347	224	150	85
Translation	100000	994	273714	0.033	1.35	48892	2470	2150
VoiceTone	578702	64300	87667	0.019	0.03	48728	1537	2498
Supertag	950028	95516	46451	0.031	0.03	60953	1864	3155
VoiceToneS	578702	64300	87191	0.010	0.004	38107	411	900

from 0 to 255. Among the 10 digits, we focus on the classification of the most difficult: 7.

The AT&T VoiceTone dataset was chosen for its large size and considerable amount of noise. In the context of customer care applications, users interact with a spoken dialog system via the telephone, speaking naturally, to ask about their bills, request a refill of a medication, ask for a change in service, or other topics depending on the application. Their responses to the open-ended prompts of the system are not constrained by the system; they may be any natural language sequence. We focused on the following binary classification problem: determine when the user requires to be transferred to a human customer care representative. The data was collected from a wide variety of industrial applications, ranging from telecommunication to banking, retailing, and health care. The data was hand-labeled differently for each application; 578,702 utterances were used for training and 64,300 for testing. On both sets, the percentage of utterances that are labeled as "Request(Customer_Care)" is around 9.5%. Compare this with the best classification accuracy we could obtain on this task (6%): this indicates a level of noise which causes learning to be a slow, complex optimization process. Features, which are binary, consist of word bigram detectors.

SuperTags are extensions of part-of-speech tags that encode morphosyntactic constraints (Bangalore and Joshi, 1999)) and are derived from the phrase-structure annotated Penn TreeBank. The most common tag is chosen for binary classification.

The machine translation (MT) dataset uses an Arabic-English corpus from the United Nations. We are attempting a brute-force lexical choice and use all morpheme trigrams in the Arabic input sentence to determine if an English word appears in the output sentence. We focus on the detection of the second most common English word: *of*.

While VoiceTone cannot be publicly released, both the Penn TreeBank and the UN Machine Translation corpus are available through the Linguistic Data Consortium (LDC).

3.7.2 Experimental Results

Table 3.5 compares two SVM learning implementations on four types of problems. LIBSVM (version 2.8) is the most commonly used open-source SVM implementation and is frequently updated. It uses the sparse dot product SDOT and traditional shrinking and caching. It represents the state of the art in traditional SVM implementations. LLAMA is the learning library used to implement the transpose matrix multiplication with either TADD or TMRG algorithms, the sparse cache, and the transpose shrinking algorithms. In all experiments, we use polynomial kernels of the type $(\langle \mathbf{x}, \mathbf{y} \rangle + 1)^p$ where p is 4 for MNIST and 2 for the other datasets. The vectors x and y are normalized to 1. Learning converges when the duality gap (a.k.a. epsilon) gets below 0.01, and we verified that the test errors and numbers of support vectors output by LLAMA and LIBSVM are similar.

LIBSVM and LLAMA speeds compare as follows, depending on the type of the problem:

Low sparsity In MNIST, about 20% of the features are nonzero. Profiling shows that LLAMA speedup is mainly due to the sparse cache algorithm.

High sparsity In VoiceTone, Supertag, and MT, only a tiny fraction of the features (around 0.01%) are nonzero, While LIBSVM takes advantage of the sparsity, LLAMA does it 23 to 31 times more efficiently. TADD works best with a large number of features (translation), but TMRG is better for the other tasks.

High sparsity and feature selection As we can see for dataset VoiceTone, only a few very common features are removed by the IG-IDF algorithm (with no impact on classification performance). The impact of the feature selection is most visible on LLAMA with the TMRG algorithm, which becomes 80 times faster than LIBSVM.

The critical ratio $\rho = \frac{1}{2}\alpha^3 N_c^2$ seems to predict well when TMRG should do better than TADD.

3.7.3 Scaling Behavior

In these experiments, we scale up the size of the training subsets from 1/32 of the VoiceTone training data (or 18,084 examples) to all the data. This enables us to determine scaling "laws."

Figure 3.3 compares LIBSVM and LLAMA with various configurations.

- Log scales are used for both axes, and the fact that scaling curves are parallel to the $y = 2x$ line confirms that learning speed scales as the square of the number of examples. This also shows that our speedups do not resolve this "quadratic scaling behavior" curse.

- The sparse cache trick alone provides considerable improvements over the dense cache used in LIBSVM, and this is especially true when feature selection allows us to make the cache even sparser and thus more compact to store. Note that for both

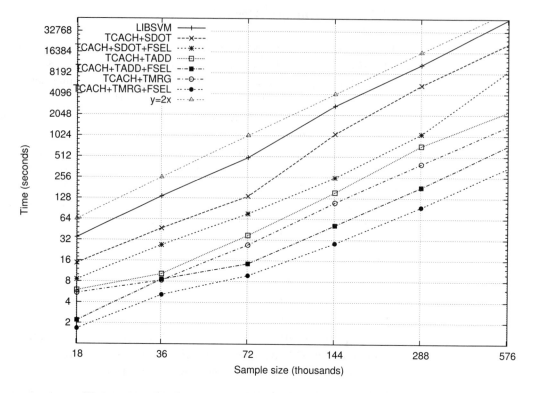

Figure 3.3 Evolution of learning time with the training set size on the VoiceTone data. TCACH indicates LLAMA with the transpose cache algorithm. The matrix multiplication in LLAMA is performed using the SDOT, TADD, or TMRG algorithms. FSEL indicates the optional feature selection algorithm.

LLAMA and LIBSVM, a cache of 2.3GB was used: the sparse cache trick allows us to store many more examples.

■ The curves obtained with the TADD and TMRG algorithms are exactly parallel (with and without feature selection). This vindicates one of the surprising findings of our "critical ratio" theory: the performance ratio between TADD and TMRG does not depend on the number of rows or training examples.

3.8 Concluding Remarks

For general applications of vector-matrix multiplication on sparse data, one should consider transpose methods, which can be *orders of magnitude* faster when both the matrix and the vector are evenly sparse. Their optimal implementations depend on the dimensions of the matrix and the sparsity structure. We prove that these methods improve kernel-based learning such as SVMs, but are inefficient on feature-based learning such as maxent. In the case of the SMO algorithm for SVMs, they can improve the leading constant in the complexity by several orders of magnitude; however, the scaling behavior remains quadratic.

We propose complexity estimates that predict well which transpose algorithm will be the fastest, depending on the sparsity ratio and the number of features.

The transpose approach is particularly successful on natural language applications and enables SVMs with vectorial kernels to handle datasets of millions of examples without sampling or parallelization. We found that their training time matches maximum entropy. However, this method is not an approximation and does not reduce the number of support vectors. At test time, we found that transpose methods can result in relatively small speed improvements when dealing with a large number of classes, or testing a large number of examples at the same time. The methods based on polynomial expansion (Kudo and Matsumoto, 2003) have been shown to be more promising.

4 Large-Scale Learning with String Kernels

Sören Sonnenburg
Gunnar Rätsch
Konrad Rieck

In genomic sequence analysis tasks, such as splice site recognition or promoter iden-tification, large amounts of training sequences are available, and indeed needed to achieve sufficiently high classification performances. In this chapter we study string kernels that can be computed in linear time w.r.t. the length of the input sequences. In particular, the recently proposed spectrum kernel, *the* weighted degree (WD) kernel, *and the* weighted degree kernel with shifts *have been successfully used for various sequence analysis tasks. We discuss extensions using data structures such as* tries *and* suffix trees *as well as modifications of a chunking algorithm for suppport vector machines (SVMs) in order to significantly accelerate their training and their evaluation on test sequences. Our simulations using the WD kernel and spectrum kernel show that large-scale SVM training can be accelerated by factors of 7 and 60 times, respectively, while requiring considerably less memory. We demonstrate that these algorithms can be effectively parallelized for further acceleration. Our method allows us to train SVMs on sets as large as 10 million sequences and solve* multiple kernel learning *problems with 1 million sequences. Moreover, using these techniques the evaluation on new sequences is often several thousand times faster, allowing us to apply the classifiers on genome-sized datasets with 7 billion test examples. We finally demonstrate how the proposed data structures can be used to understand the SVM classifiers decision function. All presented algorithms are implemented in our machine learning toolbox* SHOGUN.[1]

---

1. http://www.shogun-toolbox.org.

4.1   Introduction

Kernel-based methods such as support vector machines (SVMs) have proved to be powerful for a wide range of different data analysis problems, in particular for the analysis of texts and biological sequences. In analysis tasks like *email* or *web spam detection* (Webb et al., 2006), *splice site recognition* (Rätsch and Sonnenburg, 2004), or *promoter identification* (Sonnenburg et al., 2006c), large amounts of training sequences are available and seemingly required to achieve sufficiently high classification performances. However, training SVMs becomes prohibitively computationally expensive when using genome-sized training samples.

In this work we review and develop string kernels that are particularly well suited for sequence analysis tasks (section 4.2). We study kernels that consider the occurrence of subsequences in the sequence up to a certain length for two typical analysis problems: the analysis of the whole content of the sequences (e.g., web spam classification) and the content relative to a biological signal of interest (e.g., splice sites). We are especially interested in variants of the *spectrum kernel* (Leslie et al., 2002) and the *weighted degree (WD) kernel* (Rätsch and Sonnenburg, 2004), where the latter considers sequences of constant length and uses position dependent information which the former does not.

We will discuss strategies to efficiently compute linear combinations of sequence kernel elements which are frequently used during SVM training and testing. They exploit that the normal vector of the hyperplane in feature space is extremely sparse and build up appropriate index data structures allowing efficient operations on the nonzero elements (section 4.3). Moreover, we outline algorithms taking advantage of the properties of such kernels in order to efficiently compute the optimal SVM solution (section 4.4).

Our benchmark experiments in section 4.5 show that we can significantly speed up the training phase ($60\times$ faster for the spectrum kernel and $\approx 7\times$ faster for the WD kernel) and testing phase (often several thousand times faster). Additionally, during training the algorithms do not require much working memory, as the data structures make memory-demanding kernel caching unnecessary (Sonnenburg et al., 2006b). In section 4.6 we discuss other applications of the presented ideas. We show how one can solve *multiple kernel learning* (Sonnenburg et al., 2006b) problems with a million examples and how the data structures can be used to represent the resulting SVM classifiers in a manner comprehensible to humans.

4.2   String Kernels

Given two strings $\mathbf{x}$ and $\mathbf{x}'$, there is no obvious answer to the question: How similar are $\mathbf{x}$ and $\mathbf{x}'$? In contrast to vectors in $\mathbb{R}^d$ where a quantity inverse to $\|\mathbf{x} - \mathbf{x}'\|$ can be used, similarity of strings can be expressed in a variety of ways – each accounting and emphasizing different features and aspects.

Let us start by defining a few terms: A string (or sequence) $\mathbf{x}$ is defined as $\mathbf{x} \in \Sigma^*$, where Σ^* is the Kleene closure over all symbols from the finite alphabet Σ. The length of the string $\mathbf{x}$ is given as $l_{\mathbf{x}} := |\mathbf{x}|$. Using these definitions we can define similarity measures for use with kernel machines on strings, the so-called *string kernels*. In general there are two major types of string kernels: first, the ones that are directly defined on strings, and second, kernels that are defined on generative models (like hidden Markov models, e.g., Jaakkola et al., 2000; Tsuda et al., 2002a,b), or by using appropriately defined scores (for instance, alignment scores; e.g., Liao and Noble, 2002; Vert et al., 2004).

The following section will cover only string kernels of the first type, such as the bag-of-words (Salton, 1979; Joachims, 1998), *n*-gram (Damashek, 1995; Joachims, 1999a), locality improved (Zien et al., 2000), spectrum (Leslie et al., 2002), WD kernel (Rätsch and Sonnenburg, 2004) and WD kernel *with shifts* (Rätsch et al., 2005). For additional work that is not directly covered[2] by this work, the reader is refered to Haussler (1999), Lodhi et al. (2002), Leslie et al. (2003a), Leslie and Kuang (2004), Schölkopf et al. (2004), and Cortes et al. (2004).

4.2.1 Bag-of-Words and *n*-gram Kernels

In information retrieval a classic way to characterize a text document is to represent the text by the words it contains — the *bag of words* (Salton, 1979). The text document is split at word boundaries into contained words using a set of delimiter symbols, such as space, comma, and period. Note that in this representation the ordering of words (e.g., in a sentence) will not be taken into account. The feature space $\mathcal{F}$ consists of all possible words and a document $\mathbf{x}$ is mapped to a sparse vector $\Phi(\mathbf{x}) \in \mathcal{F}$, so that $\Phi_i(\mathbf{x}) = 1$ if the word represented by index i is contained in the document. Further alternatives for mapping $\mathbf{x}$ into a feature space $\mathcal{F}$ correspond to associating $\Phi_i(\mathbf{x})$ with frequencies or counts of contained words. The bag-of-words kernel is then computed as the inner product in $\mathcal{F}$:

$$k(\mathbf{x}, \mathbf{x}') = \langle \Phi(\mathbf{x}), \Phi(\mathbf{x}') \rangle = \sum_{i \in \text{words}} \Phi_i(\mathbf{x})\Phi_i(\mathbf{x}'), \qquad (4.1)$$

which — in practice — boils down to counting the number of words common to both documents and can thus be computed very efficiently.

Another common approach is to characterize a document by contained *n*-grams — substrings of n consecutive characters including word boundaries — where n is fixed beforehand (Suen, 1979; Damashek, 1995). The corresponding feature space $\mathcal{F}$ is spanned by all possible strings of length n. Here no dependencies other than the consecutive n characters are taken into account, which, however, might contain more than one word. The kernel is computed as in (4.1). Note that the *n*-gram

---

2. Though the `linadd` optimization trick presented here is — in some cases — also applicable.

kernel can cope with mismatches, as, for instance, a single mismatch only affects n neighboring n-grams, while keeping further surrounding ones intact.

4.2.2 The Spectrum Kernel

The spectrum kernel (Leslie et al., 2002) implements the n-gram kernel in the context of biological sequence analysis. The idea is to count how often a d-mer (bioinformatics terminology for d-gram, a contiguous string of length d) is contained in the sequences $\mathbf{x}$ and $\mathbf{x}'$. Summing up the product of these counts for every possible d-mer (note that there are exponentially many) gives rise to the kernel value which formally is defined as follows: Let Σ be an alphabet and $\boldsymbol{u} \in \Sigma^d$ a d-mer and $\#\boldsymbol{u}(\mathbf{x})$ the number of occurrences of $\boldsymbol{u}$ in $\mathbf{x}$. Then the spectrum kernel is defined as

$$k(\mathbf{x}, \mathbf{x}') = \sum_{\boldsymbol{u} \in \Sigma^d} \#\boldsymbol{u}(\mathbf{x}) \#\boldsymbol{u}(\mathbf{x}'). \tag{4.2}$$

Note that spectrum-like kernels cannot extract any positional information from the sequence which goes beyond the d-mer length. It is well suited for describing the content of a sequence but is less suitable, for instance, for analyzing signals where motifs may appear in a certain order or at specific positions. Also note that spectrum-like kernels are capable of dealing with sequences with varying length.

The spectrum kernel can be efficiently computed in $\mathcal{O}(d(l_{\mathbf{x}} + l_{\mathbf{x}'}))$ using tries (Leslie et al., 2002) and $\mathcal{O}(l_{\mathbf{x}} + l_{\mathbf{x}'})$ using suffix trees (Vishwanathan and Smola, 2003), where $l_{\mathbf{x}}$ and $l_{\mathbf{x}'}$ denote the length of sequence $\mathbf{x}$ and $\mathbf{x}'$. An easier and less complex way to compute the kernel for two sequences $\mathbf{x}$ and $\mathbf{x}'$ is to separately extract and sort the $(l_{\mathbf{x}} + l_{\mathbf{x}'})$ d-mers in each sequence, which can be done in a preprocessing step. Then one iterates over all d-mers of sequences $\mathbf{x}$ and $\mathbf{x}'$ simultaneously, counts which d-mers appear in both sequences, and finally sums up the product of their counts. For small alphabets and d-gram lengths individual d-mers can be stored in fixed-size variables, e.g., DNA d-mers of length $d \leq 16$ can be efficiently represented as 32-bit integer values. The ability to store d-mers in fixed-bit variables or even CPU registers greatly improves performance, as only a single CPU instruction is necessary to compare or index a d-mer. The computational complexity of the kernel computation is $\mathcal{O}(l_{\mathbf{x}} + l_{\mathbf{x}'})$ omitting the preprocessing step.

4.2.3 The Weighted Degree Kernel

The so-called *weighted degree* kernel (Rätsch and Sonnenburg, 2004) efficiently computes similarities between sequences while taking positional information of multiple k-mers into account. The main idea of the WD kernel is to count the (exact) co-occurrences of k-mers at corresponding positions in the two sequences to be compared. The *WD kernel of order d* compares two sequences $\mathbf{x}$ and $\mathbf{x}'$ of equal length l by summing all contributions of k-mer matches of lengths $k \in \{1, \dots, d\}$,

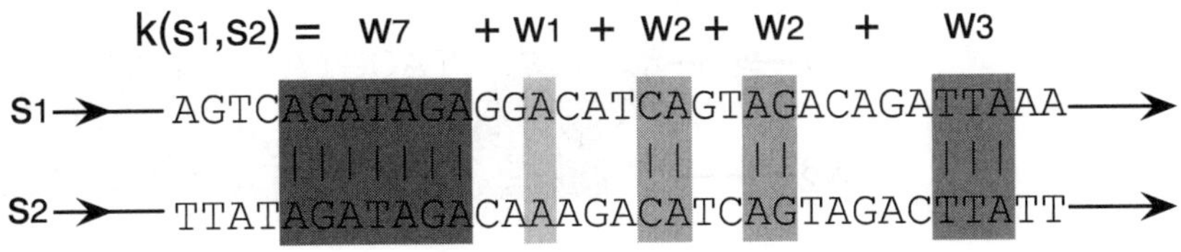

Figure 4.1 Given two sequences $\mathbf{x}_1$ and $\mathbf{x}_2$ of equal length, the kernel consists of a weighted sum to which each match in the sequences makes a contribution w_B depending on its length B, where longer matches contribute more significantly.

weighted by coefficients β_k:

$$k(\mathbf{x}, \mathbf{x}') = \sum_{k=1}^{d} \beta_k \sum_{i=1}^{l-k+1} \mathbf{I}(\boldsymbol{u}_{k,i}(\mathbf{x}) = \boldsymbol{u}_{k,i}(\mathbf{x}')). \tag{4.3}$$

Here, $\boldsymbol{u}_{k,i}(\mathbf{x})$ is the string of length k starting at position i of the sequence $\mathbf{x}$ and $\mathbf{I}(\cdot)$ is the indicator function which evaluates to 1 when its argument is *true* and to 0 otherwise. For the weighting coefficients, Rätsch and Sonnenburg (2004) proposed using $\beta_k = 2\frac{d-k+1}{d(d+1)}$. Matching substrings are thus rewarded with a score depending on the length of the substring. Note that although in our case $\beta_{k+1} < \beta_k$, longer matches nevertheless contribute more strongly than shorter ones: this is due to the fact that each long match implies several short matches, adding to the value of (4.3). Exploiting this knowledge allows for a more intuitive $\mathcal{O}(l)$ reformulation of the kernel using "block-weights" as has been done by Sonnenburg et al. (2005b) and is displayed in figure 4.1.

Note that the WD kernel can be understood as a spectrum kernel where the k-mers starting at different positions are treated independently of each other. Additionally, the WD kernel considers *substrings of length up to d*. Hence, the feature space for each position has $\sum_{k=1}^{d} |\Sigma|^k = \frac{|\Sigma|^{d+1}-1}{|\Sigma|-1} - 1$ dimensions and is additionally duplicated l times (leading to $\mathcal{O}(l|\Sigma|^d)$ dimensions). However, the computational complexity of the original WD kernel is in the worst case $\mathcal{O}(dl)$ as can be directly seen from (4.3).

4.2.4 The Weighted Degree Kernel *with Shifts*

The recognition of matching blocks using the WD kernel strongly depends on the position of the subsequence and does not tolerate any positional variation. For instance, if a consecutive block in one sequence is shifted by only one position, the WD kernel fails to discover similar blocks and returns a lower similarity score. Depending on the application in mind, this problem might lead to suboptimal results. Hence, Rätsch et al. (2005) suggested the WD kernel *with shifts* — the WDS kernel — which shifts the two sequences against each other in order to tolerate small positional variations of sequence motifs. Conceptually, it is a mixture between

Figure 4.2   Given two sequences $\mathbf{x}_1$ and $\mathbf{x}_2$ of equal length, the WD kernel with shifts consists of a weighted sum to which each match in the sequences makes a contribution $\gamma_{k,p}$ depending on its length k and relative position p, where long matches at the same position contribute most significantly. The γ's can be computed from the β's and δ's in (4.4). The spectrum kernel is based on a similar idea, but it only considers substrings of a fixed length and the contributions are independent of the relative positions of the matches to each other.

the WD and the spectrum kernel. It is defined as

$$k(\mathbf{x}, \mathbf{x}') = \sum_{k=1}^{d} \beta_k \sum_{i=1}^{l-k+1} \sum_{\substack{s=0 \\ s+i \le l}}^{S} \delta_s \, \mu_{k,i,s,\mathbf{x},\mathbf{x}'}, \tag{4.4}$$

$$\mu_{k,i,s,\mathbf{x},\mathbf{x}'} = \mathbf{I}(\boldsymbol{u}_{k,i+s}(\mathbf{x}) = \boldsymbol{u}_{k,i}(\mathbf{x}')) + \mathbf{I}(\boldsymbol{u}_{k,i}(\mathbf{x}) = \boldsymbol{u}_{k,i+s}(\mathbf{x}')),$$

where $\beta_k = 2(d-k+1)/(d(d+1))$, $\delta_s = 1/(2(s+1))$ and $\boldsymbol{u}_{k,i}(\mathbf{x})$ is the subsequence of $\mathbf{x}$ of length k that starts at position i. The idea is to count the matches between two sequences $\mathbf{x}$ and $\mathbf{x}'$ between the words $\boldsymbol{u}_{k,i}(\mathbf{x})$ and $\boldsymbol{u}_{k,i}(\mathbf{x}')$ where $\boldsymbol{u}_{k,i}(\mathbf{x}) = x_i x_{i+1} \dots x_{i+k-1}$ for all i and $1 \le k \le d$. The parameter d denotes the maximal length of the words to be compared, and S is the maximum distance by which a sequence is shifted. Note that this kernel is computationally proportional to the maximum shift l and thus much more demanding requiring $\mathcal{O}(lS)$. See figure 4.2 and (Rätsch et al., 2005) for a further discussion.

4.2.5   Summary

The string kernels revisited in this section are based on counting substrings of certain lengths. While the computational complexity is linear in the length of the input sequences, there are some significant differences: the spectrum kernel requires $\mathcal{O}(l_{\mathbf{x}} + l_{\mathbf{x}'})$, the WD kernel $\mathcal{O}(l)$, and the WDS kernel is most demanding with $\mathcal{O}(lS)$. As there is no obvious way to further speed up single kernel computations, one can try to exploit the inherent structure of learning algorithms using string kernels. One can particularly benefit from the fact that these algorithms often need to compute linear combinations of kernel elements during training and testing, which can be significantly speeded up by exploiting the sparsity of the representation in feature space. Before going into algorithmic details on how one can make use of the sparse feature space to accelerate SVM training and testing in section 4.4, we will discuss methods to represent sparse feature maps in the next section (section 4.3) as the appropriate data representation is crucial for computational efficiency.

4.3 Sparse Feature Maps

The string kernels introduced in the previous section share two important properties: (a) the mapping Φ is explicit, so that elements in the feature space $\mathcal{F}$ can be accessed directly, and (b) mapped examples $\Phi(\mathbf{x})$ are very sparse in comparison to the huge dimensionality of $\mathcal{F}$. In the following sections we illustrate how these properties can be exploited to efficiently store and compute sparse feature vectors.

4.3.1 Efficient Storage of Sparse Weights

The considered string kernels correspond to very large feature spaces, for instance, DNA d-mers of order 10 span a feature space of over 1 million dimensions. However, most dimensions in the feature space are always zero since only a few of the many different d-mers actually appear in the training sequences, and furthermore a sequence $\mathbf{x}$ can only comprise at most $l_{\mathbf{x}}$ unique d-mers. In this section we briefly discuss four efficient *data structures* for sparse representation of sequences supporting the basic operations: `clear`, `add`, and `lookup`. We assume that the elements of a sparse vector $\boldsymbol{v}$ are indexed by some index set $\mathcal{U}$ (for sequences, e.g., $\mathcal{U} = \Sigma^d$). The first operation `clear` sets $\boldsymbol{v}$ to zero. The `add` operation increases either the weight of a dimension of $\boldsymbol{v}$ for an element $\boldsymbol{u} \in \mathcal{U}$ by some amount or increases a set of weights in $\boldsymbol{v}$ corresponding to all d-mers present in a given sequence $\mathbf{x}$. Similar to `add`, the `lookup` operation either requests the value of a particular component $v_{\boldsymbol{u}}$ of $\boldsymbol{v}$ or returns a set of values matching all d-mers in a provided sequence $\mathbf{x}$. The latter two operations need to be performed as quickly as possible.

4.3.1.1 Explicit Map

If the dimensionality of the feature space is small enough, then one might consider keeping the whole vector $\boldsymbol{v}$ in memory and to perform direct operations on its elements. In this case each `add` or `lookup` operation on single elements takes $\mathcal{O}(1)$ time.[3] The approach, however, has expensive memory requirements ($\mathcal{O}(|\Sigma|^d)$), but is highly efficient and best suited, for instance, for the spectrum kernel on DNA sequences with $d \leq 14$ and on protein sequences with $d \leq 6$.

4.3.1.2 Sorted Arrays and Hash Tables

More memory efficient but computationally more expensive are sorted arrays of index-value pairs $(\boldsymbol{u}, v_{\boldsymbol{u}})$. Assuming $l_{\mathbf{x}}$ indices of a sequence $\mathbf{x}$ are given and sorted in advance, one can efficiently `add` or `lookup` a single $v_{\boldsymbol{u}}$ for a corresponding $\boldsymbol{u}$ by employing a binary search procedure with $\mathcal{O}(\log l_{\mathbf{x}})$ run-time. Given a sequence $\mathbf{x}'$

---

3. More precisely, it is $\log d$, but for small enough d (which we have to assume anyway) the computational effort is exactly one memory access.

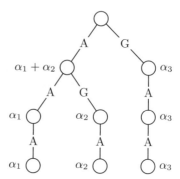

Figure 4.3 Trie containing the 3-mers AAA, AGA, GAA with weights $\alpha_1, \alpha_2, \alpha_3$. Additionally the figure displays resulting weights at inner nodes.

to look up all contained d-mers at once, one may sort the d-mers of $\mathbf{x}'$ in advance and then simultaneously traverse the arrays of $\mathbf{x}$ and $\mathbf{x}'$ in order to determine which elements appear in $\mathbf{x}'$. This procedure results in $\mathcal{O}(l_{\mathbf{x}} + l_{\mathbf{x}'})$ operations — omitting the sorting of the second array — instead of $\mathcal{O}(l_{\mathbf{x}'} \log l_{\mathbf{x}})$. The approach is well suited for cases where $l_{\mathbf{x}}$ and $l_{\mathbf{x}'}$ are of comparable size, as, for instance, for computations of single-spectrum kernel elements (Leslie et al., 2003b). If $l_{\mathbf{x}} \gg l_{\mathbf{x}'}$, then the binary search procedure should be preferred.

A tradeoff between the efficiency of explicit maps and the low memory requirements of sorted arrays can be achieved by storing the index-value pairs $(\boldsymbol{u}, v_{\boldsymbol{u}})$ in a hash table, where $\boldsymbol{u}$ is hashed to a bin in the hash table containing $v_{\boldsymbol{u}}$ (Rieck et al., 2006a). Both operations `add` and `lookup` for $\boldsymbol{u} \in \Sigma^d$ can be carried out in $\mathcal{O}(1)$ time in the best-case; however, the worst-case run-time is $\mathcal{O}(\log l_{\mathbf{x}})$, if all $\boldsymbol{u}$ of a sequence $\mathbf{x}$ are mapped to the same bin. The two opposed run-time bounds suggest that the hash table size has to be chosen very carefully in advance and also strongly depends on the lengths of the considered sequences, which makes the sorted array approach more practicable in terms of run-time requirements.

4.3.1.3   *Tries*

Another way of organizing the nonzero elements are *tries* (Fredkin, 1960; Knuth, 1973): The idea is to use a tree with at most $|\Sigma|$ siblings of depth d. The leaves store a single value: the element $v_{\boldsymbol{u}}$, where $\boldsymbol{u} \in \Sigma^d$ is a d-mer and the path to the leaf corresponds to $\boldsymbol{u}$.

To `add` an element to a trie one needs $\mathcal{O}(d)$ in order to create the necessary nodes on the way from the root to a leaf. Similar to the `add` operation, a `lookup` takes $\mathcal{O}(d)$ time in the worst-case. However, with growing d, the probability for an arbitrary $\boldsymbol{u}$ to be present in a trie decreases exponentially, so that a logarithmic run-time $\mathcal{O}(\log_{|\Sigma|} d)$ can be expected for large d. Note that the worst-case computational complexity of both operations is independent of the number of d-mers/elements stored in the tree.

Tries need considerably more storage than sorted arrays (for instance, storing

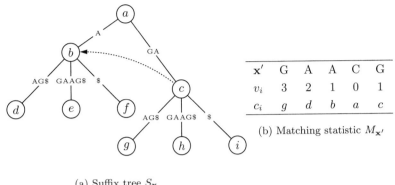

$$
\begin{array}{c|ccccc}
\mathbf{x}' & \text{G} & \text{A} & \text{A} & \text{C} & \text{G} \\
\hline
v_i & 3 & 2 & 1 & 0 & 1 \\
c_i & g & d & b & a & c \\
\end{array}
$$

(b) Matching statistic $M_{\mathbf{x}'}$

(a) Suffix tree $S_{\mathbf{x}}$

Figure 4.4   Suffix tree $S_{\mathbf{x}}$ for the sequence $\mathbf{x} = \text{GAGAAG}$ and matching statistic $M_{\mathbf{x}'}$ for $\mathbf{x}' = \text{GAACG}$ matched against $S_{\mathbf{x}}$. A sentinel symbol \$ has been added to $\mathbf{x}$, s.t. that all leaves correspond to suffixes.

edges in nodes usually requires using hash tables or balanced tree maps). However, tries are useful for the previously discussed WD kernel. Here we not only have to look up one substring $\boldsymbol{u} \in \Sigma^d$ but also all prefixes of $\boldsymbol{u}$. For sorted arrays this amounts to d separate `lookup` operations, while for tries all prefixes of $\boldsymbol{u}$ are already known when the bottom of the trie is reached. In this case the trie has to store aggregated weights in internal nodes (Sonnenburg et al., 2006b; Rieck et al., 2006a). This is illustrated for the WD kernel in figure 4.3.

4.3.1.4   *Suffix Trees and Matching Statistics*

A fourth alternative for efficient storage of sparse weights and string kernel computation builds on two data structures: suffix trees and matching statistics (Vishwanathan and Smola, 2003). A *suffix tree* $S_{\mathbf{x}}$ is a compact representation of a trie, which stores all suffixes of a sequence $\mathbf{x}$ in $\mathcal{O}(l_{\mathbf{x}})$ space and allows efficient retrieval of arbitrary subsequences of $\mathbf{x}$ (Gusfield, 1997). A *matching statistic* $M_{\mathbf{x}'}$ for a suffix tree $S_{\mathbf{x}}$ is defined by two vectors v and c of length $l_{\mathbf{x}'}$, where v_i reflects the length of the longest substring of $\mathbf{x}$ matching $\mathbf{x}'$ at position i and c_i is a corresponding node in $S_{\mathbf{x}}$ (W. I. Chang and Lawler, 1994). As an example, figure 4.4 shows a suffix tree $S_{\mathbf{x}}$ and a matching statistic $M_{\mathbf{x}'}$ for the sequences $\mathbf{x} = \text{GAGAAG}$ and $\mathbf{x}' = \text{GAACG}$.

By traversing $S_{\mathbf{x}}$ and looping over $M_{\mathbf{x}'}$ in parallel, a variety of string kernels $k(\mathbf{x}, \mathbf{x}')$ — including the spectrum and WD kernel — can be computed using $\mathcal{O}(l_{\mathbf{x}} + l_{\mathbf{x}'})$ run-time. A detailed discussion of the corresponding algorithms, weighting schemes, and extensions is given in (Vishwanathan and Smola, 2004; Rieck et al., 2006b). The approach can be further extended to support the operations `clear`, `add` and `lookup`. In contrast to sorted arrays and tries, these operations are favorably performed on the domain of *sequences* instead of single d-mers to ensure linear run-time. Starting with an empty suffix tree S obtained using `clear`, the `add`

Table 4.1 Comparison of worst-case run-times for multiple calls of `clear`, `add`, and `lookup` on a sparse vector v using explicit maps, sorted arrays, tries, and suffix trees.

	Explicit map	Sorted arrays	Tries	Suffix trees
`clear` of v	$\mathcal{O}(|\Sigma|^d)$	$\mathcal{O}(1)$	$\mathcal{O}(1)$	$\mathcal{O}(1)$
`add` of all u from $\mathbf{x}$ to v	$\mathcal{O}(l_{\mathbf{x}})$	$\mathcal{O}(l_{\mathbf{x}} \log l_{\mathbf{x}})$	$\mathcal{O}(l_{\mathbf{x}}d)$	$\mathcal{O}(l_{\mathbf{x}})$
`lookup` of all u from $\mathbf{x}'$ in v	$\mathcal{O}(l_{\mathbf{x}'})$	$\mathcal{O}(l_{\mathbf{x}} + l_{\mathbf{x}'})$	$\mathcal{O}(l_{\mathbf{x}'}d)$	$\mathcal{O}(l_{\mathbf{x}'})$

operation is realized by appending sequences and implicitly contained d-mers to S using an online construction algorithm, (e.g., Ukkonen, 1995). In order to avoid matches over multiple sequences, each sequence $\mathbf{x}_i$ is delimited by a sentinel symbol $\$_i \notin \Sigma$. Given S, the `lookup` operation for a sequence $\mathbf{x}'$ is performed by calculating $M_{\mathbf{x}'}$, so that a kernel computation can be carried out in $\mathcal{O}(l_{\mathbf{x}'})$ run-time using S and $M_{\mathbf{x}'}$.

In practice however, suffix trees introduce a crucial overhead in storage space due to the high complexity of the data structure, which makes memory-preserving data structures such as sorted arrays more attractive, especially on small alphabets. Recently, an alternative, suffix arrays, has been proposed to reduce the memory requirements; still n input symbols result in at least $19n$ bytes of allocated memory independent of the considered alphabet (Teo and Vishwanathan, 2006).

4.3.1.5 Summary

Table 4.1 coarsely summarizes the worst-case run-times for multiple calls of `clear`, `add`, and `lookup` using the previously introduced data structures. From the provided run-time bounds, it is obvious that the explicit map representation is favorable if the considered alphabet Σ and order d are sufficiently small — for instance as in several application of DNA analysis where $|\Sigma| = 4$ and $d \leq 6$. For larger alphabets and higher d, the sorted array approach is more attractive in practice. Other than tries and suffix trees, the sorted array approach is much easier to implement and its memory requirements are easier to estimate. If either Σ or d can get arbitrarily large, suffix trees are the data structure of choice as they operate linear in sequence lengths independent of Σ and d; however, as mentioned earlier, there is a large overhead in storage space due to the complexity of the suffix tree structure. The trie-based approach may not seem suitable for large-scale learning in comparison to the other methods, but the per-node augmentation of tries with additional values such as aggregated weights shown in figure 4.3 can drastically speed up computation of complex string kernels such as the WD kernel, which cannot efficiently be mapped to other approaches.

4.4 Speeding up SVM Training and Testing

As it is not feasible to use standard optimization toolboxes for solving large-scale SVM training problems, decomposition techniques are frequently used in practice. Most chunking algorithms work by first selecting Q variables (working set $W \subseteq \{1, \ldots, N\}$, $Q := |W|$) based on the current solution and then solve the reduced problem with respect to the working set variables. These two steps are repeated until some optimality conditions are satisfied, as displayed in algorithm 4.1. For

---

Algorithm 4.1 A SVM chunking algorithm (see, e.g., Joachims, 1998).

while optimality conditions are violated **do**
    select Q variables for the working set.
    solve reduced problem on the working set.
end while

---

selecting the working set and checking the termination criteria in each iteration, the vector $\mathbf{g}$ with $g_i = \sum_{j=1}^{N} \alpha_j y_j k(x_i, x_j)$, $i = 1, \ldots, N$, is usually needed. Without further assumptions, computing $\mathbf{g}$ from scratch in every iteration requires $\mathcal{O}(N^2)$ kernel computations. To avoid recomputation of $\mathbf{g}$ one typically starts with $\mathbf{g} = \mathbf{0}$ and only computes updates of $\mathbf{g}$ on the working set W

$$g_i \leftarrow g_i^{old} + \sum_{j \in W} (\alpha_j - \alpha_j^{old}) y_j k(x_i, x_j) \tag{4.5}$$

for all $i = 1, \ldots, N$. As a result the effort decreases to $\mathcal{O}(QN)$ kernel computations, which can be further accelerated by using kernel caching (Joachims, 1998). However, kernel caching is not efficient enough for large-scale problems[4] and thus most time is spent computing kernel rows for the updates of $\mathbf{g}$ on the working set W. Note, however, that this update, as well as computing the Q kernel rows, can be easily parallelized (see section 4.5.2).

Exploiting $k(\mathbf{x}_i, \mathbf{x}_j) = \langle \Phi(\mathbf{x}_i), \Phi(\mathbf{x}_j) \rangle$ and $\mathbf{w} = \sum_{i=1}^{N} \alpha_i y_i \Phi(\mathbf{x}_i)$ we can rewrite the update rule as

$$g_i \leftarrow g_i^{old} + \sum_{j \in W} (\alpha_j - \alpha_j^{old}) y_j \langle \Phi(\mathbf{x}_i), \Phi(\mathbf{x}_j) \rangle = g_i^{old} + \langle \mathbf{w}^W, \Phi(\mathbf{x}_i) \rangle, \tag{4.6}$$

where $\mathbf{w}^W = \sum_{j \in W} (\alpha_j - \alpha_j^{old}) y_j \Phi(\mathbf{x}_j)$ is the normal vector on the working set. If the kernel feature map can be computed explicitly and is sparse (as discussed before), then computing the update in (4.6) can be accelerated. One only needs to compute and store $\mathbf{w}^W$ (using the `clear` and $\sum_{q \in W} |\{\Phi_j(\mathbf{x}_q) \neq 0\}|$ `add` operations)

---

4. For instance, when using a million examples one can only fit 268 rows into 1GB. Moreover, caching 268 rows is insufficient when, for instance, having many thousands of active variables.

and performing the scalar product $\langle \mathbf{w}^W, \Phi(\mathbf{x}_i) \rangle$ (using $|\{\Phi_j(\mathbf{x}_i) \neq 0\}|$ `lookup` operations).

Depending on the kernel, the way the sparse vectors are stored (cf. section 4.3.1), and on the sparseness of the feature vectors, the speedup can be quite drastic. For instance, a single WD kernel computation (as in (4.3)) requires $\mathcal{O}(dl)$ operations. Hence, computing (4.5) N times requires $\mathrm{O}(NQld)$ operations. When using tries for computing (4.6), one needs Ql `add` operations (each $\mathcal{O}(d)$) and Nl `lookup` operations (each $\mathcal{O}(d)$). Hence, only $\mathcal{O}(Qld + Nld)$ basic operations are needed in total. When N is large enough it leads to a speedup by a factor of Q. Finally, note that kernel caching is no longer required and as Q is small in practice (e.g. $Q = 42$) the resulting trie has rather few leaves and thus only needs little storage.

The pseudocode of our `linadd` SVM chunking algorithm is given in algorithm 4.2.

Algorithm 4.2 Outline of the `linadd` chunking algorithm that exploits the fast computations of linear combinations of kernels (e.g., by tries)

INITIALIZATION
$g_i = 0, \alpha_i = 0$ for $i = 1, \ldots, N$
LOOP UNTIL CONVERGENCE
for $t = 1, 2, \ldots$ **do**
    Check optimality conditions and stop if optimal
    select working set W based on $\mathbf{g}$ and $\boldsymbol{\alpha}$, store $\boldsymbol{\alpha}^{old} = \boldsymbol{\alpha}$
    solve reduced problem W and update $\boldsymbol{\alpha}$
    `clear w`
    $\mathbf{w} \leftarrow \mathbf{w} + (\alpha_j - \alpha_j^{old}) y_j \Phi(\mathbf{x}_j)$ for all $j \in W$ (using `add`)
    update $g_i = g_i + \langle \mathbf{w}, \Phi(\mathbf{x}_i) \rangle$ for all $i = 1, \ldots, N$ (using `lookup`)
end for

4.4.1   A Parallel Chunking Algorithm

As still most time is spent in evaluating $\mathbf{g}(\mathbf{x})$ for all training examples further speedups are gained when parallelizing the evaluation of $\mathbf{g}(\mathbf{x})$. When using the `linadd` algorithm, one first constructs the data structure representing the update vector $\mathbf{w}$ and then performs parallel `lookup` operations using several CPUs (e.g., using shared memory or several copies of the data structure on separate computing nodes). We have implemented this algorithm based on multiple *threads* and gain reasonable speedups (see next section).

Note that this part of the computations is almost ideal to distribute to many CPUs, as only the updated $\boldsymbol{\alpha}$ (or $\mathbf{w}$ depending on the communication costs and size) have to be transferred before each CPU computes a large chunk $I_k \subset \{1, \ldots, N\}$ of

$$h_i^{(k)} = \langle \mathbf{w}, \Phi(\mathbf{x}_i) \rangle, \quad \forall i \in I_k, \quad \forall k = 1, \ldots, N, \text{ where } (I_1 \cup \cdots \cup I_n) = (1, \ldots, N),$$

which is transferred to a master node that finally computes $\mathbf{g} \leftarrow \mathbf{g} + \mathbf{h}$, as illustrated in algorithm 4.3.

Algorithm 4.3 Outline of the parallel chunking algorithm that exploits the fast computations of linear combinations of kernels

---

Master node
INITIALIZATION
$g_i = 0$, $\alpha_i = 0$ for $i = 1, \ldots, N$
LOOP UNTIL CONVERGENCE
for $t = 1, 2, \ldots$ **do**
    Check optimality conditions and stop if optimal
    select working set W based on $\mathbf{g}$ and $\boldsymbol{\alpha}$, store $\boldsymbol{\alpha}^{old} = \boldsymbol{\alpha}$
    solve reduced problem W and update $\boldsymbol{\alpha}$
    transfer to Slave nodes: $\alpha_j - \alpha_j^{old}$ for all $j \in W$
    fetch from n Slave nodes: $\mathbf{h} = (\mathbf{h}^{(1)}, \ldots, \mathbf{h}^{(n)})$
    update $g_i = g_i + h_i$ for all $i = 1, \ldots, N$
end for
signal convergence to slave nodes

Slave nodes
LOOP UNTIL CONVERGENCE
while not converged **do**
    fetch from Master node $\alpha_j - \alpha_j^{old}$ for all $j \in W$
    clear w
    $\mathbf{w} \leftarrow \mathbf{w} + (\alpha_j - \alpha_j^{old}) y_j \Phi(\mathbf{x}_j)$ for all $j \in W$ (using **add**)
    node k computes $h_i^{(k)} = \langle \mathbf{w}, \Phi(\mathbf{x}_i) \rangle$
        for all $i = \lceil (k-1)\frac{N}{n} \rceil + 1, \ldots, \lceil k\frac{N}{n} \rceil$ (using **lookup**)
    transfer to master: $\mathbf{h}^{(k)}$
end while

4.5   Benchmark Experiments

In this section we will perform a benchmark comparing the running times of SVMs using the proposed algorithmic optimizations.

4.5.1   Experimental Setup

To demonstrate the effect of the `linadd` SVM training optimizations (algorithm 4.2) we applied the standard and the `linadd` algorithm using 1 to 8 CPUs to a *human* splice site data set,[5] comparing it to the original WD and spectrum kernel formulation. The splice data set contains 159,771 true acceptor splice site sequences and 14,868,555 decoys, leading to a total of 15,028,326 sequences, each 141 base pairs

---

5. The splice dataset can be downloaded from `http://www.fml.tuebingen.mpg.de/` `raetsch/projects/lsmkl`.

in length. It was generated following a procedure similar to the one of Sonnenburg et al. (2005a) for *Caenorhabditis elegans*, which only contained 1,026,036 examples. Note that the dataset is very unbalanced as 98.94% of the examples are negatively labeled. For training we selected 500, 1000, 5000, 10,000, 30,000, 50,000, 100,000, 200,000, 500,000, 1,000,000, 2,000,000, 5,000,000 and 10,000,000 randomly subsampled examples and measured the time needed in SVM training. For classification performance evaluation we always use the same remaining 5,028,326 examples as a test dataset. We set the degree parameter to $d = 20$ for the WD kernel and to $d = 8$ for the spectrum kernel fixing the SVM's regularization parameter to $C = 1$. We used tries for the WD kernel and explicit maps with 2^{16} elements for the spectrum kernel as the DNA alphabet requires only 2 bits to enumerate the four symbols A, C, G, T leading to 16-bit 8th-order words.

Since the spectrum kernel is position independent it is not well suited for the splice site recognition problem that requires knowledge of the position of the substring relative to the splice site. We therefore applied this kernel to a *web spam* dataset ($d = 4$), where the task is to distinguish webpages that are maliciously tailored to achieve high ranks by search engines — so-called web spam — from normal webpages. As negative examples we obtained the Webb spam corpus[6] (Webb et al., 2006), which comprises about 350,000 pages of web spam. In order to generate normal data, we selected an initial set of popular websites (e.g., `cnn.com`; `microsoft.com`; `slashdot.org`; and `heise.de`) and recursively followed links up to a depth of 3, resulting in 250,000 downloaded webpages from more than 10,000 websites. The average length of the webpages is 20KB with a standard deviation of 25KB. We then filtered all pages that did not contain the <html> tag (case-insensitive matching) leading to 300,000 spam and 180,000 normal pages with an average size of 30KB per page and a total size of 5GB. As a sparse mapping we used sorted arrays of 64-bit unsigned integers allowing us to consider up to 8-mers, due to the fact that some of the retrieved webpages are in fact binaries (8-bit alphabet: $0 \ldots 255$). We used a random subset of 100,000 examples for training and a separate set of the same size for testing. The total size of the training and test dataset is $\approx$ 4GB, which results in $\approx$ 30GB of memory requirements using sorted arrays of 64-bit variables.

The splice and the web spam datasets are used in all benchmark experiments and SVMs are trained using the SHOGUN machine learning toolbox,[7] which contains a modified version of SVM^{light} (Joachims, 1999a). SVM^{light}'s subproblem size (parameter `qpsize`) and convergence criterion (parameter `epsilon`) were set to $Q = 42$ and $\epsilon_{SVM} = 10^{-5}$. See table 4.6 for other choices of Q. A kernel cache of 1GB was used for all kernels except the precomputed kernel and algorithms using the `linadd` extension for which the kernel cache was disabled. Experiments were performed on a PC powered by *eight* 2.4GHz AMD Opteron(tm) processors running Linux. We

---

6. Available from `http://spamarchive.org/gt/`.
7. The toolbox source code is freely available from `http://www.shogun-toolbox.org`.

Table 4.2 Speed comparison of the standard single CPU weighted degree kernel algorithm (*WD1*) in SVM^{light} training, compared to the 4 (*WD4*) and 8 (*WD8*) CPUs parallelized version, the precomputed version (*WDPre*), and the `linadd` extension used in conjunction with the standard WD kernel for 1, 4, and 8 CPUs (*LinWD1, LinWD4, LinWD8*) on the splice dataset.

N	WDPre	WD1	WD4	WD8	LinWD1	LinWD4	LinWD8
500	1	1	1	1	1	1	1
1000	2	1	1	1	3	1	1
5000	29	7	5	5	16	4	5
10,000	109	19	13	12	35	10	11
30,000	934	110	52	45	136	33	27
50,000	-	448	170	125	254	61	45
100,000	-	1233	472	386	309	101	84
200,000	-	4460	1543	1284	779	220	166
500,000	-	22229	8664	6998	2978	898	611
1,000,000	-	-	-	-	7189	2366	1474
2,000,000	-	-	-	-	-	-	4274
5,000,000	-	-	-	-	-	-	18547
10,000,000	-	-	-	-	-	-	97484

measured the training time for each of the algorithms (single, quad, or eight CPU version) and dataset sizes.

4.5.2 Benchmarking SVM

4.5.2.1 Splice Dataset

The obtained training times for the different SVM algorithms on the splice dataset are displayed in table 4.2, table 4.3 and figure 4.5. First, SVMs were trained using standard SVM^{light} with the WD Kernel precomputed (*WDPre*), the standard WD kernel (*WD1*), and the precomputed (*SpecPre*) and standard spectrum kernel (*Spec*). Then SVMs utilizing the `linadd` extension[8] were trained using the WD (*LinWD*) and spectrum (*LinSpec*) kernel. Finally, SVMs were trained on 4 and 8 CPUs using the parallel version of the `linadd` algorithm (*LinWD4, LinWD8*). *WD4* and *WD8* demonstrate the effect of a simple parallelization strategy, where the computation of kernel rows and updates on the working set are parallelized, which works with *any* kernel.

---

8. More precisely, the $\mathcal{O}(l)$ block formulation of the WD kernel as proposed by Sonnenburg et al. (2005b) was used in all WD-SVM benchmarks (potentially in addition to the `linadd` extension).

Table 4.3 Speed comparison of the spectrum kernel without (*Spec*) and with `linadd` (*LinSpec1, LinSpec4, LinSpec8*, using 1, 4, and 8 processors) on the splice dataset. *SpecPre* denotes the precomputed version. The first column shows the sample size N of the dataset used in SVM training while the following columns display the time (measured in seconds) needed in the training phase.

N	SpecPre	Spec	LinSpec1	LinSpec4	LinSpec8
500	1	1	1	1	1
1000	2	2	1	1	1
5000	27	38	4	2	3
10,000	104	117	4	5	4
30,000	915	715	33	17	13
50,000	-	1207	38	25	26
100,000	-	3982	127	64	84
200,000	-	14200	419	254	283
500,000	-	181241	3027	1719	1611
1,000,000	-	-	27350	14581	12991

The training times obtained when precomputing the kernel matrix (which includes the time needed to precompute the full kernel matrix) is in all cases larger than the times obtained using the standard WD kernel, demonstrating the effectiveness of SVM^{light}'s kernel cache. The overhead of constructing a trie on $Q = 42$ examples is visible: only starting from 50,000 examples `linadd` optimization becomes more efficient than the original WD kernel algorithm as the kernel cache cannot hold all kernel elements anymore.[9]

The `linadd` formulation outperforms the original WD kernel by a factor of 7.5 on half a million examples. The picture is similar for the spectrum kernel; here speedups of factor 59.9 on 500,000 examples are reached which stems from the fact that explicit maps (and not tries as in the WD kernel case), as discussed in section 4.3.1 were used. This led to a `lookup` cost of $\mathcal{O}(1)$ and a dramatically reduced map construction time. For that reason the parallelization effort benefits the WD kernel more than the spectrum kernel: on half a million examples the parallelization using 4 CPUs (8 CPUs) leads to a speedup of factor 3.3 (4.9) for the WD kernel, but only 1.8 (1.9) for the spectrum kernel. Thus parallelization will help more if the kernel computation is slow. Training with the original WD kernel with a sample size of 500,000 takes about 6 hours, the `linadd` version still requires about 50 minutes, whereas the 8 CPU parallel implementation requires about 2 hours, and only 20 minutes in conjunction with the `linadd` optimization. Finally, training on

9. When single precision 4-byte floating point numbers are used, caching all kernel elements is possible when training with up to 16,384 examples.

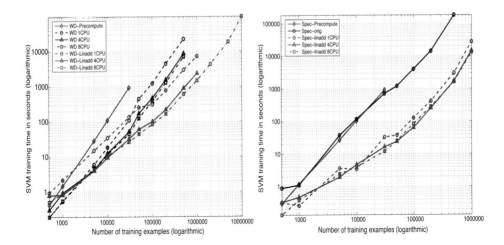

Figure 4.5   Comparison of the running time of the different SVM training algorithms using the weighted degree kernel on the splice dataset. Note that as this is a log-log plot, small-appearing distances are large for larger N and that each slope corresponds to a different exponent. In the left figure the weighted degree kernel training times are measured; the right figure displays spectrum kernel training times.

10 million examples takes about 27 hours. Note that this data set is already 2.1GB in size.

4.5.2.2   Web spam dataset

Table 4.4 lists measured run-times with and without the `linadd` optimization on the web spam dataset introduced in section 4.5.1, as well as classification accuracy. As before, we used $Q = 42$ as the quadratic subproblem size. A discussion of the subproblem size for the splice dataset can be found in section 4.5.4, suggesting that a midrange $Q = 42$ works best in most cases. Similarly to the splice dataset, the `linadd` optimization yields performance improvements for larger training sets, e.g., for 70,000 training instances of up to a factor of 2.3. The classification accuracy steadily increases with the number of training examples and finally reaches an accuracy of 98.18% and an area under the receiver operator characteristic (ROC) curve of 99.64% on 100,000 examples (for a discussion of the performance measures, see section 4.5.3).

The large alphabet, however, requires utilization of sorted arrays in contrast to the explicit map representation used for the splice dataset. Furthermore, the web spam pages are on average 200 times longer than DNA sequences in the splice dataset. As a result the speedup achieved through the `linadd` optimization is limited by maintenance of the sorted arrays and, hence, the less effective CPU cache. Note that as web documents have an average size of 30KB, training on

Table 4.4 Speed and classification accuracy comparison of the spectrum kernel without (*Spec*) and with `linadd` (*LinSpec*) on the web spam dataset. The first row shows the sample size N of the dataset used in SVM training. The next two rows display the time (measured in seconds) needed in the training phase, followed by the classification accuracy and the area under the receiver operator characteristic curve (in percent, cf. section 4.5.3)

N	100	500	1000	5000	10,000	20,000	50,000	70,000	100,000
Spec	2	97	201	1977	6039	19063	94012	193327	-
LinSpec	3	255	840	4030	9128	11948	44706	83802	107661
Accuracy	89.59	92.12	93.50	96.36	97.03	97.46	97.83	97.98	98.18
auROC	94.37	97.82	98.41	99.11	99.32	99.43	99.59	99.61	99.64

100,000 examples requires $\approx$ 15GB of memory just to store the 64-bit variables in sorted arrays.

4.5.3 Classification Performance

Figure 4.6 and table 4.5 show the classification performance[10] in terms of area under the ROC curve (Metz, 1978; Fawcett, 2003) and the area under the precision recall (PR) curve (see e.g., Davis and Goadrich, 2006) of SVMs on the human splice data set for different data set sizes using the WD kernel.

Recall the definition of the ROC and PR curves: The sensitivity (or recall) is defined as the fraction of correctly classified positive examples among the total number of positive examples, i.e., it equals the true-positive rate $TPR = TP/(TP + FN)$. Analogously, the fraction $FPR = FP/(TN + FP)$ of negative examples wrongly classified as positive is called the false-positive rate. Plotting FPR against TPR results in the ROC curve (Metz, 1978; Fawcett, 2003). Plotting the true-positive rate against the positive predictive value (also precision) $PPV = TP/(FP + TP)$, i.e., the fraction of correct positive predictions among all positively predicted examples, one obtains the PR curve (see e.g. Davis and Goadrich, 2006). Note that this is a very unbalanced dataset. Hence, the area under the ROC curve is rather meaningless, since this measure is independent of class ratios. The area under the PR curve (auPRC) seems a more sensible measure here. It steadily increases as more training examples are used for learning. Thus one should train using all available data to obtain the best results.

---

10. We omit to show the classification accuracy, as 98.94% of the examples are negatively labeled. Thus, the simplest classifier, predicting -1 for all examples, already achieves 98.94% rendering the accuracy measure meaningless.

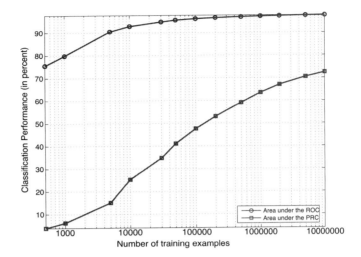

Figure 4.6 Comparison of the classification performance of the weighted degree kernel–based SVM classifier for different training set sizes. The area under the ROC curve and the area under the PR curve are displayed (in percent). Note that as this is a very unbalanced dataset, the area under the ROC curve is less meaningful than the area under the PR curve.

Table 4.5 Comparison of the classification performance of the weighted degree kernel-based SVM classifier for different training set sizes. The area under the ROC curve (*auROC*) and the area under the PR curve (*auPRC*) are displayed (in percent). Larger values are better. An optimal classifier would achieve 100%. As this is a very unbalanced dataset, the area under the ROC curve is almost meaningless. For comparison, the classification performance achieved using a fourth-order Markov chain on 10 million examples is displayed in the last row (marked *; order 4 was chosen based on model selection; orders 1-8 using several values for the pseudocount were considered).

N	auROC	auPRC		N	auROC	auPRC
500	75.55	3.94		200,000	96.57	53.04
1000	79.86	6.22		500,000	96.93	59.09
5000	90.49	15.07		1,000,000	97.19	63.51
10,000	92.83	25.25		2,000,000	97.36	67.04
30,000	94.77	34.76		5,000,000	97.54	70.47
50,000	95.52	41.06		10,000,000	97.67	72.46
100,000	96.14	47.61		10,000,000	96.03*	44.64*

Table 4.6 Influence on training time when varying the size of the quadratic program Q in SVM^{light}, when using the `linadd` formulation of the WD kernel. While training times do not vary dramatically one still observes the tendency that with larger sample size a larger Q becomes optimal. The $Q = 42$ column displays the same result as column *LinWD1* in table 4.2.

N	12	32	*42*	52	72	92	112	132	152
					Q				
500	2	1	1	2	2	1	2	2	2
1000	4	3	3	3	3	3	3	3	3
5000	22	16	16	15	15	15	16	16	17
10,000	51	**35**	**35**	**36**	39	42	43	43	43
30,000	204	**138**	136	139	148	156	165	175	**132**
50,000	397	**264**	254	266	272	290	303	315	327
100,000	449	**317**	309	368	344	374	387	721	752
200,000	1107	**771**	779	848	796	867	1573	940	1670
500,000	4691	**2754**	2978	2714	2910	3063	4369	3995	3457
1,000,000	14429	8211	**7189**	8462	8524	9857	9574	8727	9077

4.5.4 Varying the Subproblem Size Q

As discussed in section 4.4 and algorithm 4.2, using the `linadd` algorithm for computing the output for all training examples w.r.t. to some working set can be speeded up by a factor of Q (i.e., the size of the quadratic subproblems, termed `qpsize` in SVM^{light}). However, there is a tradeoff in choosing Q, as solving larger quadratic subproblems is expensive (quadratic to cubic effort). Table 4.6 shows the dependence of the computing time from Q and N. For example, choosing $Q = 42$ instead of $Q = 12$ for 1 million examples leads to a speedup of factor 2. Sticking with a midrange Q (here $Q = 42$) seems to be a good idea for this task. However, a large variance can be observed, as the SVM training time depends to a large extent on which Q variables are selected in each optimization step. For example, on the related *C. elegans* splice data set, $Q = 141$ was optimal for large sample sizes, while a mid-range $Q = 71$ led to the overall best performance. Here any $Q > 12$ leads to a similar SVM training time.

4.6   Extensions

In this section we show that the `linadd` extensions are especially helpful for multiple kernel learning (MKL) (section 4.6.1). We show that speedups of up to a factor 50 for the WD kernel are possible (using a single CPU). In section 4.6.2 we discuss methods for improving the interpretability of the classifier. We show that we can extract useful knowledge from the learned decision boundaries by using our data structures. Moreover, we illustrate that MKL can also be helpful for understanding which information is used by the SVM for discrimination. We study several toy and real-world examples for illustration.

4.6.1   Large-Scale Multiple Kernel Learning

In the MKL problem for binary classification, one is given N data points $(\mathbf{x}_i, y_i)$ $(y_i \in \{\pm 1\})$, where $\mathbf{x}_i$ is translated via K mappings $\Phi_k(\mathbf{x}) \mapsto \mathbb{R}^{D_k}$, $k = 1, \ldots, K$, from the input into K feature spaces $(\Phi_1(\mathbf{x}_i), \ldots, \Phi_K(\mathbf{x}_i))$, each of which corresponds to a different kernel. Here D_k denotes the dimensionality of the kth feature space. Now the aim is to learn a weighting over the different kernels. To do so, one solves the following optimization problem (Bach et al., 2004),[11] which is equivalent to the linear SVM for $K = 1$:[12]

MKL Primal for Classification

$$\min \quad \frac{1}{2} \left(\sum_{k=1}^{K} \|\mathbf{w}_k\|_2 \right)^2 + C \sum_{i=1}^{N} \xi_i \tag{4.7}$$

$$\text{w.r.t.} \quad \mathbf{w}_k \in \mathbb{R}^{D_k}, \boldsymbol{\xi} \in \mathbb{R}^N, b \in \mathbb{R},$$

$$\text{s.t.} \quad \xi_i \geq 0 \text{ and } y_i \left(\sum_{k=1}^{K} \langle \mathbf{w}_k, \Phi_k(\mathbf{x}_i) \rangle + b \right) \geq 1 - \xi_i, \ \forall i = 1, \ldots, N$$

Note that (4.7) is different from taking a normal SVM and adding the kernels together, as the regularizer $(\sum_k \|\mathbf{w}_k\|_2)^2$ instead of $(\sum_k \|\mathbf{w}_k\|_2^2)$ is used, leading to a feature selection over kernels.

4.6.1.1   Solving the MKL Problem

In Sonnenburg et al. (2006b) we proposed to reformulate this problem as a semi-infinite linear program (SILP), which can be derived using the dual formulation of (4.7) as suggested by Bach et al. (2004). The SILP formulation (4.8) can be solved using so-called *column generation* techniques (Hettich and Kortanek, 1993; Demiriz et al., 2002; Rätsch et al., 2002). The basic idea is to compute the optimal $(\boldsymbol{\beta}, \theta)$ for a restricted subset of constraints on $\boldsymbol{\alpha}$ of a SILP.

---

11. See (Sonnenburg et al., 2006a) for generalizations to other problem settings such as regression. Also note that very similar MKL algorithms can be found in (Weston, 1999; Bennett et al., 2002; Bi et al., 2004).
12. We assume $\text{tr}(K_k) = 1$, $k = 1, \ldots, K$ and set d_j in (Bach et al., 2004) to 1.

Semi-Infinite Linear Program (SILP)

$$\text{max} \quad \theta \tag{4.8}$$
$$\text{w.r.t.} \quad \theta \in \mathbb{R}, \boldsymbol{\beta} \in \mathbb{R}^K$$
$$\text{s.t.} \quad \mathbf{0} \le \boldsymbol{\beta}, \quad \sum_k \beta_k = 1 \text{ and}$$

$$\frac{1}{2} \sum_{i,j=1}^{N} \alpha_i \alpha_j y_i y_j \sum_{k=1}^{K} \beta_k k_k(\mathbf{x}_i, \mathbf{x}_j) - \sum_{i=1}^{N} \alpha_i \ge \theta \tag{4.9}$$

$$\text{for all } \boldsymbol{\alpha} \in \mathbb{R}^N \text{ with } \mathbf{0} \le \boldsymbol{\alpha} \le C\mathbf{1} \text{ and } \sum_i y_i \alpha_i = 0$$

Then a second algorithm generates a new, yet unsatisfied constraint determined by $\boldsymbol{\alpha}$. These two algorithms iterate until guaranteed convergence (Hettich and Kortanek, 1993). It turns out that to find the most violated constraint, one needs to solve a single-kernel SVM problem using the intermediate solution $\boldsymbol{\beta}$ (Sonnenburg et al., 2005a). Using this idea we can thus take advantage of the efficient single-kernel SVM implementations (with and without `linadd` optimization).

A more efficient version (Sonnenburg et al., 2006b) adapts the $\boldsymbol{\beta}$'s while the chunking algorithm optimizes the $\boldsymbol{\alpha}$'s. This algorithm also requires the computation of linear combinations of kernels:

$$g_i = \sum_{j=1}^{N} \alpha_j y_i \left(\sum_{k=1}^{K} \beta_k k_k(\mathbf{x}_i, \mathbf{x}_j) \right).$$

However, since the $\boldsymbol{\beta}$'s change during the optimization, one has to maintain iterates for every example *and* kernel:

$$g_{i,k} = \sum_{j=1}^{N} \alpha_j y_i k_k(\mathbf{x}_i, \mathbf{x}_j),$$

in order to compute $g_i = \sum_{k=1}^{K} \beta_k g_{i,k}$. Unfortunately, this approach is inefficient in combination with the common kernel caching strategies, since one now requires independent caching of K kernels, which considerably reduces the effectiveness when using large numbers of kernels or examples. Here, the `linadd` approach completely avoids kernel caching and can be straightforwardly applied to MKL. It turns out to be particularly effective, as will be illustrated in simulation experiments in the next subsection. More details on these concepts and algorithms can be found in Sonnenburg et al. (2006b).

4.6.1.2 Benchmarking MKL

The WD kernel of degree 20 consists of a weighted sum of 20 subkernels each counting matching d-mers, for $d = 1, \ldots, 20$. Using MKL we learned the weighting on the

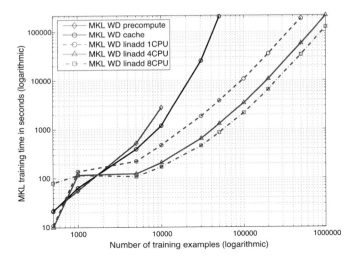

Figure 4.7 Comparison of the running time of the different MKL algorithms when used with the WD kernel. Note that as this is a log-log plot, small-appearing distances are large for larger N and that each slope corresponds to a different exponent.

splice site recognition task for 1 million examples. Focusing on a speed comparison we now show the obtained training times for the different MKL algorithms applied to learning weightings of the WD kernel on the splice site classification task. To do so, several MKL-SVMs were trained using precomputed kernel matrices (*PreMKL*), kernel matrices which are computed on the fly employing kernel caching (*MKL*), MKL using the `linadd` extension (*LinMKL1*), and `linadd` with its parallel implementation[13] (*LinMKL4* and *LinMKL8* — on 4 and 8 CPUs). In contrast to the previous experiments, the SVM's regularization parameter was set to $C = 5$ and the subproblem size was fixed at $Q = 112$. The results[14] are displayed in table 4.7 and figure 4.7. While precomputing kernel matrices seems beneficial, it cannot be applied to large-scale cases (e.g., $> 10,000$ examples) due to the $\mathcal{O}(KN^2)$ memory requirement for storing the kernel matrices.[15] On-the-fly-computation of the kernel matrices is computationally extremely demanding, but since kernel caching[16] is used, it is still possible on 50,000 examples in about 57 hours. Note that no WD kernel specific optimizations are involved here, so one expects a similar result for arbitrary kernels.

---

13. Algorithm 4.3 with the `linadd` extensions including parallelization of algorithm 4.3.
14. Erratum: a programming error caused the optimizer to terminate the MKL SVM optimization before reaching the desired accuracy $\epsilon_{SVM} = 10^{-5}$. Since this affects the `linadd` *and* vanilla formulations, the benchmark comparison is still fair.
15. Using 20 kernels on 10,000 examples requires already 7.5GB; on 30,000 examples 67GB would be required (both using single precision floats).
16. Each kernel has a cache of 1GB.

Table 4.7 Speed comparison when determining the WD kernel weight by multiple kernel learning using the chunking algorithm (MKL) and MKL in conjunction with the (parallelized) `linadd` algorithm using 1, 4, and 8 processors (*LinMKL1, LinMKL4, LinMKL8*). The first column shows the sample size N of the dataset used in SVM training while the following columns display the time (measured in seconds) needed in the training phase.

N	PreMKL	MKL	LinMKL1	LinMKL4	LinMKL8
500	22	22	11	10	80
1000	56	64	139	116	116
5000	518	393	223	124	108
10,000	2,786	1,181	474	209	172
30,000	-	25,227	1,853	648	462
50,000	-	204,492	3,849	1292	857
100,000	-	-	10,745	3,456	2,145
200,000	-	-	34,933	10,677	6,540
500,000	-	-	185,886	56,614	33,625
1,000,000	-	-	-	214,021	124,691

The `linadd` variants outperform the other algorithms by far (speedup factor 53 on 50,000 examples) and are still applicable to datasets of size up to 1 million. Note that without parallelization, MKL on 1 million examples would take more than a week, compared with 2.5 (2) days in the quad CPU (eight CPU) version. The parallel versions outperform the single processor version from the start, achieving a speedup for 10,000 examples of 2.27 (2.75), quickly reaching a plateau at a speedup factor of 2.98 (4.49) at a level of 50,000 examples and approaching a speedup factor of 3.28 (5.53) on 500,000 examples (efficiency: 82% (69%)). Note that the performance gain using 8 CPUs is relatively small as, for instance, solving the quadratic programming (QP) problem and constructing the tries is not parallelized.

4.6.1.3 MKL Applications

Multiple kernel learning can be applied to knowledge discovery tasks. It can be used for automated model selection and to interpret the learned model (Rätsch et al., 2006; Sonnenburg et al., 2006b). MKL has been successfully used on real-world datasets in the field of computational biology (Lanckriet et al., 2004; Sonnenburg et al., 2005a). It was shown to improve classification performance on the task of ribosomal and membrane protein prediction (Lanckriet et al., 2004), where a weighting over different kernels each corresponding to a different feature set was learned. In their result, the included random channels obtained low kernel weights. However, as the datasets were rather small (≈ 1000 examples) the kernel matrices could be precomputed and simultaneously kept in memory, which was not possible in (Sonnenburg et al., 2005a). There, we considered a splice site recognition task for the worm *C. elegans* and used MKL mainly to interpret the resulting classifier (Sonnenburg et al., 2005b; Rätsch et al., 2006). In the next section we will propose alternative ways to facilitate understanding of the SVM classifier, taking advantage of the discussed data representations.

4.6.2   Interpreting the SVM Classifier

One of the problems with kernel methods compared to probabilistic methods, such as position weight matrices or interpolated Markov models (Delcher et al., 1999), is that the resulting decision function is hard to interpret and, hence, difficult to use in order to extract relevant biological knowledge from it (see also Kuang et al., 2004; X. H.-F. Zhang et al., 2003). The resulting classifier can be written as a dot product between an $\boldsymbol{\alpha}$ weighted linear combination of support vectors mapped into the feature space that is often only implicitly defined via the kernel function:

$$f(\mathbf{x}) = \underbrace{\sum_{i=1}^{N_s} \alpha_i y_i \Phi(\mathbf{x}_i)}_{\mathbf{w}} \cdot \Phi(\mathbf{x}) = \sum_{i=1}^{N_s} \alpha_i y_i k(\mathbf{x}_i, \mathbf{x}).$$

In the case of sparse feature spaces, as with string kernels, we have shown how one can represent $\mathbf{w}$ in an appropriate sparse form and then efficiently compute dot products between $\mathbf{w}$ and $\Phi(\mathbf{x})$ in order to speed up SVM training or testing. This sparse representation comes with the additional benefit of providing us with means to interpret the SVM classifier. For k-mer-based string kernels like the spectrum kernel, each dimension w_u in $\mathbf{w}$ represents a weight assigned to that k-mer u. From the learned weighting one can thus easily identify the k-mers with highest absolute weight or above a given threshold τ: $\{u \mid |w_u| > \tau\}$. Note that the total number of k-mers appearing in the support vectors is bounded by dN_sL where L is the maximum length of the sequences $L = \max_{i=1,\dots,N_s} l_{x_i}$. This approach also works for the WD kernel (with and without shifts). Here a weight is assigned to each k-mer with $1 \leq k \leq d$ at each position in the sequence. While this approach will identify the k-mers contributing most to class discrimination, it is unsuitable for visualization of all possible $|\Sigma|^k$ substrings of length k per position. With growing order d, extracting all weights, especially for the WD kernel, quickly becomes infeasible: the number grows exponentially in d $(\mathcal{O}(l|\Sigma|^d))$. Thus, one would need to accept a lower-degree $\tilde{d} < d$ for visualization. However, this might lead to inferior generalization results (e.g., when using $\tilde{d}$ instead of d in training) or to an incomplete understanding of how the SVM is discriminating the sequences.

4.6.2.1   *Extracting Discriminative k-mers*

We therefore propose to choose a lower order $\tilde{d}$ just for visualization while making use of the *original* potentially higher-order SVM classifier, by computing the contributions of the k−mers with $1 \le k \le d$ to the $\tilde{d}$-mers. The idea of this *k-mer extraction* technique is to identify all k-mers with $1 \le k \le d$ overlapping with the $\tilde{d}$-mers of the trained SVM classifier. The weights of the overlapping k-mers are then marginalized by the length of the match, i.e., $w \mapsto \frac{1}{|\Sigma|^{l_p}} w$ where l_p is the length of the nonoverlapping part. The marginalized weights are then summed up and assigned to the identified $\tilde{d}$-mers.

This can be done rather efficiently for the WD (shift) kernel: The sparse representation used for the WD kernels is a suffix trie at each position in the sequence. Thus all one needs to do is to traverse the tries — one after the other while adding up contributing weights. For example, if one wants to know the weight for the trimer **AAA** at position 42 for a WD kernel of degree 10, then 10-mers **XXXXXXXXXA** ($X \in \{A, C, G, T\}$) at position 33, 10-mers **XXXXXXXAAAX** at position 36, and 10-mers **AXXXXXXXXX** at position 44, as well as all shorter overlapping k-mers ($k = 1 \ldots 9$), contribute. Thus the weights in the contributing region **AAA** are collected, marginalized, and added to the weight for **AAA** at position 42.

We have now obtained a weighting for $\tilde{d}$-mers for each position in the sequence: $W_{\boldsymbol{u},p}, p = 1 \ldots l, \boldsymbol{u} \in \mathcal{U}$. Running the algorithm for different orders (e.g. $\tilde{d} = 1 \ldots 8$), one may be interested in generating a graphical representation from which it is possible to judge where in the sequence which substring lengths are of importance. We suggest computing this scoring by taking the maximum for each order per position,[17] i.e.,

$$S_{\tilde{d},p} = \max(W_{\boldsymbol{u},p})_{\boldsymbol{u} \in \mathcal{U}}.$$

4.6.3 Illustration on Toy Data

We will now use this approach for interpreting the SVM classifier. For a proof of concept, we apply the k-mer extraction technique to two toy datasets. For one dataset we insert two motifs at fixed positions in a random DNA sequence. These motifs are to be detected by the WD kernel. The other dataset is constructed in a way that it contains a small motif at a variable position. Here we use the WDS kernel.

4.6.3.1 Motifs at Fixed Positions

For this toy dataset we generated $11,000$ sequences of length 50, where the symbols of the alphabet $\{A, C, G, T\}$ follow a uniform distribution. We choose 1000 of these sequences to be positive examples and hide two motifs of length 7: at position 10 and 30 the motifs **GATTACA** and **AGTAGTG**, respectively. To harden the problem we create different realizations of this dataset containing different amounts of noise: In the positive examples, we randomly replace $s \in \{0, 2, 4, 5\}$ symbols in each motif with

---

17. Other operators, like, for example, the mean, could also be considered.

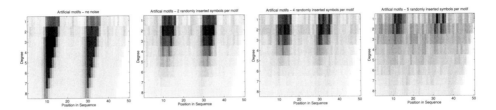

(a) Weighting **S**: Weights assigned to each $\tilde{d}$-mer at each position in the sequence for different noise levels

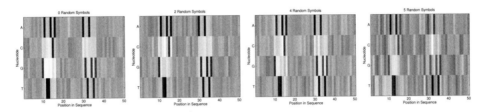

(b) Individual weights assigned to each 1-gram A,C,G,T at each position in the sequence for different noise levels

Figure 4.8   The figure illustrates positional weights **W** and **S** obtained using the k-mer extraction technique for increasing levels of noise (noise increases columnwise from left to right). (a) Plots show the weighting assigned to $\tilde{d}$-mers from 1 to 8 for each position, where the X-axis corresponds to sequence positions and the Y-axis to k-mer lengths. (b) Plots show individual weights for 1-mers listed on the Y-axis, where the X-axis corresponds to sequence positions.

a random letter. This leads to four different datasets which we randomly permute and split such that the first 1000 examples become training and the remaining 10,000 validation examples. For every noise level, we train an SVM (parameters $C = 2$, $\epsilon = 0.001$) using the WD kernel of degree 20 followed by running the k-mer extraction technique. We also apply MKL, using a WD kernel of degree 7, to learn $M = 350$ WD kernel parameters (one parameter per position and k-mer length). The results are shown in figures 4.8 and 4.9. In the figures, columns correspond to different noise levels – from no noise to five out of seven nucleotides in the motifs being randomly replaced. For the WD-SVM (figure 4.8), each figure in the upper row shows a scoring **S** where columns correspond to sequence position and rows to k-mer lengths used at that position. The lower row displays the k-mer weighting for $\tilde{d} = 1$, i.e., the weight assigned to each nucleotide A,C,G,T at each position in the sequence.

In figure 4.9 (MKL), each figure shows the obtained kernel weights $\boldsymbol{\beta}$, where columns correspond to weights used at a certain sequence position and rows to the k-mer length used at that position. In contrast to the SVM, MKL leads to

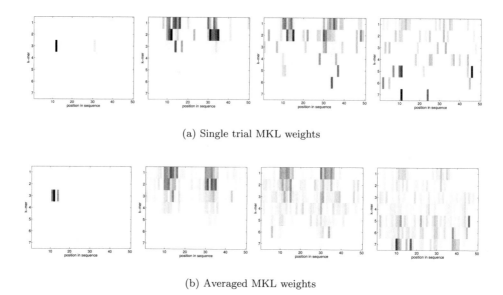

(a) Single trial MKL weights

(b) Averaged MKL weights

Figure 4.9 In this figure the columns correspond to the noise level, i.e., different numbers of nucleotides randomly substituted in the motif of the toy dataset. Each subplot shows the kernel weighting β, where columns correspond to weights used at a certain sequence position and rows to the k-mer length used at that position. While the upper row displays a single trial β, the lower row shows an averaged weighting obtained using 100 bootstrap runs, i.e. $1/100 \beta_{i=1}^{100}$.

a sparse solution implied by the 1-norm constraint on the weighting β. Hence, in the case of no noise one observes just a single 3-mer in the first motif to be sufficient to distinguish the sequences. The WD-SVM produces a rather dense solution. It exactly shows, however, that 7-mers at positions 10 and 30 have a large impact. With increasing noise level the motifs are split into smaller motifs. Thus one would expect shorter k-mers to be of importance. One indeed observes this tendency for the WD-SVM: the increased noise results in 4- and 3-mers achieving the highest weights (second column). When four out of seven nucleotides in each motif are randomly replaced, and 3- and 4-mers contribute most to discrimination. Considering the 1-gram weights with the highest scores at the positions 10-16 and 30-36 (figure 4.8(b)), the nucleotides compose the exact motifs embedded into the DNA sequences GATTACA and AGTAGTG. Note that the classification performance also drops with increased noise from 100% auROC in the first two columns to 99.8% in the third, and finally to 85% when five out of seven nucleotides in each motif are noise. At that noise level the SVM picks up random motifs from regions not belonging to the hidden motifs. However, the motifs — though a lot weaker — are still visible in the 1-gram plot. For MKL we have similar observations. However, when running the MKL algorithm on the data with two or more random nucleotides, it picks up a few unrelated k-mers. In (Sonnenburg et al., 2005a) we therefore proposed to use bootstrap replicates in order to obtain more reliable weightings (the average is shown in figure 4.9(b)) additionally combined with a statistical test such that only significant weights are detected. However, one can observe the same tendency as before: shorter k-mers are picked up with increasing noise level. In column 3, an average ROC score of 99.6% is achieved. In the last column the ROC score drops down to 83%, while random k-mer lengths are detected.

4.6.3.2 Motif at Varying Positions

In contrast to the previous paragraph, where we considered motifs at a fixed position, we will now study a dataset that contains a single motif somewhere in the interval [49, 67]. The dataset was generated in the following way: we created 5000 training and test examples which contain the letters C, G, and T (uniformly, with the exception that C appears twice as often). In the positive dataset, we inserted the motif AAA randomly in the above interval and placed three A's (in most cases nonconsecutive) in the same region for the negative examples. The task is again to learn a discrimination between the classes followed by a k-mer extraction analysis as above. While the WDS kernel is made for this kind of analysis, it is obvious that the WD kernel would have a hard time in this setup, although due to the dominance of the AAA triplet in that region it will not fail totally. In this experiment we trained two SVMs, one with the WD and one with the WDS kernel of order 20 and shift 15. We set SVM parameters to $\epsilon = 10^{-3}$ and $C = 1$. While the WD kernel achieves a respectable auROC of 92.8%, it is outperformed by the WDS kernel getting 96.6%. Running the k-mer extraction technique on the WDS-SVM result we obtain figure 4.10. One clearly observes that 3-mers are getting the highest weights and one is able to even identify the motif AAA to be of importance in the range 49 to 64.

4.6.3.3 Real-World Splice Dataset

We finally apply the same procedure to a splice dataset of (Sonnenburg et al., 2005a). This dataset contains 262,421 DNA sequences of length 141 nucleotides and was extracted by taking windows around a *C.elegans* acceptor splice site. We used a WD kernel of degree 20, trained an SVM ($\epsilon = 10^{-3}$ and $C = 1$) on the first 100,000 examples and obtained a classification performance on the remaining 162,421 examples of auROC 99.7%. We then applied the k-mer extraction technique to the WD-SVM. The obtained results are shown in figure 4.11. One observes a very focused signal in front of the acceptor splice site which is located between positions 60-61 followed by the AG consensus at positions 61 and 62 (see Sonnenburg et al., 2005a, for more details). It is also interesting to note that hexamers and pentamers are most discriminative at positions 57 and 58. Also a weak signal can be found around position 17 (33 nucleotides upstream of the splice site) which coincides with an upstream donor splice site as introns in *C.elegans* are often very short. Looking at the dinucleotide weighting one can even see an increased weighting for the GT

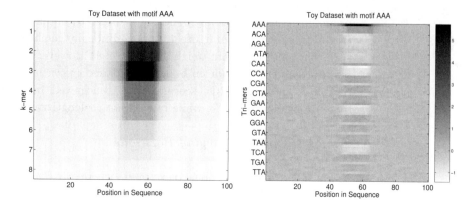

Figure 4.10 In the region $[49, 67]$ a motif `AAA` is hidden for the positive examples, and for the negative examples three `A`'s are placed in the same region, but in most cases nonconsecutive. This figure shows the result of the k-mer extraction technique applied to an SVM classifier using the WDS kernel. The left figure shows the k-mer importance per position (absolute values; darker colors correspond to higher importance). The right figure displays the weights assigned to each trimer at each position (gray values correspond to weights around zero and thus don't contribute in discrimination; white and light gray spots highlight silencers that add to a negative class label ; black and dark gray regions correspond to enhancers suggesting a positive class label).

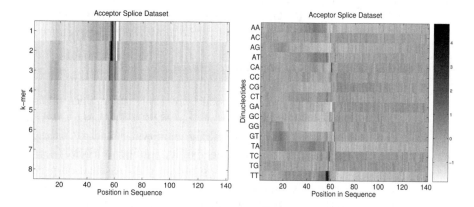

Figure 4.11 Results using the k-mer extraction technique on a splice dataset. The left figure shows the k-mer importance per position (absolute values; darker colors correspond to higher importance). The right figure displays the weights assigned to each trimer at each position (gray values correspond to weights around zero and thus don't contribute in discrimination; white and light gray spots highlight silencers that add to a negative class label; black and dark gray regions correspond to enhancers suggesting a positive class label).

consensus of the upstream donor splice site. One also recognizes the known T-rich region in front of the splice sites as well as a strong aversion against T's downstream of the splice site.

4.6.3.4 Discussion

The presented k-mer extraction technique proves very useful in understanding the SVM classifier. It is advantageous compared to MKL as one can directly use the SVM that performs best on a certain task. One does not have to retrain a MKL-SVM on a smaller dataset (MKL is computationally much more demanding) and also bootstrapping is not necessary. In addition to identifying the important k-mer lengths, the technique also highlights the locations of motifs that contribute most to discrimination. MKL will also determine the important k-mer lengths (at least when an additional statistical test is used). It is, however, not limited to kernels whose feature space is sparse and can be enumerated, but will also work with, e.g., radial basis function (RBF) kernels as was shown in Sonnenburg et al. (2006b). MKL is superior when one seeks a sparse solution and the data contains little noise. It might be necessary to incorporate the learned α into the scoring.

4.7 Conclusion

This chapter proposes performance enhancements to make practical large-scale learning with string kernels and any kernel that can be written as an inner product of sparse feature vectors. The `linadd` algorithm (algorithm 4.2) not only speeds up stand-alone SVM training but also helps to drastically reduce training times for MKL. Also, the sparse representation of the SVM normal vector allows one to look inside of the resulting SVM classifier, as each substring is assigned a weight. In a speed benchmark comparison, the `linadd` algorithm greatly accelerates SVM training. For the stand-alone SVM using the spectrum kernel, it achieves speedups of factor 60 (for the WD kernel, about 7). For MKL, we gained a speedup of factor 53. Finally, we proposed a parallel version of the `linadd` algorithm running on an 8 CPU multiprocessor system which led to *additional* speedups of factor up to 5.5 for MKL, and up to 4.9 for vanilla SVM training.

Acknowledgments

The authors gratefully acknowledge partial support from the PASCAL Network of Excellence (EU #506778), DFG grants (JA 379/13-2, MU 987/2-1), and the BMBF project MIND (FKZ 01-SC40A). We thank Alexander Zien, Bernhard Schölkopf, Olivier Chapelle, Pavel Laskov, Cheng Soon Ong, Jason Weston, and K.-R. Müller for great discussions. Additionally, we would like to express thanks to Alexander Zien for correcting and extending the visualization of contributions of k-mers for the WD-kernel.

5   Large-Scale Parallel SVM Implementation

Igor Durdanovic
Eric Cosatto
Hans-Peter Graf

We present several parallelization approaches for increasing the ability of SVM (support vector machines) to solve large-scale problems. As target systems, we consider shared memory processors, clusters of processors, vector processors, and SIMD (single instruction multiple data) processors. On a given system the speed of an SVM is limited by the compute performance of the processor as well as by the size of the memory. Efficient parallelizations have to overcome both of these limitations while not getting bogged down in communication overhead.

Modern PCs contain multicore processors, as well as SIMD accelerators, and with little programming efforts such parallelisms can be exploited to obtain substantial gains in speed. Clusters of processors offer high compute power for a modest price, but mapping an SVM onto a cluster is challenging since the calculations on the different processors have to be synchronized precisely. If this is not done judiciously the data transfers between processors can overwhelm the communication network. In the past, clusters have been used mostly in cases for such tasks as tuning of SVM hyperparameters, where many independent optimizations had to be executed. Recent parallel implementations of SVMs, such as the cascade SVM (Graf et al., 2005; J.-P. Zhang et al., 2005) or the parallel gradient projection-based decomposition technique (PGPDT) (Zanni et al., 2006; Zanghirati and Zanni, 2003), have been demonstrated for large problems with millions of training samples, but they saturate for low numbers of processors.

We highlight a new parallelization concept, the spread-kernel SVM *that solves problems with several million training vectors on a low-cost Linux cluster. This algorithm scales to hundreds of processors, providing superlinear speedup in most cases. Accelerations of over 100× are achieved with 48 machines. Since it is a parallelization of well known decomposition algorithms, all the convergence and accuracy results derived for these algorithms also hold for the spread-kernel SVM.*[1]

---

1. The code is available on `http://ml.nec-labs.com/software.php?project=milde`.

5.1   Introduction

Support vector machines (SVMs) are widely used classification and regression tools,
known for their good generalization performance, and ease of use, as well as for
their solid theoretical foundation (Vapnik, 1998). Their main limitation is a fast
increase of compute and storage requirements with the number of training vectors,
leaving many problems of practical interest beyond their reach. At the core of an
SVM is a quadratic programming (QP) problem, separating support vectors from
the rest of the training data, that scales with the cube of the number of training
vectors ($O(n^3)$; $n =$ number of training vectors). General-purpose QP solvers tend
to be rather inefficient for handling large problems, which led to the development of
several specialized algorithms for SVMs. Most of them are based on decomposition
approaches where small subsets of the training data are optimized iteratively.
Despite impressive gains in efficiency, these algorithms become impractically slow
for problem sizes on the order of $100,000$ training vectors (assuming a two-class
problem). Often the kernel matrix becomes too large to fit into main memory,
making it necessary to recompute kernel columns multiple times, which slows down
the optimization drastically.

There is a strong trend in computer design today to improve compute performance through parallelization. Other means of accelerating the compute speed,
such as increasing clock rates, are becoming more and more difficult due to fundamental physical limits. Just a few years ago parallel processors were found mostly in
esoteric high-performance architectures, but today parallel processing is used everywhere. PCs contain multicore processors and apply SIMD arrays (single-instruction,
multiple-data) to accelerate multimedia applications. Graphics processors and game
consoles are based on multiprocessor architectures, and even in cell phones multicore
processors have become common. Hence, to take advantage of these developments,
SVM algorithms must be adapted to parallel processing.

This chapter is organized as follows: In section 5.2 we give a brief overview of
recent trends in accelerating SVMs. Section 5.3 introduces the classical sequential
algorithm and discusses various optimizations that increase its speed. Often simple
optimization methods other than parallelizations can provide substantial gains
in speed, and we highlight a few such techniques as well. Sections 5.4 and 5.5
describe the spread-kernel approach to SVM parallelization and section 5.6 discusses
networking algorithms for efficient communication between processors. In section
5.7 we analyze the parallel algorithm and develop a theoretical speedup model.
Experimental results are presented in section 5.8 and in section 5.9 we discuss some
of the tradeoffs between algorithmic approaches and exploiting hardware features
for accelerating SVMs.

5.2 Accelerating SVMs: Previous Approaches

5.2.1 Decomposition

Accelerating the computation has been a concern since the first implementations of SVMs. Early attempts accelerated the QP through "chunking" (Boser et al., 1992), which starts with the optimization of a subset of the training data, followed by more data added iteratively until the global optimum is reached. Chunking has been refined in several ways (Osuna et al., 1997c; Joachims, 1999a), and led to sequential minimal optimization (SMO) algorithm (Platt, 1999; Keerthi et al., 2001). The latter, in which subsets of two vectors are optimized iteratively, is probably the most popular of these algorithms (chapter 1). The convergence properties of these schemes have been studied extensively (Keerthi and Gilbert, 2002; C.-J. Lin, 2001). The spread-kernel SVM we describe in sections 5.4 and 5.5 is a parallelization of these well-tested decomposition algorithms, and therefore convergence and accuracy guarantees derived for these methods apply also to this parallel implementation.

"Shrinking" is a popular technique to improve the speed of the optimization (section 1.7.3). Once the training is done only support vectors contribute to the result, while all other training vectors are discarded. Therefore, the goal is to develop heuristics that find and eliminate nonsupport vectors as early as possible. In the ideal case we would have to deal only with the support vectors and can expect that the computation is reduced from $O(n^3)$ to $O(ns^3)$ (n = number of training vectors; ns = number of support vectors). Typically only a small fraction of the training vectors are support vectors and therefore this should result in big savings. However, as we will discuss later in more detail, the advantages of all these heuristics remain questionable. They tend to hamper other types of speed improvements because they often introduce an irregular and unpredictable data flow.

5.2.2 Parallelizing Kernel Computations

One straightforward way of accelerating the computation is through parallelization of the kernel computation. Often the kernel values require the calculation of dot products between large vectors, an operation that can strongly dominate the total computation. Acceleration through vector units, SIMD arrays, or executing this part on a graphics processor (Steinkraus et al., 2004) can speedup an SVM considerably.

Implementations of the kernel computation in hardware have been demonstrated recently using field-programmable gate arrays (Reyna-Royas et al., 2003) and in another case with a mixed analog-digital implementation of a vector-matrix multiplier (Genov et al., 2003; Genov and Cauwenberghs, 2003). Such circuits can reach impressive performance when the computing requirements of the application match the characteristics of the circuit. But matrix-vector multipliers of a fixed size lack the flexibility required for general-purpose systems. Their efficiency drops quickly if vectors of different sizes or different resolutions have to be handled, or when an application requires sparse (homogeneous) vectors or heterogeneous vectors (e.g., combinations of numeric and symbolic values).

Acceleration of the kernel computation is most effective for testing, but less so for training. Testing is a very regular operation where a fixed number of kernel evaluations between the vector to be tested and all the support vectors have to be calculated. For example, in video surveillance, test vectors are continuously streamed and compared with the same set of support vectors. Such a regular data flow lends itself perfectly to an implementation with a fixed-size matrix-vector multiplier where special-purpose hardware is orders of magnitude faster than general-purpose processors.

For training, however, there are limits on how much an SVM can be accelerated by increasing the speed of the kernel evaluations, since even reducing this computation to zero still leaves considerable computation for other operations, for example the update of the gradients. Therefore, effective parallelization of the SVM requires careful consideration of all parts involved. In particular, storage and communication requirements have to be optimized in combination with the computation.

5.2.3   Parallelization of the Optimization

Improving the speed of the optimization through parallelization is difficult due to dependencies between the computation steps. The decomposition algorithms mentioned above work iteratively; growing the optimization sequentially, and splitting them onto multiple machines requires frequent and precisely synchronized communication between processors.

Parallelizations of SVMs have been attempted by splitting the problem into smaller subsets that can be optimized independently, either through initial clustering of the data or through a trained combination of the results from individually optimized subsets (Collobert et al., 2002a). If a problem can be structured in this way, each subset can be optimized independently, and a large problem can be mapped onto a network of processors.

Variations of the standard SVM algorithm, such as the proximal SVM (Fung and Mangasarian, 2001a), were introduced that are better suited for parallelization (Tveit and Engum, 2003; Poulet, 2003). Problems with millions of training vectors were solved with this method, but so far only with linear kernels. Moreover, these modifications introduce limitations on the dimensionality of the data, and it is not clear how to overcome them.

A parallelization scheme was developed where the kernel matrix is approximated by a block-diagonal (Dong et al., 2003). This corresponds to splitting the problem into several subsets and optimizing each of them independently. New working sets are chosen with a queue technique, instead of searching for the best candidates, which can result in considerable speedups, particularly for multiclass problems.

Parallelizing QP problems is of significance well beyond machine learning, and an active community is working on developing efficient parallel algorithms, (Migdalas et al., 2003; D'Apuzzo and Marino, 2003). Yet most of the algorithms for solving general QP problems are not effective for large SVMs. SVMs generate dense Hessian matrices of enormous sizes, something most QP solvers cannot handle efficiently. In fact, general-purpose QP solvers are often optimized for sparse Hessian matrices (for example, LOQO (Vanderbei, 1999)). Large problem sizes often quoted in the literature are reached only if they lead to very sparse Hessians.

5.2.4 Cascade SVM

The cascade SVM (Graf et al., 2005; J.-P. Zhang et al., 2005) is a parallelization concept that optimizes subproblems independently and combines the support vectors in an iterative fashion (figure 5.1). The training data are split into subsets (here eight) and each one is trained individually to identify the support vectors (first layer). The results are then combined pairwise and entered as training sets for the next layer. This process is repeated until only one set of training vectors remains. The resulting support vectors are tested for global convergence by feeding them into the first layer, together with the nonsupport vectors. The global solution is reached when the same support vectors that have been entered into the first layer come out as support vectors of the first layer (and only those). It has been proved that this process converges in a finite number of steps and reaches the solution of a single optimization.

The advantage of this approach is that the partial optimizations are completely independent of each other and communication between the processors is needed only for exchanging the support vectors. Latency in the communication is therefore not critical, and the cascade SVM is suited for networks of processors that are loosely coupled, even for grid computing. However, this parallelization concept saturates for a fairly small number of processors, since one machine has to handle all the support vectors in the last layer. Typically the cascade is efficient up to about sixteen processors.

5.2.5 Parallel Gradient Projection-Based Decomposition

An efficient parallel algorithm demonstrated recently is the parallel gradient projection-based decomposition technique (PGPBDT) (Zanni et al., 2006; Zanghirati and Zanni, 2003). The subproblems are optimized with iterative projections of the gradient, a method that can be parallelized efficiently. Subsets of variable sizes can be handled in this way, and typically the algorithm converges in a small number of iterations. Fast convergence is demonstrated and problems with several million training samples were optimized with this method on clusters with high-performance networks. Slight superlinear accelerations were obtained in a few cases, but in general it seems that the increase of memory with larger numbers of nodes cannot be exploited efficiently for caching, and the accelerations tend to saturate for more than sixteen machines.

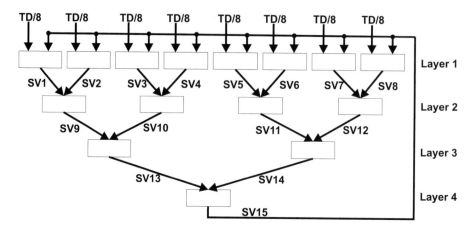

Figure 5.1 A cascade SVM implemented with eight machines. Each block represents one machine that merges two sets of vectors, performs an optimization and produces a set of support vectors. TD: training data, SV*i*: support vectors produced by the *i*th round of optimization.

5.2.6   Summary

Substantial progress has been made recently in increasing the size of problems that can be handled by SVMs, but considerable challenges remain. Several of the proposed methods introduce some constraints, either limiting the kernel types that can be used, or changing the nature of the SVM algorithm. It remains to be seen if any of these restrictions are worth the gain in speed. One of the main advantages of the SVM is the guarantee of finding the optimal solution, a feature that makes its application much easier than that of nonconvex algorithms. Any algorithm producing approximate solutions should guarantee such a behavior or provide at least reliable stopping criteria.

The cascade SVM and the PGPBDT algorithm are the only parallelizations that produce the true SVM solutions and have been shown to scale to millions of training vectors without introducing constraints on the kernel type. Both of them saturate for a relatively small number of processors (assuming clusters of machines) and further scaling in size is therefore questionable. The spread-kernel SVM introduced here shows much better scaling, which is demonstrated experimentally for up to forty-eight machines and modeling indicates the potential for scaling up to several hundred machines.

Several methods for finding approximate solutions to the SVM optimization have been proposed recently (e.g., chapter 13 and Bordes et al., 2005), that look promising for scaling SVMs to large problems. Several of the ideas developed in these papers can also be adapted to parallel processing. Yet we restrict the discussion here to algorithms that are guaranteed to find directly the optimal solution. The true SVM solution is still the gold standard and remains the most trusted solution. Methods that are able to develop the real SVM solution for large datasets are therefore of particular value.

5.3   The Sequential Algorithm

5.3.1   SVM Formulation

The (dual) formulation of the SVM algorithm is defined as a quadratic minimization problem of the objective function $W(\alpha)$:

$$W(\alpha) = \frac{1}{2}\left[\sum_{i=1}^{n}\alpha_i y_i \left[\sum_{j=1}^{n}\alpha_j y_j K(x_i, x_j)\right]\right] - \left[\sum_{i=1}^{n}\alpha_i\right], \ y_i \in \{+1, -1\}.$$

The minimization of W with respect to α is done under the following constraints:

$$\forall i \ 0 \leq \alpha_i \leq C \qquad \left[\sum_{i=1}^{n}\alpha_i y_i\right] = 0.$$

We can use the gradient of the objective function,

$$G_i = \frac{\partial W(\alpha)}{\partial \alpha_i} = y_i\left[\sum_{j=1}^{n}\alpha_j y_j K(x_i, x_j)\right] - 1,$$

to express the objective function more succinctly:

$$W(\alpha) = \frac{1}{2}\left[\sum_{i=1}^{n}\alpha_i(G_i - 1)\right].$$

5.3.2   Pseudocode

The algorithms (figures 5.2, 5.3, and 5.4) described and tested here are all based on the plain SMO algorithm (Platt, 1999; Keerthi et al., 2001). No shrinking or any other shortcuts in the optimizations are applied. Nothing in the parallelizations described later depends on the specific nature of the optimization used for solving the subproblems. Other gradient-based algorithms with different sizes of the subsets could be applied as well. Restricting the discussion to SMO makes it easy for readers to compare results and leaves no questions about the convergence behavior and the quality of the solutions.

The dominant operation is the computation of the two columns of the kernel matrix, which is required for the update of the gradient vector. Computing a kernel column has at its core a vector-matrix multiplication: $K(x_i, *) = x_i \times \mathbf{x}$, which requires $(hi - lo) \times d$ operations. This assumes that a dot product between two vectors has to be computed, which is the case for several kernel types, such as polynomial or radial basis function (RBF) kernels. A short analysis of the algorithm reveals a high degree of data independence. All the loops can be

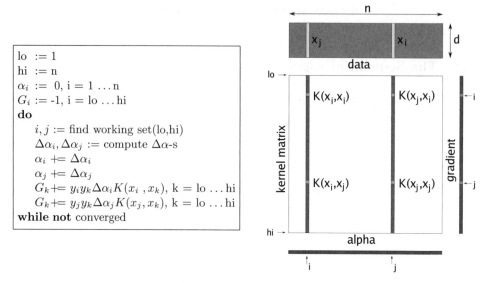

```
lo  := 1
hi  := n
αᵢ  := 0, i = 1 ... n
Gᵢ := -1, i = lo ... hi
do
     i, j := find working set(lo,hi)
     Δαᵢ, Δαⱼ := compute Δα-s
     αᵢ += Δαᵢ
     αⱼ += Δαⱼ
     Gₖ += yᵢyₖΔαᵢK(xᵢ , xₖ), k = lo ... hi
     Gₖ += yⱼyₖΔαⱼK(xⱼ, xₖ), k = lo ... hi
while not converged
```

Figure 5.2 The sequential algorithm. *Left*: The algorithm starts from a feasible solution $\alpha = 0, G = -1$, and performs gradient descent steps. In each step, a working set is chosen: the pair of points that violate the KKT conditions the most. For two points, the $\Delta\alpha$ updates can be computed analytically. Finally the gradient vector is updated. The algorithm loops until convergence: KKT violations are below a desired precision. *Right*: Schematic of the main data blocks: training data, kernel matrix, gradient values, alpha values. Indicated is also the access pattern for one optimization step: two training vectors x_i, x_j are chosen and the main computation is the calculation of two columns of the kernel matrix needed to update all gradients. The algorithm has been $lo \ldots hi$ parameterized to ease the transition to the parallel version.

parallelized by dividing them onto multiple machines and adjusting the $lo \ldots hi$ bounds appropriately. The only data dependence is contained in the loop searching for the working set. Popular selection criteria use the maximal violation of the Karush-Kuhn-Tucker (KKT) conditions. For good convergence speed it is important to find the global extrema, i.e., the extrema over the whole training set. We will discuss the consequences of this dependence in more detail in section 5.4.

The working set consists of two vectors, x_i and x_j, selected based on the first- or second-order criteria (figure 5.3) (Fan et al., 2005b).

5.3.3   Efficient Algorithm Design

Before attempting to improve the speed of SVMs by means of brute-force parallelization, one should optimize all aspects of the sequential algorithm. All the acceleration methods described in this section are independent of the acceleration obtained through parallelization with the spread-kernel algorithm (sections 5.4 and 5.5) and the different techniques can be readily combined.

$$
\begin{aligned}
&\text{find working set(lo,hi):}\\[4pt]
&\quad 1^{st}\ \text{order: } i := \underset{k=lo...hi}{arg\ max}
\begin{cases}
-G_k & : y_k > 0 \ \& \ \alpha_k < C\\
+G_k & : y_k < 0 \ \& \ \alpha_k > 0
\end{cases}\\[8pt]
&\quad 1^{st}\ \text{order: } j := \underset{k=lo...hi}{arg\ max}
\begin{cases}
+G_k & : y_k > 0 \ \& \ \alpha_k > 0\\
-G_k & : y_k < 0 \ \& \ \alpha_k < C
\end{cases}\\[8pt]
&\quad 2^{nd}\ \text{order:} j := \underset{k=lo...hi}{arg\ max}
\begin{cases}
b^2/\eta & : y_k > 0 \ \& \ \alpha_k > 0 \ \& \ b > 0\\
b^2/\eta & : y_k < 0 \ \& \ \alpha_k < C \ \& \ b > 0
\end{cases}\\[8pt]
&\qquad\qquad\text{where:}\quad
\begin{aligned}
b &= y_i\,G_i + y_k\,G_k\\
\eta &= K_{i,i} + K_{k,k} - 2\,K_{i,k}
\end{aligned}
\end{aligned}
$$

Figure 5.3 Working set selection algorithms.

$$
\begin{aligned}
&\text{compute } \Delta\alpha\text{-s:}\\
&\quad \eta := K(x_i, x_i) + K(x_j, x_j) - 2K(x_i, x_j)\\
&\quad \textbf{if } y_i = y_j\\
&\qquad \textbf{then } \Delta\alpha_i := +(G_i - G_j)/\eta\\
&\qquad\qquad\ \ \Delta\alpha_j := -\Delta\alpha_i\\
&\qquad \textbf{else }\ \ \Delta\alpha_i := -(G_i + G_j)/\eta\\
&\qquad\qquad\ \ \Delta\alpha_j := +\Delta\alpha_i\\
&\quad \text{enforce box constraints(} \Delta\alpha_i, \Delta\alpha_j \text{)}
\end{aligned}
$$

Figure 5.4 Analytical solution for α updates of the working set.

5.3.3.1 *Data Reordering*

The optimization algorithm does not depend on the order of the vectors in memory, however, the number of operations can be reduced greatly if we reorder (sort) vectors according to their labels. The effect of reordering is that the kernel matrix becomes blockwise positive/negative (figure 5.5). Therefore, we can remove $y_i y_j$ multiplications (or equality testing) from the gradient update loop (figure 5.2), resulting in less memory accesses and no branching. Furthermore, it maps efficiently to BLAS [2] library calls (`axpy`). The improvement is at least a *factor of 2* because of more efficient data transfers from memory to the CPU due to prefetching, and potentially even more since no testing and branching are involved. Prefetching, the transfer of data from memory to the CPU while executing computations with previously fetched data, is implemented in several BLAS libraries, such as Intel's

---

2. `http://www.netlib.org/blas/faq.html`.

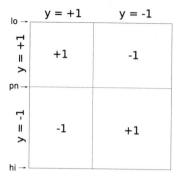

$$G_k \mathrel{+}= y_i y_k \Delta\alpha_i K(x_i, x_k)$$
$$G_k \mathrel{+}= y_j y_k \Delta\alpha_j K(x_j, x_k)$$
$$k = lo \ldots hi$$
$$becomes:$$
$$axpy(lo, pn, +y_i\Delta\alpha_i, K_i, G)$$
$$axpy(pn, hi, -y_i\Delta\alpha_i, K_i, G)$$
$$axpy(lo, pn, +y_j\Delta\alpha_i, K_j, G)$$
$$axpy(pn, hi, -y_j\Delta\alpha_i, K_j, G)$$

Figure 5.5 The signs of the elements in the kernel matrix after ordering the training vectors by their class labels.

MKL[3] BLAS/LAPACK library, AMD's CML[4] BLAS/LAPACK library, or Goto's[5] BLAS library. Therefore this acceleration can be obtained easily on any machine where such libraries are available.

More pronounced is the acceleration on a vector processor, since after reordering of the training data the gradient update loop is ideally suited for vectorization. On machines with vector processors, the BLAS library is typically implemented, taking care of all the nitty-gritty of prefetching and vectorization. Usually there is also support for vectorizing the dot product of sparse vectors. For the vectorization to be efficient on short vectors, one should consider inverting the vector-matrix multiplication order.

Notice that we do not take advantage of the symmetry in the kernel matrix. While this may, theoretically, almost double the number of stored elements, the actual amount of redundancy is rather small, because only a small fraction of the kernel matrix is really computed. The regularity in the column length facilitates storage management and vectorization that outweighs any potential gain in reduced storage requirements.

5.3.3.2 *Parallelizing Kernel Computations*

A substantial increase in speed can be obtained by using the special hardware accelerators integrated in most modern processors, such as the MMX or SSE units in Intel and AMD processors. These are SIMD-type processors that can execute the same operation on multiple data items simultaneously. Compilers typically do not support such accelerators, and assembly coding is required. But with a few short routines the most common types can be covered. Our implementation supports specialization of kernels (dot products) for particular types of vectors, dense and sparse, and several types of vector elements: bits, bytes, floats, doubles.

---

3. http://www.intel.com/cd/software/products/asmo-na/eng/perflib/index.htm.
4. http://developer.amd.com/acml.aspx.
5. http://www.tacc.utexas.edu/resources/software/.

Note The improvements are most pronounced when caching is not used or is ineffective due to the size of the problem and are twofold:

- Memory
  - Replacing floats with bits reduces memory bandwidth and size requirements by a *factor of 32*. Binary codes are often introduced to handle symbolic values, and therefore such considerations are useful for many problems.
  - Replacing floats with bytes (many image processing problems) results in a *factor of 4* improvement.
- Efficiency
  - Replacing floats with bits allows us to compute the dot product of 32(64) bit elements in parallel, resulting in a *factor of 32(64)* improvement,
  - Replacing floats with bytes allows us to compute the dot product of 4(8) byte elements in parallel (SSE/MMX), resulting in a *factor of 4(8)* improvement.

5.3.3.3   Multithreading

Most machines nowadays are equipped with dual or quad processors, and each processor can have dual or quad cores. Such machines are usually referred to as shared memory machines, since all processor cores can directly access all the memory (regardless of the underlying architecture: e.g., SMP for Intel or NUMA for AMD). Multithreading takes advantage of this type of parallelism with no need to redesign the algorithm. In contrast to this, for the distributed memory machines (often referred to as message-passing machines), where processors have direct access only to the local memory, a redesign of the algorithm becomes a necessity. Multithreading can be employed in all operations: selecting the working set, computing the kernel matrix columns, and updating the gradient vector. The achieved speedup is linear in the number of processors/cores and limited by the data bandwidth between memory and processors/cores.

Modern processors (e.g., recent Intel models) often have a feature called *hyperthreading*, in which a processor pretends to be two processors. While this may be beneficial for some applications (e.g., web servers), those where numerical operations dominate have to be mapped onto real and not virtual silicon in order to see an acceleration. Hyperthreading does not improve the performance of numerically intensive SVM algorithms and may actually be detrimental if two threads are mapped onto two virtual (instead of real) processors.

5.3.3.4   To Shrink or Not to Shrink?

We avoid shrinking or similar heuristics, because they complicate the cache design. Shrinking leads to kernel matrix columns of nonuniform lengths, resulting in memory fragmentation and the need for garbage collection. Figure 5.6 illustrates the number of training vectors that have been selected, together with the number

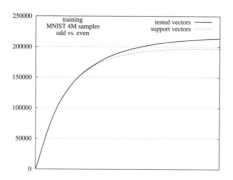 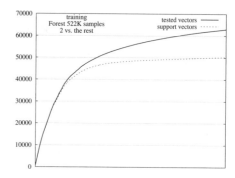

Figure 5.6 The number of vectors tested and the number of support vectors during optimization as a function of time when using the second order working set selection. *Left*: MNIST-E dataset with 4M vectors: the overhead is 8.5%. *Right*: Forest dataset with 522K vectors: the overhead is 25%.

of support vectors. Important is the use of an efficient algorithm for selecting the working set. The second-order gradient algorithm introduced in (Fan et al., 2005b) greatly improves the selection of the working set over a first-order algorithm.

For the MNIST-E problem with 4 million training samples, figure 5.6 indicates that about 214K vectors are selected for the two-vector optimization, and, consequently, 214K columns of the kernel matrix are computed. This means that less than 5.5% of all elements of the whole kernel matrix are calculated. The minimum number of columns that have to be calculated is the number of support vectors, here close to 200K. Therefore, without any shrinking tricks, the number of nonessential kernel matrix elements that are calculated are about 20K columns or less than 9% of the required ones. That means that shrinking could reduce the number of calculated kernel elements by no more than 9%. This assumes that we have perfect shrinking (selecting only support vectors), which, of course, is never the case. Due to caching the gain in speed obtained with shrinking can be larger than is suggested by this simple analysis, but in our experience the improvements are rarely much larger (compare results in table 5.1).

5.3.3.5 *Caching*

In an algorithm that uses decompositions with small working sets, such as the sequential minimal optimization (SMO) algorithm, each step improves the solution based only on a few vectors, requiring a large number of iterations. Hence the same vector may be chosen multiple times for the optimization. If we do not cache the kernel values, this would mean recomputing the same column of the kernel matrix over and over. Experimental evidence shows that a small number of (support) vectors tend to be selected often. For example, figure 5.7, left, indicates that less than 80K vectors are selected more than five times, while over 100K vectors are selected less than five times and 3.75 million never! This suggests that even modest caching will greatly improve the efficiency of the algorithm. We use a simple caching algorithm with the LRU (least recently used) strategy for discarding old entries. A qualitatively similar behavior is observed for other problems, such as Forest (figure 5.7, right).

In contrast, an algorithm like the parallel gradient projection-based decomposition technique (PGPBDT) (Zanni et al., 2006) needs only few optimization steps, but each step is essentially sequential in nature, and computationally and memorywise more expensive, making caching less effective.

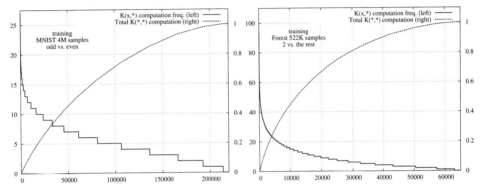

Figure 5.7 Vector access histogram: the number of times a vector is selected for the optimization (vertical axis, left scale). The increasing curve shows the cumulative kernel computations, assuming no caching, normalized to 1 (vertical axis, right scale). The horizontal axis indicates the index of the training vectors (sorted by access frequency). *Left*: MNIST-E 4M, *Right*: Forest 522K.

5.3.3.6   Sequential Results

The optimization techniques described above are not independent, and the overall accelerations obtained with a combination of them are usually less than the product of the individual accelerations. For example, an acceleration of the kernel computation through parallelization in the MMX unit may lead to a saturation of the data flow between memory and processing unit. Experimental evaluations for the well-known MNIST (see section 5.8.3) and ADULT[6] problems are shown in table 5.1, where also some comparisons with other solvers (LIBSVM, SVQP2; see chapter 1) are provided. These results show how the effects of optimized data representations and multithreading reduce the training times substantially. The effect of shrinking can be pronounced when smaller error tolerances are used for stopping, but can even be counterproductive for coarser stopping criteria (10^{-1}). The problem sizes of table 5.1 are relatively small and the effects of such optimizations as vectorization

---

6. http://leon.bottou.org/papers/bordes-ertekin-weston-bottou-2005.

Table 5.1 Comparisons of different implementations. Three different solvers are used: LIBSVM, SVQP2, MILDE. LIBSVM and SVQP2 can use shrinking, while MILDE does not. LIBSVM and SVQP2 use sparse float data representations. MILDE implements multiple representations and is tested here with sparse float and dense byte representations. Machine: Opteron 2.2GHz; the last column uses both processors of the dual machine, all other results are obtained with a single processor. Tasks: MNIST, 60k training samples, two-class problem: digit 8 against the rest; cache size: 500MB. ADULT, 32k training samples, cache size: 256MB.

MNIST 60K 8 vs. rest Cache: 500M	LIBSVM shrink sparse float	LIBSVM no-shrink sparse float	SVQP2 shrink sparse float	MILDE no-shrink sparse float	MILDE no-shrink dense byte	MILDE (2) no-shrink dense byte
RBF kernel:	$\gamma : 0.01, C : 10$			$\gamma : 0.01/256^2, C{:}10$		
Stopping (gradient error) 10^{-1}						
#iterations:	6338	6338	9050	5300	5300	5300
#Kernel $\times 10^6$	371	284	224	256	256	256
#SV	3081	3081	3031	3026	3026	3026
F2 score (%)	98.77	98.77	98.77	98.74	98.74	98.74
Time (sec)	777	535	472	484	135	79
Stopping (gradient error) 10^{-3}						
#iterations:	20820	20820	27922	19300	19300	19300
#Kernel $\times 10^6$	417	733	229	663	663	663
#SV	3151	3151	3151	3148	3148	3148
F2 score (%)	98.71	98.71	98.71	98.71	98.71	98.71
Time (sec)	816	1312	470	1292	386	207

ADULT 32K Cache: 256M	LIBSVM shrink sparse float	LIBSVM no-shrink sparse float	SVQP2 shrink sparse float	MILDE no-shrink sparse float	MILDE no-shrink dense bool	MILDE (2) no-shrink dense bool
RBF kernel	$\gamma : 0.005, C : 100$					
Stopping (gradient error) 10^{-1}						
#iterations:	33859	33821	40289	32000	32000	32000
#Kernel $\times 10^6$	616	617	578	598	598	598
#SV	11518	11447	11570	11467	11467	11467
F2 score (%)	77.74	77.77	77.78	77.67	77.67	77.67
Time (sec)	270	250	237	265	150	89
Stopping (gradient error) 10^{-3}						
#iterations:	122659	124752	150635	125300	125300	125300
#Kernel $\times 10^6$:	599	627	579	611	611	611
#SV	11345	11291	11386	11297	11297	11297
F2 score (%)	77.78	77.77	77.78	77.80	77.80	77.80
Time (sec)	271	316	269	370	246	144

Table 5.2 Sequential algorithm: results with the optimizations of section 5.3.3. Experiments were carried out on the FOREST dataset using the setup presented in section 5.8.2. The stopping criterion (gradient error) was 10^{-1}.

Training size (FOREST)	104,553	197,489	302,042	522,900
Training iterations	83,300	139,900	186,400	274,800
2x Athlon 1.5GHz, 2GB (sec)	4326	14,767	30,103	90,645
2x Opteron 2.2GHz, 4GB (sec)	1562	6365	14,374	38,455
Test accuracy (%)	95.25	96.83	97.59	98.34

are not yet pronounced. Table 5.2 shows the scaling of the training times for larger numbers of training data of the FOREST (see section 5.8.2) problem. The scaling is somewhat lower than n^2. However, it should be noted that the kernel computation for the forest problem is very small and therefore the effect of decreasing caching efficiency with increasing problem size is not pronounced. For larger vector sizes there is typically a range where the scaling is higher than n^2, due to decreasing caching efficiency (see also figure 5.23).

5.4 Spread-Kernel Optimization (Full Data) (SKOFD)

The sequential algorithm presented in section 5.3.2 exhibits a high degree of data independence, i.e., one computation can be executed without having to know what the result of another will be. Such independence can be exploited very effectively when parallelizing an algorithm. All sequential loops in the algorithm can be parallelized by executing nonoverlapping ranges $lo \dots hi$ (see figure 5.9) on different machines. In this first version of the spread-kernel algorithm, each machine is assigned a part of the kernel matrix, namely the rows $lo \dots hi$ plus the gradients in the same range (see figure 5.8). Each machine contains all the training data plus all the alpha values, hence the name "full data."

The only computation that is not independent is the search for the globally optimal working set. Each machine will find locally, within its own $lo(q) \dots hi(q)$ range, the optimal working set (i_q, j_q), but then all these locally optimal sets must be combined (synchronized) into one globally optimal working set (i, j). This is achieved with the "network max" algorithm, which will be discussed in section 5.6.1. Figure 5.9 shows the pseudocode of the SKOFD algorithm. The only difference compared to the sequential algorithm of figure 5.2 is in the selection of the working set.

Note Without merging of the local working sets, the algorithm becomes the first layer of the cascade algorithm (figure 5.1): each machine solves a subproblem independently.

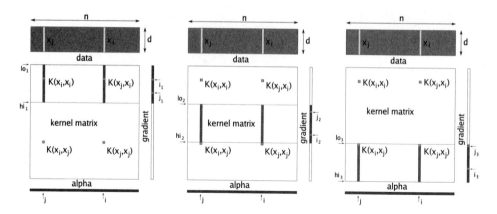

Figure 5.8 Schematic of the distribution of the data, kernel matrix, gradient values, and alphas onto three machines.

$$
\begin{aligned}
&\text{lo} := 1 + q * \lceil n/p \rceil \\
&\text{hi} := min(n, lo + \lceil n/p \rceil) \\
&\alpha_i := \ 0, \, i = 1 \ldots n \\
&G_i := -1, \, i = \text{lo} \ldots \text{hi} \\
&\textbf{do} \\
&\quad i_q, j_q := \text{find working set}(\text{lo,hi}) \\
&\quad \mathbf{i,j := network\ max(i_q, j_q)} \\
&\quad \Delta\alpha_i, \Delta\alpha_j := \text{compute } \Delta\alpha\text{-s} \\
&\quad \alpha_i \ += \ \Delta\alpha_i \\
&\quad \alpha_j \ += \ \Delta\alpha_j \\
&\quad G_k += y_i y_k \Delta\alpha_i K(x_i\,, x_k), \, k = \text{lo} \ldots \text{hi} \\
&\quad G_k += y_j y_k \Delta\alpha_j K(x_j, x_k), \, k = \text{lo} \ldots \text{hi} \\
&\textbf{while not } \text{converged}
\end{aligned}
$$

Figure 5.9 Spread-kernel optimization (full data) modification relative to the sequential optimization algorithm. The cluster-relative machine index number q starts from 0.

Discussion In the parallel version, each machine (indexed by q) works only on its $(lo(q) \ldots hi(q))$ slice of the gradient vector $\vec{G}$, for which it needs to compute a $(lo(q) \ldots hi(q))$ slice of the kernel matrix (K). The cost of computing a single kernel column is proportional to the dimensionality of the data and the size of the slice: $d \times (hi(q) - lo(q))$ (for dot product–based kernels). In the presence of a caching strategy, only slices $(\frac{1}{p})$ of the kernel matrix columns need to be cached, greatly reducing memory requirements on each machine. Note that each machine contains a complete $\vec{\alpha}$ vector. Updating the $\vec{\alpha}$ vector is such a trivial, atomic operation that it can be replicated by each machine without affecting the performance.

5.5 Spread-Kernel Optimization (Split Data) (SKOSD)

The parallelization in section 5.4 expects that each machine in the cluster has direct access to all the training data. Depending on the dimensionality d and the number of vectors this may or may not be a feasible strategy. Splitting the data, so that each machine has vectors only in its working range $(lo(q) \ldots hi(q))$, allows the parallel algorithm to solve problems that are – due to the memory constraints – *unsolvable* on a single machine. The division of data and kernel matrix is shown schematically in figure 5.10.

The modification to the algorithm is minimal. After the globally optimal working set has been determined, each machine holding vector(s) selected into the globally optimal working set sends it(them) to all other machines (operation `data_io` in the pseudocode; figure 5.11). Each machine knows where the training data is stored and waits for incoming vectors. After each machine has received the working set, the rest can be executed independently, namely the optimization step and the update of the gradients. After this is done each machine that received missing vector(s) removes it(them) from its memory (operation `data_rm` in the pseudocode; figure 5.11).

Discussion The main difference here is the necessity (in each step of the algorithm) for the machine that has vector(s) of the working set in its local memory to send it(them) to all other machines that do not have it. In section 5.6.2 we discuss how this seemingly I/O-intensive task can be achieved efficiently. Empirical evidence shows the time for sending vectors to be a small percentage (1%–2%) of the time it takes to calculate a kernel column. We can say that the cost of the I/O is amortized by the computational costs. If the vectors are large, causing a long delay in the data transfer (scales with d), then the computation will take even longer, because it scales with $(hi(q) - lo(q)) \times d$. In the presence of a cache, the communication as well as the calculation can be skipped if the required kernel column is available in the cache.

Note When the kernel columns (i, j) are cached the vectors (x_i, x_j) do not have to be sent, but kernel values $(K(x_i, x_i), K(x_j, x_j), K(x_i, x_j))$ have to be available on each machine for the computation of $\Delta \alpha_i$ and $\Delta \alpha_j$ (see figure 5.4). While the

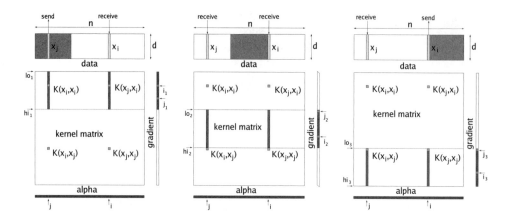

Figure 5.10 Schematic of the distribution of the data, kernel matrix, gradient values, and alphas onto three machines in the case where the training data are split. Only the data indicated by the gray areas is stored by the respective machines. Each node sends working set data it holds and receives working set data it does not hold.

$$\text{lo} := 1 + q * \lceil n/p \rceil$$
$$\text{hi} := min(n, \text{lo} + \lceil n/p \rceil)$$
$$\alpha_i := \ 0, \text{i} = 1 \ldots \text{n}$$
$$G_i := \text{-1}, \text{i} = \text{lo} \ldots \text{hi}$$
do
$\quad i_q, j_q :=$ find working set(lo,hi)
$\quad i, j :=$ network max(i_q, j_q)
$\quad$**data_io(i, j)**
$\quad \Delta\alpha_i, \Delta\alpha_j :=$ compute $\Delta\alpha$-s
$\quad \alpha_i \mathrel{+}= \Delta\alpha_i$
$\quad \alpha_j \mathrel{+}= \Delta\alpha_j$
$\quad G_k \mathrel{+}= y_i y_k \Delta\alpha_i K(x_i, x_k), \text{k} = \text{lo} \ldots \text{hi}$
$\quad G_k \mathrel{+}= y_j y_k \Delta\alpha_j K(x_j, x_k), \text{k} = \text{lo} \ldots \text{hi}$
$\quad$**data_rm(i, j)**
while not converged

Figure 5.11 Spread-kernel optimization (split data) modification relative to the spread-kernel optimization (full data).

diagonal of the kernel matrix can be precached, the off-diagonal values $(K(x_i, x_j))$ have to be sent.

5.6   Networking Overhead

5.6.1   Finding the Working Set

Finding the globally optimal working set requires merging of working sets that were determined by each machine independently. The goal is to find the working set with the largest first- or second-order gradients. We present three different algorithms here. Which one is best to use depends on the capabilities of the network.

- A *half-duplex* algorithm is the least demanding on the hardware and can be embedded into networks that support only half-duplex I/O, i.e., data can be sent only in one direction at a time. In this case the machines in the cluster are organized into a fan-tree (see figure 5.12), and the working sets are merged pairwise toward the root. The root machine ends up with the globally optimal working set and has to propagate it back to each machine. With p machines participating, the I/O cost of this algorithm is $2 \times \lceil \log_2(p) \rceil \times$ latency ($\lceil \ \rceil$ represents the ceil operator). We ignore here the time for the actual communication. Since the amount of transmitted data is small, namely just a few indices and gradient values, the time for their transmission is negligible (on the order of microseconds), compared with the latency it takes to set up the connection (on the order of milliseconds for a low-cost network).

- A *half-duplex + multicast* algorithm merges the locally optimal working sets in the same fashion as the half-duplex algorithm. But then the root machine uses a broadcast protocol (multicast) to send the globally optimal working set to all participating machines in a single step. This requires a network switch that replicates multicast packets and sends them out to all ports simultaneously. With p machines, the I/O cost of this algorithm is $(1 + \lceil \log_2(p) \rceil) \times$ latency, or almost half that of the half-duplex algorithm.

- A *full-duplex* algorithm requires the ability to send and receive messages simultaneously. Each machine, logically organized in a circle, merges locally optimal working sets with its neighbors at distances $1, 2, 4, \ldots 2^k$, where $k = \lceil \log_2(p) \rceil$. After k steps each machine has a globally optimal working set. With p machines, this algorithm is the fastest with an I/O cost of $\lceil \log_2(p) \rceil \times$ latency. It should be noted that this algorithm puts a heavy burden on the network switch, utilizing it to the maximum.

5.6.2   Data Communication for the Split Data Algorithm

The split data algorithm presented in section 5.5 is an example of parallelization-introduced data dependency: the algorithm cannot proceed before each machine has

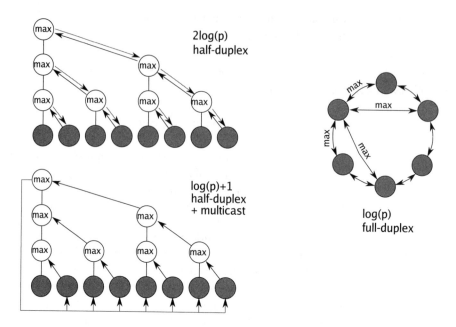

Figure 5.12 Schematic of the three network algorithms for selecting the globally optimal working set.

all the vectors for the next optimization step. This can be accomplished efficiently in two ways:

- The *half-duplex* algorithm uses a fan-tree with the machine containing the vector to be sent at its root. In $\lceil \log_2(p) \rceil$ steps, every machine has received the missing vector.

- The *multicast* approach sends it to all the participating machines in a single step. This requires a switch that supports such a protocol.

While it may seem at first glance that sending training vectors to all machines produces a bigger overhead than finding the optimal working set, in reality this is not so. The vector sending overhead is "amortized" by the computation of the kernel column. After sending d vector elements the computation of the kernel column requires $(d \times (hi - lo))$ computations. Even more important is that caching, which reduces the need for recomputing the kernel matrix columns, reduces the need for sending the missing vectors as well.

The network max is not amortized by anything and represents the real bottleneck of the parallel algorithm: when $p \to \inf$ only this overhead remains (see figure 5.14).

5.6.3   Reliable Multicast

The advantages of using a broadcast protocol for sending one-to-all messages in a single step are obvious. However, the multicast protocol is an unreliable protocol.

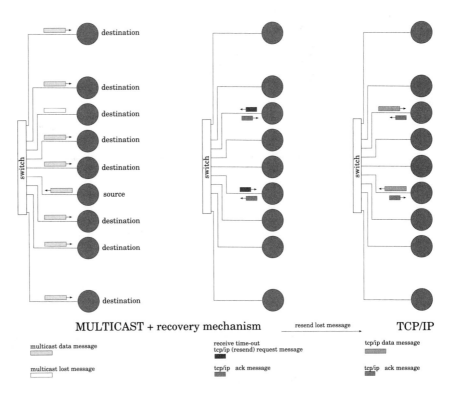

Figure 5.13   Schematic of the reliable multicast protocol. *Left*: A multicast packet is sent from the "source" to all "destinations". *Center*: One destination machine did not receive the packet and times out, requesting a resend. *Right*: The missing packet is resent via regular TCP/IP protocol.

The replication of packets puts a strain on a network switch and occasionally a packet gets lost, with rather disastrous effects on the computation, which simply stops due to a lack of data.

While it is difficult to create a reliable general-purpose multicast protocol, it is much simpler to create such a protocol tailored to a specific algorithm. The optimization algorithm presented in section 5.5 produces synchronous bursts of communications. A short analysis reveals that a small finite-state automaton, equipped with a history queue of at most four packets, is needed to implement a reliable multicast protocol for the spread-kernel algorithms. Our reliable multicast protocol (figure 5.13) is an inversion of the TCP/IP protocol. Instead of sending a confirmation packet for each received multicast packet, we send a TCP/IP retransmission request packet when the receiving multicast packet operation has timed out. The time-out threshold can usually be set very tightly since all machines in the cluster are identical and hence are running in lockstep.

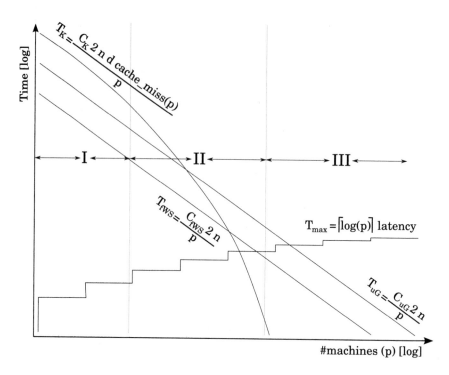

Figure 5.14 The four dominant times of the algorithm as a function of the number of machines (in log-log scale) and how they define three different speedup regions.

5.6.4 PVM, MPI

With the popularization of parallel machines, many parallel APIs have been proposed and implemented. While it is convenient to use a general communication interface, the generality of these APIs has its cost in efficiency. The spread-kernel algorithm relies on efficient implementations of one-to-all and full-duplex one-to-one message-passing functions. The PVM and MPI implementations are fan-tree–based and incur $\lceil \log_2(p) \rceil$ costs for every communication. Therefore, in order to take full advantage of modern networks, we have implemented the optimized network I/O layer – in particular the message passing functions mentioned before – ourselves. However, except for a degradation in performance, nothing precludes using PVM or MPI.

5.7   Theoretical Model

Analyzing the algorithm described in section 5.4, we can quantify the various parts and determine the influence of the number of machines on the parallelization efficiency. We neglect here the details of the kernel computation. As was shown

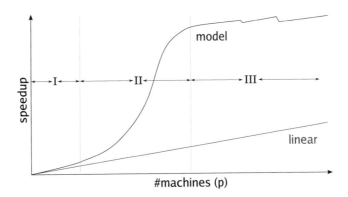

Figure 5.15 Theoretical speedup model, indicating the speedup as a function of the number of identical machines. In region **I** the time is dominated by the calculation of the kernel values. In region **II** improvements in caching efficiency dominate and a strong superlinear acceleration is observed. In region **III** the communication overhead dominates, saturating the speedup.

in section 5.2 that speed can vary substantially, depending on the details of the individual processor. But this speed is, to some extent, independent of the parallelization we model here and is approximated by a constant compute rate. We can then model the four dominating times (figure 5.14) and identify three speedup regions. Region **I** is dominated by the kernel computation time T_K. In region **II**, due to nonlinear caching effects, the kernel computation time decreases superlinearly. The latency of the network max algorithm dominates region **III**.

▪ $T_{fWS}(p)$ is the time needed to find the locally optimal working set on one machine (out of p). The time is dependent on the number of local vectors (n/p), the size of the working set (2), and some constant (C_{fWS}) that describes the compute rate. $T_{fWS}(p) = C_{fWS} \times 2 \times n/p$. This part is fully data independent and scales inverse-proportionally with the number of participating machines p: $T_{fWS}(p) = T_{fWS}(1)/p$.

▪ $T_{uG}(p)$ is the time needed to update the local portion of the gradient vector on one machine (out of p). The time depends on the number of local vectors (n/p), the size of the working set (2), and some compute rate–dependent constant (C_{uG}). $T_{uG}(p) = C_{uG} \times 2 \times n/p$. This part is fully data independent and scales inverse-proportionally with the number of participating machines p: $T_{uG}(p) = T_{uG}(1)/p$.

▪ $T_K(p)$ is the time required to compute the kernel matrix subcolumns. This time depends on the local number of vectors (n/p), the dimensionality of vectors (d), the size of the working set (2), and some compute rate–dependent constant (C_K). $T_K(p) = C_K \times 2 \times n/p \times d$. This part is fully data independent and scales inverse-proportionally with the number of participating machines p: $T_K(p) = T_K(1)/p$.
Note that the computation of kernel columns is greatly reduced in the presence of caching. The dependence on the cache size is highly nonlinear since the selection of vectors for the working set is very uneven (compare section 5.3.3.5).

But since the computation has to be executed only in the case of a cache miss, we can take this effect into account through an average cache_miss(p) rate, hence $T_K(p) = C_K \times 2 \times n/p \times d \times$ cache_miss(p).

- $\mathbf{T_{max}(p)}$ is the time needed to find the globally optimal working set, i.e., the merging of locally optimal working sets. This part does not exist in the sequential algorithm, hence it represents parallelization overhead and increases logarithmically with the number of participating machines p (compare section 5.6.2): $T_{max}(p) = \lceil \log_2(p) \rceil \times$ latency.

The time for sending the data of the working set is neglected. It is typically much smaller than the $\mathbf{T_{max}}$ (see figure 5.22).

It should be noted that cache misses happen for all machines simultaneously, so this does not cause any differences in workload for the processors and hence does not affect the synchronization of the processors. The overall time spent on optimization as a function of the number of participating machines p can now be expressed as

$$
\begin{aligned}
T(p) &= \#iter \times \left(\frac{T_{fWS}(1) + T_{uG}(1)}{p} + T_K(p) + T_{max}(p) \right), \\
&= \#iter \times \left(\frac{2n \, (C_{fWS} + C_{uG} + d \, C_K \, \text{cache\_miss}(p))}{p} + \lceil \log_2(p) \rceil \times \text{latency} \right).
\end{aligned}
$$

As can be seen in figures 5.14 and 5.15, we can distinguish three characteristic regions. For a small number of machines, the computation of the kernel columns, $\mathbf{T_K(p)}$, dominates the overall time. At this point the caching is not yet effective and most of the kernel columns have to be recomputed. Therefore we observe essentially linear acceleration. As more machines are added the cache size increases relative to the number of kernel elements on each machine, and therefore the cache efficiency improves. This leads to a sharply superlinear acceleration in region **II**. Once most of the requests for kernel values are served by the cache, adding even more machines will not improve the caching efficiency anymore. This leads to the region **III**, where saturation in the acceleration is observed due to an increase in the communication overhead (dominated by $\mathbf{T_{max}(p)} = \lceil \log_2(p) \rceil \times$ latency).

Figure 5.18 confirms experimentally the qualitative behavior of this model. The visible "kinks" in the acceleration are consequences of the parallelization overhead $\mathbf{T_{max}(p)} = \lceil \log_2(p) \rceil \times$ latency.

It has to be emphasized that this model assumes a cheap communication network where the latency for a data transfer is on the order of a millisecond. This is a typical value for low-cost Ethernet cards nowadays. Much faster networking gear is available, but it costs orders of magnitude more. The effect of such an expensive communication network would be mainly to steepen the slope of the model in region **III**. In regions **I** and **II** it is the compute performance of each node that is the limiting factor and little can be gained by a lower latency in the communication. Experimentally we are limited to forty-eight machines on our cluster, but the model shows that even with a cheap Ethernet connection the spread-kernel parallelization can be scaled to several hundred machines for a large problem.

Table 5.3   Summary of experimental results on 48 dual Athlon machines

Problem	FOREST	MNIST-E	MNIST-E	MNIST-E	MNIST-E	MNIST-E
Training size	522,765	222,411	508,368	1,016,736	2,033,472	4,066,944
# SV	50,375	25,106	41,875	63,074	97,455	196,977
Time (sec)	765	288	780	6933	29021	64958
Train iterations	271,600	55,900	97,400	157,100	253,600	552,700
Kernel requests $\times 10^9$	284	24.86	99.03	319.5	1031	4496
Accuracy (%)	98.34	98.58	98.85	99.12	99.27	99.13

5.8   Experimental Results

5.8.1   The Experimental Setup

We performed experiments on two very different datasets. One (Forest, section 5.8.2) with very short vectors ($d = 12$) and the other (MNIST-E, section 5.8.3) with relatively long vectors ($d = 784$).

All experiments have been performed on a cluster consisting of 48 identical, diskless machines. Each machine contains two Athlon, 1.53GHz processors in a shared-memory arrangement, has 2GB of RAM, and a 100Mbs Ethernet card. The network is served by a single 48-port 100Mbs switch.

In all tests we have used the second-order working set selection, and the optimization was stopped when the first-order gradient difference was < 0.1 in the last 100 iterations; all available memory has been used for caching the kernel matrix.

Table 5.3 summarizes the spread-kernel results on the full system (48 machines).

5.8.2   Forest Dataset

The Forest dataset[7] has seven classes and a dimensionality of d=54. A vector consists of 10 numerical (floating point) values and 2 bit-sets with only one bit active in each set. Hence the active bits in the bit-sets can be represented with integer values, leading to an effective dimensionality $d = 12$. The 10 numerical values have been centered and no other preprocessing has been done. We used an RBF kernel with $\gamma = 41 \times 10^{-6}$ and parameter $C = 50$ and an optimized dot product with symbolic (integer) values comparison instead of multiplication of bit-sets. In order to obtain a balanced two-class problem, we train class 2 ($254,970$ samples) versus the rest, similarly to what most other researchers, such as Collobert et al.

---

7. ftp://ftp.ics.uci.edu/pub/machine-learning-databases/covtype/.

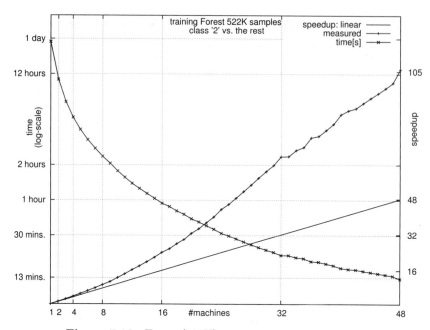

Figure 5.16   Forest (522K) training times and speedup.

(2002c), have done. The training set consists of $522,765$ samples and the test set of $58,085$.

Figure 5.16 depicts the training time for the Forest data as a function of the number of machines. Due to the small data size, the parallel algorithm has been run in full data mode (SKOFD). The acceleration is clearly superlinear, reaching a factor of 105 for 48 processors. Saturation is not yet visible in the figure, but due to the small dimensionality of the data the latency of the communication is substantial in the overall time (see figure 5.17).

5.8.3   MNIST-E

The MNIST handwritten digits dataset is widely used for benchmarking. It consists of 28×28 pixel gray-level images, with 60,000 training samples and 10,000 test samples. We treat this data as a two-class problem where the odd samples (1, 3, 5, 7, 9) are in one class and the even ones (0, 2, 4, 6, 8) in the other. The MNIST-E dataset[8] contains 4 million samples generated by warping the MNIST original samples. Vectors were encoded as dense byte vectors. We used the RBF kernel (MMX/SSE version) with $\gamma = 0.02/256^2$ and parameter $C = 10$. The original dataset with 60K samples takes only a few minutes to solve on a single machine

8. The MNIST-E data set is available at `http://ml.nec-labs.com/download/data/milde/`.

```
Data[full 0-10891 = 10891/522765][12][4]:
L0     254970 "2"
L1     267795 "R"
Kernel[522765 x Ki[10891 x vector.size()]] normal order, compact dot(x,y)
DCache[522765:0..522765]
BCache[42600][10891] = 1.7284GB, 1769.85MB, 1812330KB 1855826400B
IDX:    sec    iters / sec     obj.fun    #sv/tested cache% max:G
G0:  772.934   271600 464.5 634404.50060  50375  62965  95.43 0.096
SK:  WS1 tcpip_fd I/O:  271600 x  0.775 msec. =  210.374 sec.
SK:  WS2j tcpip_fd I/O: 271599 x  0.786 msec. =  213.446 sec.
TT:  774.00 sec or 12:54.00
I/O  423.82 sec or  7:03.82 = 54.8%
S0:  alpha:  a>0 =   a<C +   a=C, b: +0.03563515
S0:  L0    24967    20039    4928
S0:  L1    25408    20254    5154
```

Figure 5.17 Log of a training session of Forest with 522K samples on 48 machines. The solver needed 271,600 iterations before the gradient of the maximally violating pair was less than the desired accuracy of 0.1. The solver tested 62,965 vectors to determine 50,375 support vectors. Communication times for sending the working sets: WS1 (for the stopping criteria) and WS2j (for determining globally optimal working set) consumed 7 minutes (or 54.8% of the total time) while the computation required 6 minutes.

and is therefore not considered here. We have conducted several experiments on the MNIST-E dataset starting from 220K vectors up to 4M vectors. Due to the large data size, which cannot fit into the memory of a single machine, the split data version of the spread-kernel algorithm is used (SKOSD).

The MNIST-E (220K) data set demonstrates (see figure 5.18) the whole range of accelerations. A strong superlinear scaling in the range of 4 to 20 machines illustrates the increase in caching efficiency with increasing memory size and corresponds to the range **II** in figure 5.15. Above 32 machines the communication overhead becomes more and more noticeable, which grows with $\lceil \log_2(p) \rceil$ of the number of machines (p). For such a small problem the kernel submatrix (all support vectors) eventually fits into the distributed cache and the latency in the network max algorithm starts to dominate. But even for such a small problem an acceleration higher than linear can be sustained for many more machines.

The MNIST-E data size (500K) is roughly equivalent to the Forest data size (522K). The effect of caching (on 48 machines) renders the dimensionality difference irrelevant (see figure 5.19) for the overall optimization time, which becomes dependent only on the number of iterations (Forest: $274,000 = 13$ minutes vs. MNIST-E: $97,400 = 8.66$ minutes). The resulting speedup for the MNIST-E problem is greater because of the dimensionality difference (784 MNIST vs. 12 Forest). For this problem an acceleration of over 130 is achieved with forty-eight machines.

Doubling the data size from 500K to 1M (figure 5.20) requires four times as much memory (or four times as many machines) for the same caching effect. Even with

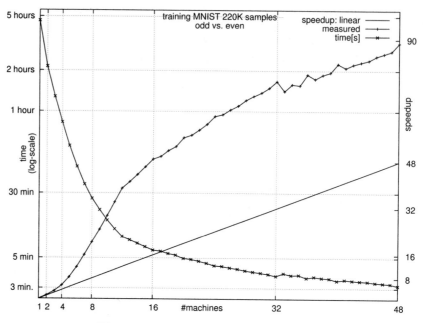

Figure 5.18   Training MNIST-E (220K).

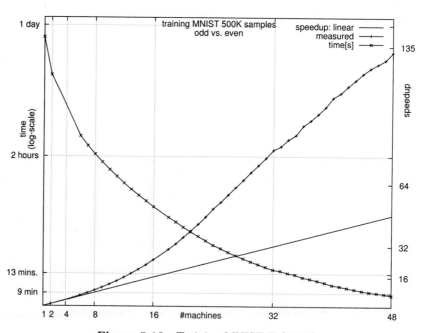

Figure 5.19   Training MNIST-E (500K).

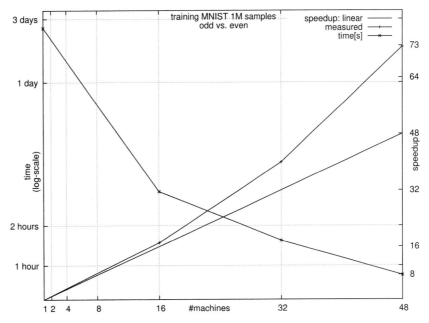

Figure 5.20   Training MNIST-E (1M).

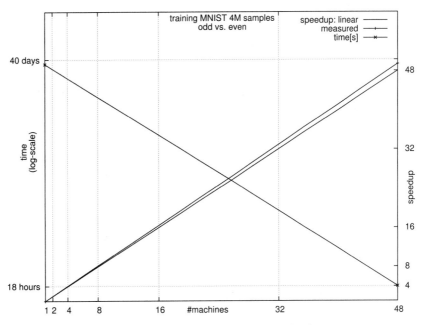

Figure 5.21   Training MNIST-E (4M).

```
Data[part 0-84728 = 84728/4066944][784][1]:
L0   1999744 "e"
L1   2067200 "o"
Kernel[4066944 x Ki[84728 x vector.size()]] normal order, compact dot(x,y)
DCache[4066944:0..84728]
BCache[4686][84728] = 1.4791GB, 1514.57MB, 1550920KB 1588141632B
IDX:     sec    iters / sec     obj.fun     #sv/tested cache% max:G
G0:  64953.0   552700 8.377 676594.48930 196977 213890    1.85 0.098
SK:  Xi   mcast    I/O: 1084589 x  0.410 msec. =  444.900 sec.
SK:  Kij  mcast    I/O:   20376 x  0.102 msec. =    2.080 sec.
SK:  WS1  tcpip_fd I/O:  552700 x  1.732 msec. =  957.399 sec.
SK:  WS2j tcpip_fd I/O:  552699 x  1.465 msec. =  809.540 sec.
TT:  64957.76 sec or 18:02:37.76
I/O   2213.92 sec or    36:53.92 = 3.4%
S0:  alpha:  a>0 = a<C + a=C, b: -2.40377766
S0:  L0    102168 73352 28816
S0:  L1     94809 65689 29120
```

Figure 5.22 Log of a training session of MNIST-E 4M samples on 48 machines. The solver needed $552,700$ iterations before the gradient of the maximally violating pair was less than the desired accuracy of 0.1. The solver tested $213,890$ vectors to determine $196,977$ support vectors. Communication times Xi (for distributing vectors), Kij (for distributing single kernel values – when kernel columns were present in the cache), WS1 (for the stopping criteria), and WS2j (for determining globally optimal working set) consumed 37 minutes (or 3.4% of the total time) while the computation consumed 17.5 hours. Note: The I/O overhead incurred by distribution of the missing vectors (Xi) (or missing kernel value (Kij) when kernel column $K(x_i, *)$ is present in the cache) is *asynchronous*: the machine that is sending the vector (kernel value) delegates that task to the network card and proceeds with the computation without delay. The receiving machine stalls until the vector is received. The reported time is the average (sending+receiving) time on one machine. This overhead constitutes 1/5 of the total I/O time. It contributes only 0.7% to the overall I/O overhead, which is dominated by the network max overhead, which is *synchronous* in nature.

forty-eight machines, the main impact of caching is not yet seen; we are only in the beginning of region **II** (compare figure 5.15). The superlinear acceleration is not as pronounced as for 500K samples, but is still over $70\times$ for 48 machines. Model estimates indicate that the superlinear acceleration would be sustained for well over 500 machines.

With a data size of 4M vectors (figure 5.21), we are even further down at the low end of region **I** (compare figure 5.15) and therefore very little superlinear acceleration is observed. Due to the limitations of the memory, the data cannot fit onto a single machine, and the total time on one machine is estimated to be 40 days, based on computational requirements. Figure 5.22 contains more detailed statistics (output log) of the run on 48 machines.

Training times and kernel requests as a function of the number of training data

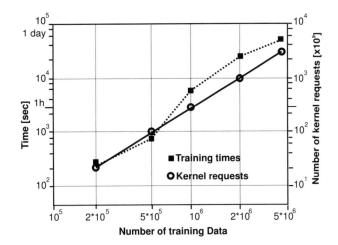

Figure 5.23 The training times (left scale) and the number of kernel requests (right scale) as a function of the number of training data for the MNIST-E problem.

are summarized in figure 5.23 for the MNIST-E problem. The number of kernel requests scales closely with n^2. The training times, on the other hand, scale lower for less than 500K training data and for more than 2M. But between 500K and 2M the problem moves from region **II** to region **I** (figure 5.14), and since the cache efficiency decreases, the training times scale higher than n^2.

Figure 5.24 shows the accelerations achieved with three different parallel algorithms, the cascade SVM (Graf et al., 2005), PGPBDT (Zanni et al., 2006, figure 5), and the spread-kernel SVM. It is clear that only the spread-kernel SVM achieves considerable superlinear accelerations and scales to a large number of processors. The spread-kernel algorithm is such an efficient strategy because it is totally symmetric. This means all processors have the same computational load that can be scheduled precisely, and all processors have the same memory requirements. Moreover, the whole memory on all processors can be used for caching. The main limitation is the latency in the communication. With more efficient communication networks this can easily be overcome, but it is actually not necessary to introduce low-latency networks in most cases. The strongest influence of the communication overhead is felt in a range where the kernel matrix is fully cached (region **III**). The highest gains in accelerations per machine are obtained in region **II** of figure 5.15. Therefore the biggest benefits of this algorithm are obtained even with a low-cost network.

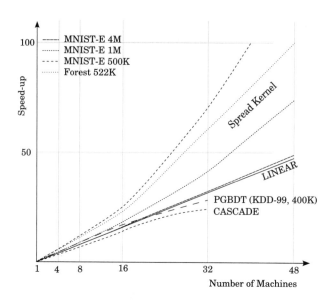

Figure 5.24 Comparison of the accelerations as a function of the number of processors. Shown are accelerations for the spread-kernel SVM, the cascade SVM and the PGPBDT (taken from Zanni et al., 2006, figure 5).

5.9   Conclusion

Parallelizing SVMs is a challenging problem, because a single QP problem has to be spread over different processors, which requires accurate synchronization between machines. As it turns out, a straightforward parallelization of well-known and widely used decomposition algorithms leads to the very efficient spread-kernel algorithm. The theoretical model of this algorithm, as well as extensive tests, confirms the good scaling to very large problems with millions of training data — problem sizes that are way beyond the reach of SVMs on a single machine. The additional accelerations of the kernel computations through multithreading and SIMD processors complement the spread-kernel algorithm well, increasing the efficiency further. The largest problems we tested are still heavily compute-starved and will scale to much larger numbers of processors, to hundreds at least and possibly to thousands. Good numerical stability was confirmed in all these tests and full convergence to the global solution is guaranteed, since the training only stops when all vectors fulfill the KKT conditions.

Extensive experiments have clearly shown that a regular data flow is an important consideration for the speed-optimization of SVMs. It may be advantageous to avoid algorithmic features that improve efficiency but introduce irregular sizes or unpredictable data flow. This is often observed when algorithms are optimized for speed. Modern processors tend to be highly pipelined at the instruction level. Unpredictable data flow, such as branches, introduces difficulties for a pipeline and requires branch prediction or speculative branch execution. Memories tend to be designed with three or more levels of hierarchy, where each higher level has a longer access time. The more predictable the data flow, the easier it is to take advantage of such features. The SVM optimization is based on a few algorithmic patterns, such as vector-matrix multiplications that have been highly optimized in many libraries. Taking advantage of these features may have more of an impact on speed than some heuristics to reduce the number of kernel computations.

Demonstrated here is a scaling to 48 machines with a total of 96 processors on a cluster. With four multipliers of the MMX unit operating in parallel on each processor, this corresponds to 384 processing units, all working in parallel. The speedup numbers in section 5.8 do not take into account the accelerations due to parallel kernel computation (multithreading, MMX); so, compared with just a single processing unit the accelerations are actually much higher. These different techniques are complementary to a large extent and can be combined with minimal interference.

The different approaches to parallelization described above require different levels of coupling between processors. Their main characteristics can be summarized as follows:

■ Parallelization of kernel computation: This type of acceleration is suited for tightly coupled processors, such as shared memory processors, SIMD arrays, and vector processors. Implementations with MMX or SSE units on modern PCs are straightforward and require little software overhead; using other accelerators, such as graphics processors or digital signal processors, can provide good accelerations, but at a higher cost of software development. Achievable accelerations depend on the dimensionality and format of the vectors. Since usually vector-vector or vector-matrix operations dominate the computation, many highly optimized libraries exist that can be exploited. Compact custom designs are suited for accelerating this type of operation. In particular, for embedded applications, which do not require training, very high accelerations are possible.

■ Spread-kernel parallelization: This approach requires only modest coupling of the processors because it produces a low communication overhead. It is suited for clusters of processors with Ethernet connections; broadcast communication is a plus, but it can tolerate fairly high latencies in the communication. This approach is efficient for a wide range of problems and scales to a large number of processors.

A recent trend is the appearance of 64 bit machines. Switching from 32 to 64 bits can accelerate the kernel evaluations, if double values are used for the computations. The main effect, however, is that the memory limitations are lifted. With 32 bit processors the practical limit on the memory size is 4GB, while with 64 bits much more can be addressed. Increasing the memory can speedup the SVM optimization considerably, yet it does not scale far. Caching efficiency rarely goes higher than 90%, and therefore the most one can hope to gain is a factor of 10 in the reduction of the kernel computation. If we assume a hypothetical single-processor machine with 96GB of main memory, the same amount as our total cluster has, the maximum acceleration we could expect is a factor of 10. What we obtain on the cluster is usually more like a factor of 100. This underlines that 64 bit machines, even with essentially unlimited amounts of memory, cannot match the accelerations possible with parallel algorithms. Only a well-balanced architecture with compute performance and storage size adjusted to the problem to be solved will provide optimal overall performance. The spread-kernel algorithm turns out to be very flexible and can handle a wide range of conditions with excellent performance.

Acknowledgment

The development of the parallel SVMs has evolved over an extended period of time at NEC Laboratories and has profited greatly from numerous discussions with several people here. In particular we want to thank Léon Bottou and Ronan Collobert, as well as Vladimir Vapnik, for their insights and comments. Jesper Traeff helped with the vectorization for the NEC SX6 processor.

6   A Distributed Sequential Solver for Large-Scale SVMs

Elad Yom-Tov

Support vector machines (SVMs) are an extremely successful class of classification and regression algorithms. Building an SVM entails solving a constrained convex quadratic programming problem, which is quadratic in the number of training samples. We introduce a parallel implementation of an iterative SVM solver. Parallelization is achieved by having each processing element compute partial updates of the Lagrange multipliers, which are then aggregated to form the complete update for each iteration. We discuss metrics for comparing parallel solvers and use them to compare the proposed algorithm to previously proposed SVM solvers, both single-node and distributed. Our comparison shows that the proposed algorithm is just as accurate as these solvers, while being significantly faster, especially for large datasets. Finally, we show that the training time of the algorithm can be accurately predicted using a simple model.

6.1   Introduction

6.1.1   Classification Using Support Vector Machines

Support vector machines (SVMs) are a class of algorithms that have, in recent years, exhibited superior performance compared to other pattern classification algorithms. There are several formulations of the SVM problem, depending on the specific application of the SVM (e.g., classification, regression, etc.). In this chapter, we consider the formulation for binary classification. Consider a training set

$$D = \{(\mathbf{x}_i, y_i), \quad i = 1, \ldots, N, \quad \mathbf{x}_i \in \Re^m, \quad y_i \in \{-1, 1\}\}. \tag{6.1}$$

The goal of the SVM is to learn a mapping from $\mathbf{x}_i$ to y_i such that the error in mapping, as measured on a new dataset, would be minimal. SVMs learn to find the linear weight vector that separates the two classes so that

$$y_i \left(\mathbf{x_i} \cdot \mathbf{w} + b \right) \geq 1 \quad for \quad i = 1, \dots, N. \tag{6.2}$$

There may exist many hyperplanes that achieve such separation, but SVMs find a weight vector $\mathbf{w}$ and a bias term b that maximize the margin, $2/\|\mathbf{w}\|$. Therefore, the optimization problem that needs to be solved is

$$\text{Minimize } J_D(\mathbf{w}) = \frac{1}{2} \|\mathbf{w}\|,$$
$$\text{subject to } y_i \left(\mathbf{x_i} \cdot \mathbf{w} + b \right) \geq 1 \quad \text{for } i = 1, \dots, N. \tag{6.3}$$

Any points lying on the hyperplane $y_i \left(\mathbf{x_i} \cdot \mathbf{w} + b \right) = 1$ are called support vectors.

If the data cannot be separated using a linear separator, a slack variable $\xi \geq 0$ is introduced and the constraint is relaxed to

$$y_i \left(\mathbf{x_i} \cdot \mathbf{w} + b \right) \geq 1 - \xi_i \quad for \quad i = 1, \dots, N. \tag{6.4}$$

The optimization problem then becomes

$$\text{Minimize } J_D(\mathbf{w}) = \frac{1}{2} \|\mathbf{w}\| + C \sum_{i=1}^{N} \xi_i,$$
$$\text{subject to } \begin{cases} y_i \left(\mathbf{x_i} \cdot \mathbf{w} + b \right) \geq 1 & \text{for } i = 1, \dots, N, \\ \xi_i \geq 0 & \text{for } i = 1, \dots, N. \end{cases} \tag{6.5}$$

Finding the weights of the linear function can be done directly or by converting the problem to a dual problem, which is usually easier to solve. Using the notation of Vijayakumar and Wu (1999), the dual problem is thus

$$\text{Maximize } L_D(\mathbf{h}) = \sum_i h_i - \frac{1}{2} \mathbf{h} \cdot \mathbf{D} \cdot \mathbf{h},$$
$$\text{subject to } \begin{cases} 0 \leq h_i \leq C & \text{for } i = 1, \dots, N, \\ \sum_{i=1}^{N} y_i h_i = 0 \end{cases} \tag{6.6}$$

where $\mathbf{D}$ is a matrix such that $D_{ij} = y_i y_j K \left(\mathbf{x}_i, \mathbf{x}_j \right)$ and $K \left(\cdot, \cdot \right)$ is either an inner product of the samples or a function of these samples. In the latter case this function is known as the kernel function, which can be any function that complies with the Mercer conditions (Schölkopf and Smola, 2002). For example, these may be polynomial functions, radial-basis (Gaussian) functions, or hyperbolic tangents. If the data is not separable, C is a tradeoff between maximizing the margin and reducing the number of misclassifications.

The classification of a new data point is then computed using the following equation

$$f(\mathbf{x}) = \text{sign} \left(\sum_{i \in SV} h_i y_i K \left(\mathbf{x}_i, \mathbf{x} \right) + b \right). \tag{6.7}$$

Following Vijayakumar and Wu (1999), we remove the explicit bias term b and instead add another dimension to the pattern vector $\mathbf{x_i}$ such that

$$\acute{\mathbf{x}}_{\mathbf{i}} = (x_1, x_2, \dots, x_N, \lambda),$$

where λ is a scalar constant. The modified weight vector which incorporates the bias term is written as $\acute{\mathbf{w}} = (w_1, w_2, \dots, w_N, b/\lambda)$. Such a modification, however, causes a change to the optimized margin. Vijayakumar and Wu (1999) discuss the effect of this modification and reach the conclusion that "setting the augmenting term to zero (equivalent to neglecting the bias term) in high dimensional kernels gives satisfactory results on real world data." We did not completely neglect the bias term, and in our experiments (which used the radial basis kernel) set it to $1/N$.

The modified weights are then found by solving the dual problem (6.6) without the equality constraint, that is,

$$\text{Maximize } L_D(\mathbf{h}) = \sum_i h_i - \frac{1}{2}\mathbf{h} \cdot \mathbf{D} \cdot \mathbf{h},$$
$$\text{subject to } 0 \leq h_i \leq C \quad \text{for } i = 1, \dots, N. \tag{6.8}$$

The resulting classifier is then computed as

$$f(\mathbf{x}) = \text{sign}\left(\sum_{i \in SV} h_i y_i K(\mathbf{x}_i, \mathbf{x}) + h_i y_i \lambda^2\right). \tag{6.9}$$

6.1.2   Methods for Single-Node SVM Solutions

There are several main methods for finding a solution to the SVM problem. See (Schölkopf and Smola, 2002, chapter 10) for a taxonomy of such methods.

Interior point algorithms solve the optimization problem by simultaneously satisfying the primal and dual feasibility conditions. These algorithms work by iteratively solving a set of equations. However, it is known that interior point algorithms have difficulty solving large-scale SVM problems due to the need to invert large matrices. A solution, albeit only approximate, can be obtained by using a low-rank approximation of the kernel matrix (Fine and Scheinberg, 2001).

Most other methods for solving the SVM problem use subset selection to reduce the problem size. The initial idea for subset selection, known as "chunking" (Vapnik, 1982), worked by storing part of the data in memory, finding the support vectors for this partial problem, and replacing all the points that are not support vectors with new data, until convergence is met. This approach works well if the whole set of support vectors can be kept in memory, but when this is not the case, chunking will converge extremely slowly, as shown below.

A slightly different approach is offered by the working set algorithms. These algorithms perform gradient descent on a subset of the variables, known as the working set, while freezing other variables. A working set algorithm was parallelized in (Zanghirati and Zanni, 2003). The working set approach is taken farthest in

Platt's sequential minimal optimization (SMO) algorithm (Platt, 1999), where the working set is comprised of two samples and the analytic update to the variables is computed. One of the main limitation of the working set algorithms for solving large SVMs is that if the working set cannot be held in memory, the algorithm might not find a feasible solution (Muske and Howse, 2003).

Iteratively updating the weights of the SVM classifier is another approach to solving SVMs. The training samples are repeatedly presented to the algorithm, which updates the weights accordingly. This can be achieved using a modified perceptron algorithm (see Duda et al., 2001, p. 263), or through algorithms such as the adatron algorithm (Frieß et al., 1998). The latter, though more efficient than the perceptron, cannot take into account slack variables. This limits its application to separable datasets. An additional drawback of such iterative algorithms is that they usually require a very high number of iterations to converge. Approximation presents a different approach to solving SVMs . The core vector machine (CVM) (Tsang et al., 2005) is an algorithm for finding an approximate solution to the SVM problem with $O(n)$ complexity. However, a recent study (Loosli and Canu, 2006) suggests that this reduced complexity sometimes comes at the cost of higher error rates.

There has been some effort to solve SVMs online. These solvers are presented once with each training point and adjust the solution accordingly. These are efficient algorithms for linear SVMs, but cannot be used for nonlinear SVMs.

Finally, there are several attempts to parallelize the SVM solution. These are addressed in the next section.

6.1.3   Distributing the Solution of Support Vector Machines

Building an SVM entails the solution of a quadratic programming (QP) problem, which is of the size of the number of training patterns, as shown in section 6.1.1. Thus, SVMs have a limited application for large datasets that occur in problems such as optical character recognition (OCR), bioinformatics, imaging, and so forth. Therefore, in recent years much work has been devoted to finding efficient algorithms for solving SVM problems. A different approach is to partition the work between multiple computing nodes and solve the problem in parallel. This is the approach we take in this chapter.

Distributing the solution process between multiple nodes has several advantages. The total amount of available memory is much larger than that available for single-node algorithms. In the latter, much of the computational effort required for the solution is devoted to repeating calculations that were previously completed, but could not be stored due to the limited amount of memory in the node. We define the fraction of excessive computations as the fraction of additional computations beyond the number of computations required to compute all entries in a full kernel matrix. This implies that this fraction can be negative, if not all matrix entries are evaluated at least once.

We tested the fraction of excessive computations on ten datasets from the

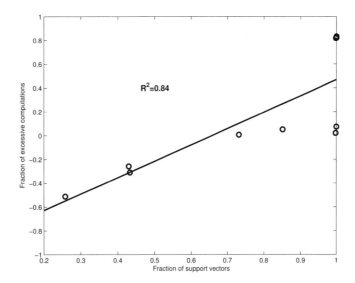

Figure 6.1   Dependence of the fraction of excessive computations on the fraction of support vectors.

UCI (University of California, Irvine) repository (Blake et al., 1998) using the SVM*light* (Joachims, 1999a) solver (using default parameters). The fraction of excess computation, limited to excess kernel computations, is shown in figure 6.1, where it is compared to the fraction of training points that are support vectors in the resulting classifiers. As can be seen there is an excellent correlation ($R^2 = 0.84$) between the fraction of excessive computations and the fraction of support vectors. This indicates that excessive computations are a major problem for datasets that are not easily separable. By utilizing the memory on multiple nodes, such excessive computations become redundant.

Another reason for distributing the computations across multiple nodes is the occurrence of instances where data cannot be gathered into a unified dataset. This can be due to privacy concerns (Yu et al., 2006), geographic reasons, or the size of the data. In such instances, it is necessary to solve the SVM problem when no single node can have access to the entire dataset.

As noted in the previous section, most SVM solvers (surveyed by Schölkopf and Smola, 2002) are not readily made parallel. In fact, little has been done to parallelize SVMs to date. A few noted exceptions are (Collobert et al., 2002b; Yu et al., 2006; Graf et al., 2005; Zanghirati and Zanni, 2003). In (Collobert et al., 2002b) the SVM solver is parallelized by training multiple SVMs, each on a subset of the training data, and aggregating the resulting classifiers into a single classifier. The training data is then redistributed to the classifiers according to their performance and the process is iterated until convergence is reached. The need to redivide the data among the SVM classifiers means that the data must be moved between nodes several times; this rules out the use of such an approach where bandwidth is a concern.

A more low-level approach is taken in (Zanghirati and Zanni, 2003), where the quadratic optimization problem is divided into smaller quadratic programs (similar to the Active Set methods), each of which is solved on a different node. The results are aggregated and the process is repeated until convergence. The performance of this method has a strong dependence on the caching architecture of the cluster.

Yu et al. (2006) developed a protocol for exchanging the training data between the storage nodes and the main computation node. Strictly speaking, this is not a parallel solution, since it requires that data, in encrypted or hashed form, arrive at a central node.

Graf et al. (2005) partition the data and solve an SVM for each partition. The support vectors from each pair of classifiers are then aggregated into a new training set, for which an SVM is solved. The process continues until a single classifier remains. The aggregation process can be iterated, using the support vectors of the final classifier in the previous iteration to seed the new classifiers. One problem with this approach is that the data must be repeatedly shared between nodes, meaning that once again the goal of data distribution cannot be attained. The second problem (which might be more severe) is that the number of possible support vectors is restricted by the capacity of a single SVM solver.

6.2   A Distributed Solution of the SVM Problem Using a Sequential Solver

Vijayakumar and Wu (1999) proposed a sequential learning algorithm for the solution of SVMs. We propose a modification of this algorithm to a batch update, instead of the original sequential update. Such a modification allows the algorithm to be parallelized, as discussed below. The MATLAB code for this algorithm is given in algorithm 6.1. The algorithm first computes the kernel matrix D, which is a function of the training data and the scalar λ, which replaces the bias term, as defined in section 6.1.1. The updates to the Lagrange multipliers are computed iteratively. The learning rate is set as in Vijayakumar and Wu (1999), divided by the number of training examples. This choice conforms to the conditions of their convergence proof. The algorithm requires several parameters: C, the slack variable; $MaxIter$, the maximum number of possible iterations; and eta, a convergence criterion. In line 8 of the algorithm, the rate of change in the optimization target function is computed. If it is small enough, the algorithm is terminated.

The sequential learning algorithm can be parallelized by dividing the training data into nodes, such that each node holds a slice of the data. Each node then computes the modified kernel matrix D for its slice of the data. This means that each node needs to see the full training set only once. If privacy is a concern, methods such as those cited by Yu et al. (2006) can be used. Once the kernel matrix is computed, the data is no longer held in memory. A master node sends an initial Lagrange multiplier vector h to the nodes. Each node computes line 5 of the algorithm for the samples for which it is responsible and sends this vector back to the master node. Once all vectors are computed, they are aggregated and the update

---

Algorithm 6.1 MATLAB code for the sequential SVM solver (see the text for an explanation of the symbols)

1: $h = zeros(1, N)$;
2: $[D]_{ij} = y_i y_j \left(K\left(x_i, x_j\right) + \lambda^2 \right)$
3: $gamma = 2/\left(N * max\left(diag\left(D\right)\right)\right)$;
4: **for** $i = 1 : MaxIter$
5:      $E = h * D$;
6:      $delta\_h = min\left(max\left(gamma * \left(1 - E\right), -h\right), C - h\right)$;
7:      $h = h + delta\_h$;
8:      **if** $delta\_h * \left(1 - E' - 0.5 * D * delta\_h\right) <= eta$
9:          $Break$;
10:     **end**
11: **end**

---

to the Lagrange multipliers is computed and added to the original vector. These steps continue until convergence is reached or the maximum number of iterations is attained. This process is depicted graphically in figure 6.2.

By parallelizing the algorithm in this way, most of the communication load is limited to the initial kernel matrix computation. Thereafter, only relatively short vectors are sent between the master node and the other nodes.

The stopping criterion for the algorithm is based on computing the update to the target function. If this value is small enough, training is terminated.

The difference between the code in algorithm 6.1 and the algorithm given by Vijayakumar and Wu (1999) is that instead of updating the Lagrange multipliers based on each sample, they are updated once every iteration, based on the updates of all samples.

The speedup in computational complexity of the distributed algorithm is dependent on both the size of the data and the number of computing nodes. Let N be the number of training data points and M the number of computing nodes (not counting the single master node required). The speedup in the computational complexity, compared to working on a single node, is $N/\lceil N/M \rceil$.

6.3 Metrics for Comparing SVMs

One of the most important factors when trying to compare the performance of different classification algorithms is the criteria by which they are measured. The most trivial parameters used to compare algorithms is the test-set error rate achieved, usually measured over several datasets, each using a cross-validation scheme (Duda et al., 2001).

Other related parameters which have been suggested for comparing the learning performance of SVM solvers are the number of support vectors in the solution and the value of the target function that each solver reaches. The number of support vectors (used as a parameter for comparison in (Tsang et al., 2005; Zanghirati and

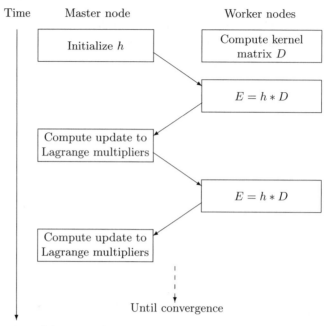

Figure 6.2 Schematic diagram of the parallel SVM solution algorithm showing the timing and the division of work between master and worker nodes.

Zanni, 2003)) is a measure of the sparsity of the solution. Sparser solution are usually preferred due to the lower computational and memory cost associated with them. The value of the optimization function is a measure of the effectiveness of the solver.

Performance measures are another set of measures by which solvers are evaluated. The most straightforward measures in this class are the time taken to converge, the number of floating point operations (flops) needed (Frieß et al., 1998), and the dependence of these measures on the size of the training set.

In distributed systems there are several additional parameters necessary for a valid comparison. These measures are not unique to machine learning algorithms. Instead, these are parameters used for measuring the performance of software on a distributed platform. Two such measures, speedup and efficiency (defined below), are the most commonly used measures. These two measures estimate the gain attained by distributing the computation across nodes.

The speedup of a distributed algorithm is defined as the ratio of the time needed to converge using a single processing element (T_S) to the time needed to converge using p processing elements (T_p):

$$sp_r(p) = \frac{T_S}{T_p}. \tag{6.10}$$

The speedup is expected to peak after a certain number of processing elements are used, and either level off or decay when more processing elements are added. This is due to clashes between the processing elements. A linear speedup ($sp_r(p) = p$)

over a wide range of processing elements is considered very good scalability, but in most cases speedup is sublinear due to communication overhead.

The relative efficiency of the distributed algorithm is the speedup normalized by the number of processing elements:

$$eff(p) = sp_r(p)/p. \tag{6.11}$$

Efficiency is a measure of how well the processing elements in the system are utilized in solving the problem, compared to the effort needed for overhead such as communication and synchronization. By definition, algorithms running on a single processor have an efficiency of 1.

Finally, it is useful to test the experimental results for statistical significance. In this chapter, we followed (Demšar, 2006) and used the Friedman test (M. Friedman, 1937, 1940) to compare multiple classifiers, and the paired two-sided test to compare two classifiers.

6.4 Simulation

This section describes performance tests of the proposed algorithm and the results of its comparison to other frequently used SVM solvers.

6.4.1 Experimental Procedure

The proposed algorithm was implemented in MATLAB. We compared its performance to that of different SVM solvers on several datasets. To obtain valid run-time estimates we compared the performance of the sequential solver to MATLAB implementations (Stork and Yom-Tov, 2004) of the cascade SVM (Graf et al., 2005), the Lagrangian SVM (Mangasarian and Musicant, 2001), and a solver using MATLAB's quadratic programming function.[1] We used five small datasets for this comparison: Iris, Wine, Vowel, Glass, and Soybean, all from the UCI repository. The performance of the sequential solver on larger datasets could not be compared to solvers implemented purely in MATLAB; therefore, we compared it to SVM*light* (Joachims, 1999a) on the following nine larger datasets: Adult, Connect-4, Isolet, Letter, Mushrooms, Nursery, Pageblocks, Pendigits, and Spambase, all from the UCI repository. The characteristics of all datasets are summarized in table 6.1

The goal in the comparison of SVM*light* to the parallel solver was not to determine which of these solvers is superior in terms of training times. Such a comparison is neither logical nor fair, as the two solvers differ in many ways: SVM*light* is fully written in C, while the parallel solver was realized in MATLAB; the combined memory size used by the parallel solver was unattainable on a single node, and

---

1. We did not compare to the SMO solver because of its highly scalar behavior, which would perform poorly on MATLAB.

thus not usable by SVM^{light}. Instead, our goal was twofold: The first was to show that the parallel solver reached solutions which are not significantly different from those of SVM^{light}, as measured by the test error. The second goal was to show how the two solvers scale as a function of the dataset size. This latter goal is important since, while hardware improves almost continuously, larger datasets will always be available, and the important question is therefore how different solvers scale as a function of dataset size, rather than their run-times on current machines.

Nominal attributes with t possible values were substituted by t binary features, where the ith binary feature was set to 1 if, and only if, the corresponding nominal attribute took the ith possible value. For each feature, we computed its average and standard deviation over the training set, and used these to normalize the data (training and testing) by subtracting the average and dividing by the standard deviation.

In order to achieve valid comparison with different solvers, we followed the methodology proposed by Rifkin and Klautau (2004) for all datasets with a training set smaller than 20,000 examples. We used tenfold cross-validation (10xCV); namely, in each fold, the union of nine out of ten equally sized random subsets were used for training, and the tenth for testing. In all our experiments, we used a radial basis function (RBF) kernel. To optimize the RBF kernel parameter σ and the classifier cost parameter C, we followed Rifkin and Klautau (2004) and used a simple greedy search via 10xCV over the training set. Initial values of σ and C were set to 1. The value of σ was then increased or decreased by a factor of 2 until no improvements were observed for three consecutive attempts. Then, σ was fixed at the best value found, and an identical optimization was performed over C. For datasets with over 20,000 training examples, we used default parameters ($\sigma = 1$, $C = 0.5$), mainly because SVM^{light} would not converge within a reasonable amount of time using other sets of parameters.

Single-node solvers were run on a 2.1GHz Intel Pentium with 2GB memory. The workers of the distributed solver were sixteen nodes of a Power 5+ processor (divided between two machines, each with 16GB memory) and four nodes of Power 5 processor (on a single machine with 2GB of memory). The master node was run on a single node of a Power 5 processor, on a different machine from that of the worker nodes. We used a shared memory space on an AFS network for passing data between the nodes. All communication was handled via a toolbox programmed in MATLAB, which used files for passing information between the master node and all other nodes.

6.4.2   Comparative Performance of Several SVM Solvers

Table 6.2 shows the errors obtained on the five datasets using the five MATLAB-based single-node solvers. The average *ranks* of the various algorithms appear in the last row of the table. Following Demšar (2006), these ranks were computed as averages of row ranks. For each row, if the errors of all algorithms are distinct, they are assigned the ranks in $\{1, \ldots, 5\}$. When algorithms share exactly the same

Table 6.1 Summary of datasets. The number of examples in parentheses is the number of test examples (if a train/test partition exists).

Dataset	Number of examples	Number of features
Iris	150	4
Wine	178	3
Vowel	528	10
Glass	214	9
Soybean	307 (376)	132
Adult	32561 (16281)	105
Connect-4	67557	127
Isolet	6238 (1559)	617
Letter	20000	16
Mushrooms	8124	117
Nursery	12960	25
Pageblocks	5473	10
Pendigits	7494 (3498)	16
Spambase	4601	57

Table 6.2 Error rates (percentages) on five small datasets using single-node solvers

Dataset	Quad. solver	Perceptron	Lagrangian	Cascade	Sequential
Iris	0.67	0.67	13.00	0.00	0.00
Wine	4.71	4.12	4.71	4.71	4.12
Vowel	2.14	0.21	32.69	0.43	0.21
Glass	30.95	17.14	29.52	14.76	16.19
Soybean	5.32	6.91	29.79	8.24	8.51
Average rank	3.5	2.3	4.6	2.5	2.1

error, they are all assigned the same average rank. For example, the rank vector for the Iris dataset is $(3.5, 3.5, 5, 1.5, 1.5)$. The best performers, in terms of ranks, are jointly perceptron, cascade SVM, and the sequential SVM solver. However, using the Friedman test (Demšar, 2006; M. Friedman, 1937, 1940)), we did not detect any statistically significant difference between the performance of the algorithms.

Run-times are reported in table 6.3. This table shows that the sequential solver and the Lagrangian solver are the fastest of the five solvers compared. In this case, the Friedman test indicates that no statistically significant difference between the Lagrangian solver, the cascade solver, and the sequential solver could be detected.

Table 6.3   Run-times (seconds) on five small datasets using single-node solvers

Dataset	Quad. solver	Perceptron	Lagrangian	Cascade	Sequential
Iris	1.51	0.10	0.06	0.26	0.03
Wine	1.61	1.16	0.05	0.36	0.04
Vowel	79.05	149.17	0.77	126.79	0.35
Glass	3.27	1.854	0.08	0.34	0.06
Soybean	39.87	4.97	0.68	5.02	1.26
Average rank	4.6	3.8	1.8	3.6	1.2

6.4.3   Performance of the Distributed Solver

We compared the performance of the sequential solver working in a distributed environment (described above) with that of SVM^{light} (Joachims, 1999a). Table 6.4 compares the error rates and run-times on nine relatively large UCI datasets. There is no statistically significant difference in either errors or run-times between the two solvers (paired, two-sided test).

However, an interesting picture emerges when the time taken to converge (from table 6.4) is plotted against the number of training points (from table 6.1), for all datasets. This is shown in figure 6.3, where a second-order polynomial model is also fitted to the data. While both training times exhibit a relatively large dependence on the size of the training set, the scaling of the sequential solver is almost linear, compared to the high influence of the squared term in the model for the behavior of SVM^{light}. The latter solver is also influenced by the separability of the dataset, as noted in section 6.1.3. This effect is not exhibited by the sequential solver, which estimates the full kernel matrix, no matter what the separability of the dataset. This implies that when datasets are known to be inseparable, the sequential solver would be more efficient than SVM^{light}. However, if the dataset is clearly separable, SVM^{light} would be a better choice. In general, however, separability cannot be estimated without classifying the data, which supports the use of the sequential solver.

Several measures for comparing the performance of distributed solvers were given in section 6.3. Figure 6.4 shows the speedup of the sequential solver as a function of the number of processing elements. This figure clearly demonstrates that twenty processing elements (or less) are sufficient for only small (under 6000 training points) datasets. In the architecture we used, datasets with more training points would benefit from additional processing elements.

As noted above, linear speedup is considered good scalability. Thus, we measured the fit of the algorithm's scalability for each dataset. In all datasets, except `Pageblocks`, there was a match of $R^2 = 0.75$ or better between the observed speedup and linear speedup. (The median of all datasets was $R^2 = 0.96$.) The slope

Table 6.4 Error rates and training times of the sequential SVM solver (working in a distributed environment) compared to that of SVM^{light}

Dataset	Error (%)		Run times (sec)	
	Sequential	SVM^{light}	Sequential	SVM^{light}
Adult	18.08	19.90	357.5	5112.6
Connect-4	2.37	34.16	497.7	10596.0
Isolet	5.77	49.97	309.1	278.0
Letter	7.34	2.30	73.0	209.1
Mushroom	0.04	0.02	120.2	95.4
Nursery	5.49	0.02	177.5	88.2
Pageblocks	3.99	2.74	15.9	10.7
Pendigits	1.37	1.57	15.3	9.7
Spambase	16.5	6.57	78.8	10.4

of the speedup had a median of 0.33. We therefore conclude that the algorithm exhibits good speedup over the range of processing elements we tested.

Figure 6.5 shows the efficiency of the processing as a function of the number of processing elements. The efficiency decreases as the number of processing elements increases. This reflects the fact that adding processing nodes reduces the training time at the cost of lower efficiency. Furthermore, with the exclusion of the Connect-4 dataset, there is a relatively high correlation (Spearman, $\rho = 0.47$) between the number of training points and the maximal efficiency achieved (using up to twenty processing nodes). This indicates that the larger the dataset, the more efficient the algorithm's performance.

6.5   A Model of the Computational Time

In this section, we describe a model for estimating the time needed for the sequential SVM solver to converge and to classify a test set. Estimating the training time of the algorithm is a useful feature, especially when trying to build a classifier for very large datasets.

We assume there are N samples in the training data, each with dimension D. The test data is comprised of N_{Test} samples of the same dimension. The classifier uses M processing nodes. The maximal number of iterations is denoted by max_iter and the time to perform a single multiplication operation by α_1.

The stages of the sequential SVM solver are:

1. Compute the kernel matrix for the training data. The time taken to complete this stage is on the order of $O(D \cdot N^2/M)$. Thus, the time taken to complete this stage is $t_{Train\_kernel} = \alpha_1 \cdot \left(D \cdot N^2/M \right)$.

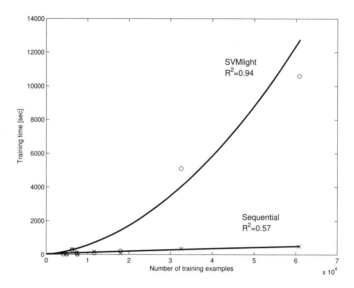

Figure 6.3   Dependence of the training time on the number of training data points. Regression lines are second-order polynomial. For run-times, circles mark those of SVM*light* and crosses mark those of the sequential SVM solver.

2. For each iteration, compute the multiplication of the kernel matrix by the Lagrange multipliers. The time taken to complete this stage is on the order of $O(N^2/M)$. Thus, the time taken to complete this stage can be bounded by $t_{Iter} \leq \alpha_1 \cdot (N^2/M) \cdot max\_iter$.

3. Compute the kernel matrix for the test data. The time taken to complete this stage is on the order of $O(D \cdot N \cdot N_{Test}/M)$. Thus, the time taken to complete this stage is $t_{Test\_kernel} = \alpha_1 \cdot (D \cdot N \cdot N_{Test}/M)$.

4. Compute the multiplication of the kernel matrix by the Lagrange multipliers. The time taken to complete this stage is on the order of $O(N \cdot N_{Test}/M)$. Thus, the time taken to complete this stage is $t_{Classifier} = \alpha_1 \cdot (N \cdot N_{Test}/M)$.

In addition, the read/write time (or in general, the data transfer time) should be taken into account. This time is bounded by $t_{RW} \leq \alpha_2 \cdot (max\_iter + 2) \cdot Nsub$, where α_2 is the read/write constant and $Nsub$ is the number of sub-problems into which the data is divided. In our work $Nsub$ was set to the maximum number of partitions needed in order to hold the kernel matrix in memory (i.e., the total number of examples, squared, divided by the largest number of elements that can be held in memory by a single node).

Thus, we hypothesize that the time it will take to train a classifier and apply it to a test set can be modeled as

$$t \leq t_{Train\_kernel} + t_{Iter} + t_{Test\_kernel} + t_{Classifier} + t_{RW}. \tag{6.12}$$

We used the training times for the nine large datasets, varying the number of

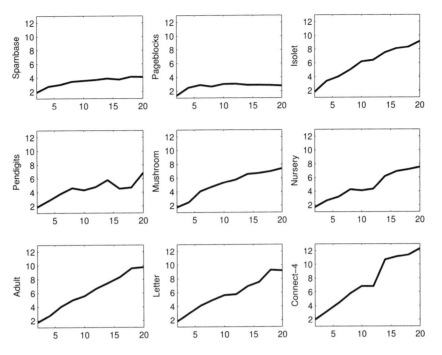

Figure 6.4 Speedup of the training as a function of the number of processing nodes. The horizontal axis is the number of processing elements. The vertical axis is the speedup. Datasets are arranged according to the number of training points, increasing from top to bottom.

processing elements between two and twenty. Thus, a total of 683 points were used to build the model (i.e., find the parameters α_1 and α_2). Using linear regression we found an excellent fit with $R^2 = 0.944$ $(p < 10^{-20})$ between the model (taking into account the actual number of iterations) and the actual training times of the classifiers. Therefore, we can deduce that, at least for the architecture we used, the training time can be bounded with extremely high accuracy using the parameters of the data, the speed of the processing elements, and the data transfer times.

Using the model it is also possible to estimate the ratio of the time the processing nodes spend computing to the time required for communication. Interestingly, the time spent performing useful computations constitutes only 41% of the time required by the classifier to converge; the remaining 59% is devoted to the communication overhead. Furthermore, as can be expected from the efficiency plots, this ratio decreases as the number of processing elements increases, resulting in an average of only 26% spent on useful computations when twenty processing nodes are used.

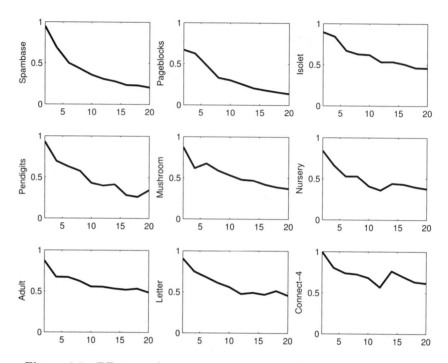

Figure 6.5 Efficiency of training as a function of the number of processing nodes. The horizontal axis is the number of processing elements. The vertical axis is the efficiency. Datasets are arranged according to the number of training points, from top to bottom.

6.6   Concluding Remarks

The construction of SVM classifiers requires a very large computational effort, quadratic in the number of training samples. Because of this drawback, much work has been devoted to making SVMs viable for large training data, either by decreasing the computational cost through approximation, or by increasing the computational resources through distribution of the solution. The latter solution has the additional attractive property that data does not have to be centrally located, thus assisting in cases where the data is simply too large to hold in a single location, or where this is undesirable due to privacy or legal issues.

In this chapter we presented an algorithm that distributes the SVM solver by making each node perform the processing associated with part of the kernel matrix. This solver, like most distributed solvers proposed so far, has the drawback that it requires the full kernel matrix to be computed. This is usually avoided by single-node classifiers when the dataset can be easily separated. However, when the data is not easily separated, such solvers usually perform repeated computations of the kernel matrix. The algorithm proposed here does not perform these repeated computations. Because it is difficult to know a priori whether the dataset is separable, this drawback is not a serious disadvantage to the proposed algorithm.

7 Newton Methods for Fast Semisupervised Linear SVMs

Vikas Sindhwani
S. Sathiya Keerthi

In this chapter, we present a family of semisupervised linear support vector classifiers that are designed to handle partially labeled sparse datasets with possibly a very large number of examples and features. At their core, our algorithms employ recently developed modified finite newton techniques. We provide a fast, multiswitch implementation of linear transductive SVM (TSVM) that is significantly more efficient and scalable than currently used dual techniques. We present a new deterministic annealing algorithm for optimizing semisupervised SVMs. This algorithm is designed to alleviate local minima problems, and is also computationally attractive. We conduct an empirical study on several classification tasks which confirms the value of our methods in large-scale semisupervised settings. Our algorithms are implemented in SVM_{lin}, a public domain software package.

7.1 Introduction

Consider the following situation: In a single web crawl, search engines like Yahoo! and Google index billions of documents. Only a very small fraction of these documents can possibly be hand-labeled by human editorial teams and assembled into topic directories. In information retrieval relevance feedback, a user labels a small number of documents returned by an initial query as being relevant or not. The remaining documents form a massive collection of unlabeled data. Despite its natural and pervasive need, solutions to the problem of utilizing unlabeled data with labeled examples have only recently emerged in machine learning literature. Whereas the abundance of unlabeled data is frequently acknowledged as a motivation in most papers, the true potential of semisupervised learning in large-scale settings is yet to be systematically explored. This appears to be partly due to the lack of scalable tools to handle large volumes of data.

In this chapter, we propose extensions of linear support vector machines (SVMs) for semisupervised classification. Linear techniques are often the method of choice in many applications due to their simplicity and interpretability. When data appears in a rich high-dimensional representation, linear functions often provide a sufficiently complex hypothesis space for learning high-quality classifiers. This has been established, for example, for document classification with linear SVMs in numerous studies.

Our methods are motivated by the intuition of margin maximization over labeled and unlabeled examples. The key idea is to bias the classification hyperplane to pass through a low data density region keeping points in each data cluster on the same side of the hyperplane while respecting labels. This formulation, first proposed in Vapnik (1998) as the *transductive SVM* (TSVM), uses an extended SVM objective function with a nonconvex loss term over the unlabeled examples to implement the cluster assumption in semisupervised learning: that points in a cluster should have similar labels. The role of unlabeled data is to identify clusters and high-density regions in the input space. Due to nonconvexity, several optimization procedures have been proposed (Joachims, 1999b; Bennett and Demiriz, 1998; Fung and Mangasarian, 2001b; Chapelle and Zien, 2005; Collobert et al., 2006; Sindhwani et al., 2006; see also chapter 12 in this book). In the discussion below, by transductive SVM, we specifically refer to the label-switching procedure of Joachims (1999b). The popular implementation of this procedure in SVM[light] software[1] is considered state of the art in text categorization, even in the face of increasing recent competition.

We highlight the main contributions of our work.

1. We outline an implementation for a variant of TSVM (Joachims, 1999b) designed for linear semisupervised classification on large, sparse datasets. As compared to currently used dual techniques (e.g., as implemented in SVM[light]), our method effectively exploits data sparsity and linearity of the problem to provide superior scalability. Additionally, we propose a multiple switching heuristic that further improves TSVM training by an order of magnitude. These speed enhancements turn TSVM into a feasible tool for large-scale applications.

2. We propose a novel algorithm for semisupervised SVMs inspired by deterministic annealing (DA) techniques. This approach generates a family of objective functions whose nonconvexity is controlled by an annealing parameter. The global minimizer is parametrically tracked in this family. This approach alleviates the problem of local minima in the TSVM optimization procedure which results in better solutions to some problems. A computationally attractive training algorithm is presented that involves a sequence of alternating convex optimizations.

3. We conduct an experimental study on many high-dimensional document classification tasks involving hundreds of thousands of examples. This study clearly shows

---

1. see http://svmlight.joachims.org.

the utility of our tools for very large-scale problems.

The modified finite Newton algorithm of Keerthi and DeCoste (2005) for fast training of linear SVMs, a key subroutine for our algorithms, is outlined in section 7.2. Semisupervised extensions of this algorithm are presented in sections 7.3 and 7.4. Experimental results are reported in section 7.5. Section 7.6 contains some concluding comments.

All the algorithms described in this chapter are implemented in a public domain software, SVM$_\text{lin}$ (see section 7.5), which can be used for fast training of linear SVMs for supervised and semisupervised classification problems. The algorithms presented in this chapter are described in further detail, together with pseudocode, in Sindhwani and Keerthi (2005).

7.2   Modified Finite Newton Linear l_2-SVM

The modified finite Newton l_2-SVM method (Keerthi and DeCoste, 2005) (abbreviated l_2-SVM-MFN) is a recently developed training algorithm for linear SVMs that is ideally suited to sparse datasets with a large number of examples and possibly a large number of features.

Given a binary classification problem with l labeled examples $\{x_i, y_i\}_{i=1}^l$ where the input patterns $x_i \in \mathbb{R}^d$ (e.g., documents) and the labels $y_i \in \{+1, -1\}$, l_2-SVM-MFN provides an efficient primal solution to the following SVM optimization problem:

$$ w^\star = \underset{w \in \mathbb{R}^d}{\operatorname{argmin}} \frac{1}{2} \sum_{i=1}^l l_2(y_i w^T x_i) + \frac{\lambda}{2} \|w\|^2, \tag{7.1} $$

where l_2 is the l_2-SVM loss given by $l_2(z) = \max(0, 1 - z)^2$, λ is a real-valued regularization parameter,[2] and the final classifier is given by $\operatorname{sign}(w^{\star T} x)$.

This objective function differs from the standard SVM problem in some respects. First, instead of using the hinge loss as the data-fitting term, the square of the hinge loss (or the so-called quadratic soft-margin loss function) is used. This makes the objective function continuously differentiable, allowing easier applicability of gradient techniques. Secondly, the bias term b is also regularized. In the problem formulation of (7.1), it is implicitly assumed that an additional component in the weight vector and a constant feature in the example vectors have been added to indirectly incorporate the bias. This formulation combines the simplicity of a least-squares aspect with algorithmic advantages associated with SVMs.

We consider a version of l_2-SVM-MFN where a weighted quadratic soft-margin

---

2. $\lambda = 1/C$ where C is the standard SVM parameter.

loss function is used:

$$\min_{w} f(w) = \frac{1}{2} \sum_{i \in J(w)} c_i l_2(y_i w^T x_i) + \frac{\lambda}{2} \|w\|^2. \qquad (7.2)$$

Here we have rewritten (7.1) using the support vector set $J(w) = \{i : y_i (w^T x_i) < 1\}$. Additionally, the loss associated with the ith example has a cost c_i. $f(w)$ refers to the objective function being minimized, evaluated at a candidate solution w. Note that if the index set $J(w)$ were independent of w and ran over all data points, this would simply be the objective function for weighted linear regularized least-squares.

Following (Keerthi and DeCoste, 2005), we observe that f is a strictly convex, piecewise quadratic, continuously differentiable function having a unique minimizer. The gradient of f at w is given by

$$\nabla f(w) = \lambda w + X_{J(w)}^T C_{J(w)} \left[X_{J(w)} w - Y_{J(w)} \right],$$

where $X_{J(w)}$ is a matrix whose rows are the feature vectors of training points corresponding to the index set $J(w)$, $Y_{J(w)}$ is a column vector containing labels for these points, and $C_{J(w)}$ is a diagonal matrix that contains the costs c_i for these points along its diagonal.

l_2-SVM-MFN is a primal algorithm that uses the Newton's method for unconstrained minimization of a convex function. The classical Newton's method is based on a second-order approximation of the objective function, and involves updates of the following kind:

$$w^{k+1} = w^k + \delta^k n^k, \qquad (7.3)$$

where the step size $\delta^k \in \mathbb{R}$, and the Newton direction $n^k \in \mathbb{R}^d$ is given by $n^k = -[\nabla^2 f(w^k)]^{-1} \nabla f(w^k)$. Here, $\nabla f(w^k)$ is the gradient vector and $\nabla^2 f(w^k)$ is the Hessian matrix of f at w^k. However, the Hessian does not exist everywhere, since f is not twice differentiable at those weight vectors w where $w^T x_i = y_i$ for some index i.[3] Thus a generalized definition of the Hessian matrix is used. The modified finite Newton procedure proceeds as follows. The step $\bar{w}^k = w^k + n^k$ in the Newton direction can be seen to be given by solving the following linear system associated with a weighted linear regularized least squares problem over the data subset defined by the indices $J(w^k)$:

$$\left[\lambda I + X_{J(w^k)}^T C_{J(w^k)} X_{J(w^k)} \right] \bar{w}^k = X_{J(w^k)}^T C_{J(w^k)} Y_{J(w^k)}, \qquad (7.4)$$

where I is the identity matrix. Once $\bar{w}^k$ is obtained, w^{k+1} is obtained from (7.3) by setting $w^{k+1} = w^k + \delta^k(\bar{w}^k - w^k)$ after performing an exact line search for δ^k,

---

3. In the neighborhood of such a w, the index i leaves or enters $J(w)$. However, at w, $y_i w^T x_i = 1$. So f is continuously differentiable in spite of these index jumps.

i.e., by exactly solving a one-dimensional minimization problem:

$$\delta^k = \operatorname*{argmin}_{\delta \geq 0} \phi(\delta) = f\left(w^k + \delta(\bar{w}^k - w^k)\right). \tag{7.5}$$

The modified finite Newton procedure has the property of finite convergence to the optimal solution. The key features that bring scalability and numerical robustness to l_2-SVM-MFN are: (a) Solving the regularized least squares system of (7.4) by a numerically well-behaved conjugate gradient scheme referred to as CGLS (Frommer and Maaß, 1999), which is designed for large, sparse data matrices X. The benefit of the least-squares aspect of the loss function comes in here to provide access to a powerful set of tools in numerical computation. (b) Due to the one-sided nature of margin loss functions, these systems are required to be solved over only restricted index sets $\jmath(w)$ which can be much smaller than the whole dataset. This also allows additional heuristics to be developed such as terminating CGLS early when working with a crude starting guess like 0, and allowing the following line search step to yield a point where the index set $\jmath(w)$ is small. Subsequent optimization steps then work on smaller subsets of the data. Below, we briefly discuss the CGLS and line search procedures. We refer the reader to (Keerthi and DeCoste, 2005) for full details.

7.2.1 CGLS

CGLS (Frommer and Maaß, 1999) is a special conjugate-gradient solver that is designed to solve, in a numerically robust way, large, sparse, weighted regularized least-squares problems such as the one in (7.4). Starting with a guess solution, several specialized conjugate gradient iterations are applied to get $\bar{w}^k$ that solves (7.4). The major expense in each iteration consists of two operations of the form $X_{\jmath(w^k)}p$ and $X_{\jmath(w^k)}^T q$. If there are n_0 nonzero elements in the data matrix, these involve $O(n_0)$ cost. It is worth noting that, as a subroutine of l_2-SVM-MFN, CGLS is typically called on a small subset, $X_{\jmath(w^k)}$ of the full dataset. To compute the *exact solution* of (7.4), r iterations are needed, where r is the rank of $X_{\jmath(w^k)}$. But, in practice, such an exact solution is unnecessary. CGLS uses an effective stopping criterion based on gradient norm for early termination (involving a tolerance parameter ϵ). The total cost of CGLS is $O(t_{cgls}n_0)$ where t_{cgls} is the number of iterations, which depends on ϵ and the condition number of $X_{\jmath(w^k)}$, and is typically found to be very small relative to the dimensions of $X_{\jmath(w^k)}$ (number of examples and features). Apart from the storage of $X_{\jmath(w^k)}$, the memory requirements of CGLS are also minimal: only five vectors need to be maintained, including the outputs over the currently active set of data points.

Finally, an important feature of CGLS is worth emphasizing. Suppose the solution w of a regularized least-squares problem is available, i.e., the linear system in (7.4) has been solved using CGLS. If there is a need to solve a perturbed linear system, it is greatly advantageous in many settings to start the conjugate gradient iterations for the new system with w as the initial guess. This is called *seeding*. If the starting residual is small, CGLS can converge much faster than with a guess of 0 vector. The utility of this feature depends on the nature and degree of perturbation. In l_2-SVM-MFN, the candidate solution w^k obtained after line search in iteration k is seeded for the CGLS computation of $\bar{w}^k$. Also, in tuning λ over a range of values, it is valuable to seed the solution for a particular λ onto the next value. For the semisupervised SVM implementations with l_2-SVM-MFN, we will seed solutions across linear systems with slightly perturbed label vectors, data matrices, and costs.

7.2.2   Line Search

Given the vectors $w^k, \bar{w}^k$ in some iteration of l_2-SVM-MFN, the line search step requires us to solve (7.5). The one-dimensional function $\phi(\delta)$ is the restriction of the objective function f on the ray from w^k onto $\bar{w}^k$. Hence, like f, $\phi(\delta)$ is also a continuously differentiable, strictly convex, piecewise quadratic function with a unique minimizer. ϕ' is a continuous piecewise linear function whose root, δ^k, can be easily found by sorting the breakpoints where its slope changes and then performing a sequential search on that sorted list. The cost of this operation is negligible compared to the cost of the CGLS iterations.

7.2.3   Complexity

l_2-SVM-MFN alternates between calls to CGLS and line searches until the support vector set $\jmath(w^k)$ stabilizes up to a tolerance parameter τ, i.e., if $\forall i \in \jmath(w^k)$, $y_i \bar{w}^{kT} x_i < 1 + \tau$ and $\forall i \notin \jmath(w^k)$, $y_i \bar{w}^{kT} x_i \geq 1 - \tau$. Its computational complexity is $O(t_{mfn}\bar{t}_{cgls}n_0)$ where t_{mfn} is the number of outer iterations of CGLS calls and line search, and $\bar{t}_{cgls}$ is the average number of CGLS iterations. The number of CGLS iterations to reach a relative error of ϵ can be bounded in terms of ϵ and the condition number of the left-hand-side matrix in (7.4) (Bjork, 1996).

In practice, t_{mfn} and $\bar{t}_{cgls}$ depend on the dataset and the tolerances desired in the stopping criterion, but are typically very small. As an example of typical behavior: on a Reuters (Lewis et al., 2004) text classification problem (top-level category CCAT versus rest) involving 804,414 examples and 47,236 features, $t_{mfn} = 7$ with a maximum of $t_{cgls} = 28$ CGLS iterations; on this dataset l_2-SVM-MFN converges in about 100 seconds on an Intel 3GHz, 2GB RAM machine.[4] The practical scaling is linear in the number of nonzero entries in the data matrix (Keerthi and DeCoste, 2005).

7.2.4   Other Loss Functions

All the discussion in this chapter can be applied to other loss functions such as Huber's Loss and rounded hinge loss using the modifications outlined by Keerthi

---

4. For this experiment, λ is chosen as in Joachims (2006); $\epsilon = \tau = 10^{-6}$.

and DeCoste (2005).

We also note a recently proposed linear time training algorithm for hinge loss (Joachims, 2006). While detailed comparative studies are yet to be conducted, preliminary experiments have shown that l_2-SVM-MFN and the methods of (Joachims, 2006) are competitive with each other (at their default tolerance parameters).

We now assume that in addition to l labeled examples, we have u unlabeled examples $\{x'_j\}_{j=1}^u$. Our goal is to extend l_2-SVM-MFN to utilize unlabeled data, typically when $l \ll u$.

7.3   Fast Multiswitch Transductive SVMs

Transductive SVM appends an additional term in the SVM objective function whose role is to drive the classification hyperplane toward low data density regions. Variations of this idea have appeared in the literature (Joachims, 1999b; Bennett and Demiriz, 1998; Fung and Mangasarian, 2001b). Since Joachims (1999b) describes what appears to be the most natural extension of standard SVMs among these methods, and is popularly used in text classification applications, we will focus on developing its large-scale implementation.

The following optimization problem is set up for standard TSVM[5]:

$$\min_{w,\{y'_j\}_{j=1}^u} \frac{\lambda}{2}\|w\|^2 + \frac{1}{2l}\sum_{i=1}^l L(y_i\, w^T x_i) + \frac{\lambda'}{2u}\sum_{j=1}^u L(y'_j\, w^T x'_j)$$
$$\text{subject to} \quad \frac{1}{u}\sum_{j=1}^u \max[0, \text{sign}(w^T x'_j)] = r,$$

where for the loss function $L(z)$, the hinge loss $l_1(z) = max(0, 1 - z)$ is normally used. The labels on the unlabeled data, $y'_1 \ldots y'_u$, are $\{+1, -1\}$-valued variables in the optimization problem. In other words, TSVM seeks a hyperplane w and a labeling of the unlabeled examples, so that the SVM objective function is minimized, subject to the constraint that a fraction r of the unlabeled data be classified positive. SVM margin maximization in the presence of unlabeled examples can be interpreted as an implementation of the cluster assumption. In the optimization problem above, λ' is a user-provided parameter that provides control over the influence of unlabeled data. For example, if the data has distinct clusters with a large margin, but the cluster assumption does not hold, then λ' can be set to 0 and the standard SVM is retrieved. If there is enough labeled data, λ, λ' can be tuned by cross-validation. An initial estimate of r can be made from the fraction of labeled examples that belong to the positive class and subsequent fine-tuning can be done based on validation performance.

---

5. The bias term is typically excluded from the regularizer, but this factor is not expected to make any significant difference.

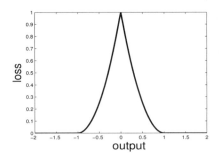

Figure 7.1 l_2 loss function for TSVM.

This optimization is implemented in (Joachims, 1999b) by first using an inductive SVM to label the unlabeled data and then iteratively switching labels and retraining SVMs to improve the objective function. The TSVM algorithm wraps around an SVM training procedure. The original (and widely popular) implementation of TSVM uses the SVM^{light} software. There, the training of SVMs in the inner loops of TSVM uses dual decomposition techniques. As shown by experiments in Keerthi and DeCoste (2005), in sparse, linear settings one can obtain significant speed improvements with l_2-SVM-MFN over SVM^{light}. Thus, by implementing TSVM with l_2-SVM-MFN, we expect similar improvements for semisupervised learning on large, sparse datasets. The l_2-SVM-MFN retraining steps in the inner loop of TSVM are typically executed extremely fast by using seeding techniques. Additionally, we also propose a version of TSVM where more than one pair of labels may be switched in each iteration. These speed-enhancement details are discussed in the following subsections.

7.3.1   Implementing TSVM Using l_2-SVM-MFN

To develop the TSVM implementation with l_2-SVM-MFN, we consider the TSVM objective function but with the l_2-SVM loss function, $L = l_2$.

Note that this objective function above can also be equivalently written in terms of the following loss over each unlabeled example x:

$$\min[l_2(w^T x), l_2(-w^T x)] = \max[0, 1 - |w^T x|]^2.$$

Here, we pick the value of the label variable y that minimizes the loss on the unlabeled example x, and rewrite in terms of the absolute value of the output of the classifier on x. This loss function is shown in figure 7.1. We note in passing that, l_1 and l_2 loss terms over unlabeled examples are very similar on the interval $[-1, +1]$. The nonconvexity of this loss function implies that the TSVM training procedure is susceptible to local optima issues. In the next subsection, we will outline a deterministic annealing procedure that is designed to deal with this problem.

The TSVM algorithm with l_2-SVM-MFN closely follows the presentation in Joachims (1999b). A classifier is obtained by first running l_2-SVM-MFN on just the labeled examples. Temporary labels are assigned to the unlabeled data by thresholding the soft outputs of this classifier so that the fraction of the total number of unlabeled examples that are temporarily labeled positive equals the parameter r. Then, starting from a small value of λ', the unlabeled data is gradually brought in by increasing λ' by a certain factor in the outer loop. This gradual increase of the influence of the unlabeled data is a way to protect TSVM from being immediately trapped in a local minimum. An inner loop identifies pairs of unlabeled examples with positive and negative temporary labels such that switching these labels would decrease the objective function. l_2-SVM-MFN is then retrained with the switched labels, starting the CGLS line search iterations with the current classifier.

7.3.2   Multiple Switching

The TSVM algorithm presented in (Joachims, 1999b) involves switching a single pair of labels at a time. We propose a variant where up to S pairs are switched such that the objective function improves. Here, S is a user-controlled parameter. Setting $S = 1$ recovers the original TSVM algorithm, whereas setting $S = u/2$ switches as many pairs as possible in the inner loop of TSVM. The implementation is conveniently done as follows:

1. Identify unlabeled examples with active indices and currently positive labels. Sort corresponding outputs in ascending order. Let the sorted list be L^+.

2. Identify unlabeled examples with active indices and currently negative labels. Sort corresponding outputs in descending order. Let the sorted list be L^-.

3. Pick pairs of elements, one from each list, from the top of these lists until either a pair is found such that the output from L^+ is greater than the output from L^-, or if S pairs have been picked.

4. Switch the current labels of these pairs.

Using arguments similar to theorem 2 of Joachims (1999b), we can show that transductive l_2-SVM-MFN with multiple-pair switching converges in a finite number of steps (see Sindhwani and Keerthi (2005) for a proof).

We are unaware of any prior work that suggests and evaluates this simple multiple-pair switching heuristic. Our experimental results in section 7.5 establish that this heuristic is remarkably effective in speeding up TSVM training while maintaining generalization performance.

7.3.3   Seeding

The effectiveness of l_2-SVM-MFN on large sparse datasets combined with the efficiency gained from seeding w in the retraining steps (after switching labels or after increasing λ') makes this algorithm quite attractive. For a fixed λ', the complexity of transductive l_2-TSVM-MFN is $O(n_{switches}\bar{t}_{mfn}\bar{t}_{cgls}n_0)$, where $n_{switches}$ is the number of label switches. Typically, $n_{switches}$ is expected to strongly depend on the dataset and also on the number of labeled examples. Since it is difficult to estimate a priori the number of switches, this is an issue that is best understood from empirical observations.

7.4   Semisupervised SVMs Based on Deterministic Annealing

The TSVM loss function over the unlabeled examples can be seen from figure 7.1 to be nonconvex. This makes the TSVM optimization procedure susceptible to local minimum issues causing a loss in its performance in many situations, e.g., as recorded by Chapelle and Zien (2005). We now present a new algorithm based on deterministic annealing (DA) that can potentially overcome this problem while also being computationally very attractive for large-scale applications.

Deterministic annealing (Bilbro et al., 1989; Peterson and Söderberg, 1989) is an established tool for combinatorial optimization that approaches the problem from information-theoretic principles. The discrete variables in the optimization problem are relaxed to continuous probability variables and a non-negative temperature parameter T is used to track the global optimum.

We begin by rewriting the TSVM objective function as follows:

$$
\begin{aligned}
w^\star \;=\; & \operatorname*{argmin}_{w,\{\mu_j\}_{j=1}^{u}} \quad \frac{\lambda}{2}\|w\|^2 + \frac{1}{2l}\sum_{i=1}^{l} l_2(w^T x_i) \\
& + \; \frac{\lambda'}{2u}\sum_{j=1}^{u}\left(\mu_j l_2(w^T x'_j) + (1-\mu_j)l_2(-w^T x'_j)\right).
\end{aligned}
$$

Here, we introduce binary-valued variables $\mu_j = (1+y_j)/2$. Let $p_j \in [0,1]$ denote the belief probability that the unlabeled example x'_j belongs to the positive class. The Ising model[6] motivates the following objective function, where we relax the binary variables μ_j to probability-like variables p_j, and include entropy terms for

---

6. A multiclass extension would use the Potts glass model. There, one would have to append the entropy of the distribution over multiple classes to a multiclass objective function.

the distributions defined by p_j:

$$
\begin{aligned}
w_T^{\star} \;=\; & \underset{w,\{p_j\}_{j=1}^{u}}{\mathrm{argmin}} \quad \frac{\lambda}{2}\|w\|^2 + \frac{1}{2l}\sum_{i=1}^{l} l_2(y_i w^T x_i) \\
& + \; \frac{\lambda'}{2u}\sum_{j=1}^{u}\left(p_j l_2(w^T x_j') + (1-p_j)l_2(-w^T x_j')\right) \\
& + \; \frac{T}{2u}\sum_{j=1}^{u}[p_j \; \log \; p_j + (1-p_j) \; \log \; (1-p_j)] \; .
\end{aligned}
\tag{7.6}
$$

Here, the "temperature" T parameterizes a family of objective functions. The objective function for a fixed T is minimized under the following class-balancing constraint:

$$
\frac{1}{u}\sum_{j=1}^{u} p_j = r \; ,
\tag{7.7}
$$

where r is the fraction of the number of unlabeled examples belonging to the positive class. As in TSVM, r is treated as a user-provided parameter. It may also be estimated from the labeled examples.

The solution to the optimization problem above is tracked as the temperature parameter T is lowered to 0.

We monitor the value of the objective function in the optimization path and return the solution corresponding to the minimum value achieved.

To develop an intuition for the working on this method, we consider the loss terms associated with an unlabeled example in (7.6) as a function of the output of the classifier, after plugging in the optimal value of the associated p variable. Figure 7.2 plots this effective loss for various values of T. As the temperature is decreased, the loss function deforms from a squared-loss shape where a global optimum is easier to achieve, to the TSVM loss function in figure 7.1. The minimizer is slowly tracked as the temperature is lowered toward zero. A recently proposed method (Chapelle et al., 2006) uses a similar idea.

The optimization is done in stages, starting with high values of T and then gradually decreasing T toward 0. For each T, the objective function in (7.6) (subject to the constraint in (7.7)) is optimized by alternating the minimization over w and $p = [p_1 \ldots p_u]$ respectively. Fixing p, the optimization over w is done by l_2-SVM-MFN with seeding. Fixing w, the optimization over p can also be done easily as described below. Both these problems involve convex optimization and can be done exactly and efficiently. We now provide some details.

7.4.1   Optimizing w

We describe the steps to efficiently implement the l_2-SVM-MFN loop for optimizing w keeping p fixed. The call to l_2-SVM-MFN is made on the data $\hat{X} = \left[X^T\ X'^T\ X'^T\right]^T$ whose first l rows are formed by the labeled examples, and the

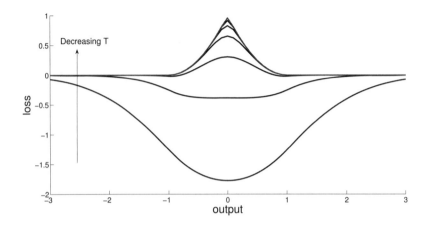

Figure 7.2 DA effective loss as a function (parameterized by T) of output on an unlabeled example.

next $2u$ rows are formed by the unlabeled examples appearing as two repeated blocks. The associated label vector and cost matrix are given by

$$\hat{Y} = [y_1, y_2...y_l, \overbrace{1,1,...1}^{u}, \overbrace{-1,-1...-1}^{u}]$$

$$C = diag \left[\overbrace{\frac{1}{l}...\frac{1}{l}}^{l}, \overbrace{\frac{\lambda' \, p_1}{u}...\frac{\lambda' \, p_u}{u}}^{u} \overbrace{\frac{\lambda'(1-p_1)}{u}...\frac{\lambda'(1-p_u)}{u}}^{u} \right]. \tag{7.8}$$

Even though each unlabeled data contributes two terms to the objective function, effectively only one term contributes to the complexity. This is because matrix-vector products, which form the dominant expense in l_2-SVM-MFN, are performed only on unique rows of a matrix. The output may be duplicated for duplicate rows. In fact, we can rewrite the CGLS calls in l_2-SVM-MFN so that the unlabeled examples appear only once in the data matrix.

7.4.2   Optimizing p

For the latter problem of optimizing p for a fixed w, we construct the Lagrangian:

$$\begin{aligned}
\mathcal{L} &= \frac{\lambda'}{2u} \sum_{j=1}^{u} \left(p_j l_2(w^T x'_j) + (1-p_j) l_2(-w^T x'_j) \right) \\
&+ \frac{T}{2u} \sum_{j=1}^{u} (p_j \, \log \, p_j + (1-p_j) \, \log \, (1-p_j)) - \nu \left[\frac{1}{u} \sum_{j=1}^{u} p_j - r \right].
\end{aligned}$$

Solving $\partial \mathcal{L}/\partial p_j = 0$, we get

$$p_j = \frac{1}{1 + e^{\frac{g_j - 2\nu}{T}}} \, , \tag{7.9}$$

where $g_j = \lambda'[l_2(w^T x'_j) - l_2(-w^T x'_j)]$. Substituting this expression in the balance constraint in Eqn. 7.7, we get a one-dimensional nonlinear equation in 2ν:

$$\frac{1}{u} \sum_{j=1}^{u} \frac{1}{1 + e^{\frac{g_i - 2\nu}{T}}} = r \, .$$

The root is computed by using a hybrid combination of Newton-Raphson iterations and the bisection method together with a carefully set initial value.

7.4.3   Stopping Criteria

For a fixed T, the alternate minimization of w and p proceeds until some stopping criterion is satisfied. A natural criterion is the mean Kullback-Liebler divergence (relative entropy) between current values of p_i and the values, say q_i, at the end of the last iteration. Thus the stopping criterion for fixed T is

$$KL(p,q) = \sum_{j=1}^{u} p_j \, \log \, \frac{p_j}{q_j} + (1 - p_j) \, \log \, \frac{1 - p_j}{1 - q_j} < u\epsilon \, .$$

A good value for ϵ is 10^{-6}. As T approaches 0, the variables p_j approach 0 or 1. The temperature may be decreased in the outer loop until the total entropy falls below a threshold, which we take to be $\epsilon = 10^{-6}$ as above, i.e.,

$$H(p) = - \sum_{j=l}^{u} (p_j \, \log \, p_j + (1 - p_j) \, \log \, (1 - p_j)) < u\epsilon \, .$$

The TSVM objective function,

$$\frac{\lambda}{2} \|w\|^2 + \frac{1}{2l} \sum_{i=1}^{l} l_2(y_i \, (w^T x_i) + \frac{\lambda'}{2u} \sum_{j=1}^{u} \max \left[0, 1 - |w^T x'_j| \right]^2 \, ,$$

is monitored as the optimization proceeds. The weight vector corresponding to the minimum transductive cost in the optimization path is returned as the solution.

7.5   Empirical Study

Semisupervised learning experiments were conducted to test these algorithms on four medium-scale datasets (aut-avn, real-sim, ccat, and gcat) and three large-scale (full-ccat, full-gcat, kdd99) datasets. These are listed in table 7.1. All experiments were performed on Intel Xeon CPU 3GHz, 2GB RAM machines.

Table 7.1   Two-class datasets. d : data dimensionality; $\bar{n}_0$: average sparsity; $l+u$: number of labeled and unlabeled examples; t : number of test examples; r : positive class ratio.

Dataset	d	$\bar{n}_0$	$l+u$	t	r
aut-avn	20707	51.32	35588	35587	0.65
real-sim	20958	51.32	36155	36154	0.31
ccat	47236	75.93	17332	5787	0.46
gcat	47236	75.93	17332	5787	0.30
full-ccat	47236	76.7	804414	-	0.47
full-gcat	47236	76.7	804414	-	0.30
kdd99	128	17.3	4898431	-	0.80

Benchmarking in this section was achieved with our SVM*lin* software package.[7]

7.5.1   Datasets

The aut-avn and real-sim binary classification datasets come from a collection of UseNet articles[8] from four discussion groups: for simulated auto racing, simulated aviation, real autos, and real aviation. The ccat and gcat datasets pose the problem of separating corporate- and government-related articles respectively; these are the top-level categories in the RCV1 training dataset (Lewis et al., 2004). full-ccat and full-gcat are the corresponding datasets containing all the 804,414 training and test documents in the RCV1 corpus. These datasets create an interesting situation where semisupervised learning is required to learn different low density separators respecting different classification tasks in the same input space. The kdd99 dataset is from the KDD 1999 competition task to build a network intrusion detector, a predictive model capable of distinguishing between "bad" connections, called intrusions or attacks, and "good" normal connections. This is a relatively low-dimensional dataset containing about 5 million examples.

For the medium-scale datasets, the results below are averaged over ten random stratified splits of training (labeled and unlabeled) and test sets. The detailed performance of SVM, DA, and TSVM (single and maximum switching) is studied as a function of the amount of labeled data in the training set. For the large-scale datasets full-ccat, full-gcat, and kdd99, we are mainly interested in computation times; a transductive setting is used to study performance in predicting the labels of unlabeled data on single splits. On full-ccat and full-gcat, we train SVM, DA, and TSVM with 100 and 1000 labels; for kdd99 we experiment with 1000 labels.

Since the two classes are fairly well represented in these datasets, we report error

---

7. SVM*lin* is available at `http://www.cs.uchicago.edu/~vikass/svmlin.html`.
8. Available at `http://www.cs.umass.edu/~mccallum/data/sraa.tar.gz`.

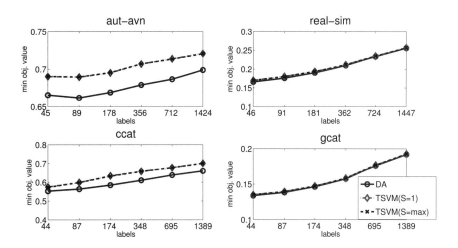

Figure 7.3 DA versus TSVM(S=1) versus TSVM(S=max): minimum value of objective function achieved.

rates, but expect our conclusions to also hold for other performance measures such as F-measure. We use default values of $\lambda = 0.001$ and $\lambda' = 1$ for all datasets except[9] for aut-avn and ccat where $\lambda' = 10$. In the outer loops of DA and TSVM, we reduced T and increased λ' by a factor of 1.5 starting from $T = 10$ and $\lambda' = 10^{-5}$.

7.5.2   Minimization of Objective Function

We first examine the effectiveness of DA, TSVM with single switching (S=1), and TSVM with maximum switching (S=u/2) in optimizing the objective function. These three procedures are labeled DA, TSVM(S=1), and TSVM(S=max) in figure 7.3, where we report the minimum value of the objective function with respect to varying numbers of labels on aut-avn, real-sim, ccat, and gcat.

The following observations can be made.

1. Strikingly, *multiple switching leads to no loss of optimization as compared to single switching.* Indeed, the minimum objective value plots attained by single and multiple switching are virtually indistinguishable in figure 7.3.

2. As compared to TSVM(S=1 or S=max), DA performs significantly better optimization on aut-avn and ccat; and slightly, but consistently better optimization on real-sim and gcat. These observations continue to hold for full-ccat and full-gcat as reported in table 7.2 where we only performed experiments with TSVM(S=max). Table 7.3 reports that DA gives a better minimum on the kdd99 dataset too.

---

9. This produced better results for both TSVM and DA.

Table 7.2 Comparison of minimum value of objective functions attained by TSVM(S=max) and DA on full-ccat and full-gcat

| | full-ccat | | full-gcat | |
l, u	TSVM	DA	TSVM	DA
100, 402,107	0.1947	0.1940	0.1491	0.1491
100, 804,314	0.1945	0.1940	0.1500	0.1499
1000, 402,107	0.2590	0.2588	0.1902	0.1901
1000, 804,314	0.2588	0.2586	0.1907	0.1906

Table 7.3 Comparison of minimum value of objective functions attained by TSVM(S=max) and DA on kdd99

l, u	TSVM	DA
1000, 4897431	0.0066	0.0063

Table 7.4 TSVM(S=max) versus DA versus SVM: error rates over unlabeled examples in full-ccat and full-gcat

| | full-ccat | | | full-gcat | | |
l, u	TSVM	DA	SVM	TSVM	DA	SVM
100, 402107	14.81	14.88	25.60	6.02	6.11	11.16
100, 804314	15.11	13.55	25.60	5.75	5.91	11.16
1000, 402107	11.45	11.52	12.31	5.67	5.74	7.18
1000, 804314	11.30	11.36	12.31	5.52	5.58	7.18

7.5.3   Generalization Performance

In figure 7.4 we plot the mean error rate on the (unseen) test set with respect to varying number of labels on aut-avn, real-sim, ccat, and gcat. In figure 7.5, we superimpose these curves over the performance curves of a standard SVM which ignores unlabeled data. Tables 7.4 and 7.5 report the corresponding results for full-ccat, full-gcat, and kdd99.

The following observations can be made.

1. Comparing the performance of SVM against the semisupervised algorithms in figure 7.5, the benefit of unlabeled data for boosting generalization performance is evident on all datasets. This is true even for a moderate number of labels, though it is particularly striking toward the lower end. On full-ccat and full-gcat too, one can see significant gains with unlabeled data. On kdd99, SVM performance with

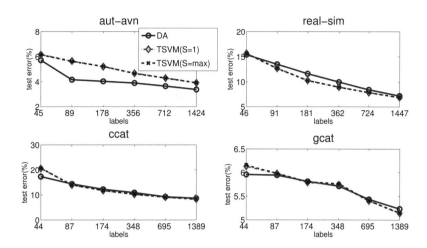

Figure 7.4   Error rates on test set: DA versus TSVM(S=1) versus TSVM(S=max).

Table 7.5   Error rates over unlabeled examples in kdd99: DA versus TSVM(S=max) versus SVM

l,u	TSVM	DA	SVM
1000, 4897431	0.48	0.22	0.29

1000 labels is already very good.

2. In figure 7.4, we see that on aut-avn, DA outperforms TSVM significantly. On real-sim, TSVM and DA perform very similar optimization of the transduction objective function (figure 7.3), but appear to return very different solutions. The TSVM solution returns lower error rates, as compared to DA, on this dataset. On ccat, DA performed a much better optimization (figure 7.3) but this does not translate into major error rate improvements. DA and TSVM are very closely matched on gcat. From table 7.4 we see that TSVM and DA are competitive. On kdd99 (table 7.5), DA gives the best results.

3. On all datasets we found that *maximum switching returned nearly identical performance as single switching*. Since it saves significant computation time, as we report in the following section, our study establishes multiple switching (in particular, maximum switching) as a valuable heuristic for training TSVMs.

4. These observations are also true for in-sample transductive performance for the medium-scale datasets (detailed results not shown). Both TSVM and DA provide high-quality extension to unseen test data.

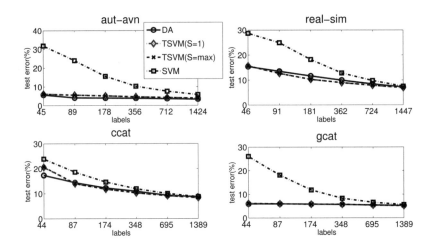

Figure 7.5   Benefit of unlabeled data.

Table 7.6   Computation times, in minutes, for TSVM(S=max) and DA on full-ccat and full-gcat (804,414 examples, 47,236 features)

	full-ccat		full-gcat	
l, u	TSVM	DA	TSVM	DA
100, 402107	140	120	53	72
100, 804314	223	207	96	127
1000, 402107	32	57	20	42
1000, 804314	70	100	38	78

7.5.4   Computational Timings

In figure 7.6 and tables 7.6 and 7.7, we report the computation time for our algorithms. The following observations can be made.

1. From figure 7.6 we see that the single-switch TSVM can be six to seven times slower than the maximum-switching variant, particularly when labels are few. DA is significantly faster than single-switch TSVM when labels are relatively few, but slower than TSVM with maximum switching.

2. In table 7.6, we see that doubling the amount of data roughly doubles the training time, empirically confirming the linear time complexity of our methods. The training time is also strongly dependent on the number of labels. On kdd99 (table 7.7), the maximum-switch TSVM took around 15 minutes to process the 5 million examples, whereas DA took 2 hours and 20 minutes.

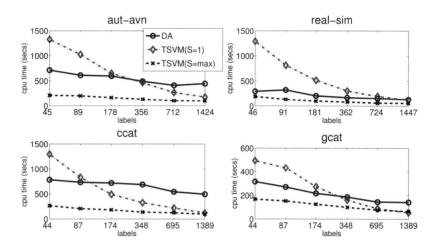

Figure 7.6 Computation time with respect to number of labels for DA and transductive l_2-SVM-MFN with single and multiple switches.

Table 7.7 Computation time, in minutes, for TSVM(S=max) and DA on kdd99 (4,898,431 examples, 127 features)

l, u	TSVM	DA
1000, 4897431	15	143

3. On medium-scale datasets, we also compared against SVM[light] which took on the order of several hours to days to train TSVM. We expect the multiswitch TSVM to also be highly effective when implemented in conjunction with the methods of Joachims (2006).

7.5.5   Importance of Annealing

To confirm the necessity of an annealing component (tracking the minimizer while lowering T) in DA, we also compared it with an alternating w,p optimization procedure where the temperature parameter is held fixed at $T = 0.1$ and $T = 0.001$. This study showed that annealing is important; it tends to provide higher-quality solutions as compared to fixed temperature optimization. It is important to note that the gradual increase of λ' to the user-set value in TSVM is also a mechanism to avoid local optima. The nonconvex part of the TSVM objective function is gradually increased to a desired value. In this sense, λ' simultaneously plays the role of an annealing parameter and also as a tradeoff parameter to enforce the cluster assumption. This dual role has the advantage that a suitable λ' can be chosen by monitoring performance on a validation set as the algorithm proceeds. In DA, however, we directly apply a framework for global optimization, and decouple annealing from the implementation of the cluster assumption. As our experiments show, this can lead to significantly better solutions on many problems. On time-critical applications, one may trade off quality of optimization against time, by varying the annealing rate.

7.6 Conclusion

In this chapter we have proposed a family of primal SVM algorithms for large-scale semisupervised learning based on the finite Newton technique. Our methods significantly enhance the training speed of TSVM over existing methods such as SVM[light] and also include a new effective technique based on deterministic annealing. The new TSVM method with multiple switching is the fastest of all the algorithms considered, and also returns good generalization performance. The DA method is relatively slower but sometimes gives the best accuracy. These algorithms can be very valuable in applied scenarios where sparse classification problems arise frequently, labeled data is scarce, and plenty of unlabeled data is easily available. Even in situations where a good number of labeled examples are available, utilizing unlabeled data to obtain a semisupervised solution using these algorithms can be worthwhile. For one thing, the semisupervised solutions never lag behind purely supervised solutions in terms of performance. The presence of a mix of labeled and unlabeled data can provide added benefits such as reducing performance variability and stabilizing the linear classifier weights. Our algorithms can be extended to the nonlinear setting (Sindhwani et al., 2006), and may also be developed to handle clustering and one-class classification problems. These are subjects for future work.

8 The Improved Fast Gauss Transform with Applications to Machine Learning

Vikas Chandrakant Raykar
Ramani Duraiswami

In many machine learning algorithms and nonparametric statistics a key computational primitive is to compute the weighted sum of N Gaussian kernel functions at M points. The computational cost of the direct evaluation of such sums scales as $O(MN)$. In this chapter we describe some algorithms that allow one to compute the same sum in $O(M + N)$ time at the expense of reduced precision, which, however, can be arbitrary. Using these algorithms can significantly reduce the run-time of various machine learning procedures. In particular we discuss the improved fast Gauss transform algorithm in detail and compare it with the dual-tree algorithm of Gray and Moore (2003) and the fast Gauss transform of Greengard and Strain (1991). As an example we show how these methods can be used for fast multivariate kernel density estimation.

8.1 Computational Curse of Nonparametric Methods

During the past few decades it has become relatively easy to gather huge amounts of data, which are often apprehensively called *massive datasets*. A few examples include datasets in genome sequencing, astronomical databases, Internet databases, experimental data from particle physics, medical databases, financial records, weather reports, audio data, and video data. A goal in these areas is to build systems which can automatically extract useful information from the raw data. *Learning* is a principled method for distilling *predictive* and therefore scientific theories from the data (Poggio and Smale, 2003).

The *parametric approach* to learning assumes a functional form for the model to be learned, and then estimates the unknown parameters. Once the model has been trained, *the training examples can be discarded*. The essence of the training examples has been captured in the model parameters, using which we can draw further inferences. However, unless the form of the model is known a priori, assuming it very often leads to erroneous inference. *Nonparametric methods* do not make any assumptions on the form of the underlying model. This is sometimes referred to as "letting the data speak for themselves" (Wand and Jones, 1995). A price to be paid is that all the available *data has to be retained* while making the inference. It should be noted that nonparametric does not mean a lack of parameters, but rather that the underlying function/model of a learning problem cannot be indexed with a finite number of parameters. The number of parameters usually grows with the size of the training data.

One of the major bottlenecks to successful inference using nonparametric methods is their computational complexity. Most state-of-the-art nonparametric machine learning algorithms have a computational complexity of either $O(N^2)$ or $O(N^3)$. This has seriously restricted the use of massive datasets. Current implementations can handle only a few thousand training examples.

In the next section we identify the key computational primitive contributing to the $O(N^3)$ or $O(N^2)$ complexity. We discuss some algorithms that use ideas and techniques from computational physics, scientific computing, and computational geometry to speed up approximate calculation of these primitives to $O(N)$ and also provide *high-accuracy guarantees*. In particular, in section 8.8 we discuss the improved fast Gauss transform (IFGT) algorithm in detail and compare it with the dual-tree algorithm of Gray and Moore (2003) and the fast Gauss transform (FGT) of Greengard and Strain (1991) (section 8.10). In section 8.11 we show how these methods can be used for fast multivariate kernel density estimation.

8.2   Bottleneck Computational Primitive: Weighted Superposition of Kernels

In most kernel-based machine learning algorithms (Shawe-Taylor and Cristianini, 2004), Gaussian processes (Rasmussen and Williams, 2006a), and nonparametric statistics (Izenman, 1991), the key computationally intensive task is to compute a linear combination of local kernel functions centered on the training data, i.e.,

$$f(x) = \sum_{i=1}^{N} q_i k(x, x_i), \tag{8.1}$$

where $\{x_i \in \mathbb{R}^d, i = 1, \dots, N\}$ are the N training data points, $\{q_i \in \mathbb{R}, i = 1, \dots, N\}$ are the appropriately chosen weights, $k : \mathbb{R}^d \times \mathbb{R}^d \to \mathbb{R}$ is the local kernel function, and $x \in \mathbb{R}^d$ is the test point at which f is to be computed.

The computational complexity to evaluate (8.1) at a given test point is $O(N)$.

For kernel machines (e.g., regularized least squares (Poggio and Smale, 2003), support vector machines (SVMs) (Cristianini and Shawe-Taylor, 2000), kernel regression (Wand and Jones, 1995)), f is the regression/classification function. This is a consequence of the well-known classical representer theorem (Wahba, 1990) which states that the solutions of certain risk minimization problems involving an empirical risk term and a quadratic regularizer can be written as expansions in terms of the kernels centered on the training examples. In the case of Gaussian process regression (Williams and Rasmussen, 1996) f is the mean prediction. For nonparametric density estimation it is the kernel density estimate (Wand and Jones, 1995).

Training these models scales as $O(N^3)$ since most involve solving a linear system of equations of the form

$$(\mathbf{K} + \lambda\mathbf{I})\xi = \mathbf{y}, \tag{8.2}$$

where $\mathbf{K}$ is the $N \times N$ Gram matrix where $[\mathbf{K}]_{ij} = k(x_i, x_j)$, λ is some regularization parameter or noise variance, and $\mathbf{I}$ is the identity matrix. For specific kernel methods then, there are many published techniques for speeding things up. However, a naive implementation would scale as $O(N^3)$.

Also, many kernel methods in unsupervised learning like kernel principal component analysis (Smola et al., 1996), spectral clustering (Chung, 1997), and Laplacian eigenmaps, involve computing the eigenvalues of the Gram matrix. Solutions to such problems can be obtained using iterative methods, where the dominant computation is evaluation of $f(x)$.

Recently, such nonparametric problems have been collectively referred to as *N-body problems in learning* by Gray and Moore (2001), in analogy with the coulombic, magnetostatic, and gravitational N-body potential problems arising in computational physics (Greengard, 1994), where all pairwise interactions in a large ensemble of particles must be calculated.

8.3 Structured Matrices and ϵ-Exact Approximation

In general we need to evaluate (8.1) at M points $\{y_j \in \mathbb{R}^d, j = 1, \ldots, M\}$,

$$f(y_j) = \sum_{i=1}^{N} q_i k(y_j, x_i) \; j = 1, \ldots, M, \tag{8.3}$$

leading to the quadratic $O(MN)$ cost. We will develop fast ϵ-exact algorithms that compute the sum (8.3) approximately in linear $O(M + N)$ time. The algorithm is ϵ-exact in the sense made precise below.

Definition 8.1. *For any given $\epsilon > 0$, $\hat{f}$ is an $\epsilon - exact$ approximation to f if the maximum absolute error relative to the total weight $Q = \sum_{i=1}^{N} |q_i|$ is upper-bounded by ϵ, i.e.,*

$$\max_{y_j}\left[\frac{|\hat{f}(y_j) - f(y_j)|}{Q}\right] \leq \epsilon. \tag{8.4}$$

The constant in $O(M + N)$, depends on the desired *accuracy* ϵ, which, however, can be *arbitrary*. In fact, for machine precision accuracy there is no difference between the results of the direct and the fast methods.

The sum (8.3) can be thought of as a *matrix-vector multiplication* $f = \mathbf{K}q$, where $\mathbf{K}$ is an $M \times N$ matrix the entries of which are of the form $[\mathbf{K}]_{ij} = k(y_j, x_i)$ and $q = [q_1, \ldots, q_N]^T$ is a $N \times 1$ column vector.

Definition 8.2. *A dense matrix of order $M \times N$ is called a* structured matrix *if its entries depend only on $O(M + N)$ parameters.*

Philosophically, the reason we will be able to achieve $O(M + N)$ algorithms to compute the matrix-vector multiplication is that the matrix $\mathbf{K}$ is a structured matrix, since all the entries of the matrix are determined by the set of $M + N$ points $\{x_i\}_{i=1}^N$ and $\{y_j\}_{i=1}^M$. If the entries of the matrix $\mathbf{K}$ were completely random, then we could not do any better than $O(MN)$.

8.4   Motivating Example: Polynomial Kernel

We will motivate the main idea using a simple polynomial kernel that is often used in kernel methods. The polynomial kernel of order p is given by

$$k(x, y) = (x \cdot y + c)^p. \tag{8.5}$$

Direct evaluation of the sum $f(y_j) = \sum_{i=1}^N q_i k(x_i, y_j)$ at M points requires $O(MN)$ operations. The reason for this is that for each term in the sum the x_i and y_j appear together and hence we have to do all pairwise operations. We will compute the same sum in $O(M + N)$ time by *factorizing* the kernel and *regrouping* the terms. The polynomial kernel can be written as follows using the binomial theorem.

$$k(x, y) = (x \cdot y + c)^p = \sum_{k=0}^{p} \binom{p}{k} (x \cdot y)^k c^{p-k}. \tag{8.6}$$

Also, for simplicity, let x and y be scalars, i.e., $x, y \in \mathbb{R}$. As a result we have $(x \cdot y)^k = x^k y^k$. The multivariate case can be handled using multi-index notation and will be discussed later. So now the sum — after suitable *regrouping* — can be written as follows:

$$
f(y_j) = \sum_{i=1}^N q_i \left[\sum_{k=0}^p c^{p-k} \binom{p}{k} x_i^k y_j^k \right] = \sum_{k=0}^p c^{p-k} \binom{p}{k} y_j^k \left[\sum_{i=1}^N q_i x_i^k \right]
$$

$$
= \sum_{k=0}^p c^{p-k} \binom{p}{k} y_j^k M_k, \tag{8.7}
$$

where $M_k = \sum_{i=1}^N q_i x_i^k$, can be called the *moments*. The moments $M_0, \ldots, M_p$ can be precomputed in $O(pN)$ time. Hence f can be computed in linear $O(pN + pM)$ time. This is sometimes known as encapsulating information in terms of the moments. Also, note that for this simple kernel the sum was computed exactly.

In general, any kernel $k(x, y)$ can be expanded in some region as

$$k(x, y) = \sum_{k=0}^{p} \Phi_k(x) \Psi_k(y) + error, \tag{8.8}$$

where the function Φ_k depends only on x and Ψ_k on y. The *truncation number* p has to be chosen such that the error is less than the desired accuracy ϵ. After suitable regrouping, the fast summation takes the form

$$f(y_j) = \sum_{k=0}^{p} A_k \Psi_k(y) + error, \tag{8.9}$$

where the moments A_k can be precomputed as $A_k = \sum_{i=1}^{N} q_i \Phi_k(x_i)$. Using series expansions about a single point can lead to large truncation numbers. We need to organize the data points into different clusters using data structures and use series expansion about the cluster centers. Also, we need to give accuracy guarantees. So there are two aspects to this problem

1. Approximation theory $\to$ series expansions and error bounds.

2. Computational geometry $\to$ effective data structures.

8.5   Sum of Gaussian Kernels: The Discrete Gauss Transform

The most commonly used kernel function is the *Gaussian kernel*,

$$k(x, y) = e^{-\|x-y\|^2/h^2}, \tag{8.10}$$

where h is called the *bandwidth* of the kernel. The bandwidth h controls the degree of smoothing, of noise tolerance, or of generalization. The sum of multivariate Gaussian kernels is known as the *discrete Gauss transform* in the scientific computing literature. More formally, for each *target point* $\{y_j \in \mathbb{R}^d\}_{j=1,\ldots,M}$ the discrete Gauss transform is defined as

$$G(y_j) = \sum_{i=1}^{N} q_i e^{-\|y_j - x_i\|^2/h^2}, \tag{8.11}$$

where $\{q_i \in \mathbb{R}\}_{i=1,\ldots,N}$ are the *source weights*, $\{x_i \in \mathbb{R}^d\}_{i=1,\ldots,N}$ are the *source points*, i.e., the center of the Gaussians, and $h \in \mathbb{R}^+$ is the *source scale* or *bandwidth*. In other words $G(y_j)$ is the total weighted contribution at y_j of N Gaussians centered at x_i each with bandwidth h. The computational complexity to evaluate the discrete Gauss transform at M target points is $O(MN)$.

8.6   Bringing Computational Tractability to the Discrete Gauss Transform

Various strategies have been proposed to reduce the computational complexity of computing the sum of multivariate Gaussians. To simplify the exposition, in this section we assume $M = N$.

8.6.1   Methods Based on Sparse Dataset Representation

There are many strategies for specific problems which try to reduce this computational complexity by searching for a sparse representation of the data (Williams and Seeger, 2001; Smola and Bartlett, 2001; Fine and Scheinberg, 2001; Y.-J. Lee and Mangasarian, 2001a; Lawrence et al., 2003; Csató and Opper, 2002; Tresp, 2000; Tipping, 2001; Snelson and Ghahramani, 2006). Most of these methods try to find a reduced subset of the original dataset using either random selection or greedy approximation. In these methods there is no guarantee on the approximation of the kernel matrix in a deterministic sense.

8.6.2   Binned Approximation based on the FFT

If the source points are on an evenly spaced grid, then we can compute the Gauss transform at an even spaced grid exactly in $O(N \log N)$ using the fast Fourier transform (FFT). One of the earliest methods especially proposed for univariate fast kernel density estimation was based on this idea (Silverman, 1982). For irregularly spaced data, the space is divided into boxes, and the data is assigned to the closest neighboring grid points to obtain grid counts. The Gauss transform is also evaluated at regular grid points. For target points not lying on the the grid the value is obtained by interpolation based on the values at the neighboring grid points. As a result there is usually no guaranteed error bound for these methods. Also, another problem is that the number of grid points grows exponentially with dimension.

8.6.3   Dual-Tree Methods

The dual-tree methods (Gray and Moore, 2001, 2003) are based on space partitioning trees for both the source and target points. This method first builds a spatial tree – kd-trees or ball trees – on both the source and target points. Using the tree data structure, distance bounds between nodes can be computed. The bounds can be tightened by recursing on both trees. An advantage of the dual-tree methods is that they work for all common kernel choices, not necessarily Gaussian. The dual-tree methods give good speedup only for small bandwidths. For moderate bandwidths they end up doing the same amount of work as the direct summation. These methods do give accuracy guarantees. The single-tree version takes $O(N \log N)$ time while the dual-tree version is postulated to be $O(N)$.

8.6.4   Fast Gauss Transform

The *fast Gauss transform* (FGT) is an ϵ-exact approximation algorithm that reduces the computational complexity to $O(N)$, at the expense of reduced precision. Given any $\epsilon > 0$, it computes an approximation $\hat{G}(y_j)$ to $G(y_j)$ such that the maximum absolute error relative to the total weight Q is upper-bounded by ϵ. The constant depends on the desired precision, dimensionality of the problem, and the bandwidth.

The FGT is a special case of the more general *fast multipole method* (Greengard and Rokhlin, 1987), adapted to the Gaussian potential. The fast multipole method has been called one of the ten most significant algorithms (Dongarra and Sullivan, 2000) in scientific computation discovered in the twentieth century, and won its inventors, Vladimir Rokhlin and Leslie Greengard, the 2001 Steele Prize. Originally, this method was developed for the fast summation of the potential fields generated by a large number of sources (charges), such as those arising in gravitational or electrostatic potential problems, that are described by the Laplace equation in two or three dimensions (Greengard and Rokhlin, 1987). The expression for the potential of a source located at a point can be factored in terms of an expansion containing the product of *multipole* functions and *regular* functions. This led to the name for the algorithm. Since then, fast multipole methods have also found application in many other problems, for example, in electromagnetic scattering, radial basis function fitting, molecular and stellar dynamics, and can be viewed as a fast matrix-vector product algorithm for particular structured matrices.

The FGT was first proposed by Greengard and Strain (1991) and applied successfully to a few lower-dimensional applications in mathematics and physics. It uses a local representation of the Gaussian based on conventional Taylor series, a far-field representation based on Hermite expansion, and translation formula for conversion between the two representations. However, the algorithm has not been widely used much in statistics, pattern recognition, and machine learning applications where higher dimensions occur commonly. An important reason for the lack of use of the algorithm in these areas is that the performance of the proposed FGT degrades exponentially with increasing dimensionality, which makes it impractical for the statistics and pattern recognition applications. The constant in the linear asymptotic cost $O(M + N)$ grows roughly as p^d, i.e., exponential in the dimension d.

8.6.5   Improved Fast Gauss Transform

In this chapter we briefly describe an *improved fast Gauss transform* (IFGT) suitable for higher dimensions (see Raykar et al., 2005, for a detailed description). For the IFGT the constant term is asymptotically polynomial in d, *i.e*, it grows roughly as d^p (see figure 8.1). The reduction is based on a new multivariate Taylor series expansion scheme combined with the efficient space subdivision using the k-center algorithm. The core IFGT algorithm was first presented in (C. Yang

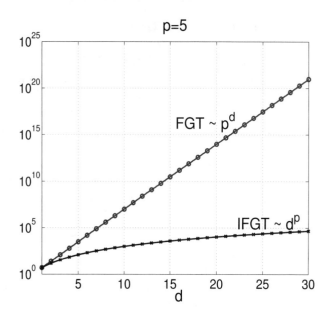

Figure 8.1   The constant term for the FGT and the IFGT complexity as a function of the dimensionality d. The FGT is exponential in d, while the IFGT is polynomial in d.

et al., 2003) and its use in kernel machines was shown in (C. Yang et al., 2005). More details of the algorithms, including the automatic choice of the algorithm parameters and a tighter error bound, can be found in (Raykar et al., 2005).

8.7   Multi-index Notation

Before we present the IFGT algorithm we will discuss the notion of multi-indices, which will be useful later.

1. A multi-index $\alpha = (\alpha_1, \alpha_2 \ldots, \alpha_d) \in \mathbb{N}^d$ is a d-tuple of non-negative integers.

2. The length of the multi-index α is defined as $|\alpha| = \alpha_1 + \alpha_2 + \ldots + \alpha_d$.

3. The factorial of α is defined as $\alpha! = \alpha_1!\alpha_2!\ldots\alpha_d!$.

4. For any multi-index $\alpha \in \mathbb{N}^d$ and $x = (x_1, x_2, \ldots, x_d) \in \mathbb{R}^d$ the d-*variate monomial* x^α is defined as $x^\alpha = x_1^{\alpha_1} x_2^{\alpha_2} \ldots x_d^{\alpha_d}$.

5. x^α is of *degree* n if $|\alpha| = n$.

6. The total number of d-variate monomials of degree n is $\binom{n+d-1}{d-1}$.

7. The total number of d-variate monomials of degree *less than or equal to* n is

$$r_{nd} = \sum_{k=0}^{n} \binom{k+d-1}{d-1} = \binom{n+d}{d}. \tag{8.12}$$

8. Let $x, y \in \mathbb{R}^d$ and $v = x \cdot y = x_1 y_1 + \ldots + x_d y_d$. Using the multi-index notation, v^n can be written as

$$v^n = (x \cdot y)^n = \sum_{|\alpha|=n} \frac{n!}{\alpha!} x^\alpha y^\alpha. \tag{8.13}$$

8.7.1   Multivariate Polynomial Kernel

Using this notation, the polynomial kernel example discussed in section 8.4 can be extended to the multivariate case.

$$
\begin{aligned}
f(y_j) &= \sum_{i=1}^{N} q_i (x_i \cdot y_j + c)^p = \sum_{i=1}^{N} q_i \left[\sum_{k=0}^{p} \binom{p}{k} c^{p-k} (x_i \cdot y_j)^k \right] \\
&= \sum_{i=1}^{N} q_i \left[\sum_{k=0}^{p} \binom{p}{k} c^{p-k} \left(\sum_{|\alpha|=k} \frac{k!}{\alpha!} x_i^\alpha y_j^\alpha \right) \right] = \sum_{i=1}^{N} q_i \left[\sum_{|\alpha| \le p} \frac{c^{p-|\alpha|} p!}{\alpha! (p-|\alpha|!)} x_i^\alpha y_j^\alpha \right] \\
&= \sum_{|\alpha| \le p} C_\alpha y_j^\alpha \left[\sum_{i=1}^{N} q_i x_i^\alpha \right] \quad \text{where,} \ C_\alpha = \frac{c^{p-|\alpha|} p!}{\alpha! (p-|\alpha|!)} \\
&= \sum_{|\alpha| \le p} C_\alpha y_j^\alpha M_\alpha \quad \text{where,} \ M_\alpha = \sum_{i=1}^{N} q_i x_i^\alpha.
\end{aligned}
\tag{8.14}
$$

The number of d-variate monomials of degree $|\alpha| \le p$ is $r_{pd} = \binom{p+d}{d}$. Hence the moments M_α can be computed in $O(r_{pd} N)$ time. Note that the computation of M_α depends on the x_i alone which can be done once and reused in each evaluation of $f(y_j)$. Hence the sum f can be computed at M points in $O(r_{pd}(M+N))$ time. Also note that we need r_{pd} space to store the moments.

Using Stirling's formula $n! \approx \sqrt{2\pi n} e^{-n} n^n$, the term r_{pd} can be simplified as follows:

$$r_{pd} = \binom{p+d}{d} = \frac{(p+d)!}{d! p!} \approx \left(1 + \frac{d}{p} \right)^p \left(1 + \frac{p}{d} \right)^d. \tag{8.15}$$

If $d \gg p$, r_{pd} is roughly polynomial in d, i.e., d^p. While not as bad as exponential growth in d, still the constant can become large for high d. This growth of the constant with d is one of the major limitations of series-based methods, which prevents them from being practical for high-dimensional datasets. For example, when $p = 5$ and $d = 10$, $r_{pd} = 53,130$.

8.7.2   Efficient Expansion of Multivariate Polynomials: Horner's Rule

Evaluating each d-variate monomial of degree n directly requires n multiplications. Hence direct evaluation of all d-variate monomials of degree less than or equal to n requires $\sum_{k=0}^{n} k \binom{k+d-1}{d-1}$ multiplications. The storage requirement is $r_{nd} = \binom{n+d}{d}$. However, efficient evaluation using Horner's rule requires $r_{nd} - 1$ multiplications. The required storage is r_{nd}.

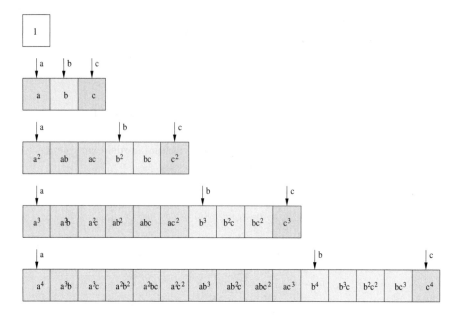

Figure 8.2   Efficient expansion of multivariate polynomials.

For a d-variate polynomial of order n, we can store all terms in a vector of length r_{nd}. Starting from the order zero term (constant 1), we take the following approach. Assume we have already evaluated terms of order $k - 1$. We use an array of size d to record the positions of the d leading terms (the simple terms such as a^{k-1}, b^{k-1}, c^{k-1}, . . . in figure 8.2) in the terms of order $k - 1$. Then terms of order k can be obtained by multiplying each of the d variables with all the terms between the variable's leading term and the end, as shown in figure 8.2. The positions of the d leading terms are updated respectively. The required storage is r_{nd} and the computations of the terms require $r_{nd} - 1$ multiplications.

8.8   The Improved Fast Gauss Transform

For any point $x_* \in \mathbf{R}^d$, the Gauss transform at y_j can be written as

$$
\begin{aligned}
G(y_j) &= \sum_{i=1}^{N} q_i e^{-\|y_j - x_i\|^2 / h^2}, \\
&= \sum_{i=1}^{N} q_i e^{-\|(y_j - x_*) - (x_i - x_*)\|^2 / h^2}, \\
&= \sum_{i=1}^{N} q_i e^{-\|x_i - x_*\|^2 / h^2} e^{-\|y_j - x_*\|^2 / h^2} e^{2(y_j - x_*) \cdot (x_i - x_*) / h^2}. \quad (8.16)
\end{aligned}
$$

In (8.16) the first exponential inside the summation, $e^{-\|x_i - x_*\|^2/h^2}$, depends only on the source coordinates x_i. The second exponential, $e^{-\|y_j - x_*\|^2/h^2}$, depends only on the target coordinates y_j. However, for the third exponential, $e^{2(y_j - x_*)\cdot(x_i - x_*)/h^2}$, the source and target are entangled. The crux of the algorithm is to separate this entanglement via Taylor series.

8.8.1   Factorization

The p-term truncated Taylor series expansion for $e^{2(y_j - x_*)\cdot(x_i - x_*)/h^2}$ can be written as (Raykar et al., 2005, corollary 2)

$$e^{2(y_j - x_*)\cdot(x_i - x_*)/h^2} = \sum_{n=0}^{p-1} \frac{2^n}{n!} \left[\left(\frac{y_j - x_*}{h} \right) \cdot \left(\frac{x_i - x_*}{h} \right) \right]^n + error_p. \tag{8.17}$$

The truncation number p is chosen based on the prescribed error ϵ. Using the multi-index notation (8.13), this expansion can be written as

$$e^{2(y_j - x_*)\cdot(x_i - x_*)/h^2} = \sum_{|\alpha| \leq p-1} \frac{2^\alpha}{\alpha!} \left(\frac{y_j - x_*}{h} \right)^\alpha \left(\frac{x_i - x_*}{h} \right)^\alpha + error_p. \tag{8.18}$$

Ignoringthe error terms for now, $G(y_j)$ can be approximated as

$$\hat{G}(y_j) = \sum_{i=1}^{N} q_i e^{-\|x_i - x_*\|^2/h^2} e^{-\|y_j - x_*\|^2/h^2} \left[\sum_{|\alpha| \leq p-1} \frac{2^\alpha}{\alpha!} \left(\frac{y_j - x_*}{h} \right)^\alpha \left(\frac{x_i - x_*}{h} \right)^\alpha \right]. \tag{8.19}$$

8.8.2   Regrouping

Rearranging the terms, (8.19) can be written as

$$\begin{aligned}
\hat{G}(y_j) &= \sum_{|\alpha| \leq p-1} \left[\frac{2^\alpha}{\alpha!} \sum_{i=1}^{N} q_i e^{-\|x_i - x_*\|^2/h^2} \left(\frac{x_i - x_*}{h} \right)^\alpha \right] e^{-\|y_j - x_*\|^2/h^2} \left(\frac{y_j - x_*}{h} \right)^\alpha, \\
&= \sum_{|\alpha| \leq p-1} C_\alpha e^{-\|y_j - x_*\|^2/h^2} \left(\frac{y_j - x_*}{h} \right)^\alpha, \tag{8.20}
\end{aligned}$$

where

$$C_\alpha = \frac{2^\alpha}{\alpha!} \sum_{i=1}^{N} q_i e^{-\|x_i - x_*\|^2/h^2} \left(\frac{x_i - x_*}{h} \right)^\alpha. \tag{8.21}$$

The coefficients C_α can be evaluated separately in $O(N)$. Evaluation of $\hat{G}_r(y_j)$ at M points is $O(M)$. Hence the computational complexity has reduced from the quadratic $O(NM)$ to the linear $O(N+M)$. A detailed analysis of the computational complexity is provided later.

8.8.3   Space Subdivision

Thus far, we have used the Taylor series expansion about a certain point x_*. However, if we use the same x_* for all the points we typically would require a very high truncation number since the Taylor series is valid only in a small open ball around x_*. We use an adaptive space-partitioning scheme — the farthest point clustering algorithm — to divide the N sources into K spherical clusters, S_k for $k = 1, \ldots, K$ with c_k being the center of each cluster. The Gauss transform can be written as

$$\hat{G}(y_j) = \sum_{k=1}^{K} \sum_{|\alpha| \leq p-1} C_\alpha^k e^{-\|y_j - c_k\|^2/h^2} \left(\frac{y_j - c_k}{h} \right)^\alpha, \tag{8.22}$$

where

$$C_\alpha^k = \frac{2^\alpha}{\alpha!} \sum_{x_i \in S_k} q_i e^{-\|x_i - c_k\|^2/h^2} \left(\frac{x_i - c_k}{h} \right)^\alpha. \tag{8.23}$$

We model the space subdivision task as a k-center problem, which is defined as follows: Given a set of N points in d dimensions and a predefined number of the clusters k, find a partition of the points into clusters $S_1, \ldots, S_k$, and also the cluster centers $c_1, \ldots, c_k$, so as to minimize the maximum radius of clusters, $\max_i \max_{x \in S_i} \|x - c_i\|$.

The k-center problem is known to be NP-hard (Bern and Eppstein, 1997). Gonzalez (1985) proposed a very simple greedy algorithm, called *farthest-point clustering*, and proved that it gives an approximation factor of 2. This algorithm works as follows: Pick an arbitrary point v_0 as the center of the first cluster and add it to the center set C. Then, for $i = 1$ to k, do the following: at step i, for every point v, compute its distance to the set C, $d_i(v, C) = \min_{c \in C} \|v - c\|$. Let v_i be the point that is farthest from C, i.e., the point for which $d_i(v_i, C) = \max_v d_i(v, C)$. Add v_i to set C. Report the points $v_0, v_1, \ldots, v_{k-1}$ as the cluster centers. Each point is assigned to its nearest center.

The direct implementation of farthest-point clustering has running time $O(Nk)$. Feder and Greene (1988) gave a two-phase algorithm with optimal running time $O(N \log k)$. Figure 8.3 displays the results of the farthest-point algorithm on a simple two-dimensional dataset.

8.8.4   Rapid Decay of the Gaussian

Since the Gaussian decays very rapidly, a further speedup is achieved if we ignore all sources belonging to a cluster if the cluster is greater than a certain distance from the target point, $\|y_j - c_k\| > r_y^k$. The cluster cutoff radius depends on the

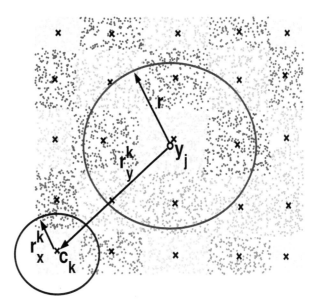

Figure 8.3 Schematic of the evaluation of the improved fast Gauss transform at the target point y_j. For the source points the results of the farthest-point clustering algorithm are shown along with the center of each cluster. A set of coefficients is stored at the center of each cluster. Only the influential clusters within radius r of the target point are used in the final summation.

desired precision ϵ. So now the Gauss transform is evaluated as

$$\hat{G}(y_j) = \sum_{\|y_j - c_k\| \le r_y^k} \sum_{|\alpha| \le p-1} C_\alpha^k e^{-\|y_j - c_k\|^2 / h^2} \left(\frac{y_j - c_k}{h} \right)^\alpha, \tag{8.24}$$

where

$$C_\alpha^k = \frac{2^\alpha}{\alpha!} \sum_{x_i \in S_k} q_i e^{-\|x_i - c_k\|^2 / h^2} \left(\frac{x_i - c_k}{h} \right)^\alpha. \tag{8.25}$$

8.8.5   Run-Time Analysis

1. Using the algorithm of Feder and Greene (1988), the farthest point clustering has a running time $O(N \log K)$.

2. Since each source point belongs to only one cluster, computing the cluster coefficients C_α^k for all the clusters is of $O(Nr_{(p-1)d})$, where $r_{(p-1)d} = \binom{p+d-1}{d}$ is the total number of d-variate monomials of degree less than or equal to $p-1$.

3. Computing $\hat{G}(y_j)$ is $O(Mnr_{(p-1)d})$ where n is the maximum number of neighbor clusters (depends on the bandwidth h and the error ϵ) which influence the target. It does not take into account the cost needed to determine n. This involves looping through all K clusters and computing the distance between each of the

M test points and each of the K cluster centers, resulting in an additional $O(MK)$ term. This term can be reduced to $O(M \log K)$ if efficient nearest neighbor search techniques are used, and this is a matter of current research.

Hence the total time is

$$O(N \log K + Nr_{(p_{max}-1)d} + Mnr_{(p_{max}-1)d} + KM). \tag{8.26}$$

Assuming $M = N$, the time taken is $O([\log K + (1+n)r_{(p_{max}-1)d} + K]N)$. The constant term depends on the dimensionality, the bandwidth, and the accuracy required. The number of terms $r_{(p-1)d}$ is asymptotically polynomial in d. For $d \to \infty$ and moderate p, the number of terms is approximately d^p.

For each cluster we need to store $r_{(p-1)d}$ coefficients. Accounting for the initial data the storage complexity is $O(Kr_{(p-1)d} + N + M)$.

8.8.6   Choosing the Parameters

Given any $\epsilon > 0$, we want to choose the following parameters,

1. K (the number of clusters),

2. p (the truncation number), and

3. $\{r_y^k\}_{k=1}^K$ (the cutoff radius for each cluster),

such that for any target point y_j, we can guarantee that $|\hat{G}(y_j) - G(y_j)|/Q \leq \epsilon$, where $Q = \sum_{i=1}^N |q_i|$. In order to achieve this we will use an upper bound for the actual error and choose the parameters based on this bound. Deriving tight error bounds is one of the trickiest and crucial parts for any series based algorithm. Also, the parameters have to be chosen automatically without any user intervention. The user just specifies the accuracy ϵ.

A criticism (D. Lang et al., 2005) of the original IFGT (C. Yang et al., 2005) was that the error bound was too pessimistic, and too many computational resources were wasted as a consequence. Further, the choice of the parameters was not automatic. An automatic way for choosing the parameters along with tighter error bounds is described in (Raykar et al., 2005).

Let us define Δ_{ij} to be the error in $\hat{G}(y_j)$ contributed by the ith source x_i. We now require that

$$|\hat{G}(y_j) - G(y_j)| = \left| \sum_{i=1}^N \Delta_{ij} \right| \leq \sum_{i=1}^N |\Delta_{ij}| \leq Q\epsilon = \sum_{i=1}^N |q_i|\epsilon. \tag{8.27}$$

One way to achieve this is to let $|\Delta_{ij}| \leq |q_i|\epsilon$, $\forall i = 1, \ldots, N$. Let c_k be the center of the cluster to which x_i belongs. There are two different ways in which a source can contribute to the error.

1. The first is due to ignoring the cluster S_k if it is outside a given radius r_y^k from

the target point y_j. In this case,

$$\Delta_{ij} = q_i e^{-\|y_j - x_i\|^2/h^2} \quad \text{if } \|y_j - c_k\| > r_y^k. \tag{8.28}$$

2. The second source of error is due to truncation of the Taylor series. For all clusters which are within a distance r_y^k from the target point, the error is due to the truncation of the Taylor series after order p. From (8.16) and (8.17) we have

$$\Delta_{ij} = q_i e^{-\|x_i - c_k\|^2/h^2} e^{-\|y_j - c_k\|^2/h^2} error_p \quad \text{if } \|y_j - c_k\| \leq r_y^k. \tag{8.29}$$

Our strategy for choosing the parameters is as follows. The cutoff radius r_y^k for each cluster is chosen based on (8.28) and the radius of each cluster r_x^k. Given r_y^k and r_x^k, the truncation number p is chosen based on (8.29) and a bound on $error_p$. More details can be seen in (Raykar et al., 2005). Algorithm 8.1 summarizes the procedure to choose the IFGT parameters. The IFGT is summarized in algorithm 8.2.

Algorithm 8.1   Choosing the parameters for the IFGT

Input   : d (dimension)
            h (bandwidth)
            ϵ (error)
            N (number of sources)

Output: K (number of clusters)
            r (cutoff radius)
            p (truncation number)

Define
$\delta(p, a, b) = \frac{1}{p!} \left(\frac{2ab}{h^2}\right)^p e^{-(a-b)^2/h^2}$, $b_*(a, p) = \frac{a + \sqrt{a^2 + 2ph^2}}{2}$, and $r_{pd} = \binom{p-1+d}{d}$;

Choose the cutoff radius $r \leftarrow \min(\sqrt{d}, h\sqrt{\ln(1/\epsilon)})$;

Choose $K_{limit} \leftarrow \min\left(\lceil 20\sqrt{d}/h \rceil, N\right)$ (a rough bound on K);

for $k \leftarrow 1 : K_{limit}$ **do**
    compute an estimate of the maximum cluster radius as $r_x \leftarrow k^{-1/d}$;
    compute an estimate of the number of neighbors as $n \leftarrow \min\left((r/r_x)^d, k\right)$;
    choose $p[k]$ such that $\delta(p = p[k], a = r_x, b = \min[b_*(r_x, p[k]), r + r_x]) \leq \epsilon$;
    compute the constant term $c[k] \leftarrow k + \log k + (1 + n)r_{(p[k]-1)d}$
end
choose $K \leftarrow k_*$ for which $c[k_*]$ is minimum. $p \leftarrow p[k_*]$.

8.9   IFGT vs. FGT

The FGT (Greengard and Strain, 1991) is a special case of the more general single-level fast multipole method (Greengard and Rokhlin, 1987), adapted to the Gaussian potential. The first step of the FGT is the spatial subdivision of the unit hypercube into N_{side}^d boxes of side $\sqrt{2}rh$ where $r < 1/2$. The sources and targets

---

Algorithm 8.2   The improved fast Gauss transform

Input :

$x_i \in \mathbf{R}^d$ $i = 1, \ldots, N$ /* N sources in d dimensions.   */
$q_i \in \mathbf{R}$ $i = 1, \ldots, N$ /* source weights.   */
$h \in \mathbf{R}^+$ $i = 1, \ldots, N$ /* source bandwidth.   */
$y_j \in \mathbf{R}^d$ $j = 1, \ldots, M$ /* M targets in d dimensions.   */
$\epsilon > 0$ /* Desired error.   */

Output: Computes an approximation $\hat{G}(y_j)$ to $G(y_j) = \sum_{i=1}^{N} q_i e^{-\|y_j - x_i\|^2/h^2}$ such that the $|\hat{G}(y_j) - G(y_j)| \leq Q\epsilon$, where $Q = \sum_{i=1}^{N} |q_i|$.

Step 0 *Define* $\delta(p, a, b) = \frac{1}{p!} \left(\frac{2ab}{h^2}\right)^p e^{-(a-b)^2/h^2}$ *and* $b_*(a, p) = \frac{a + \sqrt{a^2 + 2ph^2}}{2}$.

Step 1 *Choose the cutoff radius* r, *the number of clusters* K, *and the truncation number* p *using algorithm 8.1.*

Step 2 *Divide the* N *sources into* K *clusters,* $\{S_k\}_{k=1}^{K}$, *using the Feder and Greene's farthest-point clustering algorithm. Let* c_k *and* r_x^k *be the center and radius respectively of the kth cluster. Let* $r_x = \max_k \left(r_x^k\right)$ *be the maximum cluster radius.*

Step 3 *Update the truncation number based on the actual* r_x, *i.e., choose* p *such that* $\delta(p, a = r_x, \min [b_*(r_x, p), r + r_x]) \leq \epsilon$.

Step 4 *For each cluster* S_k *with center* c_k, *compute the coefficients* C_α^k.
$C_\alpha^k = \frac{2^\alpha}{\alpha!} \sum_{x_i \in S_k} q_i e^{-\|x_i - c_k\|^2/h^2} \left(\frac{x_i - c_k}{h}\right)^\alpha$ $\forall |\alpha| \leq p - 1$.

Step 5 *For each target* y_j *the discrete Gauss transform is evaluated as*
$\hat{G}(y_j) = \sum_{\|y_j - c_k\| \leq r + r_x^k} \sum_{|\alpha| \leq p-1} C_\alpha^k e^{-\|y_j - c_k\|^2/h^2} \left(\frac{y_j - c_k}{h}\right)^\alpha.$

---

are assigned to different boxes. Given the sources in one box and the targets in a neighboring box, the computation is performed using one of the following four methods depending on the number of sources and targets in these boxes: Direct evaluation is used if the number of sources and targets are small (in practice a cutoff of the order $O(p^{d-1})$ is introduced). If the sources are clustered in a box, then they can are transformed into a *Hermite expansion* about the center of the box. This expansion is directly evaluated at each target in the target box if the number of the targets is small. If the targets are clustered, then the sources or their expansion are converted to a local Taylor series which is then evaluated at each target in the box. Since the Gaussian decays very rapidly, only a few neighboring source boxes will have influence on the target box. If the boxes are too far apart, then the contribution will be negligible and the computation is not performed.

There are three reasons contributing to the degradation of the FGT in higher dimensions:

1. The number of the terms in the Hermite expansion used by the FGT grows exponentially with dimensionality, which causes the constant factor associated with the asymptotic complexity $O(M+N)$ to increase exponentially with dimensionality.

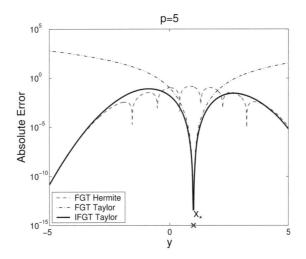

Figure 8.4 The absolute value of the actual error between the one-dimensional Gaussian $(e^{-(x_i-y)/h^2})$ and different series approximations. The Gaussian was centered at $x_i = 0$ and $h = 1.0$. All the series were expanded about $x_* = 1.0$. $p = 5$ terms were retained in the series approximation.

2. The constant term due to the translation of the far-field Hermite series to the local Taylor series grows exponentially fast with dimension making it impractical for dimensions greater than three.

3. The space subdivision scheme used by the FGT is a uniform box subdivision scheme which is tolerable in lower dimensions but grows exponentially in higher dimensions. The number of nearby boxes will be large, and the boxes will mostly be empty.

The IFGT differs from the FGT in the following three ways, addressing each of the issues above.

1. A single multivariate Taylor series expansion for a factored form of the Gaussian is used to reduce the number of the expansion terms to polynomial order.

2. The expansion acts both as a far-field and local expansion. As a result we do not have separate far-field and local expansions, which eliminates the cost of translation (figure 8.4) while achieving quickly convergent expansions in both domains.

3. The k-center algorithm is applied to subdivide the space using overlapping spheres, which is more efficient in higher dimensions.

8.10 Numerical Experiments

We compare the following four methods

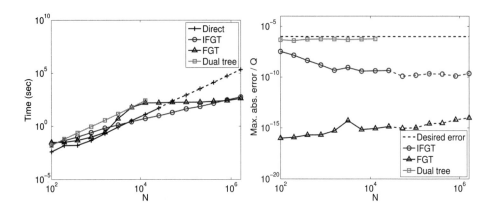

Figure 8.5 Scaling with N. The running times and the actual error for the different methods as a function of N. [$\epsilon = 10^{-6}$, $h = 0.25$, and $d = 3$].

- **Direct**: Naive $O(N^2)$ implementation of the Gauss transform.
- **FGT**: The fast Gauss Transform as described by Greengard and Strain (1991).
- **IFGT**: The improved fast Gauss transform.
- **Dual-tree**: The kd-tree dual-tree algorithm of Gray and Moore (2003).

All the algorithms were programmed in C++ or C with MATLAB bindings and were run on a 1.83GHz processor with 1 GB of RAM. See appendix 8.A for the source of different software.

8.10.1 Speedup as a Function of N

We first study the performance as the function of N for $d = 3$. N points were uniformly distributed in a unit cube. The Gauss transform was evaluated at $M = N$ points uniformly distributed in the unit cube. The weights q_i were uniformly distributed between 0 and 1. The parameters for the algorithms were automatically chosen without any user intervention. The target error was set to 10^{-6}. Figure 8.5 shows the results for all the various methods as a function of N for bandwidth $h = 0.25$. For $N > 25,600$ the timing results for the direct evaluation were obtained by evaluating the Gauss transform at $M = 100$ points and then extrapolating the results. The following observations can be made.

1. For the IFGT the computational cost is linear in N.

2. For the FGT the cost grows linearly only after a large N when the linear term $O(p^d N)$ dominates the initial cost of Hermite-Taylor translation. This jump in the performance can also be seen in the original FGT paper (see tables 2 and 4 in Greengard and Strain, 1991).

3. The IFGT shows a better initial speedup. Eventually the FGT catches up with the IFGT (i.e., the asymptotic performance starts dominating) and shows a speedup

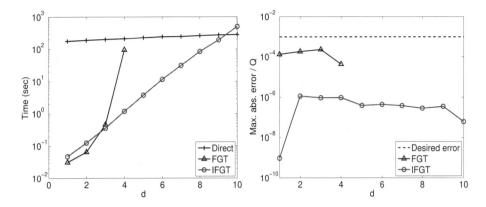

Figure 8.6 Scaling with dimensionality d. The running times and the actual error for the different methods as a function of the dimension d. [$\epsilon = 10^{-3}$, $h = 1.0$, and $N = M = 50{,}000$].

similar to that of the IFGT. However, this happens typically after a very large N which increases with the dimensionality of the problem.

4. The IFGT is closer to the target error than the FGT.

5. The kd-tree algorithm appears to be doing $O(N^2)$ work. Also, it takes much more time than the direct evaluation, probably because of the time taken to build up the kd-trees. The dual-tree algorithms show good speedups for very small bandwidths only (see also figure 8.7).

8.10.2 Speedup as a Function of d

The main advantage of the IFGT is in higher dimensions where we can no longer run the FGT algorithm. Figure 8.6 shows the performance for a fixed $N = M = 50{,}000$ as a function of d for a fixed bandwidth of $h = 1.0$.

1. The FGT becomes impractical after three dimensions with the cost of translation increasing with dimensionality. The FGT gave good speedup only for $d \leq 4$.

2. For the IFGT, as d increases, the crossover point (i.e., the N after which IFGT shows a better performance than the direct) increases. For $N = M = 50{,}000$ we were able to achieve good speedups till $d = 10$.

3. The kd-tree method could not be run for the chosen bandwidth.

8.10.3 Speedup as a Function of the Bandwidth h

One of the important concerns for N-body algorithms is their scalability with bandwidth h. Figure 8.7 shows the performance of the IFGT and the dual-tree algorithm as a function of the bandwidth h. The other parameters were fixed at $N = M = 7000$, $\epsilon = 10^{-3}$, and $d = 2, 3, 4$, and 5.

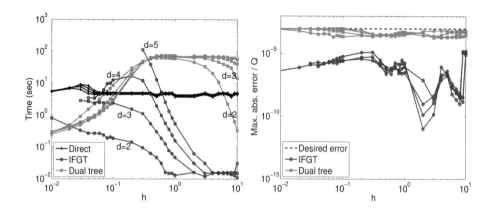

Figure 8.7   Scaling with bandwidth h. The running times and the actual error for the different methods as a function of the bandwidth h. [$\epsilon = 10^{-3}$ and $N = M = 7000$].

1. The general trend is that IFGT shows better speedups for large bandwidths while the dual-tree algorithm performs better at small bandwidths.

2. At large bandwidths the dual-tree algorithm ends up doing the same amount of work as the direct implementation. The dual-tree appears to take a longer time probably because of the time taken to build up the kd-trees.

3. There is a cutoff bandwidth h_c above which the IFGT performs better than the dual-tree algorithm. This cutoff increases as the dimensionality of the data points increases.

For small bandwidths the number of clusters and the truncation number required by the IFGT is high. The space subdivision employed by the IFGT algorithm is not hierarchical. As a result, nearest influential clusters cannot be searched effectively. When the number of clusters K is large, we end up doing a brute force search over all the clusters. In such a case it may be more efficient to directly evaluate the contribution from its neighbors within a certain radius. This is exactly what the dual-tree algorithms do, albeit in a more sophisticated way. The dual-tree algorithms suffer at large bandwidths because they do not use series expansions. It would be interesting to combine the series expansions of the IFGT with the kd-tree data structures to obtain an algorithm that would perform well at all bandwidths. A recent attempt using the FGT expansions was made by D. Lee et al. (2006). Since they used FGT series expansion, the algorithm was not practical for $d > 3$ due to the high translation costs.

8.10.4   Bandwidth as a Function of d

It should be noted that IFGT and FGT show good speedups, especially for large bandwidths. Figure 8.8 shows the performance for a fixed $N = M = 20,000$ as a function of d. In this case, we set the bandwidth $h = 0.5\sqrt{d}$ for each dimension (note

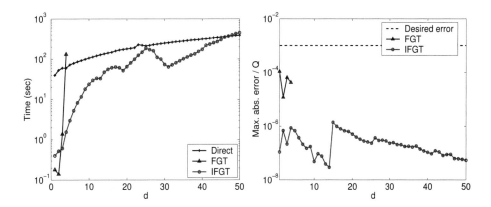

Figure 8.8 Effect of bandwidth scaling as $h = 0.5\sqrt{d}$. The running times and the actual error for the different methods as a function of the dimension d. The bandwidth was $h = 0.5\sqrt{d}$. [$\epsilon = 10^{-3}$ and $N = M = 20,000$].

that $\sqrt{d}$ is the length of the diagonal of a unit hypercube). The bandwidth of this order is sometimes used in high-dimensional data in some machine learning tasks. With h varying with dimension we were able to run the algorithm for arbitrary high dimensions. The dual-tree algorithm took more than the direct method for such bandwidths and could not be run for such large datasets.

8.10.5 Structured Data

Until now we showed results for the worst case scenario: data uniformly distributed in a unit hypercube. However, if there is structure in the data, i.e., the data is either clustered or lies on some smooth lower dimensional manifold, then the algorithms show much better speedup. Figure 8.9 compares the time taken by the IFGT and dual tree methods as a function of h for four different scenarios:

1. Both source and target points are uniformly distributed.
2. Source points are clumpy while the target points are uniform.
3. Source points are uniformly distributed while the target points are clumpy.
4. Both source and target points are clumpy.

The clumpy data was generated from a mixture of ten Gaussians. The following observations can be made:

1. For the dual-tree method, clumpiness either in source or target points gives better speedups.

2. For the IFGT, clumpiness in source points gives a much better speedup than uniform distribution. Clumpiness in target points does not matter since IFGT clusters only the source points.

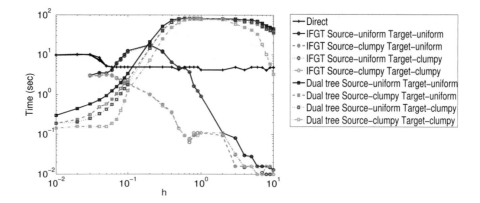

Figure 8.9 Effect of clustered data. The running times for the different methods as a function of the bandwidth h. [$\epsilon = 10^{-3}$, $N = M = 7000$, and $d = 4$]. The source and target points were either uniformly distributed (uniform) or drawn from a mixture of ten Gaussians (clumpy).

8.11   Fast Multivariate Kernel Density Estimation

The IFGT and other N-body algorithms can be used in any scenario where we encounter sums of Gaussians. A few applications would include kernel density estimation (C. Yang et al., 2003), prediction in SVMs, and mean prediction in Gaussian process regression. For training, the IFGT can also be embedded in a conjugate gradient or any other suitable optimization procedure (C. Yang et al., 2005; Y. Shen et al., 2006). In some unsupervised learning tasks the IFGT can be embedded in iterative methods used to compute the eigenvectors (de Freitas et al., 2006). While providing experiments for all applications is beyond the scope of this chapter, as an example we show how IFGT can be used to speed up multivariate kernel density estimation.

The most popular nonparametric method for density estimation is the kernel density estimator (KDE). In its most general form, the d-dimensional KDE is written as (Wand and Jones, 1995)

$$\widehat{p}_N(x) = \frac{1}{N}\sum_{i=1}^{N} K_{\mathbf{H}}\left(x - x_i\right), \quad \text{where } K_{\mathbf{H}}(x) = |\mathbf{H}|^{-1/2} K(\mathbf{H}^{-1/2}x). \qquad (8.30)$$

The d-variate function K is called the *kernel function* and $\mathbf{H}$ is a symmetric positive definite $d \times d$ matrix called the *bandwidth matrix*. In order that $\widehat{p}_N(x)$ is a bona fide density, the kernel function is required to satisfy the following two conditions: $K(u) \geq 0$ and $\int K(u)du = 1$. The most commonly used kernel is the standard d-variate normal density $K(u) = (2\pi)^{-d/2}e^{-\|u\|^2/2}$.

In general, a fully parameterized $d \times d$ positive definite bandwidth matrix $\mathbf{H}$ can be used to define the density estimate. However, in high dimensions the number of independent parameters $(d(d+1)/2)$ is too large to make a good choice. Hence the most commonly used choice is $\mathbf{H} = diag(h_1^2, \ldots, h_d^2)$ or $\mathbf{H} = h^2\mathbf{I}$. For the case when $\mathbf{H} = h^2\mathbf{I}$, the density estimate can be written as

$$\widehat{p}_N(x) = \frac{1}{N} \sum_{i=1}^{N} \frac{1}{(2\pi h^2)^{d/2}} e^{-\|x-x_i\|^2/2h^2}. \tag{8.31}$$

The computational cost of evaluating (8.31) at M points is $O(NM)$, making it prohibitively expensive. For example, a KDE with 1 million points would take around 2 days. The proposed IFGT algorithm can be used directly to reduce the computational cost to $O(N + M)$.

8.11.1   Bandwidth Selection

For a practical implementation of KDE the choice of the bandwidth h is very important. A small h leads to an estimate with small bias and large variance, while a large h leads to a small variance at the expense of an increase in the bias. Various techniques have been proposed for optimal bandwidth selection (Jones et al., 1996). The plug-in bandwidths are known to show more stable performance (Wand and Jones, 1995) than the cross-validation methods. They are based on deriving an expression for the asymptotic mean integrated squared error (AMISE) as a function of the bandwidth and then choosing the bandwidth which minimizes it. The simplest among these, known as the *rule of thumb* (ROT), assumes that the data is generated by a multivariate normal distribution. For a normal distribution with covariance matrix $\Sigma = diag(\sigma_1^2, \ldots, \sigma_d^2)$ and the bandwidth matrix of the form $\mathbf{H} = diag(h_1^2, \ldots, h_d^2)$, the optimal bandwidths are given by (Wand and Jones, 1995)

$$h_j^{ROT} = \left(\frac{4}{d+2}\right)^{1/(d+4)} N^{-1/(d+4)}\widehat{\sigma}_j, \tag{8.32}$$

where $\widehat{\sigma}_j$ is an estimate of σ_j. This method is known to provide a quick first guess and can be expected to give reasonable bandwidth when the data is close to a normal distribution. It is reported that this tends to slightly oversmooth the data. So in our experiments we only use this as a guess and show the speedup achieved over a range of bandwidths around h^{ROT}. As a practical issue we do not prefer cross-validation because we will have to do the KDE for a range of bandwidths, both small and large. We cannot use the fast methods here since the IFGT cannot be run for very small bandwidths and the dual-tree does the same work as direct summation for moderate bandwidths.

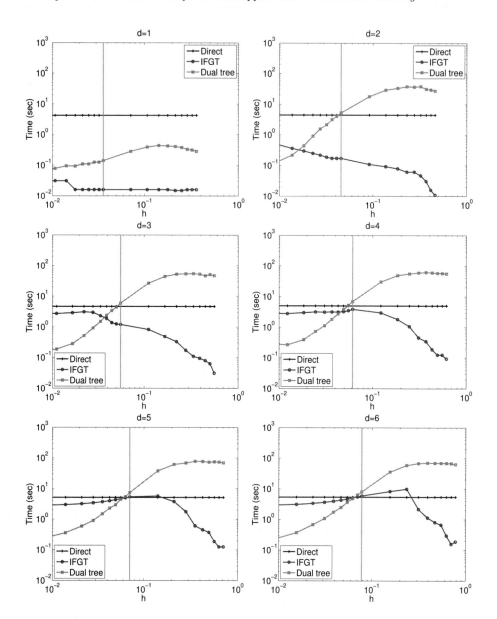

Figure 8.10   KDE results. The running time in seconds for the direct, IFGT, and the *kd*-tree method for varying dimensionality, *d*. The results are shown for a range of bandwidths around the optimal bandwidth marked by the straight line in each of the plots. The error was set to $\epsilon = 10^{-2}$. The KDE was evaluated at $M = N = 7000$ points. The IFGT could not be run across all bandwidths due to limited memory after $d > 6$.

8.11.2   Experiments

For our experimental comparison we used the SARCOS dataset.[1] The dataset contains 44,484 samples in a 21-dimensional space. The data relates to an inverse dynamics problem for a seven degrees-of-freedom SARCOS anthropomorphic robot arm. In order to ease comparisons all the dimensions were normalized to have the same variance so that we could use only one bandwidth parameter h.

Figure 8.10 compares the time taken by the direct summation, IFGT, and the kd-tree method for different dimensions. In each of the plots the KDE was computed for the first d dimensions. The results are shown for $N = 7000$ points so that the methods could be compared. The KDE was evaluated at $M = N$ points. The results are shown for a range of bandwidths around the optimal bandwidth obtained using the ROT plug-in method. An accuracy of $\epsilon = 10^{-2}$ was used for all the methods. The following observations can be made:

1. The IFGT is faster than the kd-tree algorithm at the optimal bandwidth.

2. As the bandwidth increases, the IFGT shows better speedups.

3. The kd-tree algorithm shows good performance at very small bandwidths.

4. We were able to run the IFGT algorithm till $d = 6$ due to limited memory.

5. As d increases, the speedup of the IFGT decreases. The cutoff point, i.e., the value of N for which a fast algorithm performs better than the direct summation, increases with dimension.

In the previous plot we used only 7000 points in order to compare our algorithm with the kd-tree method. For the IFGT the cutoff point — N after which IFGT is faster than the direct method — increases. As a result, for high dimensional data, better speedups are observed for large N. Table 8.1 shows the time taken by the IFGT on the entire dataset.

8.12   Conclusions

We have described the improved fast Gauss transform which is capable of computing the sums of Gaussian kernels in linear time in dimensions as high as tens for small bandwidths and as high as hundreds for large bandwidths. While different N-body algorithms have been proposed, each of them performs well under different conditions. Table 8.2 summarizes the conditions under which each algorithm performs better.

---

1. This dataset can be downloaded from the website `http://www.gaussianprocess.org/gpml/data/`.

Table 8.1 KDE results. Time taken by the direct summation and the IFGT on the entire dataset containing $N = 44{,}484$ source points in d dimensions. The KDE was evaluated at $M = N$ points. The error was set to $\epsilon = 10^{-2}$. The IFGT could not be run due to limited memory after $d > 6$.

d	Optimal bandwidth	Direct time (sec)	IFGT time (sec)	Speedup
1	0.052311	225.083000	0.240000	937.845833
2	0.070558	259.203000	1.692000	153.193262
3	0.088181	296.437000	9.864000	30.052413
4	0.104764	324.667000	48.690000	6.668043
5	0.120165	362.902000	57.152000	6.349769
6	0.134377	397.732000	91.982000	4.324020

Table 8.2 Summary of the better performing algorithms for different settings of dimensionality d and bandwidth h (assuming data is scaled to a unit hypercube). The bandwidth ranges are approximate.

	Small dimensions $d \leq 3$	Moderate dimensions $3 < d < 10$	Large dimensions $d \geq 10$
Small bandwidth $h \lesssim 0.1$	Dual-tree [kd-tree]	Dual-tree [kd-tree]	Dual-tree [probably anchors]
Moderate bandwidth $0.1 \lesssim h \lesssim 0.5\sqrt{d}$	FGT, IFGT	IFGT	
Large bandwidth $h \gtrsim 0.5\sqrt{d}$	FGT, IFGT Dual-tree	IFGT	IFGT

1. For very small bandwidths, the dual-tree algorithms give the best speedups.

2. For very large bandwidths, the IFGT is substantially faster than the other methods.

3. For moderate bandwidths and moderate dimensions, IFGT performs better than dual-tree algorithms.

4. The FGT performs well only for $d \leq 3$.

5. For moderate bandwidths and large dimensions, we may still have to resort to direct summation, and fast algorithms remain an area of active research.

Our current research is focused on combining the IFGT factorization with the kd-tree–based data structures so that we have an algorithm which gives good speedup for both small and large bandwidths.

One of the goals when designing theses kinds of algorithms is to give high accuracy guarantees. But sometimes, because of the loose error bounds, we end up doing much more work than necessary. In such a case, the IFGT can be used by just choosing a truncation number p and seeing how the algorithm performs.

Appendix

8.A N-Body Learning Software

The implementation of various N-body algorithms can be a bit tricky. However, some software is available in the public domain.

- C++ code with **MATLAB** bindings for both the FGT and the IFGT implementation is available at `http://www.umiacs.umd.edu/~vikas/Software/IFGT/IFGT_code.htm`.

- **Fortran** code for the FGT is available at `http://math.berkeley.edu/~strain/Codes/index.html`.

- C++ code with **MATLAB** bindings for the dual-tree algorithms can be downloaded from `http://www.cs.ubc.ca/~awll/nbody_methods.html`.

- **MATLAB** code for fast kernel density estimation based on N-body algorithms is also available at `http://www.ics.uci.edu/~ihler/`.

9   Approximation Methods for Gaussian Process Regression

Joaquin Quiñonero-Candela
Carl Edward Rasmussen
Christopher K. I. Williams

A wealth of computationally efficient approximation methods for Gaussian process regression have been recently proposed. We give a unifying overview of sparse approximations, following Quiñonero-Candela and Rasmussen (2005), and a brief review of approximate matrix-vector multiplication methods.

9.1   Introduction

Gaussian processes (GPs) are flexible, simple to implement, fully probabilistic methods suitable for a wide range of problems in regression and classification. A recent overview of GP methods is provided by Rasmussen and Williams (2006b). GP allow a Bayesian use of kernels for learning, with the following two key advantages:

- GPs provide fully probabilistic predictive distributions, including estimates of the uncertainty of the predictions.

- The evidence framework applied to GPs allows one to learn the parameters of the kernel.

However, a serious problem with GP methods is that the naive implementation requires computation which grows as $O(n^3)$, where n is the number of training cases. A host of approximation techniques have recently been proposed to allow application of GPs to large problems in machine learning. These techniques can broadly be divided into two classes: (i) those based on *sparse* methods, which approximate the full posterior by expressions involving matrices of lower rank $m < n$, and (ii) those relying on approximate matrix-vector multiplication (MVM) conjugate-gradient (CG) methods.

The structure of this chapter is as follows: In section 9.2 we provide an overview of GP regression. In section 9.3 we review sparse approximations under the unifying view, recently proposed by Quiñonero-Candela and Rasmussen (2005), based on inducing inputs and conditionally independent approximations to the prior. Section 9.4 describes work on approximate MVM methods for GP regression. The problem of selecting the inducing inputs is discussed in section 9.5. We address methods for setting hyperparameters in the kernel in section 9.6. The main focus of the chapter is on GP regression, but in section 9.7 we briefly describe how these methods can be extended to the classification problem. Conclusions are drawn in section 9.8.

9.2   Gaussian Process Regression

Probabilistic regression is usually formulated as follows: given a training set $\mathcal{D} = \{(\mathbf{x}_i, y_i), i = 1, \ldots, n\}$ of n pairs of (vectorial) inputs $\mathbf{x}_i$ and noisy (real, scalar) outputs y_i, compute the predictive distribution of the function values f_* (or noisy y_*) at test locations $\mathbf{x}_*$. In the simplest case (which we deal with here) we assume that the noise is additive, independent, and Gaussian, such that the relationship between the (latent) function $f(\mathbf{x})$ and the observed noisy targets y is given by

$$y_i = f(\mathbf{x}_i) + \varepsilon_i, \quad \text{where} \quad \varepsilon_i \sim \mathcal{N}(0, \sigma^2_{\text{noise}}), \tag{9.1}$$

where σ^2_{noise} is the variance of the noise, and we use the notation $\mathcal{N}(\mathbf{a}, A)$ for the Gaussian distribution with mean $\mathbf{a}$ and covariance A.

Definition 9.1. *A Gaussian process is a collection of random variables, any finite number of which have consistent[1] joint Gaussian distributions.*

Gaussian process regression is a Bayesian approach which assumes a GP prior[2] over functions, i.e., that a priori the function values behave according to

$$p(\mathbf{f}|\mathbf{x}_1, \mathbf{x}_2, \ldots, \mathbf{x}_n) = \mathcal{N}(\mathbf{0}, K), \tag{9.2}$$

where $\mathbf{f} = [f_1, f_2, \ldots, f_n]^\top$ is a vector of latent function values, $f_i = f(\mathbf{x}_i)$ and K is a covariance matrix, whose entries are given by the *covariance function*, $K_{ij} = k(\mathbf{x}_i, \mathbf{x}_j)$. Valid covariance functions give rise to positive semidefinite covariance matrices. In general, positive semidefinite kernels are valid covariance functions. The covariance function encodes our assumptions about the the function we wish to learn, by defining a notion of similarity between two function values, as a function of the corresponding two inputs. A very common covariance function is the Gaussian,

---

1. The random variables obey the usual rules of marginalization, etc.
2. For notational simplicity we exclusively use zero-mean priors.

or squared exponential:

$$K_{ij} = k(\mathbf{x}_i, \mathbf{x}_j) = v^2 \exp\left(-\frac{\|\mathbf{x}_i - \mathbf{x}_j\|^2}{2\lambda^2} \right),$$ (9.3)

where v^2 controls the prior variance, and λ is an isotropic lengthscale parameter that controls the rate of decay of the covariance, i.e., determines how far away $\mathbf{x}_i$ must be from $\mathbf{x}_j$ for f_i to be unrelated to f_j. We term the parameters that define the covariance functions *hyperparameters*. Learning of the hyperparameters based on data is discussed in section 9.6.

Note that the GP treats the latent function values f_i as random variables, indexed by the corresponding input. In the following, for simplicity we will always neglect the explicit conditioning on the inputs; the GP model and all expressions are always conditional on the corresponding inputs. The GP model is concerned only with the conditional of the outputs given the inputs; we do not model anything about the distribution of the inputs themselves.

As we will see in later sections, some approximations are strictly equivalent to GPs, while others are not. That is, the implied prior may still be multivariate Gaussian, but the covariance function may be different for training and test cases.

Definition 9.2. *A Gaussian process is called* degenerate *iff the covariance function has a finite number of nonzero eigenvalues.*

Degenerate GPs (e.g., with polynomial covariance function) correspond to *finite* linear (-in-the-parameters) models, whereas nondegenerate GPs (e.g., with the squared exponential or the radial basis function (RBF) covariance function) do not. The prior for a finite m-dimensional linear model only considers a universe of at most m linearly independent functions; this may often be too restrictive when $n \gg m$. Note, however, that nondegeneracy on its own doesn't guarantee the existence of the "right kind" of flexibility for a given particular modeling task. For a more detailed background on GP models, see, for example, Rasmussen and Williams (2006b).

Inference in the GP model is simple: we put a joint GP prior on training and test latent values, $\mathbf{f}$ and $\mathbf{f}_*$,[3] and combine it with the likelihood $p(\mathbf{y}|\mathbf{f})$ using Bayes rule to obtain the joint posterior

$$p(\mathbf{f}, \mathbf{f}_*|\mathbf{y}) = \frac{p(\mathbf{f}, \mathbf{f}_*)p(\mathbf{y}|\mathbf{f})}{p(\mathbf{y})},$$ (9.4)

where $\mathbf{y} = [y_1, \dots, y_n]$ is the vector of training targets. The final step needed to produce the desired posterior predictive distribution is to marginalize out the

---

3. We will mostly consider a vector of test cases $\mathbf{f}_*$ (rather than a single f_*) evaluated at a set of test inputs $\mathbf{X}_*$.

unwanted training set latent variables:

$$p(\mathbf{f}_*|\mathbf{y}) \;=\; \int p(\mathbf{f},\mathbf{f}_*|\mathbf{y})\mathrm{d}\mathbf{f} \;=\; \frac{1}{p(\mathbf{y})}\int p(\mathbf{y}|\mathbf{f})\,p(\mathbf{f},\mathbf{f}_*)\,\mathrm{d}\mathbf{f}\,, \tag{9.5}$$

or in words: the predictive distribution is the marginal of the renormalized joint prior times the likelihood. The joint GP prior and the independent likelihood are both Gaussian:

$$p(\mathbf{f},\mathbf{f}_*) \;=\; \mathcal{N}\!\left(\mathbf{0},\, \begin{bmatrix} K_{\mathbf{f},\mathbf{f}} & K_{*,\mathbf{f}} \\ K_{\mathbf{f},*} & K_{*,*} \end{bmatrix}\right) \quad \text{and} \quad p(\mathbf{y}|\mathbf{f}) \;=\; \mathcal{N}(\mathbf{f},\, \sigma^2_{\text{noise}}\mathbf{I})\,, \tag{9.6}$$

where K is subscript by the variables between which the covariance is computed (and we use the asterisk $*$ as shorthand for $\mathbf{f}_*$) and $\mathbf{I}$ is the identity matrix. Since both factors in the integral are Gaussian, the integral can be evaluated in closed form to give the Gaussian predictive distribution

$$p(\mathbf{f}_*|\mathbf{y}) \;=\; \mathcal{N}\!\big(K_{*,\mathbf{f}}\,(K_{\mathbf{f},\mathbf{f}}+\sigma^2_{\text{noise}}\mathbf{I})^{-1}\mathbf{y},\; K_{*,*}-K_{*,\mathbf{f}}\,(K_{\mathbf{f},\mathbf{f}}+\sigma^2_{\text{noise}}\mathbf{I})^{-1}K_{\mathbf{f},*}\big)\,. \tag{9.7}$$

The problem with the above expression is that it requires inversion of a matrix of size $n \times n$ which requires $O(n^3)$ operations, where n is the number of training cases. Thus, the simple exact implementation can handle problems with at most a few thousand training cases on today's desktop machines.

9.3   Sparse Approximations Based on Inducing Variables

To overcome the computational limitations of GP regression, numerous authors have recently suggested a wealth of *sparse* approximations. Common to all these approximation schemes is that only a subset of the latent variables are treated exactly, and the remaining variables are given some approximate but computationally cheaper treatment. However, the published algorithms have widely different motivations, emphasis, and exposition, so it is difficult to get an overview of how they relate to each other, and which can be expected to give rise to the best algorithms.

A useful discussion of some of the approximation methods is given in chapter 8 of Rasmussen and Williams (2006b). In this section we go beyond this, and provide a unifying view of sparse approximations for GP regression, following Quiñonero-Candela and Rasmussen (2005). For each algorithm we analyze the posterior, and compute the *effective prior* which it is using. Thus, we reinterpret the algorithms as "exact inference with an approximate prior," rather than the existing (ubiquitous) interpretation, "approximate inference with the exact prior." This approach has the advantage of directly expressing the approximations in terms of prior assumptions about the function, which makes the consequences of the approximations much easier to understand. While this view of the approximations is not the only one possible (Seeger, 2003, categorizes sparse GP approximations according to likelihood approximations), it has the advantage of putting all existing probabilistic sparse approximations under one umbrella, thus enabling direct comparison and revealing the relation between them.

We now seek to modify the joint prior $p(\mathbf{f}_*, \mathbf{f})$ from (9.6) in ways which will reduce the computational requirements from (9.7). Let us first rewrite that prior by introducing an additional set of m latent variables $\mathbf{u} = [u_1, \ldots, u_m]^\top$, which we call the *inducing variables*. These latent variables are values of the GP (as also $\mathbf{f}$ and $\mathbf{f}_*$), corresponding to a set of input locations $\mathbf{X_u}$, which we call the *inducing inputs*. Whereas the additional latent variables $\mathbf{u}$ are always marginalized out in the predictive distribution, the choice of inducing inputs *does* leave an imprint on the final solution. The inducing variables will turn out to be generalizations of variables which other authors have referred to variously as "support points," "active set," or "pseudo-inputs." Particular sparse algorithms choose the inducing variables in various different ways; some algorithms choose the inducing inputs to be a subset of the training set; others do not, as we will discuss in section 9.5. For now, consider any arbitrary inducing variables.

Due to the *consistency* of GP, we know that we can recover $p(\mathbf{f}_*, \mathbf{f})$ by simply integrating (marginalizing) out $\mathbf{u}$ from the joint GP prior $p(\mathbf{f}_*, \mathbf{f}, \mathbf{u})$,

$$p(\mathbf{f}_*, \mathbf{f}) \;=\; \int p(\mathbf{f}_*, \mathbf{f}, \mathbf{u}) \, \mathrm{d}\mathbf{u} \;=\; \int p(\mathbf{f}_*, \mathbf{f}|\mathbf{u}) \, p(\mathbf{u}) \, \mathrm{d}\mathbf{u}, \tag{9.8}$$

where $p(\mathbf{u}) \;=\; \mathcal{N}(\mathbf{0}, \, K_{\mathbf{u},\mathbf{u}})$.

This is an exact expression. Now, we introduce the fundamental approximation which gives rise to almost all sparse approximations. We approximate the joint prior by assuming that $\mathbf{f}_*$ and $\mathbf{f}$ are *conditionally independent given* $\mathbf{u}$ (see figure 9.1), such that

$$p(\mathbf{f}_*, \mathbf{f}) \;\simeq\; q(\mathbf{f}_*, \mathbf{f}) \;=\; \int q(\mathbf{f}_*|\mathbf{u}) \, q(\mathbf{f}|\mathbf{u}) \, p(\mathbf{u}) \, \mathrm{d}\mathbf{u} \,. \tag{9.9}$$

The name *inducing* variable is motivated by the fact that $\mathbf{f}$ and $\mathbf{f}_*$ can only communicate though $\mathbf{u}$, and $\mathbf{u}$ therefore *induces* the dependencies between training and test cases. As we shall detail in the following sections, the different computationally efficient algorithms proposed in the literature correspond to different *additional assumptions* about the two approximate *inducing* conditionals $q(\mathbf{f}|\mathbf{u})$, $q(\mathbf{f}_*|\mathbf{u})$ of the integral in (9.9). It will be useful for future reference to specify here the exact expressions for the two conditionals

training conditional:	$p(\mathbf{f}|\mathbf{u}) = \mathcal{N}(K_{\mathbf{f},\mathbf{u}} K_{\mathbf{u},\mathbf{u}}^{-1} \mathbf{u}, \; K_{\mathbf{f},\mathbf{f}} - Q_{\mathbf{f},\mathbf{f}})$,	(9.10a)
test conditional:	$p(\mathbf{f}_*|\mathbf{u}) = \mathcal{N}(K_{*,\mathbf{u}} K_{\mathbf{u},\mathbf{u}}^{-1} \mathbf{u}, \; K_{*,*} - Q_{*,*})$,	(9.10b)

where we have introduced the shorthand notation[4] $Q_{\mathbf{a},\mathbf{b}} \triangleq K_{\mathbf{a},\mathbf{u}} K_{\mathbf{u},\mathbf{u}}^{-1} K_{\mathbf{u},\mathbf{b}}$. We can readily identify the expressions in (9.10) as special (noise-free) cases of the standard predictive equation (9.7) with $\mathbf{u}$ playing the role of (noise-free) observations. Note

---

4. Note that $Q_{\mathbf{a},\mathbf{b}}$ depends on $\mathbf{u}$ although this is not explicit in the notation.

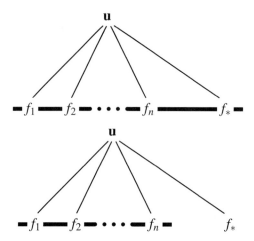

Figure 9.1   Graphical model of the relation between the inducing variables **u**, the training latent functions values $\mathbf{f} = [f_1, \ldots, f_n]^\top$, and the test function value f_*. The thick horizontal line represents a set of fully connected nodes. The observations $y_1, \ldots, y_n, y_*$ (not shown) would dangle individually from the corresponding latent values, by way of the exact (factored) likelihood (9.6). *Upper graph*: The fully connected graph corresponds to the case where no approximation is made to the full joint Gaussian process distribution between these variables. The inducing variables **u** are superfluous in this case, since all latent function values can communicate with all others. *Lower graph*: Assumption of *conditional independence* between training and test function values given **u**. This gives rise to the separation between training and test conditionals from (9.9). Notice that having cut the communication path between training and test latent function values, information from **f** can only be transmitted to f_* via the inducing variables **u**.

that the (positive semidefinite) covariance matrices in (9.10) have the form $K - Q$ with the following interpretation: the prior covariance K minus a (non-negative definite) matrix Q quantifying how much information **u** provides about the variables in question (**f** or $\mathbf{f}_*$). We emphasize that all the sparse methods discussed in this chapter correspond simply to different approximations to the conditionals in (9.10), and throughout we use the exact likelihood and inducing prior

$$p(\mathbf{y}|\mathbf{f}) \;=\; \mathcal{N}(\mathbf{f}, \, \sigma_{\text{noise}}^2 \mathbf{I}) \,, \quad \text{and} \quad p(\mathbf{u}) \;=\; \mathcal{N}(\mathbf{0}, \, K_{\mathbf{u},\mathbf{u}}) \,. \tag{9.11}$$

The sparse approximations we present in the following subsections are systematically sorted by decreasing crudeness of the additional approximations to the training and test conditionals. We will present the subset of data (SoD), subset of regressors (SoR), deterministic training conditional (DTC), and the partially and fully independent training conditional (PITC and FITC) approximations.

9.3.1   The Subset of Data Approximation

Before we get started with the more sophisticated approximations, we mention as a baseline method the simplest possible sparse approximation (which doesn't fall inside our general scheme): use only a subset of the data. The computational complexity is reduced to $O(m^3)$, where $m < n$. We would not generally expect SoD to be a competitive method, since it would seem impossible (even with fairly redundant data and a good choice of the subset) to get a realistic picture of the uncertainties when only a part of the training data is even considered. We include it here mostly as a baseline against which to compare better sparse approximations.

We will illustrate the various sparse approximations on a toy dataset, as illustrated in figure 9.4. There are $n = 100$ data points in one dimension, but for the sparse methods we have randomly selected $m = 10$ of these data points. The target function is given by $sin(x)/x$ with additive, independent, identically distributed Gaussian noise of amplitude 0.2. The training inputs lie on a uniform grid in $[-10, 10]$. For the predictions we have used a squared exponential (SE) covariance function (9.3), with slightly too short a lengthscale $\lambda = 1.2$, chosen so as to emphasize the different behaviors, and with amplitude $v^2 = 0.7$. Figure 9.4, top left, shows the predictive mean and two standard deviation error bars obtained with the full dataset. The 500 test inputs lie on a uniform grid in $[-14, 14]$.

In Figure 9.4, top right, we see how the SoD method produces wide predictive distributions when training on a randomly selected subset of ten cases. A fair comparison to other methods would take into account that the computational complexity is independent of n as opposed to other more advanced methods. These extra computational resources could be spent in a number of ways, e.g., larger m, or an active (rather than random) selection of the m points. In this chapter we will concentrate on understanding the theoretical foundations of the various approximations rather than investigate the necessary heuristics needed to turn the approximation schemes into practical algorithms.

9.3.2   The Subset of Regressors

The subset of regressors models are finite linear-in-the-parameters models with a particular prior on the weights. For any input $\mathbf{x}_*$, the corresponding function value f_* is given by

$$f_* = \sum_{i=1}^{m} k(\mathbf{x}_*, \mathbf{x}_{u_i})\, w_{u_i} = K_{*,\mathbf{u}}\, \mathbf{w}_{\mathbf{u}}\,, \quad \text{with}\ \ p(\mathbf{w}_{\mathbf{u}}) = \mathcal{N}(\mathbf{0}, K_{\mathbf{u},\mathbf{u}}^{-1})\,, \quad (9.12)$$

where there is one weight associated with each inducing input in $\mathbf{X}_{\mathbf{u}}$. Note that the covariance matrix for the prior on the weights is the *inverse* of that on $\mathbf{u}$, such that we recover the exact GP prior on $\mathbf{u}$, which is Gaussian with zero mean and covariance

$$\mathbf{u} = K_{\mathbf{u},\mathbf{u}}\,\mathbf{w}_{\mathbf{u}} \ \Rightarrow\ \langle \mathbf{u}\,\mathbf{u}^\top \rangle = K_{\mathbf{u},\mathbf{u}}\langle \mathbf{w}_{\mathbf{u}}\,\mathbf{w}_{\mathbf{u}}^\top \rangle K_{\mathbf{u},\mathbf{u}} = K_{\mathbf{u},\mathbf{u}}\,. \quad (9.13)$$

Using the effective prior on $\mathbf{u}$ and the fact that $\mathbf{w_u} = K_{\mathbf{u},\mathbf{u}}^{-1}\,\mathbf{u}$, we can redefine the SoR model in an equivalent, more intuitive way:

$$\mathbf{f}_* \;=\; K_{*,\mathbf{u}}\,K_{\mathbf{u},\mathbf{u}}^{-1}\,\mathbf{u}\,, \quad \text{with} \quad \mathbf{u} \sim \mathcal{N}(\mathbf{0},\,K_{\mathbf{u},\mathbf{u}})\,. \tag{9.14}$$

The SoR algorithm was proposed in Wahba (1990, chapter 7), and in Poggio and Girosi (1990, equation 25) via the regularization framework. It was adapted by Smola and Bartlett (2001) to propose a sparse greedy approximation to GP regression.

We are now ready to integrate the SoR model in our unifying framework. Given that there is a *deterministic* relation between any $\mathbf{f}_*$ and $\mathbf{u}$, the approximate conditional distributions in the integral in (9.9) are given by

$$q_{\mathrm{SoR}}(\mathbf{f}|\mathbf{u}) \;=\; \mathcal{N}(K_{\mathbf{f},\mathbf{u}}\,K_{\mathbf{u},\mathbf{u}}^{-1}\,\mathbf{u},\,\mathbf{0})\,, \quad \text{and} \quad q_{\mathrm{SoR}}(\mathbf{f}_*|\mathbf{u}) \;=\; \mathcal{N}(K_{*,\mathbf{u}}\,K_{\mathbf{u},\mathbf{u}}^{-1}\,\mathbf{u},\,\mathbf{0})\,, \tag{9.15}$$

with zero conditional covariance, compared to (9.10). The effective prior implied by the SoR approximation is easily obtained from (9.9), giving

$$q_{\mathrm{SoR}}(\mathbf{f},\mathbf{f}_*) \;=\; \mathcal{N}\!\left(\mathbf{0},\, \begin{bmatrix} Q_{\mathbf{f},\mathbf{f}} & Q_{\mathbf{f},*} \\ Q_{*,\mathbf{f}} & Q_{*,*} \end{bmatrix}\right)\,, \tag{9.16}$$

where we recall $Q_{\mathbf{a},\mathbf{b}} \triangleq K_{\mathbf{a},\mathbf{u}}K_{\mathbf{u},\mathbf{u}}^{-1}K_{\mathbf{u},\mathbf{b}}$. A more descriptive name for this method, would be the deterministic inducing conditional (DIC) approximation. We see that this approximate prior is degenerate. There are only m degrees of freedom in the model, which implies that only m linearly independent functions can be drawn from the prior. The $(m+1)$th one is a linear combination of the previous ones. For example, with very low noise, the posterior could be severely constrained by only m training cases.

The degeneracy of the prior can cause unreasonable predictive distributions. For covariance functions that decay to zero for a pair of faraway inputs, it is immediate to see that $Q_{*,*}$ will go to zero when the test inputs $\mathbf{X}_*$ are far away from the inducing inputs $\mathbf{X_u}$. As a result, $\mathbf{f}_*$ will have no prior variance under the approximate prior (9.16), and therefore the predictive variances far from the inducing inputs will tend to zero as well. This is unreasonable, because the area around the inducing inputs is where we are gathering the most information about the training data: we would like to be most uncertain about our predictions when far away from the inducing inputs. For covariance functions that do not decay to zero, the approximate prior over functions is still very restrictive, and given enough data only a very limited family of functions will be plausible under the posterior, leading to overconfident predictive variances. This is a general problem of finite linear models with small numbers of weights (for more details, see Rasmussen and Quiñonero-Candela, 2005). Figure 9.4, middle left panel, illustrates the unreasonable predictive uncertainties of the SoR approximation on a toy dataset.[5]

The predictive distribution is obtained by using the SoR approximate prior (9.16) instead of the true prior in (9.5). For each algorithm we give two forms of the predictive distribution, one which is easy to interpret, and the other which is economical to compute with:

$$q_{\text{SoR}}(\mathbf{f_*}|\mathbf{y}) \;=\; \mathcal{N}\big(Q_{*,\mathbf{f}}(Q_{\mathbf{f},\mathbf{f}} + \sigma_{\text{noise}}^2\mathbf{I})^{-1}\mathbf{y},$$
$$Q_{*,*} - Q_{*,\mathbf{f}}(Q_{\mathbf{f},\mathbf{f}} + \sigma_{\text{noise}}^2\mathbf{I})^{-1}Q_{\mathbf{f},*}\big) , \tag{9.17a}$$
$$=\; \mathcal{N}\big(\sigma^{-2}K_{*,\mathbf{u}}\Sigma\,K_{\mathbf{u},\mathbf{f}}\,\mathbf{y},\; K_{*,\mathbf{u}}\Sigma K_{\mathbf{u},*}\big) , \tag{9.17b}$$

where we have defined $\Sigma = (\sigma^{-2}K_{\mathbf{u},\mathbf{f}}K_{\mathbf{f},\mathbf{u}} + K_{\mathbf{u},\mathbf{u}})^{-1}$. Equation (9.17a) is readily recognized as the regular prediction equation (9.7), except that the covariance K has everywhere been replaced by Q, which was already suggested by (9.16). This corresponds to replacing the covariance function k with $k_{\text{SoR}}(\mathbf{x}_i, \mathbf{x}_j) = k(\mathbf{x}_i, \mathbf{u})\, K_{\mathbf{u},\mathbf{u}}^{-1}\, k(\mathbf{u}, \mathbf{x}_j)$. The new covariance function has rank m at most. Thus we have the following

Remark 9.1. *The SoR approximation is equivalent to exact inference in the degenerate Gaussian process with covariance function*

$$k_{\text{SoR}}(\mathbf{x}_i, \mathbf{x}_j) = k(\mathbf{x}_i, \mathbf{u})\, K_{\mathbf{u},\mathbf{u}}^{-1}\, k(\mathbf{u}, \mathbf{x}_j) .$$

The equivalent (9.17b) is computationally cheaper, and with (9.12) in mind, Σ is the covariance of the posterior on the weights $\mathbf{w_u}$. Note that as opposed to the SoD method, all training cases are taken into account. The computational complexity is $O(nm^2)$ initially, and $O(m)$ and $O(m^2)$ per test case for the predictive mean and variance respectively.

9.3.3   The Deterministic Training Conditional (DTC) Approximation

Taking up ideas contained in the work of Csató and Opper (2002), Seeger et al. (2003) recently proposed another sparse approximation to GP regression which does not suffer from the nonsensical predictive uncertainties of the SoR approximation, but that interestingly leads to exactly the same predictive mean. Seeger et al. (2003), who called the method projected latent variables (PLV), presented the method as relying on a *likelihood* approximation, based on the projection $\mathbf{f} = K_{\mathbf{f},\mathbf{u}}\, K_{\mathbf{u},\mathbf{u}}^{-1}\, \mathbf{u}$:

$$p(\mathbf{y}|\mathbf{f}) \;\simeq\; q(\mathbf{y}|\mathbf{u}) \;=\; \mathcal{N}(K_{\mathbf{f},\mathbf{u}}\, K_{\mathbf{u},\mathbf{u}}^{-1}\, \mathbf{u},\; \sigma_{\text{noise}}^2\mathbf{I}) . \tag{9.18}$$

The method has also been called the projected process approximation (PPA) by Rasmussen and Williams (2006b, Chapter 8). One way of obtaining an equivalent

---

5. Wary of this fact, Smola and Bartlett (2001) propose using the predictive variances of the SoD method, or a more accurate but computationally costly alternative (more details are given in Quiñonero-Candela, 2004, chapter 3).

model is to retain the usual likelihood, but to impose a deterministic training conditional and the exact test conditional from (9.10b):

$$q_{\mathrm{DTC}}(\mathbf{f}|\mathbf{u}) = \mathcal{N}(K_{\mathbf{f},\mathbf{u}}K_{\mathbf{u},\mathbf{u}}^{-1}\mathbf{u}, \mathbf{0}), \quad \text{and} \quad q_{\mathrm{DTC}}(\mathbf{f}_*|\mathbf{u}) = p(\mathbf{f}_*|\mathbf{u}) . \quad (9.19)$$

This reformulation has the advantage of allowing us to stick to our view of exact inference (with exact likelihood) with approximate priors. Indeed, under this model the conditional distribution of $\mathbf{f}$ given $\mathbf{u}$ is identical to that of the SoR, given in the left of (9.15). In this framework a systematic name for this approximation is the deterministic training conditional (DTC).

The fundamental difference with SoR is that DTC uses the exact test conditional (9.10b) instead of the deterministic relation between $\mathbf{f}_*$ and $\mathbf{u}$ of SoR. The joint prior implied by DTC is given by

$$q_{\mathrm{DTC}}(\mathbf{f}, \mathbf{f}_*) = \mathcal{N}\left(\mathbf{0}, \begin{bmatrix} Q_{\mathbf{f},\mathbf{f}} & Q_{\mathbf{f},*} \\ Q_{*,\mathbf{f}} & K_{*,*} \end{bmatrix}\right), \quad (9.20)$$

which is surprisingly similar to the effective prior implied by the SoR approximation (9.16). The difference is that under the DTC approximation, $\mathbf{f}_*$ has a prior variance of its own, given by $K_{*,*}$. This prior variance reverses the behavior of the predictive uncertainties, and turns them into sensible ones (see figure 9.4, middle right, for an illustration).

The predictive distribution is now given by

$$q_{\mathrm{DTC}}(\mathbf{f}_*|\mathbf{y}) = \mathcal{N}\big(Q_{*,\mathbf{f}}(Q_{\mathbf{f},\mathbf{f}} + \sigma_{\mathrm{noise}}^2\mathbf{I})^{-1}\mathbf{y},$$
$$K_{*,*} - Q_{*,\mathbf{f}}(Q_{\mathbf{f},\mathbf{f}} + \sigma_{\mathrm{noise}}^2\mathbf{I})^{-1}Q_{\mathbf{f},*}\big) , \quad (9.21\text{a})$$
$$= \mathcal{N}\big(\sigma^{-2}K_{*,\mathbf{u}}\Sigma K_{\mathbf{u},\mathbf{f}}\,\mathbf{y}, \; K_{*,*} - Q_{*,*} + K_{*,\mathbf{u}}\Sigma K_{*,\mathbf{u}}^{\top}\big) , \quad (9.21\text{b})$$

where again we have defined $\Sigma = (\sigma^{-2}K_{\mathbf{u},\mathbf{f}}K_{\mathbf{f},\mathbf{u}} + K_{\mathbf{u},\mathbf{u}})^{-1}$ as in (9.17). The predictive mean for the DTC is identical to that of the SoR approximation (9.17), but the predictive variance replaces the $Q_{*,*}$ from SoR with $K_{*,*}$ (which is larger, since $K_{*,*} - Q_{*,*}$ is positive semidefinite). This added term is the predictive variance of the posterior of f_* conditioned on $\mathbf{u}$. It grows to the prior variance $K_{*,*}$ as $\mathbf{x}_*$ moves far from the inducing inputs in $\mathbf{X_u}$.

Remark 9.2. *The only difference between the predictive distribution of DTC and SoR is the variance. The predictive variance of DTC is never smaller than that of SoR.*

Note that since the covariances for training cases and test cases are computed differently (9.20), it follows that

Remark 9.3. *The DTC approximation does not correspond exactly to a Gaussian process, as the covariance between latent values depends on whether they are considered training or test cases, violating consistency (see definition 9.1).*

The computational complexity has the same order as for SoR.

9.3.4 Partially Independent Training Conditional Approximations

The sparse approximations we have seen so far, SoR and DTC, both impose a deterministic relation between the training and inducing latent variables, resulting in inducing training conditionals where the covariance matrix has been set to zero — see (9.15) and (9.19). A less crude approximation to the training conditional is to preserve a block-diagonal of the true covariance matrix, given by (9.10a), and set the remaining entries to zero. The corresponding graphical model is shown in figure 9.2; notice that the variables in $\mathbf{f}$ are divided into k groups. Each group corresponds to a block in the block-diagonal matrix. This structure is equivalent to assuming conditional independence only for part of the training function values (those with covariance set to zero). We call this the partially independent training conditional (PITC) approximation:

$$q_{\text{PITC}}(\mathbf{f}|\mathbf{u}) \; = \; \mathcal{N}\big(K_{\mathbf{f},\mathbf{u}}\,K_{\mathbf{u},\mathbf{u}}^{-1}\,\mathbf{u}, \; \text{blockdiag}[K_{\mathbf{f},\mathbf{f}} - Q_{\mathbf{f},\mathbf{f}}]\big) \,,$$
$$\text{and} \quad q_{\text{PITC}}(f_*|\mathbf{u}) \; = \; p(f_*|\mathbf{u}) \,. \tag{9.22}$$

where blockdiag$[A]$ is a block-diagonal matrix (where the blocking structure is not explicitly stated). For now, we consider one single test input given by the exact test conditional (9.10b). As we discuss later in this section, the joint test conditional can also be approximated in various ways. The effective prior implied by the PITC approximation is given by

$$q_{\text{PITC}}(\mathbf{f}, f_*) \; = \; \mathcal{N}\left(\mathbf{0}, \; \begin{bmatrix} Q_{\mathbf{f},\mathbf{f}} - \text{blockdiag}[Q_{\mathbf{f},\mathbf{f}} - K_{\mathbf{f},\mathbf{f}}] & Q_{\mathbf{f},*} \\ Q_{*,\mathbf{f}} & K_{*,*} \end{bmatrix}\right). \tag{9.23}$$

Note that the sole difference between the DTC and PITC is that in the top left corner of the implied prior covariance, PITC replaces the approximate covariances of DTC by the exact ones on the block-diagonal. The predictive distribution is

$$q_{\text{FITC}}(f_*|\mathbf{y}) \; = \; \mathcal{N}\big(Q_{*,\mathbf{f}}(Q_{\mathbf{f},\mathbf{f}} + \Lambda)^{-1}\mathbf{y}, \; K_{*,*} - Q_{*,\mathbf{f}}(Q_{\mathbf{f},\mathbf{f}} + \Lambda)^{-1}Q_{\mathbf{f},*}\big) \tag{9.24a}$$
$$= \; \mathcal{N}\big(K_{*,\mathbf{u}}\Sigma K_{\mathbf{u},\mathbf{f}}\Lambda^{-1}\mathbf{y}, \; K_{*,*} - Q_{*,*} + K_{*,\mathbf{u}}\Sigma K_{\mathbf{u},*}\big) \,, \tag{9.24b}$$

where $\Sigma = (K_{\mathbf{u},\mathbf{u}} + K_{\mathbf{u},\mathbf{f}}\Lambda^{-1}K_{\mathbf{f},\mathbf{u}})^{-1}$ and $\Lambda = \text{blockdiag}[K_{\mathbf{f},\mathbf{f}} - Q_{\mathbf{f},\mathbf{f}} + \sigma_{\text{noise}}^2\mathbf{I}]$.

An identical expression was obtained by Schwaighofer and Tresp (2003, section 3), developed from the original Bayesian committee machine (BCM) of Tresp (2000). The BCM was originally proposed as a transductive learner (i.e., where the *test* inputs have to be known before training), and the inducing inputs $\mathbf{X_u}$ were chosen to be the test inputs.

However, it is important to realize that the BCM proposes two orthogonal ideas: first, the block-diagonal structure of the partially independent training conditional, and second, setting the inducing inputs to be the test inputs. These two ideas can be used independently and in section 9.5 we propose using the first without the second.

The computational complexity of the PITC approximation depends on the

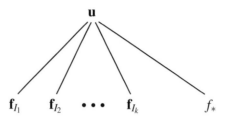

Figure 9.2 Graphical representation of the PITC approximation. The set of latent function values $\mathbf{f}_{I_i}$ indexed by the the set of indices I_i is fully connected. The PITC is more general than the FITC, (see figure 9.3) in that conditional independence is between k *groups* of training latent function values. This corresponds to the block-diagonal approximation to the true training conditional given in (9.22).

blocking structure imposed in (9.22). A reasonable choice, also recommended by Tresp (2000) may be to choose $k = n/m$ blocks, each of size $m \times m$. The computational complexity is thus $O(nm^2)$. Since in the PITC model, the covariance is computed differently for training and test cases, we have

Remark 9.4. *The PITC approximation does not correspond exactly to a Gaussian process.*

This is because computing covariances requires knowing whether points are from the training or test set, (9.23). To obtain a GP from the PITC, one would need to extend the partial conditional independence assumption to the joint conditional $p(\mathbf{f}, \mathbf{f}_*|\mathbf{u})$, which would require abandoning our primal assumption that the training and the test function values are conditionally independent, given the inducing variables.

9.3.5 Fully Independent Training Conditional

Recently, Snelson and Ghahramani (2006) proposed another likelihood approximation to speed up GP regression, which they called sparse pseudo-input Gaussian processes (SPGP). While the DTC is based on the likelihood approximation given by (9.18), the SPGP proposes a more sophisticated likelihood approximation with a richer covariance:

$$p(\mathbf{y}|\mathbf{f}) \simeq q(\mathbf{y}|\mathbf{u}) = \mathcal{N}(K_{\mathbf{f},\mathbf{u}} K_{\mathbf{u},\mathbf{u}}^{-1} \mathbf{u}, \ \mathrm{diag}[K_{\mathbf{f},\mathbf{f}} - Q_{\mathbf{f},\mathbf{f}}] + \sigma_{\mathrm{noise}}^2 \mathbf{I}) , \qquad (9.25)$$

where $\mathrm{diag}[A]$ is a diagonal matrix whose elements match the diagonal of A. As was pointed out by Csató (2005), the SPGP is an extreme case of the PITC approximation, where the training conditional is taken to be fully independent. We call it the fully independent training conditional (FITC) approximation. The corresponding graphical model is given in figure 9.3. The effective prior implied by

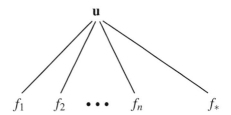

Figure 9.3 Graphical model for the FITC approximation. Compared to those in figure 9.1, all edges between latent function values have been removed: the latent function values are conditionally fully independent given the inducing variables **u**. Although strictly speaking the SoR and DTC approximations could also be represented by this graph, note that both further assume a deterministic relation between **f** and **u**. The FITC is an extreme case of PITC, with $k = n$ unitary groups (blocks); see figure 9.2.

the FITC is given by

$$q_{\mathrm{FITC}}(\mathbf{f}, f_*) \;=\; \mathcal{N}\!\left(\mathbf{0}, \; \begin{bmatrix} Q_{\mathbf{f},\mathbf{f}} - \mathrm{diag}[Q_{\mathbf{f},\mathbf{f}} - K_{\mathbf{f},\mathbf{f}}] & Q_{\mathbf{f},*} \\ Q_{*,\mathbf{f}} & K_{*,*} \end{bmatrix}\right), \tag{9.26}$$

and we see that in contrast to PITC, FITC only replaces the approximate covariances of DTC by the exact ones on the diagonal, i.e., the approximate prior variances are replaced by the true prior variances.

The predictive distribution of the FITC is identical to that of PITC (9.24), except for the alternative definition of $\Lambda = \mathrm{diag}[K_{\mathbf{f},\mathbf{f}} - Q_{\mathbf{f},\mathbf{f}} + \sigma_{\mathrm{noise}}^2 \mathbf{I}]$. The computational complexity is identical to that of SoR and DTC.

The question poses itself again for FITC, of how to treat the test conditional. For predictions at a single test input, this is obvious. For joint predictions, there are two options: either (i) use the exact full test conditional from (9.10b), or (ii) extend the additional factorizing assumption to the test conditional. Although Snelson and Ghahramani (2006) don't explicitly discuss joint predictions, it would seem that they probably intend the second option. Whereas the additional independence assumption for the test cases is not really necessary for computational reasons, it does affect the nature of the approximation. Under option (i) the training and test covariance are computed differently, and thus this does not correspond to our strict definition of a GP model, but

Remark 9.5. *Iff the assumption of full independence is extended to the test conditional, the FITC approximation is equivalent to exact inference in a nondegenerate Gaussian process with covariance function*

$$k_{\mathrm{FIC}}(\mathbf{x}_i, \mathbf{x}_j) = k_{\mathrm{SoR}}(\mathbf{x}_i, \mathbf{x}_j) + \delta_{i,j}[k(\mathbf{x}_i, \mathbf{x}_j) - k_{\mathrm{SoR}}(\mathbf{x}_i, \mathbf{x}_j)] \,,$$

where $\delta_{i,j}$ is Kronecker's delta.

A logical name for the method where the conditionals (training and test) are

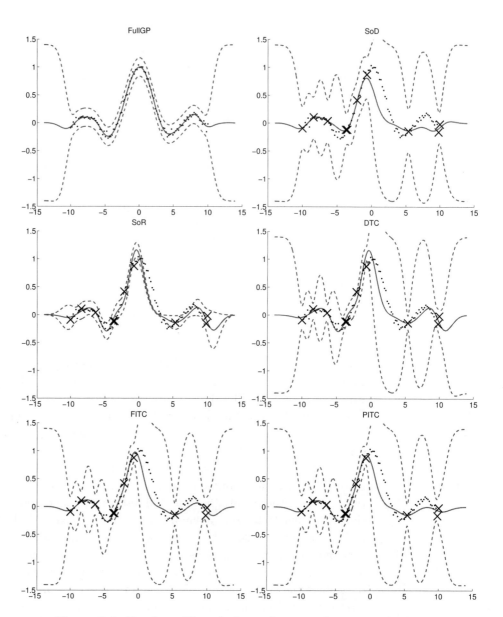

Figure 9.4 Toy data. All methods use the squared exponential covariance function, and a slightly too short lengthscale, chosen on purpose to emphasize the different behavior of the predictive uncertainties. The dots are the training points. The crosses are the targets corresponding to the inducing inputs, randomly selected from the training set. The solid line is the mean of the predictive distribution, and the dotted lines show the 95% confidence interval of the predictions. We include a full GP (top left graph) for reference.

always forced to be fully independent would be the fully independent conditional (FIC) approximation. The effective prior implied by the FIC is

$$q_{\mathrm{FIC}}(\mathbf{f}, \mathbf{f}_*) = \mathcal{N}\left(\mathbf{0}, \begin{bmatrix} Q_{\mathbf{f},\mathbf{f}} - \mathrm{diag}[Q_{\mathbf{f},\mathbf{f}} - K_{\mathbf{f},\mathbf{f}}] & Q_{\mathbf{f},*} \\ Q_{*,\mathbf{f}} & Q_{*,*} - \mathrm{diag}[Q_{*,*} - K_{*,*}] \end{bmatrix}\right). \tag{9.27}$$

In figure 9.4, bottom, we show the behavior of the predictive distribution of FITC and PITC with ten uniform blocks.

9.3.6   Summary of Sparse Approximations

Table 9.1 summarizes the way approximations are built. All these methods have been detailed in the previous subsections. The initial cost and that of the mean and variance per test case are respectively n^3, n, and n^2 for the exact GP, and nm^2, m, and m^2 for all other listed methods.

> **Table 9.1**   Summary of the way approximations are built. The "GP?" column indicates whether the approximation is equivalent to a GP. See remark 9.5 for FITC. Recall that we have defined $Q_{\mathbf{a},\mathbf{b}} \triangleq K_{\mathbf{a},\mathbf{u}} K_{\mathbf{u},\mathbf{u}}^{-1} K_{\mathbf{u},\mathbf{b}}$.

Method	$q(\mathbf{f}_*\|\mathbf{u})$	$q(\mathbf{f}\|\mathbf{u})$	Joint prior covariance	GP?
GP	exact	exact	$\begin{bmatrix} K_{\mathbf{f},\mathbf{f}} & K_{\mathbf{f},*} \\ K_{*,\mathbf{f}} & K_{*,*} \end{bmatrix}$	$\checkmark$
SoR	deterministic	deterministic	$\begin{bmatrix} Q_{\mathbf{f},\mathbf{f}} & Q_{\mathbf{f},*} \\ Q_{*,\mathbf{f}} & Q_{*,*} \end{bmatrix}$	$\checkmark$
DTC	exact	deterministic	$\begin{bmatrix} Q_{\mathbf{f},\mathbf{f}} & Q_{\mathbf{f},*} \\ Q_{*,\mathbf{f}} & K_{*,*} \end{bmatrix}$	
FITC	(exact)	fully independent	$\begin{bmatrix} Q_{\mathbf{f},\mathbf{f}} - \mathrm{diag}[Q_{\mathbf{f},\mathbf{f}} - K_{\mathbf{f},\mathbf{f}}] & Q_{\mathbf{f},*} \\ Q_{*,\mathbf{f}} & K_{*,*} \end{bmatrix}$	$(\checkmark)$
PITC	exact	partially independent	$\begin{bmatrix} Q_{\mathbf{f},\mathbf{f}} - \mathrm{blokdiag}[Q_{\mathbf{f},\mathbf{f}} - K_{\mathbf{f},\mathbf{f}}] & Q_{\mathbf{f},*} \\ Q_{*,\mathbf{f}} & K_{*,*} \end{bmatrix}$	

9.4   Fast Matrix Vector Multiplication Approximations

One straightforward method to speed up GP regression is to note that linear system $(K_{\mathbf{f},\mathbf{f}} + \sigma_{\mathrm{noise}}^2 \mathbf{I})\, \boldsymbol{\alpha} = \mathbf{y}$ can be solved by an iterative method, for example conjugate gradients. See Golub and Van Loan (1996, section 10.2) for further details on the CG method. Each iteration of the CG method requires an MVM which takes $O(n^2)$ time. The CG algorithm gives the exact solution (ignoring round-off errors) if run for n iterations, but it will give an approximate solution if terminated earlier, say after

k iterations, with time complexity $O(kn^2)$. The CG method has been suggested by Wahba et al. (1995) in the context of numerical weather prediction, and by Gibbs and MacKay (1997) in the context of general GP regression.

However, the scaling of the CG method (at least $O(n^2)$) is too slow to really be useful for large problems. Recently a number of researchers have noted that if the MVM step can be approximated efficiently, then the CG method can be speeded up. Each CG iteration involves an MVM of the form $\mathbf{a} = (K_{\mathbf{f},\mathbf{f}} + \sigma_{\text{noise}}^2 \mathbf{I})\mathbf{v}$, which requires n inner products $a_i = \sum_{j=1}^n k(\mathbf{x}_i, \mathbf{x}_j)v_j$. Each a_i is a weighted sum of kernels between source points $\{\mathbf{x}_j\}$ and target point $\mathbf{x}_i$. Such sums can be approximated using multiresolution space-partitioning data structures. For example, Y. Shen et al. (2006) suggest a simple approximation using a kd-tree, while Gray (2004) and de Freitas et al. (2006) make use of dual trees. The improved fast Gauss transform (IFGT) (C. Yang et al., 2005) is another method for approximating the weighted sums. It is specific to the Gaussian kernel and uses a more sophisticated approximation based on Taylor expansions. The IFGT and related methods are described in chapter 8 of this book. Generally, experimental results show that these fast MVM methods are most effective when the input space is low-dimensional.

Notice that these methods for accelerating the weighted sum of kernel functions can also be used at test time, and may be particularly helpful when n is large.

9.5   Selecting the Inducing Variables

We have until now assumed that the inducing inputs $\mathbf{X}_\mathbf{u}$ were given. Traditionally, sparse models have very often been built upon a carefully chosen subset of the training inputs. This concept is probably best exemplified in the popular support vector machine (SVM) (Cortes and Vapnik, 1995). Chapters 11 and 12 seek to further sparsify the SVM. In sparse GP, it has also been suggested to select the inducing inputs $\mathbf{X}_\mathbf{u}$ from among the training inputs. Since this involves a prohibitive combinatorial optimization, greedy optimization approaches have been suggested using various selection criteria like online learning (Csató and Opper, 2002), greedy posterior maximization (Smola and Bartlett, 2001), maximum information gain (Lawrence et al., 2003; Seeger et al., 2003), matching pursuit (Keerthi and Chu, 2006b), and others. As discussed in section 9.3.4, selecting the inducing inputs from among the test inputs has also been considered in transductive settings by Tresp (2000). Recently, Snelson and Ghahramani (2006) have proposed relaxing the constraint that the inducing variables must be a subset of training/test cases, turning the discrete selection problem into one of continuous optimization. One may hope that finding a good solution is easier in the continuous than the discrete case, although finding the global optimum is intractable in both cases. And it is possible that the less restrictive choice can lead to better performance in very sparse models.

Which criterion should be used to set the inducing inputs? Departing from a fully Bayesian treatment, which would involve defining priors on $\mathbf{X}_\mathbf{u}$, one could maximize the marginal likelihood (also called the evidence) with respect to $\mathbf{X_u}$, an approach also followed by Snelson and Ghahramani (2006). Each of the approximate methods proposed involves a different effective prior, and hence its own particular effective marginal likelihood conditioned on the inducing inputs

$$q(\mathbf{y}|\mathbf{X_u}) = \iint p(\mathbf{y}|\mathbf{f})\, q(\mathbf{f}|\mathbf{u})\, p(\mathbf{u}|\mathbf{X_u})\mathrm{d}\mathbf{u}\,\mathrm{d}\mathbf{f} = \int p(\mathbf{y}|\mathbf{f})\, q(\mathbf{f}|\mathbf{X_u})\mathrm{d}\mathbf{f}\ , \qquad (9.28)$$

which of course is independent of the test conditional. We have in the above equation explicitly conditioned on the inducing inputs $\mathbf{X_u}$. Using Gaussian identities, the effective marginal likelihood is very easily obtained by adding a ridge $\sigma_{\mathrm{noise}}^2\mathbf{I}$ (from the likelihood) to the covariance of the effective prior on $\mathbf{f}$. Using the appropriate definitions of Λ, the log marginal likelihood becomes

$$\log q(\mathbf{y}|\mathbf{X_u}) \;=\; -\tfrac{1}{2}\log|Q_{\mathbf{f},\mathbf{f}}+\Lambda| - \tfrac{1}{2}\mathbf{y}^\top (Q_{\mathbf{f},\mathbf{f}}+\Lambda)^{-1}\mathbf{y} - \tfrac{n}{2}\log(2\pi)\ , \qquad (9.29)$$

where $\Lambda_{\mathrm{SoR}} = \Lambda_{\mathrm{DTC}} = \sigma_{\mathrm{noise}}^2\mathbf{I}$, $\Lambda_{\mathrm{FITC}} = \mathrm{diag}[K_{\mathbf{f},\mathbf{f}} - Q_{\mathbf{f},\mathbf{f}}] + \sigma_{\mathrm{noise}}^2\mathbf{I}$, and $\Lambda_{\mathrm{PITC}} = \mathrm{blockdiag}[K_{\mathbf{f},\mathbf{f}} - Q_{\mathbf{f},\mathbf{f}}] + \sigma_{\mathrm{noise}}^2\mathbf{I}$. The computational cost of the marginal likelihood is $O(nm^2)$ for all methods, that of its gradient with respect to one element of $\mathbf{X_u}$ is $O(nm)$. This of course implies that the complexity of computing the gradient with respect to the whole of $\mathbf{X_u}$ is $O(dnm^2)$, where d is the dimension of the input space.

It has been proposed to maximize the effective posterior instead of the effective marginal likelihood (Smola and Bartlett, 2001). However, this is potentially dangerous and can lead to overfitting. Maximizing the whole evidence instead is sound and comes at an identical computational cost. For a deeper analysis, see (Quiñonero-Candela, 2004, section 3.3.5 and figure 3.2).

The marginal likelihood has traditionally been used to learn the hyperparameters of GPs in the nonfully Bayesian treatment (see, for example, Williams and Rasmussen, 1996). For the sparse approximations presented here, once you are learning $\mathbf{X_u}$ it is straightforward to allow for learning hyperparameters (of the covariance function) during the same optimization. For methods that select $\mathbf{X_u}$ from the training data, one typically interleaves optimization of the hyperparameters with selection of $\mathbf{X_u}$, as proposed, for example, by Seeger et al. (2003).

9.5.1   Augmentation

Since in the previous sections, we haven't assumed anything about $\mathbf{u}$, for each test input $\mathbf{x}_*$ in turn, we can simply *augment* the set of inducing variables by f_*, so that we have one additional inducing variable equal to the current test latent. Let us first investigate the consequences for the test conditional from (9.10b). Note that the interpretation of the covariance matrix $K_{*,*} - Q_{*,*}$ was "the prior covariance minus the information which $\mathbf{u}$ provides about f_*." It is clear that the augmented $\mathbf{u}$ (with f_*) provides all possible information about f_*, and consequently $Q_{*,*} = K_{*,*}$. An equivalent view on augmentation is that the assumption of conditional independence between f_* and $\mathbf{f}$ is dropped. This is seen trivially, by adding edges between f_* and the f_i. Because f_* enjoys a full, original prior variance under the test conditional, augmentation helps reverse the misbehavior of the predictive variances of degenerate GP priors (see Quiñonero-Candela and Rasmussen, 2005, section 8.1) for the details. Augmented SoR and augmented DTC are identical models (see Quiñonero-Candela and Rasmussen, 2005, remark 12).

Augmentation was originally proposed by Rasmussen (2002), and applied in detail to the SoR with RBF covariance by Quiñonero-Candela (2004). Later, Rasmussen and Quiñonero-Candela (2005) proposed using augmentation to "heal" the relevance vector machine (RVM) (Tipping, 2000), which is also equivalent to a degenerate GP with nonsensical predictive variances that shrink to zero far away from the training inputs (Tipping, 2001, appendix D). Although augmentation was initially proposed for a narrow set of circumstances, it is easily applied to any of the approximations discussed. Of course, augmentation doesn't make any sense for an exact, nondegenerate GP model (a GP with a covariance function that has a feature space which is infinite-dimensional, i.e., with basis functions *everywhere*).

Prediction with an augmented sparse model comes at a higher computational cost, since now f_* interacts directly with all of $\mathbf{f}$, and not just with $\mathbf{u}$. For each new test point $O(nm)$ operations are required, as opposed to $O(m)$ for the mean, and $O(m^2)$ for the predictive distribution of all the nonaugmented methods we have discussed. Whether augmentation is of practical interest (i.e., increases performance at a fixed computational budget) is unclear, since the extra computational effort needed for augmentation could be invested by the nonaugmented methods, for example, to use more inducing variables.

9.6   Approximate Evidence and Hyperparameter Learning

Hyperparameter learning is an issue that is sometimes completely ignored in the literature on approximations to GPs. However, learning good values of the hyperparameters is crucial, and it might come at a high computational cost that cannot be ignored. For clarity, let us distinguish between three phases in GP modeling:

- **Hyperparameter learning**: The hyperparameters are learned, by, for example, maximizing the log marginal likelihood.

- **Precomputation**: All possible precomputations not involving test inputs are performed (such as inverting the covariance matrix of the training function values, and multiplying it by the vector of targets).

- **Testing**: Only the computations involving the test inputs are made that could not have been made previously.

If approximations to GP regression are to provide a computational speedup, then one must, in principle, take into account *all three phases* of GP modeling.

Let us for a moment group hyperparameter learning and precomputations into a wider *training* phase. In practice, there will be situations where one of the two times, training or testing, is more important than the other. Let us distinguish between two extreme scenarios. On the one hand, there are applications for which training time is unimportant, the crucial point being that the time required to make predictions, once the system has been trained, is really small. An example could be applications embedded in a portable device, with limited CPU power. At the other extreme are applications where the system needs to be retrained often and quickly, and where prediction time matters much less than the quality of the predictions. An example could be a case where we know already that we will only need to make very few predictions, hence training time automatically becomes predominant. A particular application might lie somewhere between these two extremes.

A common choice of objective function for setting the hyperparameters is the *marginal likelihood* $p(\mathbf{y}|\mathbf{X})$. For GP regression, this can be computed exactly (by integrating out $\mathbf{f}$ analytically) to obtain

$$\log p(\mathbf{y}|\mathbf{X}) = -\tfrac{1}{2}\log|K_{\mathbf{f},\mathbf{f}}+\sigma_{\text{noise}}^2\mathbf{I}| - \tfrac{1}{2}\mathbf{y}^\top(K_{\mathbf{f},\mathbf{f}}+\sigma_{\text{noise}}^2\mathbf{I})^{-1}\mathbf{y} - \tfrac{n}{2}\log(2\pi)\,. \quad (9.30)$$

Also, the derivative of the marginal likelihood with respect to a hyperparameter θ_j is given by

$$\frac{\partial}{\partial\theta_j}\log p(\mathbf{y}|\mathbf{X}) = -\tfrac{1}{2}\mathbf{y}^\top R^{-1}\frac{\partial R}{\partial\theta_j}R^{-1}\mathbf{y} - \tfrac{1}{2}\text{tr}\left(R^{-1}\frac{\partial R}{\partial\theta_j}\right), \quad (9.31)$$

where $R = (K_{\mathbf{f},\mathbf{f}} + \sigma_{\text{noise}}^2\mathbf{I})$, and $\text{tr}(A)$ denotes the trace of matrix A. These derivatives can then be fed to a gradient-based optimization routine. The marginal likelihood is not the only criterion that can be used for hyperparameter optimization. For example, one can use a cross-validation objective (see Rasmussen and Williams, 2006b, chapter 5).

The approximate log marginal likelihood for the SoR, DTC, FITC and PITC approximations is given in (9.29), taking time $O(nm^2)$. For the SoD approximation one simply ignores all training data points not in the inducing set, giving

$$\log q_{\text{SoD}}(\mathbf{y}|\mathbf{X_u}) = -\tfrac{1}{2}\log|K_{\mathbf{u},\mathbf{u}} + \sigma_{\text{noise}}^2\,\mathbf{I}| - \tfrac{1}{2}\mathbf{y_u}^\top(K_{\mathbf{u},\mathbf{u}} + \sigma_{\text{noise}}^2\,\mathbf{I})^{-1}\mathbf{y_u}$$
$$- \tfrac{m}{2}\log(2\pi)\,, \quad (9.32)$$

where the inducing inputs $\mathbf{X_u}$ are a subset of the training inputs, and $\mathbf{y_u}$ are the corresponding training targets. The computational cost here is $O(m^3)$, instead of the $O(n^3)$ operations needed to compute the evidence of the full GP model. For all of these approximations one can also calculate derivatives with respect to the hyperparameters analytically, for use in a gradient-based optimizer.

In general we believe that for a given sparse approximation it makes most sense to both optimize the hyperparameters and make predictions under the same approximation (Quiñonero-Candela, 2004, chapter 3). The hyperparameters that are optimal for the full GP model, if we were able to obtain them, may also well be very different from those optimal for a specific sparse approximation. For example, for the squared exponential covariance function (9.3), the lengthscale optimal for the full GP might be too short for a very sparse approximation. Certain sparse approximations lead to marginal likelihoods that are better behaved than others. Snelson and Ghahramani (2006) report that the marginal likelihood of FITC suffers much less from local maxima than the marginal likelihood common to SoR and DTC.

Gibbs and MacKay (1997) discussed how the marginal likelihood and its derivatives can be approximated using CG iterative methods, building on ideas in Skilling (1993). It should be possible to speed up such computations using the fast MVM methods outlined in section 9.4.

9.7   Classification

Compared with the regression case, the approximation methods for GP classification need to deal with an additional difficulty: the likelihood is non-Gaussian, which implies that neither the predictive distribution (9.5) nor the marginal likelihood can be computed analytically. With the approximate prior at hand, the most common approach is to further approximate the resulting posterior, $p(\mathbf{f}|\mathbf{y})$, by a Gaussian. It can be shown that if $p(\mathbf{y}|\mathbf{f})$ is log-concave, then the posterior will be unimodal; this is the case for the common logistic and probit response functions. (For a review of likelihood functions for GP classification, see Rasmussen and Williams (2006b, chapter 3).) An evaluation of different, common ways of determining the approximating Gaussian has been made by Kuss and Rasmussen (2005).

For the SoR method we have $f_* = \sum_{i=1}^{m} k(\mathbf{x}_*, \mathbf{x}_\mathbf{u}^i) w_\mathbf{u}^i$ with $\mathbf{w_u} \sim \mathcal{N}(\mathbf{0},\ K_{\mathbf{u},\mathbf{u}}^{-1})$ from (9.12). For log-concave likelihoods, the optimization problem to find the maximum a posteriori (MAP) value of $\mathbf{w_u}$ is convex. Using the MAP value of the weights together with the Hessian at this point, we obtain an approximate Gaussian predictive distribution of f_*, which can be fed through the sigmoid function to yield probabilistic predictions. The question of how to choose the inducing inputs still arises; X. Lin et al. (2000) select these using a clustering method, while J. Zhu and Hastie (2002) propose a forward selection strategy.

The SoD method for GP classification was proposed by Lawrence et al. (2003), using an expectation-propagation (EP) approximation to the posterior (Minka, 2001), and an information gain criterion for greedily selecting the inducing inputs from the training set.

The DTC approximation has also been used for classification. Csató and Opper (2002) present an "online" method, where the examples are processed sequentially, while Csató et al. (2003) give an EP-type algorithm where multiple sweeps across the data are permitted.

The PITC approximation has also been applied to GP classification. Tresp (2000) generalized the use of the BCM to non-Gaussian likelihoods by applying a Laplace approximation to each of the partially independent blocks.

9.8   Conclusions

In this chapter we have reviewed a number of methods for dealing with the $O(n^3)$ scaling of a naive implementation of Gaussian process regression methods. These can be divided into two classes, those based on sparse methods, and those based on fast MVM methods. We have also discussed the selection of inducing variables, hyperparameter learning, and approximation methods for the marginal likelihood.

Probably the question that is most on the mind of the practitioner is "what method should I use on my problem?" Unfortunately this is not an easy question to answer, as it will depend on various aspects of the problem such as the complexity of the underlying target function, the dimensionality of the inputs, the amount of noise on the targets, etc. There has been some empirical work on the comparison of approximate methods, for example in Schwaighofer and Tresp (2003) and Rasmussen and Williams (2006b, chapter 8) but more needs to be done. Empirical evaluation is not easy, as there exist very many criteria of comparison, under which different methods might perform best. There is a large choice of the measures of performance: mean squared error, negative log predictive probability, etc., and an abundance of possible measures of speed for the approximations: hyperparameter learning time, precomputation time, testing time, number of inducing variables, number of CG iterations, etc. One possible approach for empirical evaluation of computationally efficient approximations to GPs is to fix a "computational budget" of available time, and see which approximation achieves the best performance (under some loss) within that time. Empirical comparisons should always include approximations that at first sight might seem too simple or naive, such as SoD, but that might end up performing as well as more elaborate methods.

Acknowledgments

We thank Ed Snelson and Iain Murray for recent, very fruitful discussions. This work was supported in part by the IST Programme of the European Community, under the PASCAL Network of Excellence, IST-2002-506778. This publication only reflects our views. Carl Edward Rasmussen was supported by the German Research Council (DFG) through grant RA 1030/1.

10 Brisk Kernel Independent Component Analysis

Stefanie Jegelka
Arthur Gretton

Recent approaches to independent component analysis (ICA) have used kernel independence measures to obtain very good performance in ICA, particularly in areas where classical methods experience difficulty (for instance, sources with near-zero kurtosis). In this chapter, we compare two efficient extensions of these methods for large-scale problems: random subsampling of entries in the Gram matrices used in defining the independence measures, and incomplete Cholesky decomposition of these matrices. We derive closed-form, efficiently computable approximations for the gradients of these measures, and compare their performance on ICA using both artificial and music data. We show that kernel ICA can scale up to larger problems than yet attempted, and that incomplete Cholesky decomposition performs better than random sampling.

10.1 Introduction

The problem of instantaneous independent component analysis (ICA) involves the recovery of linearly mixed, independent sources in the absence of information about the source distributions beyond their mutual independence (Hyvärinen et al., 2001). Classical approaches to this problem, which use as their independence criterion the sum of expectations of a fixed nonlinear function (or a small number of such functions) on each recovered source, scale well to large numbers of sources and samples. On the other hand, they only ensure local convergence in the vicinity of independence — H. Shen and Hüper (2006a) give one such analysis for FastICA — and do not guarantee independent sources are recovered at the *global* optimum of the independence criterion. Statistical tests of independence should then be applied (e.g., Ku and Fine, 2005) to verify independent sources are recovered.

Ideally, we would prefer to optimize over a criterion that exhibits a global optimum at independence. This approach is adopted in several recent algorithms, including those of (Stögbauer et al., 2004; A. Chen, 2006; Learned-Miller and Fisher, 2003), who optimize the mutual information between the sources, and (Eriksson and Koivunen, 2003; A. Chen and Bickel, 2005; Murata, 2001), who optimize characteristic function-based independence measures. We focus in particular on the kernel approaches of (Bach and Jordan, 2002; Gretton et al., 2005a,b), which are already established as yielding excellent performance in small-scale (relatively few sources and samples) linear ICA problems. Kernel methods measure independence by computing statistics on the spectrum of covariance or correlation operators defined on reproducing kernel Hilbert spaces (RKHSs). In the present study, our independence measures are the constrained covariance (COCO), which is the spectral norm of the covariance operator, and the Hilbert-Schmidt independence criterion (HSIC), which is the Hilbert-Schmidt norm of this operator.

Two difficulties arise when kernel measures of independence are used for ICA in large-scale settings. First, when there are many samples, it becomes impractical to compute and store the matrices of kernel values, especially as these evolve in the course of optimizing over the estimated unmixing matrix. Second, we are required to compute the gradient of the independence measures with respect to the mixing matrix, which is accomplished highly inefficiently in the kernel methods cited earlier: for m sources, each derivative requires $2m(m-1)$ evaluations of the independence measure (for a total cost of $O(m^4)$), which causes especially poor scaling for large numbers of sources.

To make kernel ICA relevant to large-scale problems, we must deal both with many independent sources and with a large sample size n. Our focus is on evaluating both sparse and low-rank matrix approximation techniques to efficiently compute both our independence measures and their gradients: in particular, we must avoid ever computing or storing a complete Gram matrix, since the cost of $O(n^2)$ would make the algorithm unusable. Bach and Jordan (2002) employ the incomplete Cholesky decomposition to this purpose, following Fine and Scheinberg (2001), which results in a substantial reduction in cost. An alternative approach is to compute a random subsample of the Gram matrix entries as proposed by Achlioptas and McSherry (2001), thus taking advantage of sparse matrix operations to cheaply obtain the dependence measures. As long as the spectra of the Gram matrices decay quickly, the spectral norm of the matrix product that defines COCO is well approximated by this random sampling (this is also true for the Hilbert-Schmidt norm defining HSIC, albeit to a lesser extent): in particular, error bounds established by Drineas et al. (2004) apply to our case. We also emphasize the broader implications of the problem we address, since it involves manipulating a product of Gram matrices so as to minimize its singular values: at this minimum, however, an accurate estimation of the product from low-rank approximations is at its most difficult.

Additional efficiencies can be achieved in the gradient descent algorithm on the unmixing matrix. We investigate both local quadratic approximations to the independence measures, and steps of decreasing size along consecutive directions of steepest descent. Both strategies require significantly fewer evaluations of the independence measure than the golden search used by (Bach and Jordan, 2002; Gretton et al., 2005a,b; A. Chen and Bickel, 2005).

We begin our presentation in section 10.2, where we introduce the problem of ICA. In section 10.3, we describe independence measures based on covariance operators in RKHSs, and discuss the two Gram matrix approximation strategies for these measures. We compute the gradients of our independence measures in section 10.4, and show how these may likewise be efficiently computed using our approximation strategies. We give a breakdown of the computational cost of the proposed methods in section 10.5. Finally, we present our experiments in section 10.6.

10.2   Independent Component Analysis

We describe the goal of instantaneous ICA, drawing mainly on Hyvärinen et al. (2001) and Cardoso (1998), as well as the core properties of ICA explored by Comon (1994). We are given n samples $\boldsymbol{t} := (\mathbf{t}_1, \ldots, \mathbf{t}_n)$ of the m dimensional random vector $\mathbf{t}$, which are drawn independently and identically from the distribution $\mathbf{P_t}$. The vector $\mathbf{t}$ is related to the random vector $\mathbf{s}$ (also of dimension m) by the linear mixing process

$$\mathbf{t} = \mathbf{Bs}, \tag{10.1}$$

where $\mathbf{B}$ is a matrix with full rank. We refer to our ICA problem as being *instantaneous* as a way of describing the dual assumptions that any observation $\mathbf{t}$ depends only on the sample $\mathbf{s}$ at that instant, and that the samples $\mathbf{s}$ are drawn independently and identically.

The components $\mathbf{s}_i$ of $\mathbf{s}$ are assumed to be mutually independent: this model codifies the assumption that the sources are generated by unrelated phenomena (for instance, one component might be an EEG signal from the brain, while another could be due to electrical noise from nearby equipment). Mutual independence (in the case where the random variables admit probability densities) has the following definition (Papoulis, 1991, p. 184):

Definition 10.1 (Mutual independence). *Suppose we have a random vector* $\mathbf{s}$ *of dimension* m. *We say that the components* $\mathbf{s}_i$ *are mutually* independent *if and only if*

$$\mathbf{f_s}(\mathbf{s}) = \prod_{i=1}^{m} \mathbf{f_{s_i}}(s_i). \tag{10.2}$$

It follows easily that the random variables are *pairwise* independent if they are *mutually* independent; i.e., $\mathbf{f_{s_i}}(s_i)\,\mathbf{f_{s_j}}(s_j) = \mathbf{f_{s_i,s_j}}(s_i, s_j)$ for all $i \neq j$. The reverse does not hold, however: pairwise independence does not guarantee mutual independence.

Our goal is to recover **s** via an estimate **W** of the inverse of the matrix **B**, such that the recovered vector **x** = **WBs** has mutually independent components.[1] For the purpose of simplifying our discussion, we will assume that **B** (and hence **W**) is an *orthogonal matrix*; in the case of arbitrary **B**, the observations must first be decorrelated before an orthogonal **W** is applied. We will return to the problem of gradient descent on the orthogonal group in section 10.4.5. Mutual independence is generally difficult to determine (Kankainen, 1995, gives one approach). In the case of linear mixing, however, we are able to find a unique optimal unmixing matrix **W** using only the *pairwise* independence between elements of **x**, because it is in this case equivalent to recovering the *mutually* independent terms of **s** (up to permutation and scaling). This is due to theorem 11 of Comon (1994).

10.3 Independence Measures Based on RKHS Covariance Operators

We begin in section 10.3.1 by introducing the problem variables, and describing covariance operators in RKHSs. Next, in section 10.3.2, we show how the spectral and Hilbert-Schmidt norms of the covariance operators may easily be expressed as a function of the kernels of the RKHSs, and describe the relation to other independence measures in the literature. Finally, in section 10.3.3, we cover approximation techniques based on subsampling and on the incomplete Cholesky decomposition, which will be used in computing our independence criteria and their derivatives.

10.3.1 Covariance Operators and RKHSs

In this section, we provide the functional analytic background necessary in describing covariance operators between RKHSs. Our main purpose in this section is to introduce functional covariance operators, following Baker (1973) and Fukumizu et al. (2004), who characterize these operators for general Hilbert spaces.

Consider a Hilbert space $\mathcal{F}$ of functions from $\mathcal{X}$ to $\mathbb{R}$, where $\mathcal{X}$ is a separable metric space. The Hilbert space $\mathcal{F}$ is an RKHS if at each $x \in \mathcal{X}$, the point evaluation operator $\delta_x : \mathcal{F} \to \mathbb{R}$, which maps $f \in \mathcal{F}$ to $f(x) \in \mathbb{R}$, is a bounded linear functional. To each point $x \in \mathcal{X}$, there corresponds an element $\phi(x) \in \mathcal{F}$ (we call ϕ the *feature map*) such that $\langle \phi(x), \phi(x') \rangle_{\mathcal{F}} = k(x, x')$, where $k : \mathcal{X} \times \mathcal{X} \to \mathbb{R}$ is a unique positive definite kernel. We also define a second RKHS $\mathcal{G}$ with respect to the separable metric space $\mathcal{Y}$, with feature map ψ and kernel $\langle \psi(y), \psi(y') \rangle_{\mathcal{G}} = l(y, y')$. We require

---

1. It turns out that the problem described above is indeterminate in certain respects. For instance, our measure of independence does not change when the ordering of elements in **x** is swapped, or when components of **x** are scaled by different constant amounts. Thus, source recovery takes place up to these invariances.

$\mathcal{F}$ and $\mathcal{G}$ to be universal in the sense of Steinwart (2002), since this is a requirement of theorem 10.6 (which guarantees the criteria we optimize are truly independence measures).

Let $\mathbf{P}_{\mathsf{x},\mathsf{y}}(x,y)$ be a joint measure on $(\mathcal{X} \times \mathcal{Y}, \Gamma \times \Lambda)$ (here Γ and Λ are the Borel σ-algebras on $\mathcal{X}$ and $\mathcal{Y}$, respectively), with associated marginal measures $\mathbf{P}_{\mathsf{x}}$ and $\mathbf{P}_{\mathsf{y}}$ and random variables x and y. The covariance operator $C_{xy} : \mathcal{G} \to \mathcal{F}$ is defined such that for all $f \in \mathcal{F}$ and $g \in \mathcal{G}$,

$$\langle f, C_{xy} g \rangle_{\mathcal{F}} = \mathbf{E}_{\mathsf{x},\mathsf{y}} \left[[f(\mathsf{x}) - \mathbf{E}_{\mathsf{x}} \left[f(\mathsf{x}) \right]] \left[g(\mathsf{y}) - \mathbf{E}_{\mathsf{y}} \left[g(\mathsf{y}) \right] \right] \right].$$

In practice, we do not deal with the measure $\mathbf{P}_{\mathsf{x},\mathsf{y}}$ itself, but instead observe samples drawn independently according to it. We write an i.i.d. sample of size n from $\mathbf{P}_{\mathsf{x},\mathsf{y}}$ as $\boldsymbol{z} = \{(x_1, y_1), \ldots, (x_n, y_n)\}$, and likewise $\boldsymbol{x} := \{x_1, \ldots, x_n\}$ and $\boldsymbol{y} := \{y_1, \ldots y_n\}$. Finally, we define the Gram matrices $\mathbf{K}$ and $\mathbf{L}$ of inner products in $\mathcal{F}$ and $\mathcal{G}$, respectively, between the mapped observations above: here $\mathbf{K}$ has (i,j)th entry $k(x_i, x_j)$ and $\mathbf{L}$ has (i,j)th entry $l(y_i, y_j)$. The Gram matrices for the variables centered in their respective feature spaces are shown by Schölkopf et al. (1998) to be

$$\widetilde{\mathbf{K}} := \mathbf{HKH}, \quad \widetilde{\mathbf{L}} := \mathbf{HLH},$$

where

$$\mathbf{H} = \mathbf{I} - \frac{1}{n} \mathbf{1}_n \mathbf{1}_n^{\top}, \tag{10.3}$$

and $\mathbf{1}_n$ is an $n \times 1$ vector of ones.

10.3.2   Norms of the Covariance Operator

In this section, we introduce two norms of the covariance operator, and show how these may be computed using kernels. First, the COCO (Gretton et al., 2005b).

Definition 10.2 (COCO). *Let $\mathcal{F}, \mathcal{G}$ be universal RKHSs, with F and G their respective unit balls, and $\mathbf{P}_{\mathsf{x},\mathsf{y}}$ be a probability measure. We define the* constrained covariance *as*

$$\text{COCO}(\mathbf{P}_{\mathsf{x},\mathsf{y}}; \mathcal{F}, \mathcal{G}) := \sup_{f \in F, g \in G} \left[\text{cov}(f(\mathsf{x}), g(\mathsf{y})) \right]. \tag{10.4}$$

Note that this is just the spectral norm of the covariance operator $\mathbf{C}_{xy}$.

The next lemma gives an empirical estimate of COCO.

Lemma 10.3 (Value of COCO). *Given n independent observations $\boldsymbol{z} := ((x_1, y_1), \ldots, (x_n, y_n)) \subset (\mathcal{X} \times \mathcal{Y})^n$, the empirical estimate of COCO is*

$$\text{COCO}(\boldsymbol{z}; \mathcal{F}, \mathcal{G}) = \frac{1}{n} \sqrt{\|\widetilde{\mathbf{K}}\widetilde{\mathbf{L}}\|_2}, \tag{10.5}$$

where the matrix norm $\| \cdot \|_2$ denotes the largest singular value. An equivalent unnormalized form is $\mathrm{COCO}(\boldsymbol{z}; F, G) = \max_i \gamma_i$, where γ_i are the solutions to the generalized eigenvalue problem

$$
\begin{bmatrix} \mathbf{0} & \widetilde{\mathbf{K}}\widetilde{\mathbf{L}} \\ \widetilde{\mathbf{L}}\widetilde{\mathbf{K}} & \mathbf{0} \end{bmatrix} \begin{bmatrix} \boldsymbol{\alpha}_i \\ \boldsymbol{\beta}_i \end{bmatrix} = \gamma_i \begin{bmatrix} \widetilde{\mathbf{K}} & \mathbf{0} \\ \mathbf{0} & \widetilde{\mathbf{L}} \end{bmatrix} \begin{bmatrix} \boldsymbol{\alpha}_i \\ \boldsymbol{\beta}_i \end{bmatrix}. \tag{10.6}
$$

Our second independence measure, the HSIC, is defined by Gretton et al. (2005a) as follows.

Definition 10.4 (HSIC). *Given universal RKHSs F, G and a joint measure $\mathbf{P}_{x,y}$ over $(\mathcal{X} \times \mathcal{Y}, \Gamma \times \Lambda)$, we define the* Hilbert-Schmidt independence criterion *as the squared Hilbert-Schmidt norm of the associated cross-covariance operator $\mathbf{C}_{xy}$:*

$$
\mathrm{HSIC}(\mathbf{P}_{x,y}, F, G) := \|\mathbf{C}_{xy}\|_{\mathrm{HS}}^2 \tag{10.7}
$$

To compute an empirical estimate of this norm, we need to express HSIC in terms of kernel functions. This is achieved in the following lemma:

Lemma 10.5 (HSIC in terms of kernels).

$$
\begin{aligned}
\mathrm{HSIC}(\mathbf{P}_{x,y}; F, G) \;:=\; &\mathbf{E}_{x,x',y,y'}\left[k(x,x')l(y,y')\right] + \mathbf{E}_{x,x'}\left[k(x,x')\right]\mathbf{E}_{y,y'}\left[l(y,y')\right] \\
&- 2\mathbf{E}_{x,y}\left[\mathbf{E}_{x'}\left[k(x,x')\right]\mathbf{E}_{y'}\left[l(y,y')\right]\right]
\end{aligned}
$$

Here $\mathbf{E}_{x,x',y,y'}\left[\cdot\right]$ denotes the expectation over pairs x, y and x', y' drawn independently from $\mathbf{P}_{x,y}$. A biased empirical estimate of the squared HSIC is

$$
\mathrm{HSIC}^2(\boldsymbol{z}; F, G) := \frac{1}{n^2}\mathrm{tr}(\mathbf{KHLH}).
$$

The bias in this estimate decreases as $1/n$, and thus drops faster than the variance (which decreases as $1/\sqrt{n}$).

It follows from the above lemma that the Hilbert-Schmidt norm of $\mathbf{C}_{xy}$ exists when the various expectations over the kernels are bounded. As discussed in the previous section, we only require pairwise independence for ICA: thus, we may sum either HSIC or COCO over all pairs of sources to obtain a cost function to minimize when solving for the unmixing matrix $\mathbf{W}$.

The empirical HSIC in lemma 10.5 is well established in the independence testing literature, although its description in terms of covariance operators in RKHSs is more recent. The bivariate criterion was originally proposed by Feuerverger (1993), and a multivariate generalization was established by Kankainen (1995); the original motivation of these statistics was as smoothed divergence measures between the joint characteristic function and the product of the marginal characteristic functions. Kankainen's multivariate independence measure was applied to ICA by A. Chen and Bickel (2005) and Eriksson and Koivunen (2003). The former established the consistency of ICA methods based on Kankainen's measure, and both studies proposed (different) algorithms for its optimization. Chen and Bickel's approach is closest to ours, and is further discussed in section 10.4.5. Kankainen's measure was also applied by Achard et al. (2003) to recovering sources that are first linearly mixed, and then subject to nonlinear distortion.

Note that we have omitted several additional kernel independence measures. The kernel canonical correlation (Bach and Jordan, 2002) is similar to COCO, but represents the regularized spectral norm of the functional correlation operator, rather than the covariance operator. The kernel generalized variance (Bach and Jordan, 2002) and kernel mutual information (Gretton et al., 2005b) were shown by Gretton et al. (2005b) to upper-bound the mutual information near independence (and to be tight at independence). Experiments by Gretton et al. (2005a), however, indicate that these methods do not outperform HSIC in linear ICA for large sample sizes, at least on the benchmark data of Bach and Jordan (2002). That said, it would be interesting to investigate ways to decrease the computational cost of these approaches.

Finally, we give a theorem that combines the results of Gretton et al. (2005a,b), and which justifies using both COCO and HSIC as independence measures.

Theorem 10.6 (COCO/HSIC as independence measures). *Let $\mathcal{F}, \mathcal{G}$ be two RKHSs with universal kernels on the compact metric spaces $\mathcal{X}$ and $\mathcal{Y}$, respectively. Then both* $\mathrm{COCO}(\mathbf{P}_{\mathsf{x},\mathsf{y}}; \mathcal{F}, \mathcal{G}) = 0$ *and* $\mathrm{HSIC}(\mathbf{P}_{\mathsf{x},\mathsf{y}}; \mathcal{F}, \mathcal{G}) = 0$ *if and only if* x *and* y *are independent.*

10.3.3 Gram Matrix Approximation Strategies

Both COCO and HSIC are matrix norms of a product of two centered Gram matrices. We address two main approaches to approximating these matrices. The first is sparsification by random subsampling of the matrix entries, and the second is incomplete Cholesky decomposition.

A simple and efficient approximation of matrix products was suggested by Drineas et al. (2004), based on results by Achlioptas and McSherry (2001): Replace each matrix $\mathbf{A}$ in the product by a sparse approximation $\mathbf{A}'$ with entries a'_{ij}. Assign a probability p_{ij} to each entry a_{ij} and let $a'_{ij} = a_{ij}/p_{ij}$ with probability p_{ij}, otherwise $a'_{ij} = 0$. We use a uniform probability p for all entries. The expected number of nonzero entries for an $n \times n$ matrix is then pn^2. This method is especially effective when the matrices have a strong spectral structure, since the subsampling of entries can be interpreted as adding a matrix with weak spectral structure, which will have little effect on the larger singular values of the original matrix.

Although we do not go into detail here, it is possible to provide theoretical guarantees on the closeness of both COCO and HSIC to their respective approximations (computed with this random sampling approach). Achlioptas and McSherry (2001, theorem 3) provide probabilistic bounds on both the spectral and Frobenius norms of the difference between a matrix and its sparse approximation. Drineas et al. (2004) show how to generalize this result to convergence of the difference between a *product* of two subsampled matrices and the product of the two original matrices. Thus, since COCO is a spectral norm of a matrix product, and HSIC is the

Frobenius norm of this same product, we can use the triangle inequality to obtain probabilistic bounds on the difference between the subsampled COCO and HSIC and their true values, as a function of the fraction of entries retained. Better convergence properties may be obtained by selecting matrix entries nonuniformly, with probability proportional to their size, according to the scheme of Drineas et al. (2004, theorem 4). This would require computation of the entire Gram matrix, however.

The other approach we consider, described by Williams and Seeger (2001), is to generate an index set I of length d having entries chosen without replacement from $\{1, \ldots, n\}$, and to approximate the Gram matrix as

$$\mathbf{K} \approx \mathbf{K}' := \mathbf{K}_{:,I}\mathbf{K}_{I,I}^{-1}\mathbf{K}_{I,:}, \tag{10.8}$$

where $\mathbf{K}_{:,I}$ is the Gram matrix with the rows unchanged, and the columns chosen from the set I; and $\mathbf{K}_{I,I}$ is the $d \times d$ submatrix with both rows and columns restricted to I. The question is then how to choose the subset I. Williams and Seeger (2001) propose to select the subset at random. Smola and Schölkopf (2000) greedily choose a subset of the sample points to minimize either the Frobenius norm of the difference between $\mathbf{K}$ and its approximation $\mathbf{K}'$ from these samples, or $\mathbf{tr}\,(\mathbf{K} - \mathbf{K}')$. The latter approach costs $O(pnd^2)$, where p are the number of sample points examined at each stage of the greedy search (the Frobenius approach is more expensive). Fine and Scheinberg (2001) likewise choose entries that minimize $\mathbf{tr}\,(\mathbf{K} - \mathbf{K}')$. Their incomplete Cholesky algorithm costs $O(nd^2)$: thus, we use this cheaper method.

We remark that Drineas and Mahoney (2005) generalize the approach of Williams and Seeger (2001), proposing a scheme for sampling *with* replacement from the columns of the Gram matrix. Although they provide performance guarantees for any sampling distribution (including the uniform), they find in practice that the sampling probability of a column should be proportional to its length for best performance (Drineas and Mahoney, 2005, theorem 1). They also claim that no performance guarantees are yet established for efficient, nonuniform sampling without replacement (Drineas and Mahoney, 2005, p. 2158). Since computing the column length requires computing the entire Gram matrix for each evaluation of the kernel independence measure, this approach is too expensive for kernel ICA, both in terms of time and in storage.

10.4   Gradient Descent on the Orthogonal Group

When optimizing our kernel dependence measures in ICA, a fundamental building block in the gradient is the derivative of the Gram matrix with respect to the relevant unmixing matrix entries. We provide this gradient in the case of the Gaussian kernel in section 10.4.1. We obtain the derivative of HSIC with respect to $\mathbf{W}$ in section 10.4.2, and its incomplete Cholesky approximation in section 10.4.3;

we then give the COCO derivative and its approximations in section 10.4.4. We show
how to use these free gradients to perform gradient descent on the orthogonal group
in section 10.4.5. Finally, in section 10.4.6, we describe different search strategies
along the direction of steepest descent.

10.4.1   Gradient of the Gram Matrix Entries

We begin by providing the derivative of the Gram matrix entries with respect to
a particular row $\mathbf{w}$ of the unmixing matrix, which we will require in the following
sections. This derivative clearly depends on the particular kernel used. We employ
a Gaussian kernel here, but one could easily obtain the derivatives of alternative
kernels: these can then be plugged straightforwardly into the gradients in the
following sections.

Lemma 10.7 (Derivative of a Gaussian Gram matrix). *Let* $\mathbf{K}$ *be the Gram
matrix computed with a Gaussian kernel, and let* $\mathbf{w}$ *be a* $1 \times m$ *row of the unmixing
matrix, such that*

$$k_{ij} = k(x_i, x_j) = \exp\left[\frac{-1}{2\sigma^2}\mathbf{w}^\top \mathbf{T}_{ij}\mathbf{w}\right],$$

where $\mathbf{T}_{ij} = (\mathbf{t}_i - \mathbf{t}_j)(\mathbf{t}_i - \mathbf{t}_j)^\top$*, and* $\mathbf{t}_i$ *is the ith sample of observations. Then the
derivative of any* k_{ij} *with respect to* $\mathbf{w}$ *is*

$$\frac{\partial k_{ij}}{\partial \mathbf{w}} = -\frac{k_{ij}}{\sigma^2}\mathbf{w}^\top (\mathbf{t}_i - \mathbf{t}_j)(\mathbf{t}_i - \mathbf{t}_j)^\top.$$

Since the above derivative is a vector, we must establish how to write the
derivative of the entire Gram matrix as a single matrix. This is done using the
$\mathrm{vec}(\mathbf{A})$ operation, which stacks the columns of the matrix $\mathbf{A}$ on top of each other.
Thus, the resulting differential is

$$d(\mathrm{vec}\mathbf{K}) = \underbrace{\begin{bmatrix} \partial k_{11}/\partial \mathbf{w} \\ \vdots \\ \partial k_{n1}/\partial \mathbf{w} \\ \partial k_{12}/\partial \mathbf{w} \\ \vdots \\ \partial k_{nn}/\partial \mathbf{w} \end{bmatrix}}_{\partial \mathrm{vec}(\mathbf{K})/\partial \mathbf{w}} d(\mathrm{vec}\,\mathbf{w}), \tag{10.9}$$

where obviously $d(\mathrm{vec}\,\mathbf{w}) = d\mathbf{w}$.

10.4.2   HSIC Gradient and Sparse Approximation

We next give the HSIC derivative. Since HSIC for more than two sources is computed as a sum of pairwise dependencies, we need only express the derivative for a single pair of sources: the aggregate derivative is a sum of multiple such terms.

Theorem 10.8 (Derivative of HSIC^2). *Let* $\mathbf{K}$ *and* $\mathbf{L}$ *be two* $n \times n$ *Gram matrices, corresponding to the respective rows* $\mathbf{w}$ *and* $\mathbf{v}$ *of the unmixing matrix. Then*

$$\frac{\partial \mathrm{tr}(\mathbf{KHLH})}{\partial \begin{bmatrix} \mathbf{w} \\ \mathbf{v} \end{bmatrix}} = \begin{bmatrix} \frac{\partial \mathrm{tr}(\mathbf{KHLH})}{\partial \mathbf{w}} \\ \frac{\partial \mathrm{tr}(\mathbf{KHLH})}{\partial \mathbf{v}} \end{bmatrix},$$

where

$$\frac{\partial \mathrm{tr}(\mathbf{KHLH})}{\partial \mathbf{w}} = (\mathrm{vec}(\mathbf{HLH}))^\top \begin{bmatrix} \frac{\partial k_{11}}{\partial \mathbf{w}} & \cdots & \frac{\partial k_{n1}}{\partial \mathbf{w}} & \frac{\partial k_{21}}{\partial \mathbf{w}} & \cdots & \frac{\partial k_{nn}}{\partial \mathbf{w}} \end{bmatrix}^\top.$$

We now address how this may be efficiently computed when the Gram matrices are sparsely sampled. The products in the gradients not only contain the kernel matrices but also the centered matrices $\widetilde{\mathbf{K}}$ and $\widetilde{\mathbf{L}}$. To again avoid the computation of all entries, we do not want to build sparse approximations from the centered matrices of full rank. Instead, there are two alternatives to approximate $\widetilde{\mathbf{K}}$: (i) center the sparse approximation $\mathbf{K}'$ so that $\widetilde{\mathbf{K}}' = \mathbf{HK}'\mathbf{H}$, or, (ii) approximate $\widetilde{\mathbf{K}}$ by a sparse matrix based on the sparse $\mathbf{K}'$. The expectation of the result of (i) is exactly $\widetilde{\mathbf{K}}$. However, the approximation is no longer sparse if it is explicitly computed. For a sparse approximation of $\widetilde{\mathbf{K}}$, observe that the entries of the full matrix are

$$\tilde{k}_{ij} = k_{ij} - \frac{1}{n} \sum_{q=1}^{n} k_{iq} - \frac{1}{n} \sum_{q=1}^{n} k_{qj} + \frac{1}{n^2} \sum_{q,r=1}^{n} k_{qr}, \tag{10.10}$$

i.e., the original entries of $\mathbf{K}$ minus the row and column means plus the mean of all matrix entries. Let μ_i be the mean of all nonzero elements in row i, μ^j the mean of all nonzero entries in column j, and μ the mean of all nonzero entries of the entire matrix. Then we set

$$\tilde{k}'_{ij} = \begin{cases} 0, & \text{if } k'_{ij} = 0 \\ k'_{ij} - \mu_i - \mu^j + \mu, & \text{otherwise.} \end{cases} \tag{10.11}$$

The row and column means of the resulting matrix will usually not be zero, but the matrix is sparse. With this latter scheme, we only need to compute those $\partial k_{ij}/\partial \mathbf{w}$ in the derivative in theorem 10.8 where both k'_{ij} and l'_{ij} are nonzero. Therefore we use approximate centring for the sparse HSIC derivative. In addition, the partial derivatives of $\mathbf{K}$ can be computed on the fly in the computation of the product, without being stored.

10.4.3   Incomplete Cholesky Approximation of HSIC Gradient

When computing the incomplete Cholesky decomposition so as to approximate the independence measures, we need never explicitly evaluate the matrix inverse in (10.8) (see Fine and Scheinberg, 2001, figure 2). In computing the derivative, however, we must explicitly deal with this inverse. The differential of HSIC^2 is

$$
\begin{aligned}
d\mathbf{tr}\left(\widetilde{\mathbf{K}}'\widetilde{\mathbf{L}}'\right) &= \mathbf{tr}\left(\widetilde{\mathbf{K}}'d(\mathbf{L}')\right) + \mathbf{tr}\left(\widetilde{\mathbf{L}}'d(\mathbf{K}')\right) \\
&= \mathbf{tr}\left(\widetilde{\mathbf{K}}'d(\mathbf{L}')\right) + \mathbf{tr}\left(\widetilde{\mathbf{L}}'d(\mathbf{K}_{:,I}\mathbf{K}_{I,I}^{-1}\mathbf{K}_{I,:})\right) \\
&= \mathbf{tr}\left(\widetilde{\mathbf{K}}'d(\mathbf{L}')\right) + 2\mathrm{vec}(\widetilde{\mathbf{L}}'\mathbf{K}_{:,I}\mathbf{K}_{I,I}^{-1})^{\top}\mathrm{vec}(d\mathbf{K}_{:,I}) \\
&\quad - \mathrm{vec}(\mathbf{K}_{I,I}^{-1}\mathbf{K}_{I,:}\widetilde{\mathbf{L}}'\mathbf{K}_{:,I}\mathbf{K}_{I,I}^{-1})^{\top}\mathrm{vec}(d\mathbf{K}_{I,I})\,, \qquad (10.12)
\end{aligned}
$$

where our expression for $d\mathbf{K}'$ is derived in the appendix of this chapter (we do not expand $d\mathbf{L}'$, but its expression is analogous). The matrix derivative $\partial\mathrm{vec}(\mathbf{K}_{:,I})/\partial\mathrm{vec}(\mathbf{w})$ has size $nd \times m$, and $\partial\mathrm{vec}(\mathbf{K}_{I,I})/\partial\mathrm{vec}(\mathbf{w})$ has size $d^2 \times m$, whereas the original matrix derivative from the differential (10.9) contains $n^2 \times m$ entries. If both kernel matrices are decomposed, (10.12) can be computed without ever taking a product with an $n \times n$ matrix, provided we order the matrix multiplications correctly.

We must also account for the rapid decay of the spectrum of Gram matrices with Gaussian kernels (e.g., Bach and Jordan, 2002, appendix C), since this can cause the inverse of $\mathbf{K}_{I,I}$ to be ill-conditioned. We therefore add a small ridge of 10^{-6} to $\mathbf{K}_{I,I}$, although we emphasize our algorithm is insensitive to this value.

10.4.4   COCO Gradient and Approximations

We now describe how to compute the gradient of COCO. The maximum singular value of a matrix $\mathbf{A}$ is the square root of the maximum eigenvalue of $\mathbf{A}^{\top}\mathbf{A}$. In other words, if we replace COCO by its fourth power (which has the same minimum of zero at independence), we wish to compute

$$
\mathrm{COCO}^4(z;\mathcal{F},\mathcal{G}) = \frac{1}{n^4}\lambda_{\max}\left(\widetilde{\mathbf{K}}\,\widetilde{\mathbf{L}}^2\,\widetilde{\mathbf{K}}\right)\,,
$$

where $\lambda_{\max}$ is the maximum eigenvalue. The differential of this quantity is given in the following theorem, which is proved in appendix 10.B.

Theorem 10.9 (Differential of COCO^4). *Let* $\mathbf{K}$ *and* $\mathbf{L}$ *be two* $n \times n$ *Gram matrices, corresponding to the respective rows* $\mathbf{w}$ *and* $\mathbf{v}$ *of the unmixing matrix. Then*

$$
\begin{aligned}
d\lambda_{\max}\left(\widetilde{\mathbf{K}}\,\widetilde{\mathbf{L}}^2\,\widetilde{\mathbf{K}}\right) &= \mathbf{u}^{\top}\otimes\mathbf{u}^{\top}\left(\left[\left(\widetilde{\mathbf{K}}\,\widetilde{\mathbf{L}}^2\right)\otimes\mathbf{H} + \mathbf{H}\otimes\left(\widetilde{\mathbf{K}}\,\widetilde{\mathbf{L}}^2\right)\right]d\mathrm{vec}\mathbf{K}\right. \\
&\quad \left. + \left[\left(\widetilde{\mathbf{K}}\,\widetilde{\mathbf{L}}\right)\otimes\widetilde{\mathbf{K}} + \widetilde{\mathbf{K}}\otimes\left(\widetilde{\mathbf{K}}\,\widetilde{\mathbf{L}}\right)\right]d\mathrm{vec}\mathbf{L}\right)\,,
\end{aligned}
$$

where $\otimes$ is the Kronecker product,[2] and $\mathbf{u}$ is the eigenvector of $\widetilde{\mathbf{K}}\,\widetilde{\mathbf{L}}^2\,\widetilde{\mathbf{K}}$ associated with $\lambda_{\max}$.

The above expression may be simplified further for efficient computation, giving

$$d\lambda_{\max}\left(\widetilde{\mathbf{K}}\,\widetilde{\mathbf{L}}^2\,\widetilde{\mathbf{K}}\right) = 2\mathbf{u}^\top\mathbf{H}(d\mathbf{L})\widetilde{\mathbf{K}}^2\widetilde{\mathbf{L}}\mathbf{u} + 2\mathbf{u}^\top\widetilde{\mathbf{L}}\widetilde{\mathbf{K}}(d\mathbf{K})\widetilde{\mathbf{L}}\mathbf{u}. \qquad (10.13)$$

Each entry of the above COCO gradient is a sequence of matrix-vector products. Hence we replace the kernel matrices by their sparse counterparts, and implement the multiplication by $\mathbf{H}$ as a centering operation of the vector. In addition, we need the dominant eigenvector for the product of each pair of Gram matrices. We compute this from the sparse matrices as well, so that only sparse matrix multiplications occur. Likewise, to compute the Cholesky approximation of the above gradient, we need only replace $\mathbf{K}$ and $\mathbf{L}$ with their low-rank approximations $\mathbf{K}'$ and $\mathbf{L}'$, and substitute the expressions for $d\mathrm{vec}\mathbf{K}'$ and $d\mathrm{vec}\mathbf{L}'$ from the previous section into (10.13).

10.4.5 Using the Free Gradient to Obtain a Constrained Gradient on the Orthogonal Group

In the previous two sections, we gave expressions for the free gradient of COCO and HSIC with respect to the unmixing matrix $\mathbf{W}$. We now describe how to transform these into gradients on the orthogonal group, i.e. on the manifold described by $m \times m$ matrices $\mathbf{A}$ for which $\mathbf{A}^\top\mathbf{A} = \mathbf{I}$. Gradient descent for functions defined on this manifold is described by Edelman et al. (1998). Let $f(\mathbf{W})$ be the particular dependence functional (COCO or HSIC) on which we wish to do gradient descent. We have expressions for the derivative

$$\mathbf{G} := \frac{\partial f(\mathbf{W})}{\partial \mathbf{W}}.$$

First, we compute the direction of steepest descent *on the manifold* from the free gradient $\mathbf{G}$, which is

$$\Delta_{\max} := \mathbf{G} - \mathbf{W}\mathbf{G}^\top\mathbf{W}.$$

Then, if we use t to parameterize displacement along a geodesic in the direction $\Delta_{\max}$ from an initial matrix $\mathbf{W}(0)$, the resulting $\mathbf{W}(t)$ is given by

$$\mathbf{W}(t) = \mathbf{W}(0)\exp\left(\frac{1}{2}t\mathbf{W}(0)^\top\Delta_{\max}\right),$$

which is a matrix exponential.

---

2. The Kronecker product is a special case of the tensor product for matrices, and, for $\mathbf{A} = (a_{ij})_{ij}$ and $\mathbf{B} = (b_{kl})_{kl}$, is defined in terms of block matrices as $\mathbf{A} \otimes \mathbf{B} = (a_{ij}\mathbf{B})_{ij}$.

Table 10.1   ICA performance for different line searches using the Cholesky-based gradient with 8 sources and 20,000 observations. *Golden search*: Exact line search using golden sections. *Quadratic*: Quadratic approximation of the dependence measure along the gradient. *Fixed (fl)*: Fixed scheme, t_0/j at iteration j. *Fixed (fq)*: Fixed scheme, $1.35^{-j}t_0$. The numbers are averages over 25 runs with artificial sources as described by Bach and Jordan (2002) and Gretton et al. (2005b). The average error at initialization (result from Jade) was 1.24 with a standard error of 0.06. *Eval. total*: Total number of dependence measure evaluations. *Searches*: Number of line searches (iterations). *Eval./search*: Average number of measure evaluations per line search. The fixed schemes lead to the fewest evaluations of the measure but a slightly higher error. The quadratic method is slightly more expensive in terms of measure evaluations but needs fewer iterations, i.e., fewer computations of the gradient. Golden search is most robust but also most time-consuming.

Method	Error	SD	Eval. total	Searches	Eval./search
Golden search	0.58	0.02	214.04	17.92	11.89
Quadratic (ql)	0.58	0.02	44.96	11.16	3.94
Fixed (fl)	0.60	0.02	39.04	20.00	1.90
Fixed (fq)	0.63	0.03	33.84	17.72	1.85

10.4.6   Gradient Descent Techniques

The ICA algorithm is a simple gradient descent procedure based on the code[3] provided by Bach and Jordan (2002). This code determines a good step size in the direction of the projected gradient using a golden search. In experiments, this search technique robustly finds a step width that decreases the independence measures. This robustness, however, comes with a large number of evaluations of the measure per line search (see table 10.1). Two alternatives reduce the number of measure evaluations by more than three fourth with comparable results. Note that displacement is always along the geodesic in the direction of the gradient, parameterized by the step width t.

Our first approach is to approximate the independence measure along the curve by a quadratic polynomial.[4] To do so, it suffices to evaluate the measure at three points t_1, t_2, t_3 on the curve, one of them being the current position. The minimum of the polynomial indicates the estimated best step width in the direction of the gradient. At each iteration, the distance of the t_i from the current solution decreases. This method requires at least three evaluations of the dependence measure, and possibly more if the procedure is repeated due to the polynomial being concave.

---

3. `http://www.cs.berkeley.edu/~fbach/kernel-ica/index.htm`.
4. Our approach differs from Brent's method (Brent, 1973) in that the points used to fit the polynomial are always equally spaced, i.e., we do not perform golden sections. In addition, we move to the minimum of the polynomial even if the resulting displacement is outside the interval defined by the t_i, provided the dependence measure is lower there.

In our second approach, which is even simpler, the step width is decreased by a fixed amount at each iteration. The move by the current step size along the gradient is only made if it actually reduces the dependence measure. This fixed scheme only requires evaluation of the measure at the current position and at the target of the current step. Such a method is the most efficient per iteration, but also the most sensitive with respect to the initial step width and the decrease of the width at each iteration.

Table 10.1 shows example results for the Cholesky-based gradient with golden search, a quadratic approximation of the dependence measure along the gradient, and two fixed schemes: a step width of t_0/j or $(1.35)^{-j}t_0$ at iteration j, with initial width t_0. In the case of golden search, the measure is computed more than 200 times with about 12 evaluations per search, whereas the quadratic approximation only evaluates the measure about 45 times with fewer searches and fewer evaluations per search. The fixed methods yield slightly worse results, but compute the measure least often. Note, however, that they also lead to more searches than the quadratic method and occasionally even the golden search (see figure 10.4). For each search, the gradient is recomputed if there was a move in the previous iteration. More searches may therefore mean more computations of the gradient. In summary, there is a tradeoff between robustness and time, and the quadratic approximation seems to provide a reasonable balance.

Finally, we note another approach to optimization on the orthogonal group by Eriksson and Koivunen (2003), who express $\mathbf{W}$ as a product of Jacobi rotations, solving iteratively for each rotation angle using smoothed approximations of the objective (the smoothing decreases the computational cost compared with a line search over the exact objective). This last method was only tested on small-scale problems, however, and its scaling behavior for larger problems is unclear.

10.5   Complexity Analysis

The unconstrained gradient is an $m \times m$ matrix. Its ith row corresponds to the derivative of the independence measure with respect to the ith row $\mathbf{w}_i$ of $\mathbf{W}$. We express the multiunit independence measure as the sum of pairwise measures between all $\mathbf{w}_i\mathbf{T}$ and $\mathbf{w}_j\mathbf{T}$, where $\mathbf{T}$ is the $m \times n$ matrix of observations. Therefore $m - 1$ pairwise terms of the form in theorem 10.8 contribute to the ith row of the gradient. Once the $m(m - 1)/2 = O(m^2)$ terms are computed, it takes another $O(m^2)$ to sum them up for the complete gradient. We first analyze the complexity for each pairwise term in HSIC, then we proceed to COCO.

The first factor $\widetilde{\mathbf{L}}$ in theorem 10.8 requires $O(n^2)$ time, and each of the n^2 rows of the second factor $O(m)$ time. Since matrix multiplication takes $O(nmk)$ time for an $n \times k$ by $k \times m$ multiplication, the entire term is computed in $O(n^2 + n^2m) = O(n^2m)$ time.

Now replace the kernel matrices by sparse approximations with $z \ll n^2$ nonzero elements each. A sparse first factor $\widetilde{\mathbf{L}}'$ needs $O(z)$ time, the second factor $O(mz)$, totaling in $O(mz)$ for the entire term.

The $\partial\text{vec}(\mathbf{K})/\partial\mathbf{w}_i$–type matrices in the Cholesky-based derivative (10.12) cost $O(nmd)$ if $d \ll n$ columns are retained by the incomplete decomposition. In our implementation, we reuse the Cholesky decomposition from the dependence measure computation for each of the m Gram matrices, which takes $O(nmd^2)$. The remaining terms, including matrix inversion, are computable in $O(nd^2 + d^3)$ time. In sum, this pairwise term is in $O(nmd + nd^2 + d^3)$, or $O(nmd^2 + nd^2 + d^3)$ if the incomplete decomposition is included.

Thus, the complexity for each gradient is cubic in m. If we were to use full Gram matrices, the cost would be quadratic in n. However, the number of nonzero elements z and the number of columns d are much smaller than n. The former does not grow linearly in n, and the latter can be kept almost constant. Therefore the approximations reduce the quadratic cost. In addition, the space complexity of the matrices is reduced from $O(n^2)$ to $O(z)$ and $O(nd)$, and from $O(n^2m)$ to $O(zm)$ and $O(nmd)$ for $\partial\text{vec}(\mathbf{K})/\partial\mathbf{w}_i$.

For the COCO gradient, the complexity of $\partial\text{vec}(\mathbf{K})/\partial\mathbf{w}_i$ is the same as above. Each entry in the pairwise term in theorem 10.9 further requires $O(n^2)$ for full matrices and $O(z + n)$ for sparse matrices, if the product is decomposed as matrix-vector products and $\mathbf{Hu}$ merely centers the vector $\mathbf{u}$. In total, we get $O(n^2m)$ for one pairwise term with full matrices and $O(n^2m^3)$ for the entire gradient. Sparse matrices reduce this cost to $O(m^3z + m^2(z + n)) = O(m^3z + nm^2)$.

The complexity of computing the maximum eigenvalue is more difficult to determine. The power method requires a repeated series of matrix-vector multiplications, but the speed of convergence is a function of the gap between the first and second eigenvalues (Golub and Van Loan, 1996, section 7.3.1). Nevertheless, the complexity of the multiplication in the power method is reduced by replacing the full matrices by sparse approximations.

10.6   Experiments

In this section, we test our method on the datasets described by Gretton et al. (2005b), but with a much larger number of samples and sources. We compare with classical methods suited to medium and larger-scale problems, namely Jade (Cardoso, 1998) and FastICA (Hyvärinen et al., 2001). These also provide starting points for the optimization. Comparisons of kernel ICA with several additional ICA methods are given by Gretton et al. (2005a,b).

We begin in section 10.6.1 with a measure of algorithm performance on ICA, the *Amari divergence* between the inverse of the true mixing matrix and the estimated inverse $\mathbf{W}$. After an outline of the experimental setup in section 10.6.2, we compare our methods in the following sections on 20,000 observations of mixtures of 8 artificial sources, and 20,000 observations of 8 sources representing music from various genres. We also present results for larger-scale data, i.e., 30,000 samples from 16 and 32 artificial sources.

10.6.1 Measurement of Performance

We use the Amari divergence, defined by Amari et al. (1996), as an index of ICA algorithm performance: this is an adaptation and simplification of a criterion proposed earlier by Comon (1994). Note that the properties of this quantity in lemma 10.12 were not described by Amari et al. (1996), but follow from the proof of Comon (1994).

Definition 10.10 (Amari divergence). *Let* **B** *and* **W** *be two* $n \times n$ *matrices, where* **B** *is the mixing matrix and* **W** *the estimated unmixing matrix (these need not be orthogonal here), and let* $\mathbf{D} = \mathbf{WB}$. *Then the Amari divergence between* $\mathbf{B}^{-1}$ *and* **W** *is*

$$\mathcal{D}\left(\mathbf{WB}\right) = \frac{100}{2n(n-1)} \left[\sum_{i=1}^{n} \left(\frac{\sum_{j=1}^{n} |d_{ij}|}{\max_j |d_{ij}|} - 1 \right) + \sum_{j=1}^{n} \left(\frac{\sum_{i=1}^{n} |d_{ij}|}{\max_i |d_{ij}|} - 1 \right) \right].$$

Although this measure is not a distance metric for general matrices $\mathbf{B}^{-1}$ and **W**, it nonetheless possesses certain useful properties, as shown below.

Lemma 10.11. $0 \leq \mathcal{D}\left(\mathbf{WB}\right) \leq 100$.

Note that Amari et al. (1996) define the Amari divergence on $[0, 1]$. Since the divergence was generally small in our experiments, we scaled it by a factor 100 to make the tables more readable.

Lemma 10.12. *Let* **P** *be an arbitrary permutation matrix (a matrix with a single 1 in each row and column, and with remaining entries 0), and* **S** *be a diagonal matrix of nonzero scaling factors. Then* $\mathbf{W} = \mathbf{B}^{-1}$ *if and only if* $\mathcal{D}\left(\mathbf{WB}\right) = 0$, *or equivalently* $\mathcal{D}\left(\mathbf{WBSP}\right) = 0$ *or* $\mathcal{D}\left(\mathbf{SPWB}\right) = 0$.

The above lemma is particularly useful in the context of ICA, since it causes our performance measure to be invariant to output ordering ambiguity once the sources have been demixed.

10.6.2 Experimental Setup

We replace the gradient and line search of Bach and Jordan (2002) with our gradients and line search methods. We do not apply the polishing step described by Bach and Jordan (2002) and Gretton et al. (2005b).

In all experiments, the data is generated as follows. The m sources are chosen randomly from a particular data pool (artificial or music), and n samples are generated according to each of the m distributions. The $m \times n$ data matrix is multiplied by a random mixing matrix **B** with condition number between one and two, and the resulting mixed data is then whitened. We initialize our algorithm using Jade for 8 sources, and FastICA for 16 and 32 sources. If not stated otherwise, the experiments are repeated 25 times.

All experiments employ the Gaussian kernel

$$k(x, x') = \frac{1}{\sqrt{2\pi}\sigma} \exp\left(-\frac{\|x - x'\|^2}{2\sigma^2}\right),$$ (10.14)

with a width $\sigma = 0.5$. To stabilize the inversion of $\mathbf{K}_{I,I}$ for the Cholesky-based gradient, we add a ridge of 10^{-6}. The precision for the incomplete Cholesky decomposition is set to ηn, where n is the number of samples. For the artificial sources, we set $\eta = 10^{-4}$, and for the music signals, $\eta = 10^{-6}$. The sparse matrices have an expected percentage of 0.35% nonzero entries.

We test ICA both with HSIC and COCO, and different gradients and line search methods. The gradients we test are

- HSIC with sparse kernel matrices,
- HSIC with the Cholesky-based gradient, and
- COCO with sparse kernel matrices.

For the COCO gradient, we investigate two variations: (i) using the eigenvector as in theorem 10.9, and (ii) replacing the eigenvector by a random vector. The latter saves the computation of the eigenvector, which is otherwise based on the sparse matrices (we will comment further on the consequences of this heuristic in practice). We combine these gradients with the following line search methods:

- (g) golden search,
- (ql) quadratic approximation of the dependence measure along the gradient, where at iteration j the measure is evaluated at three points that are t_0/j apart,
- (qq) quadratic approximation of the dependence measure along the gradient, where at iteration j the measure is evaluated at three points that are $2^{-j}t_0$ apart,
- (fl) fixed decay of the step width: t_0/j for iteration j,
- (fq) fixed decay of the step width: $(1.35)^{-j}t_0$ for iteration j,
- (fq2) fixed decay of the step width: $(1.1)^{-j}t_0$ for iteration j,

where t_0 is the initial step size. For the first 38 iterations, the step size is greater with (fq2) than with (fl). In the experiments presented below, there are usually less than 20 iterations. Table 10.2 summarizes the abbreviations used in the plots and tables.

10.6.3 General Mixtures of Artificial Data

We first explore performance for a collection of 18 source distributions used by Bach and Jordan (2002) and Gretton et al. (2005b). These distributions include

Table 10.2   Abbreviations for the gradients and line search methods for the tables and figures.

Gradient	
HC	HSIC, Cholesky-based (section 10.4.3)
HS	HSIC with sparse approximations (section 10.4.2)
CS	COCO with sparse approximations (section 10.4.4)
CR	COCO with sparse approximations, eigenvector $\mathbf{u}$ replaced by a random unit vector

Line Search	
g	Golden search
ql	Quadratic approximation of the dependence measure along the gradient, measure evaluated at points of distance t_0/j at iteration j with initial step size t_0
qq	Quadratic approximation of the dependence measure along the gradient, measure evaluated at points of distance $2^{-j}t_0$ at iteration j with initial step size t_0
fl	Fixed scheme: at iteration j, move t_0/j along the gradient if it improves the dependence measure
fq	Fixed scheme: at iteration j, move $(1.35)^{-j}t_0$ along the gradient if it improves the dependence measure
fq2	Fixed scheme: at iteration j, move $(1.1)^{-j}t_0$ along the gradient if it improves the dependence measure

sub- and super-Gaussian sources, near-Gaussian distributions, and both uni- and multimodal distributions.

Table 10.3 and figure 10.1 show results for 8 sources and 20,000 samples. Each gradient is combined with a line search: golden search, a quadratic approximation scheme, or a fixed scheme of step decay. We summarize the average computational cost of the various methods in figure 10.2. The measurements were repeated five times for each of 25 mixtures from the artificial sources, on cluster nodes with 64 bit Opteron CPUs running Debian/GNU Linux 3.1. Our experiments led to the following conclusions:

- The best combination of performance and cost is attained by HSIC with a Cholesky approximation and quadratic interpolation. More generally, for both HSIC and COCO, the performance of quadratic interpolation is very similar to golden search, but the cost of the former is significantly lower.

- The sparse and Cholesky HSIC approximations have a similar cost, but the Cholesky approximation performs better.

- Sparse quadratic COCO with a random vector replacing the eigenvector performs remarkably well, with similar Amari error to sparse quadratic HSIC but significantly lower cost. In general, the random vector is better than the real eigenvector, since this appears to decrease the number of critical points (with zero derivative) that arise due to the inherent difficulty in sparsely approximating a matrix with small spectrum, while retaining the minimum at independence. It even outperforms the original method of Gretton et al. (2005b), which uses an incomplete Cholesky approximation and computes the gradient via finite differences. This sparse COCO approach might be worth pursuing for very large-scale problems, where incomplete Cholesky is no longer feasible.

■ Although they are cheap, methods using fixed step widths give mixed performance when HSIC is the dependence measure, doing well with Cholesky, but poorly with random sampling. These methods are also hard to tune, being sensitive to the initial step width choice (see section 10.6.5). We were not able to obtain useful results using fixed step widths with sparse COCO.

Our methods also scale up to larger datasets. Table 10.4 shows results for 30,000 samples from 16 and 32 sources. We use FastICA with the kurtosis-based nonlinearity (similar to Jade) instead of Jade for initialization. The results demonstrate the Amari error at initialization can be halved.

10.6.4   Number of Iterations and Dependence Measure Evaluations

We now give a more detailed breakdown of the behavior of the various gradient descent procedures, as it contributes to their overall computational cost. Figure 10.3 illustrates the total number of dependence measure evaluations and iterations of the gradient descent for the results in table 10.3 and figure 10.1. Golden search is robust, but requires significantly more evaluations of the dependence measure. Performance is similar with a quadratic interpolation, but the latter computes the measure far less often. With fixed decay schemes, the measure is evaluated even fewer times.

During most iterations, we recompute the gradient, so the average number of iterations indicates how often the gradient is evaluated. Golden search is again more expensive than a quadratic approximation, except when COCO with a random vector replacing the eigenvector is used. The fixed schemes lead to more iterations than the other searches with the Cholesky-based gradient, but fewer with the sparse gradients. That said, sparse methods work poorly, or not at all, with fixed schemes.

10.6.5   Sensitivity to Step Sizes

Each line search method is initialized with a certain step size to start with. Figure 10.4 shows the sensitivity of the various methods with the Cholesky-based HSIC gradient, for initial step widths from 100 to 0.01. The results with golden search are consistent over the entire range of initial widths, because of the expensive search at each iteration. The quadratic approximation is fairly robust, except for the large start width of 100. Fixed decay schemes, on the other hand, leave little

Table 10.3 ICA performance (mean Amari error for 25 runs) for 8 sources and 20,000 observations with sparse and Cholesky-based gradients and various line searches (see table 10.2 for the abbreviations). The sparsity of the approximating kernel matrices is 0.35% and the mean error of the initialization is 1.24 ± 0.06. The Cholesky-based gradient leads to the best overall results with the lowest variance. The fixed-step approach did not work for sparse COCO.

Gradient	g	ql	qq	fl	fq	fq2
HC	0.58 ± 0.02	0.58 ± 0.02	0.59 ± 0.02	0.60 ± 0.02	0.63 ± 0.03	0.66 ± 0.04
HS	0.72 ± 0.02	0.72 ± 0.02	0.78 ± 0.02	1.21 ± 0.06	1.14 ± 0.06	1.14 ± 0.06
CS	1.17 ± 0.06	1.17 ± 0.06	1.19 ± 0.06	—	—	—
CR	0.74 ± 0.03	0.77 ± 0.03	0.72 ± 0.03	—	—	—

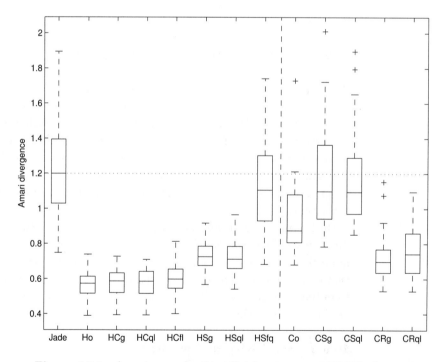

Figure 10.1 Amari error for 8 artificial sources and 20,000 observations for the sparse and Cholesky-based gradients (25 runs). For HSIC, we show the performance with golden search, one quadratic interpolation method, and one fixed decay scheme; for COCO, we display the golden and quadratic approaches. Jade was used to initialize the search. "Ho" and "Co" denote the original HSIC and COCO algorithms, respectively (golden search, gradients computed by finite differences).

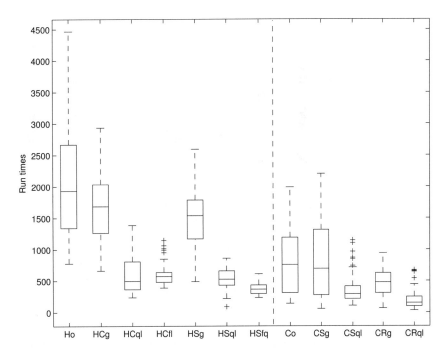

Figure 10.2 Running times for 8 sources and 20,000 observations of artificial data. The number of iterations and dependence measure evaluations are reflected in the times: golden search is usually the slowest method for a given gradient. "Ho" and "Co" refer to the original algorithms, with gradients computed via finite differences over all possible Jacobi rotations. The approximated analytic gradients compare favorably to the original method.

Table 10.4 Results for larger scale kernel ICA: Cholesky-based HSIC gradient with a quadratic approximation of the dependence measure along the gradient to find a suitable step width. The algorithm was initialized with the result of FastICA. The last two columns show the average number of iterations of the gradient descent and the average number of times the dependence measure was computed.

m	n	FastICA	HCql	Iterations	Dep. meas. eval.
16	30,000	1.12 ± 0.05	0.52 ± 0.02	18.47	74.84
32	30,000	1.10 ± 0.02	0.54 ± 0.01	20.00	80.64

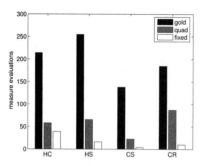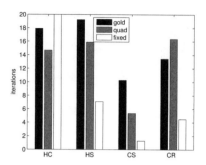

Figure 10.3   Average number of dependence measure evaluations (left) and iterations of the gradient descent (right) for the experiments in table 10.3 and figure 10.1. Golden search leads to the most computations of the dependence measure for all gradients, and the fixed decay schemes are the cheapest in this respect. Results are mixed in the case of the total number of gradient descent steps taken: there is generally little difference between the golden and quadratic algorithms, while the fixed step size requires fewer iterations in three of four cases.

freedom to adapt the step width and thus depend on a good initialization. The quadratic approximation may be a reasonable balance between good performance and parameter tuning.

10.6.6   Audio Signal Demixing

The second type of data we investigate is brief extracts from various music genres chosen and collected by Pearlmutter.[5] The music clips consist of 5 second segments, sampled at 11 kHz with a precision of 8 bits. Adjacent samples of the audio signals are certainly not independent, but ICA algorithms have still succeeded in demixing such signals. As in (Gretton et al., 2005b), the signals are randomly permuted to reduce the statistical dependence of adjacent samples.

Figure 10.5 displays results with the Cholesky-based HSIC gradient and all our line searches. We only present the best result over the variation of initial step widths. In this case, the simpler search methods lead to even better results than golden search. With the quadratic approximation, the slower decrease of the interval between the test points along the gradient (HCql) yields better results than the faster shrinking (HCqq). Likewise, the slowest converging step width decay (HCfq2) decreases the error more than the other fixed schemes. Slower convergence means more iterations in the fixed schemes. This is not true of the quadratic approximation, however, because the step width is only indirectly influenced by the shrinking: HCqq performed 10.24 iterations on average, whereas HCql only needed an average of 4.80 iterations.

---

5. http://www.bcl.hamilton.ie/ bap/demos.html.

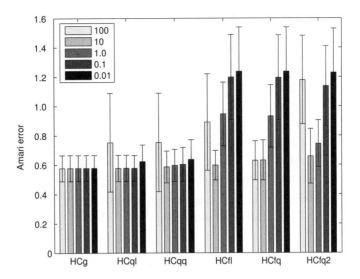

Figure 10.4 Influence of the initial step width on ICA performance for the Cholesky-based HSIC gradient (8 sources, 20,000 observations of artificial data). Golden search (HCg) is most robust with respect to the initial step size, and the quadratic approximation (HCql, HCqq) is fairly robust within a certain range. The fixed schemes of step decay (HCfl, HCfq, HCfq2) are most sensitive to step width, and may require parameter tuning. The data is averaged over 25 runs, and the error bars represent the standard deviation.

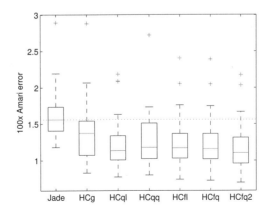

Figure 10.5 Amari error for the Cholesky-based HSIC gradient with audio signals (8 sources, 20,000 samples).

10.7   Conclusions and Future Directions

We have shown that kernel ICA may be applied to large-scale problems (up to 32 sources and 30,000 samples in our experiments), using a variety of techniques that substantially reduce its computational cost. These include the following:

▪ Efficient approximations of the independence measures and their derivatives, using both sparse approximations of the Gram matrices and incomplete Cholesky decomposition of these matrices. Prior approaches to computing the derivatives in kernel ICA were especially expensive, scaling as $O(m^4)$ (where m is the number of sources); our methods are $O(m^3)$.

▪ Better search strategies along the direction of descent, which require far fewer independence measure evaluations than the golden search used in previous implementations.

As an interesting consequence of our experiments, we observe that the Cholesky approximation performs better than sparsely sampling the matrix entries (at similar computational cost). Thus, while sparse approximation may be the only feasible option for yet larger-scale problems ($> 10^6$ samples), the greedy approximation strategy implemented via the Cholesky approach is to be preferred on the sample sizes we investigated.

A number of additional strategies exist to further reduce the cost and improve performance of kernel ICA. One could combine the approximated gradients with a rapid stochastic gradient descent algorithm, such as stochastic metadescent (SMD) by Vishwanathan et al. (2006). This should further speed convergence, since SMD includes information about the curvature. In addition, the linear cost per iteration makes SMD particularly applicable to large datasets.

Geometric optimization on the orthogonal group may also improve the algorithm. Recently, an approximate Newton-like method has successfully been applied to one-unit nonparametric ICA (H. Shen et al., 2006). The similar, fully parallelized method on the orthogonal group applies to multiunit ICA (H. Shen and Hüper, 2006b). The extension of these Newton-like geometric methods to multiunit kernel ICA is therefore of interest.

Acknowledgments

We thank Francis Bach and Aiyou Chen for providing us with their ICA implementations; Dimitris Achlioptas and Matthias Seeger for helpful discussions regarding sparse and low rank matrix approximation; and Christian Walder for providing us with his sparse matrix multiplication code.

Appendix

10.A   Differential of the Incomplete Cholesky Approximation to HSIC

In this appendix, we obtain the differential of the incomplete Cholesky approximation to HSIC^2 described in section 10.4.3. Recall that the differential of this low-rank approximation is

$$d\mathbf{tr}\left(\widetilde{\mathbf{K}}'\widetilde{\mathbf{L}}'\right) = \mathbf{tr}\left(\widetilde{\mathbf{K}}'d(\mathbf{L}')\right) + \mathbf{tr}\left(\widetilde{\mathbf{L}}'d(\mathbf{K}')\right). \tag{10.15}$$

The differential of $\mathbf{K}' = \mathbf{K}_{:,I}\mathbf{K}_{I,I}^{-1}\mathbf{K}_{I,:}$ is

$$d\mathbf{K}' = d(\mathbf{K}_{:,I})\mathbf{K}_{I,I}^{-1}\mathbf{K}_{I,:} - \mathbf{K}_{:,I}\mathbf{K}_{I,I}^{-1}(d\mathbf{K}_{I,I})\mathbf{K}_{I,I}^{-1}\mathbf{K}_{I,:} + \mathbf{K}_{:,I}\mathbf{K}_{I,I}^{-1}d(\mathbf{K}_{I,:}). \tag{10.16}$$

Making this replacement in the second term $\mathbf{tr}\left(\widetilde{\mathbf{L}}'d(\mathbf{K}')\right)$ from (10.15) yields

$$
\begin{aligned}
&\mathbf{tr}\left(\widetilde{\mathbf{L}}'d(\mathbf{K}')\right)\\
&= \mathbf{tr}\left(\widetilde{\mathbf{L}}'d\mathbf{K}_{:,I}\mathbf{K}_{I,I}^{-1}\mathbf{K}_{I,:}\right) - \mathbf{tr}\left(\widetilde{\mathbf{L}}'\mathbf{K}_{:,I}\mathbf{K}_{I,I}^{-1}(d\mathbf{K}_{I,I})\mathbf{K}_{I,I}^{-1}\mathbf{K}_{I,:}\right) + \mathbf{tr}\left(\widetilde{\mathbf{L}}'\mathbf{K}_{:,I}\mathbf{K}_{I,I}^{-1}d\mathbf{K}_{I,:}\right)\\
&= \mathbf{tr}\left(\widetilde{\mathbf{L}}'d\mathbf{K}_{:,I}\mathbf{K}_{I,I}^{-1}\mathbf{K}_{I,:}\right) - \mathbf{tr}\left(\widetilde{\mathbf{L}}'\mathbf{K}_{:,I}\mathbf{K}_{I,I}^{-1}(d\mathbf{K}_{I,I})\mathbf{K}_{I,I}^{-1}\mathbf{K}_{I,:}\right)\\
&\quad + \mathbf{tr}\left((d\mathbf{K}_{:,I}\mathbf{K}_{I,I}^{-1}\mathbf{K}_{I,:})^{\top}\widetilde{\mathbf{L}}'^{\top}\right)\\
&= \mathbf{tr}\left(\widetilde{\mathbf{L}}'d\mathbf{K}_{:,I}\mathbf{K}_{I,I}^{-1}\mathbf{K}_{I,:}\right) - \mathbf{tr}\left(\widetilde{\mathbf{L}}'\mathbf{K}_{:,I}\mathbf{K}_{I,I}^{-1}(d\mathbf{K}_{I,I})\mathbf{K}_{I,I}^{-1}\mathbf{K}_{I,:}\right) + \mathbf{tr}\left(\widetilde{\mathbf{L}}'d\mathbf{K}_{:,I}\mathbf{K}_{I,I}^{-1}\mathbf{K}_{I,:}\right)\\
&= 2\,\mathbf{tr}\left(\mathbf{K}_{I,I}^{-1}\mathbf{K}_{I,:}\widetilde{\mathbf{L}}'d\mathbf{K}_{:,I}\right) - \mathbf{tr}\left(\mathbf{K}_{I,I}^{-1}\mathbf{K}_{I,:}\widetilde{\mathbf{L}}'\mathbf{K}_{:,I}\mathbf{K}_{I,I}^{-1}d\mathbf{K}_{I,I}\right)\\
&= 2\,\mathrm{vec}(\widetilde{\mathbf{L}}'\mathbf{K}_{:,I}\mathbf{K}_{I,I}^{-1})^{\top}\mathrm{vec}(d\mathbf{K}_{:,I}) - \mathrm{vec}(\mathbf{K}_{I,I}^{-1}\mathbf{K}_{I,:}\widetilde{\mathbf{L}}'\mathbf{K}_{:,I}\mathbf{K}_{I,I}^{-1})^{\top}\mathrm{vec}(d\mathbf{K}_{I,I}),
\end{aligned}
$$

where we make use of the symmetry of the Gram matrices. The other term $\mathbf{tr}\left(\widetilde{\mathbf{K}}'d(\mathbf{L}')\right)$ in (10.15) is equivalent.

10.B   Differential of COCO

In this appendix, we obtain the differential of COCO^4 in theorem 10.9 with respect to two rows of the demixing matrix $\mathbf{W}$. We again use the formalism of Magnus and Neudecker (1999, p. 175): if $\mathbf{F}(\mathbf{X})$ is a matrix function of the matrix $\mathbf{X}$, then

$$d\mathrm{vec}\mathbf{F}(\mathbf{X}) = (\mathrm{D}\mathbf{F}(\mathbf{X}))d\mathrm{vec}\mathbf{X},$$

where $\mathrm{D}\mathbf{F}(\mathbf{X})$ is the matrix of derivatives. We also need the result of Magnus and Neudecker (1999, p. 180): if λ is an eigenvalue of a symmetric, real-valued matrix $\mathbf{A}$ with associated eigenvector $\mathbf{u}$, then

$$
\begin{aligned}
\mathrm{D}\lambda(\mathbf{A}) &= \frac{\partial\lambda}{\partial(\mathrm{vec}\mathbf{A})^{\top}}\\
&= \mathbf{u}^{\top}\otimes\mathbf{u}^{\top},
\end{aligned}
$$

where $\otimes$ is the Kronecker product. Finally, using

$$\mathrm{vec}(\mathbf{ABC}) = (\mathbf{C}^\top \otimes \mathbf{A})\mathrm{vec}\mathbf{B},$$

we compute the differential:

$$
\begin{aligned}
d\mathrm{vec}\lambda_{\max}&\left(\widetilde{\mathbf{K}}\,\widetilde{\mathbf{L}}^2\,\widetilde{\mathbf{K}}\right)\\
&= d\lambda_{\max}\left(\widetilde{\mathbf{K}}\,\widetilde{\mathbf{L}}^2\,\widetilde{\mathbf{K}}\right)\\
&= \frac{\partial}{\partial\mathrm{vec}\mathbf{A}}\,\lambda_{\max}(\mathbf{A})\big|_{\mathbf{A}=\widetilde{\mathbf{K}}\,\widetilde{\mathbf{L}}^2\,\widetilde{\mathbf{K}}}\,d\mathrm{vec}(\widetilde{\mathbf{K}}\,\widetilde{\mathbf{L}}^2\,\widetilde{\mathbf{K}})\\
&= \mathbf{u}^\top \otimes \mathbf{u}^\top \mathrm{vec}\left[\mathbf{H}\,(d\mathbf{K})\,\mathbf{H}\widetilde{\mathbf{L}}^2\,\widetilde{\mathbf{K}} + \widetilde{\mathbf{K}}\,\mathbf{H}\,(d\mathbf{L})\,\mathbf{H}\widetilde{\mathbf{L}}\,\widetilde{\mathbf{K}}\right.\\
&\qquad\qquad\qquad \left. + \widetilde{\mathbf{K}}\,\widetilde{\mathbf{L}}\mathbf{H}\,(d\mathbf{L})\,\mathbf{H}\,\widetilde{\mathbf{K}} + \widetilde{\mathbf{K}}\,\widetilde{\mathbf{L}}^2\mathbf{H}\,(d\mathbf{K})\,\mathbf{H}\right]\\
&= \mathbf{u}^\top \otimes \mathbf{u}^\top \left(\left[\left(\widetilde{\mathbf{K}}\,\widetilde{\mathbf{L}}^2\right)\otimes\mathbf{H} + \mathbf{H}\otimes\left(\widetilde{\mathbf{K}}\,\widetilde{\mathbf{L}}^2\right)\right]d\mathrm{vec}\mathbf{K}\right.\\
&\qquad\qquad\ \left. + \left[\left(\widetilde{\mathbf{K}}\,\widetilde{\mathbf{L}}\right)\otimes\widetilde{\mathbf{K}} + \widetilde{\mathbf{K}}\otimes\left(\widetilde{\mathbf{K}}\,\widetilde{\mathbf{L}}\right)\right]d\mathrm{vec}\mathbf{L}\right),
\end{aligned}
$$

where we use $\mathbf{H} = \mathbf{HH}$ to absorb the extra centering matrices.

11 Building SVMs with Reduced Classifier Complexity

S. Sathiya Keerthi
Olivier Chapelle
Dennis DeCoste

Support vector machines (SVMs), though accurate, are not preferred in applications requiring great classification speed, due to the number of support vectors being large. To overcome this problem we devise a primal method with the following properties: (i) it decouples the idea of basis functions from the concept of support vectors; (ii) it greedily finds a set of kernel basis functions of a specified maximum size ($d_{\max}$) to approximate the SVM primal cost function well; (iii) it is efficient and roughly scales as $O(nd_{\max}^2)$ where n is the number of training examples; and (iv) the number of basis functions it requires to achieve an accuracy close to the SVM accuracy is usually far less than the number of SVM support vectors.

11.1 Introduction

Support vector machines (SVMs) are modern learning systems that deliver state-of-the-art performance in real-world pattern recognition and data-mining applications such as text categorization, handwritten character recognition, image classification, and bioinformatics. Even though they yield very accurate solutions, they are not preferred in online applications where classification has to be done with great speed. This is due to the fact that a large set of basis functions is usually needed to form the SVM classifier, making it complex and expensive. In this chapter we devise a method to overcome this problem. Our method incrementally finds basis functions to maximize accuracy. The process of adding new basis functions can be stopped when the classifier has reached some limiting level of complexity. In many cases, our method efficiently forms classifiers which have an order-of-magnitude smaller number of basis functions compared to the full SVM, while achieving nearly the same level of accuracy.

11.1.1   SVM Solution and Postprocessing Simplification

Given a training set $\{(x_i, y_i)\}_{i=1}^n$, $y_i \in \{1, -1\}$, the SVM algorithm with an L_2 penalization of the training errors consists of solving the following primal problem:

$$\min \frac{\lambda}{2} \|w\|^2 + \frac{1}{2} \sum_{i=1}^n \max(0, 1 - y_i w \cdot \phi(x_i))^2 \ . \tag{11.1}$$

Computations involving ϕ are handled using the kernel function, $k(x_i, x_j) = \phi(x_i) \cdot \phi(x_j)$. For convenience the bias term has not been included, but the analysis presented in this chapter can be extended in a straightforward way to include it. The quadratic penalization of the errors makes the primal objective function continuously differentiable. This is a great advantage and becomes necessary for developing a primal algorithm, as we will see below.

The standard way to train an SVM is to introduce Lagrange multipliers α_i and optimize them by solving a dual problem. The classifier function for a new input x is then given by the sign of $\sum_i \alpha_i y_i k(x, x_i)$. Because there is a flat part in the loss function, the vector α is usually sparse. The x_i for which $\alpha_i \neq 0$ are called *support vectors*. Let n_{sv} denote the number of support vectors for a given problem. A recent theoretical result by Steinwart (2004) shows that n_{sv} grows as a linear function of n. Thus, for large problems, this number can be large and the training and testing complexities might become prohibitive since they are, respectively, $O(n\, n_{\mathrm{sv}} + n_{\mathrm{sv}}{}^3)$ and $O(n_{\mathrm{sv}})$.

Several methods have been proposed for reducing the number of support vectors. Burges and Schölkopf (1997) apply nonlinear optimization methods to seek sparse representations after building the SVM classifier. Along similar lines, Schölkopf et al. (1999b) use L_1 regularization on β to obtain sparse approximations. Downs et al. (2001) give an exact algorithm to prune the support vector set after the SVM classifier is built. Thies and Weber (2004) give special ideas for the quadratic kernel. Since these methods operate as a postprocessing step, an expensive standard SVM training is still required.

11.1.2   Direct Simplification via Basis Functions and Primal

Instead of finding the SVM solution by maximizing the dual problem, one approach is to *directly minimize the primal form* after invoking the representer theorem to represent w as

$$w = \sum_{i=1}^n \beta_i \phi(x_i) \ . \tag{11.2}$$

If we substitute (11.2) in (11.1) and solve for the β_i's, then (assuming uniqueness of solution) we will get $\beta_i = y_i \alpha_i$ and thus we will precisely retrieve the SVM solution (see chapter 2). But our aim is to obtain approximate solutions that have as few nonzero β_i's as possible. For many classification problems there exists a small subset of the basis functions[1] suited to the complexity of the problem being solved, irrespective of the training size growth, that will yield pretty much the same accuracy as the SVM classifier. The evidence for this comes from the empirical performance of other sparse kernel classifiers: the relevance vector machine (Tipping, 2001) and the informative vector machine (Lawrence et al., 2003) are probabilistic models in a Bayesian setting; and kernel matching pursuit (KMP) (Vincent and Bengio, 2002) is a discriminative method that is mainly developed for the least-squares loss function. These recent non-SVM works have laid the claim that they can match the accuracy of SVMs, while also bringing down considerably the number of basis functions as well as the training cost. Work on simplifying the SVM solution has not caught up well with those works in related kernel fields. The method outlined in this chapter makes a contribution to fill this gap.

We deliberately use the variable name β_i in (11.2) so as to interpret it as a basis weight as opposed to viewing it as $y_i\alpha_i$ where α_i is the Lagrange multiplier associated with the ith primal slack constraint. While the two are (usually) one and the same at exact optimality, they can be very different when we talk of suboptimal primal solutions. There is a lot of freedom when we simply think of the β_i's as basis weights that yield a good suboptimal w for (11.1). First, we do not have to put any bounds on the β_i. Second, we do not have to think of a β_i corresponding to a particular location relative to the margin planes to have a certain value. Going even one step further, we do not even have to restrict the basis functions to be a subset of the training set examples.

Osuna and Girosi (1998) consider such an approach. They achieve sparsity by including the L_1 regularizer $\lambda_1\|\beta\|_1$ in the primal objective. But they do not develop an algorithm (for solving the modified primal formulation and for choosing the right λ_1) that scales efficiently to large problems.

Wu et al. (2005) write w as

$$w = \sum_{i=1}^{l} \beta_i\phi(\tilde{x}_i) \ ,$$

where l is a chosen small number and optimize the primal objective with the β_i as well as the $\tilde{x}_i$ as variables. But the optimization can become unwieldy if l is not small, especially since the optimization of the $\tilde{x}_i$ is a hard nonconvex problem.

In the reduced support vector machine (RSVM) algorithm (Y.-J. Lee and Mangasarian, 2001a; K.-M. Lin and Lin, 2003), a random subset of the training set is chosen to be the $\tilde{x}_i$ and then only the β_i are optimized.[2] Because basis functions are chosen randomly, this method requires many more basis functions than needed in order to achieve a level of accuracy close to the full SVM solution; see section 11.3.

An alternative to RSVM is to use a greedy approach for the selection of the

1. Each $k(x, x_i)$ will be referred to as a basis function.
2. For convenience, in the RSVM method, the SVM regularizer is replaced by a simple L_2 regularizer on β.

subset of the training set for forming the representation. Such an approach has been popular in Gaussian processes (Smola and Bartlett, 2001; Seeger et al., 2003; Keerthi and Chu, 2006a). Greedy methods of basis selection also exist in the boosting literature (J. H. Friedman, 2001; Rätsch, 2001). These methods entail selection from a continuum of basis functions using either gradient descent or linear programming column generation. Bennett et al. (2002) and Bi et al. (2004) give modified ideas for kernel methods that employ a set of basis functions fixed at the training points.

Particularly relevant to the work in this chapter are the KMP algorithm of Vincent and Bengio (2002) and the growing support vector classifier (GSVC) algorithm of Parrado-Hernández et al. (2003). KMP is an effective greedy discriminative approach that is mainly developed for least-squares problems. GSVC is an efficient method that is developed for SVMs and uses a heuristic criterion for greedy selection of basis functions.

11.1.3   Our Approach

The main aim of this chapter is to give an effective greedy method for SVMs which uses a basis selection criterion that is directly related to the training cost function and is also very efficient. The basic theme of the method is forward selection. It starts with an empty set of basis functions and greedily chooses new basis functions (from the training set) to improve the primal objective function. We develop efficient schemes for both, the greedy selection of a new basis function, as well as the optimization of the β_i for a given selection of basis functions. For choosing up to $d_{\max}$ basis functions, the overall compuational cost of our method is $O(nd_{\max}^2)$. The different components of the method that we develop in this chapter are not new in themselves and are inspired by the above-mentioned papers. However, from a practical point of view, it is not obvious how to combine and tune them in order to get a very efficient SVM training algorithm. That is what we achieved through numerous and careful experiments that validated the techniques employed.

Table 11.1 gives a preview of the performance of our method (called SpSVM-2 in the table) in comparison with SVM on several UCI (University of California, Irvine) datasets. As can be seen there, our method gives a competing generalization performance while reducing the number of basis functions very significantly. (More specifics concerning table 11.1 will be discussed in section 11.4.)

The paper is organized as follows. We discuss the details of the efficient optimization of the primal objective function in section 11.2. The key issue of selecting basis functions is taken up in section 11.3. Sections 11.4 to 11.7 discuss other important practical issues and give computational results that demonstrate the value of our method. Section 11.8 gives some concluding remarks. The appendix gives details of all the datasets used for the experiments in this paper.

Table 11.1   Comparison of SpSVM-2 and SVM on the benchmark datasets (`http://ida.first.fraunhofer.de/~raetsch/`). For TestErate, #Basis, and n_{sv}, the values are means over ten different training/test splits and the values in parentheses are the standard deviations.

Dataset	SpSVM-2		SVM	
	TestErate	#Basis	TestErate	n_{sv}
Banana	10.87 (1.74)	17.3 (7.3)	10.54 (0.68)	221.7 (66.98)
Breast	29.22 (2.11)	12.1 (5.6)	28.18 (3.00)	185.8 (16.44)
Diabetes	23.47 (1.36)	13.8 (5.6)	23.73 (1.24)	426.3 (26.91)
Flare	33.90 (1.10)	8.4 (1.2)	33.98 (1.26)	629.4 (29.43)
German	24.90 (1.50)	14.0 (7.3)	24.47 (1.97)	630.4 (22.48)
Heart	15.50 (1.10)	4.3 (2.6)	15.80 (2.20)	166.6 (8.75)
Ringnorm	1.97 (0.57)	12.9 (2.0)	1.68 (0.24)	334.9 (108.54)
Thyroid	5.47 (0.78)	10.6 (2.3)	4.93 (2.18)	57.80 (39.61)
Titanic	22.68 (1.88)	3.3 (0.9)	22.35 (0.67)	150.0 (0.0)
Twonorm	2.96 (0.82)	8.7 (3.7)	2.42 (0.24)	330.30 (137.02)
Waveform	10.66 (0.99)	14.4 (3.3)	10.04 (0.67)	246.9 (57.80)

11.2   The Basic Optimization

Let $J \subset \{1, \ldots, n\}$ be a given index set of basis functions that form a subset of the training set. We consider the problem of minimizing the objective function in (11.1) over the set of vectors w of the form[3]

$$w = \sum_{j \in J} \beta_j \phi(x_j) \ . \tag{11.3}$$

11.2.1   Newton Optimization

Let $K_{ij} = k(x_i, x_j) = \phi(x_i) \cdot \phi(x_j)$ denote the generic element of the $n \times n$ kernel matrix K. The notation K_{IJ} refers to the submatrix of K made of the rows indexed by I and the columns indexed by J. Also, for an n-dimensional vector p, let p_J denote the $|J|$ dimensional vector containing $\{p_j : j \in J\}$.

Let $d = |J|$. With w restricted to (11.3), the primal problem (11.1) becomes the d dimensional minimization problem of finding β_J that solves

$$\min_{\beta_J} f(\beta_J) = \frac{\lambda}{2} \beta_J^\top K_{JJ} \beta_J + \frac{1}{2} \sum_{i=1}^n \max(0, 1 - y_i o_i)^2 \ , \tag{11.4}$$

---

3. More generally, one can consider an expansion on points which do not belong to the training set.

where $o_i = K_{i,J}\beta_J$. Except for the regularizer being more general, i.e., $\beta_J^\top K_{JJ}\beta_J$ (as opposed to the simple regularizer, $\|\beta_J\|^2$), the problem in (11.4) is very much the same as in a linear SVM design. Thus, the Newton method and its modification that are developed for linear SVMs (Mangasarian, 2002; Keerthi and DeCoste, 2005) can be used to solve (11.4) and obtain the solution β_J.

Newton Method

- Choose a suitable starting vector, β_J^0. Set $k = 0$.
- If β_J^k is the optimal solution of (11.4), stop.
- Let $I = \{i : 1 - y_i o_i \geq 0\}$ where $o_i = K_{i,J}\beta_J^k$ is the output of the ith example. Obtain $\bar{\beta}_J$ as the result of a Newton step or equivalently as the solution of the regularized least squares problem,

$$\min_{\beta_J} \frac{\lambda}{2}\beta_J^\top K_{JJ}\beta_J + \frac{1}{2}\sum_{i\in I}(1 - y_i K_{i,J}\beta_J)^2 \qquad (11.5)$$

- Take β_J^{k+1} to be the minimizer of f on L, the line joining β_J^k and $\bar{\beta}_J$. Set $k := k+1$ and go back to step 2 for another iteration.

The solution of (11.5) is given by

$$\bar{\beta}_J = \beta_J^k - P^{-1}g , \qquad (11.6)$$

where

$$P = \lambda K_{JJ} + K_{JI}K_{JI}^\top \quad \text{and} \quad g = \lambda K_{JJ}\beta_J - K_{JI}(y_I - o_I)$$

are the (generalized) Hessian and gradient of the objective function (11.4).

Because the loss function is piecewise quadratic, the Newton method converges in a finite number of iterations. The number of iterations required to converge to the exact solution of (11.4) is usually very small (less than five). Some MATLAB code is available online at `http://www.kyb.tuebingen.mpg.de/bs/people/chapelle/primal`.

11.2.2   Updating the Hessian

As already pointed out in section 11.1, we will mainly need to solve (11.4) in an incremental mode[4]: with the solution β_J of (11.4) already available, solve (11.4) again, but with one more basis function added, i.e., J incremented by one. Keerthi and DeCoste (2005) show that the Newton method is very efficient for such seeding situations. Since the kernel matrix is dense, we maintain and update a Cholesky factorization of P, the Hessian defined in (11.6). Even with J fixed, during the course of solving (11.4) via the Newton method, P will undergo changes due to

---

4. In our method basis functions are added one at a time.

changes in I. Efficient rank one schemes can be used to do the updating of the Cholesky factorization (Seeger, 2004). The updatings of the factorization of P that need to be done because of changes in I are not going to be expensive because such changes mostly occur when J is small; when J is large, I usually undergoes very small changes since the set of training errors is rather well identified by that stage. Of course P and its factorization will also undergo changes (their dimensions increase by one) each time an element is added to J. This is a routine updating operation that is present in most forward selection methods.

11.2.3   Computational Complexity

It is useful to ask: once the solution of (11.4) is available for some J, what is the complexity of the incremental computations needed to solve it again after one more basis element is included in J? In the best case, when the support vector set I does not change, the cost is mainly the following: computing the new row and column of K_{JJ} ($d+1$ kernel evaluations); computing the new row of K_{JI} (n kernel computations)[5]; computing the new elements of P ($O(nd)$ cost); and the updating of the factorization of P ($O(d^2)$ cost). Thus the cost can be summarized as $(n+d+1)$ kernel evaluations and $O(nd)$ cost. Even when I does change and so the cost is more, it is reasonable to take the above-mentioned cost summary as a good estimate of the cost of the incremental work. Adding up these costs till $d_{\max}$ basis functions are selected, we get a complexity of $O(nd_{\max}^2)$. Note that this is the basic cost given that we already know the sequence of $d_{\max}$ basis functions that are to be used. Thus, $O(nd_{\max}^2)$ is also the complexity of the method in which basis functions are chosen randomly. In the next section we discuss the problem of selecting the basis functions systematically and efficiently.

11.3   Selection of New Basis Element

Suppose we have solved (11.4) and obtained the minimizer β_J. Obviously, the minimum value of the objective function in (11.4) (call it f_J) is greater than or equal to $f^\star$, the optimal value of (11.1). If the difference between them is large we would like to continue on and include another basis function. Take one $j \notin J$. How do we judge its value of inclusion? The best scoring mechanism is the following one.

11.3.1   Basis Selection Method 1

Include j in J, optimize (11.4) fully using (β_J, β_j), and find the improved value of the objective function; call it $\tilde{f}_j$. Choose the j that gives the least value of

---

5. In fact this is not n but the size of I. Since we do not know this size, we upper-bound it by n.

$\tilde{f}_j$. We already analyzed in the earlier section that the cost of doing one basis element inclusion is $O(nd)$. So, if we want to try all elements outside J, the cost is $O(n^2d)$; the overall cost of such a method of selecting $d_{\max}$ basis functions is $O(n^2 d_{\max}^2)$, which is much higher than the basic cost, $O(nd_{\max}^2)$, mentioned in the previous section. Instead, if we work only with a random subset of size κ chosen from outside J, then the cost in one basis selection step comes down to $O(\kappa nd)$, and the overall cost is limited to $O(\kappa nd_{\max}^2)$. Smola and Bartlett (2001) have successfully tried such random subset choices for Gaussian process regression, using $\kappa = 59$. However, note that, even with this scheme, the cost of new basis selection ($O(\kappa nd)$) is still disproportionately higher (by κ times) than the cost of actually including the newly selected basis function ($O(nd)$). Thus we would like to go for cheaper methods.

11.3.2 Basis Selection Method 2

This method computes a score for a new element j in $O(n)$ time. The idea has a parallel in Vincent and Bengio's work on kernel matching pursuit (Vincent and Bengio, 2002) for least-squares loss functions. They have two methods, called *prefitting* and *backfitting*; see equations (7), (3), and (6) of Vincent and Bengio (2002).[6] Their *prefitting* is parallel to *basis selection method 1* that we described earlier. The cheaper method that we suggest below is parallel to their *backfitting* idea. Suppose β_J is the solution of (11.4). Including a new element j and its corresponding variable, β_j yields the problem of minimizing

$$\frac{\lambda}{2}(\beta_J^\top \ \beta_j) \begin{pmatrix} K_{JJ} & K_{Jj} \\ K_{jJ} & K_{jj} \end{pmatrix} \begin{pmatrix} \beta_J \\ \beta_j \end{pmatrix} + \frac{1}{2}\sum_{i=1}^{n} \max(0, 1 - y_i(K_{iJ}\beta_J + K_{ij}\beta_j)^2) \ . \quad (11.7)$$

We fix β_J and optimize (11.7) using only the new variable β_j and see how much improvement in the objective function is possible in order to define the score for the new element j.

This one-dimensional function is piecewise quadratic and can be minimized exactly in $O(n \log n)$ time by a dichotomy search on the different breakpoints. But a very precise calculation of the scoring function is usually unnecessary. So, for a practical solution, we can simply do a few Newton-Raphson–type iterations on the derivative of the function and get a near-optimal solution in $O(n)$ time. Note that we also need to compute the vector K_{Jj}, which requires d kernel evaluations. Though this cost is subsumed in $O(n)$, it is a factor to remember if kernel evaluations are expensive.

If all $j \notin J$ are tried, then the complexity of selecting a new basis function is $O(n^2)$, which is disproportionately large compared to the cost of including the chosen basis function, which is $O(nd)$. As in *basis selection method 1*, we can

---

6. For least-squares problems, Adler et al. (1996) had given the same ideas as Vincent and Bengio in earlier work.

simply choose κ random basis functions to try. If $d_{\max}$ is specified, one can choose $\kappa = O(d_{\max})$ without increasing the overall complexity beyond $O(nd_{\max}^2)$. More complex schemes incorporating a kernel cache can also be tried.

11.3.3 Kernel Caching

For up to medium-sized problems, say $n < 15,000$, it is a good idea to have a cache for the entire kernel matrix. If additional memory space is available and, say a Gaussian kernel is employed, then the values of $\|x_i - x_j\|^2$ can also be cached; this will help significantly reduce the time associated with the tuning of hyperparameters. For larger problems, depending on the memory space available, it is a good idea to cache as many as possible full kernel rows corresponding to j that get tried but do not get chosen for inclusion. It is possible that they get called in a later stage of the algorithm, at which time, this cache can be useful. It is also possible to think of variations of the method in which full kernel rows corresponding to a large set (as much as can fit into memory) of randomly chosen training basis is pre-computed and only these basis functions are considered for selection.

11.3.4 Shrinking

As basis functions get added, the SVM solution w and the margin planes start stabilizing. If the number of support vectors form a small fraction of the training set, then, for a large fraction of (well-classified) training examples, we can easily conclude that they will probably never come into the active set I. Such training examples can be left out of the calculations without causing any undue harm. This idea of shrinking has been effectively used to speedup SVM training (Joachims, 1999a; Platt, 1999). See also chapter 1, section 7.3 in this book.

11.3.5 Experimental Evaluation

We now evaluate the performance of basis selection methods 1 and 2 (we will call them SpSVM-1, SpSVM-2) on some sizable benchmark datasets. A full description of these datasets and the kernel functions used is given in the appendix. The value of $\kappa = 59$ is used. To have a baseline, we also consider the method Random, in which the basis functions are chosen randomly. This is almost the same as the RSVM method (Y.-J. Lee and Mangasarian, 2001a; K.-M. Lin and Lin, 2003), the only difference being the regularizer ($\beta_J^\top K_{J,J} \beta_J$ in (11.4) versus $\|\beta_J\|^2$ in RSVM). For another baseline we consider the (more systematic) unsupervised learning method in which an incomplete Cholesky factorization with pivoting (Meijerink and van der Vorst, 1977; Bach and Jordan, 2005) is used to choose basis functions.[7] For

---

7. We also tried the method of Bach and Jordan (2005) which uses the training labels, but we noticed little improvement.

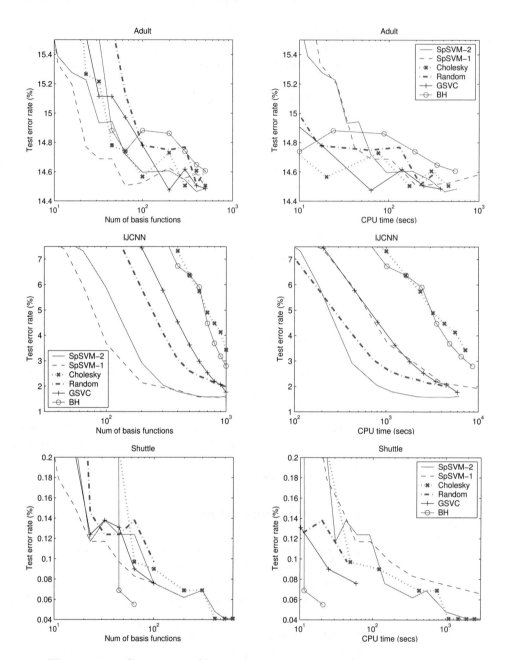

Figure 11.1 Comparison of basis selection methods on *Adult*, *IJCNN*, and *Shuttle*. On *Shuttle* some methods were terminated because of ill-conditioning in the matrix P in (11.6).

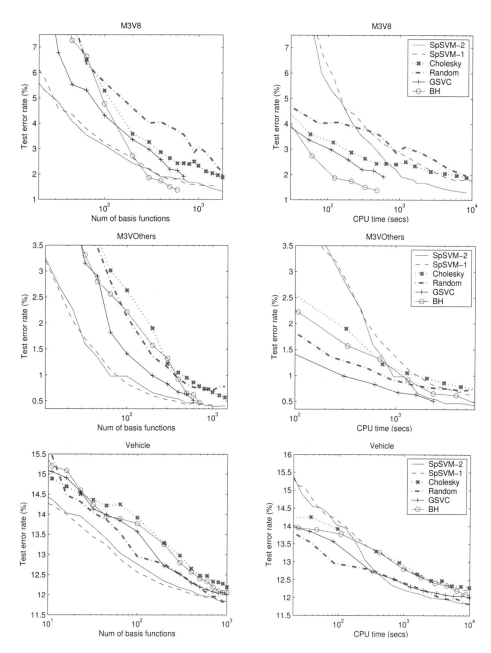

Figure 11.2   Comparison of basis selection methods on *M3V8*, *M3VOthers*, and *Vehicle*.

comparison we also include the GSVC method of Parrado-Hernández et al. (2003). This method, originally given for SVM hinge loss, uses the following heuristic criterion to select the next basis function $j^* \notin J$:

$$j^* = \arg \min_{j \in I, j \notin J} \max_{l \in J} |K_{jl}| \, , \tag{11.8}$$

with the aim of encouraging new basis functions that are far from the basis functions that are already chosen; also, j is restricted only to the support vector indices (I in (11.5)). For a clean comparison with our methods, we implemented GSVC for SVMs using quadratic penalization, $\max(0, 1 - y_i o_i)^2$. We also tried another criterion, suggested to us by Alex Smola, that is more complex than (11.8):

$$j^* = \arg \max_{j \in I, j \notin J} (1 - y_j o_j)^2 d_j^2 \, , \tag{11.9}$$

where d_j is the distance (in feature space) of the jth training point from the subspace spanned by the elements of J. This criterion is based on an upper bound on the improvement to the training cost function obtained by including the jth basis function. It also makes sense intuitively as it selects basis functions that are both not well approximated by the others (large d_j) and for which the error incurred is large.[8] Below, we will refer to this criterion as BH. It is worth noting that both (11.8) and (11.9) can be computed very efficiently.

Figures 11.1 and 11.2 compare the six methods on six datasets.[9] Overall, SpSVM-1 and SpSVM-2 give the best performance in terms of achieving good reduction of the test error rate with respect to the number of basis functions. Although SpSVM-2 slightly lags behind SpSVM-1 in terms of performance in the early stages, it does equally well as more basis functions are added. Since SpSVM-2 is significantly less expensive, it is the best method to use. Since SpSVM-1 is quite cheap in the early stages, it is also appropriate to think of a hybrid method in which SpSVM-1 is used in the early stages and, when it becomes expensive, a switch is made to SpSVM-2. The other methods sometimes do well, but, overall, they are inferior in comparison to SpSVM-1 and SpSVM-2. Interestingly, on the *IJCNN* and *Vehicle* datasets, Cholesky, GSVC, and BH are even inferior to Random. A possible explanation is as follows: these methods give preference to points that are farthest away in feature space from the points already selected. Thus, they are likely to select points which are outliers (far from the rest of the training points); but outliers are probably unsuitable points for expanding the decision function.

As we mentioned in section 11.1, there also exist other greedy methods of kernel basis selection that are motivated by ideas from boosting. These methods are usually

---

8. Note that when the set of basis functions is not restricted, the optimal β satisfies $\lambda \beta_i y_i = \max(0, 1 - y_i o_i)$.

9. Most figures given in this chapter appear in pairs of two plots. One plot gives the test error rate as a function of the number of basis functions, to see how effective the compression is. The other plot gives the test error rate as a function of CPU time, and is used to indicate the efficiency of the method.

given in a setting different from the one we consider: a set of (kernel) basis functions is given and a regularizer (such as $\|\beta\|_1$) is directly specified on the multiplier vector β. The method of Bennett et al. (2002) called MARK is given for least-squares problems. It is close to the kernel matching pursuit method. We compare SpSVM-2 with kernel matching pursuit and discuss MARK in section 11.5. The method of Bi et al. (2004) uses column generation ideas from linear and quadratic programming to select new basis functions and so it requires the solution of both the primal and dual problems.[10] Thus, the basis selection process is based on the sensitivity of the primal objective function to an incoming basis function. On the other hand, our SpSVM methods are based on computing an estimate of the decrease in the primal objective function due to an incoming basis function; also, the dual solution is not needed.

11.4 Hyperparameter Tuning

In the actual design process, the values of hyperparameters need to be determined. This can be done using k-fold cross-validation (CV). CV can also be used to choose d, the number of basis functions. Since the solution given by our method approaches the SVM solution as d becomes large, there is really no need to choose d at all. One can simply choose d to be as big a value as possible. But, to achieve good reduction in the classifier complexity (as well as computing time), it is a good idea to track the validation performance as a function of d and stop when this function becomes nearly flat. We proceed as follows. First, an appropriate value for $d_{\max}$ is chosen. For a given choice of hyperparameters, the basis selection method (say SpSVM-2) is then applied on each training set formed from the k-fold partitions till $d_{\max}$ basis functions are chosen. This gives an estimate of the k-fold CV error for each value of d from 1 to $d_{\max}$. We choose d to be the number of basis functions that gives the lowest k-fold CV error. This computation can be repeated for each set of hyperparameter values and the best choice can be decided.

Recall that, at stage d, our basis selection methods choose the $(d+1)$th basis function from a set of κ random basis functions. To avoid the effects of this randomness on hyperparameter tuning, it is better to make this κ-set to be dependent only on d. Thus, at stage d, the basis selection methods will choose the same set of κ random basis functions for all hyperparameter values.

We applied the above ideas on 11 benchmark datasets[11] using SpSVM-2 as the basis selection method. The Gaussian kernel, $k(x_i, x_j) = 1 + \exp(-\gamma \|x_i - x_j\|^2)$ was used. The hyperparameters, λ and γ were tuned using three-fold CV. The values, 2^i, $i = -7, \cdots, 7$ were used for each of these parameters. Ten different train-test partitions were tried to get an idea of the variability in generalization performance.

---

10. The CPLEX LP/QP solver is used to obtain these solutions.
11. http://ida.first.fraunhofer.de/~raetsch/.

We used $\kappa = 25$ and $d_{\max} = 25$. (The *Titanic* dataset has three input variables, which are all binary; hence we set $d_{\max} = 8$ for this dataset.)

Table 11.1 (already introduced in section 11.1) gives the results. For comparison we also give the results for the SVM (solution of (11.1)); in the case of SVM, the number of support vectors (n_{SV}) is the number of basis functions. Clearly, our method achieves an impressive reduction in the number of basis functions, while yielding test error rates comparable to the full SVM.

11.5   Comparison with Kernel Matching Pursuit

Kernel matching pursuit (Vincent and Bengio, 2002) was mainly given as a method of greedily selecting basis functions for the nonregularized kernel least-squares problem. As we already explained in section 11.3, our basis selection methods can be viewed as extensions of the basic ideas of KMP to the SVM case. In this section we empirically compare the performances of these two methods. For both methods we only consider *basis selection method 2* and refer to the two methods simply as KMP and SpSVM. It is also interesting to study the effect of the regularizer term ($\lambda\|w\|^2/2$ in (11.1)) on generalization. The regularizer can be removed by setting $\lambda = 0$. The original KMP formulation of Vincent and Bengio (2002) considered such a nonregularized formulation only. In the case of SVM, when perfect separability of the training data is possible, it is improper to set $\lambda = 0$ without actually rewriting the primal formulation in a different form; so in our implementation we brought in the effect of no-regularization by setting λ to the small value 10^{-5}. Thus, we compare four methods: KMP-R, KMP-NR, SpSVM-R and SpSVM-NR. Here "-R" and "-NR" refer to regularization and no-regularization, respectively.

Figures 11.3 and 11.4 compare the four methods on six datasets. Except on *M3V8*, SpSVM gives a better performance than KMP. The better performance of *KMP* on *M3V8* is probably due to the fact that the examples corresponding to each of the digits 3 and 8 are distributed as a Gaussian, which is suited to the least-squares loss function. Note that in the case of *M3VOthers* where the "Others" class (corresponding to all digits other than 3) is far from a Gaussian distribution, SVM does better than KMP.

The no-regularization methods, KMP-NR and SpSVM-NR, give an interesting performance. In the initial stages of basis addition we are in the underfitting zone and so they perform as well (in fact, a shade better) than their respective regularized counterparts. But, as expected, they start overfitting when many basis functions are added. See, for example, the performance on the *Adult* dataset given in figure 11.3. Thus, when using these nonregularized methods, a lot of care is needed in choosing the right number of basis functions. The number of basis functions at which overfitting sets in is smaller for SpSVM-NR than that for KMP-NR. This is because of the fact that while KMP has to concentrate on reducing the residual on all examples in its optimization, SVM only needs to concentrate on the examples violating the margin condition.

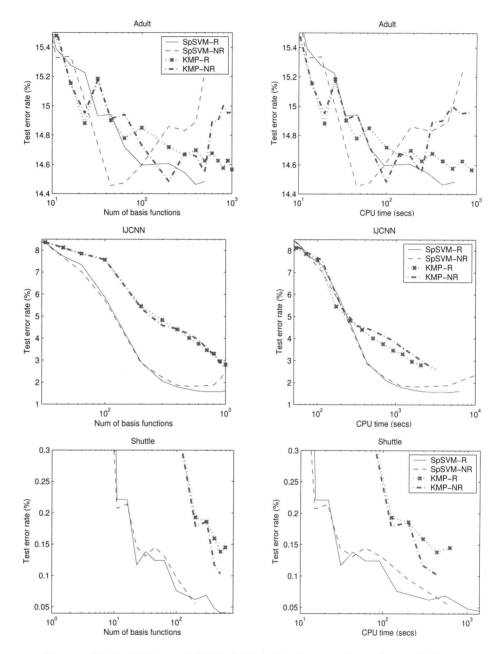

Figure 11.3 KMP vs. SpSVM (with/without regularization) on *Adult*, *IJCNN*, and *Shuttle*.

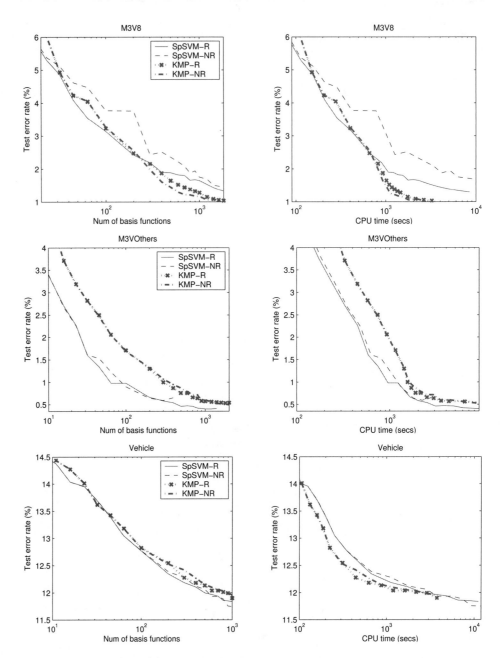

Figure 11.4 KMP vs. SpSVM (with/without regularization) on *M3V8*, *M3VOthers*, and *Vehicle*.

It is also useful to mention the method MARK[12] of Bennett et al. (2002), which is closely related to KMP. In this method, a new basis function (say the one corresponding to the jth training example) is evaluated by looking at the magnitude (the larger the better) of the gradient of the primal objective function with respect to β_j evaluated at the current β_J. This gradient is the dot product of the kernel column containing K_{ij} and the residual vector having the elements, $o_i - y_i$. The computational cost, as well as the performance of MARK, is close to that of KMP. MARK can also be easily extended to the SVM problem (11.1): all that we need to do is to replace the residual vector mentioned above by the vector having the elements $y_i \max\{0, 1 - y_i o_i\}$. This modified method (which uses our Newton optimization method as the base solver) is close to our SpSVM-2 in terms of computational cost as well as performance. Note that, if we optimize (7) for β_j using only a single Newton step, the difference between MARK (as adapted above to SVMs) and SpSVM-2 is only in the use of the second order information.

11.6 Additional Tuning

We discuss in this section the choice of κ for SpSVM, as well as the possibility of not solving (11.4) every time a new basis function is added.

11.6.1 Few Retrainings

It might be a bit costly to perform the Newton optimization described in section 11.2.1 each time a new basis function is added. Indeed, it is unlikely that the set of support vectors changes a lot after each addition. Therefore, we investigate the possibility of retraining only from time to time.

We first tried to do retraining only when $|J| = 2^p$ for some $p \in \mathbb{N}$, the set of positive integers. It makes sense to use an exponential scale since we expect the solution not to change too much when J is already relatively large. Note that the overall complexity of the algorithm does not change since the cost of adding one basis function is still $O(nd)$. It is only the constant which is better, because fewer Newton optimizations are performed.

The results are presented in figure 11.5. For a given number of basis functions, the test error is usually not as good as when we always retrain. But on the other hand, this can be much faster. We found that a good tradeoff is to retrain whenever $|J| = \lfloor 2^{p/4} \rfloor$ for $p \in \mathbb{N}$. This is the strategy we will use for the experiments in the rest of the chapter.

---

12. The basis selection idea used in MARK is also given in earlier papers (Mallat and Zhang, 1993; Adler et al., 1996) under the name *basic matching pursuit*.

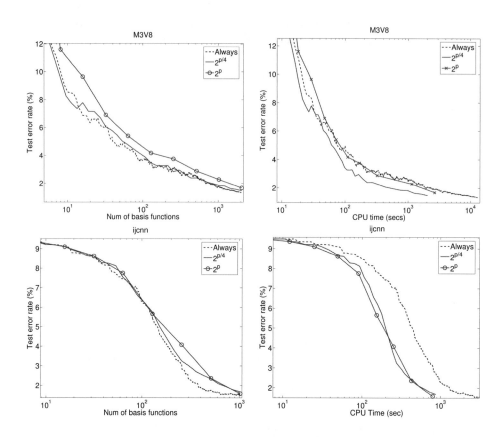

Figure 11.5 Three different possible retraining strategies showing a different tradeoff between accuracy and time: always retraining is too time-consuming; on the other hand, retraining not often enough can lead to suboptimal performances (top left plot). For these experiments, $\kappa = 100$ was used.

11.6.2   Influence of κ

The parameter κ is the number of candidate basis functions that are being tried each time a new basis function should be added: we select a random set of κ examples and the best one (as explained in section 11.3.2) among them is chosen. If $\kappa = 1$, this amounts to choosing a random example at each step (i.e., the Random method on figures 11.1 and 11.2).

The influence of κ is studied in figure 11.6. The larger κ is, the better the test error for a given number of basis functions, but also the longer the training time. We found that $\kappa = 10$ is a good tradeoff and that is the value that we will keep for the experiments presented in the next section.

Finally, an interesting question is how to choose appropriately a good value for κ and an efficient retraining strategy. Both are likely to be problem dependent,

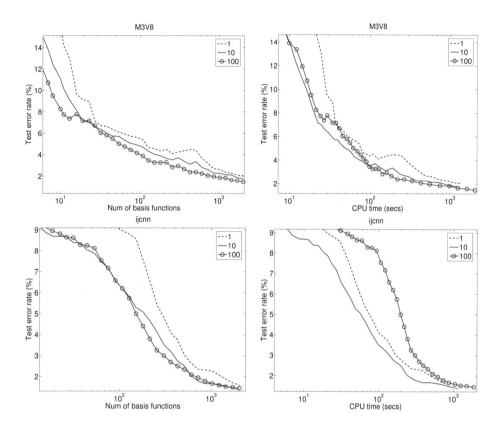

Figure 11.6   Influence of the paramter κ: when it is large, a good reduction is achieved (left column), but the computational cost is larger (right column). $\kappa = 10$ seems a good tradeoff.

and even though $\kappa = 59$ was suggested by Smola and Schölkopf (2000), we believe that there is no universal answer. The answer would, for instance, depend on the cost associated with the computation of the kernel function, on the number of support vectors, and on the number of training points. Indeed, the basic cost for one iteration is $O(nd)$ and the number of kernel calculations is $\kappa n_{\mathrm{sv}} + n$: the first term corresponds to trying different basis functions, while the second one corresponds to the inclusion of the chosen basis function. So κ should be chosen such that the kernel computations take about the same time as the training itself.

Ideally, an adaptive strategy should be designed to find κ automatically and to adjust the retraining schedule. The decay rate of the objective function and the variance of the scores produced by the basis selection scoring function are two key quantities that would be helpful in adjusting the schedule.

11.7   Comparison with Standard SVM Training

We conclude the experimental study by comparing our method with the well-known SVM solver SVM^{light} (Joachims, 1999a).[13] For this solver, we selected random training subsets of sizes from $2^{-10}n, 2^{-9}n, \ldots, n/4, n/2, n$. For each training set size, we measure the test error, the training time, and the number of support vectors. The L_2 version (quadratic penalization of the slacks) is the one relevant to our study since it is the same loss function as the one we used; note that, when the number of basis functions increases toward n, the SpSVM solution will converge to the L_2 SVM solution. For completeness, we also included experimental results of an SVM trained with an L_1 penalization of the slacks. Finally, note that for simplicity we kept the same hyperparameters for the different sizes, but that both methods would certainly gain by additional hyerparameter tuning (for instance, when the number of basis functions is smaller, the bandwith of the radial basis function (RBF) kernel should be larger).

The results are presented in figures 11.7 and 11.8. In terms of compression (left columns), our method is usually able to reach the same accuracy as a standard SVM using less than one-tenth the number of basis functions (this confirms the results of table 11.1).

From a time complexity point of view also, our method is very competitive and can reach the same accuracy as an SVM in less time. The only disappointing performance is on the *M3V8* dataset. A possible explanation is that for this dataset, the number of support vectors is very small and a standard SVM can compute the exact solution quickly.

Finally, note that when the number of basis functions is extremely small compared to the number of training examples, SpSVM can be slower than an SVM trained on a small subset (left part of the right column plots). It is because solving (11.4) using n training examples when there are few parameters to estimate is an overkill. It would be wiser to choose n as a function of d, the number of basis functions.

11.8   Conclusion

In this chapter we have given a fast primal algorithm that greedily chooses a subset of the training basis functions to approximate the SVM solution. As the subset grows, the solution converges to the SVM solution, since choosing the subset to be the entire training set is guaranteed to yield the exact SVM solution. The real power of the method lies in its ability to form very good approximations of the SVM classifier with a clear control on the complexity of the classifier (number of basis functions), as well as the training time. In most datasets, performance very

---

13. The default optimization options of SVM^{light} (Version 6.0) have been used.

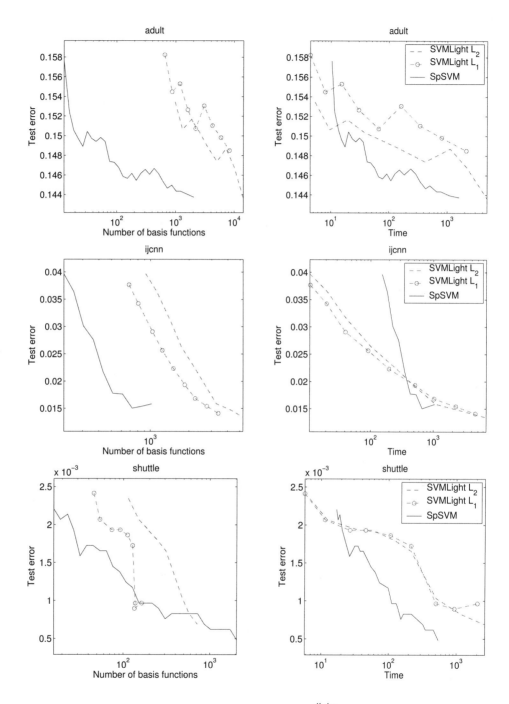

Figure 11.7 Comparison of SpSVM with SVM^{light} on *Adult*, *IJCNN*, and *Shuttle*. For SVM^{light}, "Number of basis functions" should be understood as number of support vectors.

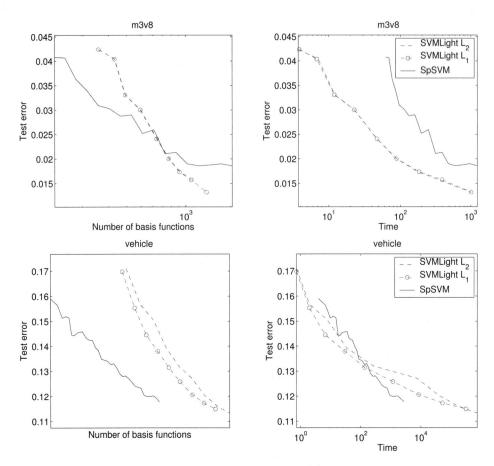

Figure 11.8 Comparison of SpSVM with SVM^{light} on *M3V8* and *Vehicle*. For SVM^{light}, "Number of basis functions" should be understood as number of support vectors.

close to that of the SVM is achieved using a set of basis functions whose size is a small fraction of the number of SVM support vectors. The graded control over the training time offered by our method can be valuable in large-scale data mining. Many times, simpler algorithms such as decision trees are preferred over SVMs when there is a severe constraint on computational time. While there is no satisfactory way of doing early stopping with SVMs, our method enables the user to control the training time by choosing the number of basis functions to use.

Our method can be improved and modified in various ways. Hyperparameter tuning time can be substantially reduced by using gradient-based methods on a differentiable estimate of the generalization performance formed using k-fold cross-validation and posterior probabilities. Improved methods of choosing the κ-subset of basis functions in each step can also make the method more effective. Also, all the ideas described in this chapter can be easily extended to the Huber loss function using the ideas in Keerthi and DeCoste (2005).

Appendix

11.A   Description of Datasets Used

As in the main text, let n denote the number of training examples. The six datasets used for the main experiments of the chapter are: *Adult, IJCNN, M3V8, M3VOthers, Shuttle,* and *Vehicle.* For *M3V8* and *M3VOthers* we go by the experience in (DeCoste and Schölkopf, 2002) and use the polynomial kernel, $k(x_i, x_j) = 1 + (1 + x_i \cdot x_j)^9$, where each x_i is normalized to have unit length. For all other datasets, we use the Gaussian kernel, $k(x_i, x_j) = 1 + \exp(-\gamma \|x_i - x_j\|^2)$. The values of γ are given below.[14] In each case, the values chosen for γ and λ are ballpark values such that the methods considered in the chapter give good generalization performance.

The *Adult* dataset is the version given by Platt in his sequential minimal optimization webpage: `http://www.research.microsoft.com/~jplatt/smo.html`. Platt created a sequence of datasets with an increasing number of examples in order to study the scaling properties of his algorithm with respect to n. For our experiments we only used *Adult-8* which has 22,696 training examples and 9865 test examples. Each example has 123 binary features, of which typically only 14 are nonzero. We used $\gamma = 0.05$ and $\lambda = 1$.

The next five datasets are available from the LIBSVM-Tools webpage `http://www.csie.ntu.edu.tw/~cjlin/libsvmtools/datasets/`.

The *IJCNN* dataset has 49,990 training examples and 91,701 test examples. Each example is described by 22 features. We used $\gamma = 4$ and $\lambda = 1/16$.

The *Shuttle* dataset has 43,500 training examples and 14,500 test examples. Each example is described by 9 features. This is a multiclass dataset with 7 classes. We looked only at the binary classification problem of differentiating class 1 from the rest. We used $\gamma = 16$ and $\lambda = 1/512$.

The *M3V8* dataset is the binary classification problem of *MNIST* corresponding to classifying digit 3 from digit 8. The original dataset has 11,982 training examples and 1984 test examples for this problem. Since the original test dataset could not clearly show a distinction between several closely competing methods, we formed an extended test set by applying invariances like translation and rotation to create a test set comprising 17,856 examples. (This dataset can be obtained from the authors.) We used $\lambda = 0.1$.

The *M3VOthers* dataset is another binary classification problem of *MNIST* corresponding to differentiating digit 3 from all the other digits. The dataset has 60,000 training examples and 10,000 test examples. We used $\lambda = 0.1$.

The *Vehicle* dataset corresponds to the "vehicle (combined, scaled to [-1,1])" version in the LIBSVM-Tools page mentioned above. It has 78,823 training examples

---

14. For both the polynomial and Gaussian kernels, the additive term "1" gives the effect of including the threshold term in the classifier and regularizing it.

and 19,705 test examples. Each example is described by 100 features. This is a multiclass dataset with three classes. We looked only at the binary classification problem of differentiating class 3 from the rest. We used $\gamma = 1/8$ and $\lambda = 1/32$.

Apart from the above six large datasets, we also used modified versions of UCI datasets available from `http://ida.first.fraunhofer.de/~raetsch/`. These datasets were used to show the sparsity that is achievable using our method; see table 11.1 of section 11.1 and the detailed discussion in section 11.4.

12   Trading Convexity for Scalability

Ronan Collobert
Fabian Sinz
Jason Weston
Léon Bottou

Convex learning algorithms, such as support vector machines (SVMs), are often seen as highly desirable because they offer strong practical properties and are amenable to theoretical analysis. However, in this work we show how nonconvexity can provide scalability advantages over convexity. We show how concave-convex programming can be applied to produce (i) faster SVMs where training errors are no longer support vectors, and (ii) much faster transductive SVMs.

12.1   Introduction

The machine learning renaissance in the 1980s was fostered by multilayer models. They were nonconvex and surprisingly efficient. Convexity rose in the 1990s with the growing importance of mathematical analysis, and the successes of convex models such as support vector machines (SVMs) (Vapnik, 1995). These methods are popular because they span two worlds: the world of applications (they have good empirical performance, ease of use, and computational efficiency) and the world of theory (they can be analyzed and bounds can be produced). Convexity is largely responsible for these factors.

Many researchers have suspected that convex models do not cover all the ground previously addressed with nonconvex models. In the case of pattern recognition, one argument was that the misclassification rate is poorly approximated by convex losses such as the SVM hinge loss or the boosting exponential loss (Freund and Schapire, 1996). Various authors proposed nonconvex alternatives (Mason et al., 2000; Perez-Cruz et al., 2002; Elisseeff, 2000), sometimes using the same concave-convex programming methods as in this chapter (Krause and Singer, 2004; Liu et al., 2005).

The ψ-learning paper (X. Shen et al., 2003) stands out because it proposes a theoretical result indicating that nonconvex loss functions yield fast convergence rates to the Bayes limit. This result depends on a specific assumption about the probability distribution of the examples. Such an assumption is necessary because there are no probability independent bounds on the rate of convergence to Bayes (Devroye et al., 1996). However, under substantially similar assumptions, it has recently been shown that SVMs achieve comparable convergence rates using the convex hinge loss (Steinwart and Scovel, 2005). In short, the theoretical accuracy advantage of nonconvex losses no longer looks certain.

On real-life datasets, these previous works only report modest accuracy improvements comparable to those reported here. None mention the potential computational advantages of nonconvex optimization, simply because everyone assumes that convex optimization is easier. On the contrary, most authors warn the reader about the potentially high cost of nonconvex optimization.

This chapter presents two examples where the *optimization of a nonconvex loss function brings considerable computational benefits* over the convex alternative.[1]

Both examples leverage a modern concave-convex programming method. Section 12.2 shows how the concave-convex Procedure (CCCP) (Yuille and Rangarajan, 2002) solves a sequence of convex problems and has no difficult parameters to tune. Section 12.3 proposes an SVM where training errors are no longer support vectors (SVs). The increased sparsity leads to better scaling properties for SVMs. Section 12.5 describes what we believe is the best known method for implementing Transductive SVMs (TSVMs) with a quadratic empirical complexity. This is in stark contrast to convex versions whose complexity grows with degree 4 or more.

12.2   The Concave-Convex Procedure

Minimizing a nonconvex cost function is usually difficult. Gradient descent techniques, such as conjugate gradient descent or stochastic gradient descent, often involve delicate hyperparameters (LeCun et al., 1998c). In contrast, convex optimization seems much more straightforward. For instance, the sequential minimal optimization (SMO) algorithm (Platt, 1999) locates the SVM solution efficiently and reliably.

We propose instead to optimize nonconvex problems using the concave-convex procedure (CCCP) (Yuille and Rangarajan, 2002). The CCCP is closely related to the "difference of convex" (DC) methods that have been developed by the optimization community during the last two decades (e.g., Tao and El Bernoussi, 1986; Tao and An, 1998). Such techniques have already been applied for dealing with missing values in SVMs (Smola et al., 2005), for improving boosting algorithms (Krause

---

1. Conversely, Bengio et al. (2006b) proposes a convex formulation of multilayer networks which has considerably higher computational costs.

and Singer, 2004), and for implementing ψ-learning (X. Shen et al., 2003; Liu et al., 2005).

Assume that a cost function $J(\boldsymbol{\theta})$ can be rewritten as the sum of a convex part $J_{vex}(\boldsymbol{\theta})$ and a concave part $J_{cav}(\boldsymbol{\theta})$. Each iteration of the CCCP procedure (algorithm 12.1) approximates the concave part by its tangent and minimizes the resulting convex function.

Algorithm 12.1 The concave-convex procedure (CCCP)

Initialize $\boldsymbol{\theta}^0$ with a best guess.
repeat

$$\boldsymbol{\theta}^{t+1} = \arg\min_{\boldsymbol{\theta}} \left(J_{vex}(\boldsymbol{\theta}) + J'_{cav}(\boldsymbol{\theta}^t) \cdot \boldsymbol{\theta} \right) \tag{12.1}$$

until convergence of $\boldsymbol{\theta}^t$

One can easily see that the cost $J(\boldsymbol{\theta}^t)$ decreases after each iteration by summing two inequalities resulting from (12.1) and from the concavity of $J_{cav}(\boldsymbol{\theta})$.

$$J_{vex}(\boldsymbol{\theta}^{t+1}) + J'_{cav}(\boldsymbol{\theta}^t) \cdot \boldsymbol{\theta}^{t+1} \leq J_{vex}(\boldsymbol{\theta}^t) + J'_{cav}(\boldsymbol{\theta}^t) \cdot \boldsymbol{\theta}^t \tag{12.2}$$

$$J_{cav}(\boldsymbol{\theta}^{t+1}) \leq J_{cav}(\boldsymbol{\theta}^t) + J'_{cav}(\boldsymbol{\theta}^t) \cdot \left(\boldsymbol{\theta}^{t+1} - \boldsymbol{\theta}^t \right) \tag{12.3}$$

The convergence of CCCP has been shown by Yuille and Rangarajan (2002) by refining this argument. The authors also showed that the CCCP procedure remains valid if $\boldsymbol{\theta}$ is required to satisfy some linear constraints. Note that no additional hyperparameters are needed by CCCP. Furthermore, each update (12.1) is a convex minimization problem and can be solved using classical and efficient convex algorithms.

12.3 Nonconvex SVMs

This section describes the "curse of dual variables," that the number of SVs increases in classical SVMs linearly with the number of training examples. The curse can be exorcised by replacing the classical hinge loss by a nonconvex loss function, the ramp loss. The optimization of the new dual problem can be solved using the CCCP.

12.3.1 Notation

In this section we consider two-class classification problems. We are given a training set $(\boldsymbol{x}_i, y_i)_{i=1\ldots L}$ with $(\boldsymbol{x}_i, y_i) \in \mathbb{R}^n \times \{-1, 1\}$. SVMs have a decision function $f_\theta(.)$ of the form $f_\theta(x) = w \cdot \Phi(x) + b$, where $\boldsymbol{\theta} = (\boldsymbol{w}, b)$ are the parameters of the model, and $\Phi(\cdot)$ is the chosen feature map, often implicitly defined by a Mercer kernel (Vapnik,

1995). We also write the hinge loss $H_s(z) = \max(0,\, s - z)$ (figure 12.1, center) where the subscript s indicates the position of the hinge point.

12.3.2 SVM Formulation

The standard SVM criterion relies on the convex hinge loss to penalize examples classified with an insufficient margin:

$$\boldsymbol{\theta} \;\mapsto\; \frac{1}{2}\|\boldsymbol{w}\|^2 + C\sum_{i=1}^{L} H_1\left(y_i\, f_{\boldsymbol{\theta}}(\boldsymbol{x}_i)\right). \tag{12.4}$$

The solution $\boldsymbol{w}$ is a sparse linear combination of the training examples $\Phi(\boldsymbol{x}_i)$, called *support vectors*. Recent results (Steinwart, 2003) show that the number of SVs k scales linearly with the number of examples. More specifically,

$$k/L \rightarrow 2\,\mathcal{B}_\Phi, \tag{12.5}$$

where $\mathcal{B}_\Phi$ is the best possible error achievable linearly in the chosen feature space $\Phi(\cdot)$. Since the SVM training and recognition times grow quickly with the number of SVs, it appears obvious that SVMs cannot deal with very large datasets. In the following we show how changing the cost function in SVMs cures the problem and leads to a nonconvex problem solvable by the CCCP.

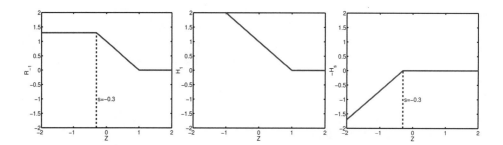

Figure 12.1 The ramp loss function $R_s(t) = \min(1 - s, \max(0, 1 - t)) = H_1(t) - H_s(t)$ (left) can be decomposed into the sum of the convex hinge loss (center) and a concave loss (right), where $H_s(t) = \max(0, s - t)$. The parameter s controls the cutoff point of the usual hinge loss.

12.3.3 Losses for SVMs

The SV scaling property (12.5) is not surprising because all misclassified training examples become SVs. This is in fact a property of the hinge loss function. Assume for simplicity that the hinge loss is made differentiable with a smooth approximation on a small interval $z \in [1-\varepsilon, 1+\varepsilon]$ near the hinge point. Differentiating (12.4) shows that the minimum $\boldsymbol{w}$ must satisfy

$$\boldsymbol{w} = -C \sum_{i=1}^{L} y_i \, H_1'(y_i) \, f_{\boldsymbol{\theta}}(\boldsymbol{x}_i)) \; \Phi(\boldsymbol{x}_i) \,. \tag{12.6}$$

Examples located in the flat area $(z > 1 + \varepsilon)$ cannot become SVs because $H_1'(z)$ is 0. Similarly, all examples located in the SVM margin $(z < 1 - \varepsilon)$ or simply misclassified $(z < 0)$ become SVs because the derivative $H_1'(z)$ is 1.

We propose to avoid converting some of these examples into SVs by making the loss function flat for scores z smaller than a predefined value $s < 1$. We thus introduce the ramp loss (figure 12.1):

$$R_s(z) = H_1(z) - H_s(z) \,. \tag{12.7}$$

Replacing H_1 by R_s in (12.6) guarantees that examples with score $z < s$ do not become SVs.

Rigorous proofs can be written without assuming that the loss function is differentiable. Similar to SVMs, we write (12.4) as a constrained minimization problem with slack variables and consider the Karush-Kuhn-Tucker conditions. Although the resulting problem is nonconvex, these conditions remain necessary (but not sufficient) optimality conditions (Ciarlet, 1990). We omit this easy but tedious derivation.

This sparsity argument provides a *new motivation for using a nonconvex loss function*. Unlike previous works (see section 12.1), our setup is designed to test and exploit this new motivation.

12.3.4 CCCP for Nonconvex SVMs

Decomposing (12.7) makes ramp loss SVMs amenable to CCCP optimization. The new cost $J^s(\boldsymbol{\theta})$ then reads

$$J^s(\boldsymbol{\theta}) = \frac{1}{2} \, \|\boldsymbol{w}\|^2 + C \sum_{i=1}^{L} R_s(y_i \, f_{\boldsymbol{\theta}}(\boldsymbol{x}_i)) \tag{12.8}$$

$$= \underbrace{\frac{1}{2} \, \|\boldsymbol{w}\|^2 + C \sum_{i=1}^{L} H_1(y_i \, f_{\boldsymbol{\theta}}(\boldsymbol{x}_i))}_{J^s_{vex}(\boldsymbol{\theta})} \underbrace{- C \sum_{i=1}^{L} H_s(y_i \, f_{\boldsymbol{\theta}}(\boldsymbol{x}_i))}_{J^s_{cav}(\boldsymbol{\theta})} \,.$$

For simplification purposes, we introduce the notation

$$\beta_i \;=\; y_i \frac{\partial J^s_{cav}(\boldsymbol{\theta})}{\partial f_{\boldsymbol{\theta}}(\boldsymbol{x}_i)} \;=\; \begin{cases} C & \text{if } y_i \, f_{\boldsymbol{\theta}}(\boldsymbol{x}_i) < s \,, \\ 0 & \text{otherwise.} \end{cases}$$

The convex optimization problem (12.1) that constitutes the core of the CCCP algorithm is easily reformulated into dual variables using the standard SVM technique. This yields algorithm 12.2.[2]

Algorithm 12.2 CCCP for ramp loss SVMs

Initialize $\boldsymbol{\theta}^0 = (\boldsymbol{w}^0, b^0)$ and $\boldsymbol{\beta}^0$ as described in the text.

repeat

- **Solve** the following convex problem (with $K_{ij} = \Phi(\boldsymbol{x}_i) \cdot \Phi(\boldsymbol{x}_j)$) and get $\boldsymbol{\alpha}^{t+1}$

$$\max_{\boldsymbol{\alpha}} \left(\boldsymbol{\alpha} \cdot \boldsymbol{y} - \frac{1}{2} \boldsymbol{\alpha}^T \boldsymbol{K} \boldsymbol{\alpha} \right) \text{ subject to } \begin{cases} \boldsymbol{\alpha} \cdot \mathbf{1} = 0 \\ -\beta_i^t \leq y_i \, \alpha_i \leq C - \beta_i^t \;\; \forall 1 \leq i \leq L \end{cases} \tag{12.9}$$

- **Compute** b^{t+1} using $f_{\boldsymbol{\theta}^{t+1}}(x_i) = \sum_{j=0}^{L} \alpha_j^{t+1} K_{ij} + b^{t+1}$ and

$$\forall i \leq L: \qquad 0 < y_i \, \alpha_i < C \implies y_i \, f_{\boldsymbol{\theta}^{t+1}}(x_i) = 1$$

- **Compute** $\beta_i^{t+1} = \begin{cases} C & \text{if } y_i \, f_{\boldsymbol{\theta}^{t+1}}(x_i) < s \\ 0 & \text{otherwise} \end{cases}$

until $\boldsymbol{\beta}^{t+1} = \boldsymbol{\beta}^t$

Convergence in a finite number of iterations is guaranteed because variable $\boldsymbol{\beta}$ can only take a finite number of distinct values, because $J(\boldsymbol{\theta}^t)$ is decreasing, and because inequality (12.3) is strict unless $\boldsymbol{\beta}$ remains unchanged.

12.3.5   Complexity

Although SVM training has a worst-case complexity of $O(L^3)$ it typically scales quadratically (see Joachims, 1999a; Platt, 1999). Setting the initial $\boldsymbol{\beta}^0$ to zero in algorithm 12.2 makes the first convex optimization identical to the hinge loss SVM optimization. Although useless SVs are eliminated during the following iterations, the whole optimization process remains quadratic, assuming a constant number of iterations (see figure 12.3).

Interestingly, we can easily give a *lower* bound on the SVM training complexity: simply verifying that a vector $\boldsymbol{\alpha}$ is a solution of the SVM quadratic problem involves computing the gradients of (12.9) with respect to $\boldsymbol{\alpha}$ and checking the Karush-Kuhn-Tucker optimality conditions (Vapnik, 1995). With L examples and S SVs, this requires a number of operations proportional to LS. With convex SVMs the number of SVs S tends to increase linearly with L, as shown in theory in section 12.3.2 and in practice in section 12.4.1 and figure 12.2: it is thus not surprising that convex SVMs are *at least* quadratic with respect to the number of training examples L.

---

2. Note that $R_s(z)$ is nondifferentiable at $z = s$. It can be shown that the CCCP remains valid when using any superderivative of the concave function. Alternatively, function $R_s(z)$ could be made smooth in a small interval $[s - \varepsilon, s + \varepsilon]$ as in our previous argument.

We can reduce the number of support vectors S even in the first iteration of algorithm 12.2 by simply choosing a better initial $\boldsymbol{\beta}^0$. We propose to initialize $\boldsymbol{\beta}^0$ according to the output $f_{\boldsymbol{\theta}^0}(\boldsymbol{x})$ of a hinge loss SVM trained on a subset of examples.

$$\beta_i^0 \;=\; \begin{cases} C & \text{if } y_i\, f_{\boldsymbol{\theta}^0}(\boldsymbol{x}_i) < s\ , \\ 0 & \text{otherwise.} \end{cases}$$

The successive convex optimizations are much faster because their solutions have roughly the same number of SVs as the final solution (see figure 12.2). We show in the experimental section 12.4.2 that this procedure is robust in practice, and its overall training time can be significantly smaller than the standard SVM training time.

12.3.6 Previous Work

The excessive number of SVs in SVMs has long been recognized as one of the main flaws of this otherwise elegant algorithm. Many methods to reduce the number of SVs are aftertraining methods that only improve efficiency during the test phase (see Schölkopf and Smola, 2002, chapter 18).

Both Elisseeff (2000) and Perez-Cruz et al. (2002) proposed a sigmoid loss for SVMs. Their motivation was to approximate the $0-1$ loss and they were not concerned with speed. Similarly, motivated by the theoretical promises of ψ-learning, Liu et al. (2005) proposes a special case of algorithm 12.2 with $s=0$ as the ramp loss parameter, and $\boldsymbol{\beta}^0 = 0$ as the algorithm initialization. In section 12.4, we show that our algorithm provides *sparse solutions*, thanks to the s parameter, and *accelerated training times*, thanks to a better choice of the $\boldsymbol{\beta}^0$ initialization.

More recently Xu et al. (2006) proposed a variant of SVMs where the hinge loss is also replaced by a nonconvex loss. Unfortunately, the resulting cost function is minimized after "convexification" of the problem, yielding to an extremely time-consuming semidefinite minimization problem.

12.4 Experiments with Nonconvex SVMs

The experiments in this section use a modified version of SVMTorch,[3] coded in C. Unless otherwise mentioned, the hyperparameters of all the models were chosen using a cross-validation technique, for best generalization performance. All results were averaged on ten train-test splits.

---

3. Experiments can be reproduced using the source code available at `http://www.kyb.tuebingen.mpg.de/bs/people/fabee/transduction.html`.

Table 12.1 Comparison of SVMs using the hinge loss (H_1) and the ramp loss (R_s). Test error rates (Error) and number of SVs. All hyperparameters including s were chosen using a validation set.

Dataset	Train	Test	Notes
Waveform[1]	4000	1000	Artificial data, 21 dims.
Banana[1]	4000	1300	Artificial data, 2 dims.
USPS+N[2]	7329	2000	0 vs rest + 10% label noise.
Adult[2]	32562	16282	As in (Platt, 1999).

[1] http://mlg.anu.edu.au/~raetsch/data/index.html
[2] ftp://ftp.ics.uci.edu/pub/machine-learning-databases

	SVM H_1		SVM R_s	
Dataset	Error	SV	Error	SV
Waveform	8.8%	983	8.8%	**865**
Banana	9.5%	1029	9.5%	**891**
USPS+N	0.5%	3317	0.5%	**601**
Adult	15.1%	11347	**15.0%**	**4588**

12.4.1 Accuracy and sparsity

We first study the accuracy and the sparsity of the solution obtained by algorithm 12.2. For that purpose, all the experiments in this section were performed by initializing the algorithm using $\boldsymbol{\beta}^0 = 0$ which corresponds to initializing the CCCP with the classical SVM solution. Table 12.1 presents an experimental comparison of the hinge loss and the ramp loss using the radial basis function (RBF) kernel $\Phi(\boldsymbol{x}_l) \cdot \Phi(\boldsymbol{x}_m) = \exp(-\gamma \|\boldsymbol{x}_l - \boldsymbol{x}_m\|^2)$. The results of table 12.1 clearly show that the ramp loss achieves similar generalization performance with much fewer SVs. This increased sparsity observed in practice follows our mathematical expectations, as exposed in section 12.3.3.

Figure 12.2 (left) shows how the s parameter of the ramp loss R_s controls the sparsity of the solution. We report the evolution of the number of SVs as a function of the number of training examples. Whereas the number of SVs in classical SVMs increases linearly, the number of SVs in ramp loss SVMs strongly depends on s. If $s \to -\infty$, then $R_s \to H_1$; in other words, if s takes large negative values, the ramp loss will not help to remove outliers from the SVM expansion, and the increase in SVs will be linear with respect to the number of training examples, as for classical SVMs. As reported on the left graph, for $s = -1$ on Adult the increase is already almost linear. As $s \to 0$, the ramp loss will prevent misclassified examples from becoming SVs. For $s = 0$ the number of SVs appears to increase like the square root of the number of examples, both for Adult and USPS+N.

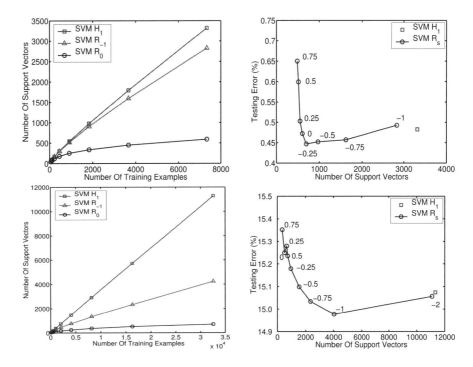

Figure 12.2 Comparison of the hinge loss and the ramp loss for `USPS+N` (top row) and `Adult` (bottom row). *Left*: Number of support vectors as a function of the training set size for the hinge loss H_1 and the ramp losses R_{-1} and R_0. *Right*: Testing error as a function of the number of support vectors for the hinge loss H_1 and various ramp losses R_s.

Figure 12.2 (right) shows the impact of the s parameter on the generalization performance. Note that selecting $0 < s < 1$ is possible, which allows the ramp loss to remove well classified examples from the set of SVs. Doing so degrades the generalization performance on both datasets.

Clearly s should be considered as a hyperparameter and selected for speed and accuracy considerations.

12.4.2   Speedup

The experiments we have detailed so far are not faster to train than a normal SVM because the first iteration ($\boldsymbol{\beta}^0 = 0$) corresponds to initializing CCCP with the classical SVM solution. Interestingly, few additional iterations are necessary (figure 12.3), and they run much faster because of the smaller number of SVs. The resulting training time was less than twice the SVM training time.

We thus propose to initialize the CCCP procedure with a subset of the training set (let's say $1/P^{th}$), as described in section 12.3.5. The first convex optimization is then going to be at least P^2 times faster than when initializing with $\boldsymbol{\beta}^0 = 0$

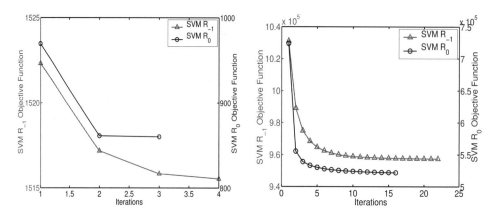

Figure 12.3 The objective function with respect to the number of iterations of the CCCP outer loop for USPS+N (left) and Adult (right).

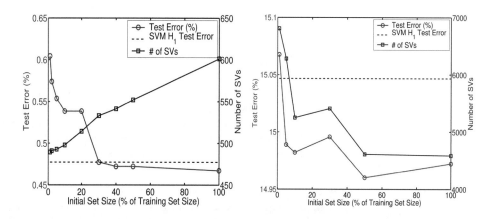

Figure 12.4 Results on USPS+N (left) and Adult (right) using an SVM with the ramp loss R_s. We show the test error and the number of SVs as a function of the percentage r of training examples used to initialize the CCCP, and compare to standard SVMs trained with the hinge loss. For each r, all hyperparameters were chosen using cross-validation.

(SVM's training time being known to scale at least quadratically with the number of examples). We then train the remaining iterations with all the data; however, compared to standard SVMs, fewer of these examples become SVs. Since the subsequent iterations involve a smaller number of SVs, we expect accelerated training times.

Figure 12.4 shows the robustness of the CCCP when initialized with a subset of the training set. On USPS+N and Adult, using respectively only one-third and one-tenth of the training examples is sufficient to match the generalization performance of classical SVMs.

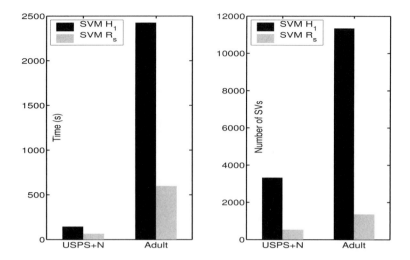

Figure 12.5 Results on `USPS+N` and `Adult` comparing hinge loss and ramp loss SVMs. The hyperparameters for the ramp loss SVMs were chosen such that their test error would be at least as good as the hinge loss SVM ones.

Using this scheme, and tuning the CCCP for speed and similar accuracy to SVMs, we obtain more than a twofold and fourfold speedup over SVMs on `USPS+N` and `Adult` respectively, together with a large increase in sparsity (see figure 12.5).

12.5 Nonconvex Transductive SVMs

The same nonconvex optimization techniques can be used to perform large-scale semisupervised learning. Transductive SVMs (Vapnik, 1995) seek large margins for both the labeled and unlabeled examples, in the hope that the true decision boundary lies in a region of low density, implementing the so-called cluster assumption (see Chapelle and Zien, 2005). When there are relatively few labeled examples and relatively abundant unlabeled examples, TSVMs can leverage unlabeled examples and give considerably better generalization performance than standard SVMs. Unfortunately, the TSVM implementations are rarely able to handle a large number of unlabeled examples.

Early TSVM implementations perform a *combinatorial* search of the best labels for the unlabeled examples. Bennett and Demiriz (1998) use an integer programming method, intractable for large problems. The SVM^{light}-TSVM (Joachims, 1999b) prunes the search tree using a nonconvex objective function. This is practical for a few thousand unlabeled examples.

More recent proposals (De Bie and Cristianini, 2004; Xu et al., 2005) transform the transductive problem into a larger *convex semidefinite programming problem*. The complexity of these algorithms grows like $(L + U)^4$ or worse, where L and U

are numbers of labeled and unlabeled examples. This is only practical for a few hundred examples.

We advocate instead the *direct optimization of the nonconvex objective function*. This direct approach has been used before. The sequential optimization procedure of Fung and Mangasarian (2001b) is the one most similar to our proposal. Their method potentially could scale well, although they only use 1000 examples in their largest experiment. However, it is restricted to the linear case, does not implement a balancing constraint (see below), and uses a special kind of SVM with a 1-norm regularizer to maintain linearity. The primal approach of Chapelle and Zien (2005) shows improved generalization performance, but still scales as $(L+U)^3$ and requires storing the entire $(L+U) \times (L+U)$ kernel matrix in memory.

12.5.1   Notation

We consider a set of L training pairs $\mathcal{L} = \{(\mathbf{x}_1, y_1), \ldots, (\mathbf{x}_L, y_L)\}$, $\mathbf{x} \in \mathbb{R}^n$, $y \in \{1, -1\}$ and an (unlabeled) set of U test vectors $\mathcal{U} = \{x_{L+1}, \ldots, x_{L+U}\}$.

12.5.2   TSVM Formulation

The original TSVM optimization problem is the following (Vapnik, 1995; Joachims, 1999b; Bennett and Demiriz, 1998). Given a training set $\mathcal{L}$ and a test set $\mathcal{U}$, find among the possible binary vectors,

$$\{\mathcal{Y} = (y_{L+1}, \ldots, y_{L+U})\} \, ,$$

the one such that an SVM trained on $\mathcal{L} \cup (\mathcal{U} \times \mathcal{Y})$ yields the largest margin.

This is a combinatorial problem, but one can approximate it (see Vapnik, 1995) as finding an SVM separating the training set under constraints which force the unlabeled examples to be as far as possible from the margin. This can be written as

$$\min_{\mathbf{w}} \quad \frac{1}{2}\|\mathbf{w}\|^2 + C \sum_{i=1}^{L} \xi_i + C^* \sum_{i=L+1}^{L+U} \xi_i$$

$$\text{subject to} \quad \begin{cases} y_i \, f_{\boldsymbol{\theta}}(\boldsymbol{x}_i) \geq 1 - \xi_i & \forall i = 1, \ldots, L \, , \\ |f_{\boldsymbol{\theta}}(\boldsymbol{x}_i)| \geq 1 - \xi_i & \forall i = L+1, \ldots, L+U \, . \end{cases}$$

This minimization problem is equivalent to minimizing

$$J(\boldsymbol{\theta}) = \frac{1}{2}\|\mathbf{w}\|^2 + C \sum_{i=1}^{L} H_1(y_i \, f_{\boldsymbol{\theta}}(\boldsymbol{x}_i)) + C^* \sum_{i=L+1}^{L+U} H_1(|f_{\boldsymbol{\theta}}(\boldsymbol{x}_i)|) \, , \tag{12.10}$$

where the function $H_1(\cdot) = \max(0, 1 - \cdot)$ is the classical hinge loss (figure 12.1, center). The loss function $H_1(|\cdot|)$ for the unlabeled examples can be seen in figure 12.6, left. For $C^* = 0$ in (12.10) we obtain the standard SVM optimization problem. For $C^* > 0$ we penalize unlabeled data that is inside the margin. This

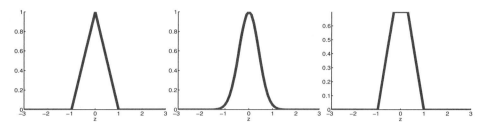

Figure 12.6 Three loss functions for unlabeled examples, from left to right: (i) the symmetric hinge $H_1(|t|) = \max(0, 1 - |t|)$, (ii) the symmetric sigmoid $S(t) = \exp(-3t^2)$, and (iii) the symmetric ramp loss $R_s(|t|) = \min(1 + s, \max(0, 1 - |t|))$. The last loss function has a plateau of width $2|s|$ where $s \in (-1, 0]$ is a tunable parameter, in this case $s = -0.3$.

is equivalent to using the hinge loss on the unlabeled data as well, but where we assume the label for the unlabeled example is $y_i = \text{sign}(f_{\boldsymbol{\theta}}(\boldsymbol{x}_i))$.

12.5.3   Losses for Transduction

TSVMs implementing formulation (12.10) were first introduced in SVM^{light} (Joachims, 1999b). As shown above, it assigns a hinge loss $H_1(\cdot)$ on the labeled examples (figure 12.1, center) and a "symmetric hinge loss" $H_1(|\cdot|)$ on the unlabeled examples (figure 12.6, left). More recently, Chapelle and Zien (2005) proposed handling unlabeled examples with a smooth version of this loss (figure 12.6, center). While we also use the hinge loss for labeled examples, we use for unlabeled examples a slightly more general form of the symmetric hinge loss, that we allow to be "nonpeaky" (figure 12.6, right). Given an unlabeled example $\boldsymbol{x}$ and using the notation $z = f_{\boldsymbol{\theta}}(\boldsymbol{x})$, this loss can be written as[4]

$$z \mapsto R_s(z) + R_s(-z) + const. \,, \tag{12.11}$$

where $-1 < s \leq 0$ is a hyperparameter to be chosen and

$$R_s(t) = \min(1 - s, \max(0, 1 - t))$$

is the ramp loss already introduced in section 12.3.3 and figure 12.1. The s parameter controls where we clip the ramp loss, and as a consequence it also controls the wideness of the flat part of the loss (12.11) we use for transduction: when $s = 0$, this reverts to the symmetric hinge $H_1(|\cdot|)$. When $s \neq 0$, we obtain a nonpeaked loss function (figure 12.6, right) which can be viewed as a simplification of Chapelle's loss function. We call this loss function (12.11) the "symmetric ramp loss".

---

4. The constant does not affect the optimization problem we will later describe.

Training a TSVM using the loss function (12.11) is equivalent to training an SVM using the hinge loss $H_1(\cdot)$ for labeled examples, and using the ramp loss $R_s(\cdot)$ for unlabeled examples, where each unlabeled example appears as two examples labeled with both possible classes. More formally, after introducing

$$
\begin{aligned}
y_i &= 1 & i &\in [L+1\ldots L+U] \\
y_i &= -1 & i &\in [L+U+1\ldots L+2U] \\
\boldsymbol{x}_i &= \boldsymbol{x}_{i-U} & i &\in [L+U+1\ldots L+2U]\,,
\end{aligned}
$$

we can rewrite (12.10) as

$$
J^s(\boldsymbol{\theta}) = \frac{1}{2}\|\mathbf{w}\|^2 + C\sum_{i=1}^{L} H_1(y_i\,f_{\boldsymbol{\theta}}(\boldsymbol{x}_i)) + C^*\sum_{i=L+1}^{L+2U} R_s(y_i\,f_{\boldsymbol{\theta}}(\boldsymbol{x}_i))\,. \tag{12.12}
$$

This is the minimization problem we now consider in the rest of the chapter.

12.5.4   Balancing Constraint

One problem with TSVM as stated above is that in high dimensions with few training examples, it is possible to classify all the unlabeled examples as belonging to only one of the classes with a very large margin, which leads to poor performance. To cure this problem, one further constrains the solution by introducing a balancing constraint that ensures that the unlabeled data is assigned to both classes. Joachims (1999b) directly enforces that the fraction of positive and negatives assigned to the unlabeled data should be the same fraction as found in the labeled data. Chapelle and Zien (2005) use a similar but slightly relaxed constraint, which we also use in this work:

$$
\frac{1}{U}\sum_{i=L+1}^{L+U} f_{\boldsymbol{\theta}}(\boldsymbol{x}_i) = \frac{1}{L}\sum_{i=1}^{L} y_i\,. \tag{12.13}
$$

12.5.5   CCCP for TSVMs

As for nonconvex SVMs in section 12.3, the decomposition (12.7) of the ramp loss makes the TSVM minimization problem as stated in (12.12) amenable to CCCP optimization. The cost $J^s(\boldsymbol{\theta})$ can indeed be decomposed into a convex $J^s_{vex}(\boldsymbol{\theta})$ and concave $J_{cav}^s(\boldsymbol{\theta})$ part as follows:

$$
\begin{aligned}
J^s(\boldsymbol{\theta}) &= \frac{1}{2} \|\boldsymbol{w}\|^2 + C \sum_{i=1}^{L} H_1(y_i \, f_{\boldsymbol{\theta}}(\boldsymbol{x}_i)) + C^* \sum_{i=L+1}^{L+2U} R_s(y_i \, f_{\boldsymbol{\theta}}(\boldsymbol{x}_i)) \\
&= \underbrace{\frac{1}{2} \|\boldsymbol{w}\|^2 + C \sum_{i=1}^{L} H_1(y_i \, f_{\boldsymbol{\theta}}(\boldsymbol{x}_i)) + C^* \sum_{i=L+1}^{L+2U} H_1(y_i \, f_{\boldsymbol{\theta}}(\boldsymbol{x}_i))}_{J_{vex}^s(\boldsymbol{\theta})} \\
&\quad \underbrace{- C^* \sum_{i=L+1}^{L+2U} H_s(y_i \, f_{\boldsymbol{\theta}}(\boldsymbol{x}_i))}_{J_{cav}^s(\boldsymbol{\theta})} .
\end{aligned}
\tag{12.14}
$$

This decomposition allows us to apply the CCCP as stated in algorithm 12.1. The convex optimization problem (12.1) that constitutes the core of the CCCP is easily reformulated into dual variables $\boldsymbol{\alpha}$ using the standard SVM technique.

We show in (Collobert et al., 2006) that enforcing the balancing constraint (12.13) can be achieved by introducing an extra Lagrangian variable α_0 and an example $\boldsymbol{x}_0$ implicitly defined by

$$
\Phi(\boldsymbol{x}_0) = \frac{1}{U} \sum_{i=L+1}^{L+U} \Phi(\boldsymbol{x}_i) ,
$$

with label $y_0 = 1$. Thus, if we note K the kernel matrix such that

$$
K_{ij} = \Phi(\boldsymbol{x}_i) \cdot \Phi(\boldsymbol{x}_j) ,
$$

the column corresponding to the example $\boldsymbol{x}_0$ is computed as follows:

$$
K_{i0} = K_{0i} = \frac{1}{U} \sum_{j=L+1}^{L+U} \Phi(\boldsymbol{x}_j) \cdot \Phi(\boldsymbol{x}_i) \quad \forall i .
\tag{12.15}
$$

The computation of this special column can be achieved very efficiently by computing it only once, or by approximating the sum (12.15) using an appropriate sampling method.

Given the decomposition of the cost (12.14) and the trick of the special extra example (12.15) to enforce the balancing constraint, we can easily apply algorithm 12.1 to TSVMs. To simplify the first-order approximation of the concave part in the CCCP procedure (12.1), we denote as in section 12.3.4

$$
\beta_i = y_i \frac{\partial J_{cav}^s(\boldsymbol{\theta})}{\partial f_{\boldsymbol{\theta}}(\boldsymbol{x}_i)} =
\begin{cases}
C^* & \text{if } y_i \, f_{\boldsymbol{\theta}}(\boldsymbol{x}_i) < s , \\
0 & \text{otherwise,}
\end{cases}
\tag{12.16}
$$

for unlabeled examples (that is $i \geq L+1$). The concave part J_{cav}^s does not depend on labeled examples ($i \leq L$) so we obviously have $\beta_i = 0$ for all $i \leq L$. After some standard derivations detailed in (Collobert et al., 2006), this yields algorithm 12.3.

This algorithm is very similar to algorithm 12.2 which we obtained in the case of nonconvex SVMs.

Algorithm 12.3 CCCP for TSVMs

Initialize $\boldsymbol{\theta}^0 = (\boldsymbol{w}^0, b^0)$ with a standard SVM solution on the labeled points.

Compute $\beta_i^0 = \begin{cases} C^* & \text{if } y_i\, f_{\boldsymbol{\theta}^0}(\boldsymbol{x}_i) < s \text{ and } i \geq L+1 \\ 0 & \text{otherwise} \end{cases}$

Set $\zeta_i = y_i$ for $1 \leq i \leq L+2U$ and $\zeta_0 = \frac{1}{L}\sum_{i=1}^{L} y_i$

repeat

- **Solve** the following convex problem (with $K_{ij} = \Phi(\boldsymbol{x}_i) \cdot \Phi(\boldsymbol{x}_j)$) and get $\boldsymbol{\alpha}^{t+1}$

$$\max_{\boldsymbol{\alpha}} \left(\boldsymbol{\alpha} \cdot \boldsymbol{\zeta} - \frac{1}{2}\boldsymbol{\alpha}^T \boldsymbol{K} \boldsymbol{\alpha} \right) \text{ subject to } \begin{cases} \boldsymbol{\alpha} \cdot \mathbf{1} = 0 \\ 0 \leq y_i\, \alpha_i \leq C \quad \forall 1 \leq i \leq L \\ -\beta_i \leq y_i\, \alpha_i \leq C^* - \beta_i \quad \forall i \geq L+1 \end{cases}$$

- **Compute** b^{t+1} using $f_{\boldsymbol{\theta}^{t+1}}(x_i) = \sum_{j=0}^{L+2U} \alpha_j^{t+1} K_{ij} + b^{t+1}$ and

$$\forall i \leq L : \qquad\qquad 0 < y_i\, \alpha_i < C \quad \Longrightarrow \quad y_i\, f_{\boldsymbol{\theta}^{t+1}}(x_i) = 1$$
$$\forall i > L : \quad -\beta_i^t < y_i\, \alpha_i < C^* - \beta_i^t \quad \Longrightarrow \quad y_i\, f_{\boldsymbol{\theta}^{t+1}}(x_i) = 1$$

- **Compute** $\beta_i^{t+1} = \begin{cases} C^* & \text{if } y_i\, f_{\boldsymbol{\theta}^{t+1}}(\boldsymbol{x}_i) < s \text{ and } i \geq L+1 \\ 0 & \text{otherwise} \end{cases}$

until $\boldsymbol{\beta}^{t+1} = \boldsymbol{\beta}^t$

12.5.6 Complexity

The main point we want to emphasize is the advantage in terms of training time of our method compared to existing approaches. Training a CCCP-TSVM amounts to solving a series of SVM optimization problems with $L + 2U$ variables. As we highlighted in section 12.3.5, SVM training has a worst-case complexity of $O((L + 2U)^3)$ but typically scales quadratically, and we find this is the case for our TSVM subproblems as well. Assuming a constant number of iteration steps, the whole optimization of TSVMs with CCCP should scale quadratically in most practical cases (see figures 12.7, 12.9, and 12.10). From our experience, around five iteration steps are usually sufficient to reach the minimum, as shown in section 12.6 and figure 12.8.

12.5.7 Previous Work

12.5.7.1 SVMLight-TSVM

Like our work, the heuristic optimization algorithm implemented in SVM^{light} (Joachims, 1999b) solves successive SVM optimization problems, but on $L + U$ instead of $L + 2U$ data points. It improves the objective function by iteratively switching the labels of two unlabeled points $\mathbf{x}_i$ and $\mathbf{x}_j$ with $\xi_i + \xi_j > 2$. It uses two nested loops to optimize a TSVM which solves a quadratic program in each step. The convergence proof of the inner loop relies on the fact that there is only a finite number 2^U of labelings of U unlabeled points, even though it is unlikely that all of them are examined. However, since the heuristic only swaps the labels of two unlabeled examples at each step in order to enforce the balancing constraint, it might need many iterations to reach a minimum, which makes it intractable for big dataset sizes in practice (cf. figure 12.7).

SVM^{light} uses annealing heuristics for the selection of C^*. It begins with a small value of C^* ($C^* = 1e - 5$), and multiplies C^* by 1.5 on each iteration until it reaches C. The numbers $1e - 5$ and 1.5 are hard coded into the implementation. On each iteration the tolerance on the gradients is also changed so as to give more approximate (but faster) solutions on earlier iterations. Again, several heuristics parameters are hard-coded into the implementation.

12.5.7.2 ∇TSVM

The ∇TSVM of Chapelle and Zien (2005) is optimized by performing gradient descent in the primal space: minimize

$$\frac{1}{2}\|\mathbf{w}\|^2 + C \sum_{i=1}^{L} H^2(y_i\, f_{\boldsymbol{\theta}}(\boldsymbol{x}_i)) + C^* \sum_{i=L+1}^{L+U} H^*(y_i\, f_{\boldsymbol{\theta}}(\boldsymbol{x}_i)),$$

where $H^2(t) = \max(0, 1 - t)^2$ and $H^*(t) = \exp(-3t^2)$ (figure 12.6, center). This optimization problem can be considered a smoothed version of (12.10). ∇TSVM also has similar heuristics for C^* as SVM^{light}-TSVM. It begins with a small value of C^* ($C^* = bC$), and iteratively increases C^* over l iterations until it finally reaches C. The values $b = 0.01$ and $l = 10$ are default parameters in the code.[5]

Since the gradient descent is carried out in the primal, to learn nonlinear functions it is necessary to perform kernel principal component analysis (KPCA) (Schölkopf et al., 1997). The overall algorithm has a time complexity equal to the square of the number of variables times the complexity of evaluating the cost function; in this case, evaluating the objective scales linearly in the number of examples, so the overall worst case complexity of solving the optimization problem for ∇TSVM is

---

5. The ∇TSVM code is available at `http://www.kyb.tuebingen.mpg.de/bs/people/chapelle/lds`.

$O((U+L)^3)$. The KPCA calculation alone also has a time complexity of $O((U+L)^3)$. This method also requires one to store the entire kernel matrix in memory, which clearly becomes infeasible for large datasets.

12.5.7.3　*CS³VM*

The work of Fung and Mangasarian (2001b) is algorithmically the closest TSVM approach to our proposal. Following the formulation of TSVMs found in (Bennett and Demiriz, 1998), the authors consider transductive linear SVMs with a 1-norm regularizer, which allows them to decompose the corresponding loss function as a sum of a linear function and a concave function. Bennett and Demiriz (1998) proposed the following formulation which is similar to (12.10):

$$\min_{\mathbf{w}}\quad ||\mathbf{w}||_1 + C\sum_{i=1}^{L}\xi_i + C^*\sum_{i=L+1}^{U}\min(\xi_i, \xi_i^*)$$

$$\text{subject to}\quad \begin{cases} y_i\, f_{\boldsymbol{\theta}}(\boldsymbol{x}_i) \geq 1 - \xi_i & \forall i = 1,\ldots,L\ , \\ f_{\boldsymbol{\theta}}(\boldsymbol{x}_i) \geq 1 - \xi_i & \forall i = L+1,\ldots,L+U\ , \\ -(\mathbf{w}\cdot\mathbf{x}_i + b) \geq 1 - \xi_i^* & \forall i = L+1,\ldots,L+U\ , \\ \xi_i \geq 0\ , \\ \xi_i^* \geq 0\ . \end{cases}$$

The last term of the objective function is nonlinear and corresponds to the loss function given in figure 12.6 (left). To deal with this, the authors suggest iteratively approximating the concave part as a linear function, leading to a series of linear programming problems. This can be viewed as a simplified subcase of the CCCP (a linear function being convex) applied to a special kind of SVM. Note also that the algorithm presented in their paper did not implement a balancing constraint for the labeling of the unlabeled examples as in (12.13). Our transduction algorithm is nonlinear and the use of kernels, solving the optimization in the dual, allows for large-scale training with high dimensionality and number of examples.

12.6　Experiments with TSVMs

12.6.1　Small-Scale Experiments

This section presents small scale experiments appropriate for comparing our algorithm with existing TSVM approaches. In order to provide a direct comparison with published results, these experiments use the same setup as (Chapelle and Zien, 2005). All methods use the standard RBF kernel, $\Phi(\mathbf{x})\cdot\Phi(\mathbf{x}') = \exp(-\gamma||\mathbf{x}-\mathbf{x}'||^2)$.

Table 12.2 lists the datasets we have used. The g50c dataset is an artificial dataset where the labels correspond to two Gaussians in a 50-dimensional space. The means of those Gaussians are placed in such a way that the Bayes error is 5%. The coil20

Table 12.2 Small-scale datasets. We used the same datasets and experimental setup in these experiments as found in (Chapelle and Zien, 2005).

Dataset	Classes	Dims	Points	Labeled
g50c	2	50	500	50
coil20	20	1024	1440	40
text	2	7511	1946	50
uspst	10	256	2007	50

Table 12.3 Results on small-scale datasets. We report the best test error over the hyperparameters of the algorithms, as in the methodology of Chapelle and Zien (2005). SVM^{light}-TSVM is the implementation in SVM^{light}. ∇TSVM is the primal gradient descent method of Chapelle and Zien (2005). CCCP-TSVM $|_{UC^*=LC}^{s=0}$ reports the results of our method using the heuristic $UC^* = LC$ with the symmetric hinge loss, that is, with $s = 0$. We also report CCCP-TSVM $|_{UC^*=LC}$, where we allow the optimization of s, and CCCP-TSVM, where we allow the optimization of both C^* and s.

	coil20	g50c	text	uspst	Number of hyperparameters
SVM	24.64	8.32	18.86	23.18	2
SVM^{light}-TSVM	26.26	6.87	7.44	26.46	2
∇TSVM	17.56	5.80	5.71	17.61	2
CCCP-TSVM $|_{UC^*=LC}^{s=0}$	16.69	5.62	7.97	16.57	2
CCCP-TSVM $|_{UC^*=LC}$	16.06	5.04	5.59	16.47	3
CCCP-TSVM	15.92	3.92	4.92	16.45	4

data is a set of gray-scale images of 20 different objects taken from different angles, in steps of 5 degrees (Nene et al., 1996). The text dataset consists of the classes mswindows and mac of the Newsgroup20 dataset preprocessed as in (Szummer and Jaakkola, 2002). The uspst dataset is the test part of the USPS handwritten digit data. All datasets are split into ten parts with each part having a small amount of labeled examples and using the remaining part as unlabeled data.

12.6.1.1   Accuracies

Following Chapelle and Zien (2005), all hyperparameters are tuned on the test set (they do this for all methods but one, LDS, for which they perform cross-validation). We should be cautious when comparing our algorithm in this way, especially

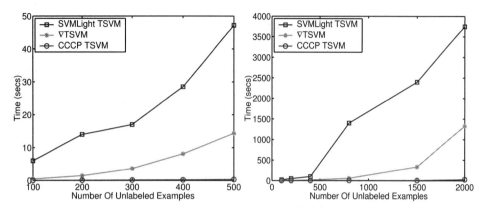

Figure 12.7 Training times for `g50c` (left) and `text` (right) for SVM^{light}-TSVMs, ∇TSVMs and CCCP-TSVMs, using the best parameters for each algorithm as measured on the test set in a single trial. For the Text dataset, using 2000 unlabeled examples, CCCP-TSVMs are **133x** faster than SVM^{light}-TSVMs, and **50x** faster than ∇TSVMs.

when the algorithms have different sets of hyperparameters. For CCCP-TSVMs, compared to the other algorithms, we have two additional parameters, C^* and s. Therefore we report the CCCP-TSVM error rates for three different scenarios:

- CCCP-TSVM, where all four parameters are tuned on the test set.

- CCCP-TSVM $|_{UC^*=LC}$, where we choose C^* using a heuristic method. We use heuristic $UC^* = LC$ because it decreases C^* when the number of unlabeled data increases. Otherwise, for large enough U no attention will be paid to minimizing the training error.

- CCCP-TSVM $|^{s=0}_{UC^*=LC}$, where we choose $s = 0$ and C^* using heuristic $UC^* = LC$. This setup has the same free parameters (C and γ) as the competing TSVM implementations, and therefore provides the most fair comparison.

The results are reported in table 12.3. CCCP-TSVM in all three scenarios achieves approximately the same error rates as ∇TSVM and appears to be superior to SVM^{light}-TSVM.

12.6.1.2 Training Times

At this point we ask the reader to simply assume that all authors have chosen their hyperparameter selection method as well as they could. We now compare the computation times of these three algorithms.

The CCCP-TSVM algorithm was implemented in C++.[6] The successive con-

---

6. Source code available at `http://www.kyb.tuebingen.mpg.de/bs/people/fabee/transduction.html`.

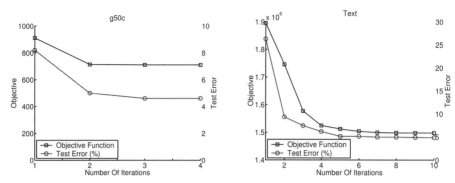

Figure 12.8 Value of the objective function and test error during the CCCP iterations of training TSVM on two datasets (single trial), g50c (left) and text (right). CCCP-TSVM tends to converge after only a few iterations.

vex optimizations are performed using a state-of-the-art SMO implementation. Without further optimization, CCCP-TSVMs run orders of magnitude faster than SVM*light*-TSVMs and ∇TSVM.[7] Figure 12.7 shows the training time on g50c and text for the three methods as we vary the number of unlabeled examples. For each method we report the training times for the hyperparameters that give optimal performance as measured on the test set on the first split of the data (we use CCCP-TSVM $|_{UC^*=LC}^{s=0}$ in these experiments). Using all 2000 unlabeled data on Text, CCCP-TSVMs are approximately *133 times faster* than SVM*light*-TSVM and *50 times faster* than ∇TSVM.

We expect these differences to increase as the number of unlabeled examples increases further. In particular, ∇TSVM requires the storage of the entire kernel matrix in memory, and is therefore clearly infeasible for some of the large-scale experiments we attempt in section 12.6.2.

Finally, figure 12.8 shows the value of the objective function and test error during the CCCP iterations of training TSVM on two datasets. The CCCP-TSVM objective function converges after five to ten iterations.

12.6.2 Large-Scale Experiments

In this section, we provide experimental results on large-scale experiments. Since other methods are intractable on such data sets, we only compare CCCP-TSVM against SVMs.

---

7. ∇TSVM was implemented by adapting the **MATLAB** LDS code of Chapelle and Zien (2005) available at `http://www.kyb.tuebingen.mpg.de/bs/people/chapelle/lds`.

Table 12.4 Comparing CCCP-TSVMs with SVMs on the RCV1 problem for different numbers of labeled and unlabeled examples. See text for details.

Method	Labeled	Unlabeled	Parameters	Test error
SVM	100	0	$C = 252.97,\ \sigma = 15.81$	16.61%
TSVM	100	500	$C = 2.597, C^* = 10,\ s = -0.2,\ \sigma = 3.95$	11.99%
TSVM	100	1000	$C = 2.597, C^* = 10,\ s = -0.2,\ \sigma = 3.95$	11.67%
TSVM	100	2000	$C = 2.597, C^* = 10,\ s = -0.2,\ \sigma = 3.95$	11.47%
TSVM	100	5000	$C = 2.597, C^* = 2.5297,\ s = -0.2,\ \sigma = 3.95$	10.65%
TSVM	100	10000	$C = 2.597, C^* = 2.5297,\ s = -0.4,\ \sigma = 3.95$	10.64%
SVM	1000	0	$C = 25.297,\ \sigma = 7.91$	11.04%
TSVM	1000	500	$C = 2.597, C^* = 10,\ s = -0.4,\ \sigma = 3.95$	11.09%
TSVM	1000	1000	$C = 2.597, C^* = 2.5297,\ s = -0.4,\ \sigma = 3.95$	11.06%
TSVM	1000	2000	$C = 2.597, C^* = 10,\ s - 0.4 =,\ \sigma = 3.95$	10.77%
TSVM	1000	5000	$C = 2.597, C^* = 2.5297,\ s = -0.2,\ \sigma = 3.95$	10.81%
TSVM	1000	10000	$C = 2.597, C^* = 25.2970,\ s = -0.4,\ \sigma = 3.95$	10.72%

12.6.2.1   RCV1 Experiments

The first large-scale experiment that we conducted was to separate the two largest top-level categories CCAT (CORPORATE/INDUSTRIAL) and GCAT (GOVERNMENT/SOCIAL) of the training part of the Reuters dataset as prepared by Lewis et al. (2004). The set of these two categories consists of 17,754 documents. The features are constructed using the bag of words technique, weighted with a TF.IDF scheme and normalized to length 1. We performed experiments using 100 and 1000 labeled examples. For model selection we use a validation set with 2000 and 4000 labeled examples for the two experiments. The remaining 12,754 examples were used as a test set.

We chose the parameter C and the kernel parameter γ (using an RBF kernel) that gave the best performance on the validation set. This was done by training a TSVM using the validation set as the unlabeled data. These values were then fixed for every experiment.

We then varied the number of unlabeled examples U, and reported the test error for each choice of U. In each case we performed model selection to find the parameters C^* and s. A selection of the results can be seen in table 12.4. The best result we obtained for 1000 training points was 10.58% test error, when using 10,500 unlabeled points, and for 100 training points was 10.42% when using 9500 unlabeled points. Compared to the best performance of an SVM of 11.04% for the former and 16.61% for the latter, this shows that unlabeled data can improve the results on this problem. This is especially true in the case of few training examples, where the improvement in test error is around 5.5%. However, when enough training data is available to the algorithm, the improvement is only on the order of 1%. Figure

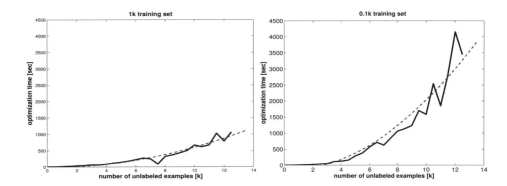

Figure 12.9 Optimization time for the Reuters dataset as a function of the number of unlabeled data. The algorithm was trained on 1000 points (left) and on 100 points (right). The dashed lines represent a parabola fitted at the time measurements.

Table 12.5 Comparing CCCP-TSVMs with SVMs on the MNIST problem for different numbers of labeled and unlabeled examples. See text for details.

Method	Labeled	Unlabeled	Parameters	Test
SVM	100	0	$C = 10, \gamma = 0.0128$	23.44%
TSVM	100	2000	$C^* = 1, s = -0.1$	16.81%
SVM	1000	0	$C = 10, \gamma = 0.0128$	7.77%
TSVM	1000	2000	$C^* = 5, s = -0.1$	7.13%
TSVM	1000	5000	$C^* = 1, s = -0.1$	6.28%
TSVM	1000	10000	$C^* = 0.5, s = -0.1$	5.65%
TSVM	1000	20000	$C^* = 0.3, s = -0.1$	5.43%
TSVM	1000	40000	$C^* = 0.2, s = -0.1$	5.31%
TSVM	1000	60000	$C^* = 0.1, s = -0.1$	5.38%

12.9 shows the training time of CCCP optimization as a function of the number of unlabeled examples. On a 64 bit Opteron processor the optimization time for 12,500 unlabeled examples was approximately 18 minutes using the 1000 training examples and 69 minutes using 100 training examples. Although the worst-case complexity of SVMs is cubic and the optimization time seems to be dependent on the ratio of the number of labeled to unlabeled examples, the training times show a quadratic trend.

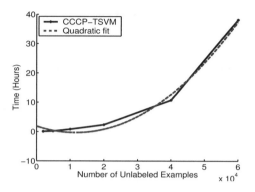

Figure 12.10 Optimization time for the MNIST dataset as a function of the number of unlabeled data. The algorithm was trained on 1000 labeled examples and up to 60,000 unlabeled examples. The dashed lines represent a polynomial of degree 2 with a least-squares fit on the algorithm's time measurements.

12.6.2.2   MNIST Experiments

In the second large-scale experiment, we conducted experiments on the MNIST handwritten digit database, as a 10-class problem. The original data has 60,000 training examples and 10,000 testing examples. We subsampled the training set for labeled points, and used the test set for unlabeled examples (or the test set plus the remainder of the training set when using more than 10,000 unlabeled examples). We performed experiments using 100 and 1000 labeled examples. We performed model selection for one-vs.-rest SVMs by trying a grid of values for σ and C, and selecting the best ones by using a separate validation set of size 1000. For TSVMs, for efficiency reasons we fixed the values of σ and C to be the same ones as chosen for SVMs. We then performed model selection using 2000 unlabeled examples to find the best choices of C^* and s using the validation set. When using more unlabeled data, we only reperformed model selection on C^*, as it appeared that this parameter was the most sensitive to changes in the unlabeled set, and kept the other parameters fixed. For the larger labeled set we took 2000, 5000, 10,000, 20,000, 40,000 and 60,000 unlabeled examples. We always measure the error rate on the complete test set. The test error rate and parameter choices for each experiment are given in table 12.5, and the training times are given in figure 12.10.

The results show an improvement over SVM for CCCP-TSVMs which increases steadily as the number of unlabeled examples increases. Most experiments in semisupervised learning only use a few labeled examples and do not use as many unlabeled examples as described here. It is thus reassuring to know that these methods do not apply just to toy examples with around 50 training points, and that gains are still possible with more realistic dataset sizes.

12.7   Conclusion

We described two nonconvex algorithms using the CCCP that bring marked scalability improvements over the corresponding convex approaches, namely for SVMs and TSVMs. Moreover, any new improvements to standard SVM training could immediately be applied to either of our CCCP algorithms.

In general, we argue that the current popularity of convex approaches should not dissuade researchers from exploring alternative techniques, as they sometimes give clear computational benefits.

Acknowledgments

We thank Hans Peter Graf, Eric Cosatto and Vladimir Vapnik for their advice and support. Part of this work was funded by NSF grant CCR-0325463.

13 Training Invariant SVMs Using Selective Sampling

Gaëlle Loosli
Léon Bottou
Stéphane Canu

In this chapter we present the combination of two approaches to build a very large support vector machine (SVM). The first method, from Loosli et al. (2005), proposes a strategy for handling invariances in SVMs. It is based on the well-known idea that small deformations of the examples should not change their class. The deformed samples are selected or discarded during learning (it is selective sampling). The second approach, from Bordes et al. (2005), is an efficient online algorithm (each training point is only seen once) that also uses selective sampling. We present state-of-the-art results obtained on a handwritten digit recognition problem with 8 millions points on a single processor. This work also demonstrates that online SVMs can effectively handle really large databases.

13.1 Introduction

Because many patterns are insensitive to certain transformations such as rotations or translations, it is widely admitted that the quality of a pattern recognition system can be improved by taking into account invariance. Very different ways to handle invariance in machine learning algorithms have been proposed (Fukushima, 1988; K. J. Lang and Hinton, 1988; Simard et al., 2000; Leen, 1995; Schölkopf et al., 1996).

In the case of kernel machines, three general approaches have been proposed. The first approach consists of learning orbits instead of points. It requires costly semidefinite programming algorithms (Graepel and Herbrich, 2004). The second approach involves specialized kernels. This turns out to be equivalent to mapping the patterns into a space of invariant features (Chapelle and Schölkopf, 2002). Such features are often difficult to construct. The third approach is the most general.

It consists of artificially enlarging the training set by new examples obtained by deforming the available input data (Schölkopf and Smola, 2002). This approach suffers from high computational costs. Very large datasets can be generated this way. For instance, by generating 134 random deformations per digit, we have increased the MNIST training set size from 60,000 to more than 8 million examples. A batch optimization algorithm working on the augmented database needs to go several times through the entire dataset until convergence. Either we store the whole dataset or we compute the deformed examples on demand, trading reduced memory requirements for increased computation time.

We propose two tools to reduce these computational costs:

- *Selective sampling* lets our system select informative points and discard useless ones. This property would reduce the amount of samples to be stored.

- Unlike batch optimization algorithms, *online learning* algorithms do not need to access each example again and again until convergence. They only consider each example once. Such repeated access is particularly costly when the deformed examples are computed on demand. This is even more wasteful because most examples are readily discarded by the selective sampling methods.

13.1.1   Large-Scale Learning

Running machine learning algorithms on very large scale problems is still difficult. For instance, Bennett and Campbell (2000) discuss the problem of scaling support vector machines (SVMs) "to massive datasets" and point out that learning algorithms are typically quadratic and imply several scans of the data. Three factors limit machine learning algorithms when both the sample size n and the input dimension d grow very large. First, the training time becomes unreasonable. Second, the size of the solution affects the memory requirements during both the training and recognition phases. Third, labeling the training examples becomes very expensive. To address those limitations, there have been a lot of clever studies on solving quadratic optimization problems (chapter 1), on online learning (Bottou, 1998; Kivinen et al., 2002; Crammer et al., 2004), on sparse solutions (Vincent and Bengio, 2002), and on active learning (Cohn et al., 1995; Campbell et al., 2000).

The notion of computational complexity discussed in this chapter is tied to the empirical performance of algorithms. Three common strategies can be distinguished to reduce this practical complexity (or observed training time). The first strategy consists in working on subsets of the training data, solving several smaller problems instead of a large one, as in the SVM decomposition method (Osuna et al., 1997a). The second strategy consists in parallelizing the learning algorithm. The third strategy tries to design less complex algorithms that give an approximate solution with equivalent or superior performance. For instance, early stopping approximates the full optimization without compromising the test set accuracy. This paper focuses on this third strategy.

13.1.2   Learning Complexity

The core of many learning algorithms essentially amounts to solving a system of linear equations of the form $A\mathbf{x} = b$ where A is an $n \times n$ input matrix, b an output vector, and x is an unknown vector. There are many classical methods to solve such systems (Golub and Van Loan, 1996). For instance, if we know that A is symmetric and semidefinite positive, we can factorize as $A = LL'$ where L is a lower triangular matrix representing the square root of A. The factorization costs $O(n^3)$ operations. Similarly to this Cholesky factorization, there are many methods for all kinds of matrices A such as QR, LU, etc. Their complexity is always $O(n^3)$. They lead to the exact solution, even though in practice some are more numerically stable or slightly faster. When the problem becomes large, a method with a cubic complexity is not a realistic approach.

Iterative methods are useful for larger problems. The idea is to start from some initial vector $\mathbf{x}_0$ (null or random) and to iteratively update it by performing steps of size ρ_k along direction d_k, that is, $\mathbf{x}_{k+1} = \mathbf{x}_k + \rho_k d_k$. Choosing the direction is the difficult part. The optimization literature suggests that the first-order gradients yield very poor directions. Finding a second-order direction costs $O(n^2)$ operations (conjugate gradients, etc.) and provides the exact solution in n iterations, for a total of $O(n^3)$ operations. However, we obtain an approximate solution in fewer steps. Therefore these algorithms have a practical complexity of $O(kn^2)$ where k is the number of steps required to have a good enough approximation. Hence we have algorithms for larger problems, but they remain too costly for really very large datasets.

Additional progress can be achieved by exploiting sparsity. The idea is to constrain the number of nonzero coefficients in vector $\mathbf{x}$. Approximate computations can indicate which coefficients will be zero with high confidence. Then the remaining subsystem can be solved with any of the previously described methods. This approach corresponds to the fact that many examples bring very little additional information. The hope is then to have a solution with an empirical complexity $O(n^d)$ with d close to 2. This idea is exploited by modern SVM algorithms.

During his optimization lecture, Nemirovski (2005) said that "*the extremely large-scale case ($n \gg 10^5$) rules out all advanced convex optimization technics.*" He argues that there is only one option left, "*first order gradient methods.*" We are convinced that other approximate techniques can exploit the specificities of learning problems (e.g., sparseness). For instance, the LASVM method (Bordes and Bottou, 2005; Bordes et al., 2005) seems considerably more efficient than the first order online SVMs discussed in (Kivinen et al., 2002).

13.1.3   Online Learning

Online learning algorithms are usually associated with problems where the complete training set is not available beforehand. However their computational properties are very useful for large-scale learning. A well-designed online algorithm needs less computation to reach the same test set accuracy as the corresponding batch algorithm (Murata and Amari, 1999; Bottou and LeCun, 2004).

Two overlapping frameworks have been used to study online learning algorithms: by leveraging the mathematics of stochastic approximations (Bottou, 1998), or by refining the mathematics of the perceptron (Novikoff, 1962). The perceptron seems a natural starting point for online SVM. Algorithms derived from the perceptron share common characteristics. Each iteration consists of two steps. First, one decides if the new point $\mathbf{x}_t$ should influence the decision rule and then one updates the decision rule. The perceptron, for instance, only updates its parameter w_{t-1} if the point $\mathbf{x}_t$ is misclassified. The updated parameters are obtained by performing a step along direction $\mathbf{x}_t$, that is, $w_t = w_{t-1} + \mathbf{y}_t \mathbf{x}_t$. Compared to maximum margin classifiers such as SVM, the perceptron runs much faster but does not deliver as good a generalization performance.

Many authors (Freund and Schapire, 1998; Frieß et al., 1998; Gentile, 2001; Li and Long, 2002; Crammer et al., 2004) have modified the perceptron algorithm to ensure a margin. Older variants of the perceptron, such as *minover* and *adatron* in (Nadal, 1993), are also very close to SVMs.

13.1.4   Active Learning

Active learning addresses problems where obtaining labels is expensive (Cohn et al., 1995). The learner has access to a vast pool of unlabeled examples, but is only allowed to obtain a limited number of labels. Therefore it must carefully choose which examples deserve the labeling expense.

Even when all labels are available beforehand, active learning is useful because it leads to sparser solutions (Schohn and Cohn, 2000; Bordes et al., 2005). Moreover, when the example selection criterion is cheap to compute, selecting and processing a few relevant examples might be as accurate and less expensive than processing all the examples.

13.1.5   Outline of the Chapter

Section 13.2 briefly presents the SVMs and describes how the LASVM algorithm combines online and active characteristics. Section 13.3 discusses invariance and presents selective sampling strategies to address them. Finally, section 13.4 reports experiments and results on a large-scale invariant problem.

13.2   Online Algorithm with Selective Sampling

This section first discusses the geometry of the quadratic optimization problem and its suitability to algorithms, such as sequential minimal optimization (SMO) (Platt, 1999), that iterate feasible direction searches. Then we describe how to organize feasible direction searches into an online learning algorithm amenable to selective sampling (Bordes et al., 2005).

Consider a binary classification problem with training patterns $\mathbf{x}_1 \ldots \mathbf{x}_n$ and associated classes $\mathbf{y}_1 \ldots \mathbf{y}_n \in \{+1, -1\}$. A soft-margin SVM (Cortes and Vapnik, 1995) classifies a pattern $\mathbf{x}$ according to the sign of a decision function:

$$f(\mathbf{x}) = \sum_i \boldsymbol{\alpha}_i \langle \mathbf{x}, \mathbf{x}_i \rangle + b \, , \tag{13.1}$$

where the notation $\langle \mathbf{x}, \mathbf{x}' \rangle$ represents the dot product of feature vectors associated with the patterns $\mathbf{x}$ and $\mathbf{x}'$. Such a dot product is often defined implicitly by means of a Mercer kernel (Cortes and Vapnik, 1995). The coefficients $\boldsymbol{\alpha}_i$ in (13.1) are obtained by solving the following quadratic programming (QP) problem[1]:

$$\max_{\boldsymbol{\alpha}} \; W(\boldsymbol{\alpha}) \;=\; \sum_i \alpha_i \mathbf{y}_i - \frac{1}{2} \sum_{ij} \boldsymbol{\alpha}_i \boldsymbol{\alpha}_j \langle \mathbf{x}_i, \mathbf{x}_j \rangle$$
$$\text{with} \quad \begin{cases} \displaystyle\sum_i \boldsymbol{\alpha}_i = 0 \\[2mm] 0 \leq \mathbf{y}_i \boldsymbol{\alpha}_i \leq C \end{cases} \tag{13.2}$$

A pattern $\mathbf{x}_i$ is called "support vector" when the corresponding coefficient $\boldsymbol{\alpha}_i$ is nonzero. The number s of support vectors asymptotically grows linearly with the number n of examples (Steinwart, 2004).

13.2.1 Feasible Direction Algorithms

Figure 1.2 in chapter 1 summarizes the geometry of the SVM QP problem (13.2). The box constraints $0 \leq \mathbf{y}_i \boldsymbol{\alpha}_i \leq C$ restrict the solutions to an n–dimensional hypercube. The equality constraint $\sum \boldsymbol{\alpha}_i = 0$ further restricts the solutions to an $(n-1)$–dimensional polytope $\mathcal{F}$.

Consider a feasible point $\boldsymbol{\alpha}_t \in \mathcal{F}$. A direction $\boldsymbol{u}_t$ indicates a *feasible direction* if the half-line $\{\boldsymbol{\alpha}_t + \lambda \boldsymbol{u}_t, \lambda \geq 0\}$ intersects the polytope in points other than $\boldsymbol{\alpha}_t$. Feasible direction algorithms iteratively update $\boldsymbol{\alpha}_t$ by first choosing a feasible direction $\boldsymbol{u}_t$ and searching the half-line for the feasible point $\boldsymbol{\alpha}_{t+1}$ that maximizes the cost function. The optimum is reached when no further improvement is possible (Zoutendijk, 1960).

The quadratic cost function restricted to the half-line search might reach its maximum inside or outside the polytope (see figure 1.3). The new feasible point $\boldsymbol{\alpha}_{t+1}$ is easily derived from the differential information in $\boldsymbol{\alpha}_t$ and from the location

---

1. Note that, in our formulation, α_i is positive when $\mathbf{y}_i = +1$ and negative when $\mathbf{y}_i = -1$.

of the bounds A and B induced by the box constraints.

$$\boldsymbol{\alpha}_{t+1} = \boldsymbol{\alpha}_t + \max\left\{A, \, \min\left\{B, C\right\}\right\} \boldsymbol{u}_t$$

$$\text{with} \quad C = \frac{d\,W(\boldsymbol{\alpha}_t + \lambda \boldsymbol{u}_t)}{d\,\lambda} \left(\frac{d^2\,W(\boldsymbol{\alpha}_t + \lambda \boldsymbol{u}_t)}{d\,\lambda^2}\right)^{-1} . \tag{13.3}$$

Computing these derivatives for arbitrary directions $\boldsymbol{u}_t$ is potentially expensive because it involves all n^2 terms of the dot product matrix $\langle \mathbf{x}_i, \mathbf{x}_j \rangle$. However, it is sufficient to pick $\boldsymbol{u}_t$ from a well chosen finite set of directions (Bordes et al., 2005, appendix), preferably with many zero coefficients. The SMO algorithm (Platt, 1999) exploits this opportunity by only considering feasible directions that only modify two coefficients $\boldsymbol{\alpha}_i$ and $\boldsymbol{\alpha}_j$ by opposite amounts. The most common variant selects the pairs (i, j) that define the successive search directions using a first order criterion:

$$
\begin{aligned}
i &= \arg\max_s \left\{ \frac{\partial W}{\partial \boldsymbol{\alpha}_s} \quad \text{s.t.} \quad \boldsymbol{\alpha}_s < \max(0, \mathbf{y}_s\, C) \right\}, \\
j &= \arg\min_s \left\{ \frac{\partial W}{\partial \boldsymbol{\alpha}_s} \quad \text{s.t.} \quad \boldsymbol{\alpha}_s > \min(0, \mathbf{y}_s\, C) \right\}.
\end{aligned}
\tag{13.4}
$$

The time required for solving the SVM QP problem grows like n^β with $2 \leq \beta \leq 3$ (Bordes et al., 2005, section 2.1) when the number of examples n increases. Meanwhile, the kernel matrix $\langle \mathbf{x}_i, \mathbf{x}_j \rangle$ becomes too large to store in memory. Computing kernel values on the fly vastly increases the computing time. Modern SVM solvers work around this problem using a cache of recently computed kernel matrix coefficients.

13.2.2   Learning is Easier Than Optimizing

The SVM quadratic optimization problem (13.2) is only a sophisticated statistical proxy, defined on the finite training set, for the actual problem, that is, classifying future patterns correctly. Therefore it makes little sense to optimize with an accuracy that vastly exceeds the uncertainty that arises from the use of a finite number of training examples.

Online learning algorithms exploit this fact. Since each example is only processed once, such algorithms rarely can compute the optimum of the objective function. Nevertheless, many online learning algorithms come with formal generalization performance guarantees. In certain cases, it is even possible to prove that suitably designed online algorithms outspeed the direct optimization of the corresponding objective function (Bottou and LeCun, 2004): they do not optimize the objective function as accurately, but they reach an equivalent test error more quickly.

Researchers therefore have sought efficient online algorithms for kernel machines. For instance, the budget perceptron (Crammer et al., 2004) demonstrates that online kernel algorithms should be able to both insert and remove support vectors from the current kernel expansion. The Huller (Bordes and Bottou, 2005) shows that both insertion and deletion can be derived from incremental increases of the

SVM objective function $W(\boldsymbol{\alpha})$.

13.2.3   The LASVM Online SVM Algorithm

Bordes et al. (2005) describe an online SVM algorithm that incrementally increases the dual objective function $W(\boldsymbol{\alpha})$ using feasible direction searches. LASVM maintains a current coefficient vector $\boldsymbol{\alpha}_t$ and the associated set of support vector indices $\mathcal{S}_t$. Each LASVM iteration receives a fresh example $(\mathbf{x}_{\sigma(t)}, \mathbf{y}_{\sigma(t)})$ and updates the current coefficient vector $\boldsymbol{\alpha}_t$ by performing two feasible direction searches named "*process*" and "*reprocess*."

- *Process* is an SMO direction search (13.3) along the direction defined by the pair formed with the current example index $\sigma(t)$ and another index chosen among the current support vector indices $\mathcal{S}_t$ using the first-order criterion (13.4). Example $\sigma(t)$ might be a new support vector in the resulting $\boldsymbol{\alpha}'_t$ and $\mathcal{S}'_t$.

- *Reprocess* is an SMO direction search (13.3) along the direction defined by a pair of indices (i, j) chosen among the current support vectors $\mathcal{S}'_t$ using the first-order criterion (13.4). Examples i and j might no longer be support vectors in the resulting $\boldsymbol{\alpha}_{t+1}$ and $\mathcal{S}_{t+1}$.

Repeating LASVM iterations on randomly chosen training set examples provably converges to the SVM solution with arbitrary accuracy. Empirical evidence indicates that a single presentation of each training example is sufficient to achieve training errors comparable to those achieved by the SVM solution. After presenting all training examples in random order, it is useful to tune the final coefficients by running *reprocess* until convergence.

Algorithm 13.1 Online LASVM

1:   Initialize $\boldsymbol{\alpha}_0$
2:   **while** there are training examples left **do**
3:       Select an unseen training example $(\mathbf{x}_{\sigma(t)}, \mathbf{y}_{\sigma(t)})$
4:       Call PROCESS$(\sigma(t))$
5:       Call REPROCESS
6:   **end while**
7:   *Finish*: Repeat REPROCESS until convergence

This single-pass algorithm runs faster than SMO and needs much less memory. Useful orders of magnitude can be obtained by evaluating how large the kernel cache must be to avoid the systematic recomputation of kernel values. Let n be the number of examples and s be the number of support vectors which is smaller than n. Furthermore, let $r \leq s$ be the number of *free support vectors*, that is, support vectors such that $0 < \mathbf{y}_i \boldsymbol{\alpha}_i < C$. Whereas the SMO algorithm requires $n\,r$ cache entries to avoid the systematic recomputation of kernel values, the LASVM algorithm only needs $s\,r$ entries (Bordes et al., 2005).

13.2.4 Selective Sampling

Each iteration of algorithm 13.1 selects a training example $(\mathbf{x}_{\sigma(t)}, \mathbf{y}_{\sigma(t)})$ randomly. More sophisticated example selection strategies yield further scalability improvements. Bordes et al. (2005) suggest four example selection strategies:

- *Random selection* : Pick a random unseen training example.

- *Gradient selection* : Pick the most poorly classified example (smallest value of $\mathbf{y}_k f(\mathbf{x}_k)$) among 50 randomly selected unseen training examples. This criterion is very close to what is done in (Loosli et al., 2004).

- *Active selection* : Pick the training example that is closest to the decision boundary (smallest value of $|f(\mathbf{x}_k)|$) among 50 randomly selected unseen training examples. This criterion chooses a training example independently of its label.

- *Autoactive selection* : Randomly sample at most 100 unseen training examples but stop as soon as 5 of them fall inside the margins (any of these examples would be inserted in the set of support vectors). Pick among these 5 examples the one closest to the decision boundary (smallest value of $|f(\mathbf{x}_k)|$.)

Empirical evidence shows that the *active* and *autoactive* criteria yield a comparable or better performance level using a smaller number of support vectors. This is understandable because the linear growth of the number of support vectors is related to fact that soft-margin SVMs make a support vector with every misclassified training example. Selecting training examples near the boundary excludes a large number of examples that are uninformative outliers. The reduced number of support vectors further improves both the learning speed and the memory footprint.

The following section presents the challenge set by invariance and discusses how the low memory requirements and the selective sampling capabilities of LASVM are well suited to the task.

13.3 Invariance

Many pattern recognition problems have invariance properties: the class remains largely unchanged when specific transformations are applied to the pattern. Object recognition in images is invariant under lighting changes, translations and rotation, mild occlusions, etc. Although humans handle invariance very naturally, computers do not.

In machine learning, the a priori knowledge of such invariance properties can be used to improve the pattern recognition accuracy. Many approaches have been proposed (Simard et al., 1993; Wood, 1996; Schölkopf et al., 1996; Leen, 1995). We first present an illustration of the influence of invariance. Then we describe our selective sampling approach to invariance, and discuss practical implementation details.

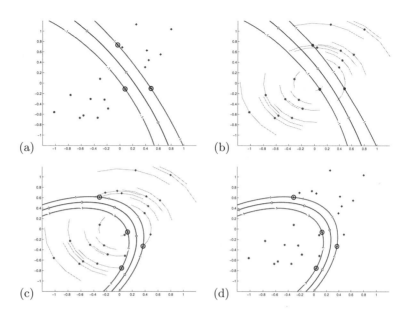

Figure 13.1   These figures illustrate the influence of point variations on the decision boundary for a toy example. Plot (a) shows a typical decision boundary obtained by only considering the training examples. Plot (b) shows "orbits" describing the possible transformations of the training examples. All these variations should be given the same label by the classifier. Plot (c) shows a decision boundary that takes into account the variations. Plot (d) shows how this boundary can be obtained by selecting representative examples for each orbit.

13.3.1   On the Influence of Invariance

Let us first illustrate how we propose to handle invariance. Consider points in the plane belonging to one of two classes and assume that there is an uncertainty on the point coordinates corresponding to some rotation around the origin. The class labels are therefore expected to remain invariant when one rotates the input pattern around the origin. Figure 13.1(a) shows the points, their classes, and a prospective decision boundary. Figure 13.1(b) shows the example orbits, that is, the sets of all possible positions reached by applying the invariant transformation to a specific example. All these positions should be given the same label by the classifier. Figure 13.1(c) shows a decision boundary that takes into account all the potential transformations of the training examples. Figure 13.1(d) shows that this boundary can be obtained by selecting adequate representatives for the orbits corresponding to each training example.

This simple example illustrates the complexity of the problem. Learning orbits leads to some almost intractable problems (Graepel and Herbrich, 2004). Adding virtual examples (Schölkopf et al., 1996) requires considerable memory to simply store the transformed examples in memory. However, figure 13.1(d) suggests that we do not need to store all the transformed examples forming an orbit. We only need to add a few well-chosen transformed examples.

The LASVM algorithm (section 13.2) displays interesting properties for this purpose. Because LASVM is an online algorithm, it does not require storing all the transformed examples. Because LASVM uses selective sampling strategies, it provides the means to select the few transformed examples that we think are sufficient to describe the invariant decision boundaries. We therefore hope to solve problems with multiple invariance with milder size and complexity constraints.

Our first approach was inspired by (Loosli et al., 2005). Each iteration randomly picks the next training example, generates a number of transformed examples describing the orbit of the original example, selects the best transformed example (see section 13.2.4), and performs the LASVM *process/reprocess* steps.

Since the online algorithm never revisits a previously seen training example, this first approach cannot pick more than one representative transformed example from each orbit. Problems with multiple invariance are likely to feature complicated orbits that are poorly summarized using a single transformed example. This major drawback can be remedied by revisiting training examples that have generated interesting variations in previous iterations. Alas, this remedy requires either recomputing the example transformations, or storing all of them in memory.

Our final approach simply considers a huge virtual training set composed of all examples and all their transformations. Each iteration of the algorithm picks a small sample of randomly transformed training examples, selects the best one using one of the criteria described in section 13.2.4, and performs the LASVM *process/reprocess* steps.

This approach can obviously select multiple examples for each orbit. It also provides great flexibility. For instance, it is interesting to bootstrap the learning process by first learning from untransformed examples. Once we have a baseline decision function, we can apply increasingly ambitious transformations.

13.3.2   Invariance in Practice

Learning with invariance is a well studied problem. Several papers explain how to apply pattern transformations efficiently (Simard et al., 1993; Wood, 1996; Schölkopf et al., 1996). We use the MNIST database of handwritten digit images because many earlier results have been reported (LeCun et al., 1998b). This section explains how we store the original images and how we efficiently compute random transformations of these digit images on the fly.

13.3.2.1   *Tangent Vectors*

Simard et al. (2000) explains how to use Lie algebra and tangent vectors to apply arbitrary affine transformations to images. Affine transformations can be described as the composition of six elementary transformations: horizontal and vertical translations, rotations, horizontal and vertical scale transformations, and hyperbolic transformations. For each image, the method computes a tangent vector for each elementary transformation, that is, the normalized pixelwise difference between an infinitesimal transformation of the image and the image itself.

Small affine transformations are then easily approximated by adding a linear combination of these six elementary tangent vectors:

$$x_{aff}(i,j) = x(i,j) + \sum_{T \in \mathcal{T}} \eta_T t_T(i,j) \, ,$$

where $\mathcal{T}$ is the set of elementary transformations, $x(i,j)$ represents the initial image, $t_T(i,j)$ is its tangent vector for transformation T, and η_T represents the coefficient for transformation T.

13.3.2.2 Deformation Fields

It turns out that the tangent vector for the six elementary affine transformations can be derived from the tangent vectors $t_x(i,j)$ and $t_y(i,j)$ corresponding to the horizontal and vertical translations. Each elementary affine transformation can be described by a vector field $[f_x^T(i,j), f_y^T(i,j)]$ representing the displacement direction of each pixel (i,j) when one performs an infinitesimal elementary transformation T of the image. The tangent vector for transformation T is then

$$t_T(i,j) = f_x^T(i,j) \, t_x(i,j) + f_y^T(i,j) \, t_y(i,j) \, .$$

This property provides for extending the tangent vector approach from affine transformations to arbitrary *elastic transformations* (Simard et al., 2003), that is, transformations that can be represented by a deformation field $[\, f_x(i,j), \, f_y(i,j) \,]$. Small transformations of the image $x(i,j)$ are then easily approximated using a linear operation:

$$x_{deformed}(i,j) = x(i,j) + \eta(f_x(i,j)t_x(i,j) + f_y(i,j)t_y(i,j)) \, .$$

Plausible deformation fields $[f_x(i,j), f_y(i,j)]$ are easily generated by randomly drawing an independent motion vector for each pixel and applying a smoothing filter. Figure 13.2 shows examples of such deformation fields. Horizontal and vertical vector components are generated independently and therefore can be used interchangeably.

We also generate transformation fields by adding a controlled amount of random smoothed noise to a transformation field representing a pure affine transformation. This mainly aims at introducing more rotations in the transformations.

13.3.2.3 Thickening

The horizontal and vertical translation tangent vectors can also be used to implement a thickening transformation (Simard et al., 2000) that erodes or dilates the

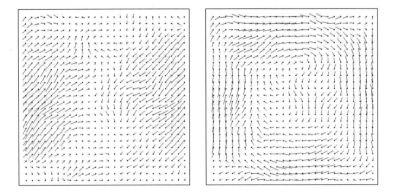

Figure 13.2   This figure shows examples of deformation fields. We represent the combination of horizontal and vertical fields. The first one is smoothed random and the second one is a rotation field modified by random noise.

digit images:

$$x_{thick}(i,j) = x(i,j) + \eta_b\sqrt{t_x(i,j)^2 + t_y(i,j)^2}\ ,$$

where η_b is a coefficient that controls the strength of the transformation. Choosing $\eta_b < 0$ makes the strokes thinner. Choosing $\eta_b > 0$ makes them thicker.

13.3.2.4   *The Infinite Virtual Training Set*

As discussed before, we cannot store all transformed examples in memory. However, we can efficiently generate random transformations by combining the above methods:

$$\begin{aligned} x_{trans}(i,j) &= x(i,j) + \eta_x f_x(i,j) t_x(i,j) \\ &+ \eta_y f_y(i,j) t_y(i,j) \\ &+ \eta_b\sqrt{t_x(i,j)^2 + t_y(i,j)^2}\ . \end{aligned}$$

We only store the initial images $x(i,j)$ along with its translation tangent vectors $t_x(i,j)$ and $t_y(i,j)$. We also store a collection of precomputed deformation fields that can be interchangeably used as $f_x(i,j)$ or $f_y(i,j)$ (in the experiments, we stored 1500 fields). The scalar coefficients η_x, η_y, and η_b provide further transformation variability.

Figure 13.4 shows examples of all the combined transformations. We can generate as many examples as we need this way, playing on the choice of deformation fields and scalar coefficients.

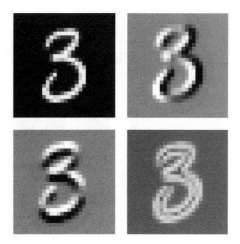

Figure 13.3 This figure shows the original digit, the two translation tangent vectors, and the thickening tangent vector.

13.3.2.5 Large Translations

All the transformations described above are small subpixel transformations. Even though the MNIST digit images are roughly centered, experiments indicate that we still need to implement invariance with respect to translations of magnitude one or two pixels. Thus we also apply randomly chosen translations of one or two pixels. These full-pixel translations come on top of the subpixel translations implemented by the random deformation fields.

13.4 Application

This section reports experimental results achieved on the MNIST database using the techniques described in the previous section. We have obtained state-of-the-art results using ten SVM classifiers in one-vs.-rest configuration. Each classifier is trained on one epoch, using 8 million transformed examples using the standard radial basis function (RBF) kernel $\langle \mathbf{x}, \mathbf{x}' \rangle = \exp(-\gamma \|\mathbf{x} - \mathbf{x}'\|^2)$. The soft-margin C parameter was always 1000.

As explained before, the untransformed training examples and their two translation tangent vectors are stored in memory. Transformed examples are computed on the fly and cached. We allowed 500MB for the cache of transformed examples, and 6.5GB for the cache of kernel values. Indeed, despite the favorable characteristics of our algorithm, dealing with millions of examples quickly yields tens of thousands of support vectors.

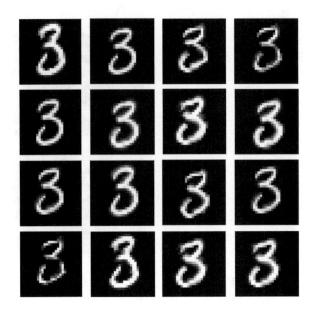

Figure 13.4 This figure shows 16 variations of a digit with all the transformations cited here.

13.4.1 Deformation Settings

One could argue that handling more transformations always increases the test set error. In fact we simply want a classifier that is invariant to transformations that reflect the typical discrepancies between our training examples and our test examples. Making the system invariant to stronger transformations might be useful in practice, but could reduce the performance on our particular test set.

We used cross-validation to select both the kernel bandwidth parameter and to select the strength of the transformations applied to our initial examples. The different parameters of the cross-validation are the deformation strength η and the RBF kernel bandwidth γ for the RBF kernel. During the same time, we have also estimated whether the thickening transform and the one- or two-pixel translations are desirable.

Figure 13.5 reports the SVM error rates measured for various configurations on a validation set of 10,000 points taken from the standard MNIST training set. The training set was composed by picking 5000 other points from the MNIST training set and applying ten random transformations to each point. We see that thickening is not a relevant transformation for the MNIST problem. Similarly, we observe that one-pixel translations are very useful, and that it is not necessary to use two-pixel translations.

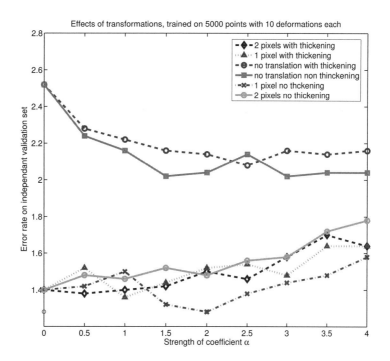

Figure 13.5 Effects of transformations on the performance. This graph is obtained on a validation set of 10,000 points, trained on 5000 points and 10 transformations for each (55,000 training points in total) with an RBF kernel with bandwidth $\gamma = 0.006$. The best configuration is elastic deformation without thickening, for $\eta = 2$ and one-pixel translations, which gives 1.28%. Note that $\eta = 0$ is equivalent to no elastic deformation. The baseline result for the validation set is thus 2.52%.

13.4.2 Example Selection

One of the claims of our work is the ability to implement invariant classifiers by selecting a moderate amount of transformed training examples. Otherwise the size of the kernel expansion would grow quickly and make the classifier impractically slow.

We implemented the example selection criteria discussed in section 13.2.4. Figure 13.6 compares error rates (left), number of support vectors (center), and training times (right) using three different selection criteria: random selection, active selection, and autoactive selection. These results were obtained using 100 random transformations of each of the 60,000 MNIST training examples. The graphs also show the results obtained on the 60,000 MNIST training examples without random transformations.

The random and autoactive selection criteria give the best test errors. The autoactive criterion, however, yields a much smaller number of support vectors and trains much faster. Therefore, we chose the autoactive selection criterion for the following experiments.

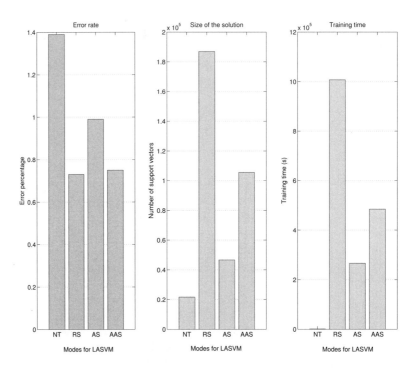

Figure 13.6 This figure compares the error rates (left), the numbers of support vectors (center), and the training times (right) of different LASVM runs. The first bar of each graph corresponds to training a regular SVM on the original 60,000 MNIST examples (NT: no transformation). The other three bars were obtained using 100 random deformations of each MNIST example, that is, 6 millions points. The second columns reports results for random selection (RS), the third for active selection (AS), and the last for auto-active selection (AAS). The deformation settings are set according to previous results (figure 13.5). The autoactive run gives the best compromise.

13.4.3   The Finishing Step

After presenting the last training example, Bordes et al. (2005) suggest tuning the final solution by running *reprocess* until convergence. This amounts to optimizing the SVM objective function restricted to the remaining support vectors. This operation is known as the "finishing step." In our case, we never see the last training examples since we can always generate more.

At first, we simply eliminated this finishing step. However we noticed that after processing a large amount of examples (between 5 and 6 million depending on the class) the number of support vectors decreases slowly. There is in fact an implicit finishing step. After a sufficient time, the *process* operation seldom does anything because hardly any of the selected examples needs to be added to the expansion. Meanwhile, the *reprocess* step remains active.

We then decided to perform a finishing step every 600,000 points. We observed the same reduction in the number of support vectors, but earlier during the learning process (see figure 13.7). These additional finishing steps seem useful for the global task. We achieved the best results using this setup. However this observation raises several questions. Is it enough to perform a single *reprocess* step after each example selection? Can we get faster and better results?

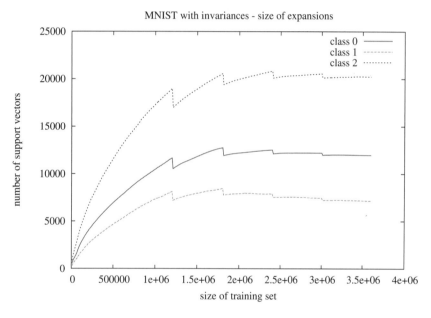

Figure 13.7   This figure shows the evolution of the expansion size during training. We used autoactive selection and performed a finishing step at regular intervals Each gap corresponds to one finishing step. Here we notice that the number of support vectors eventually decreases without fully optimizing, at least intentionally.

13.4.4   The Number of *Reprocess* Steps

As said before, the LASVM algorithm does not explicitly define how much optimization should be performed after processing each example. To explore this issue,

Table 13.1 Effects of transformations on the performance, with an RBF kernel of bandwidth $\gamma = 0.006$. The table shows a comparison for different tradeoffs between *process* and *reprocess*. We change the number of consecutive *reprocess* after each *process*, and also after each example, regardless of whether the example was selected for a *process* step.

	1R/1P	2R/1P	3R/1P	4R/1P	5R/1P
Max size	24531	21903	21436	20588	20029
Removed points	1861	1258	934	777	537
Proportion	7.6%	5.7%	4.3%	3.7%	2.6%
Train time (sec)	1621	1548	1511	1482	1441
Error rate	2.13%	2.08%	2.19%	2.09%	2.07%

	1R each	2R each	3R each
Max size	23891	21660	20596
Removed points	1487	548	221
Proportion	6.2%	2.5%	1.0%
Train time (sec)	1857	1753	1685
Error rate	2.06%	2.17%	2.13%

we ran several variants of the LASVM algorithms on five random transformations of 10,000 MNIST examples.

The variants denoted "nR/1P" consist of performing n *reprocess* steps after selecting a transformed training example and performing a *process* step. The variants denoted "nR each" consist of performing n *reprocess* steps after each example, regardless of whether the example was selected for a *process* step.

Table 13.1 shows the number of support vectors before and after the finishing step, the training times, and the test performance measured on an independent validation set of 10,000 examples. Neither optimizing a lot (last column) or optimizing very little (first column) are good setups. In terms of training time, the best combinations for this dataset are "4R/1P" and "5R/1P." These results certainly show that achieving the right balance remains an obscure aspect of the LASVM algorithm.

13.4.5   Final Results

We monitored during training the evolution of the test error along with the train error on the original 60,000 examples. In figure 13.8 we observe that learning with deformed samples decreases the error rate and does not affect the training error. It illustrates the fact that learning deformed examples does not make the machine unlearn the originals.

Table 13.2 summarizes our final results. We first bootstrapped the system using the original MNIST training and four random deformations of each example. Then

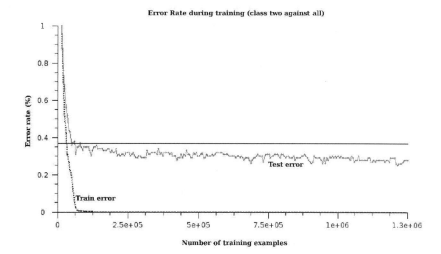

Figure 13.8 This figure shows the evolution of the training error on the 60,000 original points and the test error during training. The results are shown for class 2 against the others. We observe that training on deformed examples does not affect the performance on orginal examples but increases the performance on unseen data.

Table 13.2   Summary of our final experiment.

Number of binary classifiers	10
Number of examples for each binary classifier	8,100,000
Thickening transformation	no
Additional translations	1 pixel
RBF kernel bandwidth (γ)	0.006
Example selection criterion	auto-active
Finishing step	every 600,000 examples
Full training time	**8 days**
Test set error	**0.67%**

we expanded the database to a total of 134 random transformations, performing a finishing step every 600,000 examples. The final accuracy matches the results obtained using virtual support vectors (Schölkopf and Smola, 2002) on the original MNIST test set. Slightly better performances have been reported using convolution networks (Simard et al., 2003), or using a deskewing algorithm to make the test set easier (Schölkopf and Smola, 2002).

13.5   Conclusion

We have shown how to address large invariant pattern recognition problems using selective sampling and online algorithms. We also have demonstrated that these techniques scale remarkably well. It is now possible to run SVM on millions of examples in a relatively high dimension input space (here 784), using a single processor. Because we only keep a few thousand support vectors per classifier, we can handle millions of training examples.

Acknowledgments

Part of this work was funded by NSF grant CCR-0325463.

14   Scaling Learning Algorithms toward AI

Yoshua Bengio
Yann LeCun

One long-term goal of machine learning research is to produce methods that are applicable to highly complex tasks, such as perception (vision, audition), reasoning, intelligent control, and other artificially intelligent behaviors. We argue that in order to progress toward this goal, the machine learning community must endeavor to discover algorithms that can learn highly complex functions, with minimal need for prior knowledge, and with minimal human intervention. We present mathematical and empirical evidence suggesting that many popular approaches to nonparametric learning, particularly kernel methods, are fundamentally limited in their ability to learn complex high-dimensional functions. Our analysis focuses on two problems. First, kernel machines are shallow architectures, *in which one large layer of* simple template matchers *is followed by a single layer of trainable coefficients. We argue that shallow architectures can be very inefficient in terms of required number of computational elements and examples. Second, we analyze a limitation of kernel machines with a local kernel, linked to the curse of dimensionality, that applies to supervised, unsupervised (manifold learning), and semisupervised kernel machines. Using empirical results on invariant image recognition tasks, kernel methods are compared with* deep architectures, *in which lower-level features or concepts are progressively combined into more abstract and higher-level representations. We argue that deep architectures have the potential to generalize in nonlocal ways, i.e., beyond immediate neighbors, and that this is crucial in order to make progress on the kind of complex tasks required for artificial intelligence.*

14.1   Introduction

Statistical machine learning research has yielded a rich set of algorithmic and mathematical tools over the last decades, and has given rise to a number of commercial and scientific applications. However, some of the initial goals of this field of research remain elusive. A long-term goal of machine learning research is to produce methods that will enable artificially intelligent agents capable of learning complex behaviors with minimal human intervention and prior knowledge. Examples of such complex behaviors are found in visual perception, auditory perception, and natural language processing.

The main objective of this chapter is to discuss fundamental limitations of certain classes of learning algorithms, and point toward approaches that overcome these limitations. These limitations arise from two aspects of these algorithms: *shallow architecture* and *local estimators*.

We would like our learning algorithms to be efficient in three respects:

1. computational: number of computations during training and during recognition;

2. statistical: number of examples required for good generalization, especially labeled data; and

3. human involvement: amount of human labor necessary to tailor the algorithm to a task, i.e., specify the prior knowledge built into the model before training. (explicitly, or implicitly through engineering designs with a human-in-the-loop).

The last quarter century has given us flexible nonparametric learning algorithms that can learn any continuous input-output mapping, *provided* enough computing resources and training data. A crucial question is how efficient are some of the popular learning methods when they are applied to complex perceptual tasks, such as visual pattern recognition with complicated intraclass variability. The chapter mostly focuses on computational and statistical efficiency.

Among flexible learning algorithms, we establish a distinction between *shallow architectures* and *deep architectures*. Shallow architectures are best exemplified by modern kernel machines (Schölkopf et al., 1999a), such as support vector machines (SVMs) (Boser et al., 1992; Cortes and Vapnik, 1995). They consist of one layer of fixed kernel functions, whose role is to match the incoming pattern with templates extracted from a training set, followed by a linear combination of the matching scores. Since the templates are extracted from the training set, the first layer of a kernel machine can be seen as being trained in a somewhat trivial unsupervised way. The only components subject to supervised training are the coefficients of the linear combination.[1]

Deep architectures are perhaps best exemplified by multilayer neural networks with several hidden layers. In general terms, deep architectures are composed of multiple layers of parameterized nonlinear modules. The parameters of every module are subject to learning. Deep architectures rarely appear in the machine learning literature; the vast majority of neural network research has focused on shallow architectures with a single hidden layer, because of the difficulty of training networks with more than two or three layers (Tesauro, 1992). Notable exceptions

---

1. In SVMs only a subset of the examples are selected as templates (the support vectors), but this is equivalent to choosing which coefficients of the second layer are nonzero.

include work on convolutional networks (LeCun et al., 1989, 1998a), and recent work on deep belief networks (DBN) (Hinton et al., 2006).

While shallow architectures have advantages, such as the possibility of using convex loss functions, we show that they also have limitations in the *efficiency* of the representation of certain types of function families. Although a number of theorems show that certain shallow architectures (Gaussian kernel machines, one-hidden layer neural nets, etc.) can approximate any function with arbitrary precision, they make no statements as to the efficiency of the representation. Conversely, deep architectures can, in principle, represent certain families of functions more efficiently (and with better scaling properties) than shallow ones, but the associated loss functions are almost always nonconvex.

The chapter starts with a short discussion about task-specific versus more general types of learning algorithms. Although the human brain is sometimes cited as an existence proof of a general-purpose learning algorithm, appearances can be deceiving: the so-called no-free-lunch theorems (Wolpert, 1996), as well as Vapnik's necessary and sufficient conditions for consistency (see Vapnik, 1998), clearly show that there is no such thing as a completely general learning algorithm. All practical learning algorithms are associated with some sort of explicit or implicit prior that favors some functions over others.

Since a quest for a completely general learning method is doomed to failure, one is reduced to searching for learning models that are well suited for a particular type of task. For us, high on the list of useful tasks are those that most animals can perform effortlessly, such as perception and control, as well as tasks that higher animals and humans can do, such as long-term prediction, reasoning, planning, and language understanding. In short, our aim is to look for learning methods that bring us closer to an artificially intelligent agent. What matters the most in this endeavor is how *efficiently* our model can capture and represent the required knowledge. The efficiency is measured along three main dimensions: the amount of training data required (especially labeled data), the amount of computing resources required to reach a given level of performance, and most importantly, the amount of human effort required to specify the prior knowledge built into the model before training (explicitly or implicitly) This chapter discusses the scaling properties of various learning models, in particular kernel machines, with respect to those three dimensions, in particular the first two. Kernel machines are *nonparametric learning models*, which make apparently weak assumptions on the form of the function $f()$ to be learned. By nonparametric methods we mean methods whose capacity is allowed to increase (e.g., by hyper-parameter selection) when more data is available. This includes classical k-nearest neighbor algorithms, modern kernel machines, mixture models, and neural networks (where the number of hidden units can be selected using the data). Our arguments are centered around two limitations of kernel machines: the first limitation applies more generally to shallow architectures, which include neural networks with a single hidden layer. In section 14.3 we consider different types of function classes, i.e., architectures, including different subtypes of shallow architectures. We consider the tradeoff between the depth of the architecture and its breadth (number of elements in each layer), thus clarifying the representational limitation of shallow architectures. The second limitation is more specific and concerns kernel machines with a *local kernel*. This limitation is studied first informally in section 14.3.3 by thought experiments in the use of template matching for visual perception. Section 14.4 then focuses more formally on local estimators, i.e., in which the prediction $f(x)$ at point x is dominated by the near neighbors of x taken from the training set. This includes kernel machines in which the kernel is local, like the Gaussian kernel. These algorithms rely on a prior expressed as a distance or similarity function between pairs of examples, and encompass classical statistical algorithms as well as modern kernel machines. This limitation is pervasive, not only in classification, regression, and density estimation but also in manifold learning and semisupervised learning, where many modern methods have such locality property, and are often explicitly based on the graph of near neighbors. Using visual pattern recognition as an example, we illustrate how the shallow nature of kernel machines leads to fundamentally inefficient representations.

Finally, deep architectures are proposed as a way to escape from the fundamental limitations above. Section 14.5 concentrates on the advantages and disadvantages of deep architectures, which involve multiple levels of trainable modules between input and output. They can retain the desired flexibility in the learned functions, and increase the efficiency of the model along all three dimensions of amount of training data, amount of computational resources, and amount of human prior hand-coding. Although a number of learning algorithms for deep architectures have been available for some time, training such architectures is still largely perceived as a difficult challenge. We discuss recent approaches to training such deep networks that foreshadow new breakthroughs in this direction.

The tradeoff between convexity and nonconvexity has, up until recently, favored research into learning algorithms with convex optimization problems. We have found that nonconvex optimization is sometimes more efficient than convex optimization. Nonconvex loss functions may be an unavoidable property of learning complex functions from weak prior knowledge.

14.2   Learning Models Toward AI

The *no-free-lunch* theorem for learning algorithms (Wolpert, 1996) states that no completely general-purpose learning algorithm can exist, in the sense that for every learning model there is a data distribution on which it will fare poorly (on both training and test, in the case of finite Vapnik-Chervonenkis (VC) dimension). Every learning model *must* contain implicit or explicit restrictions on the class of functions that it can learn. Among the set of all possible functions, we are particularly interested in a subset that contains all the tasks involved in intelligent behavior. Examples of such tasks include visual perception, auditory perception, planning, control, etc. The set does not just include specific visual perception tasks (e.g., human face detection), but the set of all the tasks that an intelligent agent should be able to learn. In the following, we will call this set of functions *the AI-set*. Because we want to achieve AI, we prioritize those tasks that are in the AI-set.

Although we may like to think that the human brain is somewhat general-purpose, it is extremely restricted in its ability to learn high-dimensional functions. The brains of humans and higher animals, with their learning abilities, can potentially implement the AI-set, and constitute a working proof of the feasibility of AI. We advance that the AI-set is a tiny subset of the set of all possible functions, but the specification of this tiny subset may be easier than it appears. To illustrate this point, we will use the example first proposed by (LeCun and Denker, 1992). The connection between the retina and the visual areas in the brain gets wired up relatively late in embryogenesis. If one makes the apparently reasonable assumption that all possible permutations of the millions of fibers in the optic nerve are equiprobable, there are not enough bits in the genome to encode the correct wiring, and no lifetime long enough to learn it. The flat prior assumption must be rejected: some wiring must be simpler to specify (or more likely) than others. In what seems like an incredibly fortunate coincidence, a particularly good (if not "correct") wiring pattern happens to be one that preserves topology. Coincidentally, this wiring pattern happens to be very simple to describe in almost any language (for example, the biochemical language used by biology can easily specify topology-preserving wiring patterns through concentration gradients of nerve growth factors). How can we be so fortunate that the correct prior be so simple to describe, yet so informative? LeCun and Denker (1992) point out that the brain exists in the very same physical world for which it needs to build internal models. Hence the specification of good priors for modeling the world happen to be simple in that world (the dimensionality and topology of the world is common to both). Because of this, we are allowed to hope that the AI-set, while a tiny subset of all possible functions, may be specified with a relatively small amount of information.

In practice, prior knowledge can be embedded in a learning model by specifying three essential components:

1. The representation of the data: preprocessing, feature extractions, etc.

2. The *architecture* of the machine: the family of functions that the machine can implement and its parameterization.

3. The *loss function and regularizer*: how different functions in the family are rated, given a set of training samples, and which functions are preferred in the absence of training samples (prior or regularizer).

Inspired by Hinton (2007), we classify machine learning research strategies in the pursuit of AI into three categories. One is *defeatism*: "Since no good parameterization of the AI-set is currently available, let's specify a much smaller set for each specific task through careful hand-design of the preprocessing, the architecture, and the regularizer." If task-specific designs must be devised by hand for each new task, achieving AI will require an overwhelming amount of human effort. Nevertheless, this constitutes the most popular approach for applying machine learning to new problems: design a clever preprocessing (or data representation scheme), so that a standard learning model (such as an SVM) will be able to learn the task. A somewhat similar approach is to specify the task-specific prior knowledge in the structure of a *graphical model* by explicitly representing important intermediate features and concepts through latent variables whose functional dependency on observed variables is hard-wired. Much of the research in graphical models (Jordan, 1998) (especially of the parametric type) follows this approach. Both of these approaches, the kernel approach with human–designed kernels or features, and the graphical models approach with human–designed dependency structure and semantics, are very attractive in the short term because they often yield quick results in making progress on a specific task, taking advantage of human ingenuity and implicit or explicit knowledge about the task, and requiring small amounts of labeled data.

The second strategy is *denial*: "Even with a generic kernel such as the Gaussian kernel, kernel machines can approximate any function, and regularization (with the bounds) guarantees generalization. Why would we need anything else?" This belief contradicts the no-free-lunch theorem. Although kernel machines can represent any labeling of a particular training set, they can *efficiently represent* a very small and very specific subset of functions, which the following sections of this chapter will attempt to characterize. Whether this small subset covers a large part of the AI-set is very dubious, as we will show. In general, what we think of as generic learning algorithms can only work well with certain types of data representations and not so well with others. They can in fact represent certain types of functions efficiently, and not others. While the clever preprocessing/generic learning algorithm approach may be useful for solving specific problems, it brings about little progress on the road to AI. How can we hope to solve the wide variety of tasks required to achieve AI with this labor-intensive approach? More importantly, how can we ever hope to integrate each of these separately built, separately trained, specialized modules into a coherent artificially intelligent system? Even if we could build those modules, we would need another learning paradigm to be able to integrate them into a coherent system.

The third strategy is *optimism*: "Let's look for learning models that can be applied to the largest possible subset of the AI-set, while requiring the smallest possible amount of additional hand-specified knowledge for each specific task within the AI-set." The question becomes: Is there a parameterization of the AI-set that can be efficiently implemented with computer technology?

Consider, for example, the problem of object recognition in computer vision: we could be interested in building recognizers for at least several thousand categories of objects. Should we have specialized algorithms for each? Similarly, in natural language processing, the focus of much current research is on devising appropriate features for specific tasks such as recognizing or parsing text of a particular type (such as spam email, job ads, financial news, etc.). Are we going to have to do this labor-intensive work for all the possible types of text? Our system will not be very smart if we have to manually engineer new patches each time a new type of text or new types of object category must be processed. If there exist more general-purpose learning models, at least general enough to handle most of the tasks that animals and humans can handle, then searching for them may save us a considerable amount of labor in the long run.

As discussed in the next section, a mathematically convenient way to characterize the kind of complex tasks needed for AI is that they involve learning highly nonlinear functions with many variations (i.e., whose derivatives change direction often). This is problematic in conjunction with a prior that smooth functions are more likely, i.e., having few or small variations. We mean f to be smooth when the value of $f(x)$ and of its derivative $f'(x)$ are close to the values of $f(x + \Delta)$ and $f'(x + \Delta)$ respectively when x and $x + \Delta$ are close as defined by a kernel or a distance. This chapter advances several arguments that the smoothness prior alone is insufficient to learn highly varying functions. This is intimately related to the curse of dimensionality, but as we find throughout our investigation, it is not the number of dimensions so much as the amount of variation that matters. A one-dimensional function could be difficult to learn, and many high-dimensional functions can be approximated well enough with a smooth function, so that nonparametric methods relying only on the smooth prior can still give good results.

We call *strong priors* a type of prior knowledge that gives high probability (or low complexity) to a very small set of functions (generally related to a small set of tasks), and *broad priors* a type of prior knowledge that gives moderately high probability to a wider set of relevant functions (which may cover a large subset of tasks within the AI-set). Strong priors are task-specific, while broad priors are more related to the general structure of our world. We could prematurely conjecture that if a function has many local variations (hence is not very smooth), then it is not learnable unless strong prior knowledge is at hand. Fortunately, this is not true. First, there is no reason to believe that smoothness priors should have a special status over other types of priors. Using smoothness priors when we know that the functions we want to learn are nonsmooth would seem counterproductive. Other broad priors are possible. A simple way to define a prior is to define a language (e.g., a programming language) with which we express functions, and favor functions that have a low Kolmogorov complexity in that language, i.e., functions whose program is short. Consider using the C programming language (along with standard libraries that come with it) to define our prior, and learning functions such as $g(x) = sin(x)$ (with x a real value) or $g(x) = parity(x)$ (with x a binary vector of fixed dimension). These would be relatively easy to learn with a small number of samples because their description is extremely short in C and they are very probable under the corresponding prior, despite the fact that they are highly nonsmooth. We do not advocate the explicit use of Kolmogorov complexity in a conventional programming language to design new learning algorithms, but we use this example to illustrate that it is possible to learn apparently complex functions (in the sense they vary a lot), using broad priors, by using a nonlocal learning algorithm, corresponding to priors other than the smoothness prior. This thought example and the study of toy problems like the parity problem in the rest of the chapter also show that the main challenge is to design learning algorithms that can *discover representations of the data that compactly describe regularities in it*. This is in contrast with the approach of enumerating the variations present in the training data, and hoping to rely on local smoothness to correctly fill in the space between the training samples.

As we mentioned earlier, there may exist broad priors, with seemingly simple description, that greatly reduce the space of accessible functions in appropriate ways. In visual systems, an example of such a broad prior, which is inspired by nature's bias toward retinotopic mappings, is the kind of connectivity used in convolutional networks for visual pattern recognition (LeCun et al., 1989, 1998a). This will be examined in detail in section 14.6. Another example of a broad prior, which we discuss in section 14.5, is that the functions to be learned should be expressible as multiple levels of composition of simpler functions, where *different levels of functions can be viewed as different levels of abstraction*. Functions at lower levels of abstraction should be found useful for capturing some simpler aspects of the data distribution, so that it is possible to first learn the simpler functions and then compose them to learn more abstract concepts. Animals and humans do learn in this way, with simpler concepts earlier in life, and higher-level abstractions later, expressed in terms of the previously learned concepts. Not all functions can be decomposed in this way, but humans appear to have such a constraint. If such a hierarchy did not exist, humans would be able to learn new concepts in any order. Hence we can hope that this type of prior may be useful to help cover the AI-set, but yet specific enough to exclude the vast majority of useless functions.

It is a thesis of the present work that learning algorithms that build such deeply layered architectures offer a promising avenue for scaling machine learning toward AI. Another related thesis is that one should not consider the large variety of tasks separately, but as different aspects of a more general problem: that of learning the basic structure of the world, as seen say through the eyes and ears of a growing animal or a young child. This is an instance of multitask learning where it is clear that the different tasks share a strong commonality. This allows us to hope that after training such a system on a large variety of tasks in the AI-set, the system may generalize to a new task from only a few labeled examples. We hypothesize that many tasks in the AI-set may be built around common *representations*, which can be understood as a set of interrelated concepts.

If our goal is to build a learning machine for the AI-set, our research should concentrate on devising learning models with the following features:

- A highly flexible way to specify prior knowledge, hence a learning algorithm that can function with a large repertoire of architectures.

- A learning algorithm that can deal with deep architectures, in which a decision involves the manipulation of many intermediate concepts, and multiple levels of nonlinear steps.

- A learning algorithm that can handle large families of functions, parameterized with millions of individual parameters.

- A learning algorithm that can be trained efficiently even when the number of training examples becomes very large. This excludes learning algorithms requiring storing and iterating multiple times over the whole training set, or for which the amount of computations per example increases as more examples are seen. This strongly suggest the use of online learning.

▪ A learning algorithm that can discover concepts that can be shared easily among multiple tasks and multiple modalities (multitask learning), and that can take advantage of large amounts of unlabeled data (semisupervised learning).

14.3   Learning Architectures, Shallow and Deep

14.3.1   Architecture Types

In this section, we define the notions of shallow and deep architectures. An informal discussion of their relative advantages and disadvantage is presented using examples. A more formal discussion of the limitations of shallow architectures with local smoothness (which includes most modern kernel methods) is given in the next section.

Following the tradition of the classic book *Perceptrons* (Minsky and Papert, 1969), it is instructive to categorize different types of learning architectures and to analyze their limitations and advantages. To fix ideas, consider the simple case of classification in which a discrete label is produced by the learning machine $y = f(x, w)$, where x is the input pattern, and w a parameter which indexes the family of functions $\mathcal{F}$ that can be implemented by the architecture $\mathcal{F} = \{f(\cdot, w), w \in \mathcal{W}\}$.

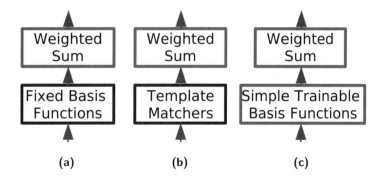

Figure 14.1   Different types of shallow architectures. (a) Type 1: fixed preprocessing and linear predictor. (b) Type 2: template matchers and linear predictor (kernel machine). (c) Type 3: simple trainable basis functions and linear predictor (neural net with one hidden layer, RBF network).

Traditional perceptrons, like many currently popular learning models, are *shallow architectures*. Different types of shallow architectures are represented in figure 14.1.

Type 1 architectures have fixed preprocessing in the first layer (e.g., perceptrons). Type 2 architectures have template matchers in the first layer (e.g., kernel machines). Type 3 architectures have simple trainable basis functions in the first layer (e.g., neural net with one hidden layer, radial basis function (RBF) network). All three have a linear transformation in the second layer.

14.3.1.1   Shallow Architecture Type 1

Fixed preprocessing plus linear predictor, figure 14.1(a): The simplest shallow architecture is composed of a fixed preprocessing layer (sometimes called features or basis functions), followed by a linear predictor. The type of linear predictor used and the way it is trained are unspecified (maximum-margin, logistic regression, Perceptron, squared error regression....). The family $\mathcal{F}$ is linearly parameterized in the parameter vector: $f(x) = \sum_{i=1}^{k} w_i \phi_i(x)$. This type of architecture is widely used in practical applications. Since the preprocessing is fixed (and handcrafted), it is necessarily task-specific in practice. It is possible to imagine a shallow type 1 machine that would parameterize the complete AI-set. For example, we could imagine a machine in which each feature is a member of the AI-set, hence each particular member of the AI-set can be represented with a weight vector containing all zeros, except for a single 1 at the right place. While there probably exist more compact ways to linearly parameterize the entire AI-set, the number of necessary features would surely be prohibitive. More importantly, we do not know explicitly the functions of the AI-set, so this is not practical.

14.3.1.2   Shallow Architecture Type 2

Template matchers plus linear predictor, figure 14.1(b): Next on the scale of adaptability is the traditional kernel machine architecture. The preprocessing is a vector of values resulting from the application of a kernel function $K(x, x_i)$ to each training sample $f(x) = b + \sum_{i=1}^{n} \alpha_i K(x, x_i)$, where n is the number of training samples, the parameter w contains all the α_i and the bias b. In effect, the first layer can be seen as a series of template matchers in which the templates are the training samples. Type 2 architectures can be seen as special forms of type 1 architectures in which the features are data-dependent, which is to say $\phi_i(x) = K(x, x_i)$. This is a simple form of unsupervised learning, for the first layer. Through the famous *kernel trick* (see Schölkopf et al., 1999a), type 2 architectures can be seen as a compact way of representing type 1 architectures, including some that may be too large to be practical. If the kernel function satisfies the Mercer condition it can be expressed as an inner product between feature vectors $K_\phi(x, x_i) = < \phi(x), \phi(x_i) >$, giving us a linear relation between the parameter vectors in both formulations: w for type 1 architectures is $\sum_i \alpha_i \phi(x_i)$. A very attractive feature of such architectures is that for several common loss functions (e.g., squared error, margin loss) training them involves a convex optimization program. While these properties are largely perceived as the magic behind kernel methods, they should not distract us from the fact that the first layer of a kernel machine is often just a series of template matchers. In most kernel machines, the kernel is used as a kind of template matcher, but other choices are possible. Using task-specific prior knowledge, one can design a kernel that incorporates the right abstractions for the task. This comes at the cost of lower efficiency in terms of human labor. When a kernel acts like a template matcher, we call it *local*: $K(x, x_i)$ discriminates between values of x that are near x_i and those that are not. Some of the mathematical results in this chapter focus on the Gaussian kernel, where nearness corresponds to small Euclidean distance. One could say that one of the main issues with kernel machines with local kernels is that they are *little more than template matchers*. It is possible to use kernels that are nonlocal yet not task-specific, such as the linear kernels and polynomial kernels. However, most practitioners have been preferring linear kernels or local kernels. Linear kernels are type 1 shallow architectures, with their obvious limitations. Local kernels have been popular because they make intuitive sense (it is easier to insert prior knowledge), while polynomial kernels tend to generalize very poorly when extrapolating (e.g., grossly overshooting). The smoothness prior implicit in local kernels is quite reasonable for a lot of the applications that have been considered, whereas the prior implied by polynomial kernels is less clear. Learning the kernel would move us to type 3 shallow architectures or to the deep architectures described below.

14.3.1.3 Shallow Architecture Type 3

Simple trainable basis functions plus linear predictor, figure 14.1(c): In type 3 shallow architectures, the first layer consists of simple basis functions that are *trainable through supervised learning*. This can improve the efficiency of the function representation, by tuning the basis functions to a task. Simple trainable basis functions include linear combinations followed by pointwise nonlinearities and Gaussian RBFs. Traditional neural networks with one hidden layer, and RBF networks belong to that category. Kernel machines in which the kernel function is learned (and simple) also belong to the shallow type 3 category. Many boosting algorithms belong to this class as well. Unlike with types 1 and 2, the output is a nonlinear function of the parameters to be learned. Hence the loss functions minimized by learning are likely to be nonconvex in the parameters. The definition of type 3 architectures is somewhat informal, since it relies on the ill-defined concept of "simple" parameterized basis function.

We should immediately emphasize that the boundary between the various categories is somewhat fuzzy. For example, training the hidden layer of a one-hidden-layer neural net (a type 3 shallow architecture) is a nonconvex problem, but one could imagine constructing a hidden layer so large that all possible hidden unit functions would be present from the start. Only the output layer would need to be trained. More specifically, when the number of hidden units becomes very large, and an L2 regularizer is used on the output weights, such a neural net becomes a kernel machine, whose kernel has a simple form that can be computed analytically (Bengio et al., 2006b). If we use the margin loss this becomes an SVM with a particular kernel. Although convexity is only achieved in the mathematical limit of an infinite number of hidden units, we conjecture that optimization of single-hidden-layer neural networks becomes easier as the number of hidden units becomes larger. If single-hidden-layer neural nets have any advantage over SVMs, it is that they can, in principle, achieve similar performance with a smaller first layer (since the parameters of the first layer can be optimized for the task).

Note also that our mathematical results on local kernel machines are limited in scope, and most are derived for specific kernels such as the Gaussian kernel, or for local kernels (in the sense of $K(u, v)$ being near zero when $||u - v||$ becomes large). However, the arguments presented below concerning the shallowness of kernel machines are more general.

14.3.1.4   Deep Architectures

Deep architectures are *compositions of many layers of adaptive nonlinear components*; in other words, they are cascades of parameterized nonlinear modules that contain trainable parameters at all levels. Deep architectures allow the representation of wide families of functions in a more compact form than shallow architectures, because they can trade space for time (or breadth for depth) while making the time-space product smaller, as discussed below. The outputs of the intermediate layers are akin to intermediate results on the way to computing the final output. Features produced by the lower layers represent lower-level abstractions that are combined to form high-level features at the next layer, representing higher-level abstractions.

14.3.2   The Depth-Breadth Tradeoff

Any specific function can be implemented by a suitably designed shallow architecture or by a deep architecture. Similarly, when parameterizing a family of functions, we have the choice between shallow or deep architectures. The important questions are: (i) how large is the corresponding architecture (with how many parameters, how much computation to produce the output); (ii) how much manual labor is involved in specializing the architecture to the task.

Using a number of examples, we shall demonstrate that deep architectures are often more efficient (in terms of number of computational components and parameters) for representing common functions. Formal analyses of the computational complexity of shallow circuits can be found in (Håstad, 1987) or (Allender, 1996). They point in the same direction: shallow circuits are much less expressive than deep ones.

Let us first consider the task of adding two N-bit binary numbers. The most natural circuit involves adding the bits pair by pair and propagating the carry. The carry propagation takes $O(N)$ steps, and also $O(N)$ hardware resources. Hence the most natural architecture for binary addition is a deep one, with $O(N)$ layers and $O(N)$ elements. A shallow architecture can implement any Boolean formula expressed in disjunctive normal form (DNF), by computing the minterms (AND functions) in the first layer, and the subsequent OR function using a linear classifier (a threshold gate) with a low threshold. Unfortunately, even for simple Boolean operations such as binary addition and multiplication, the number of terms can be extremely large (up to $O(2^N)$ for N-bit inputs in the worst case). The computer industry has in fact devoted a considerable amount of effort into optimizing the implementation of exponential Boolean functions, but the largest it can put on a single chip has only about 32 input bits (a 4Gbit RAM chip, as of 2006). This is why practical digital circuits, e.g., for adding or multiplying two numbers, are built with multiple layers of logic gates: their two-layer implementation (akin to a lookup table) would be prohibitively expensive. See (Utgoff and Stracuzzi, 2002) for a previous discussion of this question in the context of learning architectures.

Another interesting example is the Boolean parity function. The N-bit Boolean parity function can be implemented in at least five ways:

1. with $N-1$ daisy-chained XOR gates ($N-1$ layers, possibly implemented by a recurrent circuit with a single XOR gate and $N-1$ time steps);
2. with $N-1$ XOR gates arranged in a tree ($\log_2 N$ layers);
3. as a DNF formula with $O(2^N)$ minterms (two layers, $O(2^N)$ gates).

Architecture 1 has high depth and low breadth (small amount of computing elements); architecture 2 is a good tradeoff between depth and breadth; and architecture 3 has high breadth and low depth. If one allows the use of multi-input binary threshold gates (linear classifiers) in addition to traditional logic gates, two more architectures are possible (Minsky and Papert, 1969):

4. A three-layer architecture constructed as follows. The first layer has N binary threshold gates (linear classifiers) in which unit i adds all the input bits and subtracts i, hence computing the predicate $x_i = (s \geq i)$ where s is the count of nonzero inputs. The second layer contains $(N-1)/2$ AND gates that compute (x_i AND NOT x_{i+1}) for all i that are odd. The last layer is a simple OR gate.
5. A two-layer architecture in which the first layer is identical to that of the three-layer architecture above, and the second layer is a linear threshold gate (linear classifier) where the weight for input x_i is equal to $(-2)^i$.

The fourth architecture requires a dynamic range (accuracy) on the weight linear in N, while the last one requires a dynamic range exponential in N. A proof that N-bit parity requires $O(2^N)$ gates to be represented by a depth 2 Boolean circuit (with AND, NOT, and OR gates) can be found in (Ajtai, 1983). In theorem 14.3 (section 14.4.1.1) we state a similar result for learning architectures: an exponential number of terms is required with a Gaussian kernel machine in order to represent the parity function. In many instances, space (or breadth) can be traded for time (or depth) with considerable advantage.

These negative results may seem reminiscent of the classic results of Minsky and Papert (1969). This should come as no surprise: shallow architectures (particularly of types 1 and 2) fall into Minsky and Papert's general definition of a perceptron and are subject to many of its limitations.

Another interesting example in which adding layers is beneficial is the fast Fourier transform (FFT) algorithm. Since the discrete Fourier transform is a linear operation, it can be performed by a matrix multiplication with N^2 complex multiplications, which can all be performed in parallel, followed by $O(N^2)$ additions to collect the sums. However the FFT algorithm can reduce the total cost to $\frac{1}{2}N\log_2 N$ multiplications, with the tradeoff of requiring $\log_2 N$ sequential steps involving $\frac{N}{2}$ multiplications each. This example shows that, even with linear functions, adding layers allows us to take advantage of the intrinsic regularities in the task.

Because each variable can be either absent, present, or negated in a minterm, there are $M = 3^N$ different possible minterms when the circuit has N inputs. The set of all possible DNF formulae with k minterms and N inputs has $C(M, k)$ elements (the number of combinations of k elements from M). Clearly, that set (which is associated with the set of functions representable with k minterms) grows very fast with k. Going from $k - 1$ to k minterms increases the number of combinations by a factor $(M - k)/k$. When k is not close to M, the size of the set of DNF formulae is exponential in the number of inputs N. These arguments would suggest that only an exponentially (in N) small fraction of all Boolean functions require a less than exponential number of minterms.

We claim that most functions that can be represented compactly by deep architectures cannot be represented by a compact shallow architecture. Imagine representing the logical operations over K layers of a logical circuit into a DNF formula. The operations performed by the gates on each of the layers are likely to get combined into a number of minterms that could be exponential in the original number of layers. To see this, consider a K layer logical circuit where every odd layer has AND gates (with the option of negating arguments) and every even layer has OR gates. Every pair of consecutive AND/OR layers corresponds to a sum of products in modulo 2 arithmetic. The whole circuit is the composition of $K/2$ such sums of products, and it is thus a deep *factorization* of a formula. In general, when a factored representation is expanded into a single sum of products, one gets a number of terms that can be exponential in the number of levels. A similar phenomenon explains why most compact DNF formulae require an exponential number of terms when written as a conjunctive normal form (CNF) formula. A survey of more general results in computational complexity of Boolean circuits can be found in (Allender, 1996). For example, (Håstad, 1987) shows that for all k, there are depth $k + 1$ circuits of linear size that require exponential size to simulate with depth k circuits. This implies that *most functions representable compactly with a deep architecture would require a very large number of components if represented with a shallow one.* Hence restricting ourselves to shallow architectures unduly limits the spectrum of functions that can be represented compactly and learned efficiently (at least in a statistical sense). In particular, highly variable functions (in the sense of having high frequencies in their Fourier spectrum) are difficult to represent with a circuit of depth 2 (Linial et al., 1993). The results that we present in section 14.4 yield a similar conclusion: representing highly variable functions with a Gaussian kernel machine is very inefficient.

14.3.3 The Limits of Matching Global Templates

Before diving into the formal analysis of local models, we compare the kernel machines (type 2 architectures) with deep architectures, using examples. One of the fundamental problems in pattern recognition is how to handle intraclass variability. Taking the example of letter recognition, we can picture the set of all the possible images of the letter E on a 20×20 pixel grid as a set of continuous manifolds in the pixel space (e.g., one manifold for lowercase and one for cursive). The Es on a manifold can be continuously morphed into each other by following a path on the manifold. The dimensionality of the manifold at one location corresponds to the number of independent distortions that can can be applied to an image while preserving its category. For handwritten letter categories, the manifold has a high dimension: letters can be distorted using affine transforms (six parameters), distorted using an elastic sheet deformation (high dimension), or modified so as to cover the range of possible writing styles, shapes, and stroke widths. Even for simple character images, the manifold is very nonlinear, with high curvature. To convince ourselves of that, consider the shape of the letter W. Any pixel in the lower half of the image will go from white to black and white again four times as the W is shifted horizontally within the image frame from left to right. This is the sign of a highly nonlinear surface. Moreover, manifolds for other character categories are closely intertwined. Consider the shape of a capital U and an O at the same location. They have many pixels in common, many more pixels in fact than with a shifted version of the same U. Hence the distance between the U and O manifolds is smaller than the distance between two Us shifted by a few pixels. Another insight about the high curvature of these manifolds can be obtained from the example in figure 14.4: the tangent vector of the horizontal translation manifold changes abruptly as we translate the image only one pixel to the right, indicating high curvature. As discussed in section 14.4.2, many kernel algorithms make an implicit assumption of a locally smooth function (e.g., locally linear in the case of SVMs) *around each training example x_i*. Hence a high curvature implies the necessity of a large number of training examples in order to cover all the desired twists and turns with locally constant or locally linear pieces.

This brings us to what we perceive as the main shortcoming of template-based methods: a very large number of templates may be required in order to cover each manifold with enough templates to avoid misclassifications. Furthermore, the number of necessary templates can grow exponentially with the intrinsic dimension of a class-invariant manifold. The only way to circumvent the problem with a type 2 architecture is to design similarity measures for matching templates (kernel functions) such that two patterns that are on the same manifold are deemed similar. Unfortunately, devising such similarity measures, even for a problem as basic as digit recognition, has proved difficult, despite almost 50 years of active research.

Furthermore, if such a good task-specific kernel were finally designed, it may be inapplicable to other classes of problems.

To further illustrate the situation, consider the problem of detecting and identifying a simple motif (say of size $S = 5 \times 5$ pixels) that can appear at D different locations in a uniformly white image with N pixels (say 10^6 pixels). To solve this problem, a simple kernel machine architecture would require one template of the motif for each possible location, thas is, ND elementary operations. An architecture that allows for *spatially local* feature detectors would merely require SD elementary operations. We should emphasize that this spatial locality (feature detectors that depend on pixels within a limited radius in the image plane) is distinct from the locality of kernel functions (feature detectors that produce large values only for input vectors that are within a limited radius in the input vector space). In fact, spatially local feature detectors have nonlocal response in the space of input vectors, since their output is independent of the input pixels to which they are not connected.

A slightly more complicated example is the task of detecting and recognizing a pattern composed of two different motifs. Each motif occupies S pixels, and can appear at D different locations independently of each other. A kernel machine would need a separate template for each possible occurrence of the two motifs, that is, ND^2 computing elements. By contrast, a properly designed type 3 architecture would merely require a set of local feature detectors for all the positions of the first motifs, and a similar set for the second motif. The total amount of elementary operations is a mere $2SD$. We do not know of any kernel that would efficiently handle compositional structures.

An even more dire situation occurs if the background is not uniformly white, but can contain random clutter. A kernel machine would probably need many different templates containing the desired motifs on top of many different backgrounds. By contrast, the locally connected deep architecture described in the previous paragraph will handle this situation just fine. We have verified this type of behavior experimentally (see examples in section 14.6).

These thought experiments illustrate the limitations of kernel machines due to the fact that their first layer is restricted to matching the incoming patterns with global templates. By contrast, the type 3 architecture that uses spatially local feature detectors handles the position jitter and the clutter easily and efficiently. Both architectures are shallow, but while each kernel function is activated in a small area of the input space, the spatially local feature detectors are activated by a huge $(N-S)$–dimensional subspace of the input space (since they only look at S pixels). Deep architectures with spatially local feature detectors are even more efficient (see section 14.6). Hence the limitations of kernel machines are not just due to their shallowness, but also to the *local* character of their response function (local in input space, not in the space of image coordinates).

14.4   Fundamental Limitation of Local Learning

A large fraction of the recent work in statistical machine learning has focused on nonparametric learning algorithms which rely solely, explicitly or implicitly, on a *smoothness prior*. A smoothness prior favors functions f such that when $x \approx x'$, $f(x) \approx f(x')$. Additional prior knowledge is expressed by choosing the space of the data and the particular notion of similarity between examples (typically expressed as a kernel function). This class of learning algorithms includes most instances of the kernel machine algorithms (Schölkopf et al., 1999a), such as SVMs (Boser et al., 1992; Cortes and Vapnik, 1995) or Gaussian processes (Williams and Rasmussen, 1996), but also unsupervised learning algorithms that attempt to capture the manifold structure of the data, such as locally linear embedding (LLE) (Roweis and Saul, 2000), isomap (Tenenbaum et al., 2000), kernel principal component analysis (KPCA) (Schölkopf et al., 1998), Laplacian eigenmaps (Belkin and Niyogi, 2003), manifold charting (Brand, 2003), and *spectral clustering* algorithms (see Weiss, 1999, for a review). More recently, there has also been much interest in nonparametric *semisupervised learning algorithms* (e.g., X. Zhu et al., 2003; Zhou et al., 2004; Belkin et al., 2004; Delalleau et al., 2005) which also fall into this category, and share many ideas with manifold learning algorithms.

Since this is a large class of algorithms and one that continues to attract attention, it is worthwhile to investigate its limitations. Since these methods share many characteristics with classical nonparametric statistical learning algorithms — such as the k-nearest neighbors and the Parzen windows regression and density estimation algorithms (Duda and Hart, 1973) — which have been shown to suffer from the so-called *curse of dimensionality*, it is logical to investigate the following question: to what extent do these modern kernel methods suffer from a similar problem? See (Härdle et al., 2004) for a recent and easily accessible exposition of the curse of dimensionality for classical nonparametric methods.

To explore this question, we focus on algorithms in which the learned function is expressed in terms of a linear combination of kernel functions applied on the training examples:

$$f(x) = b + \sum_{i=1}^{n} \alpha_i K_D(x, x_i) , \tag{14.1}$$

where we have included an optional bias term b. The set $D = \{z_1, \ldots, z_n\}$ contains training examples $z_i = x_i$ for unsupervised learning, $z_i = (x_i, y_i)$ for supervised learning. Target value y_i can take a special missing value for semisupervised learning. The α_i's are scalars chosen by the learning algorithm using D, and $K_D(\cdot, \cdot)$ is the kernel function, a symmetric function (sometimes expected to be positive semidefinite), which may be chosen by taking into account all the x_i's. A typical kernel function is the Gaussian kernel,

$$K_\sigma(u, v) = e^{-\frac{1}{\sigma^2}||u-v||^2}, \tag{14.2}$$

with the width σ controlling how local the kernel is. See Bengio et al. (2004) to see that LLE, isomap, Laplacian eigenmaps, and other spectral manifold learning algorithms such as spectral clustering can be generalized and written in the form of (14.1) for a test point x, but with a different kernel (that is data dependent, generally performing a kind of normalization of a data-independent kernel).

One obtains the consistency of classical nonparametric estimators by appropriately varying the hyperparameter that controls the locality of the estimator as n increases. Basically, the kernel should be allowed to become more and more local, so that statistical bias goes to zero, but the effective number of examples involved in the estimator at x (equal to k for the k-nearest neighbor estimator) should increase as n increases, so that statistical variance is also driven to 0. For a wide class of kernel regression estimators, the unconditional variance and squared bias can be shown to be written as follows (Härdle et al., 2004):

$$\text{expected error} = \frac{C_1}{n\sigma^d} + C_2\sigma^4,$$

with C_1 and C_2 not depending on n nor on the dimension d. Hence an optimal bandwidth is chosen proportional to $n^{\frac{-1}{4+d}}$, and the resulting generalization error (not counting the noise) converges in $n^{-4/(4+d)}$, which becomes very slow for large d. Consider, for example, the increase in number of examples required to get the same level of error, in one dimension versus d dimensions. If n_1 is the number of examples required to get a particular level of error, to get the same level of error in d dimensions requires on the order of $n_1^{(4+d)/5}$ examples, i.e., the *required number of examples is exponential in d*. For the k-nearest neighbor classifier, a similar result is obtained (Snapp and Venkatesh, 1998):

$$\text{Expected error} = E_\infty + \sum_{j=2}^{\infty} c_j n^{-j/d} \ ,$$

where E_∞ is the asymptotic error, d is the dimension, and n the number of examples.

Note, however, that if the data distribution is concentrated on a lower-dimensional manifold, it is the *manifold dimension* that matters. For example, when data lies on a smooth lower-dimensional manifold, the only dimensionality that matters to a k-nearest neighbor classifier is the dimensionality of the manifold, since it only uses the Euclidean distances between the near neighbors. Many unsupervised and semisupervised learning algorithms rely on a graph with one node per example, in which nearby examples are connected with an edge weighted by the Euclidean distance between them. If data lies on a low-dimensional manifold, then geodesic distances in this graph approach geodesic distances on the manifold (Tenenbaum et al., 2000), as the number of examples increases. However, convergence can be exponentially slower for higher-dimensional manifolds.

14.4.1 Minimum Number of Bases Required

In this section we present results showing the number of required bases (hence of training examples) of a kernel machine with a Gaussian kernel may grow linearly with the number of variations of the target function that must be captured in order to achieve a given error level.

14.4.1.1 Result for Supervised Learning

The following theorem highlights the number of sign changes that a Gaussian kernel machine can achieve when it has k bases (i.e., k support vectors, or at least k training examples).

Theorem 14.1 (Schmitt, 2002, theorem 2). *Let $f : \mathbb{R} \to \mathbb{R}$ computed by a Gaussian kernel machine (eq. 14.1) with k bases (nonzero α_i). Then f has at most $2k$ zeros.*

We would like to say something about kernel machines in $\mathbb{R}^d$, and we can do this simply by considering a straight line in $\mathbb{R}^d$ and the number of sign changes that the solution function f can achieve along that line.

Corollary 14.2. *Suppose that the learning problem is such that in order to achieve a given error level for samples from a distribution P with a Gaussian kernel machine (14.1), then f must change sign at least $2k$ times along some straight line (i.e., in the case of a classifier, the decision surface must be crossed at least $2k$ times by that straight line). Then the kernel machine must have at least k bases (nonzero α_i).*

A proof can be found in (Bengio et al., 2006a).

Example 14.1. *Consider the decision surface shown in figure 14.2, which is a sinusoidal function. One may take advantage of the global regularity to learn it with few parameters (thus requiring few examples), but with an affine combination of Gaussians, corollary 14.2 implies one would need at least $\lceil \frac{m}{2} \rceil = 10$ Gaussians. For more complex tasks in higher dimension, the complexity of the decision surface could quickly make learning impractical when using such a local kernel method.*

Of course, one only seeks to approximate the decision surface S, and does not necessarily need to learn it perfectly: corollary 14.2 says nothing about the existence of an easier-to-learn decision surface approximating S. For instance, in the example of figure 14.2, the dotted line could turn out to be a good enough estimated decision surface if most samples were far from the true decision surface, and this line can be obtained with only two Gaussians.

The above theorem tells us that in order to represent a function that locally varies a lot, in the sense that its sign along a straight line changes many times, a Gaussian kernel machine requires many training examples and many computational elements. Note that it says nothing about the dimensionality of the input space, but we might expect to have to learn functions that vary more when the data is

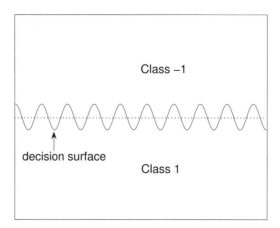

Figure 14.2   The dotted line crosses the decision surface 19 times: one thus needs at least 10 Gaussians to learn it with an affine combination of Gaussians with the same width.

high-dimensional. The next theorem confirms this suspicion in the special case of the d-bits parity function:

$$\text{parity} : (b_1, \dots, b_d) \in \{0,1\}^d \mapsto \begin{cases} 1 \text{ if } \sum_{i=1}^d b_i \text{ is even,} \\ -1 \text{ otherwise..} \end{cases}$$

Learning this apparently simple function with Gaussians centered on points in $\{0,1\}^d$ is actually difficult, in the sense that it requires a number of Gaussians exponential in d (for a fixed Gaussian width). Note that our corollary 14.2 does not apply to the d-bits parity function, so it represents another type of local variation (not along a line). However, it is also possible to prove a very strong result for parity.

Theorem 14.3. *Let $f(x) = b + \sum_{i=1}^{2^d} \alpha_i K_\sigma(x_i, x)$ be an affine combination of Gaussians with same width σ centered on points $x_i \in X_d$. If f solves the parity problem, then there are at least 2^{d-1} nonzero coefficients α_i.*

A proof can be found in Bengio et al. (2006a).

The bound in theorem 14.3 is tight, since it is possible to solve the parity problem with exactly 2^{d-1} Gaussians and a bias, for instance, by using a negative bias and putting a positive weight on each example satisfying parity$(x_i) = 1$. When trained to learn the parity function, an SVM may learn a function that looks like the opposite of the parity on test points (while still performing optimally on training points), but it is an artifact of the specific geometry of the problem, and only occurs when the training set size is appropriate compared to $|X_d| = 2^d$ (see Bengio et al.

(2005) for details). Note that if the centers of the Gaussians are not restricted anymore to be points in the training set (i.e., a type 3 shallow architecture), it is possible to solve the parity problem with only $d+1$ Gaussians and no bias (Bengio et al., 2005).

One may argue that parity is a simple discrete toy problem of little interest. But even if we have to restrict the analysis to discrete samples in $\{0,1\}^d$ for mathematical reasons, the parity function can be extended to a smooth function on the $[0,1]^d$ hypercube depending only on the continuous sum $b_1 + \ldots + b_d$. Theorem 14.3 is thus a basis to argue that the number of Gaussians needed to learn a function with many variations in a continuous space may scale linearly with the number of these variations, and thus possibly exponentially in the dimension.

14.4.1.2   *Results for Semisupervised Learning*

In this section we focus on algorithms of the type described in recent papers (X. Zhu et al., 2003; Zhou et al., 2004; Belkin et al., 2004; Delalleau et al., 2005), which are graph-based, nonparametric, semisupervised learning algorithms. Note that transductive SVMs (Joachims, 1999b), which are another class of semisupervised algorithms, are already subject to the limitations of corollary 14.2. The graph-based algorithms we consider here can be seen as minimizing the following cost function, as shown in Delalleau et al. (2005):

$$C(\hat{Y}) = \|\hat{Y}_l - Y_l\|^2 + \mu \hat{Y}^\top L \hat{Y} + \mu \epsilon \|\hat{Y}\|^2 \,, \tag{14.3}$$

with $\hat{Y} = (\hat{y}_1, \ldots, \hat{y}_n)$ the estimated labels on both labeled and unlabeled data, and L the (un-normalized) graph Laplacian matrix, derived through $L = D^{-1/2}WD^{-1/2}$ from a kernel function K between points such that the Gram matrix W, with $W_{ij} = K(x_i, x_j)$, corresponds to the weights of the edges in the graph, and D is a diagonal matrix containing indegree: $D_{ii} = \sum_j W_{ij}$. Here, $\hat{Y}_l = (\hat{y}_1, \ldots, \hat{y}_l)$ is the vector of estimated labels on the l labeled examples, whose known labels are given by $Y_l = (y_1, \ldots, y_l)$, and one may constrain $\hat{Y}_l = Y_l$ as in (X. Zhu et al., 2003) by letting $\mu \to 0$. We define a region with constant label as a connected subset of the graph where all nodes x_i have the same estimated label (sign of $\hat{y}_i$), and such that no other node can be added while keeping these properties.

Minimization of the cost criterion (14.3) can also be seen as a *label propagation* algorithm, i.e., labels are spread around labeled examples, with nearness being defined by the structure of the graph, i.e., by the kernel. An intuitive view of label propagation suggests that a region of the manifold near a labeled (e.g., positive) example will be entirely labeled positively, as the example spreads its influence by propagation on the graph representing the underlying manifold. Thus, the number of regions with constant label should be on the same order as (or less than) the number of labeled examples. This is easy to see in the case of a sparse Gram matrix W. We define a region with constant label as a connected subset of the graph where all nodes x_i have the same estimated label (sign of $\hat{y}_i$), and such that no other node can be added while keeping these properties. The following proposition then holds (note that it is also true, but trivial, when W defines a fully connected graph).

Proposition 14.4. *After running a label propagation algorithm minimizing the cost (14.3), the number of regions with constant estimated label is less than (or equal to) the number of labeled examples.*

A proof can be found in Bengio et al. (2006a). The consequence is that we will need at least as many labeled examples as there are variations in the class, as one moves by small steps in the neighborhood graph from one contiguous region of the same label to another. Again, we see the same type of nonparametric learning algorithms with a local kernel, here in the case of semisupervised learning: we may need about as many labeled examples as there are variations, even though an arbitrarily large number of these variations could have been characterized more efficiently than by their enumeration.

14.4.2   Smoothness versus Locality: Curse of Dimensionality

Consider a Gaussian SVM and how that estimator changes as one varies σ, the hyperparameter of the Gaussian kernel. For large σ one would expect the estimated function to be very smooth, whereas for small σ one would expect the estimated function to be very local, in the sense discussed earlier: the near neighbors of x have dominating influence in the shape of the predictor at x.

The following proposition tells us what happens when σ is large:

Proposition 14.5. *For the Gaussian kernel classifier, as σ increases and becomes large compared with the diameter of the data, within the smallest sphere containing the data the decision surface becomes linear if $\sum_i \alpha_i = 0$ (e.g., for SVMs), or else the normal vector of the decision surface becomes a linear combination of two sphere surface normal vectors, with each sphere centered on a weighted average of the examples of the corresponding class.*

A proof can be found in Bengio et al. (2006a).

This proposition states that a kernel classifier becomes nonlocal when σ becomes large (it approaches a linear classifier). However, this nonlocality is at the price of constraining the decision surface to be very smooth, making it difficult to model highly varying decision surfaces. This is the essence of the tradeoff between smoothness and locality in many similar nonparametric models (including the classical ones such as k-nearest neighbor and Parzen windows algorithms).

Now consider in what senses a Gaussian kernel machine is local (thinking about σ small). Consider a test point x that is near the decision surface. We claim that the orientation of the decision surface is dominated by the neighbors x_i of x in the training set, making the predictor *local in its derivative*. If we consider the α_i fixed (i.e., ignoring their dependence on the training x_i's), then it is obvious that the prediction $f(x)$ is dominated by the near neighbors x_i of x, since $K(x, x_i) \to 0$ quickly when $\|x - x_i\|/\sigma$ becomes large. However, the α_i can be influenced by all

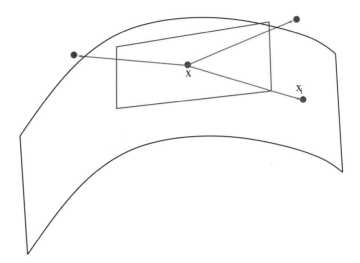

Figure 14.3 For local manifold learning algorithms such as LLE, isomap, and KPCA, the manifold tangent plane at x is in the span of the difference vectors between test point x and its neighbors x_i in the training set. This makes these algorithms sensitive to the curse of dimensionality, when the manifold is high-dimensional and not very flat.

the x_j's. The following proposition skirts that issue by looking at the first derivative of f.

Proposition 14.6. *For the Gaussian kernel classifier, the normal of the tangent of the decision surface at x is constrained to approximately lie in the span of the vectors $(x - x_i)$ with $\|x - x_i\|$ not large compared to σ and x_i in the training set.*

Sketch of the proof. The estimator is $f(x) = \sum_i \alpha_i K(x, x_i)$. The normal vector of the tangent plane at a point x of the decision surface is

$$\frac{\partial f(x)}{\partial x} = \sum_i \alpha_i \frac{(x_i - x)}{\sigma^2} K(x, x_i).$$

Each term is a vector proportional to the difference vector $x_i - x$. This sum is dominated by the terms with $\|x - x_i\|$ not large compared to σ. We are thus left with $\frac{\partial f(x)}{\partial x}$ approximately in the span of the difference vectors $x - x_i$ with x_i a near neighbor of x. The α_i being only scalars, they only influence the weight of each neighbor x_i in that linear combination. Hence, although $f(x)$ can be influenced by x_i far from x, the decision surface near x has a normal vector that is constrained to approximately lie in the span of the vectors $x - x_i$ with x_i near x. ∎

The constraint of $\frac{\partial f(x)}{\partial x}$ being in the span of the vectors $x - x_i$ for neighbors x_i of x is not strong if the manifold of interest (e.g., the region of the decision surface with high density) has low dimensionality. Indeed if that dimensionality is smaller or equal to the number of dominating neighbors, then there is no constraint at all.

However, when modeling complex dependencies involving many factors of variation, the region of interest may have a very high dimension (e.g., consider the effect of variations that have an arbitrarily large dimension, such as changes in clutter, background , etc. in images). For such a complex highly varying target function, we also need a very local predictor (σ small) in order to accurately represent all the desired variations. With a small σ, the number of dominating neighbors will be small compared to the dimension of the manifold of interest, making this locality in the derivative a strong constraint, and allowing the following curse of dimensionality argument.

This notion of locality in the sense of the derivative allows us to define a ball around each test point x, containing neighbors that have a dominating influence on $\frac{\partial f(x)}{\partial x}$. Smoothness within that ball constrains the decision surface to be approximately either linear (case of SVMs) or a particular quadratic form (the decision surface normal vector is a linear combination of two vectors defined by the center of mass of examples of each class). Let N be the number of such balls necessary to cover the region Ω where the value of the estimator is desired (e.g., near the target decision surface, in the case of classification problems). Let k be the smallest number such that one needs at least k examples in each ball to reach error level ϵ. The number of examples thus required is kN. To see that N can be exponential in some dimension, consider the maximum radius r of all these balls and the radius R of Ω. If Ω has intrinsic dimension d, then N could be as large as the number of radius r balls that can tile a d-dimensional manifold of radius R, which is on the order of $\left(\frac{R}{r}\right)^d$.

In (Bengio et al., 2005) we present similar results that apply to unsupervised learning algorithms such as nonparametric manifold learning algorithms (Roweis and Saul, 2000; Tenenbaum et al., 2000; Schölkopf et al., 1998; Belkin and Niyogi, 2003). We find that when the underlying manifold varies a lot in the sense of having high curvature in many places, then a large number of examples is required. Note that the tangent plane of the manifold is defined by the derivatives of the kernel machine function f, for such algorithms. The core result is that the manifold tangent plane at x is dominated by terms associated with the near neighbors of x in the training set (more precisely it is constrained to be in the span of the vectors $x - x_i$, with x_i a neighbor of x). This idea is illustrated in figure 14.3. In the case of graph-based manifold learning algorithms such as LLE and isomap, the domination of near examples is perfect (i.e., the derivative is strictly in the span of the difference vectors with the neighbors), because the kernel implicit in these algorithms takes value 0 for the non-neighbors. With such local manifold learning algorithms, one needs to cover the manifold with small enough linear patches with at least $d + 1$ examples per patch (where d is the dimension of the manifold). This argument was previously introduced in Bengio and Monperrus (2005) to describe the limitations of neighborhood-based manifold learning algorithms.

An example that illustrates that many interesting manifolds can have high curvature is that of translation of high-contrast images, shown in figure 14.4. The same argument applies to the other geometric invariances of images of objects.

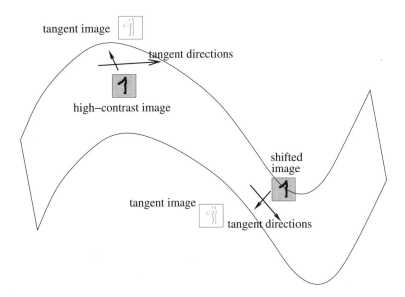

Figure 14.4 The manifold of translations of a high-contrast image has high curvature. A smooth manifold is obtained by considering that an image is a sample on a discrete grid of an intensity function over a two-dimensional space. The tangent vector for translation is thus a *tangent image*, and it has high values only on the edges of the ink. The tangent plane for an image translated by only one pixel looks similar but changes abruptly since the edges are also shifted by one pixel. Hence the two tangent planes are almost orthogonal, and the manifold has high curvature, which is bad for local learning methods, which must cover the manifold with many small linear patches to correctly capture its shape.

14.5 Deep Architectures

The analyses in the previous sections point to the difficulty of learning *highly varying functions*. These are functions with a large number of *variations* (twists and turns) in the domain of interest, e.g., they would require a large number of pieces to be well represented by a piecewise-linear approximation. Since the number of pieces can be made to grow exponentially with the number of input variables, this problem is directly connected with the well-known curse of dimensionality for classical nonparametric learning algorithms (for regression, classification, and density estimation). If the shapes of all these pieces are unrelated, one needs enough examples for each piece in order to generalize properly. However, if these shapes are related and can be predicted from each other, *nonlocal learning algorithms* have the potential to generalize to pieces not covered by the training set. Such ability would seem necessary for learning in complex domains such as in the AI-set.

One way to represent a highly varying function compactly (with few parameters) is through the composition of many nonlinearities. Such multiple composition of nonlinearities appears to grant nonlocal properties to the estimator, in the sense that the value of $f(x)$ or $f'(x)$ can be strongly dependent on training examples far from x_i while at the same time allowing the capture of a large number of variations. We have already discussed parity and other examples (section 14.3.2) that strongly suggest that the learning of more abstract functions is much more efficient when it is done sequentially, by composing previously learned concepts. When the representation of a concept requires an exponential number of elements, (e.g., with a shallow circuit), the number of training examples required to learn the concept may also be impractical.

Gaussian processes, SVMs, log-linear models, graph-based manifold learning, and graph-based semisupervised learning algorithms can all be seen as shallow architectures. Although multilayer neural networks with many layers can represent deep circuits, training deep networks has always been seen as somewhat of a challenge. Until very recently, empirical studies often found that deep networks generally performed no better, and often worse, than neural networks with one or two hidden layers (Tesauro, 1992). A notable exception to this is the convolutional neural network architecture (LeCun et al., 1989, 1998a) discussed in the next section, which has a sparse connectivity from layer to layer. Despite its importance, the topic of deep network training has been somewhat neglected by the research community. However, a promising new method recently proposed by Hinton et al. (2006) is causing a resurgence of interest in the subject.

A common explanation for the difficulty of deep network learning is the presence of local minima or plateaus in the loss function. Gradient-based optimization methods that start from random initial conditions appear to often get trapped in poor local minima or plateaus. The problem seems particularly dire for narrow networks (with few hidden units or with a bottleneck) and for networks with many symmetries (i.e., fully connected networks in which hidden units are exchangeable). The solution recently introduced by Hinton et al. (2006) for training deep-layered networks is based on a greedy, layerwise unsupervised learning phase. The unsupervised learning phase provides an initial configuration of the parameters with which a gradient-based supervised learning phase is initialized. The main idea of the unsupervised phase is to pair each feedforward layer with a feedback layer that attempts to reconstruct the input of the layer from its output. This reconstruction criterion guarantees that most of the information contained in the input is preserved in the output of the layer. The resulting architecture is a so-called deep belief networks (DBN). After the initial unsupervised training of each feedforward/feedback pair, the feedforward half of the network is refined using a gradient descent–based supervised method (backpropagation). This training strategy *holds great promise as a principle to break through the problem of training deep networks*. Upper layers of a DBN are supposed to represent more abstract concepts that explain the input observation x, whereas lower layers extract low-level features from x. Lower layers learn simpler concepts first, and higher layers build on them to learn more abstract concepts. This strategy has not yet been much exploited in machine learning, but it is at the basis of the greedy layerwise constructive learning algorithm for DBNs.

More precisely, each layer is trained in an unsupervised way so as to capture the main features of the distribution it sees as input. It produces an internal representation for its input that can be used as input for the next layer. In a DBN, each layer is trained as a restricted Boltzmann machine (RBM) (Teh and Hinton, 2001) using the contrastive divergence (Hinton, 2002) approximation of the log-likelihood gradient. The outputs of each layer (i.e., hidden units) constitute a factored and distributed representation that estimates causes for the input of the layer. After the layers have been thus initialized, a final output layer is added on top of the network (e.g., predicting the class probabilities), and the whole deep network is fine-tuned by a gradient-based optimization of the prediction error. The only difference with an ordinary multilayer neural network resides in the initialization of the parameters, which is not random, but is performed through unsupervised training of each layer in a sequential fashion.

Experiments have been performed on the MNIST and other datasets to try to understand why the DBNs are doing much better than either shallow networks or deep networks with random initialization. These results are reported and discussed in (Bengio et al., 2007). Several conclusions can be drawn from these experiments, among which the following are of particular interest here:

1. Similar results can be obtained by training each layer as an autoassociator instead of a RBM, suggesting that a rather general principle has been discovered.

2. Test classification error is significantly improved with such greedy layerwise unsupervised initialization over either a shallow network or a deep network with the same architecture but with random initialization. In all cases many possible hidden layer sizes were tried, and selected based on validation error.

3. When using a greedy layerwise strategy that is *supervised* instead of unsupervised, the results are not as good, probably because it is *too greedy*: unsupervised feature learning extracts more information than strictly necessary for the prediction task, whereas greedy supervised feature learning (greedy because it does not take into account that there will be more layers later) extracts less information than necessary, which prematurely scuttles efforts to improve by adding layers.

4. The greedy layerwise unsupervised strategy helps generalization mostly because it helps the supervised optimization to get started near a better solution.

14.6 Experiments with Visual Pattern Recognition

One essential question when designing a learning architecture is how to represent invariance. While invariance properties are crucial to any learning task, it is particularly apparent in visual pattern recognition. In this section we consider several experiments in handwriting recognition and object recognition to illustrate the relative advantages and disadvantages of kernel methods, shallow architectures, and deep architectures.

14.6.1   Representing Invariance

The example of figure 14.4 shows that the manifold containing all translated versions of a character image has high curvature. Because the manifold is highly varying, a classifier that is invariant to translations (i.e., that produces a constant output when the input moves on the manifold, but changes when the input moves to another class manifold) needs to compute a highly varying function. As we showed in the previous section, template-based methods are inefficient at representing highly varying functions. The number of such variations may increase exponentially with the dimensionality of the manifolds where the input density concentrates. That dimensionality is the number of dimensions along which samples within a category can vary.

We will now describe two sets of results with visual pattern recognition. The first part is a survey of results obtained with shallow and deep architectures on the MNIST dataset, which contains isolated handwritten digits. The second part analyzes results of experiments with the NORB dataset, which contains objects from five different generic categories, placed on uniform or cluttered backgrounds.

For visual pattern recognition, type 2 architectures have trouble handling the wide variability of appearance in pixel images that results from variations in pose, illumination, and clutter, unless an impracticably large number of templates (e.g., support vectors) are used. Adhoc preprocessing and feature extraction can, of course, be used to mitigate the problem, but at the expense of human labor. Here, we will concentrate on methods that deal with raw pixel data and that integrate feature extraction as part of the learning process.

14.6.2   Convolutional Networks

Convolutional nets are multilayer architectures in which the successive layers are designed to learn progressively higher-level features, until the last layer which represents categories. All the layers are trained simultaneously to minimize an overall loss function. Unlike with most other models of classification and pattern recognition, there is no distinct feature extractor and classifier in a convolutional network. All the layers are similar in nature and trained from data in an integrated fashion.

The basic module of a convolutional net is composed of a *feature detection layer* followed by a *feature pooling layer*. A typical convolutional net is composed of one, two, or three such detection/pooling modules in series, followed by a classification module (e.g., figure 14.5). The input state (and output state) of each layer can be seen as a series of two-dimensional retinotopic arrays called feature maps. At layer i, the value c_{ijxy} produced by the ith feature detection layer at position (x, y) in the jth feature map is computed by applying a series of convolution kernels w_{ijk} to feature maps in the previous layer (with index $i-1$), and passing the result through a hyperbolic tangent sigmoid function:

$$c_{ijxy} = \tanh\left(b_{ij} + \sum_k \sum_{p=0}^{P_i-1} \sum_{q=0}^{Q_i-1} w_{ijkpq} c_{(i-1),k,(x+p),(y+q)}\right), \tag{14.4}$$

where P_i and Q_i are the width and height of the convolution kernel. The convolution kernel parameters w_{ijkpq} and the bias b_{ij} are subject to learning. A feature detection layer can be seen as a bank of convolutional filters followed by a pointwise nonlinearity. Each filter detects a particular feature at every location on the input. Hence spatially translating the input of a feature detection layer will translate the output but leave it otherwise unchanged. Translation invariance is normally builtin by constraining $w_{ijkpq} = w_{ijkp'q'}$ for all p, p', q, q', i.e., the same parameters are used at different locations.

A feature pooling layer has the same number of features in the map as the feature detection layer that precedes it. Each value in a subsampling map is the average (or the max) of the values in a local neighborhood in the corresponding feature map in the previous layer. That average or max is added to a trainable bias, multiplied by a trainable coefficient, and the result is passed through a nonlinearity (e.g., the tanh function). The windows are stepped without overlap. Therefore the maps of a feature pooling layer are less than the resolution of the maps in the previous layer. The role of the pooling layer is to build a representation that is invariant to small variations of the positions of features in the input. Alternated layers of feature detection and feature pooling can extract features from increasingly large receptive fields, with increasing robustness to irrelevant variabilities of the inputs. The last module of a convolutional network is generally a one- or two-layer neural net.

Training a convolutional net can be performed with stochastic (online) gradient descent, computing the gradients with a variant of the backpropagation method. While convolutional nets are deep (generally five to seven layers of nonlinear functions), they do not seem to suffer from the convergence problems that plague deep fully connected neural nets. While there is no definitive explanation for this, we suspect that this phenomenon is linked to the heavily constrained parameterization, as well as to the asymmetry of the architecture.

Convolutional nets are being used commercially in several widely deployed systems for reading bank check (LeCun et al., 1998a), recognizing handwriting for tablet PCs, and for detecting faces, people, and objects in videos in real time.

14.6.3 The Lessons from MNIST

MNIST is a dataset of handwritten digits with 60,000 training samples and 10,000 test samples. Digit images have been size-normalized so as to fit within a 20×20 pixel window, and centered by center of mass in a 28×28 field. With this procedure, the position of the characters varies slightly from one sample to another. Numerous authors have reported results on MNIST, allowing precise comparisons between

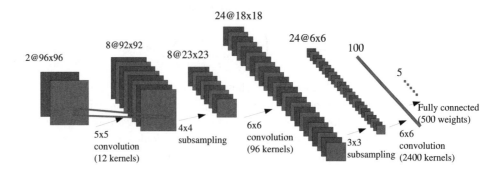

Figure 14.5   The architecture of the convolutional net used for the NORB experiments. The input is an image pair, the system extracts 8 feature maps of size 92 × 92, 8 maps of 23 × 23, 24 maps of 18 × 18, 24 maps of 6 × 6, and a 100-dimensional feature vector. The feature vector is then transformed into a 5-dimensional vector in the last layer to compute the distance with target vectors.

methods. A small subset of relevant results are listed in table 14.1. Not all good results on MNIST are listed in the table. In particular, results obtained with deslanted images or with hand-designed feature extractors were left out.

Results are reported with three convolutional net architectures: LeNet-5, LeNet-6, and the subsampling convolutional net of (Simard et al., 2003). The input field is a 32×32 pixel map in which the 28×28 images are centered. In LeNet-5 (LeCun et al., 1998a), the first feature detection layer produces six feature maps of size 28×28 using 5×5 convolution kernels. The first feature pooling layer produces six 14×14 feature maps through a 2×2 subsampling ratio and 2×2 receptive fields. The second feature detection layer produces 16 feature maps of size 10×10 using 5×5 convolution kernels, and is followed by a pooling layer with 2×2 subsampling. The next layer produces 100 feature maps of size 1×1 using 5×5 convolution kernels. The last layer produces 10 feature maps (one per output category). LeNet-6 has a very similar architecture, but the numbers of feature maps at each level are much larger: 50 feature maps in the first layer, 50 in the third layer, and 200 feature maps in the penultimate layer.

The convolutional net in (Simard et al., 2003) is somewhat similar to the original one in (LeCun et al., 1989) in that there are no separate convolution and subsampling layers. Each layer computes a convolution with a subsampled result (there is no feature pooling operation). Their simple convolutional network has 6 features at the first layer, with 5×5 kernels and 2×2 subsampling, 60 features at the second layer, also with 5×5 kernels and 2×2 subsampling, 100 features at the third layer with 5×5 kernels, and 10 output units.

The MNIST samples are highly variable because of writing style, but have little variation due to position and scale. Hence, it is a dataset that is particularly

Table 14.1 Test error rates of various learning models on the MNIST dataset. Many results obtained with deslanted images or hand-designed feature extractors were left out. NN: fully connected neural network; ConvNN: convolutional neural network; k-NN: k-nearest neighbors.

Classifier	Error	Reference
Knowledge-free methods		
2-layer NN, 800 hidden units	1.60%	Simard et al. 2003
3-layer NN, 500+300 units	1.53%	Hinton et al. 2006
SVM, Gaussian kernel	1.40%	DeCoste and Schölkopf 2002
EVM, Gaussian kernel	1.03%	Haffner 2002
DBM + final backpropagation	0.95%	Hinton et al. 2006
Convolutional networks		
ConvNN LeNet-5	0.80%	Ranzato et al. 2007
ConvNN LeNet-6	0.70%	Ranzato et al. 2007
ConvNN LeNet-6 + unsupervised learning	0.60%	Ranzato et al. 2007
Training set augmented with *affine distortions*		
2-layer NN, 800 hidden units	1.10%	Simard et al. 2003
Virtual SVM, degree 9 polynomial kernel	0.80%	DeCoste and Schölkopf 2002
ConvNN,	0.60%	Simard et al. 2003
Training set augmented with *elastic distortions*		
2-layer NN, 800 hidden units	0.70%	Simard et al. 2003
SVM Gaussian Kernel + online training	0.67%	this book, chapter 13
Shape context features + elastic k-NN	0.63%	Belongie et al. 2002
ConvNN	0.40%	Simard et al. 2003
ConvNN LeNet-6	0.49%	Ranzato et al. 2007
ConvNN LeNet-6 + unsupervised learning	0.39%	Ranzato et al. 2007

favorable for template-based methods. Yet, the error rate yielded by SVMs with Gaussian kernel (1.4% error) is only marginally better than that of a considerably smaller neural net with a single hidden layer of 800 hidden units (1.6% as reported by Simard et al., 2003), and similar to the results obtained with a three-layer neural net as reported in (Hinton et al., 2006) (1.53% error). The best result ever obtained with knowledge-free SVM-like methods on MNIST is 1.03%, using the so-called extrapolated vector machine (EVM) with early stopping (Haffner, 2002). Other authors have reported different results with SVM on MNIST, but the digits were preprocessed differently. For example, the 1.1% obtained with polynomial SVM reported in (Cortes and Vapnik, 1995) and (LeCun et al., 1998a) was obtained with digits centered by bounding box instead of by center of mass. The best result achieved by a knowledge-free method on the original MNIST set, 0.95%, was reported by Hinton et al. (2006) using a DBM initially trained with a greedy layerwise unsupervised method and refined with supervised backpropagation. By knowledge-free method, we mean a method that has no prior knowledge of the pictorial nature of the signal. Those methods would produce exactly the same result if the input pixels were scrambled with a fixed permutation.

A convolutional network uses the pictorial nature of the data, and the invariance of categories to small geometric distortions. It is a broad (low-complexity) prior, which can be specified compactly (with a short piece of code). Yet it brings about a considerable reduction of the ensemble of functions that can be learned. The best convolutional net on the unmodified MNIST set is LeNet-6, which yields a record 0.60%. As with Hinton's results, this result was obtained by initializing the filters in the first layer using an unsupervised algorithm, prior to training with backpropagation (Ranzato et al., 2007). The same LeNet-6 trained purely supervised from random initialization yields 0.70% error. A smaller convolutional net, LeNet-5, yields 0.80%. The same network was reported to yield 0.95% in (LeCun et al., 1998a) with a smaller number of training iterations.

When the training set is augmented with elastically distorted versions of the training samples, the test error rate (on the original, nondistorted test set) drops significantly. A conventional two-layer neural network with 800 hidden units yields 0.70% error (Simard et al., 2003). While SVMs slightly outperform two-layer neural nets on the undistorted set, the advantage all but disappears on the distorted set. In chapter 13, the authors report 0.67% error with a Gaussian SVM and a sample selection procedure. The number of support vectors in the resulting SVM is considerably larger than 800.

Convolutional nets applied to the elastically distorted set achieve between 0.39% and 0.49% error, depending on the architecture, the loss function, and the number of training epochs. Simard et al. (2003) report 0.40% with a subsampling convolutional net. Ranzato et al. (2007) report 0.49% using LeNet-6 with random initialization, and 0.39% using LeNet-6 with unsupervised pretraining of the first layer. This is the best error rate ever reported on the original MNIST test set without preprocessing. For comparison, we included the result of Belongie et al. (2002), obtained using a hand-built nearest neighbor method based on elastic matching of shape context feature representations.

Hence a deep network, with a small dose of prior knowledge embedded in the architecture, combined with a learning algorithm that can deal with millions of examples, goes a long way toward improving performance. Not only do deep networks yield lower error rates, they are faster to run and faster to train on large datasets than the best kernel methods. Layerwise unsupervised initialization consistenly reduces the error rate of convolutional nets by 0.1% over gradient descent from random initial conditions.

14.6.4   The Lessons from NORB

While MNIST is a useful benchmark, its images are simple enough to allow a global template matching scheme to perform well. Natural images of three-dimensional

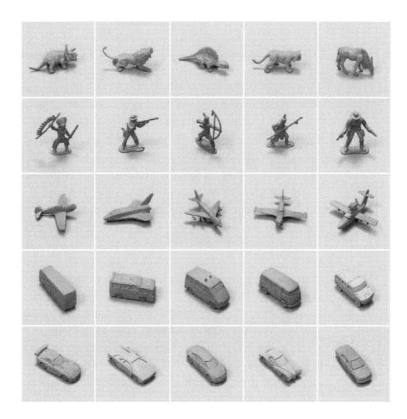

Figure 14.6 The 25 testing objects in the *normalized-uniform* NORB set. The testing objects are unseen by the trained system.

objects with background clutter are considerably more challenging. NORB (LeCun et al., 2004) is a publicly available dataset of object images from five generic categories. It contains images of 50 different toys, with 10 toys in each of the five generic categories: four-legged animals, human figures, airplanes, trucks, and cars. The 50 objects are split into a training set with 25 objects, and a test set with the remaining 25 object (see examples in figure 14.6).

Each object is captured in stereo by a pair of cameras from 162 different viewpoints (9 elevations, 18 azimuths) under 6 different illuminations. Two datasets derived from NORB are used. The first dataset, called the *normalized-uniform* set, contains images of a single object with a normalized size placed at the center of the image with a uniform background. The training set has 24,300 pairs of images of size 96×96, and another 24,300 for testing (from different object instances).

The second set, the *jittered-cluttered* set, contains objects with randomly perturbed positions, scales, in-plane rotation, brightness, and contrast. The objects are placed on highly cluttered backgrounds and other NORB objects are placed on the periphery. A sixth category of images is included: background images containing no objects. Some examples of images of this set are shown in figure 14.7. Each image in the jittered-cluttered set is randomly perturbed so that the objects are at different positions ([-3, +3] pixels horizontally and vertically), scales (ratio in [0.8, 1.1]), image-plane angles ([$-5°$, $5°$]), brightness ([-20, 20] shifts of gray scale), and contrasts ([0.8, 1.3] gain). The central object could be occluded by the randomly placed distractor. To generate the training set, each image was perturbed with 10 different configurations of the above parameters, which makes up 291,600 image pairs of size 108×108. The testing set has two drawings of perturbations per image, and contains 58,320 pairs.

In the NORB datasets, the only useful and reliable clue is the shape of the object, while all the other parameters that affect the appearance are subject to variation, or are designed to contain no useful clue. Parameters that are subject to variation are viewing angles (pose) and lighting conditions. Potential clues whose impact was eliminated include color (all images are grayscale) and object texture. For specific object recognition tasks, the color and texture information may be helpful, but for generic recognition tasks the color and texture information are distractions rather than useful clues. By preserving natural variabilities and eliminating irrelevant clues and systematic biases, NORB can serve as a benchmark dataset in which no hidden regularity that would unfairly advantage some methods over others can be used.

A six-layer net dubbed LeNet-7, shown in figure 14.5, was used in the experiments with the NORB dataset reported here. The architecture is essentially identical to that of LeNet-5 and LeNet-6, except for the sizes of the feature maps. The input is a pair of 96×96 gray scale images. The first feature detection layer uses twelve 5×5 convolution kernels to generate eight feature maps of size 92×92. The first two

Figure 14.7 Some of the 291,600 examples from the *jittered-cluttered* training set (left camera images). Each column shows images from one category. A 6-th background category is added

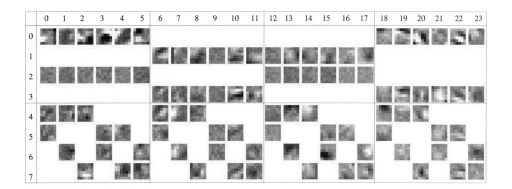

Figure 14.8   The learned convolution kernels of the C3 layer. The columns correspond to the 24 feature maps output by C3, and the rows correspond to the 8 feature maps output by the S2 layer. Each feature map draws from 2 monocular maps and 2 binocular maps of S2. Ninety-six convolution kernels are used in total.

maps take input from the left image, the next two from the right image, and the last four from both. There are 308 trainable parameters in this layer. The first feature pooling layer uses a 4×4 subsampling, to produce eight feature maps of size 23×23. The second feature detection layer uses 96 convolution kernels of size 6×6 to output 24 feature maps of size 18×18. Each map takes input from two monocular maps and two binocular maps, each with a different combination, as shown in figure 14.8. This configuration is used to combine features from the stereoimage pairs. This layer contains 3480 trainable parameters. The next pooling layer uses a 3×3 subsampling which outputs 24 feature maps of size 6×6. The next layer has 6×6 convolution kernels to produce 100 feature maps of size 1×1, and the last layer has five units. In the experiments, we also report results using a hybrid method, which consists in training the convolutional network in the conventional way, chopping off the last layer, and training a Gaussian kernel SVM on the output of the penultimate layer. Many of the results in this section were previously reported in (Huang and LeCun, 2006).

14.6.5   Results on the *Normalized-Uniform* Set

Table 14.2 shows the results on the smaller NORB dataset with uniform background. This dataset simulates a scenario in which objects can be perfectly segmented from the background, and is therefore rather unrealistic.

The SVM is composed of five binary SVMs that are trained to classify one object category against all other categories. The convolutional net trained on this set has a smaller penultimate layer with 80 outputs. The input features to the SVM of the hybrid system are accordingly 80-dimensional vectors.

The timing figures in table 14.2 represent the CPU time on a fictitious 1GHz

Table 14.2 Testing error rates and training/testing timings on the *normalized-uniform* dataset of different methods. The timing is normalized to hypothetical 1GHz single CPU. The convolutional nets have multiple results with different training passes due to their iterative training procedure.

	SVM	Convolutional network			Hybrid
Test error	11.6%	10.4%	6.0%	6.2%	5.9%
Train time (min×GHz)	480	64	448	3200	50+
Test time per sample (min×GHz)	0.95		0.03		0.04+
Fraction of SV	28%				28%
Parameters	σ=2000	Step size			dim=80
	C=40	$2 \times 10^{-5} - 2 \times 10^{-7}$			σ=5 C=40

CPU. The results of the convolutional net trained after 2, 14, and 100 passes are listed in the table. The network is slightly overtrained with more than 30 passes (no regularization was used in the experiment). The SVM in the hybrid system is trained over the features extracted from the network trained with 100 passes. The improvement of the combination is marginal over the convolutional net alone.

Despite the relative simplicity of the task (no position variation, uniform backgrounds, only six types of illumination), the SVM performs rather poorly. Interestingly, it requires a very large amount of CPU time for training and testing. The convolutional net reaches the same error rate as the SVM with eight times less training time. Further training halves the error rate. It is interesting that despite its deep architecture, its nonconvex loss, the total absence of explicit regularization, and a lack of tight generalization bounds, the convolutional net is both better and faster than an SVM.

14.6.6   Results on the *Jittered-Cluttered* Set

The results on this set are shown in table 14.3. To classify the six categories, six binary SVMs are trained independently in one-vs.-rest configuration, each with the full set of 291,600 samples. The training samples are raw 108×108 pixel image pairs turned into a 23,328-dimensional input vector, with values between 0 to 255.

SVMs have relatively few free parameters to tune prior to learning. In the case of Gaussian kernels, one can choose σ (Gaussian kernel sizes) and C (penalty coefficient) that yield best results by grid-tuning. A rather disappointing test error rate of 43.3% is obtained on this set, as shown in the first column of table 14.3. The training time depends heavily on the value of σ for Gaussian kernel SVMs. The experiments are run on a 64-CPU (1.5GHz) cluster, and the timing information is normalized into a hypothetical 1GHz single CPU to make the measurement meaningful.

For the convolutional net LeNet-7, we listed results after a different number of passes (1, 5, 14) and their timing information. The test error rate flattens out at

Table 14.3   Testing error rates and training/testing timings on the *jittered-cluttered* dataset of different methods. The timing is normalized to hypothetical 1GHz single CPU. The convolutional nets have multiple results with different training passes due to their iterative training procedure.

	SVM	Convolutional network			Hybrid
Test error	43.3%	16.38%	7.5%	7.2%	5.9%
Train time (min×GHz)	10,944	420	2100	5880	330+
Test time per sample (min×GHz)	2.2	0.04			0.06+
Fraction of SV	5%				2%
Parameters	$\sigma = 10^4$	Step size			dim=100
	C=40	$2 \times 10^{-5} - 1 \times 10^{-6}$			σ=5 C=1

7.2% after about 10 passes. No significant overtraining was observed, and no early stopping was performed. One parameter controlling the training procedure must be heuristically chosen: the global step size of the stochastic gradient procedure. Best results are obtained by adopting a schedule in which this step size is progressively decreased.

A full propagation of one data sample through the network requires about 4 million multiply-add operations. Parallelizing the convolutional net is relatively simple since multiple convolutions can be performed simultaneously, and each convolution can be performed independently on subregions of the layers. The convolutional nets are computationally very efficient. The training time scales sublinearly with dataset size in practice, and the testing can be done in real time at a rate of a few frames per second.

The third column shows the result of a hybrid system in which the last layer of the convolutional net was replaced by a Gaussian SVM after training. The training and testing features are extracted with the convolutional net trained after 14 passes. The penultimate layer of the network has 100 outputs; therefore the features are 100-dimensional. The SVMs applied on features extracted from the convolutional net yield an error rate of 5.9%, a significant improvement over either method alone. By incorporating a learned feature extractor into the kernel function, the SVM was indeed able to leverage both the ability to use low-level spatially local features and at the same time keep all the advantages of a large-margin classifier.

The poor performance of SVM with Gaussian kernels on raw pixels is not unexpected. As we pointed out in previous sections, a Gaussian kernel SVM merely computes matching scores (based on Euclidean distance) between the incoming pattern and templates from the training set. This global template matching is very sensitive to variations in registration, pose, and illumination. More importantly, most of the pixels in a NORB image are actually on the background clutter, rather than on the object to be recognized. Hence the template matching scores are dominated by irrelevant variabilities of the background. This points to a crucial deficiency of standard kernel methods: their inability to select relevant input features, and ignore irrelevant ones.

SVMs have presumed advantages provided by generalization bounds, capacity control through margin maximization, a convex loss function, and universal approximation properties. By contrast, convolutional nets have no generalization bounds (beyond the most general VC bounds), no explicit regularization, a highly nonconvex loss function, and no claim to universality. Yet the experimental results with NORB show that convolutional nets are more accurate than Gaussian SVMs by a factor of 6, faster to train by a large factor (2 to 20), and faster to run by a factor of 50.

14.7   Conclusion

This work was motivated by our requirements for learning algorithms that could address the challenge of AI, which include statistical scalability, computational scalability, and human-labor scalability. Because the set of tasks involved in AI is widely diverse, engineering a separate solution for each task seems impractical. We have explored many limitations of *kernel machines* and other *shallow architectures*. Such architectures are inefficient for representing complex, highly varying functions, which we believe are necessary for AI-related tasks such as invariant perception.

One limitation was based on the well-known depth-breadth tradeoff in circuits design (Håstad, 1987). This suggests that many functions can be much more efficiently represented with deeper architectures, often with a modest number of levels (e.g., logarithmic in the number of inputs).

The second limitation regards the mathematical consequences of the curse of dimensionality. It applies to local kernels such as the Gaussian kernel, in which $K(x, x_i)$ can be seen as a template matcher. It tells us that architectures relying on local kernels can be very inefficient at representing functions that have many variations, i.e., functions that are not globally smooth (but may still be locally smooth). Indeed, it could be argued that *kernel machines are little more than souped-up template matchers*.

A third limitation pertains to the computational cost of learning. In theory, the convex optimization associated with kernel machine learning yields efficient optimization and reproducible results. Unfortunately, most current algorithms are (at least) quadratic in the number of examples. This essentially precludes their application to very large-scale datasets for which linear- or sublinear-time algorithms are required (particularly for online learning). This problem is somewhat mitigated by recent progress with online algorithms for kernel machines (e.g., see (Bordes et al., 2005)), but there remains the question of the increase in the number of support vectors as the number of examples increases.

A fourth and most serious limitation, which follows from the first (shallowness) and second (locality), pertains to inefficiency in *representation*. Shallow architectures and local estimators are simply too inefficient (in terms of required number of examples and adaptable components) to represent many abstract functions of interest. Ultimately, this makes them unaffordable if our goal is to learn the AI-set. We do not mean to suggest that kernel machines have no place in AI. For example, our results suggest that combining a deep architecture with a kernel machine that takes the higher-level learned representation as input can be quite powerful. Learning the transformation from pixels to high-level features before applying an SVM is in fact a way to learn the kernel. We do suggest that machine learning researchers aiming at the AI problem should investigate architectures that do not have the representational limitations of kernel machines, and deep architectures are by definition not shallow and usually not local.

Until recently, many believed that training deep architectures was too difficult an optimization problem. However, at least two different approaches have worked well in training such architectures: simple gradient descent applied to convolutional networks (LeCun et al., 1989, 1998a) (for signals and images), and more recently, layer-by-layer unsupervised learning followed by gradient descent (Hinton et al., 2006; Bengio et al., 2007; Ranzato et al., 2007). Research on deep architectures is in its infancy, and better learning algorithms for deep architectures remain to be discovered. Taking a larger perspective on the objective of discovering learning principles that can lead to AI has been a guiding perspective of this work. We hope to have helped inspire others to seek a solution to the problem of scaling machine learning toward AI.

Acknowledgments

We thank Geoff Hinton for our numerous discussions with him and the Neural Computation and Adaptive Perception program of the Canadian Institute of Advanced Research for making them possible. We wish to thank Fu-Jie Huang for conducting much of the experiments described in section 14.6, and Hans-Peter Graf and Eric Cosatto and their collaborators for letting us use their parallel implementation of SVM. We thank Sumit Chopra, Olivier Delalleau, Raia Hadsell, Hugo Larochelle, Nicolas Le Roux, and Marc'Aurelio Ranzato, for helping us to make progress toward the ideas presented here. This project was supported by NSF Grants No. 0535166 and No. 0325463, by NSERC, the Canada Research Chairs, and the MITACS NCE.

References

Sophie Achard, Dinh Tuan Pham, and Christian Jutten. Quadratic dependence measure for nonlinear blind source separation. In *4th International Conference on ICA and BSS*, 2003.

Dimitris Achlioptas and Franck McSherry. Fast computation of low-rank matrix approximations. In *Proceedings of the 33rd ACM Symposium on Theory of Computing*, pages 611–618, 2001.

Jim Adler, Bhaskar D. Rao, and Kenneth Kreutz-Delgado. Comparison of basis selection methods. In *Proceedings of the 30th Asilomar Conference on Signals, Systems and Computers*, pages 252–257, 1996.

Miklos Ajtai. $\sum_1^1$-formulae on finite structures. *Annals of Pure and Applied Logic*, 24(1):48, 1983.

Eric Allender. Circuit complexity before the dawn of the new millennium. In *16th Annual Conference on Foundations of Software Technology and Theoretical Computer Science*, volume 1180 of Lecture Notes in Computer Science, pages 1–18. Springer-Verlag, 1996.

Sun-Ichi Amari, Andrzej Cichoki, and Howard Yang. A new learning algorithm for blind signal separation. In *Advances in Neural Information Processing Systems 8*, pages 757–763, Cambridge, MA, MIT Press, 1996.

Nachman Aronszajn. La théorie générale des noyaux réproduisants et ses applications. *Proceedings of the Cambridge Philosophical Society*, 39:133–153, 1944.

Francis Bach and Michael I. Jordan. Kernel independent component analysis. *Journal of Machine Learning Research*, 3:1–48, 2002.

Francis Bach and Michael I. Jordan. Predictive low-rank decomposition for kernel methods. In *Proceedings of the 22nd International Conference on Machine Learning (ICML)*, 2005.

Francis Bach, Gert R. G. Lanckriet, and Michael I. Jordan. Multiple kernel learning, conic duality, and the SMO algorithm. In *Proceedings of the 21st International Conference on Machine Learning (ICML)*, volume 69, New York, ACM Press, 2004.

Charles R. Baker. Joint measures and cross-covariance operators. *Transactions of the American Mathematical Society*, 186:273–289, 1973.

Gökhan Bakır, Léon Bottou, and Jason Weston. Breaking SVM complexity with cross-training. In Lawrence K. Saul, Yair Weiss, and Léon Bottou, editors, *Advances in Neural Information Processing Systems*, volume 17. Cambridge, MA, MIT Press, 2005.

Srinivas Bangalore and Aravind K. Joshi. Supertagging: An approach to almost parsing. *Computational Linguistics*, 25(2), 1999.

Mikhail Belkin, Irina Matveeva, and Partha Niyogi. Regularization and semi-supervised learning on large graphs. In John Shawe-Taylor and Yoram Singer, editors, *COLT'2004*. Berlin, Springer-Verlag, 2004.

Mikhail Belkin and Partha Niyogi. Using manifold structure for partially labeled classification. In Sue Becker, Sebastian Thrun, and Klaus Obermayer, editors, *Advances in Neural Information Processing Systems 15*. Cambridge, MA, MIT Press, 2003.

Serge Belongie, Jitendra Malik, and Jan Puzicha. Shape matching and object recognition using shape contexts. *IEEE Transactions on Pattern Analysis and Machine Intelligence*, 24(4):509–522, 2002.

Yoshua Bengio, Olivier Delalleau, and Nicolas Le Roux. The curse of dimensionality for local kernel machines. Technical report 1258, Département d'informatique et recherche opérationnelle, Université de Montréal, 2005.

Yoshua Bengio, Olivier Delalleau, and Nicolas Le Roux. The curse of highly variable functions for local kernel machines. In Yair Weiss, Bernhard Schölkopf, and John Platt, editors, *Advances in Neural Information Processing Systems 18*. Cambridge, MA, MIT Press, 2006a.

Yoshua Bengio, Olivier Delalleau, Nicolas Le Roux, Jean-François Paiement, Pascal Vincent, and Marie Ouimet. Learning eigenfunctions links spectral embedding and kernel PCA. *Neural Computation*, 16(10):2197–2219, 2004.

Yoshua Bengio, Pascal Lamblin, Dan Popovici, and Hugo Larochelle. Greedy layer-wise training of deep networks. In Lawrence K. Saul, Yair Weiss, and Léon Bottou, editors, *Advances in Neural Information Processing Systems 19*. Cambridge, MA, MIT Press, 2007.

Yoshua Bengio, Nicolas Le Roux, Pascal Vincent, Olivier Delalleau, and Patrice Marcotte. Convex neural networks. In Yair Weiss, Bernhard Schölkopf, and John Platt, editors, *Advances in Neural Information Processing Systems 18*, pages 123–130. Cambridge, MA, MIT Press, 2006b.

Yoshua Bengio and Martin Monperrus. Non-local manifold tangent learning. In Lawrence K. Saul, Yair Weiss, and Léon Bottou, editors, *Advances in Neural Information Processing Systems 17*. Cambridge, MA, MIT Press, 2005.

Kristin P. Bennett and Erin J. Bredensteiner. Duality and geometry in SVM classifiers. In Pat Langley, editor, *Proceedings of the 17th International Conference on Machine Learning*, pages 57–64, San Francisco, California, Morgan Kaufmann, 2000.

Kristin P. Bennett and Colin Campbell. Support vector machines: Hype or hallelujah? *SIGKDD Explorations*, 2(2):1–13, 2000.

Kristin P. Bennett and Ayhan Demiriz. Semi-supervised support vector machines. In Michael S. Kearns, Sara A. Solla, and David A. Cohn, editors, *Advances in Neural Information Processing Systems 12*, pages 368–374. Cambridge, MA, MIT Press, 1998.

Kristin P. Bennett, Michinari Momma, and Mark J. Embrechts. MARK: A boosting algorithm for heterogeneous kernel models. In *Proceedings of the 8th ACM SIGKDD International Conference on Knowledge Discovery and Data Mining*, pages 24–31, New York, ACM Press, 2002.

Adam L. Berger, Stephen A. Della Pietra, and Vincent J. Della Pietra. A maximum entropy approach to natural language processing. *Computational Linguistics*, 22 (1):39–71, 1996.

Marshall Bern and David Eppstein. Approximation algorithms for geometric problems. In D. S. Hochbaum, editor, *Approximation Algorithms for NP-Hard Problems*, pages 296–345, Boston, MA, PWS, 1997.

Dimitri P. Bertsekas. *Nonlinear Programming*. Belmont, MA, Athena Scientific, 1995.

Jinbo Bi, Tong Zhang, and Kristin P. Bennet. Column-generation boosting methods for mixture of kernels. In W. Kim, R. Kohavi, J. Gehrke, and W. DuMouchel, editors, *Proceedings of the 10th ACM SIGKDD International Conference on Knowledge Discovery and Data Mining*, pages 521–526, New York, ACM Press, 2004.

Griff Bilbro, Reinhold Mann, Thomas K. Miller, Wesley E. Snyder, and David E. Van den Bout. Optimization by mean field annealing. In David Touretzky, editor, *Advances in Neural Information Processing Systems 1*. Cambridge, MA, MIT Press, 1989.

Ake Bjork. *Numerical Methods for Least Squares Problems*. Philadelphia, SIAM, 1996.

Catherine L. Blake, Eamonn J. Keogh, and Christopher J. Merz. UCI repository of machine learning databases. Technical report, University of California, Irvine, Department of Information and Computer Sciences, 1998.

Antoine Bordes and Léon Bottou. The Huller: A simple and efficient online svm. In *Machine Learning: ECML 2005*, volume 3270 of Lecture Notes in Artificial Intelligence, pages 505–512, Berlin, Springer-Verlag, 2005.

Antoine Bordes, Seyda Ertekin, Jason Weston, and Léon Bottou. Fast kernel classifiers with online and active learning. *Journal of Machine Learning Research*, 6:1579–1619, September 2005.

Bernhard E. Boser, Isabelle M. Guyon, and Vladimir N. Vapnik. A training algorithm for optimal margin classifiers. In D. Haussler, editor, *Proceedings of the 5th Annual ACM Workshop on Computational Learning Theory*, pages 144–152, Pittsburgh, PA, ACM Press, July 1992.

Léon Bottou. Online algorithms and stochastic approximations. In David Saad, editor, *Online Learning and Neural Networks*. Cambridge, UK, Cambridge University Press, 1998.

Léon Bottou, Corinna Cortes, John S. Denker, Harris Drucker, Isabelle Guyon, Lawrence D. Jackel, Yann LeCun, Urs A. Muller, Edward Sackinger, Patrice Simard, and Vladimir N. Vapnik. Comparison of classifier methods: A case study in handwritten digit recognition. In *Proceedings of the 12th IAPR International Conference on Pattern Recognition, Conference B: Computer Vision & Image Processing.*, volume 2, pages 77–82, Piscataway, NJ, IEEE Press, October 1994.

Léon Bottou and Yann LeCun. Large scale online learning. In Sebastian Thrun, Lawrence K. Saul, and Bernhard Schölkopf, editors, *Advances in Neural Information Processing Systems 16*. Cambridge, MA, MIT Press, 2004.

Stephen Boyd and Lieven Vandenberghe. *Convex Optimization*. Cambridge, UK, Cambridge University Press, 2004.

Matthew Brand. Charting a manifold. In Sue Becker, Sebastian Thrun, and Klaus Obermayer, editors, *Advances in Neural Information Processing Systems 15*. Cambridge, MA, MIT Press, 2003.

Richard P. Brent. *Algorithms for Minimization without Derivatives*. Upper Saddle River, NJ, Prentice Hall, 1973.

Christopher J. C. Burges. A tutorial on support vector machines for pattern recognition. *Data Mining and Knowledge Discovery*, 2(2):121–167, 1998.

Christopher J. C. Burges and Bernhard Schölkopf. Improving the accuracy and speed of support vector learning machines. In Michael Mozer, Michael I. Jordan, and Thomas Petsche, editors, *Advances in Neural Information Processing Systems 9*, pages 375–381. Cambridge, MA, MIT Press, 1997.

Colin Campbell, Nello Cristianini, and Alexander J. Smola. Query learning with large margin classifiers. In *Proceedings of the 17th International Conference on Machine Learning*, pages 111–118, San Francisco, CA, Morgan Kaufmann, 2000.

Jean-François Cardoso. Blind signal separation: Statistical principles. *Proceedings of the IEEE*, 90(8):2009–2026, 1998.

Chih-Chung Chang, Chih-Wei Hsu, and Chih-Jen Lin. The analysis of decomposition methods for support vector machines. *IEEE Transactions on Neural Networks*, 11(4):1003–1008, 2000.

Chih-Chung Chang and Chih-Jen Lin. Training ν-support vector classifiers: Theory and algorithms. *Neural Computation*, 13(9):2119–2147, 2001.

William I. Chang and Eugene L. Lawler. Sublinear approximate string matching and biological applications. *Algorithmica*, 12(4/5):327–344, 1994.

Olivier Chapelle, Mingmin Chi, and Alexander Zien. A continuation method for semi-supervised SVMs. In *Proceedings of the 23rd International Conference on Machine Learning*, 2006.

Olivier Chapelle and Bernhard Schölkopf. Incorporating invariances in nonlinear svms. In Thomas G. Dietterich, Sue Becker, and Zoubin Ghahramani, editors, *Advances in Neural Information Processing Systems 14*, pages 609–616. Cambridge, MA, MIT Press, 2002.

Olivier Chapelle, Vladimir N. Vapnik, Olivier Bousquet, and Sayan Mukherjee. Choosing multiple parameters for support vector machines. *Machine Learning*, 46:131–159, 2002.

Olivier Chapelle, Jason Weston, Léon Bottou, and Vladimir N. Vapnik. Vicinal risk minimization. In *Advances in Neural Information Processing Systems 12*. Cambridge, MA, MIT Press, 2000.

Olivier Chapelle and Alexander Zien. Semi-supervised classification by low density separation. In *Proceedings of the Tenth International Workshop on Artificial Intelligence and Statistics*, pages 57–64, 2005.

Aiyou Chen. Fast kernel density independent component analysis. In *Proceedings of 6th International Conference on ICA and BSS*, volume 3889 of Lecture Notes in Computer Science, pages 24–31, Heidelberg, Springer-Verlag, 2006.

Aiyou Chen and Peter Bickel. Consistent independent component analysis and prewhitening. *IEEE Transactions on Signal Processing*, 53(10):3625–3632, 2005.

Pai-Hsuen Chen, Rong-En Fan, and Chih-Jen Lin. A study on SMO-type decomposition methods for support vector machines. *IEEE Transactions on Neural Networks*, 17:893–908, July 2006.

Fan R. K. Chung. *Spectral Graph Theory*. Providence, RI, American Mathematical Society Press, 1997.

Philippe G. Ciarlet. *Introduction à l'analyse numérique matricielle et à l'optimisation*. Paris, Masson, 1990.

David A. Cohn, Zoubin Ghahramani, and Michael I. Jordan. Active learning with statistical models. In Gerald Tesauro, David Touretzky, and Todd Leen, editors, *Advances in Neural Information Processing Systems 7*, pages 705–712. Cambridge, MA, MIT Press, 1995.

Ronan Collobert. *Large Scale Machine Learning*. PhD thesis, Université Paris VI, 2004.

Ronan Collobert, Samy Bengio, and Yoshua Bengio. A parallel mixture of SVMs for very large scale problems. *Neural Computation*, 14(5):1105–1114, 2002a.

Ronan Collobert, Samy Bengio, and Yoshua Bengio. A parallel mixture of SVMs for very large scale problems. In *Advances in Neural Information Processing Systems 14*. Cambridge, MA, MIT Press, 2002b.

Ronan Collobert, Samy Bengio, and Johnny Mariéthoz. Torch: A modular machine learning software library. Technical report 02–46, IDIAP, Martigny, Switzerland, 2002c.

Ronan Collobert, Fabian Sinz, Jason Weston, and Léon Bottou. Large scale transductive SVMs. *Journal of Machine Learning Research*, 7:1687–1712, 2006.

Pierre Comon. Independent component analysis, a new concept? *Signal Processing*, 36:287–314, 1994.

Corinna Cortes, Patrick Haffner, and Mehryar Mohri. Rational kernels: Theory and algorithms. *Journal of Machine Learning Research*, 5:1035–1062, August 2004.

Corinna Cortes and Vladimir Vapnik. Support-vector network. *Machine Learning*, 20(3):273–297, 1995.

Koby Crammer, Jaz Kandola, and Yoram Singer. Online classification on a budget. In Sebastian Thrun, Lawrence K. Saul, and Bernhard Schölkopf, editors, *Advances in Neural Information Processing Systems 16*. Cambridge, MA, MIT Press, 2004.

Nello Cristianini and John Shawe-Taylor. *An Introduction to Support Vector Machines (and Other Kernel-Based Learning Methods)*. Cambridge, UK, Cambridge University Press, 2000.

Lehel Csató, 2005. Personal communication at the 2005 Sheffield Gaussian Process Round Table, organized by Neil D. Lawrence.

Lehel Csató and Manfred Opper. Sparse online Gaussian processes. *Neural Computation*, 14(3):641–669, 2002.

Lehel Csató, Manfred Opper, and Ole Winther. TAP Gibbs free energy, belief propagation and sparsity. In Thomas G. Dietterich, Sue Becker, and Zoubin Ghahramani, editors, *Neural Information Processing Systems 14*, pages 657–663, Cambridge, MA, MIT Press, 2003.

Mark Damashek. Gauging similarity with n-grams: Language-independent categorization of text. *Science*, 267(5199):843–848, 1995.

Marco D'Apuzzo and Marina Marino. Parallel computational issues of an interior point method for solving large bound-constrained quadratic programming problems. *Journal of Parallel Computing*, 29(4):467–483, 2003.

Jesse Davis and Mark Goadrich. The relationship between precision-recall and ROC curves. Technical report #1551, University of Wisconsin, Madison, January 2006.

Tijl De Bie and Nello Cristianini. Convex methods for transduction. In Sebastian Thrun, Lawrence K. Saul, and Bernhard Schölkopf, editors, *Advances in Neural Information Processing Systems 16*. Cambridge, MA, MIT Press, 2004.

Nando de Freitas, Yang Wang, Maryam Mahdaviani, and Dustin Lang. Fast Krylov methods for n-body learning. In Y. Weiss, B. Schölkopf, and J. Platt, editors, *Advances in Neural Information Processing Systems 18*, pages 251–258. Cambridge, MA, MIT Press, 2006.

Dennis DeCoste and Bernhard Schölkopf. Training invariant support vector machines. *Machine Learning*, 46:161–190, 2002.

Olivier Delalleau, Yoshua Bengio, and Nicolas Le Roux. Efficient non-parametric function induction in semi-supervised learning. In Robert G. Cowell and Zoubin Ghahramani, editors, *Proceedings of the 10th International Workshop on Artificial Intelligence and Statistics*, pages 96–103, Savannah Hotel, Hastings, Barbados, Society for Artificial Intelligence and Statistics, January 2005.

Arthur L. Delcher, Douglas Harmon, Simon Kasif, Owen White, and Steven L. Salzberg. Improved microbial gene identification with GLIMMER. *Nucleic Acids Research*, 27(23):4636–4641, 1999.

Ayhan Demiriz, Kristin P. Bennett, and John Shawe-Taylor. Linear programming boosting via column generation. *Machine Learning*, 46:225–254, 2002.

Janez Demšar. Statistical comparisons of classifiers over multiple data sets. *Journal of Machine Learning Research*, 7:1–30, 2006.

Luc Devroye, Lázló Györfi, and Gabor Lugosi. *A Probabilistic Theory of Pattern Recognition*, volume 31 of Applications of Mathematics. New York, Springer-Verlag, 1996.

Jian-Xiong Dong, Adam Krzyzak, and Ching Y. Suen. A fast parallel optimization for training support vector machine. In *Machine Learning and Data Mining in Pattern Recognition*, pages 96–105, 2003.

Jack Dongarra and Francis Sullivan. The top ten algorithms of the century. *Computing in Science and Engineering*, 2(1):22–23, 2000.

Tom Downs, Kevin E. Gates, and Anette Masters. Exact simplification of support vector solutions. *Journal of Machine Learning Research*, 2:293–297, 2001.

Petros Drineas, Ravi Kannan, and Michael W. Mahoney. Fast Monte Carlo algorithms for matrices I: Approximating matrix multiplication. Technical report YALEU/DCS/TR-1270, Yale University, New Haven, CT, 2004.

Petros Drineas and Michael W. Mahoney. On the Nyström method for approximating a gram matrix for improved kernel-based learning. *Journal of Machine Learning Research*, 6:2153–2175, 2005.

Richard O. Duda and Peter E. Hart. *Pattern Classification and Scene Analysis*. New York, Wiley, 1973.

Richard O. Duda, Peter E. Hart, and David G. Stork. *Pattern Classification*. New York, Wiley, 2001.

Miroslav Dudik, Steven Phillips, and Robert E. Schapire. Performance guarantees for regularized maximum entropy density estimation. In *Proceedings of COLT'04*, Banff, Canada, Springer-Verlag, 2004.

Alan Edelman, Tomàs A. Arias, and Steven T. Smith. The geometry of algorithms with orthogonality constraints. *SIAM Journal on Matrix Analysis and Applications*, 20(2):303–353, 1998.

André Elisseeff. *Étude de la complexité et contrôle de la capacité des systèmes d'apprentissage: SVM multi-classe, réseaux de regularization et réseaux de neurones multi-couche*. PhD thesis, ENS-Lyon, France, 2000.

Jan Eriksson and Visa Koivunen. Characteristic-function-based independent component analysis. *Signal Processing*, 83(10):2195–2208, 2003.

Rong-En Fan, Pai-Hsune Chen, and Chih-Jen Lin. Working set selection using second order information for training SVM. *Journal of Machine Learning Research*, 6:1889–1918, 2005a.

Rong-En Fan, Pai-Hsune Chen, and Chih-Jen Lin. Working set selection using second order information for training SVM. *Journal of Machine Learning Research*, 6:1889–1918, 2005b.

Greg Fasshauer. Meshfree methods. In M. Rieth and W. Schommers, editors, *Handbook of Theoretical and Computational Nanotechnology*. Valencia, CA, American Scientific, 2005.

Tom Fawcett. ROC graphs: Notes and practical considerations for data mining researchers. Technical report HPL-2003-4, HP Laboratories, Palo Alto, CA, USA, January 2003.

Tomás Feder and Daniel Greene. Optimal algorithms for approximate clustering. In *Proceedings 20th ACM Symposium Theory of Computing*, pages 434–444, 1988.

Andrey Feuerverger. A consistent test for bivariate dependence. *International Statistical Review*, 61(3):419–433, 1993.

Shai Fine and Katya Scheinberg. Efficient SVM training using low-rank kernel representations. *Journal of Machine Learning Research*, 2:243–264, Dec 2001.

Edward Fredkin. Trie memory. *Communications of the ACM*, 3(9):490–499, 1960.

Yoav Freund and Robert E. Schapire. Experiments with a new boosting algorithm. In *Proceedings of the 13th International Conference on Machine Learning*, pages 148–146, San Francisco, Morgan Kaufmann, 1996.

Yoav Freund and Robert E. Schapire. Large margin classification using the perceptron algorithm. In J. Shavlik, editor, *Machine Learning: Proceedings of the Fifteenth International Conference*, San Francisco, Morgan Kaufmann, 1998.

Jerome H. Friedman. Greedy function approximation: A gradient boosting machine. *Annals of Statistics*, 29:1180, 2001.

Milton Friedman. The use of ranks to avoid the assumption of normality implicit in the analysis of variance. *Journal of the American Statistical Association*, 32: 675–701, 1937.

Milton Friedman. A comparison of alternative tests of significance for the problem of m rankings. *Annals of Mathematical Statistics*, 11:86–92, 1940.

Thilo-Thomas Frieß, Nello Cristianini, and Colin Campbell. The kernel-adatron algorithm: A fast and simple learning procedure for support vector machines. In *ICML'98: Proceedings of the 15th International Conference on Machine Learning*, pages 188–196, San Francisco, Morgan Kaufmann, 1998.

Andreas Frommer and Peter Maaß. Fast CG-based methods for Tikhonov-Phillips regularization. *SIAM Journal on Scientific Computing*, 20:1831–1850, 1999.

Kenji Fukumizu, Francis Bach, and Michael I. Jordan. Dimensionality reduction for supervised learning with reproducing kernel hilbert spaces. *Journal of Machine Learning Research*, 5:73–99, 2004.

Kunihiko Fukushima. Neocognitron: A hierarchical neural network capable of visual pattern recognition. *Neural Networks*, 1(2):119–130, 1988.

Glenn Fung and Olvi L. Mangasarian. Proximal support vector machine classifiers. In *KDD 2001. Proceedings of the 7th ACM SIGKDD International Conference on Knowledge Discovery and Data Mining*, pages 77–86, New York, ACM Press, 2001a.

Glenn Fung and Olvi L. Mangasarian. Semi-supervised support vector machines for unlabeled data classification. *Optimization Methods and Software*, 15:29–44, 2001b.

Roman Genov and Gert Cauwenberghs. Kerneltron: Support vector machine in silicon. *IEEE Transactions on Neural Networks*, 14(5):1426–1434, 2003.

Roman Genov, Shantanu Chakrabartty, and Gert Cauwenberghs. Silicon support vector machine with on-line learning. *International Journal of Pattern Recognition and Artificial Intelligence*, 17(3):385–404, 2003.

Claudio Gentile. A new approximate maximal margin classification algorithm. *Journal of Machine Learning Research*, 2:213–242, 2001.

Mark N. Gibbs and David J. C. MacKay. Efficient Implementation of Gaussian processes. Unpublished manuscript. Cavendish Laboratory, Cambridge, UK. http://www.inference.phy.cam.ac.uk/mackay/BayesGP.html, 1997.

Tobias Glasmachers and Christian Igel. Maximum-gain working set selection for SVMs. *Journal of Machine Learning Research*, 7:1437–1466, July 2006.

Nazli Goharian, Tarek El-Ghazawi, David Grossman, and Abdur Chowdhury. On the Enhancements of a Sparse Matrix Information Retrieval Approach. In *PDPTA'2000*, volume 2, pages 0–4, 2000.

Nazli Goharian, Ankit Jain, and Qian Sun. Comparative analysis of sparse matrix algorithms for information retrieval. *Journal of Systemics, Cybernetics and Informatics*, 2003.

Gene H. Golub and Charles F. Van Loan. *Matrix Computations*, 3rd edition. Baltimore, Johns Hopkins University Press, 1996.

Teofilo Gonzalez. Clustering to minimize the maximum intercluster distance. *Theoretical Computer Science*, 38:293–306, 1985.

Thore Graepel and Ralf Herbrich. Invariant pattern recognition by semi-definite programming machines. In Sebastian Thrun, Lawrence K. Saul, and Bernhard Schölkopf, editors, *Advances in Neural Information Processing Systems 16*, Cambridge, MA, MIT Press, 2004.

Hans Peter Graf, Eric Cosatto, Léon Bottou, Igor Durdanovic, and Vladimir Vapnik. Parallel support vector machines: The Cascade SVM. In Lawrence K. Saul, Yair Weiss, and Léon Bottou, editors, *Advances in Neural Information Processing Systems 17*, pages 521–528, Cambridge, MA, MIT Press, 2005.

Yves Grandvalet and Stéphane Canu. Adaptive scaling for feature selection in SVMs. In Sue Becker, Sebastian Thrun, and Klaus Obermayer, editors, *Neural*

Information Processing Systems 15, Cambridge, MA, MIT Press, 2002.

Alexander Gray. Fast kernel matrix-vector multiplication with application to Gaussian process learning. Technical report CMU-CS-04-110, School of Computer Science, Carnegie Mellon University, Pittsburgh, 2004.

Alexander Gray and Andrew W. Moore. N-Body problems in statistical learning. In Todd K. Leen, Thomas G. Dietterich, and Volker Tresp, editors, *Advances in Neural Information Processing Systems 13*, pages 521–527. Cambridge, MA, MIT Press, 2001.

Alexander Gray and Andrew W. Moore. Nonparametric density estimation: Toward computational tractability. In *SIAM International Conference on Data Mining*, 2003.

Leslie Greengard. Fast algorithms for classical physics. *Science*, 265(5174):909–914, 1994.

Leslie Greengard and Vladimir Rokhlin. A fast algorithm for particle simulations. *Journal of Computational Physics*, 73:325–348, 1987.

Leslie Greengard and John Strain. The fast Gauss transform. *SIAM Journal of Scientific and Statistical Computing*, 12(1):79–94, 1991.

Arthur Gretton, Olivier Bousquet, Alexander J. Smola, and Bernhard Schölkopf. Measuring statistical dependence with Hilbert-Schmidt norms. In *Proceedings of the International Conference on Algorithmic Learning Theory*, pages 63–78, 2005a.

Arthur Gretton, Ralf Herbrich, Alexander J. Smola, Olivier Bousquet, and Bernhard Schölkopf. Kernel methods for measuring independence. *Journal of Machine Learning Research*, 6:2075–2129, 2005b.

Dan Gusfield. *Algorithms on Strings, Trees, and Sequences*. Cambridge, UK, Cambridge University Press, 1997.

Patrick Haffner. Escaping the convex hull with extrapolated vector machines. In *Advances in Neural Information Processing Systems 14*. Cambridge, MA, MIT Press, 2002.

Patrick Haffner. Scaling large margin classifiers for spoken language understanding. *Speech Communication*, 48(4), 2005.

Wolfgang Härdle, Stefan Sperlich, Marlene Müller, and Axel Werwatz. *Nonparametric and Semiparametric Models*. New York, Springer-Verlag, 2004.

Johan T. Håstad. *Computational Limitations for Small Depth Circuits*. Cambridge, MA, MIT Press, 1987.

David Haussler. Convolutional kernels on discrete structures. Technical report UCSC-CRL-99 - 10, Computer Science Department, University of California Santa Cruz, 1999.

Rainer Hettich and Kenneth O. Kortanek. Semi-infinite programming: Theory, methods and applications. *SIAM Review*, 3:380–429, September 1993.

Geoffrey E. Hinton. Training products of experts by minimizing contrastive divergence. *Neural Computation*, 14(8):1771–1800, 2002.

Geoffrey E. Hinton. To recognize shapes, first learn to generate images. In Paul Cisek, Trevor Drew, and John F. Kalaska, editors, *Computational Neuroscience: Theoretical insights into brain function*, Amsterdam, Elsevier, 2007.

Geoffrey E. Hinton, Simon Osindero, and Yee Whye Teh. A fast learning algorithm for deep belief nets. *Neural Computation*, 2006.

Fu-Jie Huang and Yann LeCun. Large-scale learning with SVM and convolutional nets for generic object categorization. In *Proceedings of Computer Vision and Pattern Recognition Conference (CVPR'06)*, Piscataway, NJ, IEEE Press, 2006.

Don Hush, Patrick Kelly, Clint Scovel, and Ingo Steinwart. QP algorithms with guaranteed accuracy and run time for support vector machines. *Journal of Machine Learning Research*, 7:733–769, 2006.

Don Hush and Clint Scovel. Polynomial-time decomposition algorithms for support vector machines. *Machine Learning*, 51:51–71, 2003.

Aapo Hyvärinen, Juha Karhunen, and Erkko Oja. *Independent Component Analysis*. New York, Wiley, 2001.

Eun-Jin Im. Optimizing the performance of sparse matrix-vector multiplication. Technical report UCB/CSD-00-1104, EECS Department, University of California, Berkeley, 2000.

Alan J. Izenman. Recent developments in nonparametric density estimation. *Journal of American Staistical Association*, 86(413):205–224, 1991.

Tommi S. Jaakkola, Mark Diekhans, and David Haussler. A discriminative framework for detecting remote protein homologies. *Journal of Computational Biology*, 7:95–114, 2000.

Thorsten Joachims. Text categorization with support vector machines: Learning with many relevant features. In Claire Nédellec and Céline Rouveirol, editors, *ECML'98: Proceedings of the 10th European Conference on Machine Learning*, Lecture Notes in Computer Science, pages 137–142, Berlin, Springer-Verlag, 1998.

Thorsten Joachims. Making large–scale SVM learning practical. In Bernhard Schölkopf, Christopher J. C. Burges, and Alexander J. Smola, editors, *Advances in Kernel Methods — Support Vector Learning*, pages 169–184. Cambridge, MA, MIT Press, 1999a.

Thorsten Joachims. Transductive inference for text classification using support vector machines. In Ivan Bratko and Saso Dzeroski, editors, *Proceedings of ICML-99, 16th International Conference on Machine Learning*, pages 200–209, San Francisco, Morgan Kaufmann, 1999b.

Thorsten Joachims. Training linear SVMs in linear time. In *Proceedings of the 12th ACM SIGKDD International Conference*, New York, 2006.

M. Chris Jones, James S. Marron, and Simon J. Sheather. A brief survey of bandwidth selection for density estimation. *Journal of American Statistical*

Association, 91(433):401–407, March 1996.

Michael I. Jordan. *Learning in Graphical Models*. Dordrecht, Netherlands, Kluwer, 1998.

Annaliisa Kankainen. *Consistent Testing of Total Independence Based on the Empirical Characteristic Function*. PhD thesis, University of Jyväskylä, Finland, 1995.

S. Sathiya Keerthi and Wei Chu. A matching pursuit approach to sparse Gaussian process regression. In *Proceedings of the 18th NIPS Conference*, 2006a.

S. Sathiya Keerthi and Wei Chu. A matching pursuit approach to sparse GP regression. In Yair Weiss, Bernhard Schölkopf, and John Platt, editors, *Advances in Neural Information Processing Systems 18*. Cambridge, MA, MIT Press, 2006b.

S. Sathiya Keerthi and Dennis DeCoste. A modified finite Newton method for fast solution of large scale linear svms. *Journal of Machine Learning Research*, 6: 341–361, 2005.

S. Sathiya Keerthi and Elmer G. Gilbert. Convergence of a generalized SMO algorithm for SVM classifier design. *Machine Learning*, 46(1–3):351–360, 2002.

S. Sathiya Keerthi, Shirish K. Shevade, Chiranjib Bhattacharyya, and Krishna R. K. Murthy. A fast iterative nearest point algorithm for support vector machine classifier design. Technical report TR-ISL-99-03, Indian Institute of Science, Bangalore, 1999.

S. Sathiya Keerthi, Shirish K. Shevade, Chiranjib Bhattacharyya, and Krishna R. K. Murthy. Improvements to Platt's SMO algorithm for SVM classifier design. *Neural Computation*, 13:637–649, 2001.

George S. Kimeldorf and Grace Wahba. A correspondence between Bayesian estimation on stochastic processes and smoothing by splines. *Annals of Mathematical Statistics*, 41:495–502, 1970.

Jyrki Kivinen, Alexander J. Smola, and Robert C. Williamson. Online learning with kernels. In *Advances in Neural Information Processing Systems 14*, pages 785–793, Cambridge, MA, MIT Press, 2002.

Donald E. Knuth. *The art of Computer Programming*, volume 3. Boston, Addison-Wesley, 1973.

Nir Krause and Yoram Singer. Leveraging the margin more carefully. In *International Conference on Machine Learning, ICML*, 2004.

Chin-Jen Ku and Terence L. Fine. Testing for stochastic independence: application to blind source separation. *IEEE Transactions on Signal Processing*, 53(5):1815–1826, 2005.

Rui Kuang, Eugene Ie, Ke Wang, Kai Wang, Mahira Siddiqi, Yoav Freund, and Christina Leslie. Profile-based string kernels for remote homology detection and motif extraction. In *Computational Systems Bioinformatics Conference 2004*, pages 146–154, 2004.

Taku Kudo and Yuji Matsumoto. Fast methods for kernel-based text analysis. In *Proceedings of ACL '03*, pages 24–31, 2003.

Malte Kuss and Carl Edward Rasmussen. Assessing approximate inference for binary Gaussian process classification. *Journal of Machine Learning Research*, pages 1679–1704, 2005.

Damiel Lai, Nallasamy Mani, and Marimuthu Palaniswami. A new method to select working sets for faster training for support vector machines. Technical report MESCE-30-2003, Department of Electrical and Computer Systems Engineering, Monash University, Australia, 2003.

Gert R. G. Lanckriet, Tijl De Bie, Nello Cristianini, Michael I. Jordan, and William S. Noble. A statistical framework for genomic data fusion. *Bioinformatics*, 2004.

Dustin Lang, Mike Klaas, and Nando de Freitas. Empirical testing of fast kernel density estimation algorithms. Technical report UBC TR-2005-03, University of British Columbia, Vancouver, 2005.

Kevin J. Lang and Geoff E. Hinton. A time delay neural network architecture for speech recognition. Technical report CMU-CS-88-152, Carnegie Mellon University, Pittsburgh, 1988.

Neil D. Lawrence, Matthias Seeger, and Ralf Herbrich. Fast sparse Gaussian process methods: The informative vector machine. In Sue Becker, Sebastian Thrun, and Klaus Obermayer, editors, *Advances in Neural Information Processing Systems 15*, pages 625–632, Cambridge, MA, MIT Press, 2003.

Erik Learned-Miller and John Fisher, III. ICA using spacings estimates of entropy. *Journal of Machine Learning Research*, 4:1271–1295, 2003.

Yann LeCun, Bernhard Boser, John S. Denker, Donnie Henderson, Richard E. Howard, Wayne Hubbard, and Lawrence D. Jackel. Backpropagation applied to handwritten zip code recognition. *Neural Computation*, 1(4):541–551, 1989.

Yann LeCun, Léon Bottou, Yoshua Bengio, and Patrick Haffner. Gradient based learning applied to document recognition. *Proceedings of the IEEE*, 86(11):2278–2324, November 1998a.

Yann LeCun, Léon Bottou, Yoshua Bengio, and Patrick Haffner. Gradient-based learning applied to document recognition. *Proceedings of the IEEE*, 86(11):2278–2324, 1998b.

Yann LeCun, Léon Bottou, Genevieve B. Orr, and Klaus-Robert Müller. Efficient backprop. In Genevieve B. Orr and Klaus-Robert Müller, editors, *Neural Networks: Tricks of the Trade*, pages 9–50. New York, Springer-Verlag, 1998c.

Yann LeCun and John S. Denker. Natural versus universal probability complexity, and entropy. In *IEEE Workshop on the Physics of Computation*, pages 122–127, Piscataway, NJ, IEEE Press, 1992.

Yann LeCun, Fu-Jie Huang, and Léon Bottou. Learning methods for generic object recognition with invariance to pose and lighting. In *Proceedings of CVPR'04*.

IEEE Press, 2004.

Dongryeol Lee, Alexander G. Gray, and Andrew Moore. Dual-tree fast Gauss transforms. In Yair Weiss, Bernhard Schölkopf, and John Platt, editors, *Advances in Neural Information Processing Systems 18*, Cambridge, MA, MIT Press, 2006.

Yuh-Jye Lee and Olvi L. Mangasarian. RSVM: Reduced support vector machines. In *Proceedings of the first SIAM International Conference on Data Mining*, Philadelphia, SIAM, 2001a.

Yuh-Jye Lee and Olvi L. Mangasarian. SSVM: A smooth support vector machine for classification. *Computational Optimization and Applications*, 20(1):5–22, 2001b.

Todd K. Leen. From data distributions to regularization in invariant learning. In Gerald Tesauro, David Touretzky, and Todd Leen, editors, *Advances in Neural Information Processing Systems 7*, pages 223–230. Cambridge, MA, MIT Press, 1995.

Christina Leslie, Eleazar Eskin, and William S. Noble. The spectrum kernel: A string kernel for SVM protein classification. In Russ B. Altman, A. Keith Dunker, Lawrence Hunter, Kevin Lauderdale, and Teri E. Klein, editors, *Proceedings of the Pacific Symposium on Biocomputing*, pages 564–575, Kaua'i, HI, 2002.

Christina Leslie, Eleazar Eskin, Jason Weston, and William S. Noble. Mismatch string kernels for discriminative protein classification. *Bioinformatics*, 20(4), 2003a.

Christina Leslie and Rui Kuang. Fast string kernels using inexact matching for protein sequences. *Journal of Machine Learning Research*, 5:1435–1455, 2004.

Christina Leslie, Rui Kuang, and Eleazar Eskin. Inexact matching string kernels for protein classification. In *Kernel Methods in Computational Biology*, MIT Press series on Computational Molecular Biology, pages 95–112, Cambridge, MA, MIT Press, 2003b.

David D. Lewis, Yiming Yang, Tony G. Rose, and Fan Li. RCV1: A new benchmark collection for text categorization research. *Journal of Machine Learning Research*, 5:361–397, 2004.

Yi Li and Philip M. Long. The relaxed online maximum margin algorithm. *Machine Learning*, 46(1-3):361–387, 2002.

Li Liao and William S. Noble. Combining pairwise sequence similarity and support vector machines. In *Proceedings 6th International Conference Computational Molecular Biology*, pages 225–232, 2002.

Chih-Jen Lin. On the convergence of the decomposition method for support vector machines. *IEEE Transactions on Neural Networks*, 12(6):1288–1298, 2001.

Chih-Jen Lin. A formal analysis of stopping criteria of decomposition methods for support vector machines. *IEEE Transactions on Neural Networks*, 13(5): 1045–1052, 2002.

Kuan-Ming Lin and Chih-Jen Lin. A study on reduced support vector machines. *IEEE TNN*, 14:1449–1459, 2003.

Xiwi Lin, Grace Wahba, Dong Xiang, Fangyu Gao, Ronald Klein, and Barbara Klein. Smoothing spline ANOVA models for large data sets with Bernoulli observations and the randomized GACV. *Annals of Statistics*, 28:1570–1600, 2000.

Nathan Linial, Yishay Mansour, and Noam Nisan. Constant depth circuits, Fourier transform, and learnability. *Journal of the ACM*, 40(3):607–620, 1993.

Niko List and Hans-Ulrich Simon. A general convergence theorem for the decomposition method. Technical report, Fakultät für Mathematik, Ruhr Universität Bochum, Germany, 2004.

Yufeng Liu, Xiaotong Shen, and Hani Doss. Multicategory ψ-learning and support vector machine: Computational tools. *Journal of Computational & Graphical Statistics*, 14(1):219–236, 2005.

Huma Lodhi, Craig Saunders, John Shawe-Taylor, Nello Cristianini, and Christopher J. C. H. Watkins. Text classification using string kernels. *Journal of Machine Learning Research*, 2:419–444, 2002.

Gaëlle Loosli and Stéphane Canu. Comments on the "core vector machines: Fast SVM training on very large data sets". Technical report, INSA Rouen, France, July 2006. Submitted to JMLR.

Gaëlle Loosli, Stéphane Canu, S. V. N. Vishwanathan, and Alexander J. Smola. Invariances in classification : An efficient SVM implementation. In *ASMDA 2005 -Applied Stochastic Models and Data Analysis*, 2005.

Gaëlle Loosli, Stéphane Canu, S. V. N. Vishwanathan, Alexander J. Smola, and Manojit Chattopadhyay. Une boîte à outils rapide et simple pour les SVM. In Michel Liquière and Marc Sebban, editors, *CAp 2004 - Conférence d'Apprentissage*, pages 113–128. Presses Universitaires de Grenoble, France, 2004.

Jan R. Magnus and Heinz Neudecker. *Matrix Differential Calculus with Applications in Statistics and Econometrics*, revised edition. New York, Wiley, 1999.

Stéphane G. Mallat and Zhifeng Zhang. Matching pursuits with time-frequency dictionaries. *IEEE Transactions on ASSP*, 41:3397–3415, 1993.

Robert Malouf. A comparison of algorithms for maximum entropy parameter estimation. In *Proceedings of CoNLL-2002*, pages 49–55. Taipei, Taiwan, 2002.

Olvi L. Mangasarian. A finite Newton method for classification. *Optimization Methods and Software*, 17:913–929, 2002.

Olvi L. Mangasarian and David R. Musicant. Lagrangian support vector machines. *Journal of Machine Learning Research*, 1:161–177, 2001.

Llew Mason, Peter L. Bartlett, and Jonathan Baxter. Improved generalization through explicit optimization of margins. *Machine Learning*, 38(3):243–255, 2000.

J. A. Meijerink and Henk A. van der Vorst. An iterative solution method for linear systems of which the coefficient matrix is a symmetric M-matrix. *Mathematics of Computation*, 31:148–162, 1977.

Charles E. Metz. Basic principles of ROC analysis. *Seminars in Nuclear Medicine*, 8(4), October 1978.

Athanasios Migdalas, Gerardo Toraldo, and Vipin Kumar. Nonlinear optimization and parallel computing. *Parallel Computation*, 29(4):375–391, 2003.

Thomas P. Minka. *A Family of Algorithms for Approximate Bayesian Inference*. PhD thesis, Massachusetts Institute of Technology, Cambridge, MA, 2001.

Marvin L. Minsky and Seymour A. Papert. *Perceptrons*. Cambridge, MA, MIT Press, 1969.

Noboru Murata. Properties of the empirical characteristic function and its application to testing for independence. In *Proceedings of 3rd International Conference on ICA and Blind Source Separation*, pages 19–24, 2001.

Noboru Murata and Sun-Ichi Amari. Statistical analysis of learning dynamics. *Signal Processing*, 74(1):3–28, 1999.

Kenneth R. Muske and James W. Howse. A sequential quadratic programming method for nonlinear model predictive control. In *Large-Scale PDE-Constrained Optimization*, pages 253–267. New York, Springer-Verlag, 2003.

Jean-Pierre Nadal. *Réseaux de neurones: de la physique à la psychologie*. Armand Colin, Collection 2aI, 1993.

Arkadi Nemirovski. Introduction to convex programming, interior point methods, and semi-definite programming. Lecture at the Machine Learning, Support Vector Machines, and Large-Scale Optimization Pascal Workshop, March 2005.

Sameer A. Nene, Shree K. Nayar, and Hiroshi Murase. Columbia object image libary (coil-20). Technical report CUS-005-96, Columbia University, New York, February 1996.

Nils J. Nilsson. *Learning machines: Foundations of Trainable Pattern Classifying Systems*. New York, McGraw–Hill, 1965.

Albert B. J. Novikoff. On convergence proofs on perceptrons. In *Proceedings of the Symposium on the Mathematical Theory of Automata*, volume 12, pages 615–622. Polytechnic Institute of Brooklyn, 1962.

Cheng Soon Ong. *Kernels: Regularization and Optimization*. PhD thesis, The Australian National University, Canberra, 2005.

Edgar Osuna, Robert Freund, and Frederico Girosi. An improved training algorithm fo support vector machines. In Jose Principe, C. Lee Giles, Nelson Morgan, and Elizabeth Wilson, editors, *Neural Networks for Signal Processing VII - Proceedings of the 1997 IEEE Workshop*, pages 276–285, Cambridge, MA, 1997a.

Edgar Osuna, Robert Freund, and Frederico Girosi. Support vector machines: Training and applications. Technical report AIM-1602, MIT Artificial Intelligence Laboratory, Cambridge, MA, 1997b.

Edgar Osuna, Robert Freund, and Frederico Girosi. Training support vector machines: An application to face detection. In *Proceedings of Computer Vision and Pattern Recognition 1997*, pages 130–136, 1997c.

Edgar Osuna and Frederico Girosi. Reducing the run-time complexity of support vector machines. In *Proceedings of the International Conference on Pattern Recognition*, 1998.

Laura Palagi and Marco Sciandrone. On the convergence of a modified version of SVM*light* algorithm. *Optimization Methods and Software*, 20(2-3):315–332, 2005.

Athanasios Papoulis. *Probability, Random Variables, and Stochastic Processes*. New York, McGraw–Hill, 1991.

Emilio Parrado-Hernández, I. Mora-Jimenéz, Jerónimo Arenas-García, Aníbal R. Figueiras-Vidal, and Angel Navia-Vázquez. Growing support vector classifiers with controlled complexity. *Pattern Recognition*, 36:1479–1488, 2003.

Fernando Perez-Cruz, Angel Navia-Vazquez, Aníbal R. Figueiras-Vidal, and Antonio Artes-Rodriguez. Empirical risk minimization for support vector classifiers. *IEEE Transactions on Neural Networks*, 14(3):296–303, 2002.

Carsten Peterson and Bo Söderberg. A new method for mapping optimization problems onto neural networks. *International Journal of Neural Systems*, 1:3–22, 1989.

John Platt. Fast training of support vector machines using sequential minimal optimization. In Bernhard Schölkopf, Christopher J. C. Burges, and Alexander J. Smola, editors, *Advances in Kernel Methods — Support Vector Learning*, pages 185–208, Cambridge, MA, MIT Press, 1999.

Tomaso Poggio and Frederico Girosi. Networks for approximation and learning. *Proceedings of IEEE*, 78:1481–1497, 1990.

Tomaso Poggio and Steve Smale. The mathematics of learning: Dealing with data. *Notices of the American Mathematical Society*, 50(5):537–544, 2003.

François Poulet. Multi-way Distributed SVM algorithms. In *Parallel and Distributed computing for Machine Learning. In Conjunction with the 14th European Conference on Machine Learning (ECML'03) and 7th European Conference on Principles and Practice of Knowledge Discovery in Databases (PKDD'03)*, Cavtat-Dubrovnik, Croatia, September 2003.

Joaquin Quiñonero-Candela. *Learning with Uncertainty – Gaussian Processes and Relevance Vector Machines*. PhD thesis, Technical University of Denmark, Lyngby, Denmark, 2004.

Joaquin Quiñonero-Candela and Carl Edward Rasmussen. A unifying view of sparse approximate Gaussian process regression. *Journal of Machine Learning Research*, 6:1939–1959, 2005.

Marc'Aurelio Ranzato, Christopher Poultney, Sumit Chopra, and Yann LeCun. Efficient learning of sparse representations with an energy-based model. In Bernhard Schölkopf, John Platt, and Thomas Hofmann., editors, *Advances in Neural Information Processing Systems 19*, Cambridge, MA, MIT Press, 2007.

Carl Edward Rasmussen. Reduced rank Gaussian process learning. Technical report, Gatsby Computational Neuroscience Unit, University College London, 2002.

Carl Edward Rasmussen and Joaquin Quiñonero-Candela. Healing the relevance vector machine by augmentation. In Luc De Raedt and Stefan Wrobel, editors, *Proceedings of the 22nd International Conference on Machine Learning*, pages 689–696, 2005.

Carl Edward Rasmussen and Christopher K. I. Williams. *Gaussian processes for machine learning*, chapter Approximation methods for large datasets, pages 171–188. Cambridge, MA, MIT Press, 2006a.

Carl Edward Rasmussen and Christopher K. I. Williams. *Gaussian Processes for Machine Learning*. Cambridge, MA, MIT Press, 2006b.

Gunnar Rätsch. *Robust Boosting via Convex Optimization*. PhD thesis, University of Potsdam, Department of Computer Science, Potsdam, Germany, 2001.

Gunnar Rätsch, Ayhan Demiriz, and Kristin P. Bennett. Sparse regression ensembles in infinite and finite hypothesis spaces. *Machine Learning*, 48(1-3):193–221, 2002.

Gunnar Rätsch and Sören Sonnenburg. *Accurate Splice Site Prediction for Caenorhabditis elegans*, pages 277–298. MIT Press Series on Computational Molecular Biology. Cambridge, MA, MIT Press, 2004.

Gunnar Rätsch, Sören Sonnenburg, and Christin Schäfer. Learning interpretable SVMs for biological sequence classification. *BMC Bioinformatics, [Special Issue from NIPS workshop on New Problems and Methods in Computational Biology Whistler, Canada, 18 December 2004]*, 7:(Suppl. 1):S9, March 2006.

Gunnar Rätsch, Sören Sonnenburg, and Bernhard Schölkopf. RASE: Recognition of alternatively spliced exons in *C. elegans*. *Bioinformatics*, 21:i369–i377, 2005.

Vikas C. Raykar, Changjaing Yang, Ramani Duraiswami, and Nail A. Gumerov. Fast computation of sums of Gaussians in high dimensions. Technical report CS-TR-4767, Department of Computer Science, University of Maryland, College Park, 2005.

Roberto A. Reyna-Royas, Daniela Dragomirescu, Dominique Houzet, and Daniel Esteve. Implementation of the SVM generalization function in FPGA. In *International Signal Processing Conference, ISPC*, New York, ACM Press, March 2003.

Konrad Rieck, Pavel Laskov, and Klaus-Robert Müller. Efficient algorithms for similarity measures over sequential data: A look beyond kernels. In *Pattern Recognition, 28th DAGM Symposium*, pages 374–383, September 2006a.

Konrad Rieck, Pavel Laskov, and Sören Sonnenburg. Computation of similarity measures for sequential data using generalized suffix trees. In *Advances in Neural Information Processing Systems 19*. Cambridge, MA, MIT Press, 2006b.

Ryan Rifkin and Aldebaro Klautau. In defense of one-vs-all classification. *Journal of Machine Learning Research*, 5:101–141, 2004.

Sam Roweis and Lawrence K. Saul. Nonlinear dimensionality reduction by locally linear embedding. *Science*, 290(5500):2323–2326, December 2000.

Gerard Salton. Mathematics and information retrieval. *Journal of Documentation*, 35(1):1–29, 1979.

Craig J. Saunders, Mark O. Stitson, Jason Weston, Bottou Léon, Bernhard Schölkopf, and J. Smola, Alexander. Support vector machine reference manual. Technical report CSD-TR-98-03, Royal Holloway University of London, 1998.

Robert Schaback. Creating surfaces from scattered data using radial basis functions. In M. Daehlen, T. Lyche, and L. Schumaker, editors, *Mathematical Methods for Curves and Surfaces*, pages 477–496, Nashville, TN, Vanderbilt University Press, 1995.

Michael Schmitt. Descartes' rule of signs for radial basis function neural networks. *Neural Computation*, 14(12):2997–3011, 2002.

Greg Schohn and David Cohn. Less is more: Active learning with support vector machines. In P. Langley, editor, *Proceedings of the 17th International Conference on Machine Learning (ICML 2000)*, pages 839–846, San Francisco, Morgan Kaufmann, 2000.

Bernhard Schölkopf, Smola Alexander J, and Klaus-Robert Müller. Kernel principal component analysis. In *Artificial Neural Networks - ICANN '97, Proceedings of the 7th International Conference*, volume 1327 of Lecture Notes in Computer Science, page 583. Springer-Verlag, 1997.

Bernhard Schölkopf, Chris J. C. Burges, and Vladimir N. Vapnik. Incorporating invariances in support vector learning machines. In Christoph von der Malsburg, Werner von Seelen, Jan C. Vorbruggen, and Bernhard Sendhoff, editors, *Artificial Neural Networks – ICANN'96, Proceedings of the 6th International Conference*, volume 1112 of Lecture Notes in Computer Science, pages 47–52, Berlin, 1996.

Bernhard Schölkopf, Christopher J. C. Burges, and Alexander J. Smola. *Advances in Kernel Methods — Support Vector Learning*. Cambridge, MA, MIT Press, 1999a.

Bernhard Schölkopf, Sebastian Mika, Christopher J. C. Burges, Philipp Knirsch, Klaus-Robert Muller, Gunnar Raetsch, and A.J. Smola. Input space vs. feature space in kernel-based methods. *IEEE Transactions on Neural Networks*, 10:1000–1017, 1999b.

Bernhard Schölkopf, John Platt, John Shawe-Taylor, Alexander J. Smola, and Robert C. Williamson. Estimating the support of a high-dimensional distribution. *Neural Computation*, 13:1443–1471, 2001.

Bernhard Schölkopf and Alexander J. Smola. *Learning with Kernels*. Cambridge, MA, MIT Press, 2002.

Bernhard Schölkopf, Alexander J. Smola, and Klaus-Robert Müller. Nonlinear component analysis as a kernel eigenvalue problem. *Neural Computation*, 10: 1299–1319, 1998.

Bernhard Schölkopf, Alexanxer J. Smola, Robert C. Williamson, and Peter L. Bartlett. New support vector algorithms. *Neural Computation*, 12:1207–1245, 2000.

Bernhard Schölkopf, Koji Tsuda, and Jean-Philippe Vert. *Kernel Methods in Computational Biology*. Cambridge, MA, MIT Press, 2004.

Anton Schwaighofer and Volker Tresp. Transductive and inductive methods for approximate Gaussian process regression. In Sue Becker, Sebastian Thrun, and Klaus Obermayer, editors, *Advances in Neural Information Processing Systems 15*, Cambridge, MA, MIT Press, 2003.

Matthias Seeger. *Bayesian Gaussian Process Models: PAC-Bayesian Generalisation Error Bounds and Sparse Approximations*. PhD thesis, University of Edinburgh, 2003.

Matthias Seeger. Low rank updates for the Cholesky decomposition. Technical report, University of California, Berkeley, 2004.

Matthias Seeger, Christopher K. I. Williams, and Neil Lawrence. Fast forward selection to speed up sparse Gaussian process regression. In Christopher M. Bishop and Brendan J. Frey, editors, *Ninth International Workshop on Artificial Intelligence and Statistics, Key West, FL*. Society for Artificial Intelligence and Statistics, 2003.

John Shawe-Taylor and Nello Cristianini. *Kernel Methods for Pattern Analysis*. Cambridge, UK, Cambridge University Press, 2004.

Hao Shen and Knut Hüper. Local convergence analysis of FastICA. In *Proceedings of 6th International Conference on ICA and BSS*, volume 3889 of Lecture Notes in Computer Science, pages 893–900, Heidelberg, Germany, Springer-Verlag, 2006a.

Hao Shen and Knut Hüper. Newton-like methods for parallel independent component analysis. In *IEEE International Workshop on Machine Learning for Signal Processing (MLSP 2006)*, 2006b.

Hao Shen, Knut Hüper, and Alexander J. Smola. Newton-like methods for nonparametric independent component analysis. In *International Conference On Neural Information Processing*, 2006.

Xiaotong Shen, George C. Tseng, Xuegong Zhang, and Wing Hung Wong. On ψ-learning. *Journal of the American Statistical Association*, 98(463):724–734, 2003.

Yirong Shen, Andrew Ng, and Matthias Seeger. Fast Gaussian process regression using KD-trees. In Yair Weiss, Bernhard Schölkopf, and John Platt, editors, *Advances in Neural Information Processing Systems 18*, Cambridge, MA, MIT Press, 2006.

Jonathan R. Shewchuk. An introduction to the conjugate gradient method without the agonizing pain. Technical report CMU-CS-94-125, School of Computer Science, Carnegie Mellon University, Pittsburgh, 1994.

Bernard W. Silverman. Algorithm AS 176: Kernel density estimation using the fast Fourier transform. *Journal of Royal Statistical society Series C: Applied Statistics*, 31(1):93–99, 1982.

Patrice Simard, Yann LeCun, John S. Denker, and Bernard Victorri. Transformation invariance in pattern recognition – Tangent distance and tangent propagation. *International Journal of Imaging Systems and Technology*, 11(3), 2000.

Patrice Simard, Yann LeCun, and Denker John S. Efficient pattern recognition using a new transformation distance. In Stephen Jose Hanson, Jack D Cowan, and C. Lee Giles, editors, *Advances in Neural Information Processing Systems 5*. San Francisco, Morgan Kaufmann, 1993.

Patrice Simard, Dave Steinkraus, and John C. Platt. Best practices for convolutional neural networks applied to visual document analysis. In *Proceedings of ICDAR 2003*, pages 958–962, 2003.

Vikas Sindhwani and S. Sathiya Keerthi. Large scale semi-supervised linear svms. Technical report, Department of Computer Science, University of Chicago, 2005.

Vikas Sindhwani, S. Sathiya Keerthi, and Olivier Chapelle. Deterministic annealing for semi-supervised kernel machines. In *International Conference on Machine Learning*, 2006.

John Skilling. Bayesian numerical analysis. In Walter T. Grandy, Jr. and Peter Milonni, editors, *Physics and Probability*. Cambridge, UK, Cambridge University Press, 1993.

Alexander J. Smola and Peter L. Bartlett. Sparse greedy Gaussian process regression. In Todd K. Leen, Thomas G. Dietterich, and Volker Tresp, editors, *Advances in Neural Information Processing Systems 13*, pages 619–625, Cambridge, MA, MIT Press, 2001.

Alexander J. Smola and Bernhard Schölkopf. Sparse greedy matrix approximation for machine learning. In Pat Langley, editor, *Proceedings of the 17th International Conference on Machine Learning*, pages 911–918, San Francisco, Morgan Kaufmann, 2000.

Alexander J. Smola, Bernhard Scholkopf, and Klaus-Robert Muller. Nonlinear component analysis as a kernel eigenvalue problem. Technical report 44, Max-Planck-Institut für biologische Kybernetik, Tubingen, Germany, 1996.

Alexander J. Smola, S. V. N. Vishwanathan, and Thomas Hofmann. Kernel methods for missing variables. In *Proceedings of the 10th International Workshop on Artificial Intelligence and Statistics*, 2005.

Robert R. Snapp and Santosh S. Venkatesh. Asymptotic derivation of the finite-sample risk of the k nearest neighbor classifier. Technical report UVM-CS-1998-0101, Department of Computer Science, University of Vermont, Burlington, 1998.

Edward Snelson and Zoubin Ghahramani. Sparse Gaussian processes using pseudo-inputs. In Yair Weiss, Bernhard Schölkopf, and John Platt, editors, *Advances in Neural Information Processing Systems 18*, Cambridge, MA, MIT Press, 2006.

Sören Sonnenburg, Gunnar Rätsch, and Christin Schäfer. Learning interpretable

SVMs for biological sequence classification. In Satoru Miyano, Jill P. Mesirov, Simon Kasif, Sorin Istrail, Pavel A. Pevzner, and Michael Waterman, editors, *Research in Computational Molecular Biology, 9th Annual International Conference, RECOMB 2005*, volume 3500, pages 389–407, Berlin, Heidelberg, Springer-Verlag, 2005a.

Sören Sonnenburg, Gunnar Rätsch, and Christin Schäfer. A general and efficient multiple kernel learning algorithm. In Yair Weiss, Bernhard Schölkopf, and John Platt, editors, *Advances in Neural Information Processing Systems 18*, pages 1273–1280, Cambridge, MA, MIT Press, 2006a.

Sören Sonnenburg, Gunnar Rätsch, Christin Schäfer, and Bernhard Schölkopf. Large scale multiple kernel learning. *Journal of Machine Learning Research*, 7:1531–1565, July 2006b.

Sören Sonnenburg, Gunnar Rätsch, and Bernhard Schölkopf. Large scale genomic sequence SVM classifiers. In L. D. Raedt and S. Wrobel, editors, *ICML '05: Proceedings of the 22nd International Conference on Machine Learning*, pages 849–856, New York, ACM Press, 2005b.

Sören Sonnenburg, Alexander Zien, and Gunnar Rätsch. ARTS: Accurate recognition of transcription starts in human. *Bioinformatics*, 22(14):472–480, 2006c.

David Steinkraus, Ian Buck, and Patrice Simard. System and method for accelerating and optimizing the processing of machine learning techniques using graphics processing unit. European Patent Application EP1569128A2, 2004.

Ingo Steinwart. On the influence of the kernel on the consistency of support vector machines. *Journal of Machine Learning Research*, 2:67–93, 2002.

Ingo Steinwart. Sparseness of support vector machines. *Journal of Machine Learning Research*, 4:1071–1105, 2003.

Ingo Steinwart. Sparseness of support vector machines—some asymptotically sharp bounds. In Sebastian Thrun, Lawrence K. Saul, and Bernhard Schölkopf, editors, *Advances in Neural Information Processing Systems 16*, Cambridge, MA, MIT Press, 2004.

Ingo Steinwart and Clint Scovel. Fast rates to bayes for kernel machines. In Lawrence K. Saul, Yair Weiss, and Léon Bottou, editors, *Advances in Neural Information Processing Systems 17*, pages 1345–1352, Cambridge, MA, MIT Press, 2005.

Ingo Steinwart and Clint Scovel. Fast rates for support vector machines using Gaussian kernels. *Annals of Statistics*, 35(2), 2007.

Harald Stögbauer, Alexander Kraskov, Sergei Astakhov, and Peter Grassberger. Least dependent component analysis based on mutual information. *Physical Review E*, 70(6):066123, 2004.

David G. Stork and Elad Yom-Tov. *Computer Manual in MATLAB to Accompany Pattern Classification*, 2nd edition. New York, Wiley-Interscience, 2004.

Ching Y. Suen. N-gram statistics for natural language understanding and text processing. *IEEE Transactions on Pattern Analysis and Machine Intelligence*, 1 (2):164–172, April 1979.

Martin Szummer and Tommi Jaakkola. Partially labeled classification with Markov random walks. In *Advances in Neural Information Processing Systems 14*, Cambridge, MA, MIT Press, 2002.

Norikazu Takahashi and Tetsuo Nishi. Rigorous proof of termination of SMO algorithm for support vector machines. *IEEE Transactions on Neural Networks*, 16(3):774–776, 2005.

Pham Dinh Tao and Le Thi Hoai An. A DC optimization algorithm for solving the trust-region subproblem. *SIAM Journal on Optimization*, 8(2):476–505, 1998.

Pham Dinh Tao and Souad El Bernoussi. Algorithms for solving a class of non convex optimization problems. methods of subgradients. In Jean-Baptiste Hiriart-Urruty, editor, *Fermat Days 85: Mathematics for Optimization*, volume 129 of North-Holland Mathematics Studies, Amsterdam, Elsevier, 1986.

Yee Whye Teh and Geoffrey E. Hinton. Rate-coded restricted Boltzmann machines for face recognition. In Todd K. Leen, Thomas G. Dietterich, and Volker Tresp, editors, *Advances in Neural Information Processing Systems 13*, Cambridge, MA, MIT Press, 2001.

Josh B. Tenenbaum, Vin de Silva, and John C. L. Langford. A global geometric framework for nonlinear dimensionality reduction. *Science*, 290(5500):2319–2323, December 2000.

Choon-Hui Teo and S. V. N. Vishwanathan. Fast and space efficient string kernels using suffix arrays. In *Proceedings 23rd ICMP*, pages 939–936, New York, ACM Press, 2006.

Gerry Tesauro. Practical issues in temporal difference learning. *Machine Learning*, 8:257–277, 1992.

Thorsten Thies and Frank Weber. Optimal reduced-set vectors for support vector machines with a quadratic kernel. *Neural Computation*, 16:1769–1777, 2004.

Michael E. Tipping. The relevance vector machine. In Sara A. Solla, Todd K. Leen, and Klaus-Robert Müller, editors, *Advances in Neural Information Processing Systems 12*, pages 652–658, Cambridge, MA, MIT Press, 2000.

Michael E. Tipping. Sparse Bayesian learning and the relevance vector machine. *Journal of Machine Learning Research*, 1:211–244, 2001.

Sivan Toledo. Improving the memory-system performance of sparse-matrix vector multiplication. *IBM Journal of Research and Development*, 41(6):711–725, 1997.

Volker Tresp. A Bayesian committee machine. *Neural Computation*, 12(11):2719–2741, 2000.

Ivor W. Tsang, James T. Kwok, and Pak-Ming Cheung. Core vector machines: Fast SVM training on very large datasets. *Journal of Machine Learning Research*, 6: 363–392, 2005.

Koji Tsuda, Motoaki Kawanabe, Gunnar Rätsch, Sören Sonnenburg, and Klaus-Robert Müller. A new discriminative kernel from probabilistic models. *Neural Computation*, 14:2397–2414, 2002a.

Koji Tsuda, Taishin Kin, and Kiyoshi Asai. Marginalized kernels for biological sequences. *Bioinformatics*, 18:268S–275S, 2002b.

Amund Tveit and Håvard Engum. Parallelization of the incremental proximal support vector machine classifier using a heap-based tree topology. Technical report, IDI, NTNU, Trondheim, Norway, 2003. Workshop presentation at ECML'2003, Cavtat-Dubrovnik, Croatia.

Esko Ukkonen. Online construction of suffix trees. *Algorithmica*, 14(3):249–260, 1995.

Paul E. Utgoff and David J. Stracuzzi. Many-layered learning. *Neural Computation*, 14:2497–2539, 2002.

Robert J. Vanderbei. LOQO: An interior point code for quadratic programming. *Optimization Methods and Software*, 11:451–484, 1999.

Vladimir N. Vapnik. *Estimation of Dependences Based on Empirical Data*. Springer Series in Statistics. Berlin, Springer-Verlag, 1982.

Vladimir N. Vapnik. *The Nature of Statistical Learning Theory*. New York, Springer-Verlag, 1995.

Vladimir N. Vapnik. *Statistical Learning Theory*. New York, Wiley, 1998.

Vladimir N. Vapnik, T. G. Glaskova, V. A. Koscheev, A. I. Mikhailski, and A. Y. Chervonenkis. *Algorithms and Programs for Dependency Estimation,* in Russian. Moscow, Nauka, 1984.

Vladimir N. Vapnik and A. Lerner. Pattern recognition using generalized portrait method. *Automation and Remote Control*, 24:774–780, 1963.

Jean-Philippe Vert, Hiroto Saigo, and Tatsuya Akutsu. Local alignment kernels for biological sequences. In Bernhard Schoelkopf, Koji Tsuda, and Jean-Philippe Vert, editors, *Kernel Methods in Computational Biology*, Cambridge, MA, MIT Press, 2004.

Sethu Vijayakumar and Si Wu. Sequential support vector classifiers and regression. In *International Conference on Soft Computing*, pages 610–619, 1999.

Pascal Vincent and Yoshua Bengio. Kernel matching pursuit. *Machine Learning*, 48(1-3):165–187, 2002.

S. V. N. Vishwanathan, Nicol N. Schraudolph, and Alexander J. Smola. Step size adaptation in reproducing kernel hilbert space. *Journal of Machine Learning Research*, 7:1107–1133, 2006.

S. V. N. Vishwanathan and Alexander J. Smola. Fast kernels for string and tree matching. In Sue Becker, Sebastian Thrun, and Klaus Obermayer, editors, *Advances in Neural Information Processing Systems 15*, pages 569–576, Cambridge, MA, MIT Press, 2003.

S. V. N. Vishwanathan and Alexander J. Smola. Fast kernels for string and tree matching. In *Kernels and Bioinformatics*, pages 113–130, Cambridge, MA, MIT Press, 2004.

S. V. N. Vishwanathan, Alexander J. Smola, and M. Narasimha Murty. SimpleSVM. In *Proceedings of the 20th International Conference on Machine Learning (ICML)*, pages 760–767, 2003.

Grace Wahba. *Spline Models for Observational Data*. Philadelphia, SIAM, 1990.

Grace Wahba, Donald R. Johnson, Feng Gao, and Jianjian Gong. Adaptive tuning of numerical weather prediction models: Randomized GCV in three-and four-dimensional data assimilation. *Monthly Weather Review*, 123:3358–3369, 1995.

M. P. Wand and M. Chris Jones. *Kernel Smoothing*. London, Chapman and Hall, 1995.

Steve Webb, James Caverlee, and Calton Pu. Introducing the Webb spam corpus: Using email spam to identify web spam automatically. In *Proceedings of the 3rd Conference on Email and Anti-Spam (CEAS 2006)*, Mountain View, CA, July 2006.

Yair Weiss. Segmentation using eigenvectors: A unifying view. In *Proceedings IEEE International Conference on Computer Vision*, pages 975–982, 1999.

Jason Weston. *Extensions to the Support Vector Method*. PhD thesis, Royal Holloway University of London, 1999.

Christopher K. I. Williams and Carl Edward Rasmussen. Gaussian processes for regression. In David S. Touretzky, Michael C. Mozer, and Michael E. Hasselmo, editors, *Advances in Neural Information Processing Systems 8*, pages 514–520, Cambridge, MA, MIT Press, 1996.

Christopher K. I. Williams and Matthias Seeger. Using the Nyström method to speed up kernel machines. In Todd K. Leen, Thomas G. Dietterich, and Volker Tresp, editors, *Advances in Neural Information Processing Systems 13*, pages 682–688, Cambridge, MA, MIT Press, 2001.

David H. Wolpert. The lack of a priori distinction between learning algorithms. *Neural Computation*, 8(7):1341–1390, 1996.

Jeffrey Wood. Invariant pattern recognition: A review. *Pattern Recognition*, 29(1): 1–19, 1996.

Mingrui Wu, Bernhard Schölkopf, and Gökhan Bakır. Building sparse large margin classifiers. In *Proceedings of the 22nd International Conference on Machine Learning*, 2005.

Linli Xu, Koby Crammer, and Dale Schuurmans. Robust support vector machine training via convex outlier ablation. In *The 21st National Conference on Artificial Intelligence, AAAI*, 2006.

Linli Xu, James Neufeld, Bryce Larson, and Dale Schuurmans. Maximum margin clustering. In Lawrence K. Saul, Yair Weiss, and Léon Bottou, editors, *Advances in Neural Information Processing Systems 17*, pages 1537–1544, Cambridge, MA,

MIT Press, 2005.

Changjaing. Yang, Ramani Duraiswami, and Larry Davis. Efficient kernel machines using the improved fast Gauss transform. In Lawrence K. Saul, Yair Weiss, and Léon Bottou, editors, *Advances in Neural Information Processing Systems 17*, pages 1561–1568, Cambridge, MA, MIT Press, 2005.

Changjaing Yang, Ramani Duraiswami, Nail A. Gumerov, and Larry Davis. Improved fast Gauss transform and efficient kernel density estimation. In *IEEE International Conference on Computer Vision*, pages 464–471, 2003.

Yiming Yang and Jan O. Pedersen. A comparative study on feature selection in text categorization. In *Proceedings of the 14th International Conference on Machine Learning ICML97*, pages 412–420, 1997.

Hwanjo Yu, Jaideep Vaidya, and Xiaoqian Jiang. Privacy-preserving SVM classification on vertically partitioned data. In *Advances in Knowledge Discovery and Data Mining: 10th Pacific-Asia Conference, PAKDD 2006.*, volume 3918 of Lecture Notes in Computer Science, pages 647–656, New York, Springer-Verlag, 2006.

Alan L. Yuille and Anand Rangarajan. The concave-convex procedure (CCCP). In Thomas G. Dietterich, Sue Becker, and Zoubin Ghahramani, editors, *Advances in Neural Information Processing Systems 14*, Cambridge, MA, MIT Press, 2002.

Gaetano Zanghirati and Luca Zanni. A parallel solver for large quadratic programs in training support vector machines. *Parallel Computation*, 29(4):535–551, 2003.

Luca Zanni, Thomas Serafini, and Gaetano Zanghirati. Parallel software for training large scale support vector machines on multiprocessor systems. In *Journal of Machine Learning Research*, pages 1467–1492, 2006.

Jian Zhang, Rong Jin, Yiming Yang, and Alexander G. Hauptmann. Modified logistic regression: An approximation to SVM and its applications in large-scale text categorization. In *Proceedings of the 20th International Conference on Machine Learning*, 2003.

Jian-Pei Zhang, Zhong-Wei Li, and Jing Yang. A parallel SVM training algorithm on large-scale classification problems. In *International Conference on Machine Learning and Cybernetics*, volume 3, pages 1637–1641, 2005.

Xiang H.-F. Zhang, Katherine A. Heller, Ilana Hefter, Christina S. Leslie, and Lawrence A. Chasin. Sequence information for the splicing of human pre-mRNA identified by support vector machine classification. *Genome Research*, 13(12): 2637–2650, 2003.

Dengyong Zhou, Olivier Bousquet, Thomas Navin Lal, Jason Weston, and Bernhard Schölkopf. Learning with local and global consistency. In Sebastian Thrun, Lawrence K. Saul, and Bernhard Schölkopf, editors, *Advances in Neural Information Processing Systems 16*, Cambridge, MA, MIT Press, 2004.

Ji Zhu and Trevor Hastie. Kernel logistic regression and the import vector machine. *Journal of Computational and Graphical Statistics*, 14:185–205, 2005.

Ji Zhu and Trevor J. Hastie. Kernel logistic regression and the import vector machine. In Thomas G. Dietterich, Sue Becker, and Zoubin Ghahramani, editors, *Advances in Neural Information Processing Systems 14*, pages 1081–1088, Cambridge, MA, MIT Press, 2002.

Xiaojin Zhu, Zoubin Ghahramani, and John Lafferty. Semi-supervised learning using Gaussian fields and harmonic functions. In *Proceedings of the 20th International Conference on Machine Learning (ICML)*, 2003.

Alexander Zien, Gunnar Rätsch, Sebastian Mika, Bernhard Schölkopf, Thomas Lengauer, and Klaus-Robrt Müller. Engineering support vector machine kernels that recognize translation initiation sites. *BioInformatics*, 16(9):799–807, 2000.

Guus Zoutendijk. *Methods of Feasible Directions*. Amsterdam, Elsevier, 1960.

Contributors

Yoshua Bengio
Département d'Informatique et Recherche Opérationnelle
Université de Montréal, P.O. Box 6128, Centre-Ville Branch,
H3C-3J7, Québec, Canada
Yoshua.Bengio@umontreal.ca

Léon Bottou
NEC Labs America
Princeton, NJ 08540
leon@bottou.org

Stéphane Canu
LITIS Laboratory
INSA de Rouen
76801 Saint Etienne du Rouvray, France
stephane.canu@insa-rouen.fr

Olivier Chapelle
Yahoo! Research
Santa Clara, CA 95054
chap@yahoo-inc.com

Ronan Collobert
NEC Labs America
Princeton, NJ 08540
ronan@collobert.com

Eric Cosatto
NEC Labs America
Princeton, NJ 08540
cosatto@nec-labs.com

Dennis DeCoste
Microsoft Live Labs
Redmond, WA 98052
decoste@microsoft.com

Ramani Duraiswami
Department of Computer Science, and
Institute for Advanced Computer Studies
University of Maryland
College Park, MD 20742
ramani@umiacs.umd.edu

Igor Durdanovic
NEC Labs America
Princeton, NJ 08540
igord@nec-labs.com

Hans-Peter Graf
NEC Labs America
Princeton, NJ 08540
hpg@nec-labs.com

Arthur Gretton
Max Planck Institute for Biological Cybernetics
72076 Tübingen, Germany
arthur.gretton@tuebingen.mpg.de

Patrick Haffner
AT&T Labs–Research
Florham Park, NJ 07932
haffner@research.att.com

Stefanie Jegelka
Max Planck Institure for Biological Cybernetics
72076 Tübingen, Germany
stefanie.jegelka@tuebingen.mpg.de

Stephan Kanthak
AT&T Labs–Research
Florham Park, NJ 07932
skanthak@research.att.com

S. Sathiya Keerthi
Yahoo! Research
Burbank, CA 91504
keerthi@yahoo-inc.com

Yann LeCun
The Courant Institute of Mathematical Sciences
New York University
New York, NY 10003
yann@cs.nyu.edu

Chih-Jen Lin
Department of Computer Science
National Taiwan University
Taipei, Taiwan
cjlin@csie.ntu.edu.tw

Gaëlle Loosli
LITIS Laboratory
INSA de Rouen
76801 Saint Etienne du Rouvray, France
gaelle.loosli@insa-rouen.fr

Joaquin Quiñonero-Candela
Microsoft Research Ltd.
7 J. J. Thomson Avenue
CB3 0FB Cambridge, UK
joaquinc@microsoft.com

Carl Edward Rasmussen
Max Planck Institute for Biological Cybernetics
72076 Tübingen, Germany
carl@tuebingen.mpg.de

Gunnar Rätsch
Friedrich Miescher Laboratory of the Max Planck Society
72076 Tübingen, Germany
Gunnar.Raetsch@tuebingen.mpg.de

Vikas Chandrakant Raykar
Department of Computer Science, and
Institute for Advanced Computer Studies
University of Maryland
College Park, MD 20742
vikas@umiacs.umd.edu

Konrad Rieck
Fraunhofer Institute First
12489 Berlin, Germany
Konrad.Rieck@first.fraunhofer.de

Vikas Sindhwani
Department of Computer Science
University of Chicago
Chicago, IL 60637
vikass@cs.uchicago.edu

Fabian Sinz
Max Planck Institute for Biological Cybernetics
72076 Tübingen, Germany
`fabee@tuebingen.mpg.de`

Sören Sonnenburg
Fraunhofer Institute First
12489 Berlin, Germany
`Soeren.Sonnenburg@first.fraunhofer.de`

Jason Weston
NEC Labs America
Princeton, NJ 08540
`jaseweston@gmail.com`

Christopher K. I. Williams
Institute for Adaptive and Neural Computation
School of Informatics, University of Edinburgh
Edinburgh EH1 2QL, Scotland, UK
`c.k.i.williams@ed.ac.uk`

Elad Yom-Tov
IBM Research Laboratory in Haifa
Haifa 31905, Israel
`yomtov@il.ibm.com`

Index

Active learning, 304
AI; *see* Artificial intelligence
AI problem set, 325
Approximation
    ϵ-exact, 177
    low rank, 47, 232
    multipole, 47, *175*
    sparse, 47, 206, 231
Artificial intelligence, 323

Basis selection, *257*
Bayesian committee machine, 213
BCM; *see* Bayesian committee
        machine
BLAS, 113
Blind source separation, 225

CCCP; *see* Concave-convex
        procedure
Chunking, 13
COCO; *see* Constrained covariance
Communication overhead, 123
Comparing classifiers, 145
Concave-convex procedure, *276*, 279
Conjugate
    directions, 15, 45
    gradient, 45, 159
Constrained covariance, *229*
Convex optimization, 6, 275
Convolutional networks, 320, *348*
Core vector machine, 142
Covariance function, 204
Covariance operator, *228*
Curse of dual variables, 277
CVM; *see* Core vector machine

DC; *see* Difference of convex

Decomposition method, *16*, 83, 107,
        141
Deformations, 311, 350
Deterministic annealing, 164
Difference of convex, 276
Direction search, *13*, 305
Dual optimization, 1, 105, 139
Dual-tree methods, *180*
Duality, 6
    strong, 8
    weak, 8

Evidence, 219

Farthest point clustering, 186
Fast Gauss transform, *181*, 189
Fast matrix-vector multiplication,
        see Matrix-vector
        multiplication
Fast multipole methods, 47, *175*, 181
Feasible direction, *13*, 305
Feature selection, 67
FGT; *see* Fast Gauss transform

Gauss transform, *179*
Gaussian process, 176, *204*
Genomic sequence analysis, 73
GP; *see* Gaussian process
Gradient
    conjugate, 45, 159
    descent
        on orthogonal group, 236
        stochastic, 349
    projection, 15

Hash table, 79
Hessian, 14, 256

Hilbert-Schmidt independence
    criterion, *230*
Hinge loss, 37, 278
HSIC; *see* Hilbert-Schmidt
    independence criterion
Huber loss, 37

ICA; *see* Independent component
    analysis
IFGT; *see* Improved fast Gauss
    transform
Improved fast Gauss transform, *181*,
    189
Incomplete Cholesky decomposition,
    26, 47, *232*
Independence measure, 228
Independent component analysis,
    225, *227*
Inducing
    inputs, 207
    variables, 207, 218
Interior point methods, 141
Invariance, 301, *308*, 348
Inverted index, 51
Iterative chunking, 13

k-mers, 75, 98
Karush Kuhn Tucker, 6, 280
KDE; *see* Kernel density estimation
Kernel, 5
    cache, 12, 25, 66, 116, 259
    computation, 12
    independence measure, 228
    inverted index, *51*
    linear, 157
    local, 337
    string kernel; *see* String kernel
Kernel density estimation, 176, 196
Kernel independent component
    analysis, *225*
Kernel matching pursuit, 254, 264
KKT; *see* Karush Kuhn Tucker
KMP; *see* Kernel matching pursuit

Lagrangian duality, 7

LAPACK, 113
Large-scale learning, 2
LASVM, *307*
    example selection, 308
    finishing, 316
    process, 307
    reprocess, 307
Learning
    active, 304
    large-scale, 2
    online, 303
    semisupervised, 161, 285
    small-scale, 2
Learning architectures
    deep, 332, *345*
    shallow
        fixed preprocessing, 330
        template matching, 330
        trainable features, 331
LIBSVM, *20*, 27, 43, 69, 118
Line search, 160, 237
List merging, 58
LLAMA, *69*
Local learning, 337
LOQO, 27
Loss
    hinge, 37, 278
    Huber, 37
    nonconvex, 276
    quadratic, 34
    ramp, 279
    transduction, 287

Marginal likelihood, 219
Matching pursuit, 257, 264
Matching statistic, 81
Matrix-vector multiplication, 54,
    178, *217*, 231
    sparse, 54
Maxent, 64
Maximum violating pair, 19, *22*
MILDE, *118*
MINOS, 27
MKL; *see* Multiple kernel learning

MNIST, 69, 130, 273, 298, 310, 318, 349, *350*

Modified finite newton, 157

Modified gradient projection, 15, *15*

MPI, 126

Multicast, 124

Multiple kernel learning, 93

Multipole methods; *see* Fast multipole methods

Multithreading, 115

MVM; *see* Matrix-vector multiplication

N-body learning, 26, *177*, 201

n-mers, 75

Network overhead, 123

Newton method, 14, 34, 255

No-free-lunch theorem, 324

Nonconvex optimization, 275

NORB, 352

Numerical accuracy, 25

Online learning, 303

Optimal hyperplane, 3

Optimality criteria, 8

Optimization
    convex, 6, 275
    dual, 1, 105, 139
    nonconvex, 275
    primal, *29*

Parallel
    cascade SVM, *109*
    chunking, 84
    gradient projection, 109
    kernel, 107, 114
    scaling, 146
        linear, 150
        superlinear, 126
    sequential learning, 144
    spread kernel, 119, 121

Perceptron, 53, 142, 333
    on a budget, 306

Preconditioning, 45

Primal optimization, 29

advantages, 44

Projection on the constraints, 15

PVM, 126

QP; *see* Quadratic programming

Quadratic loss, 34

Quadratic programming, *1*, 106, 142

Ramp loss, 279

RCV1, 160, 296

Reduced kernel expansion, 47, 251, 281

Regression
    probabilistic, 204

Representer theorem, 33

Reproducing kernel Hilbert space, 5, 228

RKHS; *see* Reproducing kernel Hilbert space

Royal Holloway SVM, 27

Selective sampling, 301, 308

Semi-infinite linear programming, 93

Semi-supervised, 285

Semisupervised, 161

Sequence, 75

Sequential minimal optimization, *18*, 19, 53, 111

SHOGUN, *86*

Shrinking, *23*, 66, 115, 259

SILP; *see* Semi-infinite linear programming

SimpleSVM, 27

SMO; *see* Sequential minimal optimization

Soft margins, 5

Sorted array, 79

Sparse
    dataset, 51, 157
    expansion, *10*, 251, 279, 282
    feature maps, 79

Spread kernel
    full data, 119
    split data, 121

Stopping criterion, 20, 117, 167

String kernel, *74*
    bag-of-words, 75
    n-gram kernel, 75
    spectrum, 76
    weighted degree, 76
    weighted degree with shifts, 77
Suffix tree, 81
Support vector machine, 301
    complexity, 11, 280
    dual objective function, 5, 8, 111
    greedy optimization, *251*
    linear, 155, 157
    nonconvex, *277*, 279
    online, 304
    optimization problem, 5
    parallel solver, *105*, 139
    primal objective function, 5, 32
    primal optimization, 251
    primal training, 41
    sequential learning, 144
    solver, *1*, 29, 105, 139, 251
    transductive; *see* Transductive
        SVM
Support vectors, 10
    bounded, 10
    free, 10
    number of, 11, 278
    virtual, 320
SVM; *see* Support vector machine
SVM^{light}, *27*, 86, 270, 292
SVM*lin*, *168*
SVQP, 27
SVQP2, *27*, 118

Tangent vectors, 310
Template matching, 335
Transductive SVM
    balancing constraint, 165, 288
    CCCP, *288*
    CS^{3}VM, 292
    linear, *162*
    multiswitch, *161*
    ∇TSVM, 291
    nonconvex, *285*

SVM^{light}, 291
Tries, 80
TSVM; *see* Transductive SVM

Webb spam corpus, 86
Working set method, 13, 16, 141
Working set selection, *21*
    maximum gain, 21
    maximum violating pair, 22
    second-order schemes, 22